JEWISH LAW | HISTORY, SOURCES, PRINCIPLES | *Ha-Mishpat Ha-Ivri*

VOLUME I
PART ONE
The History and Elements of Jewish Law
and
PART TWO
The Legal Sources of Jewish Law
SECTION 1
Exegesis and Interpretation

VOLUME II
PART TWO (*continued*)
The Legal Sources of Jewish Law
SECTION 2
Legislation, Custom, Precedent, and Legal Reasoning

VOLUME III
PART THREE
The Literary Sources of Jewish Law

VOLUME IV
PART FOUR
Jewish Law in the State of Israel
and
Appendixes, Glossary, Bibliography, Indexes

A PHILIP AND MURIEL BERMAN EDITION

MENACHEM ELON

DEPUTY PRESIDENT, SUPREME COURT OF ISRAEL

JEWISH LAW

HISTORY, SOURCES, PRINCIPLES

Ha-Mishpat Ha-Ivri VOLUME II

Translated from the Hebrew
by Bernard Auerbach
and Melvin J. Sykes

THE JEWISH PUBLICATION SOCIETY Philadelphia Jerusalem 5754 / 1994

Originally published in Hebrew under the title
Ha-Mishpat Ha-Ivri
by the Magnes Press, The Hebrew University, Jerusalem

Manufactured in the United States of America

The author and publisher gratefully acknowledge the support of the Philip and Muriel Berman Book Fund of The Jewish Publication Society, sponsored by Mr. and Mrs. Philip I. Berman, Allentown, Pennsylvania, in the publication of this book.

Library of Congress Cataloging-in-Publication Data

Elon, Menachem.
[Mishpaṭ ha-ʻIvri. English]
Jewish law : history, sources, principles / Menachem Elon ; translated from the Hebrew by Bernard Auerbach and Melvin J. Sykes.
p. cm.
Includes bibliographical references and index.
Volume I, ISBN 0–8276–0385-1
Volume II, ISBN 0-8276-0386-X
Volume III, ISBN 0-8276-0387-8
Volume IV, ISBN 0-8276-0388-6
Four-volume set, ISBN 0-8276-0389–4
1. Jewish law—History. 2. Rabbinical literature—History and criticism. 3. Law—Israel—Jewish influences. I. Title.
BM520.5.E4313 1993
296.1'8'09—dc20 93–9278
CIP

Designed by Arlene Putterman

Typeset in Meridien and Perpetua by Graphic Composition, Inc.
Printed by Hamilton Printing Company

Philip and Muriel Berman Edition

The Author

JUSTICE MENACHEM ELON was first appointed to the Supreme Court of Israel in 1977 and was named Deputy President of the Court in 1988. A legal scholar and teacher, he was awarded the Israel Prize in 1979 for *Ha-Mishpat Ha-Ivri.*

Justice Elon has published many works on the history and nature of Jewish law and the relation between it and the modern State of Israel, including *The Freedom of the Person of the Debtor in Jewish Law* (1964) and *Religious Legislation in the Laws of the State of Israel and Within the Jurisdiction of the Civil and Rabbinical Courts* (1968). From 1968 to 1971 he was editor of the Jewish Law section of the *Encyclopaedia Judaica,* which was subsequently collected in his *Principles of Jewish Law* (1975). By 1984 he had edited 10 volumes of *The Annual of the Institute for Research in Jewish Law of The Hebrew University of Jerusalem* and was also editing a digest of the responsa of the medieval authorities. He has been a member of government committees for the preparation of various bills of the Israeli Civil Law Coordination.

An ordained rabbi, Justice Elon earned his diploma from the Tel Aviv School of Law and Economics in 1948, received a master's degree in humanities, and was awarded a doctor of laws degree *cum laude* from The Hebrew University of Jerusalem. He began his affiliation with The Hebrew University in 1954 as an instructor of law and was subsequently appointed teaching associate, senior lecturer, associate professor, and, in 1972, Professor of Jewish Law.

Translators

BERNARD AUERBACH, Professor of Law, University of Maryland School of Law (retired, 1992). B.A. (Yeshiva University), J.D. (New York University), LL.M. (Yale University), Rabbinic Ordination (Rabbi Isaac Elchanan Theological Seminary, Yeshiva University), Sterling Fellow, (Yale University). *Consultant:* Court of Appeals of Maryland Standing Committee on Rules of Practice and Procedure (1965–1980). *Reporter:* Maryland Judicial Conference (1967–1970). *Recipient:* Bernard Revel Memorial Award for Arts and Sciences, Yeshiva College Alumni Association. *Member:* Jewish Law Association; American Bar Association.

MELVIN J. SYKES, A.B. (Johns Hopkins University), LL.B. (Harvard University), Diplomate, Baltimore Hebrew College. *Fellow:* American College of Trial Lawyers, American College of Trust and Estate Counsel, American Bar Foundation, Maryland Bar Foundation (former president). *Member:* American Law Institute, Court of Appeals of Maryland Standing Committee on Rules of Practice and Procedure; American and Maryland State Bar Associations, Bar Association of Baltimore City. *Sole Practitioner, Baltimore, Maryland:* General practice, trial and appellate litigation, probate and trusts. *Adjunct Faculty Member:* University of Maryland School of Law.

Editorial Consultant

DANIEL D. CHAZIN, *Member:* New Jersey and New York Bars. B.A. (Yeshiva University), J.D. (New York University). *Member:* American Bar Association, New Jersey and New York State Bar Associations. Gruss Fellow, 1989–90, New York University School of Law.

Assistant Editorial Consultant

NORMAN MENACHEM FEDER, A.B., M.A. (Columbia University), J.D. (New York University). Editor-in-Chief, N.Y.U. Journal of International Law & Politics (1986–1987). Luce Scholar (1987–1988). Law Clerk to Judge Roger J. Miner, United States Court of Appeals for the Second Circuit (1988–1989). Law Clerk to Deputy President Menachem Elon, Supreme Court of Israel (1989–1990). Associate, Cleary, Gottlieb, Steen & Hamilton, New York.

SUMMARY OF CONTENTS

VOLUME II

PART TWO *(continued)*
The Legal Sources of Jewish Law
SECTION 2 *Legislation, Custom, Precedent, and Legal Reasoning*

VOLUME III

PART THREE
The Literary Sources of Jewish Law

VOLUME IV

PART FOUR
Jewish Law in the State of Israel

Appendixes, Glossary, Bibliography, Indexes

CONTENTS

 VOLUME II

PART TWO *(continued)*
The Legal Sources of Jewish Law
SECTION 2   *Legislation, Custom, Precedent,*
and Legal Reasoning

BIBLIOGRAPHICAL ABBREVIATIONS OF BOOKS AND ARTICLES FREQUENTLY CITED

H. Albeck, *Mavo la-Mishnah* [Introduction to the Mishnah], Jerusalem, 1959 = Albeck, *Mavo*.

G. Alon (or Allon), *Meḥkarim be-Toledot Yisra'el bi-Mei Bayit Sheni u-vi-Tekufat ha-Mishnah ve-ha-Talmud* [Studies in Jewish History in the Days of the Second Temple and in the Mishnaic and Talmudic Period], 2 vols., Tel-Aviv, 1957–1958 = Alon, *Meḥkarim*. (For an English version, *see Jews, Judaism and the Classical World: Studies in Jewish History in the Times of the Second Temple and Talmud*, I. Abrahams and A. Oshery trans., Jerusalem, 1977.)

——— *Toledot ha-Yehudim be-Ereẓ Yisra'el bi-Tekufat ha-Mishnah ve-ha-Talmud* [History of the Jews in the Land of Israel in the Mishnaic and Talmudic Period], 3rd ed., Tel-Aviv, 1959 = Alon, *Toledot*. (For an English version, *see The Jews in Their Land in the Talmudic Age*, G. Levi trans. and ed., Jerusalem, 1 vol., Magnes Press, 1980–1984; reprinted, Harvard University Press, 1989.)

S. Assaf, *Battei ha-Din ve-Sidreihem Aḥarei Ḥatimat ha-Talmud* [Jewish Courts and Their Procedures after the Completion of the Talmud], Jerusalem, 1924 = Assaf, *Battei Din*.

——— *Ha-Onshin Aḥarei Ḥatimat ha-Talmud* [Penal Law After the Completion of the Talmud], Jerusalem, 1922 = Assaf, *Onshin*.

——— *Tekufat ha-Geonim ve-Sifrutah* [The Geonic Period and Its Literature], Jerusalem, 1956 = Assaf, *Geonim*.

Y. Baer, *Toledot Ha-Yehudim bi-Sefarad ha-Noẓrit* [A History of the Jews of Christian Spain], 2nd ed., Tel Aviv, 1965. An English translation, *A History of the Jews in Christian Spain*, JPS, 2 vols., 1961–1966 = Baer, *Spain*.

S.W. Baron, *A Social and Religious History of the Jews*, JPS-Columbia, 18 vols. 1952–1983 = Baron, *History*.

M.A. Bloch, *Sha'arei Torat ha-Takkanot* [On Legislative Enactments], Vienna *et al.*, 7 vols., 1879–1906 = Bloch, *Sha'arei*.

P. Dykan (Dikstein), *Toledot Mishpat ha-Shalom ha-Ivri* [History of the Jewish Court of Arbitration], Tel Aviv, 1964 = Dykan, *Toledot*.

M. Elon, *Ḥakikah Datit be-Ḥukkei Medinat Yisra'el u-va-Shefitah Shel Battei ha-Mishpat u-Vattei ha-Din ha-Rabbaniyyim* [Religious Legislation in the Statutes of the State of Israel and in the Decisions of the General and Rabbinical Courts], Tel Aviv, 1968 = Elon, *Ḥakikah.*

——— "Ha-Ma'asar ba-Mishpat ha-Ivri" [Imprisonment in Jewish Law], *Jubilee Volume for Pinḥas Rosen,* Jerusalem, 1962, pp. 171–201 = Elon, *Ma'asar.*

——— *Ḥerut ha-Perat be-Darkhei Geviyyat Ḥov ba-Mishpat ha-Ivri* [Individual Freedom and the Methods of Enforcing Payment of Debts in Jewish Law], Jerusalem, 1964 = Elon, *Ḥerut.*

——— (ed.) *Principles of Jewish Law,* Jerusalem, 1975 = *Principles.*

——— "Samkhut ve-Oẓmah ba-Kehillah ha-Yehudit, Perek be-Mishpat ha-Ẓibbur ha-Ivri" [Authority and Power in the Jewish Community, A Chapter in Jewish Public Law], in *Shenaton ha-Mishpat ha-Ivri* [Annual of the Institute for Research in Jewish Law], Hebrew University of Jerusalem, III–IV (1976–1977), pp. 7ff. = Elon, *Samkhut ve-Oẓmah.* (For an English translation, *see* "Power and Authority—Halachic Stance of the Traditional Community and Its Contemporary Implications," in *Kinship and Consent, The Jewish Political Tradition and Its Contemporary Uses,* D. Elazar ed., Turtledove Publishing, 1981, pp. 183–213).

——— "Yiḥudah Shel Halakhah ve-Ḥevrah be-Yahadut Ẓefon Afrikah mi-le-aḥar Gerush Sefarad ve-ad Yameinu" [The Exceptional Character of *Halakhah* and Society in North African Jewry from the Spanish Expulsion to the Present], in *Halakhah u-Fetiḥut, Ḥakhmei Morokko ke-Fosekim le-Doreinu* [Halakhah and Open-Mindedness: The Halakhic Authorities of Morocco as Authorities for Our Own Time], 1945, pp. 15ff. = Elon, *Yiḥudah Shel Halakhah.*

J.N. Epstein, *Mavo le-Nusaḥ ha-Mishnah* [Introduction to the Text of the Mishnah], 2nd ed., Jerusalem, 1964 = Epstein, *Mavo.*

——— *Mevo'ot le-Sifrut ha-Tannaim,* [Introduction to Tannaitic Literature], Jerusalem, 1957 = Epstein, *Tannaim.*

——— *Mevo'ot le-Sifrut ha-Amoraim,* [Introduction to Amoraic Literature], Jerusalem, 1963 = Epstein, *Amoraim.*

L. Finkelstein, *Jewish Self-Government in the Middle Ages,* New York 1924 (second printing, New York, 1964) = Finkelstein, *Self-Government.*

Z. Frankel, *Darkhei ha-Mishnah* [The Methodology of the Mishnah], Leipzig, 1859 (facsimile ed., Tel Aviv, 1969) = Frankel, *Mishnah.*

——— *Mevo ha-Yerushalmi* [Introduction to the Jerusalem Talmud], Breslau, 1870 (facsimile ed., Jerusalem, 1967) = Frankel, *Mevo.*

A.H. Freimann, *Seder Kiddushin ve-Nissu'in Aḥarei Ḥatimat ha-Talmud, Meḥkar Histori-Dogmati be-Dinei Yisra'el* [Law of Betrothal and Marriage after the Completion of the Talmud: A Historical-Dogmatic Study in Jewish Law], Mosad ha-Rav Kook, Jerusalem, 1945 = Freimann, *Kiddushin ve-Nissu'in.*

L. Ginzberg, *Perushim ve-Ḥiddushim ba-Yerushalmi* [A Commentary on the Palestine Talmud] (English title by Prof. Ginzberg), New York, 1941 (facsimile ed., New York, 1971) = Ginzberg, *Perushim.*

A. Gulak, *Yesodei ha-Mishpat ha-Ivri* [The Foundations of Jewish Law], Jerusalem, 1923 (facsimile ed., Tel Aviv, 1967) = Gulak, *Yesodei.*

I. Halevy, *Dorot ha-Rishonim* [The Early Generations—A History of the Oral Law to the *Geonim*], Frankfort, 1897–1906 (facsimile ed., Jerusalem, 1957) = Halevy, *Dorot.*

I. Herzog, *The Main Institutions of Jewish Law,* 2nd ed., London, 2 vols., 1965–1967 = Herzog, *Institutions.*

D.Z. Hoffmann, *Das Buch Deuteronomium Übersetzt und Erklärt* [The Book of Deuteronomy: Translation and Commentary] = Hoffmann, *Commentary on Deuteronomy.*

Koveẓ Teshuvot ha-Rambam ve-Iggerotav [Compilation of Responsa and Epistles of Maimonides], Leipzig, 1859 = *Koveẓ ha-Rambam.*

J. Levy, *Wörterbuch über die Talmudim und Midraschim* [Talmudic and Midrashic Dictionary], 2nd ed., Berlin, 1924 = Levy, *Wörterbuch.*

S. Lieberman, *Greek in Jewish Palestine* = Lieberman, *Greek.*

——— *Hellenism in Jewish Palestine* = Lieberman, *Hellenism.*

A. Neubauer, *Seder ha-Ḥakhamim ve-Korot ha-Yamim* [Medieval Jewish Chronicles], Oxford, 1895 (facsimile ed., Jerusalem, 1967) = Neubauer, *Seder ha-Ḥakhamim.*

J.W. Salmond, *On Jurisprudence,* 12th ed., London, 1966 = Salmond.

Shenaton ha-Mishpat ha-Ivri [Annual of the Institute for Research in Jewish Law, Hebrew University of Jerusalem] = *Shenaton.*

M. Silberg, *Ha-Ma'amad ha-Ishi be-Yisra'el* [Personal Status in Israel], 4th ed., Jerusalem, 1965 = Silberg, *Ha-Ma'amad.*

H. Tykocinski, *Takkanot ha-Geonim* [Geonic Enactments], Jerusalem, 1960 = Tykocinski, *Takkanot.*

E.E. Urbach, *Ḥazal, Pirkei Emunot ve-De'ot* [The Sages: Doctrines and Beliefs], rev. ed., Jerusalem, 1971 = Urbach, *The Sages.* (For an English version *see The Sages, Their Concepts and Beliefs,* I. Abrahams trans., Magnes Press, 2 vols., Jerusalem, 1975.)

——— *Ba'alei ha-Tosafot, Toledoteihem, Ḥibbureihem ve-Shittatam* [The Tosafists, Their History, Writings and Methodology], 2nd ed, Jerusalem, 1968 = Urbach, *Tosafot.*

Z. Warhaftig, (ed.); *Osef Piskei ha-Din Shel ha-Rabbanut ha-Rashit le-Ereẓ Yisra'el* [A Compilation of the Rulings of the Chief Rabbinate of the Land of Israel], 1950, = *Osef Piskei ha-Din.*

I.H. Weiss, *Dor Dor ve-Doreshav* [The Generations and Their Interpreters—A History of the Oral Law], 6th ed., Vilna, 1915 = Weiss, *Dor Dor ve-Doreshav*.

ABBREVIATIONS USED IN CITING RABBINIC WORKS AND SCHOLARLY LITERATURE

ad loc.	*ad locum,* "at the place," used after a citation to designate commentary on the passage cited
A.M.	*anno mundi,* "in the year [from the creation] of the world"
b.	ben, bar, "son of"—as in Simeon b. Gamaliel
Baḥ	*Bayit Ḥadash,* a commentary on *Tur* by Joel Sirkes.
B.C.E.	before the common era, equivalent of B.C.
ca.	*circa,* "approximately"
C.E.	common era, equivalent of A.D.
cf.	*confer,* "compare"
EH	*Even ha-Ezer,* part of the *Shulḥan Arukh*
EJ	Encyclopaedia Judaica
ET	*Enẓiklopedyah Talmudit* [Talmudic Encyclopedia]
ḤM	*Ḥoshen Mishpat,* part of the *Shulḥan Arukh*
HUCA	*Hebrew Union College Annual*
ibn	"son of," equivalent of "b." (which *see*)
id.	*idem,* "the same," used instead of repeating the immediately preceding citation
JJGL	*Jahrbuch für jüdische Geschichte und Literatur* [Jewish History and Literature Annual]
JJLG	*Jahrbuch der jüdisch-literarischen* Gesellschaft [Jewish Literary Society Annual]
JPS	The Jewish Publication Society
JQR	*Jewish Quarterly Review*
lit.	literally
loc. cit.	*loco citato,* "in the place [previously] cited"
M	Mishnah, used to designate a Mishnaic tractate
MGWJ	*Monatsschrift für Geschichte und Wissenschaft des Judenthums* [Monthly for the History and Science of Judaism]
ms., mss.	manuscript(s)
MT	*Mishneh Torah* (Maimonides' code)

n.	note
nn.	notes
OḤ	*Oraḥ Ḥayyim,* part of the *Shulḥan Arukh*
op. cit.	*opere citato,* "in the work [previously] cited"
R.	Rabbi, Rav, or Rabban, used in the present work for the Talmudic Sages
Resp.	Responsa
Sema	*Sefer Me'irat Einayim* by Joshua Falk
Semag	*Sefer Miẓvot Gadol* by Moses of Coucy
Semak	*Sefer Miẓvot Katan* by Isaac of Corbeil
Shakh	*Siftei Kohen* by Shabbetai b. Meir ha-Kohen
Sh. Ar.	*Shulḥan Arukh*
"Shum"	Hebrew acrostic for the communities of Speyer, Worms, and Mainz
s.v.	*sub verbo, sub voce,* "under the word," designating the word or expression to which commentary is appended. Equivalent of Hebrew "d.h." (*dibbur ha-matḥil*)
Taz	*Turei Zahav* by David b. Samuel ha-Levi
TB	Talmud Bavli [Babylonian Talmud]
TJ	Talmud Yerushalmi [Jerusalem Talmud, sometimes called Palestine Talmud]
Tur	*Sefer ha-Turim* by Jacob b. Asher
v.l.	*varia lectio,* pl. *variae lectiones,* "variant reading(s)"
YD	*Yoreh De'ah,* part of the *Shulḥan Arukh*

ABBREVIATIONS USED IN CITING MODERN LEGAL MATERIALS

A.2d	Atlantic Reports, Second Series (U.S.)
A.B.A.J.	*American Bar Association Journal*
A.C.	Law Reports Appeal Cases (Eng.)
All E.R.	All England Law Reports, formerly All England Law Reports Annotated
Atk.	Atkyns English Chancery Reports (1736–1755)
Ch.	Chancery (Eng.)
C.L.R.	Current Law Reports (cases decided during the British Mandate)
Colum. L. Rev.	*Columbia Law Review*
D.C. App.	District of Columbia Court of Appeals
DK	*Divrei ha-Keneset* [The Knesset Record]
E.R., Eng. Rep.	English Reports, Full Reprint (1220–1865)
Ex.	Court of Exchequer (Eng.)
Harv. L. Rev.	*Harvard Law Review*
H.L.C.	Clark's House of Lords Cases (Eng.)
I.C.L.Q.	*International and Comparative Law Quarterly*
I.S.C.J.	Israel Supreme Court Judgments
Jur.	Jurist Reports (Eng., 18 vols.)
K.B.	King's Bench (Eng.)
L.J.	Law Journal
L.J.Q.B.	Law Journal Reports, New Series, Queen's Bench (Eng.)
L.Q.	Law Quarterly
L. Rev.	Law Review
Md. L. Rev.	*Maryland Law Review*
Minn. L. Rev.	*Minnesota Law Review*
Mod.	Modern Reports, 1669–1732 (Eng.)
N.E.2d	Northeastern Reporter, Second Series (U.S.)
Ohio App.	Ohio (Intermediate) Appellate Court reports

Osef Piskei ha-Din	a collection of rabbinical court decisions compiled by Zeraḥ Warhaftig
P.D.	*Piskei Din,* Israel Supreme Court Reports
P.D.R.	*Piskei Din Rabbaniyyim,* Israel Rabbinical Court Reports
P.L.R.	Palestine Law Reports (Court Decisions during the British Mandate)
P.M.	*Pesakim Meḥoziyyim,* Israel District Court Reports
Q.B.	Queen's Bench (Eng.)
SCJ	Supreme Court Judgments Annotated (Reports of cases in the Supreme Court of the Land of Israel during the British Mandate)
Vand. L. Rev.	*Vanderbilt Law Review*
Wis. L. Rev.	*Wisconsin Law Review*
W.L.R.	Weekly Law Reports (Eng.)

ACRONYMS AND APPELLATIONS OF HALAKHIC AUTHORITIES

Alfasi	Isaac b. Jacob ha-Kohen of Fez, Rif
Asheri	Asher b. Jehiel, Rosh
Ba'al ha-Roke'aḥ	Eliezer b. Judah
Ba'al ha-Turim	Jacob b. Asher
Baḥ	Joel Sirkes
Ḥafeẓ Ḥayyim	Israel Meir ha-Kohen
Ha-Gra	Elijah b. Solomon Zalman (Gaon of Vilna)
Ha-Kala'i	Alfasi
Ḥakham Zevi	Zevi Hirsch b. Jacob Ashkenazi
Ḥatam Sofer	Moses Sofer
Ḥayyim Or Zaru'a	Hayyim b. Isaac
Ḥazon Ish	Abraham Isaiah Karelitz
Ḥida	Ḥayyim Joseph David Azulai
Mabit	Moses b. Joseph Trani
Maharaḥ	Ḥayyim b. Isaac, also known as Ḥayyim Or Zaru'a
Maharai	Israel Isserlein
Maharal of Prague	Judah Loew b. Beẓalel
Maharalbaḥ	Levi b. Ḥabib
Maharam Alashkar	Moses b. Isaac Alashkar
Maharam Alshekh	Moses b. Ḥayyim Alshekh
Maharam of Lublin	Meir b. Gedaliah of Lublin
Maharam Mintz	Moses b. Isaac Mintz
Maharam of Padua	Meir Katzenellenbogen
Maharam of Rothenburg	Meir b. Baruch of Rothenburg
Maharash Kastilaẓ	Simeon Kastilaẓ
Maharashdam	Samuel b. Moses Medina
Maharaẓ Chajes	Ẓevi Hirsch Chajes
Mahardakh	David ha-Kohen of Corfu
Maharḥash	Ḥayyim Shabbetai of Salonika

Mahari Bruna	Israel b. Ḥayyim Bruna
Mahari Caro	Joseph Caro, also known as Maran
Mahari Minẓ	Judah Minẓ
Mahari Weil	Jacob b. Judah Weil, also known as Maharyu
Maharibal	Joseph ibn Lev
Maharif	Jacob Faraji
Maharik	Joseph b. Solomon Colon
Maharikash	Jacob b. Abraham Castro
Maharil	Jacob b. Moses Moellin
Maharit	Joseph b. Moses Trani
Maharit Algazi	Yom Tov b. Israel Jacob Algazi
Maharitaẓ	Yom Tov b. Akiva Ẓahalon
Mahariẓ	Yeḥaiah (Yaḥya, Yiḥye) b. Joseph Ẓalaḥ (Saliḥ)
Maharsha	Samuel Eliezer b. Judah ha-Levi Edels
Maharshak	Samson b. Isaac of Chinon
Maharshakh	Solomon b. Abraham
Maharshal	Solomon b. Jehiel Luria
Maharsham	Shalom Mordecai b. Moses Schwadron
Maharyu	Jacob b. Judah Weil, also known as Mahari Weil
Malbim	Meir Leib b. Jehiel Michael
Maran	Joseph Caro, also known as Mahari Caro
Neẓiv (Naẓiv)	Naphtali Ẓevi Judah Berlin
Noda bi-Yehudah	Ezekiel b. Judah ha-Levi Landau
Rabad (Rabad I)	Abraham b. David (ibn Daud) of Posquières
Rabad (Rabad II)	Abraham b. David (ibn Daud) ha-Levi
Raban	Eliezer b. Nathan of Mainz
Rabi	Abraham b. Isaac of Narbonne
Radbaz	David ibn Zimra
Ralbag	Levi b. Gershom, Gersonides
Ralbaḥ	Levi ibn Ḥabib
Ramah	Meir Abulafia
Rambam	Moses b. Maimon, Maimonides
Ramban	Moses b. Naḥman, Naḥmanides
Ran	Nissim of Gerona (Gerondi)
Ranaḥ	Elijah b. Ḥayyim
Rash	Samson b. Abraham of Sens

Rashba	Solomon b. Abraham Adret
Rashbam	Samuel b. Meir
Rashbash	Solomon b. Simeon Duran
Rashbeẓ (Rashbaẓ)	Simeon b. Ẓemaḥ Duran
Rashi	Solomon b. Isaac of Troyes
Rav Za'ir	Chaim Tchernowitz
Raviah	Eliezer b. Joel ha-Levi
Redak (Radak)	David Kimḥi
Re'em	Elijah b. Abraham Mizraḥi; Eliezer b. Samuel of Metz
Re'iyah	Abraham Isaac ha-Kohen Kook
Rema	Moses Isserles
Remakh	Moses ha-Kohen of Lunel
Reshakh	Solomon b. Abraham, Maharshakh
Rezah	Zeraḥia ha-Levi Gerondi
Ri	Isaac b. Samuel, also known as Isaac the Elder
Ri Migash	Joseph ibn Migash
Riaz	Isaac b. Moses of Vienna; Isaiah b. Elijah of Trani
Ribash	Isaac b. Sheshet Perfet
Rid	Isaiah b. Mali di Trani the Elder
Rif	Isaac b. Jacob ha-Kohen, Alfasi
Ritba	Yom Tov b. Abraham Ishbili
Riẓag	Isaac ibn Ghayyat
Rogachover	Joseph Rozin (Rosen)
Rosh	Asher b. Jehiel, Asheri
Shadal (Shedal)	Samuel David Luzzatto
Tashbaẓ (Tashbeẓ)	Samson b. Ẓadok
Tukh	Eliezer of Touques
Yaveẓ	Jacob Emden
Yaveẓ of North Africa	Jacob ibn Ẓur of Morocco

TRANSLITERATION GUIDE

LETTERS

NAME OF LETTER	SYMBOL	TRANSLITERATION	SOUND	REMARKS
aleph	א	not transliterated		
bet	בּ	b	as in *b*oy	
vet	ב	v	as in *v*alue	
gimmel	גּ, ג	g	as in *g*ate	no distinction between gimmel with *dagesh lene* and *gimmel* without *dagesh*
dalet	דּ, ד	d	as in *d*ance	no distinction between *dalet* with *dagesh lene* and *dalet* without a *dagesh*
he	ה	h	as in *h*ome	
vav	ו	v	as in *v*alve	when used as a vowel, transliterated as "o" or "u"
zayin	ז	z	as in Zion	
ḥet	ח	ḥ	ch as in German *Achtung*	no English equivalent
tet	ט	t	t as in *t*ag	
yod	י	y or i	y as in *y*es or when i, like ee in sh*ee*n	y except when vowel, and then "i"
kaf	כּ	k	k as in *k*ing or c as in *c*ome	English has no equivalent for the difference between *ḥet* and *khaf* in Hebrew
khaf	כ,ך	kh	like ch as in *Achtung*	

LETTERS (*continued*)

NAME OF LETTER	SYMBOL	TRANSLITERATION	SOUND	REMARKS
lamed	ל	l	l as in *l*ean	
mem	מ,ם	m	m as in *m*other	
nun	נ,ן	n	n as in *n*o	
samekh	ס	s	s as in *s*ing	
ayin	ע	not transliterated		indicated by apostrophe
pe	פּ	p	p as in *p*ost	
fe	פ,ף	f	f as in *f*ine	
ẓade / sade / tsade	צ,ץ	z	like ts in fi*ts*	
kof	ק	k	like ck as in lo*ck*	
resh	ר	r	r as in *r*ain	may be rolled
shin	שׁ	sh	sh as in *sh*ine	
sin	שׂ	s	s as in *s*ong	
tav / taw	תּ / ת	t	t as in *t*ame	no distinction between *tav* with *dagesh lene* and *tav* without a *dagesh*

VOWELS

NAME OF VOWEL	SYMBOL (PLACED BELOW LETTER)	TRANSLITERATION	SOUND	REMARKS
kamatz / kameẓ / kamaẓ	ָ	a	like a in f*a*ther	if "long" kamaẓ
		o	like aw in l*aw*	if "short" kamaẓ
pataḥ	ַ	a	like a in f*a*ther	
ḥataf-pataḥ	ֲ	a	like a in *a*lignment	but no precise English equivalent

VOWELS (*continued*)

NAME OF VOWEL	SYMBOL (PLACED BELOW LETTER)	TRANSLITERATION	SOUND	REMARKS
ẓere / tsere	..	e or ei	like *ai* as in pl*ai*n, ei as in "v*ei*n"	except *bet* not *beit*
segol	∵	e	like e in l*e*d	
ḥataf-segol	∵:	e	like second e in heg*e*mony	
sheva	:	e	like e in sh*e*nanigan	*sheva na* is transliterated, *sheva naḥ* is not
ḥirek / ḥireq	.	i	between ee in sh*ee*n and i in p*i*n	
holam	וֹ, ˙	o	o as in h*o*me	dot placed above letter
kubbuẓ / kibbuẓ	וּ, ⋱	u	u as in bl*ue*	

Notes

1. *Dagesh forte* is represented by doubling the letter, except that the letter *shin* is not doubled.

2. The definite article "ha" is followed by a hyphen, but although the following letter always has a *dagesh forte* in the Hebrew, it is not doubled in the transliteration. The transliteration of the definite article starts with a small "h" except in the name of Rabbi Judah Ha-Nasi, Rosh Ha-Shanah (the holiday) and the beginning of a sentence or title.

3. An apostrophe between vowels indicates that the vowels do not constitute a diphthong, but each is to have its separate pronunciation.

PART TWO (*continued*)

The Legal Sources of Jewish Law:

SECTION 2

Legislation, Custom, Precedent, and Legal Reasoning

Chapter 13
LEGISLATION: INTRODUCTION

I. THE RELATIONSHIP BETWEEN MIDRASH AND LEGISLATION

We now examine the second legal source of Jewish law—legislation.

In our discussion of midrash and exegesis, we have seen how the halakhic authorities used the various methods of interpretation to develop the different areas of the law and to solve new problems that arose as a result of changes in social and economic conditions and in the ethics of public and private life. However, midrash alone was not always adequate to supply what was missing or to make required modifications in the law. By the very nature of midrash, its creative power is confined by the content and context of the Scriptural verse or halakhic rule being interpreted.

How did the Jewish legal system solve problems that were beyond the reach of midrash? To a large and significant extent, it did so by means of legislation promulgated by halakhic authorities and other competent bodies. Unlike laws derived through midrash, legislation, as the halakhic authorities recognized, was not to be viewed as the discovery of the deeper content of a Biblical verse or a halakhic rule. To the contrary, legislative enactments were understood to be introducing something entirely new into the *Halakhah*—something not capable of being derived from any preexisting authoritative legal precept.

The law produced by midrash, according to the internal classification of the halakhic system, is "Biblical" (*mi-de-oraita,* lit. "from the Torah"),[1]

1. This is the view of most halakhic authorities, except for instances of *asmakhta,* which are held by all authorities to be rabbinic. *See supra* pp. 209–210.

whereas the law created through legislation is "rabbinic" (*mi-de-rabbanan,* lit. "from the rabbis") or "scribal" (*mi-divrei soferim,* lit. "from the words of Scribes")[2]—directly fashioned by the halakhic authorities of each era. Nevertheless, this dichotomy between Biblical and rabbinic law does not impair the unity and the uniform character of the single *corpus juris* into which Biblical law and rabbinic law have been fused. In fact, as we have seen, the halakhic authorities sometimes gave their enactments even greater force than Biblical law.[3] However, this dichotomy, which is essentially between laws whose source is midrash and laws whose source is legislation, highlights the essentially different ways these two legal sources operate as creative impulses in the *Halakhah.*

II. LEGISLATION IN JEWISH LAW AND IN OTHER LEGAL SYSTEMS

Before examining the nature of legislation in the Jewish legal system, it will be helpful to review the characteristics of legislation in other contemporary legal systems.

Legislation is defined as the promulgation of principles and rules by a competent, authoritative body for the purpose of giving those principles and rules binding legal effect.[4] There are two basic categories of legislation: supreme legislation and subordinate legislation.[5] Supreme legislation includes those legal principles and rules (whether "constitutional," "basic," or "ordinary") promulgated by the highest legislative authority of the legal system. Subordinate legislation consists of those legal principles and rules enacted by an agency of inferior rank that is subject to the system's highest legislative authority.[6]

The legal situation in the State of Israel provides a good illustration of this distinction. A law approved by the Knesset (the Israeli parliament) is supreme legislation, since the Knesset is the highest legislative body in the legal system of the state. However, an enactment by a government minister pursuant to the authority delegated to him by the Knesset to issue regulations within the scope of a particular statute is subordinate legislation, since

2. *See supra* p. 207 n. 88 and accompanying text.

3. *See supra* pp. 215–216.

4. *See* Salmond, pp. 115ff.

5. *Id.* at 116–124. *See also* C.K. Allen, *Law in the Making,* 7th ed. 1964, pp. 426ff., 531ff.

6. The subordinate agency may be more than one level below the highest legislative authority. *See* B. Akzin, *Torat ha-Mishtarim* [Theories of Government], I, pp. 102ff., 120ff., 144ff.; Salmond, pp. 83ff.

the minister's authority to issue regulations is subordinate to that of the Knesset. This illustration also shows how the subordinate legislator acquires the competence to promulgate his enactments. This competence is conferred by the delegation of power, *i.e.*, by a grant of power from the highest authority, by which a subordinate authority is authorized to promulgate legally binding rules and principles within certain limits.

An additional conclusion follows from this distinction. A legal rule enacted by the supreme legislative authority can be repealed or modified only by the very authority that enacted it—in our example, the Knesset itself. By contrast, a legal rule contained in subordinate legislation can be repealed not only by the subordinate legislator, such as the minister who promulgated the rule, but also by the supreme legislative body pursuant to whose delegated authority the subordinate legislation was enacted.[7]

This review of the general nature of legislation is helpful in understanding the similarities and differences between legislation in Jewish law and legislation in other legal systems. The Written Law (*Torah she-bi-khetav*—Scripture) is the supreme legislation of the Jewish legal system. It is the written "constitution" of Jewish law, having its ultimate source in divine revelation.[8] Every other legislated rule is subordinate legislation because the legislators derive their legislative power not from inherent authority but pursuant to formal delegation of that power—an express authorization conferred by the supreme legislation, namely, the Written Law.[9]

The basic distinction between supreme and subordinate legislation is thus common to both Jewish law and legal systems in general. However, along with this general similarity, there is also an essential difference that goes to the root of the unique character of Jewish law: in other legal systems, supreme and subordinate legislation function side by side continuously, but in the Jewish legal system, the supreme legislation is the product of divine revelation—a one-time supreme legislation that authorizes sub-

7. Salmond, pp. 83ff.; and *see* Allen, *supra* n. 5 at 531ff.

8. For further discussion of the basic norm of Jewish law, *see supra* pp. 232–234 and notes thereto.

9. The Written Law constitutes both the constitution and the supreme legislation. Legislation by the halakhic authorities is classified as subordinate legislation because their legislative power derives from authority delegated by the Written Law; *see* the text immediately following. Similarly, legislation by other bodies in Jewish law, *e.g.*, communal enactments, is classified as subordinate legislation on a level with enactments by the halakhic authorities. Although communal enactments are subject to review by the halakhic authorities in regard to a number of matters (*see infra* pp. 751–778), they should not be viewed as subordinate to legislation by the halakhic authorities, since the power to adopt communal enactments does not derive from a delegation by the halakhic authorities. The community's power to legislate, like the power of the halakhic authorities, is derived by various analogies and principles based on the Written Law. *See infra* pp. 488–489.

ordinate legislation. Subordinate legislation thus began after the supreme legislation ended; and all legislation promulgated after the revelation of the supreme legislation has been subordinate.

We have already discussed the one-time nature of the supreme legislation in the Jewish legal system, as well as the everlasting authority of that legislation that follows from the fact that a provision contained in the supreme legislation can be repealed or modified only by the same authority that enacted it.[10] Now that the Torah has been given, it is no longer in the heavens; and even the prophet who brings the word of God to humankind can no longer introduce anything new by either adding to or subtracting from the Biblical commandments. As Maimonides put it:[11]

> The Torah is clear and explicit that it is a commandment that stands forever and to all eternity, not subject to modification, subtraction, or addition; for it is written: "Be careful to observe everything which I enjoin upon you; neither add to it nor take away from it."[12] It is also written: "[What is concealed belongs to the Lord our God, but] as to what has been revealed, it is for us and our children forever to carry out all the provisions of this Torah."[13] This teaches that we are commanded to carry out the provisions of the Torah forever. It is also written: "It is a law for all time throughout the generations . . ."[14] and "It is not in heaven."[15] We thus learn that a prophet may not introduce anything new from this time, . . . inasmuch as He, blessed be His Name, commanded Moses that this commandment to us and our children is everlasting, and God, unlike man, does not speak falsely.

From this premise—that all of the provisions of the Written Law, the supreme legislation, are the product of a unique event and are everlasting—the conclusion follows that the part of the Written Law that grants authority for subordinate legislation is likewise everlasting and cannot be reversed or modified.

In short, the Written Law is the supreme legislation of the Jewish legal system; the enactments of the halakhic authorities and of others competent to legislate are the subordinate legislation. The substance of the supreme legislation is fixed, perpetual, and beyond change; and the provision of the

10. *See supra* pp. 232–234, 241–242.

11. *MT*, Yesodei ha-Torah 9:1.

12. Deuteronomy 13:1.

13. *Id.* 29:28. The 1985 JPS *Tanakh* translates this verse: "Concealed acts concern the Lord our God; but with overt acts, it is for us and our children ever to apply all the provisions of this Teaching." Our translation is much closer to the rabbinic reading and is consistent with Maimonides' point.

14. Leviticus 23:14.

15. Deuteronomy 30:12.

supreme legislation delegating power to promulgate subordinate legislation, which took effect after the supreme legislation was revealed, is similarly fixed, perpetual, and beyond change. Thus, when we speak of legislation as one of the legal sources of Jewish law (*i.e.*, a source recognized in the Jewish legal system itself as an instrument for continued halakhic creativity and development), we refer, of course, to legislation by halakhic authorities and other competent legislators. Although such legislation is subordinate legislation, we refer to it, for convenience and brevity, simply as "legislation."[16]

III. THE SOURCE IN THE WRITTEN LAW FOR THE LEGISLATIVE POWER OF THE HALAKHIC AUTHORITIES

As has been stated, the legislative power of the halakhic authorities has its source in the delegation of power made to them in the Written Law, but precisely where in the Written Law did the Sages find this delegation of power? This question has been extensively discussed in the writings of the halakhic authorities and scholars of Jewish law. In this section, we review some of that discussion.

In the Talmud[17] there is a lengthy discussion of the laws of the holiday of *Hanukkah*. A *baraita* informs us of the time and background of the enactment of the Sages establishing the eight days of the *Hanukkah* holiday:

> The Rabbis taught: On the twenty-fifth day of the month of Kislev, the eight days of *Hanukkah* begin, during which one may not eulogize the dead nor fast. When the Greeks entered the Temple, they profaned all the oil kept there; and when the Hasmonean kingdom prevailed over them and defeated them, they searched and found only one cruse of oil intact with the seal of the high priest, and it contained only enough to burn for one day. A miracle occurred, and it burned for eight days. The next year, they proclaimed those days as holidays for psalms of praise and thanksgiving.[18]

In the discussion of the laws relating to *Hanukkah*, the Talmud states that the following blessing over the *Hanukkah* lights is to be recited: "[Praise be to You, O Lord our God], Who has sanctified us by His commandments

16. For further discussion of the distinction between supreme and subordinate legislation, *see infra* pp. 499–502, regarding the view of Maimonides as to the prohibition against adding to or subtracting from Biblical law, and *infra* pp. 536–538, on the question of when subordinate legislation is *ultra vires*, *i.e.*, exceeds the authority delegated by the supreme legislation.

17. TB Shabbat 21a–23b.

18. *Id.* 21b.

and commanded us to kindle the *Hanukkah* lights." At this point the Talmud asks:

> Where did He command us? [*I.e.*, how can it be said that *God* commanded the kindling of the *Hanukkah* lights when the holiday of *Hanukkah* has its source in an enactment of the Sages?] R. Avia said: "In the verse 'You must not deviate [from the verdict—Hebrew *davar,* lit. "thing," "word," or "matter"—that they announce to you . . .].'"[19] R. Nehemiah said: "In the verse 'Ask your father, he will inform you, your elders, they will tell you.'"[20]

R. Avia found the source for the legislative authority of the Sages in the passage in Deuteronomy,[21] already discussed several times,[22] which the halakhic authorities viewed as the basic source for their continuing authority to develop and create *Halakhah.* The passage reads:[23]

> You shall act in accordance with the instructions given you and the ruling handed down to you; you must not deviate from the verdict that they announce to you either to the right or to the left.

This verse, according to R. Avia and other Sages, refers to the power of the halakhic authorities to legislate.[24] R. Nehemiah found the source for the legislative prerogative of the halakhic authorities in another verse in Deuteronomy[25] as it had been interpreted in the *Sifrei:*[26]

> "Ask your father, he will inform you"—this refers to the prophets, as it was said: "Elisha saw it and he cried out: Oh, father, father!"[27] "[Ask] your elders, they will tell you"—these are the elders of whom it was said: "Gather for Me seventy of Israel's elders. . . ."[28]

19. Deuteronomy 17:11.
20. *Id.* 32:7.
21. *Id.* 17:8–11.
22. *See, e.g., supra* pp. 236–237, 242–243, 279–280.
23. Deuteronomy 17:11.
24. *See* TB Berakhot 19b, and also *Midrash Tannaim* to Deuteronomy 17:11 (p. 103). *Pesikta Rabbati,* sec. 3, begins: "Let no one say, 'I will not observe the commandments of the elders because they are not from the Torah!' To such a man [lit. "to him"] God says, 'No, my son! No, my son! You must fulfill everything they decree upon you, as it is written, ". . . in accordance with the instructions given you."'" To the same effect are the printed editions of *Tanḥuma,* Naso, 29, where the last part reads: "God said to them, 'My sons, you may not talk in this manner; rather, you must observe everything they decree upon you, as it is written, "You shall act in accordance with the instructions given you."'" *See also supra* pp. 243–247.
25. Deuteronomy 32:7.
26. *Sifrei,* Deuteronomy, Ha'azinu, sec. 310 (p. 351).
27. II Kings 2:12.
28. Numbers 11:16.

From these two sources, we learn that the Torah commanded undeviating obedience to the enactments of the elders, *i.e.,* the halakhic authorities, and therefore it is correct to recite the blessing stating that it was God "Who has . . . commanded us to kindle the *Hanukkah* lights."

The Sages found a special source in the Torah for their authority to promulgate *gezerot.*[29] Chapter 18 of Leviticus sets forth the proscriptions of incestuous relationships, such as with a mother, sister, or daughter. At the end of this chapter,[30] it is said: "You shall keep My charge [lit. "My safeguard"] not to engage in any of the abhorrent practices that were carried on before you, lest you defile yourselves through them: I am the Lord your God." This verse was interpreted as follows:[31]

> "You shall keep My charge"—preserve a safeguard for Me and guard My charge [*i.e.,* My laws]; this is an instruction to the court.

The halakhic authorities saw in this verse a directive obligating them from time to time to establish safeguards around the law laid down in the Torah,[32] *i.e.,* to add prohibitions[33] beyond those set forth in the Torah, when necessary to ensure adherence to a Biblical prohibition. For this reason, for example, the Sages forbade marriage between more distant relatives (*i.e.,* a mother's mother, a father's mother, etc.) than those prohibited in the Torah; and these relationships, prohibited by rabbinic authority but not by Biblical law, were termed "secondary" (*sheniyyot*).[34]

Maimonides and Naḥmanides also disagreed as to the source in the Written Law for the delegation of legislative power to the halakhic authorities. Their disagreement is reminiscent of the disagreement on the same

29. For a discussion of the terms *takkanah* and *gezerah, see infra* pp. 490–492.

30. Leviticus 18:30.

31. *Sifra,* Aḥarei Mot, 13:22 (p. 86b).

32. "Make a safeguard for My charge" (R. Kahana in TB Yevamot 21a).

33. Or some other manner of safeguard; *see, e.g.,* TB Mo'ed Katan 5a.

34. TB Yevamot 21a. On *sheniyyot, see infra* pp. 552–554. The statement in TB Yevamot 21a, "It is a rabbinic law, and the verse is merely *asmakhta,*" means only that the prohibited secondary relationships were not derived from the exegesis of the verse in question, since if they were so derived, they would be considered Biblical law. However, the verse does give general legislative authority similar to the authority granted (according to R. Avia) by the verse "You must not deviate from the verdict that they announce to you" (Deuteronomy 17:11). These prohibitions may be compared to the kindling of the *Hanukkah* lights: although enacted by the Sages, the prescribed blessing states, "Praise be to You, O Lord our God, Who has sanctified us by His commandments and has commanded us to kindle the *Hanukkah* lights." The basis for attributing the commandment to God is the general grant of authority contained in the verse "You must not deviate. . . ." Similarly, the prohibition of secondary relationships is rabbinic, but the authority for that proscription is conferred by the Written Law: "You shall keep My charge." For that verse (Leviticus 18:30) as a source for the legislative power of the halakhic authorities, *see* Maimonides, *Commentary on the Mishnah,* Introduction, quoted *infra* pp. 490–491.

subject between R. Avia and R. Nehemiah. According to Maimonides, the source for this delegation of power is a passage in chapter 17 of Deuteronomy:[35]

> The High Court (Sanhedrin) in Jerusalem is the main institution of the Oral Law. The members thereof are the fount of instruction; from them issue statutes and judgments to all Israel. . . .
>
> It is immaterial whether the direction given by them concerns the Oral Law, *i.e.*, matters learned by tradition [handed down from person to person going back to Moses at Sinai], or whether it concerns interpretations that seem correct to them as a result of deduction by means of any of the canons by which the Torah is interpreted, or whether it concerns decrees (*gezerot*), enactments (*takkanot*), and practices (*minhagot*)[36]—measures devised by them to serve as a fence around the law, and designed to meet the needs of the time. Obedience to the directions given by them in all of these three categories is a positive commandment, and whoever disregards any of them [also] transgresses a negative commandment.
>
> Scripture says: "In accordance with the instructions given you"—this refers to the enactments, decrees, and practices that they promulgate in order to strengthen religion and improve the social order. "And [in accordance with] the ruling handed down to you"—this refers to laws derived through interpretation by means of any of the canons by which Scripture is expounded. "From the verdict that they announce to you"—this refers to matters of tradition transmitted orally from person to person.[37]

The legislative authority conferred by the Torah upon the halakhic authorities is thus included in that portion of the Torah which lays down general principles for solving problems that will arise in the course of time. The methods prescribed in that portion of the Torah for solving such problems are: (a) finding the answer in transmitted law, *i.e.*, in oral tradition; (b) finding the answer through Biblical interpretation; and (c) finding the solution by means of legislation to "strengthen religion and improve the social order."

In contrast to Maimonides, Naḥmanides was of the opinion that chapter 17 of Deuteronomy pertains only to solving new problems through midrash or through oral tradition known to the court and does not authorize the enactment of legislation. According to Naḥmanides, the grant of authority to legislate is found in Deuteronomy 32:7:[38]

35. *MT*, Mamrim 1:1–2.

36. For the meaning of the term *minhagot* as used by Maimonides, *see infra* p. 491 and p. 493 n. 78.

37. *See also* Maimonides, *MT*, Introduction; *id.*, *Sefer ha-Mizvot*, Shoresh 1.

38. Naḥmanides, Glosses to Maimonides' *Sefer ha-Mizvot*, Shoresh 1.

> The prohibition contained in the verse "You must not deviate . . ."[39] refers only to rulings based on Biblical interpretation . . . or on a rule contained in the oral tradition from Moses. . . . This is what is referred to in the verse, "If a case is too baffling for you to decide, be it a controversy over homicide [or] civil law [lit. "between blood and blood, between law and law"] . . . ,"[40] *i.e.*, a matter unclear to them, concerning which they differ as to what laws and prohibitions . . . the Torah prescribes. Whoever refuses to obey the decisions of the High Court of his generation and follows his own opinion violates these affirmative and negative commandments. Even if the court itself is divided on the matter, the majority is to be followed. . . . The majority view is the rule that is commanded by the Torah. . . . For the Torah was given to us by Moses our teacher (of blessed memory) in writing, and it is apparent that there will not be complete agreement on all the newly arising principles. Therefore, God decreed that we should obey the High Court in all its pronouncements, whether the judges received their interpretation from tradition or reached their conclusion on the basis of their own opinion as to the meaning and intent of the Torah; for He has given us the Torah and commanded obedience to it as construed by them.
>
> However, the *gezerot* and the *takkanot* that the Sages enacted as a safeguard for the Torah and a fence around it have only an indirect support in this [Scriptural] injunction. . . . The precepts introduced by the Sages or the prophets, such as the kindling of the *Hanukkah* lights and the reading of the Scroll of Esther [on the *Purim* holiday], do not have their authorization in the verse "If a case is too baffling for you to decide . . . ," but in the verse "Ask your father, he will inform you, your elders, they will tell you," which is a command that all Israel acknowledge the [legislative] authority of the elders.

It is thus clear that even though the halakhic authorities disagreed as to what specific verse constitutes the source of delegation of legislative authority in the Jewish legal system, there is consensus that the grant of such authority derives from Scripture, Jewish law's "constitution."[41]

39. Deuteronomy 17:11.

40. *Id.* 17:8.

41. According to both Maimonides and Naḥmanides, the delegation of authority is contained in the Written Law. This proposition is not affected by the difference of opinion between them concerning the question of whether transgression of a rabbinic law is a transgression of both a positive commandment ("You shall act in accordance with the instructions") and a negative or prohibitory commandment ("You must not deviate"). Maimonides answered this question, Yes (*MT*, Mamrim 1:1–2), and Naḥmanides, No (Glosses to *Sefer ha-Mizvot*, Shoresh 1). That difference relates to the essential nature of positive and negative commandments in the *Halakhah*. *See* G. Alon's theory (*Meḥkarim*, II, p. 239) regarding the opinion of the early Sages as to their authority to legislate; this theory requires further study. It should be pointed out that as early a work as the *Sifra*, *supra* n. 31, attributes the legislative authority of the Sages to Leviticus 18:30. In any event, it is clear that the *amoraim* derived the authority to legislate from the Written Law, just as they established

IV. LEGISLATIVE AUTHORITY OF OTHER COMPETENT BODIES AND THE SOURCE OF THAT AUTHORITY

Legislative authority was conferred by the Torah upon "the priests the Levites, and the judge of that time,"[42] *i.e.*, the halakhic authorities and the courts in every era.[43] In our later discussion of legislation in its various periods, we review various enactments attributed to the Biblical patriarchs and leaders of the nation, and study the wide-ranging legislative activity of the Great Assembly, the Sanhedrin, the later patriarchs (*nesi'im*), the courts, and the halakhic authorities in their respective historical periods.[44]

Legislative power in Jewish law is also vested in other authorized bodies. The root and origin of legislative power in agencies other than the halakhic authorities is the royal prerogative, the "king's law,"[45] which includes the power to legislate in various areas of both civil and criminal law.[46] Ac-

---

guidelines and principles as to legislative authority in general (*see infra* pp. 505ff.). In this manner, this fundamental concept crystallized and became accepted in the halakhic system.

42. *See* Deuteronomy 17:9.

43. According to Naḥmanides, *supra* n. 38, this is also the meaning of the term "elders" (*zekenim*) in Deuteronomy 32:7. For further discussion of the prerogative of the halakhic authorities in all periods, *see supra* pp. 266–267.

44. *See infra* pp. 545ff. There is a disagreement among halakhic authorities as well as academic scholars as to whether legislative authority was vested only in the highest court of each generation and only in the place where that court had its seat, such as the Sanhedrin at its seat and, later, the patriarch and his court at the place where the patriarch lived (Z.H. Chajes, *Torat ha-Nevi'im*, s.v. Lo tasur, pp. 97–111; Halevy, *Dorot*, II, pp. 46ff.), or whether "each halakhic authority and his court could issue decrees and adopt enactments, which, if they achieved broad recognition, became authoritative" (H. Albeck, "Ha-Sanhedrin u-Nesi'ah" [The Sanhedrin and its Patriarch], *Zion*, VIII, p. 169; *id.*, Commentary on M Eduyyot 1:5, and Hashlamot, p. 476). *See also* H.D. Mantel, *Studies in the History of the Sanhedrin*, pp. 80ff., and *infra* p. 501 n. 31.

An interesting comment by Rashi, Bava Meẓi'a 96b, s.v. Nim'alu bet din, also deserves mention. The Talmud there discusses the enactment adopted in Usha that if a woman sells her *melog* property during the lifetime of her husband, her husband can recover it from the purchaser, since the husband has the status of a purchaser of his wife's property (for a discussion of this subject, *see infra* pp. 568–569). The issue was, Who is guilty of sacrilege (*me'ilah*) when a husband obtains personal benefit from money inherited by his wife and consecrated to Temple use, but he is unaware that the money had been consecrated and he has received it by operation of law? One of the possibilities mentioned in the discussion, namely, that "the court is guilty of sacrilege," was explained by Rashi as follows:

> The members of the Jewish court of that generation [in which the sacrilege occurs] are responsible for the sacrilege because no legal enactments could exist without them; and it is on their authority that all previously enacted legislation continues to apply in their times. It is therefore as though they themselves enacted the legislation transferring [the property] to him, thus profaning the Temple's property.

See Z.H. Chajes, Novellae to Bava Meẓi'a, *ad loc.*

45. Deuteronomy 17:14–20; I Samuel ch. 8.

46. *See* TB Sanhedrin 20b, 48b; Maimonides, *MT*, Melakhim chs. 3–4 and 5:1–3; Gezelah va-Avedah 5:9–18; Roẓe'aḥ u-Shemirat ha-Nefesh 2:4; Sanhedrin 14:2, 18:6; Z.H.

cording to Naḥmanides, this legislative power of the king is conferred by a verse in the Torah.[47] Such legislation is promulgated by the governing authority; but the Sages viewed the acts of the king as being done in the name of the entire people, since "the leader of the generation is the entire generation"[48] and the king's "heart is the heart of the entire Israelite community."[49]

Legislation by the public and its representatives first appears in the early laws enacted by "the townspeople," and there is also evidence of an additional category of legislation by which various occupational groups governed their internal affairs.[50] There is an essential difference between legislation by the public and legislation by the halakhic authorities, both as to the persons affected and the nature of the subject matter. Legislation by the halakhic authorities is directed to all the people—the entire nation—whereas legislation by the townspeople, and even more so by occupational groups, is limited to the inhabitants of the town or the members of the

---

Chajes, *Torat ha-Nevi'im,* ch. 7, "The Law of the King of Israel" (pp. 43–49). *See also supra* pp. 55–57.

47. Leviticus 27:29. The verse is susceptible to different translations. The 1985 JPS *Tanakh* version ("No human being who has been proscribed can be ransomed; he shall be put to death") is not the reading of Naḥmanides, who read the verse as meaning, "Any proscribed thing that has been proscribed by man shall not be redeemed; whoever violates the proscription shall be put to death." Naḥmanides (*ad loc.*) interpreted "proscribed by man" as referring to the Sanhedrin or the king:

> From this verse it follows that if any king of Israel or the great Sanhedrin . . . declare[s] a ban on a city they are warring against or on anything else, whoever transgresses that ban is subject to the death penalty. That was the crime of the men of Jabesh-Gilead and Jonathan, to whom his father said, "Thus and more may God do: You shall be put to death, Jonathan!" [I Samuel 14:44]; because on what other basis than this verse did they incur liability to capital punishment? Similarly, this was Jephthah's mistake regarding his daughter [Judges chs. 11–12]. He thought that just as the death penalty is imposed for violation of a ban proclaimed by the leader of Israel on pain of death, so too a vow in time of war to make a human sacrifice of one or more persons must be carried out according to its terms. He [Jephthah] did not know that the ban of a king or the Sanhedrin applies to rebels in order to destroy them, or to anyone else who transgresses the enactments of the king or Sanhedrin; but Heaven forfend that the ban should make eligible to be a burnt-offering something that is unfit for that purpose!

Compare with this limitation on the legislative authority of the king, Maimonides, *MT,* Gezelah va-Avedah 5:9–18; and *see infra* pp. 751–778 as to review of communal enactments by the halakhic authorities to ensure that the enactments do not violate the principles of justice and equity.

48. *Numbers Rabbah* 19:17.

49. Maimonides, *MT,* Melakhim 3:6.

50. *See Tosefta* Bava Meẓi'a 11:23–26; parts of this *tosefta* are quoted in TB Bava Batra 8b and other places. *See infra* pp. 679–681.

particular group.[51] It is a fair assumption that such limited legislation was also restricted in subject matter to civil-financial regulations, such as the fixing of food prices and laborers' wages, and the regulation of public services in the town or of the internal affairs of the occupational group.[52] By contrast, legislation by the halakhic authorities encompasses all the branches and subject areas of the entire halakhic system.

In the Talmudic period, legislation by the townspeople and by occupational groups was a relatively insignificant part of the corpus of legislation in Jewish law;[53] legislation in the various areas of the law, including civil law, was enacted by the authorized central bodies. However, by the tenth century C.E., and thereafter, there no longer existed a single central authority for the entire Jewish people. Local centers arose in various diasporas, and the power of local Jewish communities increased. As a result, the importance of communal legislation (termed *takkanot ha-kahal* [communal enactments] or *haskamot ha-kahal* [communal agreements]) increased and expanded; and this type of legislation became a widespread and powerful factor in Jewish law. The geographical area to which legislation applied extended, at times, to associations of communities that included a substantial number of local communities and sometimes even entire countries;[54] and the scope of the subject matter of legislation included all branches of civil, criminal, and public law, leaving only matters of *issur* (religious law) as the exclusive domain of the halakhic authorities.[55]

Beginning with this period, the halakhic authorities dealt extensively with the basis of the authority to enact binding communal legislation. The major conceptual-legal rationale for the authority to enact communal legislation was the analogy whereby "the majority in each community stands in the same relationship to each member of the community as the High Court stood to all Israel." From this analogy followed the legal principle of *hefker ẓibbur hefker* (the community has the authority to expropriate property), parallel to the principle of *hefker bet din hefker* (the court has the authority to expropriate property).[56] Thus, the same principle served as the

51. Legislation by the king, of course, unlike communal or occupational legislation, was directed to the entire populace.

52. *See* sources *supra* n. 50. Y. Baer, "Ha-Yesodot ha-Historiyyim Shel ha-Halakhah" [The Historical Foundations of the *Halakhah*], *Zion,* XVII, pp. 24ff., argues that various provisions of civil law originated in legislation by the townspeople; *see infra* p. 1074 n. 151.

53. As to the significance of the king's law and its impact on ancient Jewish law, it is difficult to arrive at conclusions that are more than speculation and conjecture. *See infra* pp. 551–554 as to the enactments by Joshua and David.

54. *See infra* p. 672.

55. Occasionally, the community does have authority to adopt enactments that affect matters of *issur. See infra* pp. 707–712.

56. *See Resp. Rashba,* IV, #142; V, #126; *see also infra* pp. 699–707. and n. 88.

source for the legislative power of both the communal and the halakhic authorities.

Communal legislation was extensively discussed in halakhic literature from the eleventh century C.E. on; and one of the central tasks was the development of a method for maintaining compatibility between the goal and spirit of the communal enactments—even when they conflicted with some particular rule of Jewish law—and the objectives and general principles of Jewish law.[57] This communal legislation, to which a chapter is devoted later in this work,[58] is one of the major phenomena in the long course of Jewish law; and, along with the legislation of the halakhic authorities, it contributed to the solution of many fundamental problems that confronted Jewish law in the many Jewish diasporas.

As communal legislation expanded in applicability and scope, the legislation of the halakhic authorities contracted in these same respects. There was no longer a central spiritual authority, such as in the Land of Israel and later in Babylonia, which held sway over the entire Jewish diaspora during a span of time that extended into most of the geonic period. Consequently, even the legislation of the halakhic authorities was no longer directed to the entire Jewish people but only to the Jews in a particular center, such as Germany or Spain. Thus, from the tenth century C.E., legislation by the halakhic authorities was also local legislation, and the reach of its binding authority was limited to a particular center and at times to an even smaller area.[59]

A similar process also constricted the scope of the subject matter of legislation by the halakhic authorities. From the end of the geonic period, the view began to be expressed by some distinguished authorities that after the completion of the Talmud the legislative competence of the halakhic authorities in the area of family law was limited to monetary matters and did not extend to enactments affecting the validity of marriages and divorces. Geographical dispersion to different centers and communities gave rise to the fear that the adoption of different and inconsistent enactments in such a sensitive area as the validity of marriage and divorce would seriously undermine the stability and sanctity of the Jewish family; beginning with the thirteenth century, this restrictive view with regard to the legislative competence of the halakhic authorities in the area of marriage and divorce became increasingly accepted.[60]

57. This problem often arises in connection with the relationship of various creative sources in Jewish law to the objectives and general principles of Jewish law. *See supra* pp. 57, 72–73 and *infra* pp. 942–944.

58. *See infra* pp. 678ff.

59. *See infra* pp. 668–675.

60. *See infra* pp. 846–879.

The two agencies of legislation in this period—the halakhic authorities and the lay community—continued their wide-ranging legislative activity, often in concert, until the eighteenth century. The beginning of the Emancipation of Jews in modern times marked a critical turning point in legislative as well as other creative activity in Jewish law. With the end of Jewish autonomy in general, and of Jewish juridical autonomy in particular, there was no longer the same demand for Jewish law to provide the solution of actual legal problems arising out of everyday life, and Jewish legislation inevitably decreased to the point where it virtually disappeared. A limited renewal of legislative activity in the period from the 1920s to the 1950s did occur as a consequence of enactments of the Chief Rabbinate in the Land of Israel. However, legislative activity ceased almost completely after that time, and many matters in Jewish civil and public law, as well as some fundamental problems in family law, still await their sorely needed solution through the use of legislation in Jewish law.[61]

V. EXPLANATION OF TERMS

A. *Takkanah* and *Gezerah*

Halakhic legislation is sometimes called *takkanah* and sometimes *gezerah*. Many halakhic authorities and scholars of Jewish law have grappled with the questions, What is the difference between a *takkanah* and a *gezerah*, and what is the sphere of operation of each? It is difficult to arrive at a clear and precise delineation of the form and subject matter of the legislation denoted by each of these terms.[62]

Maimonides' definition of these two terms is as follows:[63]

> The fourth category consists of the rules of law that the prophets and the halakhic authorities of each generation established for the purpose of erecting a fence and protection for the Torah, and that God commanded us in general terms to enact when He said, "You shall keep My charge."[64] According to the oral tradition this means "make a safeguard for My charge."[65] These [rules] the Sages term *gezerot*.
>
> The fifth category consists of the rules of law, promulgated as a result of

61. *See infra* pp. 878–879, 1807–1809.

62. *See* M.A. Bloch, *Sha'arei Torat ha-Takkanot* [On Legislative Enactments], Vienna-Budapest, 1879–1906 (hereinafter, *Sha'arei*), I, 1st part, Introduction, par. 1.

63. *Commentary on the Mishnah*, Introduction, following the Hebrew trans. of Y. Kafaḥ, Jerusalem, 1963, p. 12. Maimonides divided Talmudic literature into five categories, of which the fourth is *gezerot* and the fifth *takkanot*. *See further* Maimonides, *MT*, Introduction.

64. Leviticus 18:30.

65. TB Yevamot 21a.

> investigation into the ordering of human relationships, that neither add to nor subtract from the laws of the Torah, as well as laws that promote the public welfare in matters of faith. All these laws are termed by the Sages *takkanot* and *minhagot.*[66] It is absolutely forbidden to violate them, since the entire nation agreed to them. . . . There are innumerable *takkanot* mentioned in the Talmud and the Mishnah, some dealing with ritual practice and others with civil law matters.

According to Maimonides' definition, the term *gezerot* includes directives designed to keep the individual at a distance from a prohibited act, to "build a fence" around the Torah. These are directives that seek to prevent a particular act. On the other hand, the term *takkanot* refers to those directives that are intended to impose an obligation to act for the advancement of communal life and the promotion of the public welfare. These are directives that create an obligation to perform a particular act.

The following illustrates this distinction:[67]

> Simeon b. Shataḥ enacted (*tikken*) [the writing of] the *ketubbah* for the wife,[68] and imposed (*gazar*) ritual impurity for metal utensils [*i.e.*, he decreed a *gezerah* imposing ritual impurity in certain circumstances on metal utensils].

With regard to the law concerning the *ketubbah*, the term used is *tikken*—a *takkanah* was enacted. With regard to ritual impurity, the term used is *gazar*—a *gezerah* was decreed.

However, this distinction is not always observed. When we examine Talmudic literature, we find that the Sages did not always use the terms *takkanah* and *gezerah* precisely in accord with this distinction.[69] The statements of the *amoraim* are particularly imprecise in this respect. A discussion in Tractate *Shabbat* contains a striking example.[70] It speaks first of six cases of doubt (concerning ritual purity) as to which *takkanot* were enacted in Usha; and subsequently, the discussion with regard to the same matter refers to a *gezerah* having been decreed in Usha.[71]

66. As to the term *minhagot*, *see infra* p. 493 n. 78.

67. TB Shabbat 14b.

68. For a discussion of this enactment, *see infra* pp. 559–561.

69. *See, e.g.*, M Gittin 4:2: "Originally, he [the husband] would appear before [lit. "convene"] a court at another place and cancel it [*i.e.*, the bill of divorcement he had sent his wife]. Rabban Gamaliel the Elder enacted [*hitkin*, "made a *takkanah*"] that, in order to promote the public welfare, this should not be done."

70. TB Shabbat 15b.

71. For further examples, *see* TB Kiddushin 17b: "Rava said: 'Under the law of the Torah, a gentile converted to Judaism does not inherit from his father . . . , but by rabbinic law he does. . . . It is an enactment (*gezerah*) that the Sages adopted lest he revert to his former ways'"; similarly TB Gittin 36a: ". . . the Sages enacted (*tekkinu*) that [the debt] should be canceled, in commemoration of the sabbatical year."

However, the amoraic use of the terms *gezerah shema* and *gezerah atu*, which are to be

It may therefore be said that, in the main, the term *gezerah* denotes legislation prohibiting the performance of a particular act that the Torah does not prohibit; the objective of a *gezerah* is to extend a prohibition established in the Torah, in order to decrease the likelihood that the Torah's prohibition will be violated. *Takkanah,* on the other hand, generally denotes an enactment that imposes a duty to perform a particular act for the benefit and welfare of the community or any of its members.[72] These general rules, however, do not always hold.

B. *Tenai Bet Din, Minhag*

At times, in Talmudic literature a *takkanah* is called *tenai bet din* ("stipulation" [or "requirement"] imposed by the court), or simply *tenai* ("stipulation" or "requirement"),[73] because the court imposes a particular requirement as a *takkanah.*[74] At times, a *takkanah* is called *minhag* (which usually means custom).[75] Sometimes, a particular *takkanah* is referred to as "an important *takkanah*" (*takkanah gedolah*) when the circumstances make it especially significant.[76]

In Talmudic literature, legislative activity is referred to by the verbs *gazar* (decreed), *tikken* or *hitkin* (enacted),[77] and sometimes also *hinhig* (established the practice).[78]

---

found in TB Bava Meẓi'a 47b, Eruvin 49a, and many other places, is irrelevant to our discussion, since the term *gezerah* there does not refer to legislation but means "lest." *See* B. De Vries, *Toledot ha-Halakhah ha-Talmudit* [A History of Talmudic *Halakhah*], pp. 97ff. For still another meaning of the term *gezerot, see* M Ketubbot 13:1 and H. Albeck's Hashlamot, *ad loc.*, p. 356; Gulak, *Yesodei,* IV, pp. 21–22. For more on the term *gezerah, see supra* p. 351.

72. Gulak (*Yesodei,* I, p. 23 n. 1), relying on Maimonides' Introduction to the *Commentary on the Mishnah,* summarized: "Therefore, in matters of *mamon* (monetary matters), *takkanot* were enacted, and in matters of *issur* (religious matters), *gezerot* were enacted." However, this is not precisely accurate inasmuch as Maimonides' own introduction to his *Commentary on the Mishnah,* when defining the term *takkanot,* said explicitly, "And [as to] those *takkanot* . . . some involve matters of *issur* and others involve matters of *mamon.*" *See further* Maimonides, *MT,* Mamrim 1:2, 2:5 and Albeck, *Mavo,* p. 25 n. 74.

73. *See, e.g.,* M Ketubbot 4:12; TB Bava Kamma 80b.

74. *See infra* p. 551 n. 28 and p. 574 n. 129 for an additional reason. Particular laws are sometimes referred to both as *takkanah* and *tenai bet din* (as in the case of the law with respect to the subjection of the husband's property to a lien as security for the payment of the wife's *ketubbah,* TB Ketubbot 82b and M Ketubbot 4:7). Sometimes a law is given the designations *takkanah, tenai bet din,* and *tenai.* With regard to Joshua's enactments, TB Eruvin 17a uses the terms *takkanta* and *tena'im.*

75. *See infra* n. 78.

76. *See, e.g.,* TB Gittin 36a; Bava Kamma 103b; Shevu'ot 45a and *Tosafot, ad loc.*, s.v. Gedolot. *See also infra* p. 617.

77. *See* Z.H. Chajes, *The Student's Guide Through the Talmud,* ch. 12 (end); *id., Imrei Binah,* par. 10; Bloch, *Sha'arei,* Introduction, par. 22. Bloch questions Chajes' distinction between the verbs *tikken* and *hitkin,* since various sources use both terms when citing the

same enactment. *See, e.g.,* TB Ketubbot 82b: ". . . until Simeon b. Shataḥ came and enacted (*ve-tikken*) that all [the husband's] possessions be subject to a lien for her [the wife's] *ketubbah*" (so also in TB Shabbat 14b, 16b). However, *Tosefta* Ketubbot 12:1 reads: ". . . Simeon b. Shataḥ enacted (*hitkin*) that the *ketubbah* should remain with the husband and that he should write for her, 'All the possessions I have are encumbered and guarantee your *ketubbah*.'"

78. *See, e.g.,* M Rosh ha-Shanah 4:1: ". . . After the Temple was destroyed, Rabban Johanan b. Zakkai enacted (*hitkin*) . . . ," and *Tosefta* Rosh ha-Shanah 2:9: "R. Joshua b. Korḥa said: 'Rabban Johanan b. Zakkai enacted [*hitkin;* ms. Erfurt has *hinhig* (established the practice of)] these things after the Temple was destroyed. . . .'" Thus, enactments are sometimes called *minhag*. *See also* TB Beẓah 4b: ". . . When the Samaritans caused trouble, they [the Sages] enacted (*hitkinu*] that messengers should go forth . . . ," concerning which the Talmud later states, "Give heed to the *minhag* of your ancestors. . . ." Similarly in TJ Ketubbot 1:5, 5b (1:5, 25c): "At first when they [the Roman government] decreed apostasy in Judea . . . , they [the Sages] enacted (*hitkinu*) that the bridegroom should cohabit with her [the bride] while she was still in her father's house. . . ." The Talmud then comments: "Although the decree compelling apostasy was annulled, the *minhag* was not abrogated." Enactments were frequently called *minhag* in the post-Talmudic period: *e.g.,* "The *minhag* was instituted by *geonim* and great authorities, and it is a fine *takkanah* . . ." (cited in B.M. Lewin, *Oẓar ha-Geonim,* Pesaḥim, Responsa, p. 6 n. 4). Also, Maimonides, *Commentary on the Mishnah,* Introduction (quoted *supra* n. 72) and *MT,* Mamrim 1:2 have: ". . . and these are the *gezerot, takkanot,* and *minhagot.*" *See further* B. Lipkin, "Samkhut ha-Ḥakikah Shel ha-Ẓibbur" [Communal Legislative Authority], *Sinai,* XXV, p. 234, and *see infra* pp. 822 n. 6, 885–888, for an explanation of the interchangeable use of *takkanah* and *minhag*.

Chapter 14
LEGISLATION: NATURE, OBJECTIVES, AND PRINCIPLES OF LEGISLATION BY THE HALAKHIC AUTHORITIES

I. THE SCOPE OF LEGISLATIVE ACTIVITY BY THE HALAKHIC AUTHORITIES

In Jewish law, as in every legal system, legislation performs two major functions. First, it fills gaps or lacunae that develop as a result of changes in social and economic conditions that produce problems for which existing law provides no solution. When performing this function, legislation generally adds to existing law; it may add a new legal norm in civil or criminal law governing the relations among individuals or between individuals and society, or it may add a new prohibition or a new affirmative precept in the religious law governing the relationship between people and God.

Second, it amends or modifies existing law when the needs of the time so require, in instances where the application of the existing law produces social, economic, or moral difficulties due to changed circumstances and conditions. The goal of legislation here is to resolve these difficulties by amending the law.

Legislation in Jewish law performs both of these functions concurrently in all of the different areas of the law; and major parts, and even entire areas, of Jewish law are based on legislation. One may point to certain areas of Jewish law that have been enormously enriched by legislation, as well as to other areas where legislation has had less effect on the growth of the law. The extent to which legislation played a part in the development of the *Halakhah* depended largely on the degree to which midrashic interpretation could be employed to find a solution to new problems. Thus, because complete sections of the Torah cover the law of torts, theft, and personal injury, it was possible to develop these legal areas through Biblical interpretation, which, as previously pointed out, is preferable to legislation.[1] Consequently, midrash is the source of a substantial part of these areas of the law. On the other hand, the law of property and contracts, for which the Biblical roots are scant and slight, developed mainly through legislation.

Both legal sources—interpretation and legislation—often operated together, with more or less equal effect, to expand and develop the *Halakhah*. This was the case, for example, in the area of family law, where many of the rules were derived by exegesis of Biblical verses and many others were created by a vast body of wide-ranging legislation.

1. *See supra* p. 287.

II. THE NATURE OF LEGISLATIVE ACTIVITY BY THE HALAKHIC AUTHORITIES; THE MEANING OF THE PROHIBITIONS "YOU SHALL NOT ADD" AND "YOU SHALL NOT TAKE AWAY"

Before examining the methodology and principles of legislation in Jewish law, a fundamental threshold question relating to halakhic legislation generally must be discussed: How is it possible to justify the power of the halakhic authorities to enact legislation designed to add to, modify, or subtract from Biblical law when the Torah itself lays down the fundamental precept, "You shall not add anything to what I command you or take anything away from it, but keep the commandments of the Lord your God that I enjoin upon you,"[2] and similarly, "Be careful to observe everything which I enjoin upon you: neither add to it nor take away from it"?[3] Does not every rule that becomes part of the halakhic system as a result of legislation either add to or take away from Biblical law, and thus violate the categorical command of the verses just quoted?[4] This question has been extensively discussed in the writings of halakhic authorities and scholars of Jewish law.

2. Deuteronomy 4:2.

3. *Id.* 13:1.

4. The solution to this fundamental problem requires an answer to the question, To what extent are addition and taking away forbidden? *Sifrei,* Deuteronomy, Re'eh, sec. 82 (p. 148) states:

> From where [do we derive] that one may not add anything to the *lulav* [palm branch taken on the *Sukkot* festival] or to the fringes [which must be attached to the corners of a four-cornered garment]? Scripture says, "You shall not add to . . . it." And from where [do we derive] that one may not take away anything from them? Scripture says, "You shall not . . . take . . . away from it." From where [do we derive] that if he [a priest] began to recite the priestly blessing, he should not say [to himself], "Since I have begun to bless, I will say, 'May the Lord, God of your fathers, increase your numbers'" [an additional blessing—contained in Scripture (Deuteronomy 1:11) but not included in the Scriptural formulation of the priestly blessing in Numbers 6:22–27]? Scripture says, "[You shall not add anything to] *ha-davar* [which can mean either "the thing," or "the word"]." You may not add even a word.

Following the *Sifrei,* Rashi (to Deuteronomy 13:1), s.v. Lo tosef alav, gave the following examples of "You shall not add": "[You may not make] five [in place of the prescribed four] compartments in the phylacteries; or five species [instead of four] in connection with the *lulav;* or four [instead of three] blessings in the priestly blessing." *See also* TB Sanhedrin 88b and Rosh ha-Shanah 28b.

This interpretation of the prohibition, *i.e.,* that it is forbidden to add to or take away from the substance of a commandment, could resolve our question, since the addition of a new commandment would not be within the prohibition. At first sight, this seems to be implied by Maharal of Prague (*Gur Aryeh* to Deuteronomy 4:2, s.v. Lo tosifu):

> "You shall not add." This should not be interpreted to refer to enactments by the Sages such as [the prohibition of marriage within the] second degree of consanguinity or additional sabbath prohibitions, because if it [the verse] were so interpreted, then, "You shall not take away" would by the same token have to mean that you may not take away an entire commandment and fail to observe it. However, it cannot mean

Two of the answers are particularly noteworthy. One denies that the question has any merit at all. That answer was given by Solomon b. Abraham Adret (Rashba), a leading halakhic authority in Spain in the thirteenth century C.E. Rashba's comments were made in connection with the statement in the Talmud[5] that "long blasts (*teki'ot*) and short blasts (*teru'ot*) [of the shofar] are to be sounded [on *Rosh Ha-Shanah*] when the congregation is seated and also when the congregation is standing, in order to confound Satan."[6] The Tosafists had queried how it is permissible to increase the number of blasts sounded by the shofar beyond the number specified by the Torah. Is this not a violation of "You shall not add . . ."?[7] Rashba responded as follows:[8]

> There really is no difficulty whatsoever; the prohibition "You shall not add . . ." was addressed only to an individual who adds on his own authority, such as a priest who adds a blessing,[9] or a person who sleeps in a *sukkah* on

---

> this because that would not be "taking away" but rather not fulfilling the commandment at all, and it [Scripture] has many times admonished that all the commandments be observed, so why would there be a need for it to tell us "You shall not take away"?
>
> Therefore, ["You shall not add" must mean that] you shall not add anything to the substance of a commandment, *e.g.*, make five fringes, or five compartments in the phylacteries, because even if one does not [thereby] intend to add [to the commandment], the commandment is nevertheless to have four fringes, and making five is adding to them. Similarly, the addition of a blessing to the priestly blessing is a transgression of "You shall not add."

However, although this analysis may narrow the scope of the basic problem, it does not provide a solution, since a significant portion of the enactments by the halakhic authorities do add to the substance of the commandments. (Indeed, Maharal himself later in his remarks had to resort to Maimonides' solution; *see infra* pp. 499–502.) Furthermore, the *Sifrei*'s interpretation is not unanimously accepted. "You shall not add" and "You shall not take away" have been interpreted literally to include in the prohibition the addition of a completely new commandment: "'You shall not add . . . or take . . . away from it'—just as one who takes away violates a commandment, so too does one who adds, such as Jeroboam b. Nevat, who created a [new] festival on his own initiative [I Kings 12:33]." *Midrash Lekaḥ Tov, Pesikta Zutrata,* Deuteronomy 4:2.

This is also Naḥmanides' opinion in his commentary on Deuteronomy 4:2, s.v. Lo tosifu: "In my opinion, the prohibition applies even if someone institutes an entirely new commandment on his own, such as creating a new festival, as Jeroboam did." Thus, the approach of the *Sifrei* leaves the problem of justifying legislation in the *Halakhah* unresolved. (For other opinions on this matter, *see* Z.H. Chajes, *Torat ha-Nevi'im,* Bal Tosif; ET, III, pp. 325–330, s.vv. Bal tigra, Bal tosif.)

5. TB Rosh ha-Shanah 16a/b.

6. "So that he should not accuse [the Jews], since when he hears that the Jewish people cherish the commandments, his words are silenced." Rashi, Rosh ha-Shanah 16b, s.v. Kedei le'arbev.

7. Tosafot, *ad loc.*, s.v. Ve-tok'in u-meri'in ke-she-hen omdin.

8. Rashba, Novellae to Rosh ha-Shanah 16a, s.v. Lamah tok'in u-meri'in.

9. To the priestly benediction, *see supra* n. 4.

the eighth day [of the *Sukkot* festival][10] with the intention of fulfilling a [self-imposed] religious requirement, and other similar acts. However, there is no violation of "You shall not add . . . ," when the halakhic authorities enact necessary legislation for the public good, for the Torah has stated: "[You shall act] in accordance with the instructions given [lit. "which they shall give"] you."[11] This conclusion is confirmed by the fact that in our day it is a rabbinic precept to dwell in a *sukkah* on the eighth day of *Sukkot,* and one eats and sleeps in the *sukkah* in observance of the precept, even though we now have the knowledge to determine in advance the date the month begins [and there is no longer any doubt about the exact day when the festival begins—which was the reason why the observance of eight rather than seven days of *Sukkot* was decreed].

The same conclusion follows with respect to the prohibition against taking away from Biblical law. That prohibition is not violated when the halakhic authorities enact necessary legislation; *e.g.,* even though the Torah requires the sounding of the shofar when the holiday of *Rosh Ha-Shanah* falls on a sabbath, the rabbis decreed for sufficient reason not to do so.[12] In our case, too, they found reason to require additional blasts of the shofar, and the obligation to obey the words of the Sages arises from the verse "You must not deviate [from the verdict that they announce to you]."[13] This is my view.

Rashba's response is remarkable for its almost revolutionary character and, perhaps on that account, also for its simplicity. He explained all of the Biblical statements against adding to or taking away from Biblical law as being intended to apply to the individual who observes the law of the Torah, for the Torah is addressing each individual Jew; each individual addressed may not act on his own to add to or take away from what the Torah says. However, the halakhic authorities, who are obligated to interpret the law and to continue halakhic creativity, are not at all within the ambit of the prohibition against adding or taking away.[14] To the contrary, their re-

10. TB Rosh ha-Shanah 28b. According to Biblical law, the commandment is to dwell in the *sukkah* for seven days. The Sages, however, enacted that outside the Land of Israel one must dwell in the *sukkah* for eight days, since news of the designation of the first day of the month of Tishri did not reach distant places in time to know precisely on which day the festival begins. The practice in the diaspora of observing each festival for an additional day is followed even today—notwithstanding that the date of the New Moon is now known by calendar—because "you have received a custom from your ancestors" (lit. "a custom of your ancestors is in your hands"), TB Beẓah 4b. *See also* the further comments of Rashba, *infra.*

11. Deuteronomy 17:11.

12. *See infra* pp. 505–506.

13. Deuteronomy 17:11.

14. Chajes, *supra* n. 4, comments that this is also the opinion of Joseph Albo (*Sefer ha-Ikkarim* 3:14) and of Rabad (Gloss to *MT,* Mamrim 2:9). *See Kol Sifrei Maharaẓ Ḥayyot* [The Collected Works of Z.H. Chajes], Jerusalem, 1958, Vol. 1, pp. 79, 96. *Query,* why Chajes did not include Rashba's opinion in his summary (*id.* at 96), inasmuch as Rashba makes the clearest statement that the two prohibitions do not apply to enactments by the halakhic authorities.

sponsibility is clearly and explicitly set forth in a passage in Deuteronomy (17:8–11) directed specifically to them, which affirmatively commands them to solve newly arising problems through specified methods, including legislation, which by its very nature involves adding to or taking away from preexisting law. Not only are they permitted to enact such legislation, but they are affirmatively commanded to do so; and every individual Jew is obligated not to deviate from the rules legislated[15] by the halakhic authorities.[16]

Most halakhic authorities adopt a different approach in answering the question dealt with by Rashba. In their opinion, the prohibition against adding to or taking away from Biblical law applies not only to the individual but also to the community, including the halakhic authorities and the courts. They contend that the solution to the problem lies in the specific manner and form that must be used by the halakhic authorities in the exercise of their legislative function; the required manner and form reflect the basic distinction between the supreme legislation of the Written Law and the subordinate legislation of the halakhic authorities.

Foremost among these halakhic authorities is Maimonides, who dealt with this problem in detail in the *Mishneh Torah* in the course of his discussion of the nature of halakhic legislation. He posed the following question:[17]

> It is the prerogative of a court to issue a decree that prohibits an act that is otherwise permissible, and its prohibition is binding on succeeding generations. It also has the power to permit temporarily the performance of a Biblically prohibited act. In light of these powers, how can we explain the Biblical injunction: "Neither add to it nor take away from it"?

His answer was:

> It is forbidden to add to or take away from Biblical law and to declare that a new law is everlasting and is a matter (Hebrew, *"be-davar"*)[18] that is part of

15. *See further* Rashba, Novellae to Nedarim 90b, s.v. Ḥazru lomar:

> . . . Whenever there is a need for a safeguard, the court may enact legislation that uproots a law of the Torah. This does not mean that the halakhic authorities may abrogate a law of the Torah on the basis of their own desire, but rather that it is a commandment of the Torah to obey whoever is judge at the time, and therefore anything they [the judges] permit for good cause is permitted by the Torah.

16. It is possible that this is also the meaning of *Sifrei, supra* n. 4, in giving *lulav* and fringes as its examples, *i.e.,* that an individual may not decide on his own to add to them. This is also implicit to some degree in the language, "From where [do we derive] that if he [a priest] began to recite the priestly blessing, he should not say, 'Since I have begun to bless . . .'?" This language suggests that during the course of the ceremony the priest decided on his own initiative to add a blessing. However, the subject requires further study.

17. *MT,* Mamrim 2:9.

18. In the Rome edition, the word *be-davar* does not appear.

the Torah, whether of the Written Law or of the Oral Law.[19] For example, it is written in the Torah:[20] "You shall not boil a kid in its mother's milk." Oral tradition taught that this verse means that one may not cook or eat meat and milk together,[21] and the prohibition applies to the meat of all animals, whether wild or domestic.[22] However, the Torah does not forbid mixing the meat of a fowl with milk.[23] If a court should declare that combining the meat of a wild beast with milk is permissible, that would be a "taking away,"[24] and if it should prohibit the meat of a fowl and assign as its reason that fowl is included in the category of "kid" and is therefore Biblically prohibited, this would be an addition.

A court, however, would not be adding to the Torah but would be constructing a fence around the Torah if it declared: "The meat of a fowl is permitted by the Torah, but we [the court] will prohibit it, and we will disclose to the people that it is a *gezerah* designed to prevent them from falling into error. [Without such a *gezerah*], some people might say, 'Fowl is permitted, since it was not explicitly mentioned in the verse, and it follows that a wild beast is also permitted for the same reason.' Others might say, 'Only goat meat is within the prohibition,' or 'Even goat meat can be boiled in cow's milk or the milk of a ewe lamb, because the verse prohibits only boiling in its mother's milk, meaning milk of its own species,' or 'The prohibition does not apply even when a kid is boiled in goat's milk, if the goat that gave the milk is not the kid's mother.' Therefore [to forestall these possibilities], we will prohibit combining milk with any meat, even the meat of fowl."

The same would likewise be true of any similar action [by the court].

19. It is also forbidden to add to or take away from laws that were transmitted to Moses orally at Mt. Sinai. *See* Maimonides, *Commentary on the Mishnah,* Introduction: "It makes no difference whether one adds to or takes away from a law based on Scriptural verses or from a law based upon the interpretation handed down by tradition" (ed. Kafaḥ, Zera'im, Hebrew translation only, p. 4; with Arabic original, p. 6). Maimonides makes the same point in his introduction to his commentary on ch. 11 (*Ḥelek*) of Tractate Sanhedrin (toward the end of the introduction, s.v. Vi-yesod ha-teshi'i; ed. Kafaḥ, Nezikin, p. 215 and *see* Kafaḥ's n. 77, *ad loc.*). *See also* Rabad, Gloss to *MT,* Mamrim 2:9.

20. Exodus 23:19.

21. TB Ḥullin 115b.

22. Many of the commentators on the *Mishneh Torah* as well as other authors and scholars have noted the conflict between this statement and that in *MT,* Ma'akhalot Asurot 9:4 to the effect that eating the flesh of a wild beast cooked in milk is not prohibited by the Torah (*see* Radbaz, *Kesef Mishneh,* and *Leḥem Mishneh,* to *MT, ad loc.*). *See also* E.S. Rosenthal, "Al Derekh ha-Rov" [On the Way of the Majority], *Perakim* (The Annual of the Schocken Institute for Judaic Research), Jerusalem, 1967/1968, I, p. 185 n. 10. Rosenthal demonstrates that the two texts are respectively a first and second version by Maimonides himself, who at first ruled contrary to R. Akiva's view stated in M Ḥullin 8:4 and later reversed himself.

23. M Ḥullin 8:4; TB Ḥullin 113a; since Scripture states "in its mother's milk," the law excludes fowl, which do not have "mother's milk."

24. From the Oral Law (*see supra* n. 19), according to which the flesh of a wild beast cooked in milk is also forbidden.

In the Introduction to the *Mishneh Torah,*[25] Maimonides expanded on the explanation of his point of view:

> There are other precepts that originated after the Torah was given and were instituted by the prophets[26] and by the Sages and accepted by all of Israel, such as: the reading of the Scroll of Esther on *Purim,* the kindling of the *Hanukkah* lights, the fast of the Ninth of [the month of] Av, the *eruv,* and the ritual impurity of hands.[27] Each of these precepts has its explanations and elaborate refinements. . . . We are bound to accept and observe all these newly established precepts, as it is stated, "You must not deviate from the verdict [that they announce to you]";[28] and they are not additions to Biblical commandments.
>
> Concerning what did the Torah warn us in providing:"Neither add to it nor take away from it"?[29] To teach us that a prophet is not permitted to establish a new law and declare that the Holy One, Blessed be He, commanded him to promulgate it as an additional Biblical commandment. Nor may he announce that one of the 613 commandments is now withdrawn. But if a court, together with the prophet living at that time, adds a precept by means of a *takkanah* . . . or a *gezerah,* this is not a prohibited addition, for they have not declared that God commanded the making of an *eruv* or the reading of the Scroll of Esther at the designated time. Were they so to declare, they would be adding to the Torah. This, then, is our position: The prophets, together with the court, enacted these laws and decreed that we read the Scroll of Esther at its designated time in order to recall the glories of God, the salvation He wrought for us, and that He was near when we cried out for help, and in order to bless and praise Him and to inform future generations of the truth of the promise in the Torah, "For what great nation is there that has a God so close at hand . . . !"[30] Every commandment that was instituted by the Scribes (*mi-divrei soferim*), whether affirmative or negative, is to be understood in the same way.[31]

This response of Maimonides and other like-minded authorities[32] penetrates to the very root and essence of legislation in Jewish law. One may

25. *MT,* Introduction, following the listing of the commandments.

26. *I.e.,* in their capacity as Sages, not as prophets. *See* the quotations from Maimonides, *supra* pp. 243, 264–265.

27. *See* TB Shabbat 15a and Eruvin 21b. *See also* H. Albeck, Tohorot, p. 473, Introduction to Tractate Yadayim.

28. Deuteronomy 17:11.

29. *Id.* 13:1.

30. *Id.* 4:7.

31. *See* Maimonides' remarks in *The Guide for the Perplexed,* part III, ch. 41, where he adds that the Torah conferred legislative power on the court possessing acknowledged authority in each generation so as to avoid the proliferation of disputes and variant opinions. This delegation is the basis for the law of the rebellious elder. For fuller treatment of the delegation of legislative authority, *see supra* p. 486 nn. 43, 44.

32. *See, e.g.,* Naḥmanides, at the end of his *Commentary on Deuteronomy* 4:2, s.v. Lo tosifu:

not add to or take away from the supreme legislation, namely, the Written Law, because the supreme legislative act as formulated at the time of the Revelation is everlasting; and it is forbidden to add to the law anything purporting to be an additional Biblical precept or to take anything away in a manner that purports to deny Biblical status to a precept explicitly commanded in the Torah. However, if the legislator makes clear that the addition or subtraction is subordinate legislation and that according to Biblical law a particular act is permitted or prohibited and there is no intent to change the Biblical rule itself but rather to prohibit or to permit by virtue of the authority the Torah itself conferred on him, and if the legislator discloses the rationale that has led to the enactment, then the legislation does not trespass upon the domain of supreme legislation but is permissible subordinate legislation.[33]

In summary, whether one prefers Rashba's or Maimonides' solution, the legislative activity of the halakhic authorities does not violate the injunction of the Torah. Indeed, when the halakhic authorities legislate, they exercise authority the Torah has specifically conferred upon them—an authority the Torah has bolstered by forbidding any deviation from the legislation that the halakhic authorities deem it necessary to enact. While, in theory, a portion of the subordinate legislation by the halakhic authorities operates as a temporary measure (*hora'at sha'ah*, lit. "a directive for the hour"), in actuality, as will be apparent later in our discussion, this "hour" during which the legislation is effective is extremely long; the vast accumulation of legislative enactments in all the various areas of the *Halakhah* has become an essential part of the entire system of Jewish law in every period of its history.

> The enactment of legislation by the Sages as a fence [around the law of the Torah], such as the [prohibition of marriage within the] second degree of consanguinity and the like, constitutes the fulfillment of a Biblical commandment as long as it is understood that the enactments were adopted as a safeguard and that they do not issue from the mouth of the Holy One, Blessed be He, in the Torah.

This is also the opinion of Maharal, *supra* n. 4:

> Every precept of rabbinic law, such as the kindling of the *Hanukkah* lights, is intended not to add to the Torah, but to be a memorial of a miracle. There is thus no addition to the Torah. No rabbinic precept constitutes an addition to the Torah, since "You shall not add" applies only when the addition is equated with the Torah itself; but fences and safeguards do not constitute additions, since they are not on a par with them [*i.e.*, with Biblical laws].

33. In addition to this theoretical difference in regard to the process of adopting enactments, there are also practical distinctions between Biblical and rabbinic law. These distinctions chiefly concern laws originating in *takkanot* and *gezerot*. *See supra* pp. 477–478. *See also* Chajes, *supra* n. 4 at ch. 2, and the conclusion of M.H. Luzzatto, *Ma'amar ha-Ikkarim* [Essay on Basic Principles], "On the Question of the Oral Law and the Talmud."

III. THE FUNDAMENTAL OBJECTIVE OF LEGISLATIVE ACTIVITY BY THE HALAKHIC AUTHORITIES

The legislative activity of the halakhic authorities in supplementing, modifying, and subtracting from preexisting law has been so comprehensive and wide-ranging that no *a priori* principles or doctrines completely succeed in explaining or accounting for all its manifestations.

In order to understand and explain not only legislation but also the other operative legal sources in the halakhic system,[34] one must keep in mind the basic principle regarding the exclusive competence of the halakhic authorities to interpret the Torah and to determine its meaning, namely, the principle that God entrusted the absolute responsibility for the Torah to the halakhic authorities.[35] This responsibility led the halakhic authorities to identify completely with the spirit and purpose of the Torah.

On the one hand, that identity in spirit and purpose required them to exercise great care and circumspection in their legislative activity; but on the other hand, it made it possible for them to adopt bold and crucial enactments when convinced that the spirit and purpose of the Torah so required. It was only because they felt they were like physicians entrusted with responsibility for the health and well-being of the *Halakhah* (a simile actually used by Maimonides)[36] that they made such far-reaching and powerful pronouncements as their interpretation of the verse[37] "It is a time to act for the Lord, for they have violated Your Torah." They interpreted this verse to mean that "when it is time to act for the Lord, Your Torah may be violated," *i.e.*, "It is better [one letter of] the Torah should be uprooted[38] so that the [entire] Torah will not be forgotten by Israel."[39] In the same vein, they declared: "There are times when setting aside the Torah is the only way to preserve it,"[40] and, "It is better that one letter of the Torah

34. *See supra* pp. 236–239.

35. *See supra* pp. 243–247.

36. *MT*, Mamrim 2:4; *see infra* p. 519.

37. Psalms 119:126.

38. This is the reading in printed editions of TB Temurah 14b; ms. Munich reads: ". . . that one letter of the Torah should be uprooted"; *see also Shittah Mekubbeẓet, ad loc.*, subpar. 5.

39. TB Temurah 14b. *See also* M Berakhot 9:5 ("And Scripture also says, 'It is a time to act for the Lord, for they have violated Your Torah.' R. Nathan said, 'When they have violated Your Torah, it is a time to act for the Lord.'"); H. Albeck, *ad loc.*, and in Hashlamot, p. 340; *Tosefta* Berakhot 6:23–24 and S. Lieberman, *Tosefta ki-Feshutah*, Berakhot, pp. 124–125; TB Berakhot 63a; TB Yoma 69a and Rashi, *ad loc.*, s.v. Et la'asot ("When a time comes to do something for the sake of God's name, it is permitted to violate the Torah."); Commentaries on Psalms 119:126 by Rashi, Meiri, and Obadiah Seforno (*Psalms with Commentaries of Joseph Javetz and Obadiah Seforno*, ed. S.J. Halpern, 1952).

40. TB Menaḥot 99a/b.

should be uprooted than that God's name should be openly profaned."[41] The same sense of responsibility also gave rise to such basic doctrines as, for example, "One shall live by them and not die because of them"[42] and "One should violate . . . one sabbath in order to enable the observance of many sabbaths."[43]

This broad view of the halakhic authorities as to their legislative power explains why there appears to have been no discussion or debate prior to the end of the tannaitic period concerning the extent of their legislative prerogative or the guidelines for its exercise. Until the end of the tannaitic period, the only explanation accompanying many *takkanot* was a recital of the factual background and the circumstances that brought about the enactment. Thus, the defilement of the oil in the Temple by the Greeks was cited as the background for the enactment establishing the holiday of *Hanukkah.*[44] Natural disasters and wars were cited as the background for the enactment concerning *agunot.*[45] The drying up of credit was cited as the reason for the enactment of the *prosbul,*[46] and the broad rationale of promoting the public welfare (*tikkun ha-olam*)[47] or public peace and tranquillity (*darkhei shalom*)[48] and other similar reasons were cited as the basis for many other enactments.[49]

Up to the end of the tannaitic period, these early enactments were introduced without any legal-halakhic explanation or foundation, and this was true for all such enactments, whether they concerned monetary or religious matters and whether or not they "uprooted" a Biblical rule either by prohibiting what the Torah commanded or by commanding what the Torah prohibited. The halakhic authorities were the guardians of the health and welfare of the *Halakhah,* and in that capacity, when convinced that the

41. TB Yevamot 79a.

42. TB Sanhedrin 74a; Yoma 85b, *et al. See also infra* p. 990.

43. TB Yoma 85b. For a similar notion, *see* TB Eruvin 32b ("Rabbi [R. Judah Ha-Nasi] believes that a *ḥaver* [one punctilious in observance of the laws of ritual purity—generally a halakhic scholar] would rather transgress a minor prohibition himself than have an *am ha-areẓ* [here, one who is not careful in observance of the laws of ritual purity; generally, one who is halakhically ignorant] transgress a major prohibition"); Gittin 38b ("When necessary in order to perform a commandment [*e.g.,* prayer in a *minyan* (quorum of ten)], the law [as to manumission of a slave, which would enable him to be counted for the *minyan*] is different [*i.e.,* relaxed]"). *See also* Z.H. Chajes, *Torat ha-Nevi'im,* Hora'at Sha'ah, p. 24b.

44. TB Shabbat 21b; *see supra* p. 481.

45. M Yevamot 16:7; Eduyyot 1:12; TB Yevamot 116b. *See infra* pp. 522–526.

46. M Shevi'it 10:3–4. *See infra* pp. 511–512.

47. M Gittin 4:2–7, 5:3, *et al.; see infra* pp. 591–592.

48. *E.g.,* M Gittin 5:8–9; *see infra* p. 628.

49. For further examples, *see Tosefta* Eruvin 3:6 (ms. Erfurt, 4:6); TB Eruvin 45a; Shabbat 60a; M Berakhot 9:5; M Rosh ha-Shanah 2:1.

times required it, they legislated to ensure that the Torah, its ways, and its precepts would not be forgotten.

IV. PRINCIPLES AND GUIDELINES FOR LEGISLATIVE ACTIVITY BY THE HALAKHIC AUTHORITIES

During the period of the *amoraim,* the Sages crystallized a number of basic principles and guidelines governing the scope and authority of their legislative activity. Most of these principles were originated by the *amoraim,* although some of them carried forward earlier formulations.[50] The fundamental doctrine that God vested responsibility for the Torah in the halakhic authorities continued to function as the basis for legislation in Jewish law,[51] but beginning with the amoraic period the halakhic authorities formulated a number of general methodological principles which served as guidelines for legislation.

A. "The Court May Direct That an Affirmative Precept of the Torah Not Be Carried Out" (*Shev ve-Al Ta'aseh*)

As is known, there are two kinds of Biblical commandments: affirmative (Biblical directives that require the performance of certain acts, such as the blowing of the shofar on *Rosh Ha-Shanah* and the taking of the *lulav* [palm branch] on the festival of *Sukkot*) and negative (Biblical injunctions that prohibit particular acts such as marrying one's mother or daughter, or another man's wife, etc.).[52] An important legislative principle states that a court may enact that an affirmative precept, obligatory according to Biblical law, should nevertheless not be performed; the court has the competence

50. The reference is to principles of legislation that were established as a result of discussions about the scope of the legislative authority of the Sages. It was the *amoraim* who first engaged in such detailed discussions and laid down principles defining this authority. As will be seen *infra,* the *amoraim* formulated most of these principles of legislation. Some of them had been formulated earlier, such as the principle stated by R. Eliezer b. Jacob that "the court may impose flogging and punishment not prescribed in the Torah—not to transgress the law of the Torah but in order to make a fence around the Torah." It may well be that the last part of this formulation, "not to transgress . . . ," was added by the *amoraim* as an explanation of the principle stated in the first part by R. Eliezer b. Jacob. *See infra* p. 515 n. 94.

51. This doctrine continued to serve especially as a basis for those enactments that direct the performance of an act prohibited by the Torah (*kum va-aseh*) even on matters of religious law. *See infra* pp. 521–533.

52. *See supra* p. 483 and *infra* p. 557.

and authority to issue a directive to "sit and not do" (*shev ve-al ta'aseh*).[53] Many instances are cited in Talmudic literature for the application of this principle.[54] A commonly cited instance is the enactment of the Sages that prohibits blowing the shofar on a day when Rosh Ha-Shanah falls on the sabbath and prohibits taking the *lulav* on a sabbath during *Sukkot*, in order to forestall the possibility that the shofar or the *lulav* be carried more than four cubits in the public domain, in violation of the Biblical prohibition against carrying on the sabbath.

As to the power of the court, in the converse situation, to adopt an enactment permitting what the Torah forbids (*kum va-aseh*, lit. "get up and do"),[55] the Babylonian *amoraim* of the third generation held conflicting views. According to Rabbah, "the court may not enact legislation uprooting a Biblical prohibition by permitting the performance of the prohibited act." However, according to R. Ḥisda, it is within the competence of the court to adopt legislation even if it thereby nullifies a prohibition of the Torah by permitting performance of an act the Torah prohibits.[56]

The outcome of this fundamental dispute was decided in favor of Rabbah's view that the court does not have the authority to adopt legislation that conflicts with a Biblical prohibition. However, the discussion in Tractate *Yevamot* concerning these two viewpoints contains an extensive array of proofs based on pre-amoraic laws of major importance that indicate that the halakhic authorities are indeed competent to adopt legislation that nullifies prohibitions in the Torah by permitting the performance of acts the Torah prohibits.[57] To resolve the difficulty and provide a rationale for all those laws that imply that a court has this power, the Talmud established three exceptions to the general principle denying this power. Each exception has its own important and respected position among the principles of legislation.[58]

53. Since, in such a case, "the abrogation [of Biblical law] is not active, by commission (lit. "by the hands"), but only passive, by omission." Rashi, Yevamot 90a, s.v. Shev ve-al ta'aseh.

54. *See, e.g.*, TB Yevamot 90a/b.

55. Such an enactment constitutes "real uprooting." Rashi, *ad loc.*, *supra* n. 53.

56. TB Yevamot 89a–90b.

57. The plain meaning of various early laws seems to corroborate R. Ḥisda's opinion that a court can indeed legislate to nullify a Biblical prohibition even to the extent of permitting performance of the prohibited act. *See* Y.D. Gilat, "Bet Din Matnin La'akor Davar min ha-Torah" [The Court May Legislate to Uproot a Biblical Law], *Bar Ilan Annual*, 1969–1970, pp. 118ff.; *infra* pp. 631, 634–636.

58. The principle that "all who marry do so subject to the conditions laid down by the Rabbis, and the Rabbis annul this marriage" (TB Yevamot 90b) has not been cited in the present chapter as a legislative principle because, in essence, it is only a logical explanation of the competence of the halakhic authorities to annul a marriage by application of the

B. "The Court Has the Power to Expropriate Property" (*Hefker Bet Din Hefker*)

The first exception is the legislative principle that establishes that in matters of civil law (*mamon*) and all other matters—even matters of religious law (*issur*)—that turn on the ownership of property, the halakhic authorities are competent to enact legislation that nullifies a Biblical law by directing performance of an act the Torah prohibits. This principle is that "the court has the power to expropriate property" (*hefker bet din hefker*).

1. THE INITIAL STAGES OF THE PRINCIPLE

The *tannaim* discussed the principle of *hefker bet din hefker* in its literal sense, *i.e.*, that the court has the power in certain circumstances to declare an individual's property forfeit. Thus, the *Tosefta* states:[59]

> On the fifteenth day of the month of Adar, the agents of the court go out and pronounce all prohibited hybrid plants (*kilayim*) to be forfeited, as the court may expropriate property, and they [the plants] are exempt from tithes.

As we learn from the Mishnah,[60] this was a decree by the court aimed at those who grew prohibited hybrid plants in their fields; it was adopted only as a last resort after all other efforts to have such plants removed were unsuccessful.[61] The agents of the court would declare the grain in the field

---

general principle of Jewish law relating to "conditions": since the validity of a marriage is subject to the approval of the halakhic authorities, those authorities are also competent to annul the marriage. The principle is discussed *infra* pp. 631–642, in connection with legislation in the amoraic period.

In Jewish law, the husband-wife relationship is effected in two stages: (1) betrothal (*kiddushin* or *erusin*) and (2) the nuptial ceremony—entrance under the canopy (*ḥuppah*, also termed *nissu'in*). Betrothal makes the couple husband and wife vis-à-vis everyone else, but as between themselves, marital obligations arise only after the *ḥuppah*. These two stages were once separate, but in the post-Talmudic period they were combined, as they are today, when the bride is betrothed by means of a ring (*kiddushin*) while under the nuptial canopy.

Under the principle that "all who marry [lit. "betroth"] do so subject to the conditions laid down by the Rabbis" (*kol di-mekaddesh ada'ata de-rabbanan mekaddesh*), it is technically the *kiddushin* (betrothal) that is annulled, but the intended reference is to the marital relationship. We have therefore translated *kiddushin*, here and elsewhere, as "marriage," except where the reference is to betrothal in the technical sense. *See, e.g.*, p. 641 n. 64.

59. *Tosefta* Shekalim 1:3.

60. M Shekalim 1:2.

61. *See* M Shekalim 1:1: "On the first day of Adar they would give warning . . . concerning prohibited hybrid plants [*i.e.*, the people would be told to go out into the fields and vineyards to uproot prohibited hybrid plantings; *see* Leviticus 19:19, Deuteronomy 22:9]. On the fifteenth of the month . . . they would go forth also with regard to prohibited hybrid plants [*i.e.*, court officials would go out to verify whether the admonition given on the first of the month to uproot the hybrids had been complied with]." *See also id.* 1:2: "R. Judah

to be forfeited. The *Tosefta* informs us that even if the owner of the field himself retakes the grain, the law deems him to have acquired ownership of abandoned grain, and he therefore does not tithe from it.[62] Such expropriation thus also affected religious law, *i.e.*, the law of tithing, because the religious obligation turns on the property ownership.

The Sages found that the principle of *hefker bet din hefker* appears as early as in the Book of Ezra:[63]

> What is the source of the principle that the court may expropriate property? It is written: "Anyone who does not come in three days, as required by the officers and elders, will have his property confiscated and himself excluded from the congregation of the returning exiles."[64]

This verse relates to the summons by Ezra and the officers and elders to those who had returned to the Land of Israel from exile in Babylonia to gather in Jerusalem and take upon themselves the obligation to send away their foreign wives; as a sanction for failure to obey this summons, it was prescribed that the property of all those who did not respond would be forfeited. From this, the Sages deduced that a court has the power to divest an individual of his rights of ownership in his money and property.[65]

2. *HEFKER BET DIN HEFKER* AS A LEGISLATIVE PRINCIPLE

The power a court possesses by virtue of the principle of *hefker bet din hefker* was interpreted by the *amoraim* to extend beyond divesting and forfeiting the proprietary rights of the lawful owners of property; the principle was expanded to effect a valid transfer of ownership of such property to other individuals. It is on the basis of this broader interpretation that a

---

said: 'At first, they [the court officials] would root them [*i.e.*, the plants] out and cast them down before the owners [and would not take the plants away]. When the number of transgressors [*i.e.*, owners who did not obey the court's admonitions but continued to grow prohibited hybrid plants and then fed the uprooted plants to their animals] increased, they [the court officials] would root out the plants and throw them onto the roads. [Finally,] they ordained that the whole field [where prohibited hybrid plants grew] should be declared forfeit [since throwing the plants onto the roads had proved ineffective, and the owners were even delighted that their fields were being weeded for them].'" This explanation of this *mishnah* follows H. Albeck's commentary, *ad loc.*

62. *See* S. Lieberman, *Tosefta ki-Feshutah*, Mo'ed, p. 659.

63. TJ Shekalim 1:2, 3a/b (1:2, 46a). *See also* TJ Pe'ah 5:1, 25a (5:1, 18d).

64. Ezra 10:8.

65. *See* TJ Shekalim and Pe'ah, *supra* n. 63, with regard to the effect of forfeiture of property as extending even to exempt the property from tithes. As to confiscation of property in Ezra's time, *see* H. Cohn, "Hefker Bet Din: Le-Shittatam Shel R. Yiẓḥak ve-Shel R. Eleazar" [The Power of the Court to Expropriate: According to the Views of R. Isaac and R. Eleazar], *Proceedings of the Fourth International Congress of Jewish Studies*, pp. 185ff.

Talmudic discussion among the *amoraim*[66] explains the law stated in a *baraita* that a husband inherits from his wife even if the marriage was invalid according to Biblical law but valid according to rabbinic law.[67] In such a case, her father's relatives are her legal heirs according to the Torah,[68] but this law contained in the *baraita* supersedes that rule of Biblical law and transfers the estate to her husband, who is an heir only by virtue of rabbinic legislation. This law is thus based on the principle of *hefker bet din hefker, i.e.,* that the court has the power to take the estate away from the legal heir and transfer ownership to someone else.

This expanded meaning was deduced not only from the verse in Ezra[69] but also by means of a midrashic interpretation of a verse in the Book of Joshua:

> R. Eleazar said: "[The deduction is made] from the following [verse]: 'These are the portions assigned by the priest Eleazar, Joshua the son of Nun and the heads of the ancestral houses [lit. 'the heads of the fathers'] of the tribes of the children of Israel.'[70] Why is the connection made between 'heads' and 'fathers' [it should have stated 'heads of the tribes of the children of Israel'—Rashi]? To tell us that just as fathers bequeath to their children whatver they wish, so, too, the 'heads' assign whatever portions they wish to the people."[71]

The action of the halakhic authorities or of the court has the same legal effect as the act of a father who bequeaths property to his children: just as a bequest transfers ownership from a father to a child, so an enactment of the halakhic authorities transfers ownership from one individual to another.[72] In this way, the principle of *hefker bet din hefker* became a legal

66. TB Yevamot 89b.

67. This refers to the case of a fatherless female minor given in marriage by her mother or brothers. Under Biblical law, neither the mother nor the brothers have the power to give her in marriage, but the Sages adopted legislation conferring such power, so that people should not treat her licentiously. TB Yevamot 89b, 112b.

68. *See* Rashi, Yevamot 89b, s.v. Mi-de-oraita avuha yareit lah.

69. The verse in Ezra is cited as the source in TB Yevamot 89b in the name of R. Isaac.

70. Joshua 19:51. Our translation differs from the JPS *Tanakh.*

71. TB Yevamot 89b.

72. The *rishonim* fully discussed the implications of the expansion of the principle of *hefker bet din hefker* resulting from R. Eleazar's exegesis. This is how Rashba put it (Novellae to Gittin 36b, s.v. Rava amar hefker bet din hefker):

> From this we learn that a court has the power to declare the property of one person forfeit and transfer ownership to another even before the latter takes possession. This is shown by the verse "These are the portions. . . ." Just as when fathers bequeath land and say, "This field shall go to So-and-so," that person owns it immediately even before he takes possession of it, so, too, the "heads" can assign [property] to whomsoever they desire and can say, "Reuben's property shall belong to Simeon"; and Simeon owns it from that moment.

doctrine permitting legislation not only to extinguish existing legal rights but also, as is the nature of legislation generally, to confer new rights.

3. SCOPE OF THE PRINCIPLE'S APPLICATION

The principle of *hefker bet din hefker* became a powerful source for the competence of the halakhic authorities throughout the history of Jewish law to enact legislation covering any part of civil law, even when proprietary rights established by Biblical law were thereby nullified.[73] A substantial and significant part of the *Halakhah* in the civil law areas of property and conveyancing, obligations, torts, wills, and intestate succession has its source in enactments by the halakhic authorities for which the basis and rationale was the principle of *hefker bet din hefker.*[74] At times, the halakhic authorities used standard forms of expression that explicitly highlighted that their enactment conflicted with a Biblical rule.[75] For example, R. Johanan stated:

> According to Biblical law, the payment of money effects the transfer of ownership of a chattel. Why then did they [the Sages] say that *meshikhah* [taking possession, lit. "pulling"] transfers ownership? Lest he [the seller] say to him [the buyer]: "*Your* wheat was burned in the loft" [emphasis supplied].[76]

See also Maharshal, *Yam Shel Shelomo,* Yevamot 10:19:

> R. Isaac said: "What is the source of the principle of *hefker bet din hefker?*" . . . R. Eleazar said, "From the following . . ." [*i.e.,* Joshua 19:51]. . . . It appears that R. Eleazar's exegesis is to be preferred, since from it we learn that they [*i.e.,* a court] can expropriate one individual's property and transfer it to another, and not merely declare property forfeit or confiscate it. . . .

See also ET, X, pp. 99–100, s.v. Hefker bet din hefker.

73. Conceptually, the principle that a court is authorized to expropriate property, as derived from the Book of Ezra, avoids the necessity of abrogating a law of the Torah directly. This is so because an enactment vesting in Reuben the ownership of a chattel that Biblical law says belongs to Simeon does not directly deny the validity of the property right granted by the Torah to Simeon. Rather, it extinguishes Simeon's right of ownership by expropriation—a sanction within the authority of the court—and then vests ownership in Reuben. *See* Rashi, Yevamot 89b, s.v. Hefker bet din hayah hefker ("Any matter involving property does not constitute uprooting"), and Rashi, Gittin 36b, s.v. Rava amar ("Enacting a safeguard or a fence in any matter involving property does not entail an uprooting of Biblical law because a court has the power to expropriate property").

74. *See* ET, X, *supra* n. 72 at 97–99. Many of the enactments of different periods, discussed in subsequent chapters of the present work, are based on the principle of *hefker bet din hefker.*

75. Such as, "According to Biblical law. . . . Why then did the Sages say . . . ?"; TB Kiddushin 28b; Gittin 55a/b; Bava Batra 175b; Sanhedrin 32a. *See also* Gulak, *Yesodei,* I, p. 26 n. 24.

76. TB Kiddushin 28b *et al.*

In other words, according to R. Johanan, under Biblical law, ownership of chattels is acquired by payment of money, *i.e.*, the buyer pays the money to the seller, and thereby the ownership of the chattel passes from the seller to the buyer. What is the reason for the enactment of the Sages? It is that if ownership passes to the buyer as soon as the money is paid even if the chattel remains in the possession and control of the seller who no longer owns it, the seller has no incentive to take sufficient precautions for the safety of the chattel if, for example, a fire breaks out in the seller's house. Therefore, the Sages enacted that the chattel is not acquired by the buyer and ownership does not pass to him until he grasps (lit. "pulls") the chattel and takes actual possession of it. This is an example of an enactment concerning civil law which prescribes performance of an affirmative act that effectively nullifies a Biblical law. According to the Torah, taking possession of the chattel (by *meshikhah*) has no effect on ownership; only the payment of money effects a transfer. The Sages, however, enacted that even if money is paid, the seller and not the buyer is still the owner, and that it is the buyer's taking possession by *meshikhah*, even without any monetary payment, that passes ownership from the seller to the buyer.[77]

4. APPLICATION OF THE PRINCIPLE TO A RELIGIOUS QUESTION TURNING ON THE OWNERSHIP OF PROPERTY; ENACTMENT OF THE *PROSBUL*

As already mentioned, when a particular halakhic rule turns on the issue of who owns property, the halakhic authorities employ the principle of *hefker bet din hefker* as the basis of their authority to enact legislation even in areas outside the civil law.

An illustration is the well-known *takkanah* of Hillel instituting the *prosbul*. The Torah states:[78]

> Every seventh year you shall practice remission of debts. This shall be the nature of the remission: every creditor shall release the debt that he claims from his fellow. He shall not dun his fellow or his kinsman, for the remission proclaimed is of the Lord.

Later[79] the Torah adds:

> Beware lest you harbor the base thought, "The seventh year, the year of remission is approaching," so that you are unaccommodating to your needy kinsman and give him nothing.

77. *See further supra* pp. 297–298 and *infra* p. 581 on *meshikhah* as a mode of acquisition.
78. Deuteronomy 15:1–2.
79. *Id.* 15:9–10.

If he cries out to the Lord against you, you will incur guilt. Give to him readily and have no regrets when you do so, for in return the Lord your God will bless you in all your efforts and in all your undertakings.

The Torah thus directs the remission of monetary debts in the seventh (sabbatical) year and expressly admonishes that concern over such remission should not deter prospective lenders from extending credit. The creditor is commanded to lend, notwithstanding that the sabbatical year will wipe out the debt; and the Torah promises the creditor that he will be blessed in all his undertakings.

But the Mishnah says:[80]

[A debt incorporated in] a *prosbul* is not released. This is one of the *takkanot* of Hillel the Elder. [He instituted the *prosbul*] when he saw that the people were refraining from lending to one another and were transgressing what is written in the Torah, "Beware lest you harbor the base thought, etc."[81] This is the text of the *prosbul:* "I give into your charge, judges [naming them] in [naming the place], that every debt due to me I may collect whenever I may desire," and the judges or the witnesses subscribe their signatures.

Hillel thus enacted that if before the sabbatical year the creditor writes a *prosbul,*[82] the sabbatical year would not cancel that debt; consequently, the creditor has the right to collect the debt even after the end of the sabbatical year.

The social and economic background of this enactment is set out in the same *mishnah*. The people of means did not obey the Torah's admonition not to let their concern for the seventh year deter them from making loans, and this caused distress to those who did not receive the credit they needed. To prevent the wealthy from transgressing the Biblical admonition not to refrain from giving loans, and to provide the needy with necessary credit, Hillel enacted the *takkanah* of the *prosbul,* which, when complied with, would prevent the debt from being canceled in the seventh year.[83]

During the fourth amoraic generation, the question was raised as to how Hillel could enact legislation directing the performance of an act the

80. M Shevi'it 10:3–4.

81. Deuteronomy 15:9.

82. The word is of Greek derivation. *See* H. Albeck, Zera'im, Hashlamot, p. 383; TB Gittin 36b. As to the enactment of the *prosbul, see* H. Albeck, *supra* at 382–383; M. Silberg, *Talmudic Law and the Modern State,* New York, 1973, pp. 38ff.

83. The *prosbul* enactment expressly states as its rationale that it sets aside one Torah law (the remission of debts) in order to preserve another (the prohibition against refraining from lending). In the final analysis, this rationale is consonant with the *dictum* of the Sages, quoted at the beginning of the present discussion, that "it is better that one letter of the Torah should be uprooted so that the [entire] Torah will not be forgotten by Israel"; *see supra* pp. 503–505.

Torah forbids: According to his enactment, the creditor has the right to demand the payment of the debt and the debtor is obligated to pay it, whereas under Biblical law the creditor is forbidden to demand payment and the debtor does not have to pay. "How is it possible, when the Torah says the seventh year cancels the debt, that Hillel enacted that it should not be canceled?"[84]

The Talmud records two answers to this question.[85] The first, the answer of Abbaye, was that Hillel as well as other Sages was of the opinion that in his time, during the period of the Second Temple, the Biblical law of the sabbatical year was no longer in effect and observance of the sabbatical year was required only by rabbinic legislation; consequently, Hillel had the authority to enact a *takkanah* reversing an earlier *takkanah* of the Sages. The second answer, that of Rava, argued that even if one adopts the view that the observance of the sabbatical year at that time was required by Biblical law, Hillel's enactment was valid on the basis of the principle of *hefker bet din hefker:* the Sages declared that the debtor's money, to the amount of the debt, becomes the property of the creditor. Therefore, the law prohibiting collection of a debt after the sabbatical year does not apply, since the creditor is merely demanding money that has become his own by virtue of the *prosbul.* There is thus no violation of the Biblical commandment prohibiting the creditor from collecting his debt from funds of the debtor after the seventh year.[86]

Other Talmudic illustrations of the application of the principle of *hefker bet din hefker* occur even in the area of religious law when the issue turns on who owns property. An excellent example is the halakhic authorities' annulment of a marriage in various situations through expropriation of the money (*i.e.,* thing of value, usually a ring) given by the groom to the bride to effect the marriage.[87] Even in this vital area of religious law, the enact-

84. TB Gittin 36a.

85. *See* Rashi, *ad loc.,* s.v. Ba-shevi'it ba-zeman ha-zeh; Rashba, *ad loc.,* s.v. Rava amar hefker bet din hefker; and other *rishonim.*

86. *See further* TJ Shevi'it 10:1(end)–2(beginning), 29a/b (10:2 [end]—3 [beginning], 39c): "'You must remit whatever is due you from your kinsman' [Deuteronomy 15:3], but not if one delivers the loan documents to the court. From here [*i.e.,* from this exegesis] they supported the *prosbul* as being from the Torah." TJ then asks: "But is *prosbul* a Biblical law [it being clear that it originated in an enactment]?" TJ responds: "When Hillel enacted it, they [*i.e.,* the Sages] connected it to the law of the Torah [*i.e.,* supported the legislation with a Scriptural verse]." *See supra* pp. 300–305 and n. 50, and *infra* p. 526 n. 140. The *prosbul* was further liberalized in the course of time. *See* Gulak, *Yesodei,* II, pp. 115–116. For the form of the *prosbul* document, *see id., Oẓar ha-Shetarot,* pp. 215–216. *See also infra* p. 642 n. 66 in regard to the views of Samuel and R. Naḥman concerning the justification for the *prosbul* enactment.

87. Rashbam, Bava Batra 48b, s.v. Teinaḥ de-kaddesh be-khaspa ("The Sages can annul the marriage because the court has the right to expropriate property, and it is as though he [the groom] had given her stolen property to effect the marriage, in which case

ment is effective to permit a "married" woman to marry someone else, because the groom must be the owner of the money given to the bride to effect the marriage.[88]

5. *HEFKER BET DIN HEFKER* AND COMMUNAL ENACTMENTS

The principle of *hefker bet din hefker* became the broadest and most inclusive principle of legislation in Jewish law, in regard both to its absolute binding force[89] and to the scope of the subject matter of the legislation enacted pursuant to it. In the course of time, as communal enactments became an increasingly important form of legislation in Jewish law, this principle became even more broadly and extensively applied as a guideline for legislation.[90]

---

the marriage is invalid . . ."); *Tosafot, ad loc.*, s.v. Teinaḥ de-kaddesh be-khaspa. *See also infra* pp. 631–642, 846–879.

88. For the use of the principle of *hefker bet din hefker* even in enactments that abrogate religious commandments and prohibitions, *see further* ET, *supra* n. 72 at 100–105. A good indication of the extent to which the principle was employed even in those purely religious matters that turn on property rights can be found in Rashba, Novellae to Shabbat 18b, s.v. Gigit ner u-kederah. The Talmud there inquires whether the School of Shammai took the view that even a Jew's possessions, such as utensils, must not "work" on the sabbath as a matter of Biblical law: "[If yes,] why did the School of Shammai allow a barrel, a lamp, a pot, or a spit [to be used on the sabbath, since they thus 'work'?" *See* Rashi, *ad loc.*, s.v. Gigit]. The answer given by the Talmud is: "They were made ownerless!" This answer is difficult for many reasons. (*See, e.g., Tosafot, ad loc.*, s.v. De-mafkar lehu afkorei; Rashba and other commentaries, *ad loc.*)

Rashba commented as follows:

> It seems to me that the reference is [not to the owner's abandonment of the utensils but] to the court's expropriation, because the court desires to issue such a decree so that the people should not transgress the prohibition. The reference must be to the court, since not everybody knows of the School of Shammai's view, and especially since the School of Hillel disagrees.

According to this view, the court declares that the utensils are ownerless and thus the utensils do not belong to their "owners," who therefore are not bound to prevent their "working."

89. In contrast to other legislative principles discussed *infra,* which are accompanied by various formal reservations (such as "It is a temporary measure" or [it is enacted] "to safeguard the matter"), the halakhic authorities are empowered to expropriate property permanently (*Nimmukei Yosef* to Alfasi, Yevamot 90b). The same point is made in the novellae of Ritba to Yevamot 90b, s.v. Ve-nigmar mineih, and in *Resp. Ritba* #180. Others, however, disagree. *See* commentaries on TB Gittin 36a/b; *Piskei ha-Rosh,* Gittin, ch. 4, #13, and *Korban Netanel, ad loc.,* subpar. 4. Similarly, the rule that one court may not overturn the legislation of another court unless greater than the other in both number and wisdom does not apply to the principle of *hefker bet din hefker* (*Tosafot,* Yevamot 79b, s.v. Bi-mei Rabbi bikshu lehattir netinim. For further details, *see Penei Yehoshu'a,* Gittin 36b, s.v. Gemara ella i amret).

90. The authority of the majority over individual members of a community was compared to that of the Sanhedrin over the entire Jewish people in both civil and criminal law:

C. "The Court May Impose Punishment Not Prescribed in the Torah"

The second exception to the general principle that denies the power to permit performance of what the Torah prohibits is the legislative principle that authorizes the halakhic authorities to enact *takkanot* in criminal law, even in capital cases and even if these enactments prescribe action the Torah prohibits. This authority is limited to instances where the felt necessities of the time require such an enactment, as the Babylonian *amoraim* put it, "as a protective measure" (*le-migdar milta,* lit. "to safeguard the matter").[91]

This legislative principle was stated by the *tanna* R. Eliezer b. Jacob:[92]

> It was taught: R. Eliezer b. Jacob said: "I have heard that the court may impose flogging and punishment not prescribed in the Torah (*bet din makkin ve-onshin she-lo min ha-Torah*)[93]—not to transgress the law of the Torah but in order to make a fence around the Torah."[94]

"The majority in each town is to each of the townspeople as the High Court is to the entire Jewish people" (*Resp. Rashba,* V, #126). It therefore became an accepted maxim, patterned after *hefker bet din hefker,* that "the community has the authority to expropriate property" (*hefker ẓibbur hefker*); *id.,* IV, #142. *See supra* p. 489 and *infra* pp. 685–688.

91. *See* TB Yevamot 90b. For the full meaning of this term, *see infra* pp. 533–536.

92. TB Sanhedrin 46a; Yevamot 90b.

93. *Makkin* refers to flogging; *ve-onshin* refers to the death penalty. Both sentences can be imposed even in cases where under the law of the Torah the defendant could not be convicted or punished. *See* Rashi, Sanhedrin 46a, s.v. She-bet din, and *infra* n. 94.

94. The phrase "not to transgress the law of the Torah" presents difficulties, as various commentators have remarked. *See* commentaries on Yevamot 90b; Sanhedrin 46a. *See also Shittah Mekubbeẓet,* Bava Kamma 96b, s.vv. Katav ha-Rif z.l. and Ve-zeh leshon ha-Ram mi-Sarkeseta z.l. The version in *Kesef Mishneh* to *MT,* Mamrim 2:4 is: "R. Eliezer b. Jacob said: 'I have heard that the court may impose flogging and punishment not prescribed in the Torah—not to transgress the law of the Torah, *i.e.,* not to establish a fixed and permanent rule of law, but in order to make a fence around the Torah, as a temporary measure.'" In parallel sources this addition is missing. TJ Ḥagigah 2:2, 11b (2:2, 78a) reads: "It was taught, R. Eliezer b. Jacob said: 'I have heard that they may impose punishment not prescribed in the *Halakhah* and that they may impose punishment not prescribed in the Torah.'" This statement appears to refer both to laws explicit in the Torah and to laws based on the Oral Law. *Shittah Mekubbeẓet* (to TB Bava Kamma 96b) gives a similar explanation for the version of the text in TB.

Megillat Ta'anit says:

> On the 22d [of the month of Elul] they resumed executing apostates. Because the gentiles ruled the Land of Israel, the Jews could not take steps against the wicked among themselves until they [the gentiles] left. After they left, they [the Jewish courts] waited three days [to see] if they [the wrongdoers] would repent. When they saw that they did not repent, they determined what to do with them and executed them. The day they executed them was declared a holiday. R. Eliezer b. Jacob said: "I have heard that the court may impose flogging and execute a sentence of death not prescribed in the Torah." Bet Levi said in the name of R. Simeon: "I have heard that the court may impose fines and flogging not prescribed in the Torah, not because it is so written in

In the discussion that follows the quoted statement of R. Eliezer b. Jacob, two incidents (*ma'asim*)[95] are reported in which the Sages acted in accordance with this legislative principle:

> Once a man rode a horse on the sabbath in the time of the Greeks, and he was brought to the court and stoned, not because this was the legally prescribed punishment[96] but because the exigencies of the time so required ["because sinfulness was rife, for, seeing the oppression and persecution of Israel by the Greeks, people were contemptuous of the commandments"—Rashi].
>
> On another occasion, a man "thrust" his wife under a fig tree [had sexual intercourse with her in a public place] and he was brought to the court and flogged, not because this was the legally prescribed punishment but because the exigencies of the time so required. [Biblical law does not impose the punishment of flogging for this act, but it was a repugnant and immoral act that the Sages sought to curb].[97]

---

the Torah, but because it is written, 'You will sweep out evil from your midst' [Deuteronomy 21:21]." (*See* H. Lichtenstein, "Die Fastenrolle" [The Fast Scroll, *i.e., Megillat Ta'anit*], *HUCA,* VIII–IX (1931–1932), pp. 305–306, 336.)

In this version of R. Eliezer b. Jacob's statement, "execute a sentence of death" is specifically stated instead of the more general "impose . . . punishment," as in TB and TJ. Also of interest is the Scriptural source to which this legislative principle was attached—the general directive of the Written Law, "You will sweep out evil from your midst." It is possible that the passage "not to transgress the law of the Torah . . . " is a later addition by the *amoraim* to the original statement by R. Eliezer b. Jacob, which was only that the court may impose flogging and punishment not prescribed in the Torah. Such an addition would accord with the reservation laid down by the *amoraim* in Yevamot 90b and other places that the authority to impose punishment not prescribed in the Torah is only "to safeguard the matter, *i.e.,* the Torah." It is also possible that the passage "not to transgress the law of the Torah . . ." should be seen as identical to the conclusion in *Megillat Ta'anit,* "not because it is so written in the Torah, but because it is written, 'You will sweep out evil from your midst.'" The subject bears further study.

95. For an explanation of the term *ma'aseh, see infra* pp. 945–948.

96. The prohibition against riding a horse on the sabbath is not Biblical, but only rabbinic—"because of *shevut,*" a term denoting certain rabbinic prohibitions relating to the sabbath (M Beẓah 5:2). There is, therefore, no basis for the death penalty for violation of this prohibition. TJ, however, indicates that riding a horse on the sabbath transgresses a positive Scriptural commandment (TJ Beẓah 5:2, 20a [5:2, 63a]). The Book of Jubilees is to the same effect, as is also the Karaite view. *See* Alon, *Meḥkarim,* I, p. 104; H. Albeck, Mo'ed, Hashlamot, p. 484; TJ Ḥagigah, quoted *infra* n. 97.

97. TJ Ḥagigah 2:2, 11b (2:2, 78a) reads: "It happened that on the sabbath a person set out on a journey riding on a horse, and he was brought to the court and stoned. But was it not [only] a *shevut* [*i.e.,* a rabbinic prohibition]?! [Yes,] but the exigencies of the time so required. It also happened that a man set out on a journey with his wife and went behind a hedge and had intercourse with her, and he was brought to the court and flogged. But was she not his wife?! [Yes,] but he behaved disgracefully." In *Megillat Ta'anit, supra* n. 94, the ending of the second incident reads: "[Yes,] but the exigencies of the time required so, so that others should learn, because they [*i.e.,* the husband and wife] acted lewdly." *See further* Alon, *supra* n. 96, and H. Lichtenstein, *supra* n. 94.

Imposing these criminal punishments in effect nullified Biblical law by permitting conduct the Torah prohibits: the Torah prohibits the flogging of any person who has not committed a transgression for which the Torah prescribes this punishment;[98] and, certainly, Biblical law does not condone executing someone whom the Torah has not subjected to the death penalty. Indeed, David ibn Zimra (Radbaz) has pointed out that such an execution would violate the commandment "You shall not murder."[99] Nevertheless, the halakhic authorities held themselves competent to legislate additions and modifications to Jewish criminal law, in order to be able to react to the changes occurring from time to time in the social, religious, and moral circumstances of the people.[100]

In the fourth generation of *amoraim* in the Land of Israel, there was a debate on the question of just how broad this principle is:[101]

> To what extent [is it permitted to impose punishment not provided for by Biblical law]? R. Eleazar b. R. Yose stated: "Even in the case of a 'buzz' (*zimzum*)" [*i.e.*, even when there is no direct evidence but only hearsay or circumstantial evidence].[102] R. Yose stated: "When there are witnesses but no prior warning" [*i.e.*, punishment cannot be inflicted unless there are eyewitnesses, but prior warning, required by Biblical law,[103] may be dispensed with].

Many enactments and practices in criminal law during the Talmudic period were based on this flexible and far-reaching principle, when the times so required.[104]

98. *See* Maimonides, *MT*, Sanhedrin 16:12; *Sefer ha-Miẓvot*, Negative Commandments, #300.

99. Radbaz to *MT*, Mamrim 2:4.

100. Halakhic authorities have variously resolved the contradiction between their authority to impose the death penalty and monetary fines in the post-Temple period, and such rulings in the Talmud as those that abolished capital punishment forty years before the destruction of the Temple and denied to the halakhic authorities in Babylonia jurisdiction to impose fines. *See* I.M. Ginsburg, *Mishpatim le-Yisra'el* [Laws for Israel], pp. 14ff., 19, 81 and n. 6. Some halakhic authorities limited this authority in theory but not in practice. *See* Ran, Novellae to Sanhedrin 46a, s.v. Bet din makkin ve-onshin, to the effect that full authority in criminal law is given only to "a court of ordained expert judges, such as Simeon b. Shataḥ and his colleagues," and that this authority in the diaspora is exercised only by virtue of a license granted by the government. *See also infra* and n. 105.

101. TJ Ḥagigah 2:2, 11b (2:2, 78a).

102. The word *zimzum* (lit. "buzzing") means "rumor"; *see* S. Lieberman, "Tikkunei Yerushalmi" [Emendations in TJ], *Tarbiẓ*, V (1934), pp. 97ff. (at p. 99). Apparently, the meaning is that there is no direct, but only circumstantial, evidence.

103. M Sanhedrin 5:1; TB Sanhedrin 41a, *et al.*

104. *E.g.*, imprisonment (*hakhnasah le-khippah*), M Sanhedrin 9:5 (for details, *see* Elon, *Ma'asar*, pp. 176–178). Simeon b. Shataḥ provides another example. He hanged eighty women in Ashkelon on a single day, notwithstanding the law that "two capital cases cannot be tried on one day, but the times demanded it in order to teach others." *See Sifrei*,

This legislative principle was used by the halakhic authorities in all periods as an extremely valuable and important tool in governing Jewish society. To the extent permitted by the degree of juridical autonomy conferred on various Jewish centers, this principle was instrumental in the development of an extensive body of legislation throughout the field of criminal law and procedure.[105] This legislation conferred broad authority to impose criminal sanctions and to adopt rules of criminal procedure that would meet the societal needs of the time, while strictly guarding against any undue infringement of the dignity of the human being, who was created in God's image. After first describing this broad power of the halakhic authorities in the area of criminal law,[106] Maimonides summarized their responsibility in regard to how their authority is to be exercised:

> All these matters apply to the extent that the judge deems appropriate and necessary for the needs of the time. In all matters, he shall act for the sake of Heaven [*i.e.*, with no selfish motive] and not regard human dignity lightly, for consideration for human dignity may warrant setting aside rabbinic injunctions.[107] This applies even more so to the dignity of the children of Abraham, Isaac, and Jacob, who follow the true law. He must be careful not to destroy their dignity; rather he must act solely to increase the honor of God, for anyone who scorns the Torah will himself be dishonored by the people,

---

Deuteronomy, Ki Teẓe, sec. 221 (p. 253); TB Sanhedrin 45b and Rashi, *ad loc.*, s.v. Ein danin shenayim be-yom eḥad (explaining that the punishment was imposed "because Jewish women widely practiced sorcery"); TJ Ḥagigah, *supra* n. 94. *Megillat Ta'anit, supra* n. 94, reads: "Simeon b. Shataḥ hanged eighty women in Ashkelon. But were they legally subject to be killed and hanged? [No,] but the times required it so that others should learn from it and [so that] all Israel should hear and be afraid." *See also* Meiri, *Bet ha-Beḥirah*, Sanhedrin 52b (ed. Sofer, p. 212); *Resp. Rashba Attributed to Naḥmanides* #279; *Resp. Asheri* 18:13; *Tur* and Sh. Ar. ḤM ch. 2.

105. *See* the statement of Judah b. Asher (Asheri's son), in *Resp. Zikhron Yehudah* #79:

> . . . It is well known that the new cases that arise all the time are innumerable and that it is impossible to list them and specify all laws applicable to them. Therefore, the Sages wrote for us a general principle [of criminal law] that includes many matters, and they thereby empowered the court to institute safeguards whenever circumstances so require, as is stated in ch. "Nigmar ha-Din": "It was taught: R. Eleazar [Eliezer] b. Jacob said: 'I have heard that the court may impose flogging and punishment not prescribed by the law—not to transgress the law of the Torah, but in order to make a fence around the Torah.'"

As to some of this wider-ranging legislation in criminal law, *see* Assaf, *Onshin;* I.M. Ginsburg, *supra* n. 100, especially at 22ff.; Elon, *Ma'asar*, pp. 171–201; ET, VIII, pp. 521–525, s.v. Hora'at sha'ah; *supra* pp. 10–11, 47, 488, 517 n. 100, and *infra* pp. 688–698.

106. *MT*, Sanhedrin 24:4–9.

107. *I.e.*, rabbinic laws based on the prohibition "You must not deviate" (Deuteronomy 17:11; *see supra* p. 482), which are set aside out of considerations of human dignity. *See* TB Berakhot 19b; Maimonides, *MT*, Evel 3:14.

> and whoever honors the Torah will himself be honored by the people; and the Torah is honored only when its statutes and laws are carried out in practice.[108]

D. Temporary Measures to Restore the People to the Faith

The third exception to the general principle that the halakhic authorities may not permit performance of what the Torah prohibits is the legislative principle that vests competence in the halakhic authorities to adopt legislation permitting conduct forbidden by the Torah—even in purely religious matters—if they deem such a temporary measure (*hora'at sha'ah*) to be a necessary precaution to restore the people to the observance of the faith.

This legislative competence of the halakhic authorities was summarized by Maimonides on the basis of Talmudic sources as follows:[109]

> If they [the court] should deem it necessary temporarily to set aside a positive commandment or to nullify a negative commandment in order to restore the people to the faith or to save many Jews from becoming lax in other matters, they may act as the needs of the time dictate. Just as a physician amputates a hand or foot to save a life, so a court in appropriate circumstances may decree a temporary violation of some of the commandments to preserve all of them,[110] in line with the approach of the early Sages who said:[111] "One should violate . . . one sabbath in order to enable the observance of many sabbaths."[112]

108. *MT,* Sanhedrin 24:10. *See also Exodus Rabbah* 30:23: "Because the Holy One, Blessed be He, gave you the Torah only on condition that you follow the laws." *See also Resp. Rashba,* V, #238:

> . . . There must be deliberation, agreement, and consultation. This will encourage the public to do the will of Heaven, for the more important the case and the greater the force involved, the more care and composure are required. The judge must take care not to become so zealous for the glory of God that he fails to perceive the fair and right solution. Therefore, when the opportunity for avenging [God's glory] comes, he should not immediately eat it [*i.e.,* implement it] lest he eat it raw. Let him cook it and sweeten it with the advice of elders and upright men.

109. *MT,* Mamrim 2:4.

110. "From the master's words it seems that the simile points up that the commandments are parts of a single organism and that the court may 'amputate' part in order to preserve the rest" (Radbaz to *MT, ad loc.*).

111. TB Yoma 85b.

112. *See also MT,* Shabbat ch. 2 and particularly par. 3:

> Any hesitation about violating the sabbath for a dangerously sick person is forbidden, as it is written [Leviticus 18:5], "By the pursuit of . . . [My laws] man shall live"—and not die because of them. Thus you learn that the commandments of the Torah were not intended to be an act of vengeance . . . but an act of mercy, grace, and peace.

See further infra p. 990–991.

The halakhic authorities derived this legislative competence from the incident involving the prophet Elijah at Mount Carmel. Elijah offered a sacrifice on Mount Carmel to return the people from worship of Baal to the worship of God.[113] The Torah forbids a sacrificial offering anywhere but in the Temple in Jerusalem,[114] and whoever sacrifices elsewhere transgresses two Biblical prohibitions;[115] but Elijah permitted himself to offer the sacrifice on Mount Carmel, as this was the method then available to him to bring back to the worship of God those who were wavering.[116] From this incident involving Elijah, the halakhic authorities derived their competence to nullify a Biblical law when the exigencies of the time require such action "to safeguard the matter."[117]

113. I Kings 18:19–46.

114. Deuteronomy 12:13–14.

115. *See* Rashi, Yevamot 90b, s.v. Kegon Eliyahu be-har ha-Carmel.

116. *See Sifrei,* Deuteronomy, Shofetim, sec. 175 (p. 221) and TB Yevamot 90b: "'Him shall you heed' [the full verse, Deuteronomy 18:15, reads: 'The Lord your God will raise up for you a prophet from among your own people, like yourself; him shall you heed']—even if he tells you to transgress one of the commandments stated in the Torah, as did Elijah on Mt. Carmel, as a temporary measure, heed him."

117. In TB Yevamot 90b, R. Ḥisda relied on the quotation from *Sifrei, supra* n. 116, to support his view that as a general principle a court may abrogate a law of the Torah even to the extent of permitting performance of an act the Torah prohibits. (As to the dispute between R. Ḥisda and Rabbah on this point, *see supra* p. 506.) The Talmud first responded: "That case [involving Elijah] was different, because it is written, '. . . him shall you heed.'" [*I.e.,* a prophet is so empowered, since the Scriptural injunction ". . . him shall you heed" explicitly applies to a prophet and includes instances of temporary abrogation of a Biblical law.] The Talmud then asked: "Then should we not learn from him [*i.e.,* should we not analogize the Sages to the prophets]?" To which the answer was, "'To safeguard the matter,' [*i.e.,* to "make a fence" to rectify the situation, as occurred in that case] is different" (for by so doing Elijah brought back the people from idolatry—Rashi).

As to the question of the Talmud suggesting that the prophet's authority be used as a precedent for the halakhic authorities, the Tosafists (*ad loc.,* s.v. Ve-ligmar mineih) asked: "How can a prophet who delivers a divine message that has come to him from God in a vision be analogous to a halakhic authority whose enactment is not of divine origin?" The answer was: "Since such abrogation is permitted for temporary needs when there is a divine command [to abrogate], so, too, it should be permitted when there is no such divine command, because a prophet is no longer authorized to innovate. . . ." As to a prophet's authority to abrogate a law of the Torah temporarily—which is the only prerogative of legal creativity possessed by the halakhic authorities that a prophet also enjoys—*see MT,* Yesodei ha-Torah 9:3. *See also supra* pp. 242–243.

This discussion in the Talmud is similarly interpreted by Naḥmanides, Rashba, Ritba, and Meiri in their novellae to TB Yevamot, *ad loc.,* and by *Tosafot,* Sanhedrin 89b, s.v. Eliyahu be-har ha-Carmel (expressing the view that in temporarily abrogating a law of the Torah, a prophet acts not by divine command but on his own authority). Rashba and Ritba also offer another interpretation of the Talmudic discussion. Rabad, in his gloss to *MT,* Mamrim 2:9, indicates that this principle, which is derived from Elijah's action on Mt. Carmel, is also subsumed under the general precept, "It is a time to act for the Lord, for they have violated Your Torah" (Psalms 119:126).

E. The Court in Special Circumstances and "Where There Is Good Cause" May Permit Performance of an Act the Torah Prohibits (*Kum va-Aseh*) Even in Matters of Religious Law

The discussion to this point has noted the essential distinction, going back to the amoraic period, between legislation of halakhic authorities permitting performance of an act prohibited by the Torah (*kum va-aseh*) and legislation prohibiting the performance of an act mandated by the Torah (*shev ve-al ta'aseh*);[118] and it has also noted three legislative principles pursuant to which the halakhic authorities, under certain circumstances, may even enact legislation permitting the performance of an act prohibited by the Torah. A study of amoraic literature and legislation further reveals that these three legislative principles do not mark the limits of the competence of the halakhic authorities to abrogate a Biblical prohibition even in the sphere of religious law.

The law of marriage provides excellent illustrations of such competence. At times, the *amoraim* explicitly emphasized the authority of the Sages to annul a marriage on the basis of their legislative power. At other times, although the amoraic discussion does not explicitly refer to that authority, it is reasonable to conclude, as did some of the leading *rishonim*, that the likely basis for legislating on this subject is the prerogative of the halakhic authorities, in special circumstances and "where there is good cause," to permit performance of an act forbidden by the Torah even in a matter of religious law.

1. ANNULMENT OF MARRIAGES "IMPROPERLY EFFECTED"

The Talmud sets forth the law applicable when a man obtains by duress a woman's consent to marry him: If, by the time the marriage takes place, the woman has fully and freely consented, the general requirements of Jewish law relating to consent and coercion pose no obstacle to the legal validity of the marriage. Nevertheless, the halakhic authorities declared such a marriage void;[119] and they likewise invalidated a marriage, notwithstanding the woman's consent to be married, if the man had previously forcibly abducted her.[120]

The rationale stated for the annulment was that in these two cases the marriage was "improperly effected," *i.e.*, it took place following coercion or

118. *See supra* p. 506 n. 57. *See also infra* pp. 634–636 to the effect that the *amoraim* of the Land of Israel also held that in certain circumstances the halakhic authorities may permit conduct that is prohibited by the Torah. For a summary of these legislative guidelines as crystallized by the Babylonian *amoraim*, *see* Ritba, Novellae to Yevamot 91b, s.v. Venigmar mineih, and *Nimmukei Yosef* to Alfasi, Yevamot 91b, s.v. Tanya amar R. Eliezer b. Jacob.

119. TB Bava Batra 48b; for further details, *see infra* pp. 636–637.

120. TB Yevamot 110a; for further details, *see infra* pp. 638–639.

abduction; and the halakhic authorities have the power to annul a marriage tainted by such clearly improper conduct, even though as a matter of strictly technical law the marriage would be valid. We consider these cases in detail in connection with our later discussion of the substance of legislation in the amoraic period, since it is more appropriate to consider them together with another principle of marriage law that originated in the teachings of the Babylonian *amoraim.*[121] It is sufficient here to cite these cases where the halakhic authorities invalidated "improperly effected" marriages as an instance—in one of the most sensitive areas of religious law—where legislation permits affirmative conduct (the woman's later marriage to another man) forbidden by the Torah (according to which she is already married to the man who had abducted or coerced her).[122]

2. LEGISLATION CONCERNING *AGUNOT*

Another illustration of where good cause was found to permit the performance of an act the Torah prohibits is the legislation relating to *agunot* (sing. *agunah,* lit. "anchored" or "bound" wife). This legislation, consisting of a number of enactments, deals with women whose husbands have disappeared under circumstances where there is insufficient evidence under Biblical law to prove the husband's death so as to enable the woman to remarry. These are among the most essential and important *takkanot* in Jewish law, both for their social and humanitarian quality and for what they tell us about the nature of legislation in Jewish law.

According to Biblical law, the testimony of at least two witnesses is necessary to establish any material fact,[123] and it is therefore impossible to free a wife to remarry by reason of her husband's death unless two witnesses prove his death. The hardship of this rule in real-life situations became apparent even in ancient times when, time and again, cases arose where a husband died as a result of natural catastrophe or war, but two

121. Annulment of "improperly effected" marriages is connected in the Talmud to the principle that "all who marry do so subject to the conditions laid down by the Rabbis and the Rabbis annul this marriage." Under this principle, the annulment is not based on the Sages' legislative authority but on the premise that the marriage took place subject to the condition that the Sages agree to it; and its validity is, therefore, dependent on their approval. In certain circumstances, the Sages withhold their consent, so that the marriage is invalidated by virtue of the law governing "conditions" generally, as in the case, for example, where the husband, after having sent a bill of divorcement to his wife, cancels it without her knowledge. For further discussion, *see supra* n. 58 and *infra* pp. 631–642.

122. According to the *amoraim* of the Land of Israel, the annulment of a marriage when a husband cancels a bill of divorcement in the absence of the wife also stems from the Sages' legislative authority. *See infra* pp. 634–636, which also discusses another example of the Sages' legislative authority to abrogate a law of the Torah by permitting what the Torah prohibits, namely the enactment relating to setting aside *terumah* of olives for olive oil.

123. Deuteronomy 19:15; TB Gittin 2b.

witnesses could not be found to testify confirming his death. Under Biblical law, the wife was an *agunah*, "bound" to her absent husband for the rest of her life; but the halakhic authorities came to her aid through various means utilizing the legal sources of Jewish law. The most important of these was legislation.

The primary sources indicate that the earliest such legislation was the enactment that permitted a woman to remarry on the sole basis of her own testimony, without requiring any other witnesses.[124] The factual background for the enactment has been preserved by a tradition going back to the beginning of the amoraic period:[125]

> What are the facts of the incident?[126] R. Judah said in the name of Samuel: "It was at the end of the wheat harvest, and ten men went to harvest the wheat. A serpent bit one of them, and he died. His wife came and related this to the court, which investigated and found that it was true. Thereupon [lit. "at that time"], they declared:[127] 'A woman who testifies, "My husband has died," may remarry, and [if there are no children] the law of levirate marriage applies.'"

This incident, which, as will be seen later, in all probability occurred at a much earlier time than the date of R. Judah's report of it, proved to the

124. There was no disagreement as to the proposition that the testimony of a woman who says, "My husband has died" sufficiently establishes his death. On the other hand, a related rule that the testimony of a single witness is sufficient to establish the husband's death was still the subject of dispute as late as the second generation of *tannaim*, as will be seen *infra*.

As to the wife's testimony, disagreement among the Sages was limited to various details, such as whether her testimony is sufficient only when she comes from the harvest, there have been good relations between the spouses, there is peace throughout the area, and she has appeared weeping and with her garments torn. *See* M Yevamot 15:1–2; M Eduyyot 1:12; *Tosefta* Eduyyot 1:6. It follows, therefore, that the basic law that the wife's testimony is sufficient was an early undisputed enactment. TJ Yevamot 15:1, 77a (15:1, 14d) also supports this conclusion:

> Not only according to the later *mishnah* that a single witness can release her [from her status as a married woman], but even under the rule stated in the original *mishnah* that a single witness cannot release her, she can release herself. What is the distinction between her and a[ny other] single witness? The single witness may be suspected of an intention to taint her [*i.e.*, bring her to transgress the prohibition against adultery]; she is not suspected of a desire to taint herself.

125. TB Yevamot 116b.

126. This refers to the incident described in M Yevamot 15:2: "The School of Hillel said: 'We have heard so only when she comes from the harvest in the same country and when the facts are similar to those in the actual case.' The School of Shammai said to them, 'The law applies whether [or not] she comes from the harvest .'" *See supra* p. 402.

127. The formula "at that time they declared" is generally used in connection with laws for which the legal source is legislation. *See, e.g.*, "At that time they declared: 'A man may not go forth in a nailed sandal'" (TB Shabbat 60a); "When the Hasmonean kings besieged . . . , at that time they declared: 'Cursed be the man who rears swine.'" (TB Sotah 49b; Bava Kamma 82b).

Sages that a woman is extremely careful in giving details of the death of her husband: in this particular case, they investigated her testimony (which was verifiable because there were other people present) and found that her testimony was true. On the basis of their experience in this case, they enacted a general *takkanah* that a husband's death may be established by the testimony of his wife alone;[128] this enactment also met the needs for solving other even more complex problems involving women whose husbands had disappeared. The circumstances to which the enactment applies was a matter of dispute between the schools of Shammai and Hillel until the School of Hillel reversed itself and agreed with the School of Shammai. The Mishnah states:[129]

> These are the subjects on which the School of Hillel reversed itself and taught in accordance with the view of the School of Shammai. A woman who comes from abroad [lit. "the region of the sea"] and declares, "My husband has died," may remarry, and [if there are no children] the law of levirate marriage applies. The School of Hillel said: "We have heard so only when she comes from the harvest" [as occurred in the incident mentioned above]. The School of Shammai said to them: "The law applies whether she comes from the harvest or the olive grove or from abroad; the harvest was mentioned only because it is the usual situation." The School of Hillel thereupon reconsidered and adopted the view of the School of Shammai.

Since the legislation was enacted against the background of an actual incident, there was at first a difference of opinion among the Sages as to whether the enactment governed cases beyond the narrow factual circumstances of that incident; but they ultimately were unanimous that the enactment was broad and general rather than limited to the specific facts of the incident that gave rise to it.[130]

The enactment permitting the court to credit a woman's testimony that her husband has died did not, however, fully meet the needs of the time.

128. *See Tosafot,* Yevamot 116b, s.v. Be-otah sha'ah amru ha-ishah she-amrah met ba'ali, and other commentaries, *ad loc. See also Resp. Binyamin Ze'ev* #1 (end). For an interesting insight, *see* E. Klatzkin, *Sefer Devar Halakhah,* p. 9: "Although there were ten persons present [when the man died], not one of them came forward to inform the court, and only his wife informed the court. It thus became clear to the Sages that if the woman's testimony is not accepted she will surely be an *agunah,* and that unless a wife's testimony is accepted under similar circumstances, there would be many more *agunot,* since no one else would come forward to clarify the matter." *See* I.Z. Kahane, *Sefer ha-Agunot,* Jerusalem, 1954, p. 45 and explanations and nn., *ad loc.*

129. M Eduyyot 1:12, and parallel in M Yevamot 15:2, with v.l.; *see* v.l. and H. Albeck, *ad loc.* Apparently, the version in M Eduyyot is the earlier; M Yevamot already includes additional refinements, *e.g.,* R. Judah's statement in M Yevamot 15:1 that the wife must come in tears and with her clothes torn.

130. *See further* TB Yevamot 116b: "It was taught: The School of Shammai said to them. . . ." On this dispute between the two schools, *see further supra* p. 402.

Often, and especially in time of war, women do not accompany their husbands and are unable to testify to the husband's death. In such cases, there is often no more than a single witness, and it became necessary to accept such testimony as sufficient to free the woman from her "chains" as an *agunah*. Consequently, an additional enactment was adopted to cover this situation. The Mishnah states:[131]

> R. Akiva stated: "When I went down to Nehardea [in Babylonia] to declare a leap year [at a time when the Roman Empire prohibited the performance of Jewish religious practices and the years could not be intercalated in the Land of Israel],[132] I met Nehemiah of Bet Dali.[133] He said to me: 'I have heard that in the Land of Israel no one except R. Judah b. Bava permits a woman to remarry on the testimony of [only] one witness.' I said to him, 'That is so.' He said to me, 'Tell them in my name: You know that the country is in a chaotic condition because of the raiding parties.[134] I have a tradition from Rabban Gamaliel the Elder that a woman may remarry on the strength of the testimony of one witness.' [R. Akiva continued]: When I came and recounted the conversation to Rabban Gamaliel [II], he rejoiced to hear my words and exclaimed, 'We have found a colleague for R. Judah b. Bava.'"
>
> As a result of the conversation, Rabban Gamaliel recollected that some men had been killed at Tel Arzah,[135] and Rabban Gamaliel the Elder had permitted their wives to remarry on the strength of the testimony of one witness. And the law was established that a woman may remarry on the strength of the testimony of one witness.

This is an enlightening and detailed description of the enactment of an additional essential *takkanah* on the problem of *agunot*. This problem was particularly acute during the period of war and religious persecution by the Romans in the century following the destruction of the Temple. Many men

131. M Yevamot 16:7.

132. *See* H. Albeck, *ad loc.*, and Hashlamot, p. 344. According to Alon, *Toledot*, I, pp. 153–154, R. Akiva went to Babylonia to intercalate the year not because it was a time of emergency but because intercalation by the Sages of the Land of Israel was performed in Babylonia for the benefit of the Jews there and in order to strengthen their ties with the Land of Israel. *But see* H.D. Mantel, *Studies in the History of the Sanhedrin*, pp. 179–184.

133. Scholars disagree as to the exact location of Bet Dali, R. Nehemiah's residence in the Land of Israel before he emigrated to Babylonia. It has been speculated that it is to be identified with Daliyat al-Karmil. *See* S. Klein, "Zur Ortsnamenkunde Palastinas" [On the Study of Palestinian Place Names], *MGWJ*, 1920, pp. 188–189; J. Neusner, *A History of the Jews in Babylonia*, I, p. 50 n. 1; *Encyclopaedia Judaica* (Berlin), IV, p. 398.

134. Obadiah Bertinoro, M Yevamot 16:7, s.v. Meshubeshet bi-geyasot, explains: "I am therefore unable to go to the Land of Israel and testify before the Sages there." *Melekhet Shelomo, ad loc.*, s.v. Ve-namti lo (end), explains: "The country is in a chaotic condition because of the raiding parties and it is not always possible to find two witnesses." Both explanations are based on TB Yevamot 115a. *See also* Alon, *supra* n. 132; Mantel, *supra* n. 132 at 185 and n. 60.

135. For the nature of this war, *see* S. Klein, *supra* n. 133 at 189 n. 1.

who took part in the wars and rebellions were missing, and it was not always possible to find two witnesses to prove the death of a husband so as to release a woman from her "chains" as an *agunah*. Only one Sage, R. Judah b. Bava, believed (apparently following the earlier *takkanah* of Rabban Gamaliel the Elder) that the testimony of one witness is sufficient to free her.[136] R. Akiva brought with him on his return from Babylonia to the Land of Israel an important tradition attributed to Rabban Gamaliel the Elder, according to which a woman may remarry on the strength of the testimony of only one witness.[137] (This attribution is reasonable because Rabban Gamaliel the Elder was heavily involved in enacting significant legislation in the area of family law.)[138]

This *mishnah* also sets out the background and the need for this enactment in the time of Rabban Gamaliel the Elder: it was a time of war, there were casualties at Tel Arzah, and there was only a single witness to give the evidence of death necessary before the wives could remarry. After the time of Rabban Gamaliel the Elder, this enactment was possibly forgotten, or perhaps not everyone agreed to it. In any event, among the Sages in the Land of Israel in the generation of Rabban Gamaliel II (of Yavneh), only R. Judah b. Bava agreed to this enactment; R. Eliezer and R. Joshua explicitly disagreed with it.[139] When R. Akiva reported this tradition to Rabban Gamaliel of Yavneh, Rabban Gamaliel recollected the case of those who were killed at Tel Arzah, in which his grandfather had freed their wives on the strength of the testimony of only one witness. Thus, from the combination of these two legal sources—legislation and precedent—the earlier enactment that the testimony of a single witness is sufficient to permit a woman to remarry was again accepted and thus "the law was established that a woman may remarry on the strength of the testimony of one witness."[140]

136. *See also* M Eduyyot 6:1: "R. Judah b. Bava testified to five things: That they may [at times] instruct women who married while they were minors to exercise a right of disaffirmance [*mi'un*, lit. "refusal"] and that a woman may remarry on the testimony of one witness. . . ."

137. This testimony of R. Akiva is also recorded in M Eduyyot 8:5: "R. Akiva testified in the name of Nehemiah of Bet Dali that a woman may remarry on the basis of the testimony of one witness."

138. *See, e.g.*, M Gittin 4:2–3 and *infra* pp. 563–566.

139. M Yevamot 16:7.

140. The quoted language is missing from the *mishnah* in TJ Yevamot 16:7, 84b (16:8, 15c) and in various editions of TB. *But see Melekhet Shelomo, ad loc.*, s.v. Ve-hissi Rabban Gamaliel ha-Zaken, proving the correctness of this reading, which is also quoted by many *rishonim*. In order to give greater force to this law, which originated in a legislative enactment, the Sages connected it with a Scriptural verse. *Midrash Tannaim*, Deuteronomy 19:15, p. 115, states: "'A single witness may not validate against a person [lit. "man"] [any guilt or blame for any offense that may be committed]'—he may not validate 'any guilt or blame,' but he may validate to benefit a woman. On this basis [lit. "from here"], R. Akiva declared:

This enactment is also an example of legislation that abrogates a Biblical prohibition in the sphere of religious law: the enactment permits a woman to remarry although under Biblical law she is still bound to her prior marriage. Considerable effort was expended in the amoraic period to provide a legal basis for this legislation. The background and policy rationale for the enactment is given in the statement of the *amoraim* that "the Rabbis relaxed the law because [of the plight] of the *agunah*."[141]

The various legal justifications are summarized in the rationale, "A woman is careful [to ascertain that her husband has died] before she remarries";[142] if it should turn out that her husband is alive she would be the one to suffer since she would be required to leave both her first and second husbands, and her children by the second husband would be *mamzerim* (offspring of a union that is incestuous or adulterous under Jewish law).[143] Still another rationale is the general rule of evidence that "people will not lie about a matter whose truth is sure to be discovered,"[144] *i.e.*, it need not

---

'A woman may remarry on strength of the testimony of one witness.'" The phrase "from here, they declared" is commonly used in the sense of "because of this they declared," as in TB Pesaḥim 99a: "From here, the Sages declared, 'Silence befits Sages . . .'" (*see* Rashi, *ad loc.*, s.v. Mi-kan amru); and as in M Avot 1:5: "From here, the Sages declared, 'Whenever a man converses excessively with a woman. . . .'"

A similar exegesis appears in *Sifrei*, Deuteronomy, Shofetim, sec. 188 (p. 228) in the name of R. Judah: "'A single witness may not validate against a man . . . .' The verse speaks only of testimony involving a man; whence do we derive that it also applies to testimony involving a woman? Scripture says [Deuteronomy 19:15] '. . . any guilt or blame for any offense that may be committed.' If ultimately women are included, why did Scripture specify 'man'? [This teaches that] a single witness is not sufficient to prove an offense, but is sufficient to permit a woman to remarry."

A similar connection between an enactment and a Scriptural verse was noted as to the *prosbul*, *see supra* p. 513 n. 86.

141. TB Yevamot 88a.

142. TB Yevamot 25a, 93b, 115a, 116b. Some of the *rishonim* saw this as a sufficient reason for the wife's testimony to have the same credence as the testimony of two witnesses under Biblical law: "Because the Sages saw that a woman is careful to ascertain that her husband has died before she remarries, it [her testimony] is as good as two witnesses, because she certainly will not lie"; *Tosafot Yeshanim*, Yevamot 88a. This is also the opinion of Ritba in his novellae, *ad loc.*, s.v. Mi-tokh ḥomer. However, apart from the very novelty of this proposition, the great difficulty with it is that the discussion in the Talmud explicitly emphasizes that the rule is based on legislation ("The Rabbis relaxed the law because [of the plight] of the *agunah*") and that under Biblical law her testimony is insufficient. Ritba, *loc. cit.*, was himself aware of this difficulty. *See also infra* nn. 144, 152.

143. TB Yevamot 87b *et seq.*

144. *Id.* 93b, 115a, 116b. Some post-Talmudic halakhic authorities strove to find in this rationale an adequate basis for a ruling that a single witness is sufficient even according to Biblical law; *see, e.g.*, Ritba, Novellae to Yevamot 88a, s.v. Mi-tokh ḥomer she-heḥemarta aleha be-sofah, and *Yam Shel Shelomo*, Yevamot 10:1. Other *rishonim*, however, disagreed; *see, e.g.*, Rashba, Novellae to Yevamot 88a, s.v. Ha de-amrinan ella sevara hi; *Tosafot*, Yevamot 88a, s.v. Mi-tokh ḥomer she-heḥemarta aleha be-sofah; and *Tosafot* quoted *infra*, text

be feared that people will lie about a matter where the truth is bound to come out; and here in the course of time it will surely become known whether or not the husband is living.

These legal justifications, however, are not in themselves a full and compelling basis for permitting a woman to remarry. It was the Tosafists[145] who aptly formulated the rationale providing the basis for the power of the halakhic authorities to enact legislation concerning *agunot:* "Even if the halakhic authorities generally lack competence to permit conduct prohibited by the Torah, there is a clear consensus that they possess such authority when there is good cause to permit such conduct" (in another place[146] *Tosafot's* formulation is, "when they have a measure of reason and justification for doing so").[147]

The number of laws enacted on the subject of *agunot* continually increased until these laws became a large and multifaceted segment of Jewish family law. As early as in the tannaitic period,[148] and thereafter in the

---

at n. 145. The plain meaning of the discussion in the Talmud is that the adequacy of a single witness is the result of a rabbinic enactment: "If a single witness says, 'He died,' the Sages give his testimony the same credence as the testimony of two witnesses" (TB Ketubbot 22b). The view of Ritba and those who follow him would explain only the enactment that a single witness is sufficient but not other rules relaxing evidentiary requirements such as that hearsay evidence is acceptable. *See also supra* n. 142.

145. TB Nazir 43b, s.v. Ve-hai met mizvah hu.

146. *Tosafot,* Yevamot 88a, s.v. Mi-tokh ḥomer she-heḥemarta aleha be-sofah.

147. *See also Tosafot,* Yevamot 89b, s.v. Keivan de-la yartei lah karya ve-la anu lah. Some *rishonim* attempted to base the enactments concerning *agunot* on the principle that "all who marry do so subject to the conditions laid down by the Rabbis." *See* Rashba, quoted in *Shittah Mekubbezet,* Ketubbot 3a, s.v. Ve-ha-Rashba z.l. katav; Meiri, *Bet ha-Beḥirah,* Yevamot 87b; and Rashi, Shabbat 145b, s.v. Le-edut ishah, regarding acceptance of hearsay evidence. This principle could explain the authority to enact such *takkanot* in the amoraic period, since the principle was formulated in that period (*see infra* p. 631). However, this explanation is questionable. One of the provisions of the enactment is that if, after the woman has remarried, it is established that the first husband did not in fact die, she is to be divorced by both men. If the basis of the enactment is that the first marriage has been annulled, then why should she be divorced from her second husband? Rashba dealt with this question, but his solution is very forced. For other reasons why, even in the amoraic period, the enactments could not have been based on the principle "All who marry do so subject to the conditions laid down by the Rabbis . . . ," *see* Ritba, Novellae to Yevamot 88a, s.v. Mi-tokh ḥomer; and *infra* p. 641 n. 65. For all these reasons, it is apparent that the Talmud does not view the enactments as being based on this principle.

148. M Yevamot 16:7: "The law was established that a woman may remarry on the basis of hearsay testimony, or the testimony of a slave, a woman, or a maidservant [all of whom are generally not competent witnesses]. . . ." *See also* M Yevamot 16:5; *Tosefta* Yevamot 14:7 (even if the witness only heard the sound of wailing in lamentation for the dead or on the testimony of a gentile who gives information, oblivious to its legal significance); M Yevamot 16:6 ("They may give evidence [of identity, even if they have only seen the corpse] by the light of a lamp or by the light of the moon, and a woman may be allowed to remarry on the strength of a *bat kol* [lit. a voice from afar, or an echo]").

amoraic[149] and in all succeeding periods to the present,[150] the law has continued to be increasingly further relaxed, either by means of midrashic interpretation or by rulings in particular cases, to permit the remarriage of an *agunah*.

The significant legislation that has been discussed here is summarized by Maimonides. His statement of the general rule concerning sufficiency of evidence is as follows:

> No case is to be decided on the testimony of a single witness, neither a civil nor a capital case, . . . [except] in two instances [where] the Torah accepts the testimony of one witness . . . and by rabbinic enactment that a woman may remarry on the strength of the testimony of one witness that her husband is dead; and whenever a single witness is sufficient, that witness may be a woman or a witness who would otherwise be incompetent to testify.[151]

Maimonides explained this special rule with regard to *agunot:*

> Do not be surprised that, as we have explained, the Sages relaxed the law in the area of forbidden sexual relationships, which are ordinarily dealt with strictly, to accept without inquiry and examination the testimony of a woman or slave or maidservant or gentile who gives information, oblivious to its legal significance, as well as hearsay and documentary evidence. The Torah was careful to require the testimony of two witnesses and the other safeguards of the rules of evidence only for facts not provable except through the testimony of these witnesses, such as the fact that A killed B or A lent money to B. But if the truth of a matter can be discovered without this witness and the witness cannot escape the consequences if it is not true, *e.g.*, if a witness testifies that A is dead, the Torah was not so strict, as it is unlikely that the witness will testify falsely. Therefore, the Sages were liberal on this matter and accepted, without inquiry and examination, a single witness, the testimony of a maidservant, and documentary evidence in order that the daughters of Israel not remain *agunot.*[152]

149. TJ Yevamot 16:7, 84b (16:7, 16a): "If they found a legal document in which was written, 'So-and-so died' or 'So-and-so was killed,' R. Jeremiah says, 'They may allow his wife to remarry . . .'"; TB Rosh ha-Shanah 22a: "R. Ashi said: 'This means that persons deemed robbers under rabbinic law are competent to testify regarding the status of a woman.'"

150. *See* Kahane, *supra* n. 128, *passim; id.*, *Le-Takkanat Agunot* [On Solving the Problem of *Agunot*], Jerusalem, 1947.

151. *MT,* Edut 5:1–3.

152. *MT,* Gerushin 13:29. Despite Maimonides' genius in supplying logical and rational reasons, his own discussion reveals how difficult he found it to explain the legal basis for these enactments relaxing the law governing forbidden sexual relationships.

In *MT,* Edut, as at the beginning and the end of his statement of the law in *MT,* Gerushin, Maimonides referred to "rabbinic enactment" and to the Sages who relaxed the law and ruled leniently. However, in the course of his remarks in *MT,* Gerushin, he also stated that "the Torah was not so strict"; *see Leḥem Mishneh, ad loc. Rishonim* and *aḥaronim*

Rabad in his gloss to this statement of Maimonides added a further rationale: "In addition, a woman will be very careful not to remarry unless she is certain that her husband is not alive."[153]

---

alike have noted this discrepancy; *see* Kahane, *supra* n. 128 at 16–19 for an extensive discussion.

153. Halakhic authorities in different periods have made many significant comments on the background and rationale of the legislation concerning *agunot.* Of particular interest is the comment of Maharsha in his novellae at the end of Tractate *Yevamot* with regard to various enactments concerning family law generally and the question of *agunot* in particular.

Tractate *Yevamot* concludes (TB Yevamot 122b):

> R. Eleazar said in the name of R. Ḥanina: "Disciples of the Sages increase peace in the world, as it is written [Isaiah 54:13], 'And all Your children will be learned of the Lord, and great will be the peace of Your children.'

Maharsha, in explaining why the tractate concludes in this manner, states:

> This tractate contains laws which, at first sight, are surprising, for they appear to abrogate Biblical law. For in ch. "Ha-Ishah [Rabbah" (TB Yevamot 89b)], the Talmud queries whether the court can adopt enactments abrogating Biblical law regarding several matters, and the Talmud then responds. *Tosafot, ad loc.*, at the beginning of the chapter (Yevamot 88a, s.v. Mi-tokh ḥomer she-heḥemarta), in connection with the statement that the Sages relaxed the law on *agunot,* remarks, "This does not constitute abrogation of a law of the Torah because the testimony is inherently credible. . . ." However, the explanation is forced. Also, as to the subject under discussion [Yevamot 122b], how could they be so lenient regarding a married woman as to uproot a law of the Torah when the Torah requires full inquiry and examination of the witness? [*See infra* p. 609.]
>
> Furthermore, in the first chapter [Yevamot 15a] it is said: "As to [certain] fellow-wives (*ẓarot*) [whose husbands died childless and who have, without *ḥaliẓah,* married someone other than the *levir,* which is permitted] according to the School of Hillel, what should be done [to satisfy the School of Shammai, who require levirate marriage or *ḥaliẓah* in such a case]? If we insist that they undergo *ḥaliẓah,* they will become distasteful in the eyes of their husbands. If you answer, 'Let them become distasteful!,' [that cannot be, since] its [the Torah's] ways are pleasant ways."
>
> Similarly, at the end of ch. "Yesh Mutarot" (Yevamot 87b), it is said: "[With regard to levirate marriage], an inference *a fortiori* should lead to the conclusion that a child who has died [after his father's death] should not be treated as a surviving child; [and the widow should have to undergo *ḥaliẓah* even though she has remarried]. However, Scripture says, 'Its ways are pleasant ways.'"
>
> This is a puzzling argument. Can we absolve a woman of the requirement to undergo *ḥaliẓah* simply in order not to make her distasteful [to her husband]? . . . [As to this, *see supra* p. 390].
>
> This tractate [Yevamot] therefore concludes with the statement that the disciples of the Sages increase peace in the world . . . to indicate that no law of the Torah is being uprooted, because these matters are connected with the ideal of peace. . . . The woman should not be made to undergo either a levirate marriage or *ḥaliẓah,* because this will cause strife—perhaps the brother will not agree to grant her *ḥaliẓah,* and she will not agree to marry him, thus becoming an *agunah.* This is not peace. . . . Scripture says, "Great peace will be granted to those who love Your Torah." It is not an uprooting but rather furthers the ideal of peace to ensure that a woman should not be an *agunah.* It is also written, "Its ways are pleasant ways . . . ," and, finally [Psalms 29:11], "May the Lord grant [lit. also, "the Lord will grant"] strength to His people."

3. EXTENSION OF THIS PRINCIPLE TO LEGISLATION IN CRIMINAL LAW

At times, the halakhic authorities made use in the criminal law of the principle that permits conduct prohibited by Biblical law "when there is good cause" to do so, although the same result could have been reached in that area of the law by means of the principle that "the court may impose punishment not prescribed in the Torah." An interesting illustration is found in a responsum by one of the leading Tosafists, Isaac b. Samuel (Isaac the Elder, Ri), to a question referred to him by Asher b. Meshullam with regard to the law relating to informers:[154]

> You are surprised at the taking of the life of a Jew who is an informer for monetary gain. . . . Do not be surprised, for there is an important reason here, since an informer is often a danger to the lives of many. An informer who has no regard for the life of his fellow man and who is suspected of robbing and killing at every opportunity [certainly constitutes such a danger]. Even [an informer concerning whom] we do not have absolute proof [of violent disposition] may properly be put to death, since most who act as he does [*i.e.*, inform] are likely to [have committed acts of violence. All this applies] even if he is not actually engaged in informing when apprehended.
>
> There is possibly a [Biblical] verse that supports this [conclusion], but even if there is no such verse, it is unanimously held that the halakhic authorities have the power to permit conduct prohibited by Biblical law when there is a measure of justification for doing so, because in that case the Torah is not being "uprooted." With regard to the opinion expressed in chapter *Ha-Ishah Rabbah*[155] that this power to prescribe rules contrary to those of the Torah exists only for legislation prohibiting what the Torah commands but not permitting what the Torah prohibits, this is true only when there is no sufficient cause to justify legislation of the latter type.
>
> It is my view that all agree that when there is good cause, a Biblical rule may be set aside, and there are many proofs for this; the rationale is that in such a case it is not deemed an "uprooting"!

These statements, although made with reference to a particular issue of criminal law, contribute greatly to the understanding of the rationale for

---

All this does not constitute the uprooting of a law of the Torah, because the Almighty gave strength and power to His people, *i.e.*, the halakhic authorities, to relax the law in this matter, for "the Lord will bless His people with peace," as it is written, "All its ways are peace," and there will be no peace if a woman is an *agunah*. This is how the verse [Numbers 6:26] is to be interpreted: "May the Lord lift up His countenance to you" even when you abrogate a law of the Torah, so that the Lord will grant you peace.

154. *Temim De'im* #203; *see* the end of the responsum as to its attribution to Isaac the Elder.

155. TB Yevamot 89a–90b.

this legislative principle. When there is "sufficient cause to justify legislation" to make such a change from Biblical law, a *takkanah* mandating conduct forbidden by the Torah may be enacted because "in such a case it is not deemed an 'uprooting.'" This rationale can be understood only on the basis of the fundamental guideline that it is better for one letter of the Torah to be "uprooted" rather than risk the danger of uprooting the entire Torah, and on the basis of similar guidelines quoted at the beginning of this discussion of this subject.

The halakhic authorities provide additional illustrations of such far-reaching legislation even in the area of religious conduct, showing how broadly the doctrine authorizing such legislation for "good cause" is applied.[156] Still, it was settled that this legislative authority was subject to a

156. For example, TB Avodah Zarah 13a states: "When a man buys and sells in a market devoted to idolatry, if [he buys] an animal, it must be mutilated; if [he buys] produce, utensils, or clothes, they must be left to rot; if coins or metal utensils, they must be thrown into the Dead Sea." The Talmud asks, "An animal . . . must be mutilated? But does that not involve violation of the prohibition against inflicting pain on it?!" Abbaye answered: "Scripture says, 'You shall hamstring their horses'" [Joshua 11:6]. *Tosafot, ad loc.*, s.v. Amar Abbaye amar kera, states:

> Rabbi Elhanan questioned [this response as follows]: "To those who maintain that inflicting pain on animals is Biblically prohibited [TB Shabbat 128b], what proof does the verse from Joshua provide [that pain may be inflicted on animals]? Perhaps Joshua's case was different because it was a direct divine command, whereas here, we are discussing a penalty imposed by rabbinic law, and is it not true that the Sages lack the power to abrogate a Biblical law?" It can be answered that the Sages certainly may exercise such power when they see good cause to do so, as is shown in ch. "Ha-Ishah Rabbah" [TB Yevamot 89b] with regard to allowing a woman to remarry on the testimony of only one witness.

A further instructive example is contained in the following law, set forth by Maimonides in *MT*, Nedarim 3:9:

> A person who vows to fast on the sabbath or on a festival must do so, because vows are valid even where they affect the performance of a commandment. . . . Similarly, if a person vows to fast every Sunday or Tuesday for the rest of his life, and a festival or the eve of the Day of Atonement coincides with one of those days, he is still required to fast on that day. . . . However, if *Hanukkah* or *Purim* [which are rabbinic holidays] coincides with one of the days [to which his vow applies], his fast must be set aside, since fasting on those holidays is forbidden by the Scribes [*i.e.*, by rabbinic enactment] and their enactments must be reinforced, so the fulfillment of the vow is set aside because of the rabbinic enactment.

Joseph Caro, in *Kesef Mishneh, ad loc.*, s.v. U-le-inyan, was surprised by this ruling of Maimonides that the fast is set aside for *Hanukkah* and *Purim:*

> But the conclusion in ch. "Ha-Ishah Rabbah" [TB Yevamot 90b] is that the Sages can abrogate a Biblical law only by prohibiting action required by the Torah, but not by affirmatively permitting action proscribed by the Torah; and yet here, according to the master [Maimonides], oaths and vows are not applicable on *Hanukkah* and *Purim,* and this goes so far as to affirmatively require [Biblically prohibited] action, since we tell him to eat!

The following is one of two answers Caro advances (the other answer is discussed *infra* n. 177):

basic and significant limitation, namely, that the halakhic authorities do not have the power to eliminate completely the obligation to fulfill a Biblical commandment: "We have not found that the court may uproot a single commandment completely from the Torah."[157]

V. THE TERMS *LE-MIGDAR MILTA* (TO SAFEGUARD THE MATTER), *LEFI SHA'AH* (TEMPORARILY), *HORA'AT SHA'AH* (A TEMPORARY MEASURE), ETC.

Analysis of the principles and guidelines governing legislation by the halakhic authorities reveals that those authorities are empowered and directed to take action pursuant to these principles and guidelines[158] when necessary as a protective measure (*le-migdar milta,* lit. "to safeguard the matter")[159] or because "the time (lit. "hour") requires it" (*ha-sha'ah ẓerikhah le-khakh*).[160] The legislation is applicable only "temporarily" (*lefi sha'ah*),[161] or as "a temporary measure" (*hora'at sha'ah*),[162] and "does not establish a rule for all generations."[163]

It is also possible to argue, as indeed *Tosafot* has written in ch. "Sheloshah Minim" [Nazir 43b, s.v. Ve-hai met miẓvah hu], that although the Sages do not [generally] have the power to abrogate a law of the Torah by permitting action prohibited by the Torah, all will agree that they can do so when there is good cause for it; and here the reinforcement of rabbinic enactments is certainly good cause.

On this theory, the "good cause" that brings into play the power of the Sages to permit the performance of an act prohibited by the Torah is indeed very broad. The general principle that rabbinic enactments should be reinforced is premised on the fact that a given law is a rabbinic enactment. Thus, in the final analysis, the rabbinic character of an enactment is the very justification for the exercise of the power of the halakhic authorities to abrogate a Biblical law. *See also* Akiva Eger, *Gilyon ha-Shas,* Yevamot 88a, s.v. Tosafot s.v. Mi-tokh; *Tosafot R. Akiva Eger,* M Gittin ch. 4, #35; Z.H. Chajes, *Torat ha-Nevi'im,* Hora'at Sha'ah, pp. 40ff.; *id. The Student's Guide Through the Talmud,* ch. 13, pp. 105ff.; N.Z.J. Berlin, *Ha'amek She'elah,* She'ilta 58, par. 14.

157. *Peri Ḥadash* to Sh. Ar. OḤ 588:5; *see also Magen Avraham, ad loc.*, subpar. 4.

158. Except for the principle of *hefker bet din hefker.* According to most halakhic authorities, the restrictions on legislative power under principles such as "to safeguard the matter" (*le-migdar milta*) do not apply, even in theory, to the principle of *hefker bet din hefker. See supra* p. 514 n. 89 and accompanying text.

159. *See* TB Yevamot 90b, as to legislation (derived from the incident of the prophet Elijah on Mt. Carmel) designed to return the people to the faith, and legislation based on the principle that "the court may impose punishment not prescribed in the Torah."

160. *See id.*, as to the cases cited in connection with the imposition of punishment not prescribed in the Torah.

161. *See id.*, as to the legislation (derived from Elijah) designed to return the people to the faith; Maimonides, *MT,* Mamrim 2:4, 9.

162. Maimonides, *MT,* Mamrim 2:4, Sanhedrin 24:4, as to the imposition of punishment not prescribed in the Torah.

163. Maimonides, *MT,* Sanhedrin 24:4, Mamrim 2:4, 9.

Although, on the surface, these formulas appear to limit the time during which legislation may continue to be in force, it is apparent from an examination of the substance of the legislation of the halakhic authorities throughout all the areas of the law that in fact there is generally no such limitation. The enactments concerning *agunot,* for example,[164] which are among the most far-reaching exercises of the legislative prerogative of the halakhic authorities, have become permanent parts of Jewish law, and hundreds of their provisions and rules constitute an essential part of Jewish family law.

Another example is the enactment permitting the Oral Law to be put in writing. As has been pointed out,[165] it was originally provided that "matters transmitted orally you are not at liberty to recite from a writing."[166] However, when the Sages saw that the Jewish people could not continue to live with this rule, inasmuch as their tribulations had tremendously increased and people were in danger of forgetting the Torah,[167] they enacted that the Oral Law may be put in writing; and they interpreted the verse, "It is a time to act for the Lord, for they have violated Your Torah,"[168] to mean that "when it is time to act for the Lord, Your Torah may be violated," *i.e.,* that "it is better that one letter of the Torah should be uprooted so that the [entire] Torah will not be forgotten by Israel."[169] This *takkanah,* which was enacted because of the exigencies of the time,[170] became a permanent rule of law with regard to the entire Oral Law and is still effective today. Similarly, the wrongdoing in the case illustrating the principle that a court may impose punishment not prescribed in the Torah (the act of the man and his wife under the fig tree, which resulted in his punishment by flogging), in order "to safeguard the matter" and because "the time requires it,"[171] became permanently designated as a transgression punishable by disciplinary flogging (*makkot mardut*).[172]

164. *See supra* pp. 522–530.

165. *Supra* p. 224.

166. TB Gittin 60b; Temurah 14b.

167. *See* Rashi, Gittin 60a, s.v. Keivan de-lo efshar, and Maimonides, *MT,* Introduction.

168. Psalms 119:126.

169. TB Terumah 14b, and *see supra* pp. 226, 503.

170. *See supra* text at n. 167; *see also* Rashi, Gittin 60a, s.v. Et la'asot la-shem: "When it was necessary to adopt an enactment for the sake of Heaven, they abrogated Torah laws for as long as necessary."

171. TB Yevamot 90b.

172. *I.e.,* flogging imposed by rabbinic enactment. Maimonides, *MT,* Issurei Bi'ah 21:14, summarized the law as follows:

> A man may not have intercourse with his wife in the market place, in the street, in a garden, or in an orchard, but only in a dwelling house, so that the act should not look like fornication and the people become inured to lewdness. If a person has intercourse with his wife in those places, he is to be punished by disciplinary flogging.

The results have been similar throughout all of the vast body of legislation in criminal and religious law enacted in every era in consequence of different religious, social, economic and moral circumstances; this legislation is treated in halakhic literature as an integral part of the halakhic system.

What then is the "temporary" character of the legislation by the halakhic authorities? To answer this question, it is necessary to return to the point made at the beginning of our discussion of this subject,[173] namely, that the halakhic authorities are empowered to act only by way of subordinate legislation; they may not enact legislation that adds to or takes away from the supreme legislation by purporting to be part of the Written Law. Every law and commandment in the Written Law "stands forever, not subject to being changed or diminished."[174] It is not temporary, but eternal. By contrast, while the halakhic authorities may enact legislation that may in practical effect be permanent, they may not "declare that a new law is everlasting and is a part of the Torah,"[175] and they must "disclose to the people that it is a *gezerah* designed to prevent them from falling into error."[176]

Acting "to safeguard the matter" and enacting a "temporary" measure do not therefore mean that legislation may not be permanent in the practical sense. Those expressions rather connote the subordinate position of legislative enactments in the hierarchy of norms in the Jewish legal system. Biblical laws are supreme legislation, to which concepts such as "temporary" and making a "safeguard" are inapplicable. The laws originating in the legislation of the halakhic authorities, however, are subordinate legislation whose objective is "to safeguard the matter" and to fulfill the needs

---

This law is also codified in *Tur* EH 25:20 and Sh. Ar. EH 25:4. A similar law is set forth by Maimonides later in the same paragraph: "Similarly, one who effects a marriage by means of sexual intercourse or who marries a woman in the market place or without having been previously engaged to her is to be punished by disciplinary flogging."

This latter law, which is repeated in *MT,* Ishut 3:21, is based on the passage in TB Yevamot 52a and Kiddushin 12b: "Rav would flog any man who effected a marriage by means of sexual intercourse or who married in the market place or without having been previously engaged to his bride." Marriage effected by means of sexual intercourse is valid under Biblical law (Deuteronomy 24:1; M Kiddushin 1:1; TB Kiddushin 4b, 9b; Maimonides, *MT,* Ishut 3:20–21). Rav's ruling that this means of effecting a marriage is wrongful and punishable by flogging can be explained as constituting a temporary measure to "safeguard the matter." However, this "temporary measure" became a permanent part of the law and is codified as such in *Tur* EH 26:7 and Sh. Ar. EH 26:4. Nevertheless, such a marriage remains valid *post factum* (*MT,* Ishut 3:21).

173. *Supra* pp. 479–481, 499–502.

174. Maimonides, *MT,* Yesodei ha-Torah 9:1.

175. Maimonides, *MT,* Mamrim 2:9; *see supra* p. 499 for a variant reading.

176. *Id.*

of "the hour." Nevertheless the "safeguard" for "the matter" is not merely transitory;[177] "the hour" may be long, and the supreme legislation itself commands that the subordinate legislation be undeviatingly obeyed.[178]

VI. LEGISLATION IN JEWISH LAW AND THE PROBLEM OF *ULTRA VIRES*

Our study of the nature of halakhic legislation and of the competence of the halakhic authorities to enact legislation going so far as to impose obligations that conflict with the Torah naturally gives rise to the question: Does not all this disprove the hypothesis set forth at the beginning of our discussion, namely, that legislation in Jewish law should be classified as subordinate? Is it not axiomatic that subordinate legislation must not exceed the authority delegated by the supreme legislation and that, therefore, subordinate legislation in conflict with a precept in the supreme legislation is *ultra vires* and consequently null and void?

This question has a ready answer. It is indeed correct that in other legal systems, generally speaking, a law enacted by subordinate legislation may

177. A most far-reaching view of the breadth of the concept *le-migdar milta* ("to safeguard the matter"), even with regard to the degree of permanence of enactments based on that principle, appears in the comments of Joseph Caro, the main thrust of which was discussed *supra* n. 156. As there noted, Caro queried Maimonides' ruling that a vow to fast every Sunday or Tuesday for the rest of one's life must be complied with on Biblically ordained festivals but may not be complied with on *Hanukkah* or *Purim* (which are rabbinic holidays). Caro pointed out that the exception for *Hanukkah* and *Purim* abrogates a law of the Torah by directing the performance of an act the Torah prohibits. In his first answer (the second answer is quoted *supra* n. 156), Caro greatly expanded the definition of "to safeguard the matter":

> It can be answered that we do conclude there [TB Yevamot 90b] that in "safeguarding the matter," the Sages are empowered to abrogate a law of the Torah even by directing the performance of an act the Torah prohibits. The reinforcement of rabbinic enactments even in those cases that do not, strictly speaking, involve "safeguarding the matter" will lead to the better observance of those measures designed to create such a safeguard, because if people fail to respect one rabbinic enactment, they will ultimately lose respect for all of them. Therefore, anything that reinforces a rabbinic enactment comes within the ambit of "safeguarding the matter."

In addition to the novelty of this definition of "to safeguard the matter" as including the notion of the safeguarding and strengthening of rabbinic enactments, this answer of Caro introduces a new meaning for this expression with regard to the degree of permanence of such a safeguard. As Z.H. Chajes (*Torat ha-Nevi'im,* Hora'at Sha'ah, p. 40) concluded:

> The master [Caro] has shown us a new principle, that although "safeguarding the matter" is meant to be only temporary, nevertheless as long as the cause which led the Sages to abrogate the Biblical law continues to exist, so long will the enactment continue to be valid.

178. On *le-migdar milta* and *hora'at sha'ah, see further* Chajes, *supra* n. 177 at 40–43; Ginsburg, *supra* n. 100 at 45–55, 90 par. 14 and nn., *ad loc.*

not conflict with laws established by the supreme legislation,[179] whereas in Jewish law, such a conflict is permissible. Nevertheless, this greater latitude of subordinate legislation in Jewish law does not mean that *takkanot* and *gezerot* are any the less subordinate legislation. The basic criterion for determining whether a particular law is properly classified as subordinate legislation is whether the authority to promulgate that law arises out of a delegation of power contained in the supreme legislation.[180] The fact that the delegation of power is broad and includes the right to go beyond other provisions contained in the supreme legislation cannot take away from the enactments promulgated pursuant to this delegation their character as subordinate legislation.

That this is indeed true can be seen from the way subordinate legislation actually works in other legal systems. In those systems, not only are there instances when the law delegating legislative power expressly provides that the subordinate legislation may deviate from provisions of the law conferring the power and even from the laws in general,[181] but there also exists a specific type of legislation in which "wholesale" deviations from the supreme law are sanctioned *ab initio* by constitution or statute, either with or without limitation.[182] An Israeli statute permitting such deviation in the form of "emergency regulations" is the Law and Administration Ordinance, 1948, Section 9 of which provides:

> (a) If the Provisional Council of State deems it expedient, it may declare that a state of emergency exists in the State, and upon publication of such declaration in the *Official Gazette,* the Provisional Government may authorize the Prime Minister or any other Minister to make such emergency regulations as may seem to him expedient in the interests of the defense of the State, the public security, and the maintenance of supplies and essential services.
>
> (b) An emergency regulation may alter, modify, or suspend the effect of any law, and may also impose or increase taxes or other obligatory payments.

This section thus states that the supreme legislator of the State of Israel (then the Provisional Council of State and now the Knesset) authorizes the subordinate legislator (the executive) to enact subordinate legislation (decree emergency regulations) once the Knesset determines that a state of emergency exists; and this subordinate legislation may amend or suspend any law, or may prescribe conditions under which the law is to apply. The

179. Even this general rule has its exceptions. Not infrequently, a specific statute may provide that regulations promulgated under its authority may deviate from other provisions of that statute or even from provisions of the law in general. *See* B. Akzin, *Torat ha-Mishtarim* [Theory of Government], I, p. 139 n. 22. *See also* C.K. Allen, *Law in the Making,* pp. 563ff.

180. *See supra* pp. 478–479.

181. *See supra* n. 179.

182. Akzin, *supra* n. 179.

fact that an emergency regulation may change a law contained in the supreme legislation cannot, of course, take away from the emergency regulation its character as subordinate legislation; the authority of the government to enact such an emergency regulation—even if it deviates from a provision of the supreme legislation—itself flows from a delegation contained in the supreme legislation, namely, the Law and Administration Ordinance, which was enacted by the Knesset.[183]

In summary, the binding character of legislation in Jewish law, however far it deviates from Biblical law, is based on a delegation of power to the halakhic authorities by the Written Law (the supreme legislation), and consequently such enactments by the halakhic authorities may be properly and unqualifiedly classified as subordinate legislation. The subordinate character of this legislation is underscored by the reason for conferring legislative power on the halakhic authorities in the first place. The entire purpose of conferring authority broad enough to enact legislation that can deviate from Biblical law is to assure that "the Torah will not be forgotten by Israel." The "uprooting" of "one letter" of the Torah has the goal of preventing the entire Torah from being uprooted. The goal of the subordinate legislation is thus to protect the supreme legislation, the entire Torah; a change in even so much as a single letter or detail is not permitted unless it is made to preserve the supreme legislation as a whole.

VII. THE ROLE OF THE PUBLIC IN THE LEGISLATIVE ACTIVITIES OF THE HALAKHIC AUTHORITIES

The previous discussion has established that the right to initiate and enact legislation was vested first and foremost in the halakhic authorities, who have led the nation and determined the course of its laws and practices. To a certain extent, however, legislative power was also vested in governmental entities—the king, the townspeople, and the community (*kehillah*). The initiative and power of the public manifested itself in legislation by the

183. The Law and Administration Ordinance, 1948, sec. 9(c) provides:

> An emergency regulation shall expire three months after it is issued, unless it is extended, or revoked at an earlier date, by an Ordinance of the Provisional Council of State, or revoked by the regulation-making authority.

Clearly, this subsection is not an essential for the effective operation of secs. 9(a) and 9(b). From a juridical point of view, subsec. (c) could have contained different provisions or could have been entirely omitted. In other words, there is no necessary connection between the substance of the statutory provision authorizing an emergency regulation to amend an existing law, as provided in subsec. (b), and the requirement that after three months the emergency regulation must be extended as provided in subsec. (c) if the regulation is to continue in effect. Subsec. (b) can stand without subsec. (c).

townspeople and—to a progressively increasing extent from the eleventh century C.E. onward—the community.

The question arises: What is the proper role of the public in legislation that emanates not from the community, but from the halakhic authorities? Is the role of the public in regard to such legislation purely passive? Must the public simply accept and obey the enactments promulgated by its leaders, the halakhic authorities, or is it entitled to exert influence on the extent to which enactments legislated on its behalf are to be accepted and become binding?

Upon analysis, it becomes clear that even when legislation emanates from the halakhic authorities, the public does have a decisive influence on this important and substantial source for creating and developing Jewish law; but the time when this influence is brought to bear is not the same as in the case of legislation in other legal systems. In other systems, the public plays its role before the legislation is enacted, whereas in the case of legislation by the halakhic authorities, the influence of the public operates afterward.

In other legal systems, the public (whether directly, as in the Roman public assemblies, or through its representatives) is the legislator; the public is the source of legislative authority. This is also true in the case of communal enactments in Jewish law. The situation is otherwise when the halakhic authorities legislate: the courts and the halakhic authorities do the legislating, but after the legislation is enacted, the public determines whether the legislation will continue in force. Actually, this ultimate effectiveness of communal power means that the influence of the public operates to an extent even before legislation is enacted, because the legislator must first carefully investigate whether the public will be able to conform to any enactment to be adopted on its behalf. This need for the halakhic authorities to investigate before they legislate is a consequence of the decisive power possessed by the public after the legislation has been enacted.

The significant role of the public in legislation by halakhic authorities is expressed in a principle laid down by two of the leading Sages in the fourth generation of the tannaitic period. This principle has two versions.

The Babylonian Talmud states:[184]

> Rabban Simeon b. Gamaliel [the Patriarch, *i.e.*, the head of the legislative body in the fourth generation of the *tannaim*] and R. Eleazar b. Ẓadok said: "No legislation (*gezerah*) should be imposed on the public unless the majority can conform to it."

184. TB Avodah Zarah 36a.

In the Jerusalem Talmud,[185] this principle is expressed differently:

> R. Johanan said: "I have a tradition from R. Eleazar b. Ẓadok that any *gezerah* enacted by a court but not accepted by the majority of the public is no *gezerah.*"

We may thus conclude from both versions of this principle that: (1) before legislating, the legislator must examine and investigate whether a majority of the public will be able to conform to the proposed enactment, and (2) if, after the legislation is enacted, it appears that a majority of the public do not accept it, the legislation is legally ineffective.[186]

This fundamental principle[187] guided all legislative activity by the halakhic authorities.[188] Maimonides summarized it, on the basis of a number of Talmudic sources, as follows:[189]

> A court that sees fit to enact a *gezerah* or a *takkanah* or to institute a practice must consider the matter and know beforehand whether or not the majority of the public can conform to it; no *gezerah* is ever imposed on the public unless the majority can conform to it.
>
> If the court has enacted a *gezerah,* believing that the majority of the public can conform to it, and thereafter the people resist it[190] and a majority of the public do not conform to it, it is void and it is not permissible to compel the people to observe it.
>
> If, after a *gezerah* had been enacted, the court was of the opinion that it was universally accepted by the entire Jewish people, and this remained the situation for many years, but a long time later another court inquires into the

185. TJ Avodah Zarah 2:8, 16a (2:9, 41d).

186. *See* Bloch, *Sha'arei,* Introduction, par. 7, discussing this twofold version of the principle as the source for Maimonides' ruling quoted *infra.* M. Rath, *Resp. Kol Mevasser,* I, #3, makes the same point.

187. The term *gezerah,* which appears in this principle, denotes the whole body of rabbinic legislation, both *gezerot* and *takkanot,* and is not limited to *gezerot* in the technical sense (as to which *see supra* pp. 490–492). *See* the examples cited *infra* n. 188, and the terminology of TJ and *Tosefta. See also* Maimonides, quoted *infra.*

188. For various examples of the application of the principle that no legislation should be imposed on the public unless the majority can conform to it, *see* TB Bava Batra 60b and *Tosefta* Sotah 15:10; TB Bava Kamma 79b and *Tosefta* Shevi'it 3:13 (where the reading is: "They only erected a fence [*i.e.,* made a safeguard] that was able to stand)"; TJ Shevi'it 4:2, 10b (4:2, 35b) (where the reading is: "They only decreed to erect a fence that could be lived with"). *See also Tosefta* Sanhedrin 2:13; *Tosefta* Shevi'it 3:11, 13; S. Lieberman, *Tosefta ki-Feshutah,* Zera'im, p. 518. For the application of this principle to communal enactments, *see infra* pp. 762–763.

189. *MT,* Mamrim 2:5–7.

190. The Hebrew for "resist" (*pikpeku*) connotes doubt as to correctness of the enactment and lack of respect for it; *cf.* M Eduyyot 5:6.

conduct of the Jewish people and discovers that the *gezerah* is not generally accepted, that court, even if it is inferior to the first court in wisdom and number, is empowered to declare the legislation no longer binding.[191]

VIII. "ONE COURT MAY NOT OVERTURN THE LEGISLATION OF ANOTHER UNLESS GREATER THAN THE OTHER IN WISDOM AND NUMBER"

To put the foregoing quotation from Maimonides in full perspective, another principle of legislation by the halakhic authorities must be reviewed, namely, the principle that one court may not overturn the legislation of another court unless greater than the other in wisdom and number.[192]

The Mishnah states:[193]

> Why do we [*i.e.*, why does the Mishnah] cite dissenting views, seeing that the law follows the view of the majority? Because a court may agree with the dissenting view and follow it. One court may not overrule another court unless it [the overruling court] is greater than the other in wisdom and number.[194] If greater in wisdom but not in number, or in number but not in wisdom, it cannot overturn the act of the first court. It must be greater in both wisdom and number.[195]

It appears from the Talmudic sources that the principle that one court may not overrule another court unless the overruling court is greater in wisdom and number was construed as applicable only to the exercise of a court's legislative function.[196] As to a law derived by means of midrashic

191. *See* commentaries on *MT*, Mamrim 2:5–7; Ritba, Novellae to Avodah Zarah 35a, s.v. Mikhlal de-ikka man de-shari; ET, I, pp. 281–282.

192. The halakhic authorities and the scholars of Jewish law have discussed this principle at length. Here, we treat briefly only a few of its main aspects. *See* Bloch, *Sha'arei*, Introduction, par. 8; Weiss, *Dor Dor ve-Doreshav*, pp. 57–61; ET, I, pp. 279–281.

193. M Eduyyot 1:5.

194. For the interpretation of "greater in wisdom" and "greater in number," *see* Maimonides' commentary on M Eduyyot 1:5 and *MT*, Mamrim 2:2; Rabad's commentary on M Eduyyot 1:5; H. Albeck's commentary on M Eduyyot 1:5 and Hashlamot, pp. 475–476; ET, I, p. 279.

195. *See also* R. Judah's rationale in M Eduyyot 1:6. There are varying opinions as to whether a later court not greater in either wisdom or number may abrogate an enactment and follow the view of a judge who dissented from the original enactment. *See* commentaries of Maimonides, Rabad, and Samson of Sens on M Eduyyot 1:5, and *infra* pp. 1070–1072.

196. *See* TJ Shevi'it 1:1, 1a (1:1, 33a); Avodah Zarah 2:8, 16a (2:9, 41d); Shabbat 1:4, 10b (1:8, 3d); TB Gittin 36b; Megillah 2a; Mo'ed Katan 3b; Avodah Zarah 36a; TJ Shabbat 6:2, 34a (6:2, 8a). In all these sources, the principle is cited only in connection with laws for which legislation was the legal source.

interpretation, a later court may properly arrive at a different conclusion through a different interpretation of a Biblical verse or of the preexisting law.[197] There is no such power, however, with regard to a law of legislative origin. This limit on the power to nullify rabbinic legislation gave subordinate legislation in Jewish law the same stability and effectiveness as that possessed by the supreme legislation—the laws of the Torah.

As a result of research and analysis of the changes and developments in many laws created by legislative enactments, the *amoraim* ascertained that various earlier enactments had been nullified in the course of time by subsequent legislation. To reconcile the inconsistency between this fact and the principle that one court may not overrule another unless greater than the other in wisdom and number, a number of exceptions were established pursuant to which a court may repeal the enactment of another court even if the repealing court is not greater in wisdom and number. These exceptions produced a measure of flexibility in the legislative process. The major exceptions are the following:[198]

1. Where the enacting court at the time of the original enactment expressly stipulates that any court that wishes to nullify the enactment may do so;[199]
2. Where it first appears that the enactment had been accepted by the people, but it is later discovered that a majority of the people did not accept it;[200] and
3. Where the original rationale and purpose of the enactment[201] no longer hold.[202]

197. Maimonides, *MT,* Mamrim 2:1.

198. *See further supra* n. 195.

199. M Ma'aser Sheni 5:2; TB Mo'ed Katan 3b. *See Tosafot,* Bava Kamma 82b, s.v. Ata ihu ve-tikken afillu le-divrei Torah. This is perhaps also the correct interpretation of Gittin 36b: "He enacted it for his generation," *i.e.,* any later authority who so wishes may repeal it. *See also* Meiri, *Bet ha-Beḥirah,* Gittin 36b (ed. Schlesinger, p. 159); Weiss, *Dor Dor ve-Doreshav,* p. 59 n. 2. *See further Tosafot,* Beẓah 5a, s.v. Kol davar she-be-minyan ẓarikh minyan aḥer le-hattiro; *Yam Shel Shelomo,* Beẓah, 1:9; *Resp. Ribash* #119.

200. *See supra* pp. 540–541.

201. *E.g.,* TJ Shabbat 6:2, 34a (6:2, 8a) as to the enactment regarding the nailed sandal: "But did they not adopt the *gezerah* at the time of the persecution?! Now that the persecution has passed, should it not be permitted? [No, because] no court arose and abrogated it." *I.e.,* since the enactment was not explicitly abrogated by a court, it does not automatically become void even if the rationale and purpose for which it was adopted no longer hold. However, a court is permitted in such circumstances to abrogate the enactment. *See* Rattner, *Ahavat Ẓiyyon vi-Yerushalayim* to TJ, *ad loc.* (p. 73).

See also TB Beẓah 5a/b ("The produce of the fourth year of the vineyard was taken to Jerusalem . . . ," as interpreted by Rabad in his gloss to *MT,* Mamrim 2:2, Meiri, *Bet ha-Beḥirah,* Beẓah 5a, s.v. Kol davar she-ne'esar be-minyan, and Rashi, Beẓah 5a, s.v. Mina amina lah); TJ Shevi'it 4:2, 10b (4:2, 35b); Shabbat 2:1, 25b (1:1, 4c); *Tosafot Yom Tov,* M

The purpose of the legislative principle that one court may not overturn the legislation of another unless greater than the other in wisdom and number is to put legislation by the halakhic authorities on a par with, but not above, the laws of the Torah itself in stability and effectiveness. Consequently, all principles and guidelines concerning the power of the halakhic authorities to legislate on matters covered by Biblical law manifestly apply also to their authority to legislate with regard to rules originating in earlier enactments by the halakhic authorities. Maimonides has pointed this out:[203]

> A court may abrogate [lit. "uproot"] even these things [legislation of another court] temporarily even if it has a lower standing than the first court, so that such enactments will not be given greater force than Biblical law itself, since every court has the power to abrogate even a law of the Torah as a temporary measure.

The discussion of legislation up to this point has sought to portray the nature, objectives, and principles of legislation in Jewish law. Legislation has been one of the major sources of creativity in every area of the law. The halakhic authorities and the leaders of the people well realized both the vastness of their power and the corresponding weight of their responsibility

---

Ma'aser Sheni 5:2, subpar. 5; Gulak, *Yesodei,* I, pp. 27–28; H. Albeck, Commentary on M Eduyyot 1:5 and Hashlamot, pp. 475–476.

Magen Avraham to Sh. Ar. OḤ 9, subpar. 7, states as to *ẓiẓit* (fringes) of linen on a linen garment that if the reason for the prohibition is known and is no longer applicable, the prohibition *ipso facto* lapses. According to Maimonides, however, even if the rationale is no longer applicable, only a court greater in wisdom and number can repeal the enactment (*MT,* Mamrim 2:2). *See also* other *rishonim* and the lengthy discussion in ET, VI, pp. 698–705.

202. Within the recent past, Z.P. Frank, the Rabbi of Jerusalem, was asked an interesting question with regard to this rule. According to the Talmud, it is forbidden to rear small animals, such as sheep, in the Land of Israel—and in Babylonia—because they usually cause damage. It was ruled, however, that the prohibition applies only when most fields are under Jewish ownership (*Tur* ḤM ch. 409), and therefore in the post-Talmudic period the prohibition lapsed. The question was whether "the prohibition has now been revived" since most of the fields in the Land of Israel are again owned by Jews.

Rabbi Frank ruled that the original *takkanah* no longer applies: "Since the prohibition lapsed in the course of time and Jews were permitted to rear small animals in the Land of Israel, it cannot be revived." His rationale was that "once an enactment by the halakhic authorities has ceased to be binding, the prohibition is completely abrogated and forever void; and further legislative action is required if the prohibition is to take effect once again. So long as the prohibition is not reenacted, it remains like any other legislative proposal not yet enacted, which we cannot enact on our own" (*Har Ẓevi, Tur* ḤM ch. 409). *See also* his proofs and queries from TB Rosh ha-Shanah 18b in connection with the four fast days.

203. *MT,* Mamrim 2:4.

to use their legislative prerogative to develop and fashion the *Halakhah*. This authority and responsibility enabled them to utilize legislation as an instrument that, although indeed temporarily adding to, changing, or nullifying "one letter" of the Torah, nevertheless in the long run protected the existence, perpetuation, and continuity of the Torah as a whole. The following chapters review how this was accomplished and examine more closely the substantial and wide-ranging legislative activity that took place in the Jewish legal system throughout its various periods.

Chapter 15

LEGISLATION: ENACTMENTS THROUGH THE END OF THE TANNAITIC PERIOD

I. INTRODUCTION

Legislation in Jewish law began immediately after the Revelation at Sinai[1] and has never stopped. There were periods when legislation flourished and periods when it declined, periods when it was a powerful force enriching the Jewish legal system and periods in which the halakhic authorities were reluctant to legislate, periods in which the courts and the halakhic authorities played the major part in legislating and periods in which the predominant mode of legislation was direct enactment by the Jewish public at large—the Jewish community and its representatives.

Zacharias Frankel divides the halakhic activity of the Sages up to the end of the tannaitic period into two consecutive segments:

> The Sages of the Mishnah and the *Baraita* are generally divided into legislators (*metakkenei takkanot ve-gozrei gezerot*) and jurists (*ḥakhmei ha-Halakhah*). The Sages who legislated were the early generations until Hillel and Shammai. . . . The jurists started with the generations of the *tannaim* who were the disciples of Hillel and Shammai (referred to as the School of Hillel and the

1. Talmudic tradition also attributes the adoption of various enactments to the Biblical patriarchs. *See infra* p. 550.

> School of Shammai) and continued until R. Judah Ha-Nasi and his generation. These generations examined and investigated the *Halakhah* through study and reasoning. . . . And between these boundaries that we have drawn, Hillel and Shammai stand in the center and are considered to be both legislators and jurists; yet even after them there were public leaders who occupied themselves primarily with legislation.[2]

Asher Gulak correctly observed[3] that even if there is a certain historical basis for Frankel's distinction generally, his sharp demarcation of two periods—one in which the Sages were legislators and the other in which their method was interpretation and legal reasoning—cannot be supported. Although it is true that there were certainly many important legislative enactments during the period of the early Sages when the Sanhedrin was the supreme legislative authority, the Sages even then were heavily occupied with exegetical interpretation, especially from the time of Ezra the Scribe; and they explained the Torah and solved through midrashic interpretation many halakhic problems that claimed their attention from time to time.[4] Moreover, it is clear that very many enactments were added to Jewish law in the period after Hillel and Shammai. Some of them were attributed to the court and the *nasi* (patriarch) of that period, and a considerable portion that are of unknown authorship and date of origin (which constitute the majority of the legislation in the halakhic system) also surely originated in the period after Hillel and Shammai.[5]

Legislative activity continued in full force in the amoraic period in the Land of Israel and in Babylonia, and thereafter in the days of the *geonim* in Babylonia. From the end of the geonic period, extensive legislative activity continued in the different centers of the Jewish diaspora. From that time forward, such legislative activity was characterized by a parochial quality, *i.e.*, *takkanot* were enacted not for the entire Jewish people, but only for a particular Jewish center. This local legislation, too, enriched Jewish law with extremely significant enactments; the halakhic leaders in each locality enacted *takkanot* in all the areas of the law, and most of this legislative activity was in the area of *mishpat ivri*.[6] However, over the course of time, the local character of legislation also caused a certain reduction of legislative activity; and the halakhic authorities did not deem it appropriate to enact legislation that would affect the validity of marriage and divorce.[7] From the

2. Z. Frankel, *Mishnah*, p. 29. *See also* E.E. Urbach, "Ha-Derashah ki-Yesod ha-Halakhah u-Va'ayat ha-Soferim" [Interpretation as a Basis for the *Halakhah* and the Problem of the Scribes], *Tarbiz*, XXVII (1959), pp. 168, 171.

3. Gulak, *Yesodei*, I, p. 24.

4. *See supra* pp. 309–314.

5. Frankel himself pointed this out at the end of the passage quoted *supra*.

6. *See infra* pp. 780ff.

7. *See infra* pp. 846–879.

tenth century C.E. on, there was a progressive increase in the legislation originating in the public and its representatives—*i.e., takkanot ha-kahal* (communal enactments)—in the areas of public, civil, and criminal law. Often, both halakhic agencies—the halakhic authorities and the public—were joint participants in the legislative process on matters within the area of *mishpat ivri.*[8]

From the end of the eighteenth century, legislative activity—especially in the European centers—sharply declined. This decline was comparable to the changes that from then on also affected the functioning of the other legal sources of Jewish law. With the return of a certain measure of Jewish juridical autonomy to the halakhic authorities in the Land of Israel at the beginning of the twentieth century, there was some creative legislative activity by the Chief Rabbinate of the Land of Israel, but this too subsided after a short while.[9]

The following chapters discuss examples of legislation and the unique features of the legislation of different periods,[10] and reveal the enormous development that occurred in Jewish law through the use of legislation as a legal source. First, however, some preliminary observations are appropriate. Many more laws in the Jewish legal system are based on legislation than are expressly identified as such. Many laws are stated in the form of Biblical exegesis (midrash), but their actual source is legislation; the exegesis is only integrative, *i.e.,* its function is to connect the enactment with a Biblical verse. At times, the Sages themselves pointed this out,[11] and at times the integrative nature of the exegesis can be discerned from a comparison of other sources that deal with the same subject.[12] By the same

8. *See infra* chs. 19 and 20.

9. *See infra* pp. 824–835.

10. Elijah Galipapa, an eighteenth-century Turkish halakhic authority, collected in his book *Yedei Eliyahu* some of the laws stemming from legislation. This volume sets out 172 enactments in the order they appear in Maimonides' *Mishneh Torah.* Some enactments are also listed by Z.H. Chajes in his *The Student's Guide Through the Talmud,* from ch. 7 on, where they are presented in chronological order. The most comprehensive compilation of enactments that antedate the final redaction of the Talmud is found in Bloch, *Sha'arei.* This excellent work contains a very large proportion of the laws known to have originated in legislation, as well as a significant proportion of the Talmudic and post-Talmudic textual sources pertaining to specific subjects. For compilations of post-Talmudic enactments, *see infra* p. 646 n. 8, and pp. 782–783 nn. 4–7.

11. *E.g.,* in connection with the support found in a Scriptural verse for the *prosbul* enactment, *see supra* p. 513 n. 86.

12. For example, M Bava Meẓi'a 2:7 states:

> If he [the claimant] said what the lost article was but did not supply the identification marks, he [the finder] should not give it to him. And if [the claimant is] a swindler, then even if he did supply the identification marks, he should not give it to him, as it is written, "until your fellow claims it" [lit. "searches it out" (Deuteronomy 22:2),

token, it is possible that a law whose legal source is identified as custom, case law, or legal reasoning actually first entered Jewish law through legislation.[13] It is sometimes possible, through comparison with other literary sources, to prove that legislation is the source of a law for which the legal source is not expressly stated.[14] For the most part, however, if a particular law is set forth with no attribution of legal source, there is virtually no way to determine whether the source of that law is legislation or some other legal source.[15]

As will be seen later, Talmudic tradition attributes different enactments to different periods and Sages. Sometimes there is a discussion in the Talmud as to the identity of the legislator who promulgated a particular enactment,[16] and sometimes the attribution of an enactment to an individual or a particular period appears to be the result of an exegesis of a Biblical verse or an inference from events connected with that period.[17] Sometimes one

---

> which is to be interpreted as] "until you search out [*i.e.*, investigate] your fellow [*i.e.*, the claimant to ascertain] whether he is a swindler or not."

This *mishnah* indicates that the source of the rule is midrash—Biblical exegesis. However, *Tosefta* Bava Meẓi'a 2:16 states:

> Originally, anyone who came and supplied the article's identification marks could take it, but when swindlers became numerous, they [the Sages] enacted that the claimant was required not only to supply identification marks but also to prove that he was not a swindler.

This text is cited in TB Bava Meẓi'a 28b and shows that the rule originated in legislation and that the connection with the verse is *asmakhta*—an attempt to find Scriptural support for the rule that originated in legislation.

13. Occasionally, the Sages themselves differed as to whether the source of a particular rule was legislation or custom. *See* TB Sukkah 44a concerning the rite of the *aravah* (willow twig).

14. The following are example of laws that one text sets forth with no attribution to any legal source and another text attributes to legislation. M Bava Meẓi'a 2:6 states that the finder of lost property must give public notice of his find so that his neighbors will be aware of it, whereas *Tosefta* Bava Meẓi'a 2:17 (TB Bava Meẓi'a 28b is to the same effect) states: "From the 'time of the danger' [*sakanah, i.e.*, oppression] and thereafter, they enacted that he should inform his neighbors." M Ketubbot 9:9 includes Rabban Simeon b. Gamaliel's rule that from the "time of the danger" and thereafter, a woman could claim her *ketubbah* without producing her *get* (bill of divorcement), whereas the same law is reported in *Tosefta* Ketubbot 9:6 as a *takkanah*. M Bava Kamma 7:7 states: "One may not rear small animals in the Land of Israel," whereas *Tosefta* Shevi'it 3:13 reads: "Small animals may not be reared in the Land of Israel, but large animals may, because they [*i.e.*, the Sages] enacted only such legislation [lit. "built fences"] that could be conformed to." *See also supra* p. 526 n. 140.

15. *See further supra* p. 297 and *infra* p. 946.

16. *See, e.g., infra* p. 552 n. 31 on Joshua's enactments. For further examples, *see* Bloch, *Sha'arei*, Introduction. *See also infra* nn. 44, 49.

17. *See* H. Albeck, *Mavo*, p. 29, and *infra* pp. 553, 556 on the enactments of Joshua and Ezra.

Talmudic source attributes an enactment to a particular individual, and a different source cites the enactment without attribution.[18]

Sometimes a particular legal institution was created through legislation in successive stages, reflecting the social and economic circumstances and the problems that arose from time to time. Such a development in the creation of a particular legal doctrine may be explicitly revealed by the sources[19] or may be discerned from an examination of the relevant parallel sources.[20] The *amoraim* are noteworthy for indicating the existence of different stages of legal development in a particular subject area by pointing out that a number of enactments were adopted in that area over the course of time.[21]

II. EARLIEST LEGISLATION

Talmudic tradition attributes various enactments to the very earliest periods: to the Biblical patriarchs;[22] to Moses, Joshua, Samuel, Boaz, David, Solomon, and Jehoshaphat; to "the prophets" as a group; to Haggai, Zechariah, Malachi, and others. Certain enactments are explicitly mentioned in the books of the Prophets and the Hagiographa.[23] The following are two illustrations of such early legislation.

18. For examples, *see* Bloch, *Sha'arei*, Introduction and Preface (before the introduction to the sections) for his comments and his reliance on statements by the Sages as to who promulgated which enactments and when.

19. *See, e.g.*, TB Shabbat 123b in regard to moving utensils on the sabbath; *Tosefta* Niddah 9:18 and *Tosefta* Ma'aser Sheni 1:9 as to the ritual impurity of hands in connection with *besar ta'avah* (meat of an animal that has not been a sacrificial offering); M Shevi'it 4:1 and *Tosefta* Shevi'it 3:8–9 as to agricultural labor in the sabbatical year.

20. *See infra* pp. 559–561 concerning Simeon b. Shataḥ's enactment in regard to the *ketubbah*.

21. *See infra* p. 622 and n. 1. There were occasions in particular periods when the Sages sought to enact a *takkanah* but were unable to do so, and it was not until later that the enactment was adopted. *See, e.g.*, TB Yevamot 13b, 27a: ". . . as in the case of R. Johanan b. Nuri, who said: 'Come, let us enact a *takkanah*' . . . , but before they succeeded in concluding the matter, the times worsened, [and it was impossible to adopt the enactment]." However, "R. Naḥman b. Yiẓḥak said: 'After his time, they returned and enacted [the *takkanah*]'" (*id.* 27b). Similarly in *Tosefta* Shevi'it 3:10: "As to a field that has been made ready for planting [in the sabbatical year] . . . , Shammai the Elder said: 'If the time permitted, I would decree that it may not be sown [in the eighth year].' A court enacted after his time that it may not be sown." R. Judah Ha-Nasi laid down the rule accordingly in M Shevi'it 4:2: "A field . . . that has been made ready for planting or used for penning cattle [in the sabbatical year] may not be sown in the eighth year."

22. Abraham, Isaac, and Jacob, who instituted the morning, afternoon, and night prayers, respectively; TB Berakhot 26b.

23. For various of these enactments, *see* Bloch, *Sha'arei*, I, pp. 1–106; H. Albeck, *Mavo*, pp. 29–37; B.Z. Dinur, "Le-Mashma'utah Shel Massekhet Avot ke-Makor Histori" [On the Significance of Tractate *Avot* as a Historical Source], *Zion*, XXXV (1970), p. 15 n. 53.

A. The Enactments of Joshua Concerning the Relationship between the Individual and the Public in Property Matters

A *baraita*[24] attributes to Joshua the promulgation of ten enactments at the time of the conquest of the Land of Israel and the allocation of the land among the Israelite tribes.[25] The Talmudic discussion deals with the explanation of these enactments. Maimonides summarized the enactments as follows:[26]

> Joshua and his court[27] promulgated ten enactments [*tena'im,* lit. "conditions" or "stipulations"][28] when he allocated the land, and they are:
>
> 1. Small cattle may graze in a forest [even when the forest belongs to another] where the trees are large [so that any damage would not be perceptible], but large cattle may not graze there. However, in a forest of small trees [where there is danger of serious damage to the trees], no cattle, whether large or small, may graze, except with the consent of the owner of the forest.
>
> 2. Anyone may gather wood from another's field provided that it is taken from growths of negligible value, akin to thorns, such as prickly shrubs and thistles, and provided also that the wood is moist [since, if it is dry, the wood has value to the owner of the field as fuel] and attached to the ground [since if it is not attached, it is assumed that the owner of the field cut it for

24. TB Bava Kamma 80b–81b. *See also* TB Eruvin 17a/b; TJ Bava Batra 5:1, 15b (5:1, 15a) *et seq.*

25. Talmudic literature attributes to Joshua various other enactments that are also mainly connected with the allocation and agricultural settlement of the Land of Israel. *See Tosefta* Bava Kamma 10:27 and TB Bava Kamma 81b and 114b as to the rule that if a swarm of bees settles on land owned by another, the owner of the bees, in order to recover them, may enter the land and cut off the branch on which the swarm has settled. *See also Tosefta* Bava Meẓi'a 11:8 and TB Bava Kamma 81b as to the rule that at the time of the year when manure is put out, a person may pile up his manure in the public thoroughfare at the entrance to his house for 30 days. TJ Bava Batra 5:1, 15b (5:1, 15a) refers to four enactments (lit. "stipulations") that Joshua adopted. With regard to the ten enactments referred to in the *baraita,* the Talmud (TB Bava Kamma 81b) asks: "But are they ten? Are they not eleven?"

26. *MT,* Nizkei Mamon 5:3.

27. TB Bava Kamma 80b and other Talmudic sources do not have "and his court."

28. This is the reading in TB Bava Kamma 80b. *Tenai* is synonymous with *takkanah, see supra* p. 492 nn. 73–74. *See also* TB Eruvin 17a: "This *takkanta* [Aramaic for *takkanah*] was by Joshua"; and *Tosefta* Bava Kamma 10:27 on the rescue of a swarm of bees (*supra* n. 25): "It is a *tenai bet din* [lit. 'stipulation of the court'] that a person may cut down the branch to rescue his swarm, because it was subject to this condition that Joshua apportioned the land to Israel" (also, with certain textual variations, in TB Bava Kamma 114b). These sources explain that the terms *tenai* and *tenai bet din* were used to designate Joshua's enactments because those enactments stipulated the conditions on which he apportioned the land to the Israelites. The use of the term *tenai bet din* for enactments concerning the *ketubbah* can be similarly explained as meaning that the marriage is entered into subject to those conditions. However, in the case of the *ketubbah,* contractual stipulations between the parties to the marriage preceded those laid down by the court. *See infra* n. 129.

his own use] and that he does not tear out the roots. Other wood, however, is forbidden.

3. Anyone may pick grasses growing wild anywhere [even in another's field, to feed his own animals] except in a field of trefoil clover that has been sown for animal fodder [since grasses intermingled with the clover are beneficial to the clover and are good animal fodder].

4. One may take a cutting from a tree [*i.e.*, cut a branch from a tree for planting or grafting] anywhere [even from a tree that belongs to another], except from the branches of an olive tree [*i.e.*, an old olive tree that has been cut down, leaving two branches that sprout again and produce shoots]. One may take cuttings only up to the size of an egg from an olive tree, and only above the joint from reeds and vines, and from the side branches but not from the central part of any other tree. Permission to take cuttings applies only to a newly grown branch that does not produce fruit but not to old branches that do produce fruit, and one may take cuttings only from a part that does not face the sun.

5. If a spring begins to flow [*i.e.*, a new spring is discovered],[29] the inhabitants of the town within whose boundaries it emerges may use it even though its source is not in the public domain [*i.e.*, despite the fact that the spring emerges from a field owned by one of the townspeople, the water belongs to all the townspeople]; but no others [from outside that town] can use it with them.

6. Anyone may catch fish in Lake Tiberias (Kinneret) [even though it is located in the territory of the tribe of Naphtali], provided he uses only a fishhook [so as not to interfere with the movement of boats]; only members of the tribe in whose territory the lake is located may catch fish by spreading a net [posing an obstacle to navigation] or may keep a boat there.[30]

7. Anyone who must relieve himself may leave the road, go behind the nearest fence, and do so there, even if it is a field of saffron. He may also take a pebblestone from there and wipe himself clean.[31]

8. Anyone who is lost among vineyards or a similar place may cut his

29. "And certainly ancient springs that have existed since Joshua's time"—Rashi, Bava Kamma 81a, s.v. Ba-teḥillah.

30. According to *Tur* ḤM 274:6, members of those tribes in whose territory the lake is located could fish with nets, but even they were forbidden "to spread the type of net that obstructs navigation."

31. A *baraita* in TB Bava Kamma 81a sets out at this point an additional enactment that in the summer (when no produce is growing in the fields) travellers may take a short cut through privately owned fields until the rains of the "second quarter" (*i.e.*, the rains that usually begin on the 23rd of the month of Ḥeshvan. After that date, the seeds begin to grow, and trampling would damage them). However, the Talmud states (*id.* 81b) that King Solomon was the author of that enactment; and support for this view was found in Proverbs 3:27: "Do not withhold good from one who deserves it when you have the power to do it [for him]." On the basis of this Scriptural support, Maimonides, *MT*, Nizkei Mamon 5:4, also attributed this enactment to Solomon.

way through and go up or down until he comes out on his way [*i.e.*, he may cut the vines that block the way in order to make a path].

9. Whenever a public road becomes very muddy or waterlogged, travelers may go to the sides of the road and walk there even though they traverse private property.

10. A *met mizvah* [a person found dead without relatives to attend to him; it is a religious commandment (*mizvah*) that whoever finds him must attend to his burial] acquires title to his place [*i.e.*, the place where he is found] and must be buried where he is found [even if this place is the private property of another], provided that he is not lying across the boundary [*i.e.*, on the public path] or within the bounds of a town. If he is found across the boundary or within the bounds of a town, he must be taken to a cemetery.

These enactments pertain for the most part to the relation between an individual and the public, and particularly to the problem of the rights of the public in property belonging to an individual or a particular group. It was reasonable for these enactments to have been promulgated at the time when the land was allocated among the tribes and then further apportioned among the families within each tribe. The Book of Joshua stresses particularly how Joshua established a legal order: "On that day at Shechem, Joshua made a covenant for all the people and he made *ḥok u-mishpat* [fixed rules, lit. "statute and law"] for them,"[32] which, according to the commentary of Naḥmanides,[33] refers "not to laws and statutes of the Torah but to administrative regulations for the settlement of the country, such as the enactments promulgated by Joshua and mentioned by the Sages, and similar rules."[34]

32. Joshua 24:25. The JPS *Tanakh* translates *ḥok u-mishpat* as "a fixed rule."

33. Naḥmanides, *Commentary on Exodus* 15:25, which tells of Moses in the wilderness of Shur: "There he made for them *ḥok u-mishpat*."

34. According to the *amora* Samuel (TB Bava Kamma 81b), these enactments apply even outside the Land of Israel—a view that was codified as law in Maimonides, *MT*, Nizkei Mamon 5:5, and in *Tur* ḤM 274:1. Originally, they were enacted only for the Land of Israel, as appears from explicit statements to that effect about several of Joshua's *takkanot:* ". . . because it was subject to this condition that Joshua apportioned the land to Israel" (*see supra* n. 28). However, once the enactments were accepted, they became an integral part of Jewish law and applied everywhere. *See also Bayit Ḥadash* to *Tur* ḤM 274, subpar. 1, and *Sema* to Sh. Ar. ḤM 274, subpar. 2. Even the matter of putting out manure (*see supra* n. 25) was codified as law in *MT*, Nizkei Mamon 13:15 and in Sh. Ar. ḤM 404:2.

Joseph Caro did not codify Joshua's ten enactments in the *Shulḥan Arukh* nor did he address himself to them in his *Bet Yosef* to the *Turim*—a fact about which Rema in his gloss to Sh. Ar. ḤM ch. 274 made this interesting comment:

> Joshua promulgated ten enactments in the Land [of Israel] and all of them apply outside the Land as well. Maimonides included them in chapter 5 of [*MT*,] Nizkei Mamon, as did the *Turim* in chapter 274, and I do not know why this author [*i.e.*, Caro] omitted them. Perhaps its was because the conditions under which they apply

B. Military Legislation by King David

The first Book of Samuel, chapter 30, describes the victory of David and his men over the Amalekite troops. When the battle started, David left behind two hundred of his men to guard his army's equipment; and he and the rest of his soldiers engaged the Amalekites. When the victors returned from the battle carrying spoils of their enemies, some of the men who had fought along with David sought to prevent those who had remained to guard the equipment from sharing in the spoils; but David rejected their demand:

> How could anyone agree with you in this matter? The share of those who remain with the equipment shall be the same as the share of those who go down to battle; they shall share alike.[35]

This enactment of David[36] providing that the same rules apply to the noncombat soldier as to the soldier who does battle became a part of the legal system, as stated in the very next verse (I Samuel 30:25): "So from that day on it was made a fixed rule for Israel, continuing to the present day."

III. LEGISLATION AT THE TIME OF EZRA AND THE GREAT ASSEMBLY

A. The Men of the Great Assembly

Ezra the Scribe and Nehemiah and those who entered into the covenant to observe the laws of the Torah[37] are called, according to the tannaitic tradi-

---

occur infrequently, inasmuch as most of them apply only where Jews own fields and vineyards, and such ownership is unusual in the diaspora.

The extent to which legal rules develop and are the subject of debate and discussion depends on the degree of their practical relevance. *See further infra* pp. 1326–1327.

35. I Samuel 30:24.

36. The rationale underlying David's enactment appears in the Torah in connection with the war against Midian: ". . . [D]ivide the booty equally between the combatants who engaged in the campaign and the rest of the community" (Numbers 31:27), but in that case the whole community participated in the division, as indeed also was the case with David, *see* I Samuel 30:27 *et seq.* and Seforno's commentary on Numbers, *ad loc.* The text of the verse emphasizes that it was David who instituted the division of spoil between those who fought and those who guarded the equipment, and that he made it into a fixed rule.

In the *Aggadah,* this rule was attributed to a much earlier source—the patriarch Abraham in his war with the four kings. This attribution was based on interpretation of Genesis 14:24: "For me, nothing but what my servants have used up; as for the share of the men who went with me—Aner, Eshkol, and Mamre—let them take their share." *See Genesis Rabbah* 43:14, cited in Rashi, Genesis, *ad loc.*, s.v. Ha-ne'arim.

37. *See* Ezra ch. 10; Nehemiah chs. 8, 10.

tion, "The Men of the Great Assembly" (*Anshei Keneset ha-Gedolah*). Our discussion of midrash has noted the great importance of this period (the latter half of the fifth century B.C.E.), which was a critical turning point in the *Halakhah*.[38] The people returned to the study of the Torah and to living according to its precepts, and this naturally led to a surge of creativity in Jewish law. To a considerable extent, this creative function was performed by midrash; but simultaneously with the functioning of midrash, and especially when exegesis could not solve the problems requiring solution, legislation provided the necessary assistance.

Clear information is lacking concerning the specific functions of the Great Assembly (which during its existence was the supreme institution of the Jewish people),[39] nor is it known precisely how its membership was selected. Even the number of its members is disputed. According to one tradition, the Great Assembly had 120 members, whereas according to another tradition, its membership was only eighty-five.[40] Despite the lack of precise information concerning the functions of the Great Assembly, it is clear that one of its major tasks was legislation.

This function of the Great Assembly is described in the Mishnah, Tractate *Avot* (*Ethics of the Fathers*):[41] "They (the Men of the Great Assembly) said three things: 'Be deliberate in judgment, raise up many disciples, and make a fence around the Torah.'" "Raise up many disciples" involves the dissemination of the Torah to the entire people. "Make a fence around the Torah" refers to legislative enactments (*gezerot* and *takkanot*), which are described as "a fence around the Torah."[42] "Be deliberate in judgment" was a necessary and important admonition in this significant period of creativity.

The Talmudic tradition attributes to this period many enactments relating to a broad range of different areas in the life of the people,[43] including *mishpat ivri*. The following are two illustrations of legal enactments that originated in this period.

38. *See supra* pp. 309–314.

39. *See* Finkelstein, *Ha-Perushim ve-Anshei ha-Keneset ha-Gedolah* [The Pharisees and the Men of the Great Assembly]; Alon, *Toledot*, II, pp. 223–224.

40. TB Megillah 17b; TJ Megillah 1:5, 6b (1:7, 70d); Berakhot 2:4, 17a (2:4, 4d). *See also* Ginzberg, *Perushim*, I, pp. 327–330.

41. M Avot 1:1.

42. *See* Maimonides, *Commentary on the Mishnah*, Avot 1:1, and *see supra* pp. 490–492 for the definition of *takkanah* and *gezerah*.

43. "The men of the Great Assembly enacted for Israel benedictions and prayers, liturgy for the sanctification of sabbaths and festivals (*kedushot*), and liturgy to mark the ending of these holy days (*havdalot*)" (TB Berakhot 33a); "They wrote the Scroll of Esther" (TB Bava Batra 15a), and "They enacted that it should be read in public" (TB Megillah 2a); *etc.* For fuller discussion, *see* Bloch, *Sha'arei*, I, 1st maḥberet, pp. 107–273, 2nd maḥberet, pp. 1–287. *See also* Alon, *Toledot*, II, pp. 223–224.

B. Sessions of Court

Among the ten enactments attributed to Ezra[44] is one providing that "the court shall sit on Mondays and Thursdays." This enactment established fixed times for the sessions of court. Nachman Krochmal has observed[45] that the document which the king gave to Ezra, as recorded in the Book of Ezra, strongly supports the tradition that Ezra promulgated legislation concerning the designation of court sessions. This document stated:[46]

> And you, Ezra, by the divine wisdom you possess, appoint magistrates and judges who know the laws of your God to judge all the people . . . beyond the River and teach those who do not know them.

Ezra received special authority from the king of Persia to appoint magistrates and judges; and it reasonably follows that in connection with such appointments Ezra also prescribed rules of procedure, including the scheduling of court sessions. There was a great need for this enactment in that period because the return of the people to the life of the Torah gave rise to many problems that required solution and it was necessary to designate fixed times for court sessions in order to solve these problems of both individual and national concern.[47]

C. Extension of the Proscription of Incestuous Relationships from the First to the Second Degree of Consanguinity

Another enactment from this period is the extension of the proscription of incestuous relationships from the first to the second degree of consanguin-

44. TB Bava Kamma 82a and TJ Megillah 4:1, 29a/b (4:1, 75a). TB Sanhedrin 19a attributes one of the enactments listed in TJ (that women should converse with each other while in the lavatory, so that men should not intrude) to R. Yose in Sepphoris. The enactment concerning men who had an emission is listed in TJ Shabbat 1:4, 9a (1:8, 3c) among the "eighteen things" that the schools of Shammai and Hillel enacted.

45. *Kitvei Reb Naḥman Krochmal* [The Collected Writings of Nachman Krochmal], ed. Rawidowicz, p. 63.

46. Ezra 7:25.

47. TB Bava Kamma 82a connects the enactment fixing Mondays and Thursdays as the days for holding court with another of Ezra's enactments, namely, that the Torah should be read in public on Mondays and Thursdays. The Talmud points out that since the public assembles on Mondays and Thursdays to hear the Torah reading, it is convenient for people to bring to court on those days any matters requiring adjudication. Indeed, the connection between these two enactments—Torah reading days and court days—is not merely technical but is substantive. The point of assembling the people for the reading of the Torah was for the people to learn the Torah, as stated with regard to Ezra and the Levites, "They read from the scroll of the Torah of God, translating it and giving the sense; so they understood the reading" (Nehemiah 8:8), *i.e.,* the reading was accompanied by study and learning by way of midrash (*see supra* pp. 312–313). This practice aroused the need for clarification and for solution to various problems and led to the establishment of fixed days for court sessions.

ity (*sheniyyot mi-divrei soferim*).[48] The import of this prohibition is that in addition to the incestuous relationships forbidden by the Torah, the Scribes prohibited sexual unions between persons of the "second degree" of consanguinity.[49] Under Biblical law,[50] the prohibition of incestuous relationships applies only to sexual relations with those relatives listed in the Torah, such as: mother, sister, daughter, and daughter's daughter. In order to "make a fence" around the Torah, the Scribes also interdicted more distant relatives, termed "relatives of the second degree." There is a detailed listing in the *Tosefta:*[51] "Relatives of the second degree by enactment of the Scribes are: mother's mother, father's mother, the wife of a father's father, the wife of a mother's father, the wife of a mother's brother by his father; the wife of a father's brother by his mother; the wife of a son's son and the wife of a daughter's son." A review of these family relationships explains why the term "second degree" was part of the title of the enactment: the Scribes prohibited relatives one degree further than those expressly prohibited in the Torah.

In the course of time, other prohibited relationships were added by the halakhic authorities, until they reached the number of twenty,[52] some of which do not have any generational limits.[53] In practice, when prohibitions were added that in certain circumstances "do not have any limits," the specific meaning of the term "second degree" was lost, since these additional prohibitions do not stop with the second degree of consanguinity. However, since the term "second degree" was accepted in its time, all prohibited sex-

48. M Yevamot 2:4; *Tosefta* Yevamot 3:1; TJ Yevamot 2:4, 11b (2:4, 3d) *et seq.*; TB Yevamot 20a *et seq.*

49. Incestuous relations prohibited by rabbinic law between persons related by consanguinity in the second degree are also referred to as "forbidden by virtue of a commandment" (*issur mizvah,* M Yevamot 2:4) because "it is a commandment to heed the words of the Sages" (TB Yevamot 20a). *See also* TB Yevamot 21a, where the opinion of R. Judah and others is cited to the effect that King Solomon was the author of the enactment forbidding sexual union between parties related by second degree of consanguinity. However, TB Eruvin 21b does not list this among Solomon's enactments. *See also Tosafot,* Yevamot 21a, s.v. Rav Yehudah amar.

50. Leviticus chs. 18, 20.

51. *Tosefta* Yevamot 3:1; *see also* TJ Yevamot 2:4, 12a (2:4, 3d); TB Yevamot 21a; S. Lieberman, *Tosefta ki-Feshutah,* Yevamot, p. 21.

52. *See* Maimonides, *MT,* Ishut 1:6, following TB Yevamot 21a/b; Sh. Ar. EH ch. 15.

53. *I.e.,* "there is no limit" in this prohibition, *e.g.,* "in the case of a mother's mother there is no limit; even the great-great-grandmother and as far back as it is possible to go is forbidden." Similarly, "in the case of a son's daughter-in-law [one's own daughter-in-law is forbidden by the Torah] there is no limit, but even the daughter-in-law of the great-great-grandson and of future descendants to the end of the world, is forbidden—so much so that each of our wives [Maimonides was speaking of his own generation] is considered to be of second degree of consanguinity to the patriarch Jacob" (Maimonides, *MT,* Ishut 1:6).

ual relationships that were added in the course of time continued to be so designated.[54]

IV. THE SANHEDRIN

A. The Sanhedrin as a Legislative Body

Although the nature and composition of the Sanhedrin and the changes that occurred in the course of its history have been the subject of considerable scholarly research, there is no clear consensus on any conclusions as to these matters.[55] It is clear, however, that the Sanhedrin, in addition to its function as the highest judicial tribunal, was the ultimate legislative authority in the Jewish legal system:

> The great Sanhedrin was authorized to enact *takkanot* and to decree *gezerot* as fixed laws. Although as a general rule the tradition attributes *takkanot* to the patriarchs (*nesi'im*)—Simeon b. Shataḥ, Hillel the Elder, Rabban Gamaliel the Elder, etc.—in fact, the *takkanot* were enacted and promulgated by the Sanhedrin and the patriarchs in the same way that, after the destruction of the Temple, the patriarch and his court together enacted *takkanot* and *gezerot* that were considered absolutely binding on all Jews. These new laws were considered to be secondary to Biblical law and to be only temporary promulgations. However, in actuality they broadened the sphere of the law. Thus, the Sanhedrin, entrusted with this authority, carried out the functions of a legislative body.[56]

The *takkanot* enacted by the Sanhedrin and the patriarchs, as well as those enacted by the patriarchs and their courts after the destruction of the Temple, were substantive legislation that determined the developmental pattern of Jewish law; they shaped and fashioned its character and mode of development for future generations. Many of these enactments dealt with matters of *mishpat ivri.* By far the largest part of the enactments of the Sanhedrin have reached us in anonymous form, because they were adopted by the Sanhedrin as a legislative body. Only a small portion bear the name of the Sage who was the head of the Sanhedrin when the *takkanah* was en-

54. It is possible to interpret "second degree" as referring to the stringency of prohibition and not to the degree of consanguinity, *i.e.,* the primary prohibitions are those listed in the Torah, and all the prohibitions of rabbinic origin are secondary.

55. *See* Hoffmann, *Commentary on Deuteronomy* 17:8–11 (vol. II, pp. 315–325); *id., Der Oberste Gerichtshof* [The Supreme Tribunal], 1878; Alon, *Toledot,* I, pp. 114–128; S.B. Hoenig, *The Great Sanhedrin,* 1953; H.D. Mantel, *Studies in the History of the Sanhedrin,* Cambridge, Mass., 1965, pp. 54–139.

56. Alon, *Toledot,* I, p. 125.

acted. The following are a few examples of enactments of the Sanhedrin in the area of *mishpat ivri*.

B. The Enactment of Simeon b. Shataḥ Concerning the *Ketubbah*

A number of enactments relating to different areas of the law and to the educational system[57] are attributed to Simeon b. Shataḥ, a member of the second of the *Zugot* ("pairs").[58] One of his enactments concerned the *ketubbah*:[59]

> At first, the practice was to write in the *ketubbah* the sum of two hundred *zuz* for a virgin and one hundred for a widow [but there was no lien for the *ketubbah* on the husband's property—Rashi]. As a result, they grew old and did not take wives [*i.e.*, the women did not wish to marry them, saying: "when he dies or divorces me there will be nothing to collect from, as the heirs will conceal the money they inherit"—Rashi].[60]
>
> It was then enacted that it [the amount stipulated in the *ketubbah*] was to be deposited with the wife's father [the wife was therefore assured that she would find assets from which to collect]; but even so, whenever the husband was angry at her he would tell her, "Go to your *ketubbah*" [and it tended to encourage impulsive and ill-considered divorce (lit. "made it a light thing in his eyes to divorce her")].[61]
>
> It was therefore enacted that the amount stipulated in the *ketubbah* was to be deposited with her father-in-law [at the house of the husband—Rashi]; wealthy women [the amount of whose *ketubbah* was substantial—Rashi] would convert it into baskets of silver or gold; poor women would convert it into a [more modest] vessel (*avit*)[62] [*i.e.*, they would convert the assets into utensils that were useful and could also be pledged as security whenever nec-

57. *See* TB Shabbat 14b and 16b; TJ Ketubbot 8:11, 50b (8:11, 32c).

58. *See infra* p. 1043.

59. TB Ketubbot 82b. The *baraita* there describes in detail all the stages of the legislation on the *ketubbah*. Other sources—*see Tosefta* Ketubbot 12:1; TJ Ketubbot 8:11, 50b (8:11, 32b/c)—do not mention the first stage of this series of enactments. There are also other differences in the various sources. *See also* Bloch, *Sha'arei*, II, 1st maḥberet, pp. 45ff.; S. Lieberman, *Tosefta ki-Feshutah*, Nashim, pp. 369–370.

60. For another interpretation, *see* Lieberman, *supra* n. 59 at 370.

61. *Tosefta* Ketubbot 12:1 and TJ Ketubbot 8:11, 50b (8:11, 32b). At that time, the law was that a woman could be divorced without her consent, and the Sages sought ways to discourage hasty divorce. *See infra* pp. 785–786.

62. Current printed editions of the Talmud read: *avit shel mei raglayim* (a chamber pot), but the last three Hebrew words were not in the original text, which reads "*avit*" (a pot); *see* Rashi, *ad loc.*, who quotes the text as reading "*avit*" and adds by way of explanation "for urine." *Tosafot, ad loc.*, states: "The correct reading is '*avit shel neḥoshet*' (a brass pot) in which grapes were taken to the treading floor. A similar use [of *avit*] appears in ch. 'Eizehu Nesh-

essary; and it was not easy for the husband to give them up in the event of divorce when she would come to take possession of the utensils as payment for her *ketubbah*];[63] still, when the husband would be angry at her, he would tell her, "Take your *ketubbah* and go" [as they were nevertheless specific utensils that were at hand].

Simeon b. Shataḥ then enacted that the husband must write in the *ketubbah:* "All my property is subject to a lien for your *ketubbah*" [*i.e.,* he does not specify any personalty but rather designates all of his assets as security for the wife's *ketubbah;* and since he does not have the money for her *ketubbah* in hand inasmuch as he makes use of it, he will have to sell his property at the time of a divorce to pay for the *ketubbah,* and he will thus be discouraged from being overly hasty in divorcing her].[64]

We may draw several conclusions from this *baraita* with regard to legislation in Jewish law. One is that the basic law requiring the giving of a *ketubbah* to a woman at the time she marries—two hundred *zuzim* for a virgin and one hundred for a widow[65]—has its source in a very early enactment,[66] for it appears that even before Simeon b. Shataḥ the Sages had promulgated two enactments in connection with the *ketubbah,* which itself had already become an established and accepted legal institution. The first of these enactments required that the stipulated amount be left with the wife's father, and the second required that it be left with her father-in-law.[67]

---

ekh' [M Bava Meẓi'a 5:7; TB Bava Meẓi'a 72b]: 'and on the *avit* of grapes.' This is Rabbenu Tam's opinion."

63. *See* TJ Ketubbot 8:11, 50b (8:11, 32 b/c) and *Tosafot,* Ketubbot 82b, s.v. Batehillah hayu kotevim la-betulah matayim.

64. *See* TJ Ketubbot 8:11, 50b (8:11, 32c):

> They dealt with the subject again and enacted that a man could do business with [the assets designated for] his wife's *ketubbah,* because in so doing he may lose it, and it would be difficult for him to divorce her. And Simeon b. Shataḥ enacted three things: that a man may do business with his wife's *ketubbah,* that children should go to school, and that glass vessels are subject to ritual impurity.

Thus, Simeon b. Shataḥ's enactment that all of the husband's property is subject to the lien of his wife's *ketubbah* is stated in TJ as being to the effect that the husband may use the assets designated for his wife's *ketubbah* for his own business purposes. The two formulations represent the two aspects of the same enactment.

65. This law is set forth in M Ketubbot 1:2.

66. The *tannaim* disagreed as to whether the *ketubbah* is Biblical or rabbinic (TB Ketubbot 10a, 110b; TJ Ketubbot 13:11, 72a [13:11, 36b]), but it is most likely a very early *takkanah. See* Maimonides, *MT,* Ishut 16:9 (". . . like the conditions of the *ketubbah,* enacted by the Great Sanhedrin"). *See also supra* pp. 211, 215–217; H. Albeck, Commentary on M Nashim, pp. 77–81. The sums of two hundred and one hundred *zuzim* respectively are minimum amounts, which the husband may supplement; *see* M Ketubbot 5:1.

67. In TB Shabbat 14b and 16b it is stated: "Simeon b. Shataḥ enacted (*tikken*) the *ketubbah* for the wife." This cannot mean that he legislated the institution of the *ketubbah* providing for two hundred *zuzim* and one hundred *zuzim,* but rather that he promulgated

Also presented here is a full description of different stages of the legislative development of a particular legal institution. We can discern here how the Sages used the legislative process from time to time in different periods to adjust and modify the *ketubbah* as experience following particular stages of the legislation demonstrated the need to do so. After the basic early enactment that instituted the *ketubbah* itself, the Sages promulgated three additional enactments on the subject, each one changing the law set forth in the preceding *takkanah,* all with the central purpose of deterring hasty and ill-considered divorces to the greatest possible extent.[68]

C. The Enactments of Hillel

There are extant two important enactments in the sphere of *mishpat ivri* in the name of Hillel the Elder (a member of the fifth "pair"), whose role in the development and crystallization of the canons of interpretation has already been discussed. It is likely that this halakhic giant was also quite active in the area of legislation and that others of his enactments have reached us in an anonymous form.[69]

The two enactments of Hillel just referred to were prompted by similar economic and social forces. The *prosbul* was enacted to remedy the denial of credit to the needy in consequence of concern of prospective lenders that the loan would be cancelled in the seventh or sabbatical year. This enactment has been discussed in detail.[70] The second enactment concerns the redemption of a house in a walled city; its purpose was to aid a seller to redeem and reclaim for himself a home he had been forced to sell.

---

an enactment relating to the *ketubbah. See* Rashi, Shabbat 14b, s.v. Tikken ketubbah, explaining that "he enacted the *ketubbah, i.e.,* that he [the husband] should write for her, 'All my property is subject to a lien for the *ketubbah.*' . . ." *See also* S. Lieberman, *Tosefta ki-Feshutah,* Nashim, p. 369, interpreting the word *tikken*—usually translated as "enacted"—as meaning "edited" or "redacted," as in the expression in TB Yevamot 64b: "*Matnitan man takkin? Rabbi*" (Who redacted our *mishnah?* Rabbi [Judah Ha-Nasi]).

68. Both the basic liability for the *ketubbah* and the lien of the *ketubbah* on the husband's assets exist by virtue of legislation, even if the husband never expressly agrees to assume the obligation. Thus, M Ketubbot 4:7 states:

> Even if he does not write her a *ketubbah,* a virgin may collect two hundred *zuz* and a widow one hundred *zuz,* because it is a stipulation [*tenai*] of the court [*i.e.,* a *takkanah, see supra* p. 492]. If he designates for her a field worth one hundred *zuz* as security for the two hundred *zuz* and does not write for her, "All my property is subject to the lien of your *ketubbah,*" he is still liable [for the two hundred *zuz* and all his property is subject to a lien for that amount] because it is a stipulation of the court.

See further Maimonides, *MT,* Ishut 16:9.

69. This can be deduced from M Shevi'it 10:3 regarding the *prosbul* enactment: "This is one of the *takkanot* of Hillel the Elder." *See further* Bloch, *Sha'arei,* II, 1st maḥberet, pp. 117–118.

70. *See supra* pp. 511–513.

With regard to the redemption of a house in a walled city, the Torah states[71] that if an individual sells a dwelling located in a walled city, he is entitled to redeem it from the buyer during the first year following the sale; if he fails to do so, the house belongs permanently to the buyer. The reason is that "inasmuch as the sale of a person's home is an act of extreme gravity, and he is humiliated when he sells it, the Torah sought to have him redeem it during the first year."[72]

Concerning this, the Mishnah states:[73]

> At first, he would hide himself on the last day of the twelve months so that it might become his permanently [*i.e.*, the buyer would conceal himself when the end of the year approached, so that the seller could not find him to redeem the house from him]; Hillel the Elder enacted that he [the seller] could deposit his money in the chamber [of the treasury in the Temple][74] and that he could break down the door and enter [*i.e.*, after the seller deposited the money for the benefit of the buyer, the seller could forcibly reenter his house]; and whenever he [the buyer] wished, he could come and take his money.

The purpose of Hillel's enactment was thus to prevent the buyer from evading Biblical law by concealing his whereabouts and thereby preventing the seller from redeeming his house. Legally, the seller had to deliver his money directly to the buyer and the buyer had to be willing to accept it, because the governing rule in that situation was that "delivery to another against his will" is legally ineffective.[75] Hillel enacted an important change—in this situation, the seller may deposit the money in a place where it will be safeguarded by public authority[76] for the benefit of one who, although required by law to accept the payment, nevertheless refuses to do so; and this deposit is the equivalent of fully effective legal delivery.[77]

71. Leviticus 25:29–30.

72. Naḥmanides, *Commentary on Leviticus* 25:29.

73. M Arakhin 9:4.

74. The chamber of the Temple treasury served as a sort of central bank where deposits by various people, including widows and orphans, were placed for safekeeping; *see* II Maccabees 3:10, 22–24. *See also* L. Blau, *MGWJ*, LXIII (1919), pp. 154–155; H. Albeck, Commentary on M Arakhin, p. 218. The present-day practice of depositing funds in court is similar in concept.

75. *See* TB Arakhin 31b–32a; Gittin 74b–75a.

76. *See* Maimonides, *MT*, Shemittah ve-Yovel 12:7: "If the last day of the twelfth month came and the purchaser was not available so as to permit [the house] to be redeemed from him, he [the seller] could deposit his funds in court, break down the door [of the house], and re-enter. When the purchaser appears, he can come and take his money."

77. On the basis of this law as to houses in a walled city, the Talmud derives rules applicable to other similar cases. *See* TB Arakhin 31b–32a; Gittin 74b–75a; *MT*, Gerushin 8:21; Sh. Ar. EH 143:4. *Tosafot Yom Tov* to M Arakhin 9:4, s.v. Hitkin Hillel ha-zaken,

D. The Enactments of Rabban Gamaliel the Elder

Significant legislation, especially in the area of family law, was enacted by Rabban Gamaliel the Elder, the grandson of Hillel the Elder. Rabban Gamaliel the Elder[78] lived in the first century C.E.; he was the patriarch of the Sanhedrin, and his enactments had a decisive influence on the development of Jewish law. Following is a discussion of three of them.

1. WRITING OF NAMES IN A *GET* (BILL OF DIVORCEMENT)

The Mishnah states:[79]

> Originally, a husband would change his and his wife's name and the name of his town and his wife's town. Rabban Gamaliel the Elder enacted that he should write: "The man named So-and-so" and [then list] every other name by which he has been known, "the woman named So-and-so" and [then list] every other name by which she has been known, in order to promote the public welfare.

Before this enactment, when a man changed his name or there was a change in the name of his town, only the new name would be written in the *get*.[80] Rabban Gamaliel the Elder enacted that the husband must write in the *get* not only his present name and that of his town but also his previous names and the previous names of his town, and the same with regard to his wife[81]—"to promote the public welfare," *i.e.*, to preclude the possibility that after the wife remarries, it would be said that the *get* in her possession is that of a different woman, and the stigma of being *mamzerim* (offspring of a union that is incestuous or adulterous under Jewish law) would attach to her children by her second husband.

---

explains that this enactment of Hillel is based on the same principle used by the *amoraim* to explain the enactment of the *prosbul*, namely, *hefker bet din hefker* (the court has the power to expropriate property). *See supra* p. 513.

78. Rabban Gamaliel, too, is called "the Elder" to distinguish him from his grandson, Rabban Gamaliel of Yavneh, also known as Rabban Gamaliel II.

79. M Gittin 4:2.

80. In that historical period, it was common practice for a conqueror to change the names of cities he conquered. Personal names were also often changed. *See* the *baraita* quoted *infra* in the text at n. 82.

81. Some of the *rishonim* understood the enactment as having provided that the *get* should read "The man named So-and-so and every other name by which he has been known" and that it was not necessary to list those other names (*Tosafot*, Gittin 34b, s.v. Ve-khol shum she-yesh lo; Meiri, *Bet ha-Beḥirah*, Gittin 34b, ed. Schlesinger, p. 144). However, in light of the plain meaning and manifest purpose of the enactment, Rabban Gamaliel probably intended that each of the names by which the parties have been known should be set forth in the *get*.

A tradition from the beginning of the amoraic period[82] indicates the social and historical background of this enactment:

> R. Judah said in the name of Samuel: "The inhabitants of the 'region of the sea' [those residing overseas or outside of the Land of Israel] sent the following inquiry to Rabban Gamaliel: 'If a man comes from there to here [from the Land of Israel to a foreign land] whose name is Joseph but he is called Johanan, or his name is Johanan and he is called Joseph, how should he divorce his wife?' [*I.e.,* what name should be written in the *get* to avoid subsequent problems?] Rabban Gamaliel thereupon enacted a *takkanah* that they should write: 'The man named So-and-so' and [then list] every other name by which he has been known, 'the woman named So-and-so' and [then list] every other name by which she has been known, in order to promote the public welfare."

The above-quoted *baraita* indicates that when people changed their residence, they would be influenced by their new environment to change their name, thus causing the problem necessitating the enactment.

2. NULLIFICATION OF A *GET* SENT TO A WIFE THROUGH AN AGENT

Another enactment of Rabban Gamaliel the Elder also concerns the subject of divorce. The Mishnah states:

> If a man, after sending a *get* to his wife by an agent, meets the agent or sends a messenger after him and tells him, "The *get* I gave you is canceled," it is canceled. If he [the husband] meets his wife first, or he sends a messenger to her and he tells her, "The *get* I sent to you is canceled," it is canceled. Once the *get* reaches her, he may no longer cancel it.[83]

The Mishnah establishes that if a husband sends a *get* to his wife through an agent, he may cancel the *get* as long as it has not been delivered to his wife. The succeeding *mishnah* continues:

> Originally he would appear before [lit. "convene"] a court at another place and cancel it. In order to promote the public welfare, Rabban Gamaliel the Elder enacted that this should not be done.

In other words, originally the husband could cancel the *get* before it reached his wife if he appeared for that purpose before a court, even though the court sat in a locality other than where his wife lived. Rabban Gamaliel the Elder nullified this method of canceling the *get,* because of the danger

82. TB Gittin 34b.
83. M Gittin 4:1.

that the agent and the wife would be unaware of the cancellation, the wife would remarry, and her children born as a result of her second marriage would be *mamzerim.*[84] The purpose of the enactment of Rabban Gamaliel the Elder was to prohibit the husband from canceling the *get* except in the presence of his wife.

There was an important controversy concerning the scope of this *takkanah* between two leading legislators at the end of the tannaitic period—R. Judah Ha-Nasi and Rabban Simeon b. Gamaliel:

> The Rabbis taught: If he canceled it, it is legally canceled; this is the view of R. Judah Ha-Nasi [*i.e.,* R. Judah Ha-Nasi was of the opinion that if the husband did cancel the *get* before a court although his wife was not present, then notwithstanding that he acted contrary to Rabban Gamaliel's *takkanah,* the *get* is effectively canceled and she is not divorced]. Rabban Simeon b. Gamaliel holds: He may neither cancel it nor add any conditions [*i.e.,* the act of the husband in canceling it in violation of the *takkanah* is of no legal effect, nor can he add any conditions to the *get*], for otherwise, of what value is the authority of the court [to legislate]?[85]

It was the opinion of R. Judah Ha-Nasi that, since under Biblical law a cancellation in the absence of the wife is legally effective, the *get* is nullified by cancellation in this manner even though the cancellation contravenes the enactment of Rabban Gamaliel the Elder. However, Rabban Simeon b. Gamaliel's view was that once legislation had been enacted to the effect that a *get* may not be canceled in this manner, a cancellation that contravenes that legislation is not effective. Otherwise, Rabban Simeon b.

84. TB Gittin 33a; TJ Gittin 4:2, 20b (4:2, 45c). These sources also give an additional reason, namely, to prevent women from becoming *agunot.*

85. TB Gittin 33a; Yevamot 90b. In *Tosefta* Gittin 4:1 and in TJ Gittin 4:2, 20b (4:2, 45c) the clause "for otherwise, of what value is the authority of the court?" is missing. TB's version seems correct because the clause fits well into the context as the rationale for Rabban Simeon b. Gamaliel's opinion, which appears to be premised on the principle stated in TJ Gittin 4:2 that the Sages are empowered to adopt legislation abrogating a law of the Torah (as opposed to the rationale stated in TB Yevamot 90b and Gittin 33a that the enactment is based on the principle that all who marry do so subject to the conditions laid down by the Rabbis). *See further infra* pp. 634–636.

See also D. Ha-Livni, *Mekorot u-Masorot* [Sources and Traditions], pp. 531–532, arguing that the clause was added under the influence of M Ketubbot 11:5, where Rabban Simeon b. Gamaliel is reported in another connection as having raised the same query in identical language. The argument is not convincing. This query—"Of what value is the authority of the court?"—is clearly relevant to legislation, which is the subject of TB Gittin 33a and Yevamot 90b. It is the court that adopts enactments, which are sometimes called "stipulations imposed by the court." *See supra* p. 492. Moreover, Ha-Livni's argument notwithstanding, the query "Otherwise, of what value is the authority of the court?" is apposite only if action taken in contravention of the enactment is void *ex post* (*be-di-avad*), and the enactment is not merely prohibitory *ex ante* (*le-khateḥillah*). *See also* A. Weiss, *Le-Ḥeker ha-Talmud* [On Research of the Talmud], p. 389 n. 366.

Gamaliel reasoned, of what value is the legislative authority of the court if legislation is not fully effective against one who violates it? And, he concluded, since the cancellation is not effective, the *get* is valid, and the wife may remarry.

The *amoraim* raised the query whether the rationale "Of what value is the authority of the court?" was sufficient to establish that a *get* legally canceled under Biblical law is effective to permit the wife to marry another man. In answer to this question, the Babylonian *amoraim* explained that the legislation was valid on the basis of the principle that the Sages have full authority to dissolve marriages, since marriages are entered into subject to the conditions laid down by them. The *tannaim* did not see any need for this explanation, and the rationale based on the institutional authority of the Sanhedrin ("Otherwise, of what value is the authority of the court?") was regarded as sufficient.[86]

3. ENACTMENT CONCERNING *AGUNOT*

Another enactment of Rabban Gamaliel the Elder, concerning *agunot*, has already been discussed above in detail.[87]

E. The Enactments of Usha

The Sanhedrin continued to legislate even after the destruction of the Temple. Talmudic literature tells of the enactments of Rabban Johanan b. Zakkai (who lived in the period of the destruction of the Temple)[88] and of Rabban Gamaliel of Yavneh (who lived in the succeeding generation and was the patriarch at the end of the first and beginning of the second centuries C.E.).[89] In the middle of the second century C.E., a long series of enactments known as the "*Takkanot* of Usha" were enacted by the Sanhedrin while it was sitting at Usha in the Galilee.[90]

86. *See infra* pp. 631–642 for the discussions by the *amoraim* of Babylonia and the Land of Israel concerning the enactment of Rabban Gamaliel the Elder. Theretofore, the rationale based on the institutional authority to legislate had been considered sufficient.

87. *Supra* pp. 522ff. *See supra* pp. 525–526 for the enactment of Rabban Gamaliel the Elder that the testimony of only one witness as to the death of the husband is sufficient to permit the wife to remarry.

88. As to Rabban Johanan b. Zakkai's enactments, *see* Bloch, *Sha'arei*, II, 1st maḥberet, pp. 211–251.

89. As to Rabban Gamaliel of Yavneh's enactments, *see id.* at 251–252.

90. According to most scholars, the *takkanot* of Usha should be attributed to the Sanhedrin sitting at Usha after the Bar Kokhba war. *See id.* at 253–255; Gulak, *Yesodei*, II, pp. 68–69, III, pp. 68–69. For a more detailed discussion, *see* H.D. Mantel, *supra* n. 55 at 146–174. Mantel (pp. 365–369 of the Hebrew edition of his book, Tel Aviv, 1969) is of the opinion that all but two of the *takkanot* of Usha (*Tosefta* Shevi'it 4:21 and TB Shabbat 15b) date from the beginning of the amoraic period and were enacted by the local court of Usha

These were difficult times for the people in the Land of Israel—times of war and suffering—immediately following the decrees of the Emperor Hadrian. The harsh economic situation brought in its wake social crises and a weakening of the financial ties between spouses and between parents and minor children. A considerable portion of the *Takkanot* of Usha, two of which are next discussed, were aimed at ameliorating these social problems.

1. OBLIGATION OF CHILD SUPPORT

At first,[91] a father had no legal obligation to support and maintain his children. The father's moral and religious duty to care for his children was sufficient to assure that the needs of the children would be met. However, with the intensification of economic hardships, especially after the defeat of the Bar Kokhba revolt and after the Hadrianic edicts, there were cases where fathers stopped supporting their children and the children became public charges. To stem this, the Sages employed legislation to transform the moral obligation into an enforceable legal obligation.

The Talmud states:[92]

> R. Ilaa said in the name of Resh Lakish, who had heard it from R. Judah[93] b. Ḥanina: "It was enacted in Usha that a man must support his sons and daughters when they are young."

The Talmudic and post-Talmudic sources reflect the controversy concerning the substance of this enactment and the extent to which the public accepted it. According to one view, this enactment of Usha originally was intended to impose a duty to support a son until the age of thirteen years and one day, and a daughter until twelve years, six months and one day,[94] but the enactment was not accepted in its full extent; instead, a father's duty of support was limited to children up to the age of six years—"minors of a very young age." Another view is that the entire enactment was rejected until the amoraic period, and then it was accepted only to a limited extent,

---

for the residents of Usha. According to Mantel, this explains why the *amoraim* had doubts about whether these *takkanot* were binding and therefore did not fully recognize them. This theory requires a great deal of study.

91. *See supra* p. 116.

92. TB Ketubbot 49b.

93. This is the correct reading as in the printed editions and not as emended by *Masoret ha-Shas* to read: "R. Yose b. Ḥanina," who was a disciple of R. Johanan. *See* A. Hyman, *Toledot Tanna'im ve-Amora'im* [A History of the *Tannaim* and *Amoraim*], II, p. 724.

94. A girl has an intermediate period of puberty (*na'arut*) between the age of twelve years and one day and the age of twelve years, six months and one day. *See* Maimonides, *MT*, Ishut 2:1–2.

i.e., a duty to support children until the age of six.[95] It is likely that beginning approximately at the end of the third century, the enactment was accepted in this limited form, and the obligation to support children above the age of six continued to be rooted in the obligation to give charity.[96]

2. SALE BY A WIFE OF HER USUFRUCT (*MELOG*) PROPERTY

An additional *takkanah* enacted at Usha increased the rights of the husband in his wife's property. The Talmud states:[97]

> R. Yose[98] b. Ḥanina said: "It was enacted in Usha that if a woman sold usufruct (*melog*) property during the lifetime of her husband and then she died, the husband may retake the property from the purchaser."

As will be seen later,[99] according to an early enactment, the husband has the right to the usufruct of the *melog* property of his wife, *i.e.*, the right to receive the income from the property his wife brings with her from her father's house at the time of the marriage or that she acquires (*e.g.*, by inheritance) after her marriage; the principal remains in the wife's ownership but the income belongs to the husband. There was an additional early enactment that the husband has priority over the other heirs to the wife's estate. Under this second enactment, the husband inherits the property that remains in her possession and ownership at the time of her death, *i.e.*, the property that she does not sell during her lifetime. If the wife sells the property during her lifetime, the sale does not terminate the husband's right to receive the income from the property so long as she lives, and the husband retains the right to use the property during the marriage. However, ownership of the property is transferred to the purchaser, *i.e.*, the sale of the principal is immediately effective; and after the death of the wife, the right to the actual use of the property also passes to the purchaser.

The purpose of the enactment of Usha was to strengthen the rights of the husband in his wife's property. "The Sages strengthened the husband's rights" by providing that even if the wife sells her *melog* property during her lifetime, the principal and income pass at her death not to the purchaser but rather to the husband because "the husband may retake the property from the purchaser."[100] This enactment changed the legal status of the hus-

95. Rashi, Ketubbot 49b, s.v. Ke-she-hen ketannin, and *Tosafot, ad loc.*, s.v. Ke-she-hem ketannim; *Tosafot*, Ketubbot 65b, s.v. Aval zan ketanei ketannim. *See also* Bloch, *Sha'arei*, II, 1st maḥberet, pp. 283–287; Gulak, *Yesodei*, II, pp. 68–69, III, pp. 68–69.

96. *See supra* pp. 116–117.

97. TB Ketubbot 50a.

98. *See supra* n. 93.

99. *See infra* p. 572 and n. 118.

100. The commentators had difficulty with the word "retake" (*moẓi*), which implies that ownership of *melog* property passes to the purchaser as soon as the wife sells it. *See*

band with regard to his wife's property from that of an heir to that of a purchaser. It conferred on the husband the same status as if he had bought the wife's property at the time of the marriage; he was in effect the first purchaser, with priority over all other purchasers. After this enactment, the only instance in which the purchaser can ever enjoy the *melog* property sold to him by a married woman is when her husband predeceases her.

One reason given for this *takkanah* was "to prevent enmity" between them,[101] *i.e.*, to prevent ill feeling and suspicion between husband and wife. There is a further rationale in the Talmud:[102] "They brought the loss on themselves [*i.e.*, the purchasers themselves caused their own loss]; she has a husband, and they should not have bought from a woman who lives with her husband."

Thus, it was the erosion of family ties that provided the background for the enactment of this *takkanah*. There were occasions when a wife sold property to remove it from the reach of her husband, thus causing enmity and quarreling between them; and the elimination of that possibility strengthened normal family relationships.[103]

V. ANONYMOUS ENACTMENTS IN VARIOUS FIELDS OF LAW

The overwhelming majority of enactments up to the end of the tannaitic period were not handed down in the name of the bodies or individuals who promulgated them.[104] As a result, it is difficult to establish with certainty

---

Shittah Mekubbezet, Ketubbot 78b, s.v. Ve-khen pershu talmidei Rabbenu Yonah, to the effect that "retake" means to remove from any claim of right by the purchaser (implying that the purchaser does not acquire ownership as a result of the sale). However, Maimonides, *MT*, Ishut 22:7, indicates that the property itself passes to the ownership of the purchaser simultaneously with the sale but that the income from it belongs to the husband. *See further* Sh. Ar. EH 90:9 and commentaries, *ad loc.*, as to the effect of the passage of ownership to the purchaser simultaneously with the sale.

101. Rashi, Bava Kamma 88b, s.v. Be-Usha hitkinu. As to this rationale, which was given by the *amoraim*, *see infra* p. 628.

102. TB Bava Batra 139b.

103. The later *tannaim* continued to promulgate legislation. *See* Bloch, *Sha'arei*, II, 1st maḥberet, pp. 300–326, for the enactments of R. Yose b. Ḥalafta in Sepphoris and of R. Judah Ha-Nasi. The enactments of the latter and his court concerning purchases from the *sikerikon* (*sicarii*, bandits) is of special legal interest; *see* M Gittin 5:6 and H. Albeck, *ad loc.*; Bloch, *Sha'arei*, *supra* at 314–320.

104. Occasionally, parallel sources offer evidence of the identity of the author of an enactment. For example, with regard to the enactment of Simeon b. Shataḥ, discussed *supra* pp. 559ff., M Ketubbot 4:7 records a law, not attributed to any named source, that whether the husband designates in the *ketubbah* a field worth one hundred *zuzim* as security for the two

even to what period a considerable portion of the enactments should be ascribed. It is possible to prove in various ways (*i.e.,* their style or the sources in which they are first mentioned) that some of these enactments are of early origin, but even as to these, it is difficult to establish with certainty in what period they were enacted.

These anonymous enactments cover entire fields of Jewish law: family law, succession, property, contracts, torts, procedure, evidence, and labor law. Following are examples from each of these areas of the law.

A. Legislation Concerning Family Law and the Law of Succession

A large and significant part of family and succession law is based on legislation enacted in all periods of Jewish law, and a considerable portion of this legislation was enacted before the end of the tannaitic period.

1. SPOUSAL SUPPORT

According to some Sages, the obligation of the husband to support his wife is based on legislation:

> The Rabbis taught: Her right to support was enacted in return for her handiwork (*ma'aseh yadeha*) [*i.e.,* the Sages enacted that the husband is obligated to support his wife in return for her domestic services to which, pursuant to legislative enactment, the husband is entitled].[105]

This view of the legislative origin of the husband's duty of support was shared by Rav and Samuel and other *amoraim.*[106] In contrast to this view, a few *tannaim,* such as R. Eleazar and others,[107] were of the opinion that the legal source of the obligation of support is not legislation, but the Torah, *i.e.,* Biblical exegesis. According to these latter *tannaim,* the duty of support

---

hundred *zuzim* of the *ketubbah* or provides for no security, his property is nevertheless subject to the lien for the full two hundred *zuzim,* since it is a stipulation of the court. From the *baraita* quoted in TB Ketubbot 82b, it can be inferred that it was Simeon b. Shataḥ who promulgated the enactment that all the husband's assets are subject to the lien of the wife's *ketubbah.*

The following is a further example: M Rosh ha-Shanah 1:14 states, "The sabbath may be violated with regard to two months," *i.e.,* witnesses who have seen the New Moon for the months of Nisan and Tishri may violate the laws of the sabbath to travel to Jerusalem to give testimony as early as possible. A *baraita* cited in TB Rosh ha-Shanah 21b describes this law as an enactment of Rabban Johanan b. Zakkai.

105. TB Ketubbot 47b.

106. *Id.* 58b–59a.

107. *Id.* 47b; *see also id.* 48a, *Tosafot,* s.v. R. Eliezer b. Ya'akov omer.

is deduced from the statement in the Torah with regard to the rights of the maidservant who is betrothed to the master's son: "If he marries another, he shall not diminish her *she'er,* her *kesut* (clothing), or her *onah.*"[108] According to one opinion, *she'er* refers to support,[109] and *onah* refers to conjugal duty;[110] according to R. Eleazar, *she'er* refers to conjugal duty[111] and *onah* to support.[112]

These differences among the Sages with regard to the legal source of the husband's duty to support his wife continued in the post-Talmudic period. Maimonides was of the opinion that the obligation of support is Biblical;[113] Naḥmanides' view was that it is a rabbinic enactment.[114]

2. THE WIFE'S HANDIWORK; WAIVER OF RIGHTS CONFERRED BY LEGISLATION

It is universally agreed that the legal source for the husband's right to the wife's handiwork (*ma'aseh yadeha*) is legislation. This right was given to the husband in return for the obligation imposed on him to support his wife. The rationale was "to prevent enmity,"[115] *i.e.,* the ill feeling that might occur between husband and wife if the law were to be that the husband is obligated to support his wife and yet the wife is not required to participate in the management of the household.

As a consequence of the reciprocal relationship between a husband's right to his wife's handiwork and his duty to support her, a general principle was laid down that an individual for whose particular benefit an enactment is adopted may waive the benefit the enactment confers:

> Rav Huna said in the name of Rav: "A woman may say to her husband: 'I will not be supported nor shall I perform [any handiwork].'" He [Rav Huna in the name of Rav] is of the opinion that the Rabbis established support for the wife as the primary obligation, and the husband was given the right to

108. Exodus 21:10.

109. Following Micah 3:3: "You have eaten My people's flesh (*she'er ami*)."

110. Following Genesis 31:50, Laban's statement to Jacob: "If you ill-treat [*te'aneh, cf. onah*] my daughters or take other wives besides my daughters. . . ." For a different explanation of the word *onah* as referring to conjugal relations, *see* Ibn Ezra, *Commentary on Exodus* 21:10, s.v. Ve-onatah.

111. Following Leviticus 18:6: "None of you shall come near anyone of his own flesh [*she'er besaro*] to uncover nakedness."

112. Following Deuteronomy 8:3: "He subjected you to the hardship [*va-ye'ankha, cf. onah*] of hunger and then gave you manna to eat, which neither you nor your fathers had ever known. . . ."

113. *MT,* Ishut 12:2. *See also Maggid Mishneh, ad loc.,* s.v. Ke-she-nose adam, and *Kesef Mishneh, ad loc.*

114. Naḥmanides, *Commentary on Exodus* 21:10, and *see* C. Chavel's note, *ad loc.,* s.v. Takkinu lah rabbanan.

115. TB Ketubbot 58b. *See also supra* n. 101 and accompanying text.

her handiwork to prevent enmity; thus, she has the right to say: "I will not be supported nor shall I perform [any handiwork]."[116]

In other words, the primary legislation is the enactment imposing the duty on a husband to support his wife. It is only on the basis of this obligation and in exchange for it that legislation was enacted giving a husband the right to his wife's handiwork; therefore, the wife may waive her right to support, in which event the right of the husband to her handiwork automatically lapses.[117]

3. RANSOM OF THE WIFE; USUFRUCT OF *MELOG* PROPERTY

Another reciprocal relationship in family law is the relationship between a husband's duty to ransom his wife from captivity and his entitlement to the usufruct of her *melog* property.[118] Thus, the Talmud states:[119] "The duty of ransoming her[120] was enacted in exchange for the usufruct [*i.e.*, in return for the right to the usufruct of the *melog* property]."[121]

116. TB Ketubbot 58b.

117. Since the primary enactment was for the benefit of the wife, *i.e.*, to provide that her husband must support her, only she can waive her right. The husband cannot say, "Go out and let your earnings from your handiwork be your support"; TB Ketubbot 70b; Maimonides, *MT*, Ishut 12:4; Sh. Ar. EH 69:4.

118. The assets a woman brings to her marriage are divided into two main categories: 1. *Nikhsei ẓon barzel* (lit. "property of the iron flock") are her assets that she and her husband have agreed should be in his almost absolute ownership. The husband undertakes to be responsible for any loss or diminution in value of such property; the agreement is that the value of the assets as of the time of the marriage will be preserved like "iron," which endures. 2. *Nikhsei melog* (*melog* property, lit. "plucked property," *i.e.*, usufruct property) are assets that the wife continues to own but the income from them is the husband's. The husband is not responsible for loss or damage to *melog* property. There is a third category of a wife's property, of which both principal and income belong solely to her. Examples of this type of property are: a gift to the wife from a third party on the express condition that the husband is to have no rights in it, and a gift to the wife from her husband after the marriage. *See also* B. Schereschewsky, *Dinei Mishpaḥah* [Family Law], pp. 153ff. For the etymology of *melog*, *see* Levy, *Wörterbuch*, III, pp. 123–124, s.v. Melog.

119. TB Ketubbot 47b.

120. In that period, taking prisoners or kidnapping, particularly of women, was a common occurrence at times of war or unrest. A woman's legal rights in this situation are still relevant even today; *see* Schereschewsky, *supra* n. 118 at 151–152.

121. *See further supra* pp. 568–569 on the *takkanah* of Usha concerning sale of *melog* property by a wife. The husband's right to the income of *melog* property is only for "the well-being of the household" (TB Ketubbot 80a/b); therefore, when such income is more than is required for maintenance of the household, the husband is obligated to reinvest the excess in such a manner that it becomes capital, which will then belong to the wife and not the husband (TB Ketubbot 79b, 83a/b; Sh. Ar. EH ch. 85; *Bet Shemu'el, ad loc.*, subpar. 38), because his right to the income is meant to ensure "that they will both be supported in dignity from the income that the property will generate daily" (*Shittah Mekubbeẓet*, Ketubbot 80a, s.v. Iba'ya lehu). *See* Elon, *Ḥakikah*, pp. 37ff.

4. THE HUSBAND'S RIGHT OF INHERITANCE AND THE WIDOW'S RIGHT TO MAINTENANCE

Under Jewish law, a husband is the heir of his wife. The Sages disagreed as to whether this right of inheritance is Biblical (derived from Biblical exegesis) or rabbinic (based on legislation).[122] This disagreement continued into the post-Talmudic period.[123]

On the other hand, a wife does not inherit from her husband;[124] therefore, the Sages adopted an enactment designed to assure complete support for a widow out of the assets of her husband's estate during her widowhood. Concerning this, the Mishnah states:[125]

> Even if he [the husband] did not agree in writing that "You may dwell in my house and be supported in my house out of my estate throughout the duration of your widowhood," he is so obligated, as it is a stipulation of the court. The men of Jerusalem did so write. The men of Galilee wrote the same as the men of Jerusalem. The men of Judea wrote, "until the heirs wish to give you your *ketubbah*"; therefore, if the heirs wish to do so, they may give her the amount of her *ketubbah* and have no further obligation to her.

The enactment provides that during her widowhood, the widow may live in the marital home and be supported out of the estate. This enactment automatically obligates every husband at the time of his marriage, even if he has not explicitly so obligated himself in the *ketubbah.*

The latter part of the *mishnah* reveals that there were two forms of *ketubbah* with regard to the rights of a widow in her husband's estate, and the difference in their language produced differences in her rights. According to one form, used in Jerusalem and Galilee, the right of the widow to support from the estate exists so long as she remains a widow and does not voluntarily collect the amount of her *ketubbah;*[126] and the heirs may not

122. M Bava Batra 8:1; TB Bava Batra 109b and 111b (where the husband's right of inheritance is derived by way of Biblical exegesis); Bekhorot 52b; Ketubbot 83b–84a.

123. According to Maimonides, the husband inherits from his wife by virtue of rabbinic law (*MT,* Ishut 12:3, 9; Naḥalot 1:8). According to Rabad, the husband's right of inheritance is Biblical (Gloss to *MT,* Naḥalot 1:8), which is also the opinion of most authorities. *See Maggid Mishneh* and *Kesef Mishneh* to *MT,* Naḥalot 1:8.

124. M Bava Batra 8:1; Maimonides, *MT,* Naḥalot 1:8. Various enactments were adopted in the post-Talmudic period entitling the wife to a portion of her husband's estate. *See infra* pp. 841–842.

125. M Ketubbot 4:10, 12.

126. TB Ketubbot 97b. According to R. Judah in the name of Samuel, the widow's right to support is terminated as soon as she claims her *ketubbah* in court even though she has not yet recovered the proceeds; *see, e.g.,* TB Ketubbot 54a. By claiming or recovering the proceeds of her *ketubbah* on her own initiative, the widow demonstrates that she is severing her connection with her late husband's family, and she is therefore no longer entitled to maintenance.

escape their duty of support by paying her the amount of her *ketubbah* against her will. However, according to the second form, used in Judea, the heirs may satisfy her claim to the amount of the *ketubbah* even against her wishes, and may thereby terminate any further obligation to support her out of the estate.

The question arises: If the legal source of the widow's right to support from the estate is based on legislation, how did it happen that there are two different forms, each used by a different segment of the population? Does this indicate that the legislation was enacted not by a single central legislative body but by different courts in Judea and Galilee?

Apparently, the answer to this question is to be found in the particular background of these types of enactments: the legislation was enacted in light of prior customs that had already become entrenched among the people. The practice developed that, at the time of the marriage, the wife or her father requested an explicit undertaking by the husband that if he predeceased his wife, she would have the right to support from his property. In the first stage of the development of the custom, it was a private agreement between husband and wife; under Jewish law there is no barrier to such agreements.[127] This custom developed in one form in Jerusalem and Galilee, and in a different form in Judea. The difference reflected the influence of different economic and social factors in the two areas.[128] After these private agreements became the customary practice of most of the people, the court, *i.e.*, the legislative body, saw fit to "adopt" the practice and to transform it into binding law so as to make it obligatory for all couples, including those who made no such explicit agreement.[129] The legislation, since it was based on customary practice, gave binding effect to the custom as it had developed in the different areas of the country—in Jerusalem and in Galilee on the one hand, and in Judea on the other.

5. SUPPORT OF DAUGHTERS OUT OF THEIR FATHER'S ESTATE

The section of the Torah on inheritance[130] states that when there is a son, a daughter does not inherit. In order to assure the support of a daugh-

127. *See supra* pp. 123–127.

128. *See* TJ Ketubbot 4:14, 31a (4:15, 29b): "The Galileans were concerned about their honor and not about their money; the men of Judea were concerned about their money and not about their honor." For details of these differences in custom—which persisted for many generations—and their background, *see* the judgment of S. Assaf, J., in the Supreme Court of Israel, Miller v. Miller, 5 *P.D.* 1301, 1305ff. (1949).

129. It is possible that this background is reflected in the term "stipulation of the court (*tenai bet din*)," which was the designation given to these enactments. The designation indicates that these enactments originated from a condition, or stipulation, which the court imposed on the basis of prior private agreements between the parties.

130. Numbers 27:8; *see* M Bava Batra 8:2.

ter after her father's death, the Sages adopted an enactment providing that a daughter has the right to support from her father's estate:

> Even if he [the father] did not agree in writing that "the daughters who will be born from our marriage shall dwell in my house and be supported out of my property until they are married by men" (*ad de-tinasevan le-guvrin*), he is so obligated, as it is a stipulation of the court.[131]

There are two versions of this enactment from the period of the *amoraim*. One version is the one in the *mishnah* just quoted. The second version states: "until they become of age" (*ad de-tibageran*) instead of "until they are married," *i.e.*, that the right of the daughters to support from the estate lasts only until they become of age.[132]

The Sages differed with regard to the measure of the daughter's right:

> If one dies and leaves sons and daughters, and the estate is substantial, the sons inherit and the daughters receive support. If the estate is small, the daughters receive support and the sons go begging [*i.e.*, the entire estate is devoted to the support of the daughters, and the sons receive no inheritance nor do they receive support from the estate]. Admon said: "Should I lose out because I am male?" Rabban Gamaliel stated: "I see the justice of Admon's statement."[133]

Admon's "protest" in behalf of the sons did not prevail. The law was settled that when the estate is small, all of it is devoted to the support of the daughters, and the sons receive nothing.[134]

6. ENACTMENT CONCERNING INHERITANCE RIGHTS OF THE WIFE'S SONS; ENSURING DAUGHTERS A SHARE IN THEIR FATHER'S PROPERTY

As early as in the Talmudic period,[135] there were a number of enactments designed to give a daughter a share in her father's property even when there is a surviving son. One such enactment related to the clause in the *ketubbah* concerning the wife's sons (*ketubbat benin dikhrin*):

131. M Ketubbot 4:10, 11. Current printed editions of the Mishnah (TB Ketubbot 52b) read: "Until they will be taken by men (*ad de-tilakhun le-guvrin*)." *See infra* n. 132.

132. TB Ketubbot 53b: "Rav read [the *mishnah*]: 'Until they will be taken by men'; Levi read it: 'Until they become of age.'"

133. M Ketubbot 13:3; M Bava Batra 9:1.

134. Maimonides, *MT,* Ishut 19:17; Sh. Ar. EH 112:11. This principle of the right to maintenance from the estate was adopted in Israel's Succession Law, 1965, as a suitable way of providing for the needs of the heirs. *See* M. Elon, "The Sources and Nature of Jewish Law and its Application in the State of Israel" (Part IV), 4 *Israel Law Review* 80, 130–132 (1969), and *infra* pp. 1678–1680.

135. For the enactments in the post-Talmudic period concerning a daughter's inheritance rights, *see infra* pp. 842–846. *See also infra* pp. 1683–1684.

> Even if he [the husband] did not agree in writing that "the sons to be born from our marriage shall inherit the money of your *ketubbah* in addition to their shares with their brothers," he is so obligated, as it is a stipulation of the court.[136]

The law is that a husband is first in the order of succession from his wife, taking priority over all other heirs.[137] If the wife dies, and the husband then dies after having inherited her property, his sons would inherit his estate, including the portion that he had inherited from his wife. Thus, at the husband's death, all of his sons by all of his wives would inherit from him, with the result that the sons by one wife would inherit the property of another wife;[138] and property that a woman brings with her from her father's house at the time of her marriage would not devolve exclusively upon her own sons or even remain entirely within her family. Instead, her property would pass to a different family as a result of being distributed among her sons' half-brothers.

In order to ensure that a woman's property remains within her family, the enactment "concerning the wife's sons" was adopted. Pursuant to this enactment, when a husband dies and his estate includes property brought by his wife at the time she married him, his sons by that wife are the sole heirs to that property; only the remaining property is shared equally with their father's other sons. Thus, the possibility that the wife's property would pass to a different family was eliminated.

The Sages' desire to encourage fathers to give a portion of their property to their daughters played an important role in the adoption of this enactment. Thus, the Talmud states:[139]

> R. Johanan said in the name of R. Simeon b. Yoḥai: "Why was the *takkanah* concerning the wife's sons enacted? To encourage a man to give to his daughter as much as he gives to his son" [*i.e.*, to encourage a father to give to his daughter at the time of her marriage the same portion of his property that he leaves to his son, since he is assured that the property will remain with his daughter's sons and he need not fear that it might pass to a different family].

An interesting query was raised in the course of the Talmud's discussion of R. Simeon b. Yoḥai's rationale:

136. M Ketubbot 4:10.

137. *See* references *supra* n. 123.

138. The husband may have had children by another wife whom he married after the death of the wife whose property he inherited, or, since polygamy was still permitted in the Talmudic era, by another wife to whom he was married during the lifetime of the deceased wife.

139. TB Ketubbot 52b.

> Seeing that the Torah declared that "a son shall be an heir and a daughter shall not," how could the rabbis legislate to make the daughter an heir? [The objective of this *takkanah* is to encourage fathers to give a daughter the same portion as he gives to a son, but the result is that the son is deprived of the property that should belong to him under Biblical law.]

The response was:

> This also has Biblical sanction [*i.e.*, to give part of the property to a daughter is also Biblical law], as it is written:[140] "Take wives and beget sons and daughters; and take wives for your sons and give your daughters to husbands. . . ." Granted that with respect to sons, it is within one's power to carry this out; but is it within one's power to carry it out with respect to daughters? [*I.e.*, the prophet instructs the father to make certain that his son will take a wife and that his daughter will take a husband; the instruction that the son should take a wife is easy to carry out because it is "the manner of a man to seek out a woman" (Rashi), but is the instruction concerning the daughter within the power of the father? Is it not true that "it is not the way of a woman to seek out a man"? (Rashi)] Therefore, what the prophet is instructing us is that a father must provide his daughter with clothing and property so that she will be desirable as a marriage partner.

The query and the response in this discussion both warrant further comment. On the one hand, the question is hardly overpowering, inasmuch as the enactment concerning the wife's sons does not abrogate any Biblical law: it does not *require* the father to give anything to his daughter but only indirectly encourages him to do so; and, in any case, what the daughter receives from her father is a gift and not a portion of an inheritance. On the other hand, the response, based on the verse in Jeremiah, is also not convincing. How can it be deduced from this verse in Jeremiah that, contrary to the explicit Biblical law that a son has priority over a daughter, there is another Biblical law that requires that property be given also to a daughter?[141]

However, we must view this discussion—both the question and the response—not as a debate concerning the abrogation of an explicit Biblical law (which is not the situation here at all) but as a discussion in connection with the adoption of an enactment inconsistent with the policy of favoring sons over daughters that is expressed in the section of the Torah on inheri-

140. Jeremiah 29:6.

141. As has been noted, there is also a rule that law cannot be derived from the Prophets or the Hagiographa; *see supra* p. 204. For further discussion of the enactment concerning the wife's sons, *see* S. Assaf, "Bittulah Shel Ketubbat Benin Dikhrin" [The Abrogation of the *Ketubbah* Clause Concerning the Wife's Sons], *Ve-Zot li-Yehudah* [Jubilee Volume in Honor of Y.A. Blau], pp. 18–20. With regard to the abrogation of the clause, *see infra* p. 655.

tance. The justification given in the response is that the needs connected with a daughter's marriage require her father to give her a portion of his property. There is here, therefore, no inconsistency with the policy of the Torah with regard to priority in inheritance, but rather the satisfaction of economic and social needs that indirectly results in the receipt by a daughter of a portion of her father's property.

However, the status of a daughter as an heir even when there is also a son became more direct and substantial as a result of the enactment discussed next—the enactment of "one-tenth of the estate."

7. ENACTMENT OF "ONE-TENTH OF THE ESTATE"; THE DAUGHTER'S STATUS AS AN HEIR

The enactment of "one-tenth of the estate" (*isur nekhasim*) also deals with the right of a daughter to a portion of her father's property, and there is reason to believe that it was based on the enactment concerning the wife's sons. Under the enactment of "one-tenth of the estate," a daughter obtains a right in the nature of a true, albeit limited, right of succession, even when there are surviving sons.

The Talmud states:[142]

> Was it not taught: R. Judah Ha-Nasi says: "A daughter who is maintained by her brothers receives one-tenth of the estate"?

Under this enactment, a daughter has the right to receive, in addition to her support, a one-tenth share of her father's estate. As the Talmudic sources and their commentaries indicate, the object of this enactment, too, was to furnish the material resources necessary to enable a daughter to marry. However, the enactment also reflects the beginning of a recognition that a daughter has some right in her father's estate. The enactment concerning the wife's sons did not create any legal right for a daughter to a particular share in her father's property. The objective of that enactment was to encourage a father's voluntary act during his lifetime; that enactment did not require the father to give part of his property, but only indirectly encouraged this result. On the other hand, the enactment of "one-tenth of the estate" wrought a far-reaching change: it conferred upon a daughter the legal right to demand a fixed and definite portion of her father's estate, and this legal right has many of the characteristics of a right of succession.

142. TB Ketubbot 68a. *Isur* in *isur nekhasim* comes from *asarah* ("ten"), and is not related to *issur* ("prohibition"), which is often used as a synonym for "religious" as distinguished from monetary or civil law. The two words, although they sound alike, are spelled differently in Hebrew.

This enactment was extensively discussed in the Talmud. Some of the *amoraim* were of the opinion that a daughter is not entitled to the fixed portion of one-tenth of her father's estate under all circumstances, but only when it is not possible to ascertain how much the father would have intended to give his daughter for a dowry; if such ascertainment is possible, then the portion her father would have given her if he were still alive, whether more or less than one-tenth, is the measure of her entitlement.[143] Similarly, some of the *amoraim* sought to limit to a tenth of the father's property the amount that a father may give his daughter during his lifetime pursuant to the enactment concerning the wife's sons.[144] However, notwithstanding these differences of opinion, it is clear that the essential thrust of the enactment of "one-tenth of the estate" is the explicit prescription of a daughter's right to a specified portion of her father's estate even when there are surviving sons.

There are some fundamental and interesting differences of opinion at the close of the period of the Babylonian *amoraim* with regard to the legal nature of a daughter's right to a tenth of her father's property:[145]

> Ameimar said: "A daughter has the status of an heir" [*i.e.*, the tenth of the estate is given to her by the *takkanah* as an inheritance—Rashi].
>
> Rav Ashi said to Ameimar: "If the sons wish to settle her claim by paying her ten percent in money rather than in kind, do you hold that they are not entitled to do so?" He responded: "Yes." [Rav Ashi further asked]: "If they wish to settle her claim with a single plot of land [rather than by a pro rata distribution of one-tenth of each asset], do you hold that they are not entitled to do so?" He responded: "Yes," [for if she wishes, she may take her portion of every parcel of land and they cannot satisfy her share by making her take any other property instead—Rashi].
>
> Rav Ashi said: "A daughter has the status of a creditor." [*I.e.*, according to Rav Ashi the legal status of a daughter with regard to her right to one-tenth of the property is comparable to the status of a creditor and not to the status of an heir, and it is therefore possible to settle the claim of the daughter by paying money or giving a particular plot of land, as the sons wish.]

This difference of opinion among the Sages relates to the legal character of a daughter's right conferred by the enactment of "one-tenth of the estate." According to Ameimar, the enactment established a daughter as an heir, so that her right to a tenth of the property is governed by all of the laws applicable to any other heir. Thus, one may not say to an heir: "Take money instead of your share of the inheritance," or, "Take this part of the

143. *Id.*
144. *Id.* 52b.
145. *Id.* 69a.

property but no other part." In contrast to this opinion, Rav Ashi held that the enactment did not establish the daughter as an heir but only as a creditor, whom the debtor may satisfy by the payment of money or whatever property the debtor chooses to apply to payment of the debt.[146]

These two enactments, concerning the wife's sons and one-tenth of the estate, demonstrate that, by way of legislation, a daughter was treated like an heir,[147] albeit to a limited extent, even when there were sons.[148]

B. Legislation Concerning Modes of Acquisition (*Kinyan*)

Most of the methods of acquiring property (*kinyan*) in Jewish law originated in legislation by the halakhic authorities. Modes of acquisition are those legal acts by means of which are created rights of ownership in property, *i.e.*, the rights which an individual acquires in property as against the entire world. The fact that Jewish law cast obligations in a distinctly property mold by creating a lien of the creditor on the debtor's property[149] meant that contractual obligations were created by the very same methods through which ownership rights in property were acquired. This result followed from the fact that a contractual obligation entailed proprietary rights in the debtor's property. While the basis for the formation of a contract between the parties was the intention of each party to be bound, the only legally recognized way of manifesting the necessary intent was to use one of the modes of acquisition of property. Therefore, in contrast to Roman law, under which a contract may be created orally, in Jewish law, as a general rule, spoken words alone cannot create obligations entailing legally

146. In the course of the Talmudic discussion, *id.*, the *amora* R. Manyumi b. R. Niḥumi asserted that Ameimar had retracted his view that a daughter has the status of an heir. R. Manyumi's assertion was based on a case in which Ameimar was a judge. Regarding this proof, *see Tosafot, ad loc.*, s.v. Ve-ishtik, and other commentaries, *ad loc.*

147. The daughter's status underwent further development in the post-Talmudic period; *see infra* pp. 842–846.

148. Much of the law of succession originated in legislation. An excellent example involves gifts by a person facing imminent death (*shekhiv me-ra*). Jewish law does not recognize a will that becomes effective after the death of a testator; therefore a will, by Jewish law, has the character of a gift *inter vivos* and becomes effective during the lifetime of the donor. However, the Sages provided by legislation for a will similar in character to wills in other legal systems. Such a will is a gift by a person facing imminent death, which becomes effective after the death of the testator ("The Sages made it like inheritance") and does not require an act of acquisition (*kinyan*) but "his [the testator's] words are as though written and delivered." *See* TB Bava Batra 147a/b. Ritba to Bava Batra 147b, s.v. Shema titaref da'ato, bases the enactment on the court's power to expropriate property pursuant to the principle of *hefker bet din hefker.* As to the law concerning gifts by a person in good health and wills by a *shekhiv me-ra, see* Gulak, *Yesodei,* III, pp. 113ff.

149. *See infra* pp. 590–591.

enforceable consequences;[150] breach of purely oral undertakings is subject only to religious or moral sanctions.[151]

The early modes of acquisition were characterized by a tangible and formal quality; they could not satisfy the needs for the acquisition and conveyance of property rights and were even less suitable for the creation and assignment of contractual rights in a progressively developing economy with commerce crossing geographical boundaries and expanding beyond barter transactions. Consequently, the Sages created—through legislation as the legal source—modes of acquisition that on the one hand retained the "real" character of Jewish modes of acquisition but on the other hand were more convenient, less cumbersome, and more consonant with the needs of time and place.

1. ACQUISITION BY "PULLING" (*KINYAN MESHIKHAH*)

We have already discussed the mode of acquisition known as *kinyan meshikhah* (taking possession, lit. "pulling"), which is based on an enactment of the Sages.[152] The motive for the enactment was not the superior convenience of this mode; rather, the enactment resulted from the concern that the seller will not take proper care of the property if ownership passes to the purchaser while the seller retains possession.[153] The major disadvantage of this mode is the need, at the time of the transaction between the parties, for the physical presence of the chattel that is the subject of the transaction; it is difficult to meet this requirement in a developed state of commercial life. To correct this defect and others, various other modes of acquisition were enacted, some of which are discussed in the following sections.

2. ACQUISITION BY BARTER (*KINYAN ḤALIFIN*) AND ACQUISITION BY SYMBOLIC BARTER (*KINYAN SUDAR*)

Acquisition by barter (*kinyan ḥalifin*), *i.e.*, the exchange of one chattel for another, is one of the earliest modes of acquisition in Jewish law. Through this mode, when A performs an act of acquisition with regard to a chattel he wishes to acquire—such as taking physical possession of it by

150. TB Bava Meẓi'a 94a. There are exceptions to the rule; under certain circumstances, obligations can be created by oral undertakings. For details, *see* M. Elon, EJ, V, pp. 923–933, s.v. Contract (reprinted in *Principles*, pp. 246–256). Creation of obligations by oral agreement is also possible on the basis of custom. *See infra* pp. 917–920.

151. M Bava Meẓi'a 4:2; TB Bava Meẓi'a 49a. *See also supra* p. 148.

152. *See supra* pp. 297–298, 510–511. *See further* TB Bava Meẓi'a 99a: "Just as they enacted *meshikhah* for purchasers, so did they enact *meshikhah* for bailees."

153. TB Bava Meẓi'a 47a; *see also supra* pp. 297–298, 510–511.

"pulling"—B automatically acquires the chattel given in exchange, even though B did not engage in any act of acquisition of that chattel:

> As soon as one party takes possession of whatever can be used as payment for another object [whatever is given in place of money to obtain another object], he becomes obligated for what is to be given in exchange. For example, if one exchanges an ox for a cow or an ox for an ox, as soon as one party takes possession, he becomes obligated for what is to be given in exchange [*i.e.*, when the owner of the ox takes possession of the cow, the owner of the cow automatically acquires the ox even without taking possession of the ox; and if from that time the ox is stolen, he and not the previous owner will suffer the loss].[154]

Acquisition by *sudar* (symbolic barter) developed from acquisition through barter. The removal of a sandal, mentioned in the Book of Ruth,[155] has a distinct similarity to acquisition by *sudar:*

> Now this was formerly done in Israel in cases of redemption or exchange: to validate any transaction, one man would take off his sandal and hand it to the other.

However, the removal of a sandal was mainly a symbolic act for a particular acquisition; acquisition by *sudar,* on the other hand, is based on the concept of acquisition through barter, but developed from it as a much more convenient, simple, and practical method. In acquisition by *sudar,* the buyer gives the seller any symbolic object (the *sudar,* generally a kerchief) belonging to the buyer; and by acquiring this symbolic object, the seller in exchange automatically transfers to the buyer the chattel that is the subject of the transaction. Although the basis of acquisition by *sudar* is the concept of acquisition through barter, *i.e.*, an exchange of the buyer's *sudar* for the subject of the transaction belonging to the seller, acquisition by *sudar* does not have the disadvantages of acquisition through barter. Instead of the physical presence of the purchased article, as required for acquisition through barter, the physical presence of the *sudar* is sufficient; and it may be any object of merely symbolic value, generally carried by everyone on his person and readily at hand for the buyer to use in the act of acquisition. In addition, the symbolic object is transferred to the seller only temporarily; after the completion of the acquisition, the object is returned to the buyer. When the seller takes possession of the *sudar,* there is an automatic transfer of ownership of the purchased article, no matter how valuable and no matter how far its location from where the transaction takes place.

154. M Kiddushin 1:6.
155. Ruth 4:7. *See* TJ Kiddushin 1:5; 16a (1:5, 60d).

The *sudar* has also been used to the same extent to create contractual obligations, *i.e.*, the obligee gives the obligor a symbolic object belonging to the obligee, and in exchange for this object the obligor assumes the obligation.[156]

Acquisition by *sudar* has become the most widely used mode of acquisition because of its convenience and the ease with which it may be effected; and, as the usual and customary mode of acquisition,[157] it is referred to in Talmudic and post-Talmudic literature simply as *kinyan*.[158]

3. ACQUISITION OF PERSONALTY INCIDENTAL TO ACQUISITION OF LAND (*KINYAN AGAV KARKA*)

Kinyan agav karka ("acquisition incidental to land," also called *kinyan agav*, "incidental acquisition") is another mode of acquisition designed to avoid the difficult requirement of the presence of the chattel to be acquired, but this mode does not have all of the ease and convenience of *kinyan sudar*.[159]

Under *kinyan agav karka*, an individual transfers to another any parcel of land, and incidental to the transfer of the land he may also transfer chattels without limitation as to quantity or value. The nature of the land transaction and that of the transaction with respect to the chattels may be entirely different; *e.g.*, one may be a sale and the other a gift. There is also no need for any contextual or physical connection between the chattels and the land; there is no requirement, for example, that the chattels be on the land. The purpose of this mode of acquisition is to facilitate transactions in chattels without the necessity of having the chattels present at the place of the transaction, and this mode is effective even with the smallest possible parcel of land.[160] In the Talmudic period, this requirement presented no particular difficulty, since almost everyone owned at least some land. When this situation changed in the post-Talmudic period, an additional enactment was adopted under which chattels could sometimes be transferred incidental to land even when the transferor did not own any land. The transfer was

156. In later periods, this was called *kabbalat kinyan*, "the acceptance of an obligation."

157. *See also* Gulak, *Yesodei*, I, pp. 121–125.

158. TB Ketubbot 102b; Bava Meẓi'a 94a; Bava Batra 3a; Maimonides, *MT*, Mekhirah 5:5, *et al.*

159. According to many of the *rishonim*, *kinyan agav* is effective by rabbinic law; *see Tosafot*, Bava Kamma 12a, s.v. Ana matnita yada'na; *Piskei ha-Rosh*, *ad loc.*, #14; Rashba, *ad loc.*, s.v. Me-ha de-amrinan. Other *rishonim* believe it to be based on Biblical law; *see Tosafot*, Kiddushin 5a, s.v. She-ken podin bo hekdeishot u-ma'aser, and Bava Kamma 104b, s.v. Agav asipa de-veiteih.

160. M Pe'ah 3:7; M Kiddushin 1:5; TB Kiddushin 26a *et seq.*; *see* Gulak, *Yesodei*, I, pp. 118–120; ET, I, pp. 54–58, s.v. Agav.

effective on the theory that the entire Jewish people are concurrent owners of the Land of Israel, and every Jew is deemed to own four cubits there.[161]

4. "A MEETING OF THE THREE"

"A meeting of the three" (*ma'amad sheloshtan*) is the title of an enactment of the Sages designed to enable the oral assignment of proprietary or contractual rights without any act of acquisition; the assignment is required to be made at "a meeting of the three," *i.e.,* in the presence of the obligor, the obligee, and the assignee.[162] This method was summarized by Maimonides as follows:[163]

> If the three people were standing together and the first said to the second: "Give this person the *maneh* [a sum of money] that I have with you as a bailment" (or "as a loan"), he [the third person] acquires it and none of the three can retract.[164]

The Sages struggled to find a legal explanation for this far-reaching enactment and viewed it as *hilkheta be-lo ta'ama,* "a law that has no rationale."[165] The purpose of the enactment, however, is clear and easy to understand; it was the facilitation of commerce. "It is 'a law that has no rationale' as to how it is effective as a transfer, but there is good reason why the Sages enacted it: they did so in order to make it unnecessary for people to have to take the trouble to perform acts of acquisition."[166]

Many additional enactments were adopted concerning modes of acquisition in the Talmudic and post-Talmudic periods; and if none of these could provide a satisfactory solution for a particular situation, custom was the legal source that came to the aid of legislation, especially in this area of Jewish law.[167]

161. *See infra* pp. 649–651 as to this enactment. *See also* ET and Gulak, *supra* n. 160, for differences of opinion as to whether the acquisition of chattels incidental to four cubits in the Land of Israel is available generally or only in certain specific instances, such as for powers of attorney.

162. TB Gittin 13b–14a.

163. *MT,* Mekhirah 6:8, Zekhiyyah u-Mattanah 3:3.

164. Similarly, it is possible to transfer money to a woman for the purpose of betrothal by way of *ma'amad sheloshtan;* TB Kiddushin 48a; Maimonides, *MT,* Ishut 5:17.

165. TB Gittin 14b; *see also* commentaries, *ad loc.,* and Maimonides, *MT,* Mekhirah 6:8. *But see* Rashi, Gittin 14a, s.v. Ke-hilkheta be-lo ta'ama, stating; "As though Moses received it at Sinai, so there is no need to give a rationale for it." It is implicit in Rashi's further discussion (*id.,* s.v. Epitropia) that he bases this enactment on the principle of *hefker bet din hefker, i.e.,* the power of the court to expropriate property. To the same effect, *see Tosafot Rid, ad loc.*

166. *Tosafot,* Gittin 14a, s.v. Ke-hilkheta be-lo ta'am.

167. *See infra* pp. 913–920; Gulak, *Yesodei,* I, pp. 87–127, II, pp. 31–57, 96–104.

5. LEGAL CAPACITY

The age at which an individual achieves legal capacity in Jewish law, *i.e.*, the age of majority, is thirteen years and one day for a male and twelve years and one day for a female. All the legal acts of one who has reached the age of majority are fully binding.[168] The legal acts of an individual below this age have no binding effect; such an individual can neither enter into a contract nor transfer property. Similarly, neither a mental incompetent nor a deaf mute (*i.e.*, one who can neither speak nor hear)[169] has legal capacity. With reference to the minor and the deaf mute, the Sages enacted exceptions to the rule of lack of legal capacity in connection with certain transactions. These enactments will be discussed to the extent that they concern the modes of acquisition and the creation of obligations.

The Mishnah states:[170]

> A deaf mute may act by gestures [*i.e.*, he may gesture with his hand or his head, and others may similarly gesture to him; and his acts done by means of gestures are effective]. Ben Bathyra says: "He may also use lip motions (*kofeẓ ve-nikfaẓ*)"[171] when chattels are involved.[172] The purchase or sale of chattels by young children is legally effective.

The Talmud states the rationale for this enactment:[173]

> What is the reason? R. Abba b. Jacob said in the name of R. Johanan: "So that they may procure necessaries."

If the transaction of a deaf mute[174] or a young child were not binding, no one would sell them food or other necessaries or would buy from

168. *See* M Niddah 5:3 *et seq.;* Maimonides, *MT,* Ishut ch. 2, Mekhirah 29:12. As to a girl's intermediate period of puberty, *na'arut, see supra* n. 94.

169. M Terumot 1:1–2; the rule deals with a deaf mute from birth who, because of congenital impairment, was never able to learn, or to appreciate the nature of his conduct.

170. M Gittin 5:7.

171. *See* Rashi, Gittin 59a, s.v. Kefiẓah ("This means *akimat sefatayim* [lip motions], as it is written, *'kafẓah piha'* ['the mouth is shut'—Job 5:16]; and this is less noticeable than gestures"); *Tosafot Rid,* Gittin 59a. *See also* Isaiah 52:15; Psalms 107:42. Others interpret the term as meaning "jumping" on his legs and conclude that Ben Bathyra was more stringent than the first *tanna* and would require more than gestures. *See* Maimonides, *Commentary on the Mishnah, ad loc.*; Meiri, *Bet ha-Beḥirah,* Gittin 59a (ed. Schlesinger, pp. 244–245); H. Albeck, *Commentary on the Mishnah, ad loc.*

172. The clause "when chattels are involved" applies to the statements of both the first *tanna* and Ben Bathyra, and means that, according to both of them, the enactment of the Sages, even with regard to the deaf mute, applies to chattels only (Maimonides, *MT,* Mekhirah 29:2). Rabad, in his gloss to *MT, ad loc.*, was of the opinion that according to the first *tanna,* gestures by a deaf mute are effective even for the transfer of real property.

173. TB Gittin 59a.

174. The rationale "so that they may procure necessaries" also applies to the enactment concerning the deaf mute; *see* Rashi, Gittin 59a, s.v. Ka mashma lan.

them.[175] Therefore, the Sages enacted a *takkanah* giving legally binding effect to certain transactions of a young child and of a deaf mute.[176]

What is the age of a "young child"? The Talmud[177] mentions various ages (from six to ten), and the standard finally established was: "Each according to his intelligence," *i.e.*, the case of each young child should be dealt with in accordance with the degree of his acuity and intelligence; the standard is thus individual and not absolute.

Maimonides summarized this law as follows:[178]

> There are three categories of persons whose sales and purchases are not valid under Biblical law: the deaf mute, the mental incompetent, and the minor; but the Sages enacted that the transactions of the deaf mute and the minor are valid so that they may procure necessaries.[179]
>
> The transfer of ownership by a minor less than six years old has no validity. From the age of six until he matures, if he understands the nature of business transactions, his purchase, sale, or gift is valid regardless of whether a large amount or small amount is involved, and regardless of whether at the time of the gift he is in good health or a *shekhiv me-ra* [a person terminally ill or facing imminent death]. This is an enactment of the Sages . . . so that he will not become idle or face a situation where no one will sell to him or buy from him. All this applies to chattels but not to land, which he cannot sell or give as a gift until he matures.[180]

Just as the Sages, in consideration of the material and social needs of a minor, enacted legislation to give legal effect to his transactions entered into before he has reached the age of general legal capacity, they also enacted that with regard to certain transactions, the age of general legal capacity is not sufficient if the character of the particular transaction requires a greater and fuller maturity.

175. Rashi, *ad loc.*, s.v. Mishum kedei ḥayyav.

176. *See also* Naḥmanides, Novellae to Gittin, *ad loc.*: "This, too, is for the public welfare, as stated in the Talmud, 'so that they may procure necessaries.'"

177. TB Gittin 59a.

178. *MT*, Mekhirah 29:1, 6.

179. No enactment was adopted with reference to the mental incompetent, since he is not responsible for his actions at all: "With regard to the mental incompetent, his purchases, sales, and gifts are not effective. The court appoints a guardian for a mental incompetent just as for a minor"; Maimonides, *MT*, Mekhirah 29:4, and *see id.* 29:5 with regard to a person who is mentally incompetent but has lucid intervals; his acts while he is of sound mind have full legal effectiveness.

180. Similarly, the minimum age with regard to the law of finders was lowered, and the law with regard to findings by mental incompetents was also liberalized: "[Taking away] the findings of deaf mutes, mental incompetents, and minors is deemed an act of theft, in order to promote peace and tranquillity" (*mipenei darkhei shalom*); M Gittin 5:8. The theory was that if they are deprived of their findings, family quarrels will result. These rules were codified in Maimonides, *MT*, Gezelah va-Avedah 17:12, and Sh. Ar. ḤM 270:1.

Maimonides summarized this enactment[181] on the basis of the Talmudic discussion,[182] as follows:

> If a minor has matured and has exhibited signs of puberty [lit. "two pubic hairs"], in the case of males after reaching the age of thirteen and in the case of females after reaching the age of twelve, then even if such a person does not understand the nature of business transactions, his purchases, sales, and gifts of chattels are valid; but his acts with regard to land have no validity even after he becomes of age until he understands the nature of business transactions.
>
> To what does this rule apply? To his own land; but his sale of land he inherited from his ancestors or from others is not effective until he reaches the age of twenty, even if he exhibits signs of puberty and understands the nature of business transactions, lest he sell cheaply because his nature is to desire money and he has not yet matured in knowledge of the ways of the world.[183]

C. Legislation Concerning the Law of Obligations

Jewish law relating to obligations is predominantly legislative in origin. Many enactments are connected with *shi'bud nekhasim* (security interests, lit. "the encumbrance of property"), which in its nature, scope, and purpose is unique to the Jewish legal system. In order to understand the nature of this legal institution, the Jewish law of obligations must first be briefly reviewed.

1. NATURE OF THE LAW OF OBLIGATIONS; PERSONAL AND REAL CHARACTER OF OBLIGATIONS IN JEWISH LAW

The law of obligations concerns the rights of one individual against another, as distinguished from the law of acquisitions, which deals with an individual's right to property as against the entire world. As is generally the case in other legal systems, obligations in Jewish law are created mainly in two ways: (a) obligations *ex contractu, i.e.,* arising out of contract, as a result of agreement, whereby one party acquires a claim of right against another, and the other obligates himself to carry out a corresponding duty; (b) obligations *ex delicto, i.e.,* arising out of tort by which an individual or his prop-

181. *MT,* Mekhirah 29:12, 13.

182. TB Bava Batra 155a–156a.

183. This is an enactment of the Sages, as indicated by the rationale. *See* Rashbam, Bava Batra 155b, s.v. Hashta u-mah zevini de-ka-shakil zuzi: "Even so, the Sages enacted that his sale should not be effective until he reaches the age of twenty. . . ." In post-Talmudic times, additional enactments were adopted concerning the minimum age for specific types of transactions, such as signing promissory notes, for which the minimum age was set at 25. *See* Elon, *supra* n. 134 at 121–122.

erty causes damage to the person or property of another and, as a consequence, the victim acquires a claim against the tortfeasor to make good the damage and the tortfeasor becomes obligated to satisfy this claim.

Jewish law distinguishes between the obligations created in each of these two ways. Among the differences is the manner of payment of the claim if the obligor fails to make payment either in cash or chattels: obligations for damages arising from a tort are recoverable from the best of the tortfeasor's land, while damages for breach of contractual obligations are recoverable from the obligor's land of medium quality.[184] An obligation (*ḥiyyuv*)[185] places on one party, called the *ḥayyav*[186] (debtor or obligor), the duty of fulfilling the obligation. The *ḥayyav* grants to the other party, called *ba'al ḥov* (creditor, lit. "owner of the obligation," or "obligee"),[187] the right to demand the fulfillment of the obligation. In addition to the designations *ba'al ḥov* and *ḥayyav,* the terms *malveh* (lender) and *loveh* (borrower) are also used. The latter terms are used in Jewish law not only for an obligation arising out of a loan but also to designate the two parties to any obligation even if the obligation does not arise out of a loan. This reflects the tendency of Jewish law to express abstract legal norms in concrete terms;[188] thus the term "loan," which is a concrete example of a common and well-understood type of obligation, is used to designate obligations in general.[189]

Many ancient legal systems allowed a creditor to enslave his debtor and even members of the debtor's family in order to secure the payment of

184. *See* M Gittin 5:1 to the effect that the wife's *ketubbah* is collected from the poorest land. *See also supra* pp. 301–303. As to other categories of obligations, *see* M. Elon, EJ, XII, pp. 1310–1316, s.v. Obligations, law of (reprinted in *Principles,* pp. 241–246).

185. The term *ḥiyyuv* is derived from the word *ḥov* (obligation) and signifies both the duty of the debtor or obligor (M Bava Batra 10:6: "He who has repaid part of his debt [*ḥovo*]") and the right of the creditor or obligee (M Bikkurim 3:12: "And the creditor or obligee [*ba'al ḥov*] can take them to satisfy his debt [*ḥovo*]"; M Gittin 8:3: "[If] his creditor or obligee [*ba'al ḥovo*] said to him, 'Throw me [the amount of] my debt [*ḥovi*]'"). The term *ḥov* generally refers to a debt of money only, while *ḥiyyuv* generally also includes the obligation to perform an act beyond merely paying money. *Ḥiyyuv* is parallel to the Roman-law *obligatio.*

186. *E.g.,* "When the debtor (*ḥayyav*) admits [his obligation]"; TB Bava Meẓi'a 12b.

187. *See supra* n. 185. Occasionally, *ba'al ḥov* is also used in the sense of "one who has a debt [to pay]," *i.e.,* the debtor; *see* S. Abramson, *Leshonenu* [Our Language], XVI (1949), pp. 165–166; S. Lieberman, *Greek in Jewish Palestine* (hereinafter *Greek*), p. 156 n. 78; Elon, *Ḥerut,* p. 1 n. 1. This dual and contradictory usage requires extreme caution in the use of the term *ba'al ḥov* in Jewish law.

188. *E.g.,* "horn" (*keren*), "tooth" (*shen*), and "pit" (*bor*), which signify the main categories of tort; there are many further examples. *See supra* pp. 79–80.

189. The discussion that follows includes a few examples of this usage of the terms *malveh* (lender), *loveh* (borrower), and cognate words in the more general sense. Chs. 97–106 of Sh. Ar. ḤM are called "The Laws of Debt [*milvah*] Collection," but they also treat the enforcement of obligations other than loans.

the debt.[190] According to the Roman law of the Twelve Tables, under the *legis actio per manus iniectionem* the creditor was even entitled, after certain procedural steps, to put the defaulting debtor to death; and if the debtor had several creditors, each creditor had the right to take his proportionate share of the debtor's body. This "right" was abrogated by the Lex Poetelia in the year 313 (326?) B.C.E. and was replaced by the right to imprison the defaulting debtor.[191] By contrast, Jewish law did not recognize a right to any form of servitude in the debtor's person,[192] and the creditor was strongly admonished to act mercifully toward the debtor, not to take in pledge implements that were necessary for the preparation of food, and even not to enter the debtor's home to retake a pledge.[193] However, in practice, the law was not always strictly observed; and due to the influence of the practices of other neighboring legal systems, there were incidents when an individual was sold into slavery for a debt.[194] The prophets vehemently condemned this heinous practice,[195] and it appears that after the strong reaction of Nehemiah,[196] defaulting debtors were no longer sold into slavery.[197]

190. This was the case under the laws of Babylonia, Assyria, and Eshnunna, among others. *See* Elon, *Ḥerut,* pp. 3–8.

191. Elon, *Ḥerut,* pp. 11–12. As to imprisonment for debt in Jewish law, *see id.* at 2, 16ff., 111ff.

192. According to the Torah, servitude could come about only in two instances: (1) a thief who could not pay for what he stole (Exodus 22:2); (2) a voluntary sale of oneself because of extreme poverty (Leviticus 25:39).

193. Exodus 22:24–26; Deuteronomy 24:6, 10–13.

194. II Kings 4:1; Isaiah 50:1 *et al.*

195. Amos 2:6, 8:4–6.

196. Nehemiah 5:1–13.

197. Elon, *Ḥerut,* pp. 8–10. The limitations on the enforcement of creditors' rights against the person of the debtor under Jewish law led, in the second half of the fourth century C.E., to a significant difference of opinion as to the nature of the personal obligation of the debtor to repay a loan. There was no dissent as to the existence of a clear legal obligation to restore a bailed chattel or a stolen article to its owner, since the bailor or the person from whom the article was stolen has a proprietary right even though the property is in the hands of the bailee or the thief. However, in the case of a loan of money, which is made in the first instance on the basis that the borrower will disburse the money for his own purposes, the obligation to repay is only, according to R. Papa, a religious commandment, in that a person has a religious obligation to keep his word (Rashi, Ketubbot 86a, s.v. Peri'at ba'al ḥov miẓvah); but there is no element of legal obligation. On the other hand, R. Huna b. R. Joshua was of the opinion that repayment of a loan of money is also a legal obligation, and his view was concurred in by most Sages and has become accepted as law. *See supra* pp. 117–119.

In the Talmud, the personal aspect of an obligation is called *sha'beid nafsheih* (lit. "he has obligated himself"; *see, e.g.,* TB Gittin 13b, 49b; Bava Kamma 40b; Bava Meẓi'a 94a; Bava Batra 175b). In the post-Talmudic period, apparently from the eleventh century C.E. on, the personal aspect of an obligation was called *shi'bud ha-guf* (lit. "the encumbrance of

The impossibility of securing the payment of a debt by enslaving the debtor's person created a need for Jewish law to give effective security to the creditor by subjecting the debtor's assets to a lien in favor of the creditor. The debtor's land was well suited for this purpose, because land has perpetual existence and is not subject to depreciation or concealment. Simultaneously with the creation of a debt, the creditor acquires a lien on all the debtor's real estate, so that the debt not only creates a personal right of action against the debtor, but also a right *in rem* to a lien on all the debtor's real estate.[198] Real estate is called "property bearing responsibility" (*nekhasim she-yesh lahem aḥarayut*)[199] because it was responsible for and secured the debtor's obligation,[200] and because recourse to it to collect the debt is based not on the personal claim of the creditor against the debtor but on the creditor's lien on the land, which arises simultaneously with the debt.[201]

---

the body"). The latter term was apparently first used by Alfasi, quoted in *Resp. Maharam of Rothenburg* (ed. Cremona) #146, and more fully explained by Rabbenu Tam, quoted in Ran to Alfasi, Ketubbot 85b, s.v. Ha-mokher shetar ḥov (p. 44b in printed eds.). *See also* M. Elon, EJ, V, pp. 923–933, s.v. Contract (reprinted in *Principles*, pp. 246–256).

198. The lien is on all the debtor's property and becomes effective automatically when the obligation arises. Such a lien is unique to Jewish law. As in other legal systems, Jewish law also has liens which the parties limit to specific property of the obligor, such as the *apotiki* (where the encumbered property remains in the control of the obligor) or *mashkon* (pledge or security, where the encumbered property passes to the control of the obligee). *See further* M. Elon, EJ, XI, pp. 227–232, s.v. Lien (reprinted in *Principles*, pp. 287–294); *id.*, XIII, pp. 636–644, s.v. Pledge (reprinted in *Principles*, pp. 294–301).

199. M Kiddushin 1:5; *see also* M Bava Meẓi'a 1:6.

200. TB Bava Batra 174a: "A person's assets are responsible for him [*i.e.*, for his debts]."

201. The concept "responsibility of property" (*aḥarayut nekhasim*) is already reflected in the enactment of Simeon b. Shataḥ's time pursuant to which the husband writes in his wife's *ketubbah* that all his property is subject to a lien for the obligation of the *ketubbah* (TB Ketubbot 82b; *see supra* pp. 559–561); and it may be assumed that such "responsibility" then existed with regard to other obligations as well. In the third century C.E., the *amoraim* Ulla and Rabbah differed as to whether such "responsibility" is Biblical or created by rabbinic legislation (*see infra* pp. 594–595).

According to a few *rishonim* (*Tosafot*, Bava Batra 175b, s.v. Devar torah ba'al ḥov dino be-ẓibburit, and Meiri, *Bet ha-Beḥirah, ad loc.*, ed. Sofer, p. 726), this difference of opinion concerns only the enforcement of the lien against property transferred to a third party; but there was no disagreement that the lien on property still in possession of the obligor is Biblical.

Other *rishonim* were of the opinion that the disagreement as to whether the lien is Biblical or rabbinic extends even to the situation where the property remains in the obligor's possession. The disagreement goes to the fundamental question of whether the right to collect from such property flows only from the personal aspect of the obligation (as in the case of collection from the personalty of the obligor) or whether the creditor has additional rights *in rem* against the realty itself (Rashbam, quoted in *Tosafot, supra;* Rashba, Novellae to Bava Batra 175b, s.v. Amar Rava; Ritba, Novellae to Kiddushin 13b. *See further* Elon, *Ḥerut*, p. 21). The law was settled to the effect that "the lien is Biblical." Maimonides, *MT*, Malveh ve-Loveh 11:4; Sh. Ar. ḤM ch. 111 and *Sema, ad loc.*, subpar. 1.

By contrast, the debtor's chattels, which are subject to concealment and depreciation, could not serve as security for the debtor's obligation and are therefore called "property bearing no responsibility" (*nekhasim she-ein lahem aḥarayut*);[202] recourse to them to collect the debt is based on the personal claim of the creditor against the debtor.[203]

The lien that a creditor acquires in the debtor's land does not preclude the debtor from transferring ownership of the land to a third party, but the creditor may seize such land from the transferee to enforce payment of the debt. However, the creditor has no property right in the debtor's personalty; any recourse to such property was based solely on the personal obligation of the debtor.[204] Consequently, when the debtor's personalty is transferred out of the debtor's ownership, the creditor has no right to seize the personalty from the transferee.[205]

2. LEGISLATION CONCERNING LIENS ON PROPERTY

The general encumbrance of the real property of the debtor (*shi'bud nekhasim*) created many problems with regard to the protection of the rights of a third party who acquires such property from the debtor, since it could be anticipated that the creditor would seize the property from the third party on the strength of the creditor's prior lien. Many *takkanot* were enacted to regulate this situation. A discussion of some of them follows.

a. ENCUMBERED PROPERTY SOLD BY THE DEBTOR CAN BE SEIZED ONLY IF THE DEBTOR HAS NO OTHER ASSETS

"A debt may not be satisfied out of encumbered property (*nekhasim meshu'badim*) [sold by the debtor to a third person] when there remains free property (*nekhasim benei ḥorin*) [in the hands of the debtor] even if of inferior quality . . . in order to promote the public welfare."[206]

202. M Kiddushin 1:5.

203. TB Bava Kamma 11b: "From him—even from the shirt on his back." To meet the requirements of expanding commerce, contractual obligations in the post-Talmudic period underwent a substantial change, from an essentially real (*i.e.*, relating to property) to a primarily personal obligation in which the property aspect of the obligation was secondary. This change was related to the need to make it possible to create obligations with respect, *e.g.*, to something not yet in existence, or to something in which the obligor had no existing rights. For fuller discussion, *see* M. Elon, EJ, s.v. Contract, *supra* n. 197; *id.*, s.v. Lien, *supra* n. 198.

204. "With regard to chattels . . . the creditor does not rely on them. . . . The fact that he collects from them in the debtor's lifetime . . . is not by virtue of any right of lien"; Meiri, *Bet ha-Beḥirah*, Bava Batra 175b (ed. Sofer, p. 726).

205. TB Ketubbot 92a. In the course of time, with the changes in the economic conditions of Jewish life, significant changes occurred in regard to this distinction between personalty and real property. *See* M. Elon, EJ, s.v. Lien, *supra* n. 198.

206. M Gittin 5:2; the phrase "in order to promote the public welfare" (*mipenei tikkun ha-olam*) appears at the end of *mishnah* 3, but it also refers to *mishnah* 2. The phrase "even

The import of this enactment is that the creditor may not recover out of encumbered property that the debtor has sold, so long as the debtor still has other assets ("free property"), even if the remaining assets are of a quality inferior to those to which the creditor is entitled (*e.g.*, where the assets remaining are of a medium quality and the debt arose out of a tort, which is to be paid from property of the best quality). This enactment was adopted to "promote the public welfare," *i.e.*, to promote the security of trade and commerce. Similarly, if the debtor has sold property to several purchasers, the creditor must first seize the property from the last purchaser, since an earlier purchaser could argue: "I left you room to recover from him,"[207] *i.e.*, "I did not buy all of the debtor's property, but I left property with him from which you, the creditor, may recover."

Maimonides gave the following example of the operation of this enactment:[208]

> For example, Reuben injured Simeon and became obligated to him [to pay for the injury]; and afterwards, Reuben sold his property of the highest quality, and property of the lowest quality remained with him. Simeon is to recover compensation for his injury from the inferior property Reuben still has that is "free," and he [Simeon] cannot argue: "The law allows me to collect from the superior property; you sold it after you became obligated to me, and I may seize it from the purchaser." For we do not permit this unless Reuben has no other assets from which payment can be made.

b. ENCUMBERED PROPERTY CANNOT BE SEIZED IF THE DEBT IS UNLIQUIDATED

Another limitation is found in the following enactment:[209]

> There shall be no recovery from encumbered property for consumed produce, for improvement to the land, or for the support of a widow or daughters, in order to promote the public welfare.[210]

---

if of inferior quality" was included in *mishnah* 2 because of the rule in *mishnah* 1 that tort damages are to be paid out of land of the best quality, debts out of land of medium quality, and a wife's *ketubbah* out of the poorest land. *See supra* p. 588.

207. TB Bava Kamma 8a.

208. *Commentary on the Mishnah*, Gittin 5:2.

209. M Gittin 5:3.

210. The nature of the claim of the wife and daughters for support is clear and has been discussed *supra* pp. 570–571, 574–575. The claims for consumed produce (*akhilat perot*) and for improvement to the land (*shevaḥ karka'ot*) arise where A has stolen B's field, consumed its produce and, after a period of time, sold the field to C. B, the lawful owner of the field, then recovers it from C. According to the law, B is entitled to recover the field "as is," including any produce that may be on it, upon payment to C of the amount of C's actual expenses in working the field, but no more. This situation then gives rise to two possible claims:

Why is the public welfare promoted by the rule against recovery from encumbered property for these claims? There is a difference of opinion among the *amoraim* on this question.[211] According to the view which has become accepted law,[212] the promotion of the public welfare lies in the fact that "they are unliquidated amounts," *i.e.*, claims in an amount which, unlike a loan, are not determinable in advance.[213] Thus, a potential buyer of land cannot calculate in advance how much in "free" assets to leave in the possession of the debtor from which the debtor may pay his debt; and if the creditor could recover these debts from the purchaser by seizing the encumbered property, people would refrain from buying property, and commerce consequently would be inhibited.

c. ENCUMBERED PROPERTY CAN BE SEIZED FOR A DEBT EVIDENCED BY A DOCUMENT BUT NOT FOR A DEBT CREATED ORALLY

If one has lent money to another on the strength of a promissory note [which witnesses signed], he may collect from encumbered property. If the loan was made in the presence of witnesses [without a note], he may collect from free property only. If one produces against another a note in the other's handwriting [written and signed by the debtor without the signatures of any wit-

---

(1) B, the lawful owner, can claim from A, the thief, the value of the produce of the field which A consumed when it was in his control. This claim is called "a claim for consumed produce" (there are also other explanations of the nature of this claim; *see* commentators, *ad loc.*).

(2) C, the purchaser, can claim from A, the thief, the return of the sum C paid A for the field plus the value of the produce that grew in the field and that B recovered, along with the field, from C (*i.e.*, the difference between the actual value of the produce and the amount recouped from B for C's expenses in working the field). This claim is called "a claim for improvement to the land," *i.e.*, a claim to compensation for that part of the value of the land due to produce for which the purchaser was not compensated by the original owner.

211. TB Gittin 50b.

212. Maimonides, *MT*, Malveh ve-Loveh 21:1.

213. According to tannaitic *Halakhah*, a tort victim could recover damages from encumbered property (*Tosefta* Ketubbot 2:2: "Damages, half-damages [for injury by an "innocuous" ox], double damages [for theft], and quadruple and quintuple damages [for theft and slaughter or sale of an ox or a sheep] can all be recovered from encumbered property even though they are not based on a written instrument (*shetar*)." However, the *amoraim* differed as to whether an obligation imposed by law has the same effect as an obligation created by a written instrument, *i.e.*, whether "an obligation pursuant to the Torah is like a loan evidenced by a promissory note." *See* TB Bekhorot 49b *et al.* In view of the enactment that an unliquidated claim may not be collected from encumbered property, there was good reason to rule that damages in tort should also not be recovered from encumbered property, since tort obligations are generally also unliquidated. However, this question remains a matter of dispute among the halakhic authorities (*see, e.g., Tosafot,* Bava Kamma 8a, s.v. Kulan nikhnesu taḥat ha-ba'alim; *Tur* ḤM 119:4 and *Bet Yosef, ad loc.*).

> nesses] evidencing the indebtedness, he may collect from the debtor's free property only.[214]

This enactment is an additional significant step in securing to a purchaser the property he has bought. Under this enactment, only when a debt satisfies two conditions—that it is in writing and that the note is signed by two witnesses—may the creditor recover from encumbered property.[215] The rationale for these conditions is that the note and the signatures of the witnesses provide public notice that A owes B a particular sum of money; and as a result of this publicity, purchasers who buy property from A will make sure that sufficient assets remain with him to pay the debt. However, a debt created in the presence of witnesses but without a written instrument, or a debt created through a writing—even if handwritten and signed by the debtor himself—but without witnesses, has no notoriety, and the purchaser will not know of its existence. There is, therefore, no justification for dispossessing the purchaser, and the creditor may execute only against the free assets in the debtor's possession. The *amoraim* disagreed on a basic question regarding this law:[216]

> Ulla said: "Under Biblical law, both an oral loan and a loan evidenced by a note may be collected from encumbered property. Why is this so? [Because] the lien is Biblical [*i.e.,* the principle of property encumbrance is Biblical and applies to all kinds of debts, whether oral or in writing]; but why did they say [*i.e.,* what is the reason for the enactment by the Sages] that 'an oral loan can be collected only from free property'? To prevent loss to the purchaser."
>
> If so, should this not also apply to a loan evidenced by a note? [*I.e.,* a loan evidenced by a note with witnesses will also cause a loss for the purchaser if the creditor may seize the property from him.]
>
> In that case [where a loan was made in the presence of witnesses and with a note], the purchaser has brought the loss on himself [since he could have ascertained the existence of the loan through a brief investigation and should not have bought the property without leaving the debtor sufficient assets to pay the debt].
>
> Rabbah said: "Under Biblical law, both an oral loan and a loan evidenced by a note may be collected only from free property. Why is this so? [Because] there is no property encumbrance under Biblical law. Why did the Sages enact that 'a loan evidenced by a note may be collected from encumbered property'? So that the door should not be closed to borrowers."
>
> If so, should not this also apply to an oral loan? [*I.e.,* the rationale of

214. M Bava Batra 10:8.

215. The terms "loan by promissory note" (*milvah bi-shetar*) and "loan in the presence of witnesses" (*milvah al yedei edim*) apply to all obligations and not only to obligations arising from loans. *See supra* p. 588.

216. TB Bava Batra 175b.

not closing the door to borrowers applies also to oral loans, which should therefore also be collectible from encumbered property.] In that case, there is no notoriety [*i.e.*, in the case of an oral loan, there is no public knowledge of the transaction].

There is thus a disagreement as to the legal classification of liens on property and, consequently, also as to the rule distinguishing between a debt evidenced by a note and a debt created without a writing. In Ulla's opinion, the lien on property is created by Biblical law,[217] pursuant to which a lien attaches to property not only as a result of a debt evidenced by a note but also as a result of a debt created orally. The source of the rule that a debt created orally can be collected only from free property and not from encumbered property is an enactment of the Sages designed to prevent loss to the purchaser by limiting the lien on encumbered property to cases where the loan is evidenced by a note signed by witnesses.

Rabbah took the opposite view as to how liens on property should be classified. In his view, the rule that a loan evidenced by a note signed by witnesses can be collected from encumbered property has its source in rabbinic legislation; it was the Sages who established the lien on property.[218] Their reason was that giving the creditor the right to collect from the debtor's property even after the debtor has transferred title to someone else assured the creditor that he would be repaid. It was necessary to provide such assurance to the creditor so that "the door should not be closed to borrowers," *i.e.*, that people would not refrain from extending credit.[219] However, the Sages did not make this enactment applicable to oral loans because such loans have no notoriety, and therefore the legal situation as to such loans remained as it was before the enactment, *i.e.*, the creditor cannot collect from property of the debtor that has been sold to a third person.

217. Ulla derived the law of liens by interpretation of Deuteronomy 24:11: "You must remain outside, while the man to whom you made the loan brings the pledge out to you"; *see* Rashbam, Bava Batra 175b, s.v. Shi'buda de-oraita. *See also supra* n. 201 and sources cited there.

218. The *rishonim* differed as to whether Rabbah held that there was no lien at all on property as a matter of Biblical law or whether he was of the opinion that there was such a lien but it was unenforceable against property in the possession of a purchaser; *see supra* n. 201.

219. The need to impose an automatic general lien on all the obligor's real estate in order to secure the creditor's rights arose because the creditor had no right to enforce payment by subjecting the debtor to involuntary servitude or to other deprivation of personal liberty. *See supra* pp. 589–590. L. Auerbach has conjectured that the special need for such a strong measure to secure the creditor's rights resulted from the creditor's inability to profit from the loan because in Jewish law the taking of interest is prohibited; thus, if even the principal were not secured, people might refuse to make loans. In his opinion, this security, which originally related only to loans, was later applied to other types of obligations. *See* L. Auerbach, *Das Jüdische Obligationenrecht* [The Jewish Law of Obligations], I, 1870, p. 172.

Later in the discussion, R. Papa stated:

> The law is that an oral loan may be collected from [property in the hands of] heirs, but not from [property in the hands of] purchasers. It may be collected from the heirs, so as not to close the door to borrowers; but it may not be collected from purchasers, as there is no notoriety.

According to R. Papa, a lien on property arises even from an oral loan but only if the third parties are heirs of the debtor and not purchasers from the debtor. The reason is that permitting collection by a creditor from property whose ownership has passed to heirs will have no effect on commerce, inasmuch as the heirs invested no money to obtain the property. In such a case, the economic interest in "not closing the door to borrowers" outweighs the personal interest of the debtor's heirs.[220] However, one may not collect from purchasers if the loan was oral, because the policy against causing loss to the purchasers should prevail in view of the lack of publicity of the debt.[221]

The principle in the enactment that one may collect from encumbered property only if there is public notice of the debt[222] was basic to the entire law of liens on property and influenced various categories of obligations in different directions.[223]

3. MARKET OVERT

The problem of protecting the "third party" assumed increasingly greater importance with the increasing expansion and development of commerce and led to a significant enactment known as *takkanat ha-shuk* (market overt, lit. "enactment for the market"). The purpose of this enactment was to protect the rights of a purchaser of a chattel if it becomes

220. According to Rav (TJ Bava Kamma 10:1, 42a [10:1, 7b]; Bava Meẓi'a 1:6, 4b [1:6, 8a]; and TB Bava Batra 175a), an oral loan cannot be collected even from the debtor's heirs. This is also Samuel's view (TB Bava Batra 175a).

221. The law was settled to this effect. *See* Maimonides, *MT,* Malveh ve-Loveh 11:4; Sh. Ar. ḤM 107:1.

222. Various enactments were adopted in the post-Talmudic period providing that a debt could not be collected from encumbered property unless the instrument creating the obligation had been written and signed by a scribe and signed by witnesses specially designated for the purpose (*see Tur* ḤM 61:1). Thus, the maximum possible notice was given to warn prospective purchasers—a function similar to the recording of liens in modern land record systems.

223. *E.g.,* with regard to the sale of land, if property is recovered from a purchaser by a creditor of the seller or, if the land was stolen, by the lawful owner, the purchaser, even though his purchase was not by deed but only in the presence of witnesses, may recover his purchase price from subsequent purchasers from the seller. The reason is that the sale of land (as distinguished from a loan) in the presence of witnesses is accompanied by publicity, even without a written instrument (TB Bava Batra 41b). *See further* M. Elon, EJ, s.v. Lien, *supra* n. 198; *id.,* s.v. Obligations, law of, *supra* n. 184.

known after the purchase that the article had been stolen and its owner claims it from the purchaser.

Thus, the Mishnah states:[224]

> If one identifies his utensils or books in the possession of another person, and it is known in the town that there was a burglary of his [the owner's] home, the purchaser takes an oath as to how much he paid and is to be reimbursed [by the owner]; but if this is not so [*i.e.*, if there is no public knowledge of the theft], he [the one who claims his property had been stolen] is not believed, as it is presumed that he sold them to another and the third party purchased them from him [*i.e.*, from the person to whom the original owner is presumed to have sold them].

When an individual finds his utensils or his books in another's possession, proves that the articles belong to him, and claims that they were stolen from him, and it had indeed become known in the town that utensils or books had been stolen from him, the law is that the purchaser takes an oath as to how much he paid for the articles, and only after he recovers this amount from the owner is the purchaser obligated to return the articles to the owner. But if there was no public report that the articles had been stolen from the original owner, the claimant's statement that they belong to him is not accepted; even if he proves that the articles were once his, he is presumed to have sold them to someone from whom the third party purchased them.

Under Biblical law, a purchaser from a thief, even if he purchased in good faith and without knowledge of the theft, must return the article to its owner.[225] This rule that the owner could demand the return of the stolen property became a burden on commerce, since every purchaser had reason to fear that someone would appear and prove that the article was his and had been stolen from him, in which case the purchaser would lose both the article and the money he paid for it. Consequently, the enactment prescribed that before the purchaser returns the article he may demand that the owner-claimant reimburse him for the purchase price. This enactment is known in the Talmud[226] as *takkanat ha-shuk* (market overt) "because the purchaser bought it in the open market not realizing that it was stolen; a *takkanah* was enacted for his benefit that the owner should pay him back

224. M Bava Kamma 10:3.

225. According to the original law, if the owner abandoned hope of regaining his property, his abandonment made the property ownerless, and there was no obligation to return it to him. In the post-Talmudic period, it was established that even if the owner has abandoned hope and the article has passed into someone else's possession, it must be returned to the original owner; Rema to Sh. Ar. ḤM 356:7. *See also infra* n. 237.

226. TB Bava Kamma 115a.

his [purchase] money."[227] The objective of the enactment was to permit the free flow of commerce:

> The reason for the *takkanah* of market overt is that if anyone who misses an article and finds it in the possession of someone else could take it back without paying, nobody would buy anything from anyone, for he [the potential buyer] would say, "Soon its owner will appear and seize it."[228]

Therefore, as above stated, the *takkanah* was enacted requiring the owner of the article to reimburse the purchaser for the purchase price. The purchaser must take an oath as to the purchase price; his statement of the amount is not accepted without an oath even though the article is in his possession. The reason is given in the Jerusalem Talmud:[229]

> R. Ba [Abba] b. Memel said: "Under strict law, he need not take an oath [but his unsworn statement as to how much he paid for the chattel is accepted because it is in his possession—*Penei Moshe*]. Why was it enacted that he swear? So that householders should not deal with thieves" [but rather will say: 'Tomorrow it will be taken from me and I will have to take an oath in order to be reimbursed'—*Penei Moshe*].

The enactment was adopted for the case where the thief cannot be found and there is no other way the purchaser can be reimbursed. What is the law if the thief is located and the purchaser has the opportunity to claim his money from the thief? Does the market overt enactment apply to entitle the purchaser to demand reimbursement from the owner even in this situation, or can the owner in such case refuse to reimburse the purchaser for the purchase price and relegate the purchaser to an action against the thief for recovery of the purchase money?

The early *amoraim* differed on this question:[230]

> It was stated: If an article was stolen and sold by the thief, who was then identified, Rav in the name of R. Ḥiyya said: "The claim [of the purchaser] is against the first party [the thief]." R. Johanan in the name of R. Yannai said: "The claim is against the second party [the owner]."

227. Rashi, Bava Kamma 115a, s.v. Takkanat ha-shuk.

228. *Hilkhot Re'u,* cited in *Oẓar ha-Ge'onim,* Bava Kamma, Responsa, p. 110. *See Shakh,* Sh. Ar. ḤM 356, subpar. 4: "They established market overt, because otherwise no person would purchase anything, for fear that it had been stolen"; similarly, *Arukh ha-Shulḥan,* ḤM 356:2: "They enacted this on account of market overt because otherwise people would refrain from buying, and commerce would be brought to a halt."

229. TJ Bava Kamma 10:3, 43b (10:3, 7c).

230. TB Bava Kamma 115a.

Subsequently, this dispute was explained by R. Papa:

> Rav in the name of R. Ḥiyya said that he must claim against the thief: [where the thief has been identified], the law is that the purchaser is to be reimbursed by the thief, and the market overt enactment does not apply in this case.
>
> R. Johanan in the name of R. Yannai said that he may claim against the owner, [because] the law is that [even if the thief is identified] the purchaser is to be reimbursed by the owner [who may then proceed against the thief], and the market overt enactment does apply in this case.

All authorities agree that if the thief is identified but is judgment-proof (*i.e.,* there is no possibility of recovering anything from him), the market overt enactment applies, and the purchaser is to be reimbursed by the owner. The subsequent discussion in the Talmud makes this clear:

> Does Rav really maintain that [if the thief is identified] the market overt enactment does not apply? R. Huna was a disciple of Rav [and it is assumed that he followed the opinion of Rav], and when Ḥanan the Scoundrel stole a garment and sold it, and he was brought before R. Huna, did not R. Huna say to that party [from whom the garment had been stolen]: "Go and redeem your pledge" [*i.e.,* you must reimburse the purchaser for the cost of the garment in order to redeem it from him]?

We might conclude from this incident that even if the identity of the thief is known—like Ḥanan the Scoundrel, whose reputation was common knowledge—the owner must reimburse the purchaser for the purchase price of the stolen article as a condition of redeeming it from him. The response in the Talmud to this was:

> Ḥanan the Scoundrel is different; since it is impossible to get any payment from him [as he had no assets], it is as if the thief is not identified.

Thus, Rav agreed that if the purchaser has no reasonable possibility of recovering his money from the thief, the enactment gives the purchaser the right to demand his money from the owner.[231]

In the fourth generation of *amoraim,* an important limitation was placed on this enactment, namely, that it applies only if the article was bought in good faith and the purchaser did not know that it was stolen. "Rava said: 'If the thief is notorious, the market overt enactment does not

231. The law was settled in accordance with the view that R. Johanan stated in the name of R. Yannai, *i.e.,* that even if the thief is located and is financially responsible, the owner must reimburse the purchaser for the purchase price and then pursue his claim against the thief. *See* Maimonides, *MT,* Genevah 5:1–3 (quoted *infra*) and Sh. Ar. ḤM 356:2.

apply.'"[232] In other words, if the purchaser bought from a person known in the community as a thief, the enactment will not benefit the purchaser, since he should have taken care not to buy articles from anyone with such a reputation.

How much notoriety is necessary to prevent the application of the enactment for the benefit of the purchaser? The subsequent discussion in the Talmud provides the answer:

> Was not Ḥanan the Scoundrel notorious, and yet the *takkanah* of market overt was applied to his case [as we saw above in the decision of R. Huna]? [The *takkanah* was applied because] although he [Ḥanan] was known for his evil deeds, he did not have a reputation as a thief.[233]

The law of market overt was summarized by Maimonides as follows:[234]

> (a) It is forbidden to buy from a thief any article that he has stolen, such purchase being a grave transgression since it encourages criminals and causes the thief to steal other property, for a thief who finds no buyer will not steal.[235] Of this, Scripture states: "He who shares with a thief is his own enemy" [lit. "hates his own soul"].[236]
>
> (b) If one steals an article and sells it and the owner has not abandoned hope of recovering it, and subsequently the thief is identified and witnesses testify that "the article that this man sold, he stole in our presence," the article is restored to its owner, who, pursuant to the rule of market overt, must reimburse the purchaser for the price paid to the thief; the owner may then claim against the thief. If he was a notorious thief, the rule of market overt does not apply, and the owner need not pay anything to the purchaser; but the purchaser may claim against the thief and recover from him the money paid to him.
>
> (c) If the owner abandons hope of recovering the stolen article, whether he first abandons hope and then the thief sells it, or he abandons hope after the thief has sold it, the purchaser acquires title to it as a result of the change in possession and the owner's abandonment of hope of recovery, and the purchaser need not return the stolen property itself to the owner. If the purchaser bought it from a notorious thief, he must give the owner its value; but if the seller was not a notorious thief, the purchaser gives the owner noth-

232. TB Bava Kamma 115a.

233. According to some authorities, even a person who makes a purchase from a known thief is considered a bona fide purchaser and within the protection of the market overt enactment, unless he had actual knowledge that the article he bought was stolen; *see Piskei ha-Rosh*, Bava Kamma, ch. 10, #18; *Tur* ḤM 356:4; Rema to Sh. Ar. ḤM 356:2.

234. *MT*, Genevah 5:1–3.

235. *I.e.*, a purchaser from the thief not only assists the thief in the particular crime but also encourages him to perpetrate other thefts, because "the real thief is not the mouse but the hole [in which the mouse hides itself and its booty]" (TB Gittin 45a).

236. Proverbs 29:24.

ing—neither the property nor its value—because he has the benefit of the rule of market overt.[237]

D. Legislation Concerning the Law of Torts

The field of Jewish tort law also received the benefit of considerable development through legislation. A number of illustrations are next discussed.

1. ENACTMENT FOR THE ENCOURAGEMENT OF PENITENTS

Various enactments were adopted by the Sages to encourage penitence and rehabilitation (*takkanat ha-shavim*). The earliest of these related to the manner of returning a stolen article. It is a basic principle that every thief is obligated to restore the stolen article itself; the thief cannot discharge his responsibility by paying the value of the article. The source of this rule is the verse in the Torah:[238] "He [shall] . . . restore that which he got through robbery. . . ."[239] This rule may at times tend to discourage the thief from repenting, and the schools of Shammai and Hillel differed on the need to enact legislation for these particular circumstances:

> The Rabbis taught: If a man steals a beam and incorporates it in a palace, the School of Shammai rules [that] he must demolish the entire palace and restore the beam to its owner; the School of Hillel rules [that] the owner can claim only the value of the beam, so as to encourage penitents.[240]

According to the School of Shammai, the thief must restore the stolen article itself, even if he must demolish the entire building in order to do so; however, according to the School of Hillel, it is sufficient in the particular

237. According to Maimonides, notwithstanding the fact that abandonment and change of possession effectively terminate the ownership of the lawful owner, the law obligates the purchaser to pay the owner the value of the article. However, the market overt enactment absolves the purchaser from that obligation if he bought from a thief not known as such. Other authorities disagree with Maimonides on this point and hold that if the purchase was effected after abandonment, the law no more requires the purchaser to pay the value of the article to the lawful owner than it requires the purchaser to restore the article itself. *See* the opinion of Isaac b. Samuel (Ri) cited in *Tur* ḤM 353:5 and 356:5; *Bet Yosef* to *Tur* ḤM 353:5.

It should be pointed out that according to the law as it was later settled, "By virtue of *dina de-malkhuta* (the law of the land), one should return any stolen article, even after abandonment and change of possession" (Rema to Sh. Ar. ḤM 356:7). *See also infra* p. 688 n. 35, to the effect that this strict obligation to return stolen property was enacted by a *takkanah* dating as early as the tenth century C.E. *See also Shakh,* Sh. Ar. ḤM 356, subpar. 10. On the market overt enactment generally, *see* Z. Warhaftig, *Ha-Ḥazakah ba-Mishpat ha-Ivri* [Possession in Jewish Law], pp. 135ff.

238. Leviticus 5:23.

239. TB Bava Kamma 66a.

240. TB Gittin 55a.

circumstances if the thief restores only the value of the stolen article and not the article itself, "since, if you require him to demolish the building and to return the beam itself, he will not repent."[241] By the beginning of the tannaitic period, the enactment for the encouragement of penitents obtained acceptance,[242] and the view of the School of Hillel prevailed.[243]

2. LATENT DAMAGE

Under Biblical law, one who damages another's property must pay compensation whether the tort is intentional or merely negligent; when an individual personally causes damage, the Torah makes no distinction between intentional and negligent acts. The principle is: "A person is always deemed forewarned [and thus legally responsible for the damage he does] whether he acts inadvertently or deliberately."[244] However, this applies only to damage that is physical and perceptible. If one causes damage that is not perceptible, but the value of the property has been diminished (*e.g.*, if one's ritually pure object is made impure), there is no liability under Biblical law. However, it was difficult in practice to abide by this rule, since sometimes

241. Rashi, TB Gittin 55a on the *mishnah*, s.v. Mipenei takkanat ha-shavim.

242. M Gittin 5:5, citing the testimony of R. Johanan b. Gudgada. The law was so codified. *See* Maimonides, *MT*, Gezelah va-Avedah 1:5; Sh. Ar. ḤM 360:1. *See also* Ravina's statement (TB Sukkah 31a) to the effect that the same law applies if the thief stole a beam and used it in building his *sukkah* for the festival of *Sukkot*. If the owner claims his beam during the festival, he can only collect its value, but if he claims it after the festival, the thief must return the beam itself. This is also stated as the law in *MT* and Sh. Ar., *loc. cit.*

243. In R. Judah Ha-Nasi's time, another enactment was adopted, which provided that if the stolen article no longer exists and the thief voluntarily offers to pay an amount equal to its value, "the Sages are displeased with him," *i.e.*, with the person who accepts such restitution; TB Bava Kamma 94b. Rashi, *ad loc.*, interprets the statement "the Sages are displeased with him" as meaning "such a person does not possess the spirit of wisdom and piety." According to Rabbenu Tam (*Tosafot, ad loc.*, s.v. Bi-mei rabbi nishneit mishnah zu), the enactment applied to that generation only, because of a particular incident. (*See* Bava Kamma 94b for the story of a man who wanted to repent of his crimes. His wife said to him "If you are going to make restitution, even your girdle will not remain yours," and he therefore did not repent.) As to subsequent generations, Rabbenu Tam held that the enactment did not apply, "as is evident from the fact that every day we accept restitution from robbers and adjudicate cases of robbery."

However, most *rishonim* accepted this enactment, too, as being permanently applicable and ruled that restitution should be accepted only if the thief does not repent of his own volition (Maimonides, *MT*, Gezelah va-Avedah 1:13). The object of the rule is to make it easier to repent and turn over a new leaf in the future. According to the *Shulḥan Arukh* and Rema, the enactment applies only with regard to "a notorious professional thief for whom repentance would be difficult [if he made good all that he stole in the past]"; but restitution may be accepted from an ordinary thief even if the thief repents of his own volition; Sh. Ar. ḤM 366:1.

As to the incorporation of the Jewish law on the encouragement of penitents into Israeli legislation, *see infra* pp. 1707–1709.

244. M Bava Kamma 2:6; Maimonides, *MT*, Ḥovel u-Mazzik 1:11; Sh. Ar. ḤM 421:3.

damage that does not change the appearance of an object can be real, substantial, and severe. The *Tosefta* states:[245]

> Originally they ruled that one who defiles [the ritually pure articles of another such as priestly tithes (*terumah*)] or mixes [*terumah* with another's ordinary food, the mixture of which may not be eaten by an Israelite, *i.e.*, one who is not a priest]—and later they included also one who uses [another's] wine as a libation for idolatry [which causes the wine to become prohibited]—is not liable if his act was inadvertent; but if the act was intentional, he is liable, in order to promote the public welfare.[246]

In the three instances mentioned in this passage from the *Tosefta*, damage is caused even though the appearance of the property remains in all respects exactly as it was before the damage. Under Biblical law, the actor is not liable; however, the Sages, in order to promote the public welfare, enacted that there is liability if the damage was intentional:

> Under Biblical law, there is no liability whether the act was done inadvertently or intentionally. Why is this so? Damage that is not perceptible is not considered damage. Why was it enacted that if one acts intentionally he is liable? To prevent people from intentionally defiling the ritually pure articles of another and then saying, "I am not liable."[247]

Maimonides summarized this enactment as follows:[248]

> If one causes latent damage to another's property, he is not liable to pay compensation under Biblical law, inasmuch as the property has not been altered and its appearance has not been adversely affected; however, by enactment of the Scribes (*mi-divrei soferim*), it was provided that inasmuch as he has reduced its value, he is liable to pay for the loss.
>
> For example, if one defiles another's ritually pure food, or mixes *terumah* with another's ordinary food, or mixes a drop of forbidden libation wine into his ordinary wine, causing all of it to be forbidden, or [if one] causes

245. *Tosefta* Gittin 4(3):5.

246. So also in M Gittin 5:4, except that the phrase "in order to promote the public welfare" is missing. On the basis of the *Tosefta*'s reference to the promotion of the public welfare, it is fair to conclude that legislation was the source of the law in the Mishnah as well.

247. TB Gittin 53a (R. Johanan's view). In the Talmudic discussion, Hezekiah and R. Johanan disagreed on the basic question of whether damage not physically perceptible is considered compensable damage under Biblical law. According to Hezekiah, it is; and the enactment absolved from liability the person who unintentionally caused such damage. The purpose of the enactment was to encourage the person who caused the damage to inform the owner that the produce has become forbidden, and thus prevent the owner from inadvertently eating it.

248. *MT*, Ḥovel u-Mazzik 7:1–3.

similar damage, the loss in value is assessed; and he must, like all tortfeasors, pay for the full damage from the best of his property.

This is a penalty imposed by the Sages to prevent evildoers from habitually defiling another's ritually pure things and then saying, "I am not liable."

3. EXEMPTION FROM LIABILITY FOR DAMAGE INADVERTENTLY CAUSED BY A PERSON ACTING PURSUANT TO PUBLIC AUTHORITY

In the case of latent damage, the objective of the Sages' enactment was to expand tort liability. However, in certain instances, the Sages considered it desirable to limit tort liability. An example of this is damage caused by a person acting pursuant to public authority:

> An agent of the court who strikes anyone [by administering the punishment of flogging] under the authority of the court and causes injury is not liable if [the injury is] inadvertent; if [the injury is] intentional, he is liable—in order to promote the public welfare. If a qualified physician who is engaged in healing under the authority of the court[249] causes injury, he is not liable if inadvertent; if [the injury is] intentional, he is liable—in order to promote the public welfare.
>
> If one performs an abortion under the authority of the court[250] and causes injury [to the mother], if inadvertent, he is not liable; if [the injury is] intentional, he is liable—in order to promote the public welfare.[251]

In all these instances, under strict law generally applicable to tortfeasors, the court's agent and the physician are liable for the injury they cause, even if the injury is inadvertent. However, the Sages enacted, "in order to promote the public welfare," that they are not liable for damage done in the course of their occupations if they act inadvertently; "if a qualified physician who acts under authority of the court is not absolved when he acts inadvertently, he will refrain from healing."[252] The definition of an "intentional" injury by one acting by permission of public authority is that "he intentionally inflicted a wound that was greater than necessary."[253] Moreover, although they are absolved when the injury was not caused intention-

249. *I.e.,* he was licensed by the court to practice medicine. At that time, the courts also performed such administrative functions. The same was true with regard to performing those abortions that were permitted by Jewish law. *See* M. Elon, EJ, II, pp. 98–101, s.v. Abortion (reprinted in *Principles,* pp. 482–486), supplemented in *Enziklopedyah Ivrit,* 1985 Supp., s.v. Happalah.

250. As in the case of a pregnancy endangering the mother; *see Resp. Tashbeẓ,* III, #82.

251. *Tosefta* Gittin 4(3):6–7.

252. *Resp. Tashbeẓ,* III, #82.

253. *Tosefta* Bava Kamma 9:11; *see also Resp. Tashbeẓ, supra* n. 252.

ally, "their judgment is committed to the decision of Heaven"[254]—this, too, being a sanction in the halakhic system.[255]

E. Legislation Concerning Criminal Law

The previous discussion of legislative methods has noted the legislative principle the Sages laid down for criminal law—that the court may impose punishment, although not prescribed in the Torah, in order to build "a fence around the Torah." The legislative activity of the halakhic authorities in the area of criminal law, being particularly sensitive to the social and moral changes that take place from one period of time to another, has been extremely broad, and some examples of this legislation have been noted in our prior discussion of this legislative principle.[256]

F. Legislation Concerning the Law of Procedure and Evidence

Legislation accomplished much in the development and broadening of Jewish law not only in substantive areas but also in the law of procedure and evidence. Following are some examples.

1. INQUIRY AND EXAMINATION OF WITNESSES

The Mishnah in Tractate *Sanhedrin* states:[257] "Both civil and capital cases require thorough inquiry and examination (*derishah va-ḥakirah*), as it is written:[258] 'You shall have one standard. . . .'" In other words, the judges must conduct a thorough inquiry and examination of the witnesses in both civil and capital cases.

Jewish law does not require that a witness take an oath to tell the truth; just as the third commandment prohibits false swearing, the ninth commandment prohibits false testimony, and one who is suspected of violating the prohibition against testifying falsely will also be suspected of violating the prohibition against swearing falsely.[259] Therefore, instead of

254. *Tosefta* Bava Kamma 6:17; *see also Resp. Tashbeẓ, supra* n. 252.

255. *See supra* pp. 145–146.

256. *Supra* pp. 515–519.

257. M Sanhedrin 4:1.

258. Leviticus 24:22.

259. In the post-Talmudic period, beginning in the fourteenth century C.E. (*see Resp. Ribash* #170; *Resp. Tashbeẓ*, III, #15), the law was settled that "if the court sees a temporary need to swear the witnesses to tell the truth, it may [require the oath]"; Rema to Sh. Ar. ḤM 28:2. For a more detailed discussion, *see infra* pp. 1697–1702; Elon, *supra* n. 134 at 106–107.

swearing a witness, the court admonishes the witness to testify truthfully and, in the course of the admonition, explains to the witness the enormity of the punishment awaiting a false witness.[260] In addition, the witness is rigorously interrogated along seven lines of inquiry and examination in order to determine how accurate and precise the testimony is.[261] Although the need for inquiry and examination of witnesses is mentioned in the Torah solely in connection with capital cases,[262] the above-quoted *mishnah* states the principle that inquiry and examination of witnesses are also required in civil cases. This rule is deduced by an interpretation of the verse "You shall have one standard . . . ," *i.e.*, in this respect, namely, examination of witnesses, there is no distinction between different branches of the law.

The Talmud[263] questions this mishnaic rule, citing a number of other statements in the Mishnah and *Baraita* that indicate that there is no need for such rigorous inquiry and examination in civil cases. The Talmud then sets forth three solutions by *amoraim* of different periods to resolve the inconsistency. From these, we may deduce the nature, scope, and objective of the Sages' legislation concerning inquiry and examination of witnesses.

a. THE SOLUTION OF R. ḤANINA

R. Ḥanina's solution was as follows:

> Under Biblical law, both civil and capital cases require thorough inquiry and examination, as it is written: "You shall have one standard. . . ."
>
> Why did they [the Sages] enact that inquiry and examination are not required for civil cases? So that the door should not be closed to borrowers. [*I.e.*, if it is necessary to interrogate the witnesses in this way in civil cases, people will refrain from lending money, for fear that the witnesses will not be able to give consistent testimony in the face of the strict interrogation, and if the borrower denies the loan, the lender will have lost his money.]
>
> But if so [*i.e.*, if you prevent inquiry and examination in civil cases], and they [the judges] err, they should not have to pay. [*I.e.*, you should also provide that if the judge errs in his decision, he should not be liable for the damage caused to the losing party, since the judge could argue that if he had closely interrogated the witnesses he would have decided the case correctly.][264]

260. M Sanhedrin 4:5.

261. *Id.* 5:1–2.

262. *See, e.g.*, Deuteronomy 13:15 as to the law regarding an idolatrous town. *See also supra* p. 275.

263. TB Sanhedrin 32a/b.

264. According to Jewish law, a judge who errs in his decision is liable, in certain circumstances, for the damage caused to one of the parties because of the error; *see* TB

This would close the door even tighter to borrowers. [*I.e.*, if you provide that the judge is not liable to pay for the damage caused to the losing party on account of his error, you would certainly be closing the door to borrowers, because people would refrain from lending for fear that the judge will err in his decision and that they will not be compensated for their damage.]

R. Ḥanina's resolution of the inconsistency between the *mishnah* in Tractate *Sanhedrin* and the other sources was that the *mishnah* in *Sanhedrin* that requires inquiry and examination of witnesses in civil as well as criminal cases describes the legal situation under Biblical law, whereas the other sources speak of the law as it was after the Sages changed it by enacting that in civil cases there is no requirement of inquiry and examination of witnesses.

b. THE SOLUTION OF RAVA

Rava propounded the following solution:

The *mishnah* here [in Tractate *Sanhedrin*] speaks of a penalty case [a civil case where a penalty, such as double payment for theft, is imposed], while the others speak of admissions and loans [*i.e.*, the other sources deal with the usual type of civil cases, such as admissions (witnesses who testify that A admitted that he owes B a sum of money) and loans (witnesses who testify to a loan)].

According to Rava's solution, both the *mishnah* in *Sanhedrin*, which requires inquiry and examination of witnesses in civil cases, and the other tannaitic sources, which do not so require, deal with the law after the Sages' enactment (and in this Rava differed from R. Ḥaninah). However, the *mishnah* in *Sanhedrin* is concerned with the type of civil case that involves a penalty; in such a case, the judge must conduct a rigorous inquiry and examination of the witnesses just as in capital cases. By contrast, the other tannaitic sources deal with the usual type of civil cases, as to which the legislation abolished the requirement for such inquiry and examination of witnesses "so that the door should not be closed to borrowers."

c. THE SOLUTION OF R. PAPA

R. Papa proposed a third solution:

Both deal with admissions and loans [*i.e.*, both the *mishnah* in *Sanhedrin* and the other sources deal with the same matter, the usual type of civil case]. In

---

Bekhorot 28b; Sanhedrin 5a; Maimonides, *MT*, Sanhedrin 6:1–2; Sh. Ar. ḤM ch. 25. *See also* Elon, *supra* n. 134 at 103–104.

the *mishnah* in *Sanhedrin,* the claim is suspected of being fraudulent; in the other sources, there is no suspicion of dishonesty in the claim.

In other words, if the court receives the impression from the arguments that the claim is fraudulent, although there is no clear proof of fraud, the court is required to conduct an inquiry and examination of the witnesses even in civil cases; but if the court has no reason to suspect that the claim is fraudulent, there is no need for such an interrogation in civil cases.

Integrating these three responses gives a good picture of the nature of this significant procedural enactment. Biblical law requires inquiry and examination of witnesses even in civil cases. However, legislation by the Sages abolished this requirement in civil cases in order to prevent the disturbance of the orderly functioning of economic life ("so that the door should not be closed to borrowers") that would result if legal proceedings became cumbersome as a result of excessive interrogation of witnesses. On the basis of this rationale, the enactment was applied to the usual range of matters involved in civil cases—not only loans but also sales, gifts, etc.—since these are also common economic transactions; but the enactment was not applied to civil cases involving penalties. Not only is the rationale for the enactment inapplicable to such cases, but it is a basic requirement that in all such matters very careful investigation is necessary before any decision is reached. Consequently, if one even suspects that a claim is fraudulent, the enactment does not apply, and a careful inquiry and examination of the witnesses must be conducted. Maimonides summarized this enactment as follows:[265]

> Both civil and capital cases require thorough inquiry and examination, as it is written: "You shall have one standard. . . . " But the Rabbis enacted that in order not to close the door to borrowers there need not be such inquiry and examination of witnesses in civil cases. For example, if the witnesses testified, "A lent B one hundred *zuz* in such-and-such a year in our presence," their testimony is valid even though they did not specify the month, the place where the loan was made, or the specific coinage.
>
> This enactment applies only to testimony concerning admissions, loans, gifts, sales, etc. However, cases involving penalties, and certainly cases involving flogging and banishment,[266] require inquiry and examination; similarly, if the judge has grounds for suspicion that a claim is dishonest, inquiry and examination are necessary.

265. Maimonides, *MT,* Edut 3:1–2.

266. *I.e.,* offenses for which the penalty is flogging (*see MT,* Sanhedrin ch. 16), or banishment in the case of an unintentional homicide for which the manslayer is banished to a city of refuge (Numbers 35:9–34).

Some *tannaim* were of the opinion that this enactment also applies to certain matters in the area of family law. Thus, the Talmud states:[267]

> It was taught: Witnesses who testify to a husband's death in order to permit his wife to remarry are not subject to interrogation by inquiry and examination—this is the view of R. Akiva. R. Tarfon says they are interrogated.

The subsequent Talmudic discussion clarifies the disagreement between R. Akiva and R. Tarfon:

> Their disagreement involves R. Ḥanina's pronouncement.[268] R. Ḥanina said: "Under Biblical law, both civil and capital cases require thorough inquiry and examination, as it is written: 'You shall have one standard. . . . ' Why did they [the Sages] enact that inquiry and examination are not required for civil cases? So that the door should not be closed to borrowers."
>
> What is their disagreement? One master [R. Akiva] maintains: Since payment is to be made under the *ketubbah*, it is like a civil case. [*I.e.*, since the witnesses' testimony that permits the woman to remarry also results in the woman's recovering the amount of her *ketubbah* from the husband's estate, and the *ketubbah* is a matter of civil law, the witnesses are not subject to inquiry and examination.] The other master [R. Tarfon] argues: Since we permit the woman to remarry, it is like a capital case. [*I.e.*, since the witnesses' testimony permits a woman to remarry, it is a matter of capital law (adultery being subject to capital punishment); therefore, one must conduct a thorough inquiry and examination of the witnesses.]

R. Akiva thus expanded into the area of family law the application of the enactment abolishing the requirement of inquiry and examination. He accomplished this by classifying rules of family law as civil laws so far as this enactment is concerned. R. Tarfon opposed this expansion, since the purpose of the testimony is to permit a woman to remarry, and therefore he viewed the case as one of capital law. The law was settled in accordance with the view of R. Akiva.[269]

267. TB Yevamot 122b.

268. *I.e.*, R. Akiva and R. Tarfon disagreed on a principle which was later formulated by R. Ḥanina. It can obviously not mean that R. Akiva and R. Tarfon, who lived midway through the tannaitic period, disputed a statement of R. Ḥanina, an *amora* who lived afterwards.

269. Maimonides (*MT*, Gerushin 13:28) offered another rationale for this result: "We do not subject to inquiry and examination witnesses who come to testify concerning the status of a woman; the reason is that the Sages did not intend to be strict in this matter, but to be lenient, so as to free the *agunah*." This is the general rationale applicable to all the other evidentiary leniencies designed to free for remarriage women whose husbands have died. Maimonides also gave this rationale in his responsa (ed. Blau, #350). Maimonides apparently believed that the rationale given in the Talmud (that the issue also involves the

2. AUTHENTICATION AND CERTIFICATION OF LEGAL INSTRUMENTS

The nature and import of the legislation concerning authentication and certification of legal instruments (*kiyyum shetarot*) is the subject of a disagreement between the majority of the halakhic authorities, on the one hand, and Maimonides, on the other, that also touches on basic rules of evidence and legal instruments. The Torah states:[270]

> A single witness may not validate against a person any guilt or blame for any offense that may be committed; a case can be valid only on the testimony of two witnesses or more [lit. "by the mouth of two witnesses or three witnesses"].

The Sages deduced from the words "by the mouth of two witnesses or three witnesses" a basic principle of the law of evidence: that testimony must be oral ("by their mouths") and may not be written.[271] Testimony is admissible only if the judge hears the witness directly; the witness's written statement is not sufficient.[272]

---

ketubbah) is not sufficient to transform the case into a civil matter. Therefore, he grounded the result on the general rationale of freeing the *agunah*. On this rationale, the Sages had gone so far as to permit a woman to remarry on the basis of the testimony of a single witness or of otherwise incompetent witnesses or on the basis of hearsay evidence (*see supra* pp. 522–530).

Apparently, the Talmud could not explain R. Akiva's opinion as resting on this general rationale of freeing the *agunah*, because, although he too allowed a woman to remarry on the testimony of a single witness, he required that the witness be legally competent to testify (M Yevamot 16:7), and, therefore, in R. Akiva's view, this general rationale is not strong enough to justify relaxation of the requirement of inquiry and examination. However, since Maimonides held that a woman may remarry on the basis of testimony of witnesses generally not competent to testify (*MT*, Gerushin 13:29), he was able to rely on the general rationale of freeing the *agunah* to justify dispensing with the need for inquiry and examination. This seems to be the answer to the question raised by *Leḥem Mishneh, ad loc.*, as to why Maimonides did not mention the rationale stated in the Talmud, as well as to the additional question of why the Talmud did not refer to the general rationale of facilitating remarriage of an *agunah*. *See* Maharsha to TB Yevamot (end), quoted *supra* p. 530 n. 153, also referring to the general rationale of promoting peace as justifying dispensing with inquiry and examination in the situation here discussed.

270. Deuteronomy 19:15.

271. TB Gittin 71a.

272. TJ Yevamot 16:7, 84b (16:7, 16a) is to the same effect: "'By the mouth of . . . witnesses,'—not by their written statements, nor through an interpreter." This is why witnesses cannot send their testimony to the court in writing; *see* Rashi on Deuteronomy 19:15, s.v. Al pi shenei edim. However, Isaac b. Samuel (Ri) cites Rabbenu Tam to the effect that "nowadays it is customary for witnesses to send their testimony to the court in their own handwriting; and we do not consider this as contravening the rule, 'By their mouths, and not by their written statements,' since they remember their testimony [and therefore could testify in person]." *See Tosafot*, Yevamot 31b, s.v. De-ḥazu bi-khetava ve-atu u-mesahadi. In

This principle gives rise to the question: What good, then, are the witnesses' signatures on a legal instrument? Are not the signatures of the witnesses written testimony? And inasmuch as written testimony is not admissible, how can the signatures of the witnesses prove that an instrument is authentic?

Rashi's response to this question was as follows:

> "By their mouths"—on the basis of two witnesses who testify orally in court and not through a writing; this is not the same as a document that they sign contemporaneously with its execution, because that is the way legal instruments are executed.

Rashi thus distinguished between witnesses to an occurrence, who testify in open court, and witnesses who authenticate the contents of a document. The distinction is based on the fact that by the very nature of the authentication of documents, the only practical method is for the authenticating witnesses to sign the document. Not only are their signatures on a document valid and acceptable evidence, but the principle under Biblical law is that the court presumes that the signatures are not forged or fraudulent. "Witnesses whose signatures appear on a document are deemed [as reliable] as if their testimony had withstood thorough inquiry by the court";[273] *i.e.*, their signatures are viewed as having the same effect as if they had testified in person and been found credible by the court. The presumption is that "people are not so brazen as to perpetrate a forgery"[274]—no one is likely to be so brazen as to forge a signature on a document.[275]

With the changes in the times and in the social and moral climate, it became impossible to continue to treat every document signed by witnesses as authentic and unchallengeable on the ground of forgery. The presumption that "people are not so brazen as to perpetrate a forgery" did not stand up under the critical test of experience, and the Sages therefore adopted a

---

Yevamot 31b, the principle "'By their mouths' . . ." is the basis for the rule that a witness must testify from memory and not from what he wrote in a document. *See also infra* n. 285.

273. Resh Lakish in TB Gittin 3a and Ketubbot 18b.

274. Rashi, Gittin 3a, s.v. Na'asah ke-mi she-neḥkerah edutan be-vet din.

275. *See also Tosafot,* Ketubbot 92b, s.v. Dina hu de-azil Reuven u-mafzei leih:

> The Torah requires no authentication for a document, since the witnesses whose signatures appear on the document are deemed [as reliable] as if their testimony had withstood inquiry by the court. Even if the document is produced by a known thief, it does not appear to me that it needs authentication. We cannot assume that he forged the signatures; although he is suspect in money matters, he would be afraid to write a forged document lest the court discover his forgery.

See also Rashbam, Bava Batra 170a, s.v. Ein ẓarikh le-kayyemo: "Jews are not to be suspected of forging documents, but the Sages were stringent and required authentication when a document is challenged."

specific enactment known as *takkanat kiyyum shetarot.*[276] Under this enactment, one who bases a claim, or otherwise relies, upon a legal instrument must prove the authenticity of the signatures on it. This burden is placed on the claimant in various situations, *e.g.,* where the debtor specifically raises forgery as a defense, or where the creditor seeks to recover on the instrument in the absence of the debtor, or from a third party who has purchased the debtor's property, or from the orphan children of the debtor.[277]

A document may be authenticated in various ways, the primary methods being:

i. The witnesses who signed the instrument testify to the authenticity of their signatures.
ii. Other witnesses testify to the authenticity of the signatures, *i.e.,* that they recognize the signatures as those of the authenticating witnesses, or they testify that the authenticating witnesses signed in their presence.
iii. If no witnesses are available to authenticate the document, authentication is accomplished by comparing the signatures on the document with the signatures of the same witnesses on other documents (this method is called "their handwriting is determined from a different place").[278]

An additional enactment made it possible for the holder of a legal instrument to certify it immediately upon its execution, before any legal proceeding. This enactment was designed to provide a remedy where the holder was apprehensive that when the document would be needed, witnesses would not be available to authenticate it. Consequently, it was enacted that the holder may appear before a court (which for this purpose may consist entirely of three laymen) and authenticate the document by one of the three methods set forth above. After the signatures of the witnesses had been authenticated, the court would write on the document, adjacent to the witnesses' signatures, the following certification: "Sitting as a court of three, before us appeared A and B and testified to the authenticity of their own signatures (or the signatures of C and D), and having concluded that their signatures are authentic, we have properly validated and

276. TB Ketubbot 21b, 28a; Gittin 3a; and *see* Rashbam's statement, *supra* n. 275. This enactment is ancient and in any event, as can be concluded from the Talmudic sources, was applied during the period of the Temple. *See* Bloch, *Sha'arei,* II, 3rd maḥberet, p. 101. *See also Shakh,* Sh. Ar. ḤM 46, subpar. 9 for the opinion of Avigdor ha-Kohen that when it is explicitly claimed that a document is forged, authentication, in certain circumstances, is required by Biblical law, and *Shakh*'s own objections to this view.

277. *See further* Bloch, *Sha'arei,* II, 3rd maḥberet, pp. 67–76.

278. *See* Maimonides, *MT,* Edut ch. 6; Bloch, *Sha'arei,* II, 3rd maḥberet, pp. 76–86.

certified the document." The members of the court would then sign the certification.[279] This certification is also called *asharta* or *henpek.*[280]

The foregoing is the view of the majority of halakhic authorities. Maimonides' view as to the nature of the legislation concerning the authentication and certification of legal instruments is original and unique. In his opinion, the Biblical principle that only oral testimony is admissible also applies to evidence in the form of signatures on a document. It therefore follows that the basic rule that witnesses' signatures on a document are accepted as proof of the content and authenticity of the document is solely the result of legislation by the Sages enacted to the end that "the door should not be closed to borrowers." Because economic life could not properly function if every document had to be authenticated orally before a court, the Sages enacted that a document attested by the signatures of witnesses has full legal validity.

Maimonides formulated this principle as follows:[281]

> Under Biblical law, no testimony is admissible in either civil or capital cases unless it is given orally, as it is written:[282] "By the mouth of two witnesses," [which implies that] the testimony must be oral and not in writing. However, by enactment of the Scribes (*mi-divrei soferim*) it was provided that civil cases can be decided on the basis of evidence in a legal instrument even though the witnesses are unavailable, so that the door should not be closed to borrowers.[283] The signatures of witnesses will not render a legal instrument admissible in cases involving penalties, and it goes without saying [that the same rule applies] in cases involving flogging and banishment;[284] the testimony [in such cases] must be oral and may not be in writing.[285]

279. Sh. Ar. ḤM 46:3, following TB Ketubbot 21a–22a; *see Be'ur ha-Gra, ad loc.*, subpar. 13.

280. The term *asharta* is related to *ishur* (validation); and *henpek* derives from the Aramaic *nafak* (to go out, or issue) because the formula of certification contains the clause "This document has issued [from] before us . . ."; *see Sefer he-Arukh,* s.v. Henpek.

281. Maimonides, *MT,* Edut 3:4.

282. Deuteronomy 17:6.

283. *See Be'ur ha-Gra* to Sh. Ar. ḤM 28, subpar. 56, citing TB Gittin 36a: "The Sages enacted that witnesses should sign documents in order to promote the public welfare, because the witnesses may die or leave the country." This rationale was given with reference to a *get* (bill of divorcement), and Maimonides believed that it applies to all legal instruments.

284. *See supra* n. 266 and accompanying text.

285. *See also Leḥem Mishneh, ad loc.*, to the effect that it is possible that Maimonides agreed with Rabbenu Tam (*see supra* n. 272) that testimony in writing may be sent to the court as long as the witnesses are alive and in a position to testify orally, and that written testimony is inadmissible only when the witnesses are dead. However, the plain meaning of the quotation from Maimonides is not consistent with *Leḥem Mishneh*'s contention.

From Maimonides' starting point, which differed from the approach of the majority of the halakhic authorities as to the legal source for the evidentiary validity of witnesses' signatures on legal instruments, he also arrived at a different rationale with regard to the legislation concerning authentication and certification of such instruments. In Maimonides' view, this legislation did not operate on Biblical law, as most other authorities believed, but it supplemented earlier legislation that recognized the basic evidentiary validity of the document. Maimonides therefore stated[286] that the reason for the legislation providing for the authentication and certification of documents is "that the door should not be closed to borrowers," which is the very same rationale that he used in order to justify the basic evidentiary validity of the document itself. According to Maimonides, authentication of documents by subscribing witnesses is founded entirely on legislation, which was enacted by the Sages in two stages: the first stage established the evidentiary validity of a document attested by subscribing witnesses, which was contrary to Biblical law, under which no testimony in writing is admissible; the second stage established that a legal instrument may be authenticated and certified on the basis of proof of the genuineness of the attesting witnesses' signatures.[287]

G. Legislation Concerning Labor Law; Enactment That the Laborer May Take an Oath and Receive His Wages

Labor law is one of the richest and most extensive subjects of Jewish law, and a considerable portion of it is of legislative origin.[288] An instructive illustration is a significant enactment relating to both labor law and evidence, namely, the enactment giving a laborer the right to take an oath and receive his wages.

The oath in Jewish law is one of the evidentiary methods by which a claimant may prove the truth of his claim. The Jewish law of oaths passed through different stages, in each of which different objectives and forms of the oath were prescribed.[289] Before an examination of the laborer's oath, a brief survey of the Biblical oath is necessary.

286. Maimonides, *MT*, Edut 6:1.

287. According to Maimonides, Resh Lakish's statement, quoted *supra* p. 611 at n. 273 (that the witnesses whose signatures appear on a document are deemed as reliable as if their testimony had withstood thorough inquiry by the court), expresses the rabbinic law according to the Sages' first enactment, which validated documents signed by witnesses, notwithstanding that the attestation is "by their written statements and not by their mouths." *See also* Bloch, *Sha'arei*, II, 3rd maḥberet, p. 66.

288. *See* S. Warhaftig, *Dinei Avodah ba-Mishpat ha-Ivri* [Labor Law in Jewish Law], 1969. *See infra* pp. 1629–1634 concerning Israeli labor legislation based on Jewish law.

289. *See* Gulak, *Yesodei*, IV, pp. 129–149.

There are three instances when a Biblical oath is required:

i. *When part of a claim is admitted*

Plaintiff, P, makes a claim against defendant, D, for the payment of a debt, but has no witnesses to prove his claim. D admits that he owes part of the amount claimed, but denies liability for the balance. In this situation, D must take an oath that he does not owe any amount greater than he admits, and he is then not liable for the balance. If he does not swear, he must also pay the portion he denies owing. The theory is that admission of part of the claim raises a substantial suspicion that the defendant owes the entire amount but is seeking to escape payment of a part of the claim at the time demand is made.

ii. *When a plaintiff's claim is supported by one witness*

Plaintiff, P, produces only one witness for his claim; but there can be no recovery from the defendant, D, on the strength of this testimony (because "a case can be valid only on the testimony of two . . . witnesses . . ."). However, the testimony of one witness imposes on D the burden of taking an oath to contradict the testimony of the witness, and if D takes such an oath, he is not liable.

iii. *When a bailee asserts a defense to liability*

The four types of bailees (the unpaid bailee, the hirer [lessee], the paid bailee, and the borrower) who assert facts that absolve them from liability for property they had in their possession (such as an unpaid bailee who claims that the property was stolen, or a paid bailee who claims that it was lost as a result of *force majeure*) must take an oath that their defense is true in order to absolve themselves from liability for the damage.

In these three instances of the Biblical oath, the oath absolves the defendant from the obligation of payment. Under Biblical law, the probative force of an oath is not sufficient to support recovery by a plaintiff who swears that his claim is meritorious. The power of an oath is sufficient only to absolve a defendant who swears to the facts constituting his defense. This principle finds expression in the rule: "All those who take a Biblical oath swear and do not pay."[290]

The Sages adopted an enactment that for certain important claims the oath has evidentiary force sufficient to enable a plaintiff to recover on his claim even in the absence of any other supporting evidence. Such an oath belongs in the category of oaths called "swear and take" (*i.e.*, the oath proves the claim and does not merely establish a defense) and is referred to

290. M Shevu'ot 7:1.

in Talmudic literature as the "Mishnaic Oath"—an oath based on an enactment of the Sages recorded in the Mishnah.

Thus, the Mishnah states:[291]

> All who take a Biblical oath swear and do not pay. The following swear and take: the laborer, the victim of a robbery, the victim of an assault and battery, a person whose adversary is suspected of taking a false oath, and a shopkeeper with his account book.

Later in the same chapter, the Mishnah explains the law of the oath of the robbery victim and the other cases mentioned. The Mishnah's explanation for the laborer's oath is as follows:

> What is the case of the laborer? He [the laborer] said to him [the employer]: "Pay me the wages that you owe me." He [the employer] said: "I have paid," and he [the laborer] said: "I have not received it." He [the laborer] swears and takes. R. Judah says: "There must be a partial admission [for this rule to apply]." What would be such a case? If he [the laborer] said to him [the employer]: "Give me the wages of fifty *denarii* [of silver] that you owe me," and he [the employer] said: "You have received a *denar* of gold [which is twenty-five *denarii* of silver]." [Thus, according to R. Judah, the laborer swears and takes only when the employer admits part of the laborer's claim, but not if the employer denies the entire amount.]

The laborer is thus given the right to take an oath that his claim is valid and to obtain all his wages even though the employer disputes his claim and argues that the laborer has already been paid his wages. Under Biblical law, if the defendant denies the entire claim, he is absolved both from taking an oath and from payment so long as the claimant brings no proof to support his claim. However, in this instance, the Sages enacted that the laborer should be able to obtain judgment solely on the basis of an oath, even though under Biblical law the employer is not liable and cannot be made liable by the laborer's oath. This is the opinion not only of the Sages who held that the laborer swears and recovers a judgment even if the employer denies his entire claim, but also of R. Judah, who held that the laborer's right to recover judgment is limited to the case where the employer admits at least part of the laborer's claim.

What is the background for the adoption of this far-reaching enactment? The answer to this question is found in the Talmudic discussion explaining the legislation:[292]

291. *Id.*
292. TB Shevu'ot 45a.

Why is the laborer different that the Rabbis enacted that he should swear and take? [*I.e.*, in what way does the laborer differ from other claimants to cause the Sages to legislate in his favor that he may take an oath and receive his wages?]

R. Judah said in the name of Samuel: "They taught here important *halakhot* [*i.e.*, laws based on tradition]." But are these *halakhot?*[293] Rather, say they taught important *takkanot* here. Important? Do you imply that there are unimportant ones?[294] Rather, R. Naḥman said in the name of Samuel: "They taught here *takkanot kevu'ot* (permanent or established enactments)."[295]

The Rabbis uprooted the oath from the employer and placed it on the laborer for the sake of his livelihood.[296] [*I.e.*, the Sages took the oath away from the employer and allowed the laborer to take an oath and receive his wages, since the laborer needs his wages for his livelihood.][297]

293. The parallel passage in TB Bava Meẓi'a 112b reads: "But are these *halakhot?* These are *takkanot.*" *See* Rashi, *ad loc.*, s.v. Hani halakhah ninhu: "But are they laws from Moses at Sinai? Are they not *takkanot* of the Sages?" *See also* Rashi, Shevu'ot 45a, s.v. Hani hilkhata ninhu.

294. *See Tosafot,* Shevu'ot 45a, s.v. Gedolot mi-kelal de-ikka ketannot, asking why the query is raised only here, inasmuch as the statement that "they enacted an important *takkanah*" occurs in other Talmudic passages. *Tosafot* explains that the reason for the Talmud's query is that our text reads, "They taught important *takkanot* here," which implies that they did so "here" but nowhere else. *See also Tosafot,* Bava Meẓi'a 112b, s.v. Mi-kelal de-ikka ketannot.

295. Rashi (Bava Meẓi'a 112b, s.v. Takkanot kevu'ot) explains: "It is appropriate to make them permanent (*keva*)." Ri Migash (Shevu'ot 45a, s.v. Hani nishba'in ve-notelin) explains: "They are called 'established' (*kevu'ot*) because it [the oath] was uprooted from one place [*i.e.*, from applying to the employer] and established elsewhere [*i.e.*, placed on the laborer]."

296. TB Bava Meẓi'a 112b reads: "The oath is the employer's, but the Rabbis uprooted it and placed it on the laborer, for the sake of the laborer's livelihood."

297. The commentators struggled with the interpretation of the statement "The Rabbis uprooted the oath from the employer." What oath was applicable to the employer? Under Biblical law, when a defendant denies the entire claim, no oath on his part is necessary to establish his freedom from liability. Most *rishonim* explain that the point is that it might have seemed more appropriate to enact that the employer take an oath and be absolved from liability (since the general rule where the Biblical oath applies is that "they [the defendants] swear and do not pay"), but the Sages eliminated (*akru*, lit. "uprooted") that possibility for wage claims and permitted the laborer to take the oath "because of his livelihood." *See* Ri Migash to Shevu'ot 45a, s.v. Hani nishba'in ve-notelin; *Tosafot,* Shevu'ot 45a, s.v. Akaruha rabbanan shevu'ah mi-ba'al ha-bayit, Bava Meẓi'a 112b, s.v. Shekaluha rabbanan li-shevu'ah mi-ba'al ha-bayit ve-shadyuha asakhir; Ran to Shevu'ot 45a and Bava Meẓi'a 112b, s.v. Akaruha rabbanan.

Rashi, Bava Meẓi'a 112b, s.v. Takkanot kevu'ot, explains: "It is appropriate to make them [the *takkanot*] permanent (*keva*) and to abrogate a Biblical law; for under Biblical law, it is the one who has to pay who takes an oath . . . but in this case they [the Sages] saw fit to take the oath from the employer and place it on the laborer." Meiri, *Bet ha-Beḥirah* (Bava Meẓi'a 112b, ed. Schlesinger, p. 418) implies that, at first, legislation by the Sages did in fact impose the obligation of the oath on the employer.

This was not the end of the colloquy. The discussion continued:

> Should we penalize the employer for the sake of the laborer's livelihood?[298] [*I.e.,* out of concern for the livelihood of the laborer, should we cause deprivation to the employer as if we are fining him?]
>
> The employer himself is satisfied that the laborer should take the oath and receive his wages so that laborers will hire themselves out to him.[299]
>
> On the contrary! Would not the laborer be satisfied that the employer should take the oath and be absolved, so that the employer should hire him next time?[300] The employer must of necessity hire laborers. [*I.e.,* the laborer need not be concerned that the employer will not hire him for work, because it is necessary for the employer to hire laborers.]
>
> Does not the laborer also need to be employed? [*I.e.,* the laborer also must hire himself out for work as he must have a livelihood; thus, the employer need not be concerned about finding laborers!]

The Talmud then suggests another answer:

> Rather, it is because the employer is busy with his workers. ["He pays wages to a number of laborers and he thinks that he has paid this one too"—Rashi.][301] Then should he not give it to him without an oath?[302] [*I.e.,* if so, should he not give the wages to the laborer even without the laborer's having to swear that he did not receive his wages?][303]

298. TB Bava Meẓi'a 112b reads: "Should we cause [the employer] a loss?"

299. *See* Rashi, Shevu'ot 45a, s.v. Ki heikhi de-litaggeru leih po'alim: "If he [the employer] takes an oath and the laborers lose [their pay], he will no longer be able to find laborers to work for him, because they will be afraid to work for him, since he denies his laborers their wages."

300. Rashi, s.v. Ki heikhi de-litaggerei ba'al ha-bayit: "So that he [the employer] should not suspect him [the laborer] of claiming his wages after he has received them."

301. TJ Shevu'ot 7:1, 33b (7:1, 37c) reads: "R. Avin said: 'Because the employer's business affairs are extensive, they enacted that the laborer could take an oath and take [his wages].'" According to this version, the employer is preoccupied with his business affairs even if he has only one employee, since "his business affairs are extensive." *See also Tosafot,* Shevu'ot 45a, s.v. Ba'al ha-bayit tarud be-fo'alav, explaining that no distinction is to be made between one employee or many and relying on TJ, *supra.* Ran to Bava Meẓi'a 112b, s.v. Akaruha rabbanan, takes the same position.

302. TB Bava Meẓi'a 112b reads: "If that is the case, we should give it to him without an oath."

303. Since the employer is occupied with his business affairs, we presume that he does not remember whether he has already paid the wages, and his legal position is as though he claims, "I do not know whether I have paid him the wages." Since it is undisputed that the laborer did work for the employer and that the employer is liable to pay the laborer his wages, the case is similar to one where A claims against B, "You have one hundred *zuz* of mine," and B replies, "I do not know whether I returned them to you," in which case B must pay. *See also Tosafot,* Shevu'ot 45a, s.v. Ve-neitav leih be-lo shevu'ah, and Bava Meẓi'a 112b, s.v. I hakhi neitav leih be-lo shevu'ah.

[The purpose of the oath is] to satisfy the mind of the employer. [*I.e.,* the laborer must take an oath to set the employer's mind at rest, because the employer claims that he already paid the laborer his wages.]

Let him pay him in the presence of witnesses! [*I.e.,* would it not be better to adopt an enactment that the employer should pay laborers their wages in the presence of witnesses, and there would then be no necessity for any oath?] That would be too troublesome. [*I.e.,* such an enactment would impose too much of a burden.]

Let him pay him at the beginning! [*I.e.,* would it not be better to adopt an enactment that the employer should pay laborers their wages before the work begins, so that no question will arise at the completion of the work as to whether the wages have already been paid?]

Both desire credit. [*I.e.,* both the laborer and the employer desire that wages should be paid after the completion of the work and not at the beginning.]304

In this discussion, we are presented with an instructive description of the social and economic factors, as elucidated by the *amoraim,* that produced this highly significant enactment. Under Biblical law, the employer owes nothing to the laborer—neither money nor an oath—since the employer claims that he has already paid, and the plaintiff-laborer who claims that the employer did not pay seeks to recover money from the defendant-employer and thus has the burden of proof. The employer, however, is occupied with his business matters and it is reasonable to conclude that he mistakenly believes that he paid the laborer's wages, whereas the only "matter" in which the laborer is interested is his pay, and he undoubtedly clearly remembers whether or not he has been paid. Moreover, the laborer's pay is his livelihood, whereas to the employer it is only a business expense. For all these reasons,305 the Sages enacted legislation departing from Biblical law and providing that the laborer may take an oath that he did not receive his wages; and on the strength of the oath alone, the laborer may recover his wages from the employer.

Of special interest is the Talmud's discussion of possible alternative approaches. Other arrangements were suggested: that the employer should

304. Rashi, Shevu'ot 45a, s.v. Sheneihem roẓim be-hakafah, gives the following rationale: "The employer, because he sometimes does not have the money available in the morning; the laborer, to ensure he will not have spent before the end of the day the money needed for his livelihood." In Rashi, Bava Meẓi'a 112b, s.v. Sheneihem roẓim be-hakafah, the rationale is: "The employer, because sometimes he has no money; the laborer, because of concern that he might lose the money."

305. According to Ran (Bava Meẓi'a 112b, s.v. Akaruha rabbanan), the rationale "for the sake of his livelihood" was withdrawn after the Talmud adduced the rationale that the employer is busy with his workers. Maimonides (*MT*, Sekhirut 11:6, quoted in the text at n. 308 *infra*) disagreed. Apparently, all these factors played a part in bringing about the enactment.

pay his laborers in the presence of witnesses, or that he should pay the wages of his laborers in advance. From the point of view of the preservation of Biblical law, these alternatives are undoubtedly superior, as they do not "uproot" a Biblical rule. However, inasmuch as these alternative suggestions were not economically feasible, the Sages preferred to adopt an enactment departing from Biblical law,[306] in order to satisfy the social and economic requirements of the employer-employee relationship.[307]

The law was settled in accordance with the majority view of the Sages, and the laborer may take an oath and obtain his wages even if the employer completely denies the claim. Maimonides summarized the law as follows:[308]

> Where a laborer who has been hired in the presence of witnesses makes a timely demand[309] and the employer says, "I have given you your wages," and the laborer says, "I have received nothing," the Sages enacted that the laborer may take an oath while holding a sacred object[310] and recover in accordance with the law applicable to all who swear and take, because the employer is busy with his employees and the laborer looks to his wages for his livelihood.

As stated, the Sages enacted the oath of "he swears and takes" in a number of other instances.[311] However, because of their special solicitude for the laborer, they were also lenient in his favor as to the procedure for taking the oath.[312]

Maimonides codified this aspect of the law as follows:[313]

> A laborer who takes an oath is not to be treated with strictness, and no other ancillary oath (*gilgul shevu'ah*) may be required;[314] he swears only that he did

306. *See* Rashi, Bava Meẓi'a 112b, quoted *supra* n. 297.

307. Talmudic law prescribes many additional rules relating to this enactment that "the laborer swears and takes." One example is the rule that if the time limit has passed for payment of the wages as required by the law of the Torah that "the wages of a laborer shall not remain with you until morning" (*see supra* pp. 336–337), the laborer's claim that he has not received his pay is no longer believed, even on oath, because we presume that the employer will not transgress a Biblical prohibition and that the laborer will not delay so long in making his claim. TB Shevu'ot 45b; Bava Meẓi'a 112b–113a. The commentators and codifiers differ as to the length of the period during which the laborer is entitled to swear and take. *See* S. Warhaftig, *supra* n. 288 at I, 389–395.

308. *MT,* Sekhirut 11:6.

309. *See supra* n. 307.

310. The person taking the oath holds a sacred object, such as a Torah scroll, phylacteries, or a book containing God's name. *See* Maimonides, *MT,* Shevu'ot 11:8,12; Sh. Ar. ḤM 87:14–15 and Rema, *ad loc.*

311. M Shevu'ot ch. 7. *See supra* pp. 615–616.

312. TB Shevu'ot 48b–49a.

313. Maimonides, *MT,* Sekhirut 11:9. *See also* Ran to Alfasi, s.v. Lifto'aḥ, for an explanation of Alfasi's interpretation of R. Huna's and R. Ḥisda's statements in TB Shevu'ot 49a.

314. A person obligated to take an oath can ordinarily be required by the other party to broaden the oath to cover all other claims the other party has against him, including

> not receive his wages, and he is to be paid. All others who take the oath are not to be treated with leniency. Only the laborer is so treated, and the court takes the initiative for him by saying to him: "Do not have qualms. Swear and take."

We have discussed a considerable number of examples of enactments adopted in different periods and in different areas of Jewish law through the end of the tannaitic period. The laws for which legislation was the legal source are not compiled in one place, and Talmudic literature has no compendium of enactments for particular areas of the law. However, in a few instances, a number of enactments having a common rationale were grouped together, such as certain enactments to promote the public welfare[315] or in the interests of peace and tranquillity.[316] This diffuseness does not make it easy to draw conclusions with regard to the number of laws in the entire halakhic system that are legislative in origin. However, the illustrations that have been discussed—and many others that could be added[317]—enable us to appreciate the significant role that legislation played in creating and expanding Jewish law in the tannaitic period.

---

claims which, standing alone, would not require an oath. *See* Maimonides, *MT,* To'en ve-Nit'an 1:12.

315. M Gittin 4:2 through 5:3; *Tosefta* Gittin ch. 4(3).

316. M Gittin 5:8–9; *Tosefta* Gittin 5(3):4–5.

317. *See supra* p. 548 n. 10.

Chapter 16
LEGISLATION IN THE AMORAIC PERIOD

I. INTRODUCTION

The *amoraim* dealt in their characteristic manner with previously adopted legislative enactments: they clarified them and resolved various difficulties in connection with the substance of their provisions and the identity of their promulgators.[1] In addition, as has been discussed,[2] the *amoraim* grounded the authority for halakhic legislation on a number of principles, on the basis of which they also explained the legislative activity of their predecessors. In addition, the *amoraim* continued to engage in wide-ranging legislative activity of their own in order to solve the problems of their own time and place.[3]

This chapter examines two major features characteristic of the legislative activity of the *amoraim:* (1) the formulation of general principles to serve as guidelines for legislating, not only in regard to establishing the limits of legislative authority but also in regard to the policy objectives of

1. *See, e.g.,* TB Shabbat 14a–15b; Avodah Zarah 35b–36b. Occasionally, the *amoraim* resolved such difficulties by positing that legislation concerning a specific subject had been adopted in stages, *i.e.,* that a number of different enactments relating to that subject were adopted in different periods. *See* TB Shabbat and Avodah Zarah, *loc. cit. See also supra* pp. 549–550.

2. *See supra* pp. 505–533.

3. Like the *tannaim,* the *amoraim* legislated in all areas of the law: acquisition and obligations, procedure, divorce and *ḥaliẓah,* financial relations between spouses, torts, and legal instruments. *See* the various enactments discussed *infra* and the detailed discussion in Bloch, *Sha'arei,* III.

legislation, and (2) the explanation and grounding of various enactments on the basis of general legal principles of the total halakhic system. This approach of crystallizing rules and principles to govern halakhic legislation is characteristic of the general approach of the *amoraim* to other aspects of halakhic study and to the ongoing process of halakhic creativity.[4]

II. PRINCIPLES OF LEGISLATION

A. "Do What Is Right and Good"

The Torah states:[5]

> Be sure to keep the commandments, decrees, and laws that the Lord your God has enjoined upon you. Do what is right and good in the sight of the Lord, that it may go well with you and that you may be able to possess the good land that the Lord your God promised on oath to your fathers.

There were conflicting views among the *tannaim* with regard to the conclusions to be drawn from the words "Do what is right and good." The specific situation giving rise to this dispute related to the person who entered the Temple office to gather into baskets (*kuppot*) the half-shekels that had been contributed by the people and had accumulated there.[6] According to one view:[7]

> When he entered to gather [the money] from the Temple office, he would be searched on entering and on leaving; and they would engage him in conversation from the time that he entered until the time that he left, in order to fulfill what Scripture states: "You shall be clear before the Lord and before Israel."[8]

In other words, they would search the body and clothing of the person who entered the office, so that he would not be able to claim that he brought his own money with him if money were found on his person when he left. According to another view:[9]

4. *See infra* pp. 992–998, 1090–1091.
5. Deuteronomy 6:17–18.
6. "How did they gather the half-shekels? One of them entered the inner chamber, and the guards remained outside. He said to them, 'Shall I gather them?' and they answered him, 'Gather them! Gather them! Gather them!'—three times . . ."; Maimonides, *MT*, Shekalim 2:5.
7. *Tosefta* Shekalim 2:2.
8. Numbers 32:22.
9. M Shekalim 3:2.

> The collector may not enter dressed in a loose-hanging garment [with sleeves in which money can be concealed—so that he would not be suspected of stealing from the Temple office] nor wearing boots or sandals or phylacteries or an amulet [in which money can be hidden], lest he become impoverished and people will say that he became impoverished because of his transgression in the Temple office [*i.e.*, stealing its money], or lest he become rich and people will say that he enriched himself from the money in the Temple office. For a person must be as blameless before his fellow man as before God, as Scripture states: "You shall be clear before the Lord and before Israel," and "You will find favor and approbation in the eyes of God and man."[10]

Under the latter view, the person who enters is not to be subjected to demeaning searches of his clothing and his body; it is sufficient if he takes care not to enter the office wearing clothing and objects that could possibly make him suspect.

The *Tosefta* explains the disagreement among the *tannaim* as follows:[11] The opinion that the person's clothing should not be searched was that of R. Akiva, who stated: "'What is right and good in the sight of the Lord'[12] means what is good in the sight of Heaven and what is right in the sight of man"; *i.e.*, it is necessary for man to do what is good in the sight of God and also to be clear in the eyes of the people and to try to be beyond suspicion; but it is also essential to be right in the sight of man, and therefore there should be no searches, since a body search of a person is demeaning and not right in the sight of man. On the other hand, R. Ishmael took the first view because "One must also be 'right' in the sight of Heaven";[13] *i.e.*, not only the word "good" but also the word "right" in the verse relates to the sight of Heaven, and whatever is right and good in the sight of Heaven is *ipso facto* good and right in the sight of man; therefore, the search is necessary, as stated, to make certain that the person has not stolen any of the money in the office.[14] The view of R. Akiva was accepted as the law.[15]

This general precept "Do what is right and good" became a principle establishing that the law ("the decrees and laws") sometimes requires sup-

10. Proverbs 3:4.
11. *Tosefta* Shekalim 2:2.
12. Deuteronomy 6:18.
13. *Tosefta* Shekalim 2:2.
14. We have followed the interpretation of S. Lieberman, *ad loc.*, and in *Tosefta Ki-Feshutah,* Mo'ed, pp. 676–678. This difference of opinion between R. Akiva and R. Ishmael as to the meaning of "right and good" also appears in *Sifrei,* Deuteronomy, Re'eh, sec. 79 (ed. Finkelstein-Horowitz, p. 145); *see also* Finkelstein's explanation, *ad loc.* In *Sifrei,* the dispute is centered on Deuteronomy 12:28: "For you will be doing what is good and right. . . ." As to "good and right," *see also* Urbach, *The Sages,* p. 332; E.S. Rosenthal, "Al Derekh ha-Rov" [On the Way of the Majority], *Perakim* [Annual of the Schocken Institute for Judaic Research], I, 1967/8, pp. 189ff.
15. Maimonides, *MT,* Shekalim 2:10.

plementation through provisions dictated by social and economic justice. Sometimes these supplementary provisions are promulgated as fully binding legal rules, and sometimes they are only ethical precepts.[16]

In the amoraic period, "Do what is right and good" became a basic principle of legislative policy in Jewish law, which generated rules having full legal force. It is a reasonable assumption that many enactments were adopted on the basis of this principle even when the Talmud contains no express statement to that effect. The following sections examine two instances of legislation where it was explicitly pointed out that this principle was the basis of the enactment.

1. THE ADJOINING LANDOWNER'S PREEMPTIVE RIGHT

The *takkanah*[17] of the adjoining landowner's preemptive right (*din bar meẓra*) provides that if A owns land contiguous to B's and sells it to a third party, B is entitled to recover the land from the purchaser upon reimbursing him for the purchase price: "He [the purchaser] is ousted on the basis of the law of the adjoining landowner's preemptive right, in accordance with the verse 'Do what is right and good,'"[18] because it is right and good to give

16. *See* Naḥmanides, *Commentary on Deuteronomy* 6:18:

> The meaning here is that He [God] first says that you should obey His laws and decrees that He commanded you; and immediately afterwards He says that even in regard to matters as to which He did not command you, you should be scrupulous to do what is good and right in His eyes because He loves goodness and equity. This is a matter of great consequence, inasmuch as it is impossible for the Torah to mention explicitly all the ways in which people relate to their neighbors and fellows and to cover all the types of business transactions and all the things necessary for the proper ordering of society and government. It mentioned a great many such things . . . and then stated generally that in all things one should do what is right and good. This is the basis for compromise (*pesharah*), for behaving more generously than the law requires (*lifnim mi-shurat ha-din*), for what was set forth in connection with giving a preemptive right to adjoining landowners, and even for what the Sages called a pleasant demeanor and a mild manner of speech toward other people so as to become known as a guileless and upright person.

Thus, according to Naḥmanides, the principle "Do what is right and good" applies both to precepts that have no legal consequences and to rules that have full legal effect, such as the preemptive right of the adjoining landowner. To the same effect is *Maggid Mishneh* to *MT*, Shekhenim 14:5, s.v. Kadam eḥad ve-kanah:

> . . . The Sages wrote down some of the specific practical applications of these general principles [*i.e.*, the principles "You shall be holy" and "Do what is right and good"]. Some they established as binding law, others [as ethical precepts] for proper and pious behavior.

See also supra p. 160; Naḥmanides, *Commentary on Deuteronomy* 12:28.

17. This is how the law is referred to in the sources. *See* Assaf, *Mi-Sifrut ha-Geonim* [From the Geonic Literature], p. 103; *Resp. Avraham b. ha-Rambam* #78; *Piskei ha-Rosh*, Bava Meẓi'a, ch. 9, #24; *et al. See also* Maimonides, *MT*, Shekhenim 12:5, quoted *infra* p. 626.

18. TB Bava Meẓi'a 108a.

priority to a neighbor to obtain this land that is contiguous to his own rather than to allow a stranger to acquire it.[19] Maimonides stated this enactment, on the basis of the various Talmudic sources, as follows:[20]

> If a man sells his land to another, the neighbor whose land is contiguous to the purchased land may reimburse the purchaser and oust him. . . . The law of the adjoining landowner's preemptive right applies whether the land is sold by the owner, by his agent, or by the court. Even if the purchaser is a halakhic scholar, a neighbor, or a relative of the seller, and the owner of the contiguous land is an ignorant person and not a relative, he [the adjoining landowner] has priority and can oust the purchaser. This is the law because it is written, "Do what is right and good"; and the Sages said that since any sale is the same [to the seller],[21] it is right and good that the adjoining owner, rather than someone more remote, should buy this property.

This principle of doing the right and good, which was the basis for this enactment, gave the enactment considerable flexibility; its application depended on the particular circumstances of each case. Thus, for example, the rule was laid down[22] that the preemptive right does not apply where the sale is to an orphan or to a woman:

> If one sells to orphans, the preemptive right does not apply, because the good and the right in doing kindness to them outweighs the interest of the owner of the contiguous land. Likewise, if one sells to a woman, the preemptive right does not apply, because she does not often trouble herself with buying [real estate]; now that she has bought, it is a kindness to her to let her keep the land.[23]

19. *See* Rashi, *ad loc.*, s.v. Va-asita ha-yashar ve-ha-tov. According to Rashi, *ad loc.*, s.v. Lo mesalkinan leih, R. Naḥman disagreed with the enactment relating to the adjoining landowner's preemptive right, whereas according to *Tosafot, ad loc.*, s.v. Hai man de-aḥazik be-rakta de-nehara, the enactment was unanimously accepted. The view of *Tosafot* accords with the plain meaning of the Talmud and was concurred in by most *rishonim. See Piskei ha-Rosh, ad loc.*, ch. 9, #20; *Nimmukei Yosef, ad loc.*, s.v. Lo mesalkinan leih (in printed editions of Alfasi, fol. 64a), and *Shittah Mekubbeẓet, ad loc.*, s.v. I mishum dina de-bar meẓra.

20. *MT*, Shekhenim 12:5.

21. *I.e.*, it is immaterial to the seller who the buyer is; the seller will not lose in any event, since he receives his price no matter who purchases. For a slightly different interpretation, *see* Rashi, Bava Meẓi'a 108a, s.v. Ve-asita ha-yashar ve-ha-tov.

22. TB Bava Meẓi'a 108b.

23. Maimonides, *MT*, Shekhenim 12:13–14. *See also* Rashi, Bava Meẓi'a 108b, s.v. Le-ishah u-le-yatmei u-le-shutafei. As to the laws concerning the preemptive right of the adjoining landowner generally, *see* Sh. Ar. ḤM ch. 175; ET, IV, pp. 168–195, s.v. Bar meẓra; M. Silberg, *Talmudic Law and the Modern State*, pp. 100–104.

2. THE DEBTOR'S RIGHT TO REDEEM LAND SEIZED TO SATISFY A DEBT

Another enactment on the basis of the principle "Do what is right and good" provides that property seized in satisfaction of a debt is redeemable by the debtor (*shuma hadra*, lit. "return of appraised property").[24]

Under the rules of Jewish law relating to execution of judgments,[25] when a debt is due and unpaid, the court, after granting an extension of time and after certain procedural steps, appraises the debtor's real property and seizes it for the creditor, to be applied to payment of the debt. The enactment *shuma hadra* provides that if the debtor obtains money to pay the debt after the land has been seized by the court, the debtor may demand the return of the seized land even though its legal ownership passed from the debtor to the creditor as soon as the land was seized.

This enactment is explained on the same basis as the enactment relating to adjoining landowners:[26]

> According to the strict law, the land need not be returned, but because of "Do what is right and good in the sight of the Lord" the Rabbis enacted that it should be returned.

It was indeed right and good—especially in that period when land was the major source of livelihood—that the land should be returned to the debtor when he became financially able to pay his debt.

Some of the *amoraim* limited the duration of the debtor's right under the enactment to only twelve months from the date the land was seized, whereas others held that this right of the debtor is unlimited as to time.[27] The rule was also established that after the creditor sold the seized land to a third party, the debtor could no longer redeem it. The very same principle of doing right and good requires that the right of the third party to continue to possess the land which he legally bought should prevail over the claim of the debtor to demand its return from him.[28] Similarly, other restrictions

24. TB Bava Meẓi'a 16b, 35a/b. *See also* A. Gulak, *Ha-Ḥiyyuv ve-Shi'budav* [Obligations and Their Liens], p. 125.

25. For a detailed discussion, *see* M. Elon, EJ, VI, pp. 1007–1020, s.v. Execution (civil) (reprinted in *Principles*, pp. 621–633).

26. TB Bava Meẓi'a 16b.

27. TB Bava Meẓi'a 16b, 35a. The latter opinion was already accepted as law in the Talmud (*id.*) and by the codifiers (Maimonides, *MT*, Malveh ve-Loveh 22:16; Sh. Ar. ḤM 103:9).

28. The Talmud (Bava Meẓi'a 35a) explains this on the basis that "the purchaser went in [to the property] with the intention of [keeping] the land"; *i.e.*, he bought the land in order to have land and not in order to receive money for it. This is the distinction between the purchaser and the creditor with regard to the debtor's right to redeem the land: "In the

and limitations were established on the right of the debtor to redeem his land.[29]

B. Prevention of Strife and Enmity

As previously noted, the goal of maintaining "the public peace and tranquillity" was one of the guidelines for the legislative activity of the *tannaim.*[30] The *amoraim* used this rationale, expressed somewhat differently, both as one of the explanations for pre-amoraic enactments and as a guideline for their own legislative activity.

The rationale given by the *amoraim* for a long series of enactments adopted by the *tannaim* in various areas of the *Halakhah* was that they were intended "to prevent enmity" (*mishum eivah*).[31] These enactments concerned, *inter alia,* the legal relations between husband and wife,[32] father and children,[33] and Jews and non-Jews.[34] With regard to other enactments, the rationale given was that they were intended to prevent contention and strife. The enactment that a person acquires an object located within a radius of four cubits around him was explained as having been enacted "to

---

case of [redemption from] the creditor, 'Do what is right and good' is satisfied because we can say [to the creditor]: 'Your only claim against him [the debtor] is for money, and here it is available for you,' but they [*i.e.,* a purchaser or donee] acquired land" (Rashi, *ad loc.,* s.v. Ada'ata de-ar'a neḥut).

29. *See* TB Bava Meẓi'a 35b. There is a difference of opinion among the *amoraim* with regard to a debtor who voluntarily surrenders his land to his creditor in satisfaction of the debt without any judicial enforcement proceedings. In the post-Talmudic period, additional limitations were established; *see* Sh. Ar. ḤM 103:9. For a comparison of this right of a debtor under the enactment of *shuma hadra* with the common law's equitable right of redemption, *see* Custodian of Abandoned Property v. Na'im and Khalil Abud, 16 *P.D.* 2649, 2655 (1962). *See also* M. Silberg, *Talmudic Law and the Modern State,* pp. 95–104.

30. *Supra* p. 504. *See* M Gittin 5:8–9; similarly, *Tosefta* Pe'ah 3:1; *Tosefta* Ḥullin 10:13; TB Bava Meẓi'a 102a.

31. This phrase, "to prevent enmity," occurs as early as in a statement of R. Judah Ha-Nasi with reference to a man who betroths a woman on condition that the betrothal is to become effective after her husband dies or after her sister [to whom he is already married] dies: "R. Judah says: 'Under strict law the [conditional] betrothal is valid. Then why was it ruled that it is not valid? In order to prevent enmity!'" The enmity referred to is that of the woman's spouse or sister whose death would make the betrothal take effect. TB Kiddushin 63a, and *see* Rashi, *ad loc.,* s.v. Mishum eivah.

32. Such as the enactment relating to a husband's right to his wife's handiwork (TB Ketubbot 58b; *see also supra* pp. 571–572) and his right to property found by her (M Bava Meẓi'a 1:5; TB Bava Meẓi'a 12b).

33. Such as the enactment relating to a father's right to property found by a son or daughter (M Ketubbot 4:4; TB Ketubbot 47a; M Bava Meẓi'a 1:5; TB Bava Meẓi'a 12b).

34. TB Avodah Zarah 26a; Bava Meẓi'a 32b. The same rationale was given for other rulings, *e.g.,* the acceptability of testimony from an ignorant or illiterate person (*am ha-areẓ*); *see* TB Ḥagigah 22a.

prevent strife."[35] Maimonides set forth this law, on the basis of the Talmudic sources, as follows:[36]

> The area around a person within a radius of four cubits can acquire property for him, and if a lost article is within his four cubits, he acquires it [and another may not take it]. The Sages enacted this rule in order to prevent finders from quarreling with each other. This rule applies in an alleyway, at the sides of the public domain [where people do not push against one another], or in an ownerless field. But if one stands in the public domain [where, because of the large number of people using it, no one has his own four cubits and quarreling will occur in any case] or in another's field [where the owner of the field has the sole right to acquire property], the four cubits do not acquire property for him, and he cannot acquire a lost article there unless he takes it in his hand.

An interesting example of a legislative enactment by the *amoraim* to prevent strife and breach of the peace deals with liability for torts between husband and wife. Under Jewish law, a husband who injures his wife is liable to pay her full compensation; and the husband has no rights in the money so paid or in the income from it, notwithstanding that he is entitled to the income from certain other property of his wife. A wife is similarly liable if she tortiously injures her husband.[37] As a consequence, the *amoraim* of the Land of Israel raised a question that is recorded in the Jerusalem

35. TB Bava Meẓi'a 10a. The rule was stated by Resh Lakish in the name of Abba Kohen Bardela. *See* TJ Gittin 8:3 for a contrary opinion of R. Johanan. *See also* Bloch, *Sha'arei,* II, 3rd maḥberet, pp. 1ff., attributing this enactment to the *tannaim.*

36. *MT,* Gezelah va-Avedah 17:8–9.

37. TB Bava Kamma 32a, 89a/b; Maimonides, *MT,* Ḥovel u-Mazzik 4:16–18; Sh. Ar. EH 83:2, ḤM 421:12, 424:10–11. The common law on this issue (which is totally different from Jewish law) is based on its interpretation of Genesis 2:24—"Hence a man leaves his father and mother and clings to his wife, so that they become one flesh"—as leading to the conclusion that "by marriage, husband and wife are one person in law." The common law thus denied the possibility of legal transactions such as contracts between spouses, and afforded immunity from liability for interspousal torts. *See* G. Williams, "Husband and Wife," 10 *Modern Law Review* 16–31 (1947). In the course of time, the harsh legal consequences of this "legal identity" of husband and wife were mitigated; but some of its effects, such as interspousal immunity from tort claims, still exist in various common-law jurisdictions. Currently, the trend in the common law is away from the notion of legal identity of husband and wife (*see, e.g.,* Gottliffe v. Edelston, [1930] 2 K.B. 378, 384).

Following the common law, Israeli law (Civil Wrongs Ordinance, 1944–1947, sec. 9; Civil Wrongs Ordinance [New Version], 1968, sec. 18) provided that no claim could be made by one spouse against another for damages that occurred before or during the marriage. The Supreme Court of Israel interpreted this statute strictly and contrary to the common law, holding that the statute was not intended to introduce the substantive principle of the legal identity of husband and wife into Israeli law, but rather that it had only a procedural effect, *i.e.,* that although there was interspousal liability, it was not legally enforceable. Epstein v. Aharoni, 15 *P.D.* 682, 694–695 (1960). The Litigation Between Spouses (Regu-

Talmud as follows:[38]

> If she [a wife] breaks household utensils, what should be done with her [*i.e.*, what is the extent of her liability for the damage]? Is she analogous to an unpaid bailee [since she receives no wages, she should not be liable unless she has been negligent],[39] or is she analogous to a paid bailee [since she performs her duties in exchange for her support, she is similar to a paid bailee and should be exempt from liability only in the case of *force majeure*]? Logically, the law applicable to her should be that of a paid bailee. But we say that she is not even considered to be an unpaid bailee, since if you held her even to that standard, there never would be peace in the household.[40]

Maimonides summarized this law as follows:[41]

---

lation) Law, 1969, repealed sec. 9 and substituted a provision substantially similar to the thrust of the decision of the Israeli Supreme Court.

Justice H. Cohn, speaking for the Court in Epstein v. Aharoni, *supra*, commented on the source from which the common law drew the notion of the legal identity of spouses (15 *P.D.* at 699):

> The concept of the legal identity of husband and wife . . . was never part of Jewish law. This is one of several examples of Biblical interpretation by Christian judges in England that differ from the interpretation of the same verse in the Jewish tradition. It would hardly be in good taste for us to adopt as our operative legal rule the Christian interpretation and ignore the traditional Jewish interpretation.

See also 15 *P.D.* at 699–700.

Landau, J., in Barnet v. Barnet, 12(i) *P.D.* 565, 577 (1957), stated:

> In England, the injustice done to women by the common law in regard to matters of property used to be explained on the basis of . . . the Biblical concept that husband and wife were "one flesh." Currently, this way of thinking, which is somewhat hypocritical, has been supplanted by a more modern and more truthful rationale: that it is not proper for a married couple to turn to the courts to resolve their disputes, and that such litigation is likely to disrupt domestic harmony.

See also Berinson, J., in Hananiah v. Friedman, 18(iii) *P.D.* 25 (1964), commenting that the clause "so that they become one flesh" was the basis for the early English rule that a husband and wife have only one vote between them in a business association.

Genesis 2:24 has indeed been interpreted variously by halakhic authorities and Jewish Bible commentators, but none of them has seen in that verse any basis for inferring legal identity of husband and wife.

38. TJ Ketubbot 9:4, 52b (9:4, 33a).

39. An unpaid bailee is not liable unless he is guilty of at least negligence; a paid bailee is also liable in case of theft or loss and is excused from liability only in case of *force majeure*.

40. The same reason is cited in TJ, *supra* n. 38, to explain the opinion of the Sages in M Ketubbot 9:4 that a wife is not required to give an accounting under oath of her management of the household.

41. *MT*, Ishut 21:9.

42. In the discussion in TJ, it is not stated that it is only when she is performing her work that she is not liable. *See also Ḥelkat Meḥokek* to Sh. Ar. EH ch. 80, subpar. 29. Apparently, Maimonides' interpretation is based on his rationale that "she would take excessive care and refrain from doing most of her work."

A wife who breaks utensils while she is performing her work[42] in her home is not liable. This is not the original law (*min ha-din*) but is a *takkanah,* enacted because otherwise there would never be peace in the household; she would take excessive care and refrain from doing most of her work, and matrimonial strife would result.

III. "ALL WHO MARRY DO SO SUBJECT TO THE CONDITIONS LAID DOWN BY THE RABBIS, AND THE RABBIS ANNUL THIS MARRIAGE"

As previously stated, the second feature characteristic of the amoraic approach to legislation is that the *amoraim* explained and grounded various enactments on the basis of general principles of Jewish law rather than on principles specifically related to the legislative authority of the Sages.[43] On the one hand, this approach involved some limitation on legislative authority from a theoretical point of view; on the other hand, it produced important techniques and principles for the solution of various problems within Jewish law.

An interesting example of this approach is the principle enunciated by the Babylonian *amoraim* that "All who marry do so subject to the conditions laid down by the Rabbis, and the Rabbis annul this marriage (*kol di-mekaddesh ada'ata de-rabbanan mekaddesh ve-afke'inhu rabbanan le-kiddushin mineih*)." The previous discussion of the enactments of Rabban Gamaliel the Elder reviewed the *takkanah* prohibiting the cancelling of a *get* (bill of divorcement) in the absence of the wife. Under Biblical law, a husband who sends a *get* to his wife may cancel it even in her absence if it has not yet reached her. Rabban Gamaliel the Elder promulgated an enactment prohibiting the cancellation of the *get* except in the wife's presence, "in order to promote the public welfare," since if she married someone else in the interim, her children from the second marriage would be *mamzerim* (offspring of a union that is incestuous or adulterous under Jewish law).

At the end of the tannaitic period, there was a dispute with regard to the scope of this enactment. According to R. Judah Ha-Nasi, if the enactment was violated and the *get* was cancelled in the wife's absence, the cancellation was nevertheless effective, and the woman could not remarry. The view of Rabban Simeon b. Gamaliel was that a cancellation that violated the enactment had no effect, as otherwise "of what value is the authority of the court [to legislate]?" The divorce was therefore valid, and the woman could remarry.[44]

43. *E.g.,* the rules governing when the court may "uproot" a law of the Torah. *See supra* pp. 505–506.

44. M Gittin 4:1–2; TB Gittin 33a; Yevamot 90b. *See also supra* p. 565 and n. 85.

The *amoraim* raised the following question concerning Rabban Simeon b. Gamaliel's view:[45]

> Is it possible that because of [the rationale] "of what value is the authority of the court?" we permit a married woman to [marry] another man on the strength of a divorce that has been canceled under Biblical law?
>
> Yes, all who marry do so subject to the conditions laid down by the Rabbis,[46] and the Rabbis annul this marriage.
>
> Ravina said to R. Ashi: "This is understandable if he [the groom] effected the marriage by means of money [*i.e.,* anything of value, such as a ring], but what can be said if the marriage was effected by means of sexual intercourse?" [*I.e.,* this explanation is satisfactory if the man married the woman by giving money to her, since in such case the annulment is accomplished by the Sages' retroactive expropriation of the money from the man. This renders the marriage void *ab initio,* for a man cannot marry a woman by means of money that does not belong to him; but if he marries her by means of intercourse, how can the marriage be annulled?][47]

45. TB Gittin 33a.

46. "The marriage is effective pursuant to the law of Moses and Israel in accordance with the enactments of the Sages of Israel"—Rashi, *ad loc.*, s.v. Ada'ata de-rabbanan mekaddesh. The phrase "pursuant to the law of Moses and Israel" is part of the husband's betrothal declaration. *See also Tosafot, ad loc.*, s.v. Kol di-mekaddesh ada'ata de-rabbanan mekaddesh; *Tosefta* Ketubbot 4:9; TJ Ketubbot 4:8, 29a (4:8, 28d–29a), where the formula is: "pursuant to the law of Moses and the Jews."

47. The *rishonim* expressed surprise at this query of the Talmud. If the marriage is annulled because it was entered into subject to the conditions laid down by the Rabbis, and if the Rabbis annulled the marriage *ab initio* by withholding their consent to it because the husband canceled a *get* contrary to their enactment, why should it make any difference whether the marriage was effected by means of money or by means of sexual intercourse? *See Shittah Mekubbeẓet,* Ketubbot 3a, s.v. Od katav, and other commentaries, *ad loc.* Furthermore, even the annulment of a marriage that has been effected by means of money does not need to be explained by the expropriation of the money when the reason is that marriages are entered into subject to the conditions laid down by the Rabbis, and in this case the Rabbis withheld their consent. *See* Naḥmanides, quoted in *Shittah Mekubbeẓet,* Ketubbot 3a, s.v. Hateinaḥ de-kaddesh be-khaspa. Our text follows the interpretation of the Talmud adopted by the *rishonim; see* Rashi *et al.*

It would seem that, as various scholars have suggested, the question is really pertinent to TB Yevamot 110a and Bava Batra 48b, where the annulment of the marriage is based on the Sages' legislative authority to annul marriages brought about through improper means (and not on the basis of the fact that the marriage was conditional, as in the Talmudic passage we have been considering; *see infra*). Where legislative power is the basis for the annulment, it is apposite to raise the point that a marriage effected by means of money can be annulled by the exercise of the court's power to expropriate the money but that such an explanation is not applicable to marriage effected by means of sexual intercourse (*see Tosafot,* Bava Batra 48b, s.v. Teinaḥ de-kaddesh be-khaspa). *See* Bezalel ha-Kohen, *Mar'eh Kohen* [Glosses to the Talmud], Yevamot 90b and, for a detailed discussion, A. Weiss, *Le-Ḥeker ha-Talmud* [On Research into Talmud], p. 393; D. Ha-Livni, *Mekorot u-Masorot le-Seder Nashim* [Sources and Traditions Pertinent to the Order of *Nashim*], p. 530 n. 2; Y.D. Gilat, "Bet Din Matnin La'akor Davar min ha-Torah" [The Court May Legislate to Uproot a Biblical Law], *Bar Ilan Annual,* 1969–1970, p. 120.

[R. Ashi responded:] "The Rabbis declared his intercourse to be fornication." [The Sages annulled the marriage by determining that the act was to be deemed merely carnal and not for the purpose of marriage.]

The Babylonian *amoraim* thus grounded the enactment of Rabban Gamaliel the Elder, as interpreted by Rabban Simeon b. Gamaliel, on a general legal-halakhic rationale taken from the law relating to conditional transactions, which they applied to the subject of marriage. Since all marriages are entered into "pursuant to the law of Moses and Israel," they are subject to the approval and consent of the halakhic authorities. These authorities, like anyone else whose approval and consent are required for the validity of a transaction, may declare that under certain conditions they do not consent, and thus the marriage is annulled *ab initio*.[48] It was on the basis of this principle—that a marriage requires the consent of the Rabbis and is therefore retroactively annulled when their consent is withdrawn—that Rabban Gamaliel the Elder's enactment, permitting the wife's remarriage despite the husband's prior cancellation of the divorce in her absence, was not regarded as abrogating Biblical law. The enactment did not give effect to a Biblically invalid divorce but was consistent with the general rule of Jewish law with regard to juristic acts performed subject to conditions. This same legal construction was also utilized by the Babylonian *amoraim* to explain other basic laws in the area of marriage and divorce.[49]

48. Since the annulment of the marriage here is based on the general rules applicable to conditional transactions, the post-Talmudic halakhic authorities extended the principle so that its new formulation stated: "All who marry do so subject to the conditions laid down by the community in its enactments." *See Resp. Ribash* #399 and others. *Resp. Maharam Alashkar* #48 explains:

> It can also be said that just as all who marry do so subject to the conditions laid down by the Rabbis, so all who marry do so subject to the conditions laid down in communal legislation. It is like the case where the groom says to his bride, "You are hereby betrothed to me subject to my father's consent," in which case there is no marriage unless the father consents. Conditions to which all agree are effective even if not expressed; and although they are left unsaid, it is as though they had been expressly stated.

See further infra pp. 856–859, 864–869.

49. In TB Ketubbot 2b–3a Rava ruled that "*force majeure* is immaterial in the law of divorce." This is contrary to the rule, accepted in all other areas of Jewish law, that every legal transaction is void where there is *force majeure* or an act of God beyond a party's control. The example given in TB Ketubbot 2b–3a is set forth by Maimonides in *MT*, Gerushin 9:8, as follows:

> If a man gives a divorce to his wife on the stated condition that it should be effective if he does not reach a designated country within thirty days, and he sets out [for that country] within the thirty days but falls ill or is delayed at a river-crossing and does not arrive until after the thirtieth day, the divorce is effective. Even if [within the thirty-day period] he stands [on the other side of the river] and screams, "I am constrained by circumstances beyond my control!" [the divorce is effective], because in the law of

The Jerusalem Talmud, which contains the teachings of the *amoraim* of the Land of Israel, does not contain this rationale that the marriage is annulled retroactively on the basis that all who marry do so subject to the conditions laid down by the Rabbis. The *amoraim* of the Land of Israel explained Rabban Simeon b. Gamaliel's view—namely, that a cancellation in violation of the enactment is of no effect—as resting on the legislative authority conferred upon the Sages to "uproot" even Biblical law.

Thus, the Jerusalem Talmud states:[50]

> If he canceled it, it is legally canceled; this is the view of R. Judah Ha-Nasi. Rabban Simeon b. Gamaliel holds: He may neither cancel it nor add any conditions. Rabban Simeon b. Gamaliel's view would seem to be correct.
>
> What is the rationale of R. Judah Ha-Nasi? The rationale is that under Biblical law, it [the divorce] is canceled. Yet they [the Sages] declared that it is not cancelled. Can their declaration abrogate Biblical law? [*I.e.*, the Sages have no power to abrogate Biblical law, pursuant to which the divorce is canceled.]
>
> [But the Sages do indeed have the power to abrogate Biblical law, as the following example demonstrates.] Is it not Biblical law that one may set aside *terumah* [priestly tithe, which may not be used or enjoyed by anyone other than a priest] of olives for oil and grapes for wine? [*I.e.*, under Biblical law the requirement of giving *terumah* of oil is satisfied by giving olives from which oil can be made. The same is true of *terumah* of grapes for wine.] Yet, they [the Sages] declared that this should not be done, to prevent robbing the

---

divorce *force majeure* is immaterial even though he has made it clear that he does not want to divorce her.

The Talmud's rationale for this special rule in the area of divorce is "because of meticulous women and imprudent women," *i.e.*, if the ruling were to be that *force majeure* voids the divorce, it might happen that the husband would deliberately not arrive within the thirty days because he wants the divorce to be effective, yet his wife, if a meticulous woman, might fear that he was delayed by circumstances beyond his control and refrain from remarrying for a protracted period. On the other hand, if the wife is imprudent it may very well happen that she would remarry immediately after the expiration of the thirty days, yet there may in fact have been circumstances beyond the husband's control that prevented his arrival in time, in which case the divorce would be invalid and the woman would still be married at the time her marriage to someone else is performed. In order to prevent such unfortunate occurrences, Rava ruled that *force majeure* does not void a divorce and that if the husband does not arrive within the thirty days the divorce is effective under all circumstances. Here too, the Talmud (TB Ketubbot 3a) queries: "But how can it be that notwithstanding that Biblical law invalidates the divorce [because of *force majeure*] we permit a married woman to marry someone else 'because of meticulous women and imprudent women'?" The Talmud's answer is: "All who marry do so subject to the conditions laid down by the Rabbis, and the Rabbis annul this marriage." For a further example, *see* TB Gittin 73a regarding a divorce by a *shekhiv me-ra* (someone terminally ill or facing imminent death).

50. TJ Gittin 4:2, 20b (4:2, 45c).

priests [olive oil being more valuable than unrefined olives, and wine more valuable than grapes].[51] Moreover, they even said: "If one transgressed and gave [olives for oil or grapes for wine], his contribution of *terumah* is invalid." [*I.e.*, under Biblical law, giving *terumah* of olives for oil and grapes for wine is valid after the fact; yet the Sages enacted that this should not be done because it causes loss to the priests; and if someone transgressed and in fact gave olives for oil or grapes for wine as *terumah*, it does not have the status of *terumah*, and a nonpriest is permitted to eat it.][52]

R. Oshaia b. Abba said to R. Judah Nesiah [the grandson of R. Judah Ha-Nasi]: "Who can adequately explain your grandfather's statement to us?" [*I.e.*, the statement is surprising. Why should an enactment by the Sages not have the power to establish that even if the husband canceled the *get*, the *get* nevertheless continues to be effective even though this result abrogates a Biblical law?][53]

According to the Jerusalem Talmud, Rabban Gamaliel the Elder's enactment, as interpreted by Rabban Simeon b. Gamaliel (*i.e.*, that the husband's purported cancellation of the divorce is ineffective), is explained on the basis that the Sages have the authority in certain circumstances to adopt even an enactment that abrogates a Biblical law. The existence of such authority is implicit in the ruling of the School of Hillel that giving olives for

51. Ed. Venice reads: "Is it not Biblical law that one may set aside *terumah* of oil for olives and grapes for wine [even if it constitutes] robbing the priests, but they [the Sages] declared that this should not be done?" *See* Weiss, *supra* n. 47 at 392.

52. *See* M Terumot 1:4,10 to the effect that under Biblical law it is forbidden to set aside *terumah* of olives for oil, because doing so constitutes giving "an unfinished product for a finished product"; however, according to this reasoning, the *terumah* would be valid *post factum* (*id.* 1:10), whereas, following the School of Hillel (*id.* 1:4), the law is that when olives are given for oil, the *terumah* is invalid even *post factum*, in order to prevent loss to the priests (TJ Terumot 1:8, 7a *et seq.* [1:8, 40d *et seq.*]). Such olives revert to the status of untithed produce, which may not be consumed by anyone; and if *terumah* and the other tithes (*ma'aser*) are subsequently set aside from other olives for them, anyone may consume them. This change in the status of such produce, whereby nonpriests may consume produce forbidden to them under Biblical law, thus constitutes the "uprooting" of Biblical law through a rabbinic enactment which, in order to prevent loss to the priests, permits what Biblical law prohibits. *See further* Gilat, *supra* n. 47.

53. R. Naḥman in TB Gittin 33b–34a ruled according to R. Judah Ha-Nasi that "if he canceled it, it is legally canceled" and distinguished between *mamon*, *i.e.*, monetary matters, where it is possible to apply the principle of *hefker bet din hefker* (the court may expropriate an individual's property), and *issur*, religious or ritual matters pertaining to the personal status of a married woman, as to which a Biblically valid marriage cannot be annulled. It would be desirable to clarify whether in R. Naḥman's time the principle that "all who marry do so subject to the conditions laid down by the Rabbis" had already been formulated and R. Naḥman rejected it, or whether R. Naḥman's ruling addressed only the rationale that the Sages have the legislative power to "uproot" a law of the Torah, as is indeed the plain meaning of Rabban Simeon b. Gamaliel's statement and the explanation of the passage in TJ.

oil is not effective as *terumah* even though that ruling abrogates a Biblical law.[54] According to this rationale, the marriage is not annulled *ab initio* but dissolved on the strength of the *get* given by the husband. The legislation that the husband may not cancel the divorce in the absence of the wife was enacted by the Sages "in order to promote the public welfare"; and it is within their authority to prescribe further that if the husband violates their enactment and purports to cancel the divorce, the cancellation has no effect—the divorce is valid, and on the strength of it the woman may marry another man.[55]

Even the Babylonian *amoraim* did not contend that the Sages lacked inherent authority to annul a marriage or that it was only the premise that the marriage was entered into subject to their approval that permitted annulments. However, it was their view that the Sages made use of this inherent authority only when the marriage itself, although technically valid under Biblical law, took place as the result of conduct contrary to elementary propriety, as where the marriage took place following duress or abduction.

Under Talmudic law, a sale under duress is valid if the seller accepts the purchase price and ultimately expresses his consent to the sale. However, if the seller makes a declaration before two witnesses who have knowledge of the details of the duress that he is about to sell the property because he is under duress, the sale is invalid.[56]

This is not the law with regard to the marriage of a woman under duress. "Whenever it is known that because of duress by the man, she said

54. *See supra* n. 52. For a discussion of this authority of the Sages, *see supra* pp. 503–505, 522–530. To the same effect is R. Ḥisda's explanation in TB Yevamot 89a/b of the statement in the *mishnah,* "One may not set aside *terumah* for ritually pure produce from produce that is ritually impure, and if he has done so . . . knowingly, his act is ineffective" (lit. "he has done nothing"). According to R. Ḥisda, this means "his act has no effect whatsoever in that [not only is the ritually pure produce prohibited for consumption but] even what was designated as *terumah* reverts to the status of untithed produce. Why? Lest the owner will wrongfully fail to give *terumah* [for the ritually pure produce]." Although under Biblical law, the *terumah* set aside from the impure produce is valid *terumah,* R. Ḥisda was of the opinion that the court can abrogate a law of the Torah even by permitting an act that the Torah forbids, *i.e.,* consumption of Biblically valid *terumah* by a nonpriest. On the difference of opinion between R. Ḥisda and Rabbah, who held that the court can abrogate a law of the Torah only to the extent of forbidding what the Torah permits, but not *vice versa, see supra* p. 506.

55. This seems to be the correct interpretation of TJ's approach, which makes no reference to the annulment of marriage and which explains Rabban Simeon b. Gamaliel's opinion as being based on the principle that the Sages are authorized to adopt legislation abrogating Biblical law.

56. TB Bava Batra 47b–48b; Bava Kamma 62a; Maimonides, *MT,* Mekhirah 10:1; Sh. Ar. ḤM 205:1; and *see* additional qualifications in Sh. Ar., *loc cit. See also* Gulak, *Yesodei,* I, pp. 57–62.

'I consent' and the marriage was performed, the marriage is invalid."[57] This law is explained in the Talmud as follows:[58]

> Mar bar R. Ashi[59] said: "The marriage is certainly not valid; he acted improperly, therefore the Rabbis treat him 'improperly' and annul his marriage." [*I.e.*, the Rabbis annul the marriage even though it is technically valid under Biblical law.]
>
> Ravina said to R. Ashi: "This is understandable if he effected the marriage by means of money, but what can be said if the marriage was effected by means of sexual intercourse?"
>
> He replied: "The Rabbis declared his intercourse to be fornication."

This explanation does not premise the Sages' annulment of the marriage on the principle that "all who marry do so subject to the conditions laid down by the Rabbis," as was done in the cases previously discussed. Here, the Sages invalidated the marriage because "he acted improperly" in forcing the woman to marry him, notwithstanding that in the end she may have consented. This is an application of the principle that "the Sages have the power to uproot a Biblical law" and annul the marriage.[60] Moreover, it is impossible in this case to view the marriage as having been intended to be "subject to the conditions laid down by the Rabbis," since a coerced marriage does not have the consent of the Rabbis when it takes place, and is in fact contrary to their will. This distinguishes the case of marriage under duress from the cancellation of a divorce in the absence of the wife. In the latter case there was no defect in the marriage, which thus had the consent of the Sages when it took place. Therefore, according to the Babylonian *amoraim*, the Sages have no inherent authority to invalidate the marriage and thus abrogate Biblical law; they can annul that marriage only on the theory that it was intended to be subject to their approval and that the husband's cancellation of the *get* contrary to their will results in the retraction of their original consent and consequently in the retroactive invalidation of the marriage.[61]

57. Meiri, *Bet ha-Beḥirah*, Bava Batra 48b, s.v. Ha-ishah einah mitkaddeshet al korḥah (ed. Sofer, p. 267).

58. TB Bava Batra 48b; *see also* Ameimar's opinion, *id.*, disagreeing and holding that the law is that even such a marriage is valid.

59. *See Dikdukei Soferim*, *ad loc.*, Letter *mem*, noting that many versions read "R. Ashi" and not "Mar bar R. Ashi." "R. Ashi" seems to be the correct reading, as indicated by the later version of the incident at Naresh in TB Yevamot 110a, quoted *infra*.

60. *Tosafot*, Bava Batra 48b, s.v. Teinaḥ de-kaddesh be-khaspa.

61. All this is explained in detail in *Tosafot*, *supra* n. 60. Rashbam, *ad loc.*, s.v. Mar bar Rav Ashi amar (his first explanation), similarly explains the annulment of a coerced marriage:

This conclusion is supported by the following account of an incident discussed in the Talmud involving abduction:[62] In Naresh (a Babylonian city), a girl was betrothed while still a minor. When she became of age, her fiancé made preparations to finalize the marriage—by entry under the *ḥuppah*—but she was forcefully abducted from him and later married by the man who carried her off. R. Bruna and R. Hananel (who were both disciples of Rav) ruled that the marriage to the kidnapper was invalid and there was no need for a divorce. Legally, her marriage to the kidnapper should have been valid, since her betrothal while still a minor was not effective and she was therefore not a married woman; and since there was no duress at the time of the marriage, she was legally married to the kidnapper. The Talmud therefore sought a rationale for the ruling by R. Bruna and R. Hananel that a divorce from the kidnapper was unnecessary:

> R. Ashi said: "He acted improperly; therefore the Rabbis treat him 'improperly' and annul his marriage."
>
> Ravina said to R. Ashi: "This is understandable if he effected the marriage by means of money, but what can be said if the marriage was effected by means of sexual intercourse?"
>
> [R. Ashi responded]: "The Rabbis declared his intercourse to be fornication."

Here, too, the annulment of the marriage was not explained on the ground that "all who marry do so subject to the conditions laid down by the Rabbis," since the marriage, which followed a kidnapping, was not entered into on the basis of the Sages' consent. The rationale was that "the Sages have the power to abrogate a Biblical law," and they annulled the marriage by

---

> The Rabbis enacted that the marriage is not valid because he behaved improperly in that he forced her. Therefore, they [the Rabbis] behaved "improperly" toward him, and depart from the strict law, in that even though the marriage is valid under Biblical law, the Rabbis invalidated it. . . .

Similarly, Meiri, *Bet ha-Beḥirah, ad loc.*, states:

> Although she said, "I consent," nevertheless he behaved improperly, and so the Sages treated him "improperly" and annulled his marriage. If the marriage was effected by means of money, they expropriated it, and if effected by means of sexual intercourse, they ruled it to be an act of fornication.

The same explanation is found in Rashba's novellae, *ad loc.*, s.v. De-ha ishah: ". . . because even R. Ashi agrees that under Biblical law the woman is married; but we punish him [the man] and annul his marriage." These *rishonim* do not here rely on the rationale that "all who marry do so subject to the conditions laid down by the Rabbis," but rather explain that the Sages annulled the marriage because of the impropriety by which it was brought about. Other *rishonim,* as well as the second explanation of Rashbam, *ad loc.*, use in this case the rationale based on the conditional nature of the marriage. *See Shittah Mekubbeẓet,* Ketubbot 3a.

62. TB Yevamot 110a.

exercising that power because there was impropriety in the way the marriage had been brought about.[63]

63. *See Tosafot, ad loc.*, s.v. Lefikhakh asu lo she-lo ke-hogen ve-afke'inhu le-kiddushei mineih:

> Ri [Isaac b. Samuel] was in doubt whether the basis for the annulment is that "all who marry do so subject to the conditions laid down by the Rabbis" or whether it is that the Sages are empowered to abrogate a Biblical law. [His doubt arose] because in this passage, unlike all the other [similar] passages, no mention is made of the principle that "all who marry do so subject to the conditions laid down by the Rabbis."

Although Ri was in doubt, it would appear from the thorough reasoning contained in *Tosafot*, Bava Batra 48b, in connection with the case of a woman married under duress, that the marriage is annulled by virtue of the Sages' legislative authority to annul it. This is also evident from Meiri, *Bet ha-Beḥirah*, Yevamot 110a (ed. Dickman, pp. 414–415):

> Another man came and abducted her from the first, and they [the Rabbis] did not require a divorce from the second; because he behaved improperly, they treated him "improperly" and annulled his marriage. If it was effected by means of money, they annulled it by expropriating that money, with the result that he had given her nothing; if [the marriage was effected] by means of sexual intercourse, [they annulled it] by treating that intercourse as an act of fornication. If the marriage was effected by means of a document, I do not know how it can be annulled.

Meiri does not mention at all the principle that "all who marry do so subject to the conditions laid down by the Rabbis." This resolves an apparent inconsistency between his comments here and his explanation of TB Ketubbot 3a, s.v. Zo she-sha'alu (ed. Sofer, p. 14). In his commentary on the passage in TB Ketubbot concerning the rule that *force majeure* is immaterial in matters of divorce (*see supra* n. 49), Meiri states that the marriage in that case is annulled by virtue of the principle that "all who marry do so subject to the conditions laid down by the Rabbis"; if the marriage was effected by means of money, they expropriated the money, if by means of sexual intercourse, they treated that act as fornication; and "the same applies even if the marriage was effected by means of a document, since their [the Rabbis'] intention was that in any such case the marriage should have no validity whatsoever." In his comments on the passage in Yevamot, however, Meiri states that he does not know how a marriage effected by means of a document can be annulled.

The resolution of the inconsistency is that in the case discussed in TB Ketubbot the marriage was entered into subject to the consent of the Rabbis; and if the Rabbis determine in a particular case to withhold their consent, the marriage will be annulled whatever the means by which it was effected, since it was conditional and the condition was not fulfilled. However, in the case in TB Yevamot, the Sages annulled the marriage on the basis of their authority to invalidate legal transactions. The exercise of this authority requires recourse to the accepted legislative principles governing the permissibility of abrogating particular laws, and there is no such principle permitting abrogation in the case of marriage effected by means of a document. (*See* A. Sofer's note to *Bet ha-Beḥirah*, Ketubbot [n. 4], and S. Dickman's note to *Bet ha-Beḥirah*, Yevamot [n. 176], both of whom noted the inconsistency but failed to give an adequate explanation.) Other *rishonim*, chief among them Rashi, explain that the case in Yevamot also rests on the principle that "all who marry do so subject to the conditions laid down by the Rabbis." *See* Rashi, Yevamot 110a, s.v. Ve-ka afke'inhu le-kiddushin mineih, and s.v. Shavyuha li-ve'ilato be'ilat zenut; *Shittah Mekubbeẓet*, Ketubbot 3a. *See also supra* pp. 521–522.

Ribash's approach to the case of marriage under duress and the incident at Naresh requires examination. He (*Resp. Ribash* #399) based the authority of the Sages and the community to adopt an enactment invalidating a marriage celebrated without at least ten being present, not on the principle that "all who marry do so subject to the conditions laid

To summarize: Rabban Simeon b. Gamaliel's view that Rabban Gamaliel the Elder's enactment (which prohibited a husband from canceling a *get* in the wife's absence) made the *get* effective even after the husband's purported cancellation and authorized the wife to remarry on the strength of it was explained in the Jerusalem Talmud on the basis of the Sages' legislative authority to abrogate a Biblical law and give effect to a *get* even if Biblical law regards the *get* as canceled. In contrast to this, the Babylonian *amoraim* explained this enactment not as giving effect to the divorce and thus setting aside Biblical law, but rather as retroactively annulling the marriage on the basis of the principle they enunciated to the effect that all who marry do so subject to the conditions laid down by the Rabbis, and the Rabbis' consent may be withdrawn in certain situations, such as violation of their enactment relating to cancellation of a *get*. The result is that the marriage is necessarily annulled and the woman is free to marry someone else. Consequently, such a case involves no "uprooting" of any Biblical law, but rather the application of an already existing rule of Jewish law relating to conditional transactions.

However, even the Babylonian *amoraim* agreed that in special circumstances when a marriage is brought about through improper means, the halakhic authorities are empowered to invalidate the marriage even if their enactment abrogates Biblical law, under which the marriage is valid. The meaning of "improper means" is, however, limited to serious misconduct,

---

down by the Rabbis," but rather on the power to expropriate the groom's money, thus rendering the marriage effected with money that does not belong to him. Ribash stated:

> In the case of marriage under duress discussed in ch. "Ḥezkat" [Bava Batra], where it is also stated that because he acted improperly, they [the Sages] treated him "improperly" and annulled his marriage, and in Yevamot, ch. "Bet Shammai," in the case of the woman whom they sat on the bridal chair, where the same reason is given, there is no mention of the principle that "all who marry do so subject to the conditions laid down by the Rabbis." In these cases, since the marriage was not entered into on the basis of the Sages' consent and was in fact contrary to their will, they annulled it by expropriating the money given to the woman to effect the marriage and transforming it into a gift [to her]. However, the principle that "all who marry do so subject to the conditions laid down by the Rabbis" is required for the concluding part, which states that if the marriage was effected by means of sexual intercourse, the Rabbis declared his act to be fornication, because otherwise, on what ground could they annul a marriage effected by means of sexual intercourse?

Ribash's opening remarks are understandable; they are based on the fact that in neither of the two Talmudic passages under discussion is there mention of the rationale of "all who marry. . . ." However, that rationale is not mentioned in the concluding part either, so how can that rationale be assigned as the basis for annulling a marriage effected by means of sexual intercourse? However, according to Ri, quoted *supra*, the primary rationale—that the Sages are empowered to enact legislation that abrogates Biblical law—would apply whether the marriage was effected by means of money or by means of sexual intercourse.

such as kidnapping or duress. In such cases, the impropriety is not cured even if by the time the marriage takes place the woman consents.[64]

The rationale of the *amoraim* that a marriage may be annulled *ab initio* in certain circumstances on the basis of the principle that "all who marry do so subject to the conditions laid down by the Rabbis" was a significant innovation. It gave rise to many questions by the leading *rishonim*[65] and

64. *See, e.g.*, M Kiddushin 3:1: "If a man says to his fellow, 'Go and be my agent to betroth So-and-so,' and he [the agent] goes and betroths her to himself, her betrothal [to the agent] is valid." TB Kiddushin 58b quotes a *baraita:* "What he has done is done, but he has acted dishonestly" (so also in *Tosefta* Yevamot 4:4). The betrothal to the agent is effective because the woman, who was unmarried, agreed to be betrothed to him; but the agent acted dishonestly, since he was commissioned to betroth the woman for his principal and not for himself. As to the rule stated in the *mishnah*, the *rishonim* ask, "Is this a new rule [which needs to be stated]? It is obvious [that she is betrothed to the agent]!" (*Tosafot*, Kiddushin, *ad loc.*, s.v. Ha-omer ve-halakh ve-kiddeshah le-aẓmo mekuddeshet). Rashba, in his novellae, *ad loc.*, s.v. Ve-halakh ve-kiddeshah, answered: "It could be argued that since he [the agent] acted dishonestly and behaved improperly, they [the Sages] should act toward him 'improperly' and should annul his betrothal, as in the case of TB Yevamot . . . where another [man] came and snatched her [the bride] away. Therefore it [the *mishnah*] tells us [that this is not the law]."

In other words, although the betrothal here followed a dishonest act, that act is not sufficiently egregious to justify the annulment of a betrothal valid under Biblical law. The same point was made by Ran to Alfasi, Kiddushin, *ad loc.*, s.v. Ha-omer le-ḥavero (fol. 23b in printed editions of Alfasi). *See also* Weiss, *supra* n. 47 at 392. *Resp. Rashba*, I, #1185 gives the same explanation and adds that this is also the reason why a marriage is not annulled where the witnesses to the marriage are incompetent by rabbinic law. However, Rashba held that not only the cases of improper behavior justifying annulment but also the cases to which the principle "all who marry . . . " may be applied are limited to those instances explicitly specified in the Talmud; *see also infra* pp. 852–855.

65. The fact that a marriage is annulled *ab initio*, as if it had never taken place, must, of necessity, raise many questions regarding the period during which the "marriage" existed until it was annulled. For instance, on what basis can any married woman who commits adultery be punished? The law is that to be guilty, an accused must have been warned, categorically and unequivocally, immediately before the prohibited act, that the proposed conduct is unlawful; and surely, any warning given to a woman about to commit adultery would not be categorical or unequivocal, since it may turn out that her marriage will be annulled and thus she was never really married. Also, with the possibility of retroactive annulment, a man could protect his "sister's daughter" to whom he was married and who committed adultery, by causing the marriage to be retroactively annulled. In a similar manner, *mamzerim* could be "purified." For further discussion, *see Shittah Mekubbeẓet*, Ketubbot 3a, in the name of various commentators; *Tosafot*, Gittin 33a, s.v. Ve-afke'inhu rabbanan le-kiddushin mineih; Rashba, Novellae to Gittin 33a, s.v. Kol di-mekaddesh; *Tosafot Yeshanim*, Yevamot 90b, s.v. Shavyuhu rabbanan li-ve'ilato be'ilat zenut.

Some commentators are of the opinion that even in the case of such an annulment, the marriage is dissolved only prospectively, from the date of the annulment. *See Shittah Mekubbeẓet*, Ketubbot 3a, s.v. U-ve-shittah katuv (ed. Ẓioni, p. 48). However, most *rishonim* disagree, and the plain meaning of the Talmudic passages is inconsistent with merely prospective invalidity. According to many *rishonim*, such annulment is available only where there is at least some sort of bill of divorcement (*serekh shel get*) and not when there is no

subsequently provided one of the major methods for solving many problems in the law of marriage and divorce in the post-Talmudic period.[66]

---

bill of divorcement at all—such as in the cases recorded in TB Ketubbot 3a and Gittin 33a and 73a—and it is therefore not available to free *agunot. See Shittah Mekubbeẓet,* Ketubbot 3a, and particularly the statement of Rashba quoted there, s.v. Ve-ha-Rashba z.l. katav (ed. Ẓioni, p. 50); Meiri, *Bet ha-Beḥirah,* Ketubbot 3a, s.v. Kol she-amru (ed. Sofer, p. 14). *See also supra* p. 528 n. 147. Many additional questions concerning the principle "all who marry . . ." arose in the course of its use in the post-Talmudic period. *See* Freimann, *Kiddushin ve-Nissu'in,* pp. 13–14, and the discussion *infra* pp. 846–879.

66. *See infra* pp. 656–665, 846–879. It should be pointed out that in the amoraic period there was not always unanimity as to the need or justification for specific enactments. *See, e.g.,* the enactment of the *prosbul* (*supra* pp. 511–513) which, according to Samuel (TB Gittin 36b), constitutes an act of usurpation on the part of the court, whose taking of the debtor's money is against the law, since Biblical law provides that the sabbatical year cancels the debt. Therefore, Samuel said, "If I had the power and authority, I would abrogate it [*i.e.,* Hillel's enactment]." (*Id.*) R. Naḥman, however, took the opposite view and considered Hillel's enactment good and useful legislation: "But R. Naḥman said, 'I would uphold it.'" He even extended it by an enactment that every loan should be considered as having been made on a promissory note filed with the court, so that even if the creditor did not write a *prosbul,* the result would be the same as if he had—the debt would not be canceled by the sabbatical year.

Chapter 17
LEGISLATION IN THE GEONIC PERIOD

I. INTRODUCTION

During the geonic period, which lasted from the end of the savoraic period (*i.e.*, from the end of the sixth or middle of the seventh century C.E.) until the middle of the eleventh century,[1] far-reaching changes took place in the economic condition of Babylonian Jewry:

> In this period, the economic structure of Babylonian Jewry completely changed. Farming, which had been the economic mainstay of Babylonian Jews, was increasingly abandoned. Like their brethren in the other lands of the diaspora, almost all of them became artisans or engaged in commerce. There were many reasons for this, including government expropriation of Jewish-owned lands for allotment among retired soldiers, officers, and government officials. In addition, heavy taxes, recurring wars, rebellions, and disorders played their part in contributing to the decline of agriculture among the population as a whole and particularly among Jews.[2]

The commerce of Babylonian Jews was not confined to Babylonia; in the wake of the great Moslem conquests in the geonic period, it expanded across North Africa and other countries. New Jewish settlements were es-

1. *See supra* pp. 42–43.
2. Assaf, *Geonim*, pp. 14–15.

tablished in those lands, and the Babylonian scholars and laymen corresponded and transacted business with them. The expansion of commerce brought with it changes in the nature of credit. Moneylending, which formerly served mainly as a means of financial aid and support and was generally confined within a narrow geographical area, was transformed into a mechanism for the extension of credit, which increasingly played a substantial role in international commercial life.

Along with the economic changes came social changes and changes in mores. The expansion of commerce made it more difficult to discover the financial condition of debtors and easier for debtors to conceal their property from creditors. A debtor's plea of inability to pay was not always made because of distress and poverty; at times, it was motivated by a desire to make use of other people's money by hindering, delaying, and defrauding creditors in the multitude of subtle ways possible in a developed commercial system.[3]

The change from rural to urban life also produced moral upheavals in the Jewish family.[4] These economic, social, and moral changes presented the halakhic authorities with many problems demanding legal solution. A substantial part of the process by which these problems were solved involved legal interpretation, which is reflected in one of the important literary sources of Jewish law—the responsa literature, which was then beginning to develop.[5]

In this period, generally speaking, Babylonia was still the most important and authoritative center for the entire Jewish people. From all over the world, Jews turned to the Babylonian authorities for answers to all halakhic questions; and the *geonim* attempted in their responsa to solve the problems by interpreting the existing law. However, when interpretation of the *Halakhah* could not provide a solution, the *geonim* used the other legal method designed for this very situation, namely, legislation.

The *geonim* adopted their enactments cooperatively with the various other agencies active in the leadership of Jewish communal life:

> In order to enact a *takkanah*, the *geonim* who headed the two academies [Pumbedita and Sura], apparently together with the leading scholars in the academies, would confer with the exilarch. They included the exilarch not only so that he would lend to the *takkanah* the force of his political power but also because the exilarch and the *geonim* had joint authority over the regula-

3. *See infra* pp. 651–654 regarding the oath "I have nothing" (*ein li*). *See also* Elon, *Ḥerut*, pp. 38–39, and *infra* pp. 646–648 as to collection of debts out of personalty, and pp. 649–651 as to the enactment relating to the appointment of an agent to conduct litigation.

4. *See, e.g., infra* pp. 658–665 as to the enactment relating to the grant of a divorce to a *moredet* (wife who refuses to cohabit with her husband).

5. *See infra* pp. 1468–1473.

tion of legal affairs in the lands of the great Baghdad Caliphate. In the territory of the caliphate, there were, as is known, three "domains" or spheres of influence, namely, Sura, Pumbedita, and the exilarch. In all the Jewish communities, the judges were appointed by that *gaon* to whom they were subject [*i.e.*, Sura or Pumbedita] or by the exilarch; and these authorities would also remove any judge upon well-founded complaints against him. In order to present a unified front in any legal activity, it was therefore necessary to include the exilarch.

When all three participants agreed to an enactment, they would publish it in letters sealed with the exilarch's ring and "the four seals of the domains," and they would add that any judge who would not follow it "shall be removed and an order divesting and transferring his authority shall be recorded against him." The enactments were binding and administratively enforceable within the territory of the caliphate. However, the geonic enactments were recognized far beyond the boundaries of Babylonia and were given effect in all Jewish courts—even in places where the *geonim* had no political power, such as the countries of Christian Europe.[6] In this respect, the power of the *geonim* was greater than the power of the exilarch.[7]

6. As will be demonstrated *infra* (pp. 651, 661–665, 668), not all geonic enactments were accepted by all Jewish centers or all halakhic authorities; this fact distinguishes geonic from Talmudic enactments. This distinction is especially emphasized by Maimonides in his attitude to the various geonic enactments (*see, e.g., MT,* Ishut 14:14, 16:7–9; Sheluḥin ve-Shutafin 3:7). Maimonides, *MT,* Introduction, states:

> Thus, Ravina and R. Ashi and their colleagues were the last of the great Sages of Israel who recorded the Oral Law, issued decrees (*gezerot*), adopted enactments (*takkanot*), and instituted customs (*minhagot*). Their decrees, enactments, and customs were recognized by the entire Jewish people wherever they lived. After the redaction of the Talmud by R. Ashi's court and the completion of that task in the lifetime of his son, the Jews became dispersed throughout the world. . . . After the completion of the Talmud, when a court in any country issued decrees, adopted enactments, or instituted customs for the Jews of its own country or of a number of countries, its rulings did not gain acceptance by the entire Jewish people, because of the distances between the [Jewish] settlements and the difficulties of communication.
>
> Since the court of any particular country is composed of individuals [whose authority has not been universally accepted], and since the High Court of seventy-one [members] had already ceased to exist many years before the redaction of the Talmud, the residents of one country cannot be compelled to conduct themselves according to the custom and practice of another country, nor is a court in one country under any obligation to issue a decree that has been issued by a court of another country. . . . This applies to laws, decrees, enactments, and customs that originated after the Talmud had been redacted; but everything in the Babylonian Talmud is binding on all Israel. (*Rambam la-Am,* Mosad Ha-Rav Kook, pp. 12–13.)

See also infra p. 1228 n. 138. Notwithstanding this clear distinction between the Talmudic and post-Talmudic periods, the Jewish centers throughout the world during most of the geonic period did recognize the authority of the rules and enactments promulgated by the Babylonian *geonim.* It was only from the tenth century C.E. on that legislation for the most part took on an essentially local character. *See infra* pp. 668–669.

7. Assaf, *Geonim,* p. 62. Not all enactments were adopted simultaneously by the two academies and the exilarch; some were adopted by one academy and later accepted by the

During the geonic period, enactments were adopted in various areas of Jewish law—obligations, property acquisition, family law, procedure, evidence, and criminal law.[8] The source of our knowledge of these enactments is the halakhic literature of the geonic and subsequent periods. There are also many enactments that cannot be attributed with any certainty to the geonic period. It should be remembered that even the use of the title *gaon* does not necessarily establish that the person called by that title was a halakhic scholar who lived in the geonic period.[9] On the other hand, it is reasonable to assume, even though there is no conclusive evidence, that there are many laws known to us from the post-geonic period that have their legal source in legislation enacted during the geonic period.[10]

II. ENACTMENTS OF THE *GEONIM*

A. Equalizing Real and Personal Property for the Satisfaction of Debts

According to Talmudic law, a widow may recover the amount of her *ketubbah* only from the real property of her deceased husband's estate. Similarly, a creditor who seeks to collect his debt from the debtor's heirs can collect only from the real property inherited from the decedent. Thus, the Talmud states:

---

other authorities. Occasionally, a particular enactment was not accepted unanimously; *see infra* pp. 655–656, as to the abrogation of the *ketubbah* clause concerning inheritance rights of the wife's sons, and *see* H. Tykocinski, *Takkanot ha-Geonim* [Geonic Enactments] (hereinafter, *Takkanot*), p. 124.

8. H. Tykocinski devoted an entire volume to geonic enactments—*Die Gaonäischen Verordnungen,* Berlin, 1929, translated into Hebrew by M. Ḥavaẓelet in 1960 and cited herein according to the Hebrew edition. *See also* Weiss, *Dor Dor ve-Doreshav,* IV, pp. 177–184; Assaf, *Geonim,* pp. 62–64; I. Schepansky, "Takkanot ha-Geonim" [Geonic Enactments], *Ha-Darom,* XXIV (1967), pp. 135–197 (with regard to this article, *see Ha-Darom,* XXVI (1968), pp. 203–210); M. Ḥavaẓelet, "Yaḥas ha-Rambam le-Takkanot ha-Geonim" [Maimonides' Attitude to Geonic Enactments], *Talpiot,* VII (1958), pp. 99–125. The geonic enactments quoted in the responsa of the Spanish and North African halakhic authorities from the eleventh to the fifteenth century are collected in M. Elon (ed.), *Digest of the Responsa Literature of Spain and North Africa, Legal Digest,* II (1986), pp. 542–543.

9. *See, e.g.,* the comments of Maimonides in *MT,* Introduction (*Rambam la-Am, supra* n. 6 at 14): "All the halakhic authorities who lived after the redaction of the Talmud, who built upon it and were renowned for their wisdom and scholarship, are called *geonim.* All these *geonim* who flourished in the Land of Israel, Babylonia, Spain, and France. . . ." The *geonim* are also occasionally called by other appellations, such as *rabboteinu* ("our teachers") and even *rabbanan savorai* ("our savoraic rabbis"). *See* Elon, *Ḥerut,* p. 46 n. 42.

10. *See* Tykocinski, *Takkanot,* p. 124; Schepansky, *supra* n. 8 at 174ff., 192–193.

> Rava said: "The law is that payment may be exacted from real property but not from personal property, whether for a *ketubbah*, for support, or for outfitting for marriage [*i.e.*, dowry]."[11]

In the Talmudic period, when land was the major and common form of wealth, this rule was consistent with economic reality: the widow and the creditor were assured of collecting their debt from the estate because the estate generally included real property; in fact, they never relied on personal property to assure satisfaction of their claim. In the geonic period, when land was no longer the common form of wealth, it became necessary to permit creditors to collect their debts from the personal as well as the real property of the deceased debtor's estate, in order to promote the free flow of credit and "so that the door should not be closed to borrowers."[12] This change in the law of creditors' rights was accomplished by an enactment adopted at the beginning of the geonic period[13] and extensively discussed both in that period and later.[14]

A responsum on this subject was written by the Gaon Moses b. Jacob, who headed the *yeshivah* (academy) in Sura in the first half of the ninth century C.E. The responsum provides an enlightening perspective on the general approach of the *geonim* to legislation. The question concerned the collection of a *ketubbah* or a debt from personal property. Moses b. Jacob responded:[15]

> It is not now customary to include in a *ketubbah* a clause saying, "It may be collected from real or personal property in my lifetime and after my death"; and although a promissory note includes the language "from real or personal property," it does not state "in my lifetime and after my death." Nevertheless, the Rabbis enacted that a *ketubbah* owed to a woman and a debt owed to a creditor may be collected even from the personal property [inherited by the heirs], since here [in Babylonia] most people [in the Jewish community] do not have land, and the later Rabbis enacted a *takkanah* to prevent the closing of the door to borrowers and to assure a woman that her *ketubbah* will be paid. They patterned this enactment on previous legislation enacted by the prior Sages in every generation, and they relied on a number of reasons that need not be mentioned here.

11. TB Ketubbot 51a, 69b.

12. As to this rationale generally, *see supra* pp. 605–608.

13. For a detailed discussion of the probable date of this enactment, *see* Tykocinski, *Takkanot*, pp. 43ff.

14. *See* Tykocinski, *Takkanot*, pp. 30ff; B.M. Lewin, *Oẓar ha-Geonim*, Ketubbot, Responsa, pp. 210–213.

15. *Ḥemdah Genuzah* #65; *see also* #62 under the heading, "Mar Rav Moshe Gaon"; *Oẓar ha-Geonim*, *supra* n. 14 at 210.

> However, in other places, where most people do own land, if there is no clause stating "from personal property in my lifetime and after my death," then the *ketubbah* of a woman and the debt of a creditor may be collected only from land; if there is such a clause, . . . they may also collect from the personal property of the decedent.

The enactment gained quick acceptance, and the *geonim* and the exilarch required all judges to follow it: "Any judge who does not permit collection by a creditor or for a woman's *ketubbah* from personal property shall be removed, and an order divesting and transferring his authority shall be recorded against him."[16]

In the geonic period, there was still disagreement as to the types of obligations to which the enactment applied; but the enactment was finally accepted as being applicable to various obligations—such as the *ketubbah*, a debt resulting from a loan, and the payment of compensation for injury or theft—and it introduced a substantial change in the Jewish law of creditors' rights.[17] In contrast to the original Talmudic law that a debt could be recovered only from the decedent's land in the possession of the heirs,[18] it was now possible for a debt to be collected from personal property as well, thus providing the creditor additional assurance that the debt would be paid.[19]

16. *Oẓar ha-Geonim, supra* n. 14 at 212.

17. *See* Maimonides, *MT*, Malveh ve-Loveh 11:11; Ishut 16:7–9, 17:5–6, 19:17–18; Nizkei Mamon 8:12; Gezelah va-Avedah 5:6. Maimonides attests to the fact that the geonic enactment had spread "throughout all Jewish courts" (Nizkei Mamon 8:12), "throughout all the Jewish courts in the world" (Malveh ve-Loveh 11:11), and "throughout most of Israel" (Ishut 16:7). However, Maimonides limits the binding effect of the enactment and distinguishes between the authoritativeness of that enactment and the authoritativeness of Talmudic enactments (*see MT*, Malveh ve-Loveh 11:11, Ishut 16:9).

18. The Talmud itself mentions situations in which it was possible to recover from personalty in the possession of heirs, because of reliance by the creditor (*see* TB Ketubbot 67a and Rashi, *ad loc.*, s.v. Asmakhtaihu alaihu); but these were isolated cases and did not substantially modify the general procedures for collection of debts. *See also Tosafot, ad loc.*, s.v. Gemalim shel aravya ishah govah parna mehem; Rashbam, Bava Batra 174a, s.v. Rav Huna bereih de-Rav Yehoshu'a amar, also attesting to the practice in his time (twelfth century C.E.): "It seems to me that nowadays when people do not ordinarily own land, even though the basic law is that the decedent's creditor has no lien on the heirs' personalty, the rule presently applied is that he can recover [his debt] from the personalty their father left them." Further on in his discussion, Rashbam cited the geonic enactment and TB Ketubbot 67a, cited *supra*.

19. For further developments concerning this enactment and for a general discussion of the question of satisfaction of debts from personalty, *see* M. Elon, EJ, XI, pp. 227–232, s.v. Lien (reprinted in *Principles*, pp. 287–294).

B. Power of Attorney from the Plaintiff to Litigate against the Defendant; "Four Cubits in the Land of Israel"

Another important enactment resulting from the wider scope and increased sophistication of commercial life permitted a plaintiff to authorize an agent to litigate against the defendant.

According to Talmudic law, if the plaintiff does not appear in person at the trial but sends an agent to conduct the case for him, the defendant may plead against the agent: "You are not my adversary." In order to overcome this preliminary objection, the plaintiff had to assign the claim to the agent, thus establishing the agent as the adversary of the defendant. This assignment was a fiction solely for the purpose of the litigation; when the agent recovered from the defendant, it was the real plaintiff, the principal, who was entitled to the recovery.

Because the effectiveness of a power of attorney to conduct the case on behalf of the plaintiff was based on an assignment of the claim to the agent, it followed that the power of attorney could be used only in cases in which the claim was legally assignable. There were convenient methods to convey land or transfer ownership of articles deposited with the defendant; a claim for the payment of funds deposited with the defendant could be transferred incidental to a conveyance of land. However, if the object of the litigation was to recover money borrowed by means of an oral loan transaction, there was no way of assigning the claim to an agent in the absence of the debtor.[20] In the Talmudic period, it was thus possible to give a power of attorney to conduct litigation to recover deposited chattels or specific funds, but there was no way to give a power of attorney to conduct litigation to recover intangible property, such as a loan.[21]

This legal situation no longer satisfied the needs of commercial and economic life. Commerce transcended the boundaries of cities and countries, and transactions were entered into between people at a distance from each other. If a debtor lived far away from the creditor, the creditor could not sue without traveling to the debtor's residence and personally bringing suit there—a considerable hardship that impeded healthy economic devel-

20. Assignment of a debt can be effected in two ways: "A meeting of the three" (*ma'amad sheloshtan, see supra* p. 584), for which the presence of the debtor is required, or delivery of a written assignment of the promissory note, which is possible, of course, only if the loan was documented by a note. Maimonides, *MT,* Sheluḥin ve-Shutafin 3:7.

21. *See* Maimonides, *MT,* Sheluḥin ve-Shutafin 3:1–7. For various opinions on the matter, *see* commentaries to *MT, ad loc.*, and *Tosafot,* Bava Kamma 70a, s.v. Ametaltelin de-kafreih, and commentaries, *ad loc. See also* Gulak, *Yesodei,* I, p. 120, IV, pp. 54–56. *Cf.* the resistance of the common law that had to be overcome before choses in action finally became assignable.

opment. The situation was rectified by a geonic enactment.[22] Maimonides summarized this enactment and described the legal situation that preceded it and the factors that brought about its adoption as follows:[23]

> If one has deposited money with another and wishes to authorize an agent to recover it for him, its transfer by a *kinyan* [*i.e.,* its acquisition by *kinyan sudar*—a symbolic barter] is not effective because money cannot be acquired by barter. What then can he do? He can convey to the agent the smallest piece of land and transfer ownership of the money incidental to the conveyance, so that the agent may recover the money; [this power of attorney is thereupon effective and] the agent then can proceed to sue the defendant and recover. If, however, the claim is for repayment of a loan, the creditor cannot write a power of attorney for it.
>
> Such is the law as it appears to me from the Talmud. The *geonim,* however, enacted that one may write a power of attorney even when the claim is for repayment of a loan. This was done so that no one will take another's money and then go off to another country.[24]

The most effective method of assigning a claim for the purpose of litigation was a transfer incidental to the conveyance of land. As we have seen, however, Babylonian Jews in this period did not generally own land, and it was therefore difficult to use that method of transfer. In order to overcome this difficulty, some of the *geonim* adopted an additional interesting enactment—that every individual Jew, even if he owns no land, may nevertheless assign his claim to his agent incidental to the conveyance of the four cubits in the Land of Israel which, in theory, every Jew owns:

> With regard to these four cubits, when one actually owns no land, the Rabbis have affirmed that there is no Jew who does not own four cubits in the Land of Israel. If you argue that it was taken away many generations ago [when the Land of Israel was taken away from the Jews], it is the law that land can never be effectively stolen,[25] and it therefore still belongs to the people of Israel, as it is written: "The earth [lit. "land"] is the Lord's."[26]

22. For sources, *see* Tykocinski, *Takkanot,* pp. 81ff.

23. *MT,* Sheluḥin ve-Shutafin 3:7.

24. A similar rationale is given by Rava for permitting recovery by a creditor in the absence of the debtor: "So that no one will take another's money and leave and settle in another country, which would lead to the door being closed to borrowers" (TB Ketubbot 88a). The geonic enactment paved the way in Jewish law for the use of a power of attorney for any kind of claim, ". . . since, after the enactment of the *geonim,* there is no matter for which a power of attorney may not be written" (*Arukh ha-Shulḥan,* ḤM 123:3).

25. *See, e.g.,* TB Bava Kamma 95a.

26. Exodus 9:29 (another version, following Exodus 19:5, has: "Indeed all the earth is Mine." *See Oẓar ha-Geonim,* Kiddushin, Responsa, p. 62). The responsum as quoted in the text is from Assaf, *Teshuvot ha-Geonim* #105 (p. 95). *See also Oẓar ha-Geonim,* Kiddushin,

The legal fiction on which this enactment was based aroused strong opposition in the geonic period and thereafter. Maimonides wrote:[27]

> They [the *geonim*] further provided that if a principal authorizes an agent to recover money that he [the principal] has deposited with another or to sue another for the payment of a debt, and he [the principal] has no land, he can transfer to him [the agent] four cubits of land from his [the principal's] share in the Land of Israel and, incidental to the land, transfer to him [the agent] ownership of the money. The basis for this enactment is extremely tenuous and flimsy.[28]

This second geonic enactment, providing for assignment of a claim incidental to the conveyance of four cubits in the Land of Israel, was not accepted. However, the assignment of a claim incidental to the conveyance of land at a time when ownership of land was rare throughout the diaspora became possible in the course of time by means of a different legal fiction.[29]

C. The Oath "I Have Nothing" in Proceedings to Enforce Civil Judgments

The procedure for the enforcement of judgments in Jewish law is extremely solicitous of the debtor's personal freedom and the basic necessities for the debtor's survival. This fundamental approach rests on many Biblical verses admonishing creditors not to act harshly toward debtors, not to enter a debtor's home to recover a pledge, not to take in pledge the lower or upper millstone that a debtor needs for his livelihood, etc.[30] These rules are exten-

---

Responsa, p. 60; Tykocinski, *Takkanot*, pp. 85–86. In another source (*Oẓar ha-Geonim, supra* at 63) the reading is: "For there is no Jew who does not own land in the Land of Israel, because the gentiles who are in possession do not own [the land], since the rule is that land can never be effectively stolen; and the Land of Israel is thus in our ownership forever, even though we do not control it."

27. *MT*, Sheluḥin ve-Shutafin 3:7.

28. *See Kesef Mishneh, ad loc.*, to the effect that Maimonides is referring only to the enactment concerning the four cubits in the Land of Israel. *See also Oẓar ha-Geonim*, Kiddushin, Responsa, p. 60.

29. The rule was established that inasmuch as the transferor represents that he owns land, he is estopped to deny ownership by virtue of the principle that the admission of a party is as effective as a hundred witnesses. *See Tosafot*, Bava Batra 44b, s.v. De-lo havah leih ar'a me-olam:

> It seems to Rabbenu Tam that the reason is as follows: Since he represents that he owns land—and the representation is against his interest because it is by means of the land that he makes the transfer to the other party—even if a number of witnesses deny [that he owns land], the admission of a party is equal to a hundred witnesses, and we do not have to fear any apparent untruthfulness on his part.

See also Sh. Ar. ḤM 113:2 and commentaries thereto, *ad loc.*

30. Exodus 22:24–26; Deuteronomy 24:6,10–13.

sively discussed in Talmudic sources[31] and are summarized by Maimonides as follows:[32]

> The rule of Biblical law is that when a creditor demands payment, and the debtor is found to have assets, his [the debtor's] needs are to be arranged for[33] and the remainder is given to the creditor, as we have stated.[34] If no assets belonging to the debtor are found, or if only exempt assets are found, the debtor may go free; he is not to be imprisoned,[35] nor is he told to "bring proof that you are poor," nor is he subjected to an oath [that he has nothing]—as is the practice among non-Jews—for it is written: "Do not act toward him as a creditor."[36] The creditor, however, is told, "If you know of assets belonging to the debtor, you may seize them."

A developed economic and commercial system could not survive under this idyllic state of law, as many sources from the geonic period confirm. In one responsum, Hai Gaon observed[37] that when promissory notes of certain merchants were presented and the court ordered payment, the merchants pleaded: "We have nothing of our own, and the merchandise in our possession belongs to others and not to us." The *gaon* ruled that there is no basis for a presumption of poverty for such people that would absolve them from paying the obligations they indisputably owe.

The *geonim* therefore sought a method of facilitating the collection of debts. One such measure, apparently enacted at the beginning of the geonic period,[38] was the requirement that a debtor who claims that he has no assets with which to pay a debt must take "the oath 'I have nothing'" (*shevu'at ein li*) or, as it was also called, "the oath of suspicion" (*shevu'at ha-ḥashad*). This enactment appears in many sources[39] and was summarized by Maimonides as follows:[40]

31. For details, *see* Elon, *Ḥerut,* pp. 1–37.

32. *MT,* Malveh ve-Loveh 2:1.

33. *I.e.,* the debtor is left with the minimum necessities for his livelihood. For details, *see* M. Elon, EJ, VI, pp. 1007–1020, s.v. Execution (civil) (reprinted in *Principles,* pp. 621–633).

34. *MT,* Malveh ve-Loveh 1:7.

35. Jewish law rejected enslavement or imprisonment for debt. Imprisonment for debt was applied in Jewish law only from the fourteenth century C.E. on, as a result of social conditions that made it necessary, but even then only against a debtor who concealed his assets from his creditors. It was forbidden to impose any form of imprisonment on a debtor too poor to repay his debt. For a detailed discussion, *see* Elon, *Ḥerut,* pp. 1–37, 111–237; *id.,* EJ, VIII, pp. 1303–1309, s.v. Imprisonment for debt (reprinted in *Principles,* pp. 633–640). *See also infra* pp. 1635–1637.

36. Exodus 22:24.

37. Harkavy, *Zikkaron la-Rishonim* #182 (mistakenly printed as #184; *see id.* at 357); Elon, *Ḥerut,* pp. 40ff.

38. Elon, *Ḥerut,* p. 39 text and notes.

39. *See* Tykocinski, *Takkanot,* pp. 51ff.; Elon, *Ḥerut,* pp. 46ff.

40. *MT,* Malveh ve-Loveh 2:2.

> When the first *geonim* after the redaction of the Talmud[41] saw that deceivers had multiplied and that the door had become closed to borrowers [*i.e.*, people refrained from lending money to others on account of apprehension that at the time payment would fall due the debtor would secrete his assets and claim "I have nothing" and the creditor would have no sanction against him], they enacted that a debtor, while holding a sacred object,[42] is to be subjected to a strict oath, similar to the Biblical oath, that he has nothing over and above his exemption, that he has not secreted anything with others, and that he has made no gift on condition that it be returned to him.
>
> He is to include in this oath that whatever he will earn or will come into his possession or control as his own he will not spend on food, clothing, or support of his wife and children[43] or give away as a gift to any person whatsoever, but that he will take out of whatever he obtains only enough to satisfy his personal need for food for thirty days and clothing for twelve months. It is not to be the food of gluttons or drunkards or what is served before kings, nor the clothing of nobles or high officers, but it must be consistent with his own station in life. Whatever is over and above his own needs, he must continually keep paying to his creditor until the entire debt has been paid. At the beginning, a ban is to be pronounced[44] against anyone who knows of property, visible or concealed, belonging to the debtor and does not notify the court.

Public morality weakened, deceivers multiplied, and it was no longer possible to maintain the Biblical rule that a debtor pleading poverty must be deemed to be credible and may not be subjected to an oath. Consequently, the *geonim* enacted that the debtor should be subjected to a strict oath, similar to a Biblical oath, to verify that his plea is true. At first, this oath was imposed even on a debtor who was generally known to be poor, on the theory that the oath does not involve any sanction but is merely for the purpose of proof and clarification. However, with the passage of time, Maimonides,[45] and subsequently other authorities, determined the law to be as follows:

> If one is generally known to be poor, honest, and a person of integrity, this being manifest and known to the judge and to the majority of the people,

41. *See* Elon, *Ḥerut,* p. 46 n. 42.

42. The person taking the oath holds a sacred object, such as a Torah scroll or phylacteries. *See also supra* p. 620 n. 310.

43. According to Hai Gaon, the arrangement made for the debtor includes the needs of his wife and children, and this was the practice in Kairouan. *See* Elon, *Ḥerut,* p. 47 n. 43; *id.*, EJ, VI, pp. 1007–1020, s.v. Execution (civil) (reprinted in *Principles,* pp. 621–633).

44. This is the "ordinary" ban imposed in connection with various civil claims; this ban was also enacted by the *geonim. See* Tykocinski, *Takkanot,* pp. 90–98.

45. *MT,* Malveh ve-Loveh 2:4.

and his creditor seeks to subject him to an oath under this *takkanah,* and it is clear that it is not enough for the creditor that the debtor is poor but the creditor desires to torment him with this oath, to cause him distress, and to disgrace him in public so as to take revenge on him, or to force him to go to a non-Jew to borrow money, or to use his wife's property[46] to pay the debt in order to be spared this oath, then it seems to me that a God-fearing judge is forbidden to subject him to this oath.

If he [the creditor] does demand the oath, he violates the negative commandment of the Torah, "Do not act toward him as a creditor." Moreover, it is fitting for the judge to reprimand the creditor and expel him [banish him from the judge's presence] because he acts out of callousness and ill will. For the *geonim* enacted this *takkanah* only because of the deceivers, and it is written,[47] "Until your fellow claims it [lit. "searches it out"][48]—this means 'search him out,' [*i.e.,*] see whether he is attempting to deceive you or or not." Since he is known to be poor and not a deceiver,[49] it is forbidden to subject him to the oath.[50]

46. There is no lien on a wife's property (whether *melog* or *ẓon barzel*) in favor of her husband's creditors, and the creditors cannot collect from such property. *See* Sh. Ar. ḤM 97:26. As to *melog* and *ẓon barzel* property, *see supra* p. 572 n. 118.

47. TB Bava Meẓi'a 28a.

48. Deuteronomy 22:2.

49. *See further MT,* Malveh ve-Loveh 2:4 for the reverse situation:

> I also say that [if the debtor is] a person known to be a deceiver and one whose business methods are dishonest and he is reckoned to have assets although he claims to have none and is eager to take the oath provided for by this enactment, the oath should not be administered to him. [*See Be'ur ha-Gra,* ḤM 87, subpar. 113, citing a source for this from *Leviticus Rabbah* 6:3: "We do not administer an oath to one who is eager to swear"; *see* n. 29 in *MT,* ed. *Rambam la-Am, ad loc.*]. If a judge has the power to compel such a person to pay his creditor or to impose a ban on him until he pays, he should do so, since he is reckoned [to have assets from which to pay], because payment of a debt is a religious obligation [TB Ketubbot 86a, and *see supra* pp. 117–119]. The general rule is that a judge is permitted to take any of these steps as long as his only motive is to pursue justice as we have been commanded to pursue it [Deuteronomy 16:20, interpreted in TB Sanhedrin 32b as referring to a dishonest claim] and not to favor one of the parties; and he will be rewarded as long as his actions are for the sake of Heaven.

See Maggid Mishneh and *Leḥem Mishneh* and notes in ed. *Rambam la-Am, ad loc.,* as to this last-quoted passage.

50. Close to the end of the geonic period, Hai Gaon instituted the sanction of a severe ban, involving total ostracism from Jewish society, to be imposed on the debtor for a fixed period of ninety days. This sanction was not imposed on debtors known to be poor but on those who claimed to have no assets and who were suspected of secreting their assets to evade payment of debts. However, by the eleventh century C.E., this sanction met with strong opposition and was never incorporated into Jewish law. *See* Elon, *Ḥerut,* pp. 38–46.

D. Abrogation of the *Ketubbah* Clause Concerning Inheritance Rights of a Wife's Sons

Another enactment responding to changes in social outlook in the geonic period was the enactment abrogating the *ketubbah* clause concerning the wife's sons (*ketubbat benin dikhrin*).

We have previously discussed[51] the early enactment involving the clause in the *ketubbah* concerning the wife's sons. The clause was designed to assure that the property given by a father to his daughter at the time of her marriage would remain in her family and would not pass to a different family as a result of her husband's inheriting it from her. This early enactment provided that only her own sons inherit the property with which she came into the marriage and that the husband's sons by other wives do not share in this property. The purpose of the enactment was to encourage fathers to give dowries to their daughters—"to encourage a man to give to his daughter as much as he gives to his son."[52] A father would be more inclined to give property to his daughter if assured that it would pass at her death to her children and not to a different family.

Various sources indicate that particularly in the first part of the geonic period there were *geonim* who nullified the clause concerning the wife's sons. A number of reasons are given,[53] the main one apparently being a change in society's attitude toward gifts of property by a father to his daughter. Mattathias Gaon (Pumbedita, second half of the ninth century C.E.) is quoted as saying: "At this time, the clause concerning the wife's sons is not used because the only reason for it was to encourage a man to give to his daughter as much as to his son, and now the custom is to give more and more."[54] In other words, in this period, the practice was to give "more and more" to a daughter regardless of whether or not the *ketubbah* contained the clause, and there no longer was any need for legislative encouragement of such gifts. A more detailed analysis is contained in a responsum of Hananiah b. Judah Gaon (Pumbedita, second half of the tenth century C.E.):[55]

> Our direction and communication to you on this matter came at the time that we invoked the *ketubbah* clause concerning the wife's sons. But, for a number of years, this clause has been abrogated in our *yeshivah* (academy), and we do not make use of it. . . . And why was the clause concerning the wife's sons abrogated? Because it is questionable for a number of reasons. . . . In addi-

51. *Supra* pp. 575–578.
52. TB Ketubbot 52b.
53. *See* the responsum of Hananiah Gaon, quoted immediately *infra*.
54. *Piskei ha-Rosh*, Ketubbot, ch. 4, #24; *Oẓar ha-Geonim*, Ketubbot, Responsa, p. 138.
55. *Sha'arei Ẓedek*, Part IV, Sha'ar 4, #17; *Oẓar ha-Geonim*, *supra* n. 54 at 139–140.

> tion, the only purpose of the enactment was to encourage a man to give to his daughter as much as to his son, and today would that a man should give to his son as much as to his daughter! Most people leave their sons without sustenance and provide amply for their daughters. On a number of occasions, it was necessary to place under a ban all those who gave too lavish gifts and dowries to their daughters. When the halakhic authorities saw this, they abrogated the *ketubbah* clause concerning the wife's sons.

Not only was it no longer necessary to encourage giving to a daughter as much as to a son, but the opposite was true; fathers gave most of their property to their daughters and it was necessary to find ways to assure that sons would not be deprived of their proper share—"Would that a man should give to his son as much as to his daughter!"[56]

E. Legislation on Marriage and Divorce

The legislative activity of the *geonim* also extended to the rules governing the validity of marriage and divorce. The *geonim* relied, sometimes explicitly and sometimes implicitly, on the principle that "all who marry do so subject to the conditions laid down by the Rabbis," as it was formulated in the Babylonian Talmud.[57] From these enactments, too, we may note the changes in society and social mores that occurred in this period and provided the background and the impetus for the adoption of far-reaching enactments in this sensitive area of Jewish law.

1. ENACTMENT CONCERNING THE MANNER OF EFFECTING BETROTHAL

At the beginning of the tenth century C.E., an enactment was promulgated by Judah Gaon (the grandfather of Sherira Gaon) designed to prevent impulsive and hasty betrothals that frequently gave rise to disputes between the parties about such issues as the validity of the betrothal itself. Judah Gaon did not confine himself to establishing procedures to prevent such betrothals; he also included in the enactment a far-reaching sanction for its

56. It is evident from statements of other *geonim,* even after Hananiah Gaon, that the clause concerning the wife's sons was still in use; *see, e.g.,* Sherira Gaon and Hai Gaon quoted in *Resp. Ribash* #106. For details, *see* Assaf, "Bittulah Shel Ketubbat Benin Dikhrin" [The Abrogation of the *Ketubbah* Clause Concerning the Wife's Sons], *Ve-Zot li-Yehudah* [Jubilee Volume in Honor of Y.A. Blau], pp. 20–24; Tykocinski, *Takkanot,* pp. 74–77; *Ozar ha-Geonim, supra* n. 54 at 138–142. However, because of the abrogation of the clause during the geonic period (*see* Hananiah Gaon's statement, "When the halakhic authorities saw this, they abrogated the *ketubbah* clause concerning the wife's sons"), the original enactment became a nullity in the course of time, first in Spain and then in Northern France and Germany. For details, *see* Assaf, *supra* at 24–30, and Tykocinski, *supra.*

57. *See supra* pp. 631–633.

violation, namely, that a betrothal not effected in accordance with the procedure established by the enactment is completely void. Thus, a responsum states:[58]

> Hai Gaon wrote: "Take notice that you are causing great harm to yourselves in that it is your custom to permit betrothals without simultaneously writing a *ketubbah* or a betrothal document. Although a woman may [legally] be betrothed even in the marketplace in the presence of two witnesses, there is harm in this practice. Such a practice has not been heard of in Babylonia for a hundred years, and a betrothal at a time other than at the signing of the *ketubbah* is completely unknown.
>
> "Over a hundred years ago there was a practice in Chorosan for a man to betroth a woman by means of a ring at parties and similar occasions. The disputes multiplied; there were claims in favor of and against the validity of the betrothals, and much harm resulted. Our forefather, teacher, and rabbi, Judah Gaon, enacted that a woman must be betrothed under the Babylonian procedure with the writing of the *ketubbah,* the signatures of the witnesses, and the betrothal benedictions, and that whenever this procedure is not followed, the betrothal is invalid on the basis of the principle that 'all who marry do so subject to the conditions laid down by the Rabbis, and the Rabbis annul this marriage.'[59]
>
> "You, too, should do away with such a practice [as yours], and whoever betroths a woman at a time other than at the writing of the *ketubbah* and the document of betrothal should be punished [lit. "fined"] until he rectifies the matter."[60]

Under strict law, a woman is betrothed when a man places a ring on her finger in the presence of two witnesses and declares to her, "You are hereby betrothed to me according to the law of Moses and Israel"; the surrounding circumstances are irrelevant. Judah Gaon promulgated an enactment that a betrothal requires a public ceremony that includes the writing of a *ketubbah* containing the signatures of witnesses and is publicized through the recital of the betrothal benedictions in the presence of a large number of people. This procedure prevents disputes as to whether the betrothal has fulfilled the requirements of the law and is valid. In order to put

58. Assaf, *Teshuvot ha-Geonim* #113 (p. 101); *Oẓar ha-Geonim,* Ketubbot, Responsa, pp. 18–19.

59. TB Ketubbot 50a, *et al. See supra* pp. 631–633.

60. This sentence should not be interpreted as referring to the imposition of a fine rather than annulment of the marriage; the "fine" is the annulment, or there is a fine in addition to the annulment. For this usage of the term *kenas* ("fine"), *see* Rashba, Novellae to Bava Batra 48b: ". . . But we punish him (*kansinan leih* [lit. "fine him"]) and annul his marriage (quoted *supra* p. 637 n. 61). *See also* Freimann, *Kiddushin ve-Nissu'in,* pp. 21–22 and sources cited in nn., *ad loc.*; M. Ḥavaẓelet's supplements to Tykocinski, *Takkanot,* pp. 127–128.

teeth in his enactment, he provided that any betrothal not effected in accordance with the procedure established in the enactment is void; the basis of the enactment was the principle that all who marry do so subject to the conditions laid down by the Rabbis, *i.e.*, the halakhic authorities of each generation. Thus, any betrothal effected contrary to the procedure laid down by the halakhic authorities of the time lacks their consent[61] and is therefore automatically annulled.[62]

2. ENACTMENT CONCERNING THE GRANT OF A DIVORCE TO A *MOREDET* (WIFE WHO REFUSES TO COHABIT WITH HER HUSBAND)

One of the significant enactments of the *geonim* is the *takkanah* compelling a husband to give a divorce to a *moredet*. The terms *moredet* ("rebellious wife") and *mored* ("rebellious husband"), as defined in the Talmud and subsequent law, signify a refusal by the wife or the husband to live together conjugally. Various rules were established concerning the granting

61. The formula "All who marry do so subject to the conditions laid down by the Rabbis" signifies that the annulment of a marriage is effected because the consent of the Rabbis is a necessary condition and not because of any general authority in the Rabbis to legislate. For details, *see supra* pp. 631–642. Athough other sources that quote Judah Gaon's enactment state simply, "The betrothal of any person who does not follow this procedure is totally invalid" (*see* Freimann, *Kiddushin ve-Nissu'in*, p. 19), which is language indicating exercise of legislative authority, it seems likely that this is an abbreviated version of the original language quoted in our text.

62. Freimann, *Kiddushin ve-Nissu'in*, p. 21, quotes from a responsum in *Resp. Bet Yosef*, Dinei Kiddushin #10, ed. Salonika, 1598 (on the basis of which the 1960 Jerusalem edition was printed. The responsum is printed as #10 following #9(2) on p. 59. Another #10 is printed on p. 65):

> I saw an explicit statement by one of the *geonim* in a responsum that the annulment of marriages by the Rabbis is limited to cases that are specified [in the Talmud].

Freimann concluded from this that as early as the geonic period there were those who believed that after the completion of the Talmud the halakhic authorities are not empowered to apply the principle "all who marry do so subject to the conditions laid down by the Rabbis" except in cases expressly specified in the Talmud.

It is, however, doubtful whether such a conclusion can be drawn from the passage quoted. The expression "one of the *geonim* " does not necessarily mean a halakhic authority of the geonic period, since, as is well known, the appellation *gaon* was also used for the *rishonim* (*see supra* p. 646 and n. 9). Furthermore, even if the reference is not to Rashba (*see* Freimann, *supra* at n. 19), other halakhic authorities limited the principle to the cases expressly specified in the Talmud. (*See infra* pp. 848–878 for the opinion of Rabbenu Tam and others). Moreover, *Resp. Bet Yosef*, quoted above, reads, "the annulment of marriages by the Rabbis . . . ," *i.e.*, annulment by virtue of the Rabbis' authority to legislate and not by virtue of the principle "all who marry . . . ," pursuant to which a marriage is conditional on the agreement of the halakhic authorities, so that if they withhold their consent, the marriage is automatically annulled. As we have noted, annulment based on the conditional nature of marriage is more easily accomplished than annulment based on legislative authority. *See supra* pp. 631–642 and *infra* pp. 846–847.

of a divorce and monetary rights in cases of a *mored* or *moredet.*[63] In light of the changes in the social and moral climate in Babylonia, the *geonim* enacted at the beginning of the geonic period[64] that a husband is to be compelled to deliver forthwith a divorce to a wife who is a *moredet.* This enactment represented a substantial change in the essential nature and validity of the process of divorce and subsequently gave rise to many disputes. The following is a brief review of the enactment and the debate to which it gave rise.

A responsum of Sherira Gaon, which appears in one of the sources dealing with this enactment,[65] states:

> Your question is: A woman lived with her husband and told him, "Divorce me; I do not wish to live with you." Must he give her any part of her *ketubbah?* In such a case, is she a *moredet?*
>
> [Response:] This is our opinion: The law originally provided that a husband is not compelled to divorce his wife when she demands a divorce, except in those instances where the Sages specifically declared that he is compelled to divorce her. . . . [66] Afterwards, another *takkanah* was enacted, which provided that a public proclamation should be made concerning her on four consecutive sabbaths and that the court should inform her: "Take notice that you have even forfeited one hundred *maneh* of your *ketubbah*. . . . " Finally, they enacted that public proclamation is to be made concerning her on four sabbaths and she forfeits the entire amount [of her *ketubbah*]; nevertheless, they did not compel the husband to grant her a divorce. . . .
>
> They then enacted that she should remain without a divorce for twelve months in the hope that she would become reconciled, and after twelve months they would compel her husband to grant her a divorce.
>
> After the time of the *savoraim,* Jewish women attached themselves to non-Jews to obtain a divorce through the use of force against their husbands; and some husbands, as a result of force and duress, did grant a divorce that might be considered coerced and therefore not in compliance with the requirements of the law [as under the law one may not use duress to force the giving of a divorce].
>
> When the disastrous results became apparent, it was enacted in the days of Mar Rav Rabbah b. Mar Hunai[67] that when a *moredet* requests a divorce,

63. *See* M Ketubbot 5:7; TB Ketubbot 63a *et seq.*; Maimonides, *MT,* Ishut ch. 14; *Tur* and Sh. Ar. EH ch. 77.

64. *See* Tykocinski, *Takkanot,* p. 24.

65. *Teshuvot ha-Geonim, Sha'arei Ẓedek,* IV, Sha'ar 4, #15, and other sources. The responsum is Sherira Gaon's. *See also Oẓar ha-Geonim,* Ketubbot, Responsa, pp. 191–192, which is the version followed in the present work, and which also contains minor v.l. in the various sources.

66. M Ketubbot 7:10; TB Ketubbot 77a *et seq.*

67. The correct reading is "and Mar Rav Hunai." *See* Tykocinski, *Takkanot,* p. 15; *Oẓar ha-Geonim,* Ketubbot, Responsa, p. 192 n. 15.

> all of the guaranteed dowry that she brought into the marriage (*nikhsei ẓon barzel*) should be paid to her—and even what was destroyed and lost is to be replaced—but whatever the husband obligated himself to pay [beyond the basic *ketubbah* amount], he need not pay, whether or not it is readily available. Even if it is available and she seizes it, it is to be taken from her and returned to her husband; and we compel him to grant her a divorce forthwith and she receives one hundred or two hundred *zuz* [the basic *ketubbah* amount]. This has been our practice for more than three hundred years, and you should do the same.

This responsum describes in detail the different stages of development of the law of the *moredet.* Under the law as it originally stood, her husband was not compelled to divorce her. It was then enacted that the wife forfeits her *ketubbah* and that she is given a warning, but the husband was still not obligated to give her a divorce. Afterward, a substantial change occurred: it was enacted that the wife had to wait for twelve months. If at the end of this "cooling off" period she still had not become reconciled with her husband, he was compelled to give her a divorce.[68] In the geonic period, this approach of compelling the husband to give a divorce reached its high point: since women were then utilizing the pressure of the Moslem government to coerce their husbands to give them a divorce,[69] it was feared that a divorce given after such pressure would likely be invalid because it would be in violation of the law forbidding coercion to compel the granting of a divorce.[70] For this reason, the *geonim* enacted that the husband is immediately compelled by the Jewish court to divorce a *moredet;* and this compulsion does not invalidate the divorce, because the compulsion is effected pursuant to law.

This enactment was still being adhered to at the end of the geonic period, both in Babylonia and elsewhere;[71] and it was accepted by some

68. *See* TB Ketubbot 63a–64a. Sherira Gaon explains the statement there (64a), "We delay her divorce for twelve months," as meaning that after that period the husband is compelled to divorce her. Thus, the innovation of the geonic enactment is not that it compelled divorce, but rather that it did so immediately. *See* Naḥmanides, Novellae to Ketubbot, *ad loc.*, and *infra* pp. 661–662 for Rabbenu Tam's discussion. According to other commentators, the Talmudic rule is that the husband is legally obligated to divorce after twelve months but no judicial compulsion is applied to enforce the obligation.

69. The reference is to indirect pressure by the government or by violent individuals, but not by the non-Jewish judicial authorities, since the Jewish community enjoyed judicial autonomy. In other sources, an additional rationale is given—the fear that the women may leave the Jewish faith. *See* Tykocinski, *Takkanot,* p. 25.

70. *See* TB Gittin 88b.

71. *E.g.,* by Sherira Gaon and Hai Gaon, *see Oẓar ha-Geonim,* Ketubbot, Responsa, pp. 191–193; by Rabbenu Gershom, Alfasi, and others, *see* Alfasi to Ketubbot 63a (printed eds., p. 27a of Alfasi); *Piskei ha-Rosh,* Ketubbot, ch. 5, #35; and gloss to *Piskei ha-Rosh, ad loc.*

halakhic authorities in the twelfth and even in the thirteenth century C.E.[72] However, there is evidence from the twelfth century C.E. that the enactment had not been accepted by most Jewish communities;[73] in this period, one of the leading authorities[74] denied that the *geonim* had the power to adopt an enactment validating a divorce that was invalid under Talmudic law. Although most halakhic authorities did not concur with this fundamental challenge to the authority of the *geonim,* they did agree that this particular geonic enactment should not be followed in their own time. They reached this conclusion on various grounds, but primarily on the same rationale that in its time had brought about the adoption of the enactment itself, namely, that the social and moral situation in their own time was different from what it had been previously.

The fundamental challenge to the authority of the *geonim* to adopt an enactment purporting to validate an otherwise invalid divorce was expressed by Rabbenu Tam:[75]

> Rabbenu Samuel has written that the *geonim* enacted that the divorce is not deferred for twelve months [which was the period required by the enactment of the *amoraim*] but is immediately compelled.
>
> Far be it from him to increase *mamzerim* [offspring of a union which is incestuous or adulterous under Jewish law] among the Jews! The accepted rule is, "Legislation (*hora'ah*) ended with Ravina and R. Ashi" [*i.e.,* the authority to enact *takkanot* on this subject terminated with Ravina and R. Ashi].[76]
>
> Although the *geonim* could legislate that a woman's *ketubbah* may be collected from personal property on the basis of either accepted law or their own view [of sound policy] because that kind of legislation involves money, we do not have the power from the time of R. Ashi until the advent of the Messiah to validate an invalid divorce. And this is an invalid divorce! Since we learn in the Talmud[77] that a divorce may not be compelled until the expiration of twelve months, and they [the *geonim*] advanced the time for the compulsion of the divorce, it is clear that the divorce is invalid even if he [the husband] should declare, "I consent"!
>
> As R. Naḥman stated at the end of Tractate *Gittin:*[78] "A divorce given under compulsion exercised by a Jewish court with good legal ground is

72. Rashbam, Ri mi-Trani, and others; *see Sefer ha-Yashar* of Rabbenu Tam quoted *infra,* text accompanying n. 75; *Resp. Maharam of Rothenburg,* ed. Berlin, #337-#339 (p. 285) (ed. Prague, #865; ed. Lemberg, #136).

73. Maimonides, *MT,* Ishut 14:14.

74. Rabbenu Tam; *see infra.*

75. *Sefer ha-Yashar le-Rabbenu Tam,* Responsa, ed. Rosenthal, #24 (p. 40).

76. TB Bava Meẓi'a 86a.

77. TB Ketubbot 64a.

78. TB Gittin 88b.

> valid; without good legal ground, [it] is invalid"; and this, being within the twelve-month period, is without good legal ground.[79]

According to Rabbenu Tam, the *geonim* did not have legislative authority to validate a divorce that is invalid under Talmudic law. Rabbenu Tam agreed that, according to the Talmud, a divorce in the case of a *moredet* may be compelled, but only after twelve months, whereas the *geonim* enacted that the divorce should be immediately compelled, and in this respect, according to Rabbenu Tam, they exceeded their authority.

As stated, most halakhic authorities held that the *geonim* did have authority to legislate even on matters of marriage and divorce, and even to adopt enactments that deviated from Talmudic law. However, most of these authorities nevertheless held that the geonic enactment concerning a divorce for a *moredet* should not be followed. Thus, Naḥmanides ruled:[80]

> God forbid that I should dispute a *takkanah* of the *geonim,* for who am I to disagree with and change the practice of the *geonim,* who are my teachers? Moreover, I disapprove of those who say that their [*i.e.,* the *geonim*'s] enactments are not worthy of being followed and that only the law of the Talmud is binding. It is indeed proper to obey them and to follow their enactments, and whoever is careful in doing this is not acting improperly.
>
> However, the Talmud states the law that compulsion is not to be used, and this is fundamental and well known. At present, it is appropriate to be extremely careful not to follow the *takkanah* at all, as it has already been nullified because of the licentiousness of the generation.

Asheri's view was the same as Naḥmanides', and his words not only fully reveal how the situation had changed by their time but also set forth an important additional reason for not following the geonic enactment.[81]

First, Asheri set forth the practice in his day with regard to a divorce for a *moredet:*

> With regard to the compulsion of a divorce, it is the practice of our Rabbis, the halakhic authorities of Germany and France, to avoid the use of all possible means of compelling a husband to give a divorce to his wife who rejects him, as they agree with Rabbenu Tam and his main arguments, and they are worthy of being relied on.

79. Rabbenu Tam then concluded: "[And this is so] even according to the interpretation of Rabbenu Shelomo [Rashi] regarding the *moredet.*" Apparently, the reference is to Rashi's statement quoted in *Shiltei Gibborim* to Alfasi, *ad loc.*, that even according to the Talmud the husband would be compelled to divorce his wife after twelve months. S.P. Rosenthal's statements, *supra* n. 75 at n. 12, are difficult to understand.

80. Naḥmanides, Novellae to Ketubbot 63b, s.v. U-maẓinu bi-Yerushalmi (in regular editions printed as Rashba's novellae to Ketubbot).

81. *Resp. Asheri* 43:8.

Then Asheri discussed the nature and binding force of the geonic enactment:

> In the generations that succeeded the Talmudic Sages, in the days of the *geonim* in the Babylonian academies, it was realized that there was a temporary need in their time to diverge from the law of the Torah and to create a fence and safeguard. They accordingly enacted that a man should be compelled to divorce his wife when she declares, "I do not want this man," so that she should not attach herself to a non-Jew and so that Jewish women should not fall into evil ways. They relied on the principle that all who marry do so subject to the conditions laid down by the Rabbis, and the Rabbis decided to annul the marriage when a wife rejects her husband.

After Asheri clarified the nature of the geonic enactment and the reason for its binding effect in its time,[82] he stated his first reason why he felt it should no longer be followed:

> That enactment was not accepted by all the Jewish communities, and even if there are places that engaged in compulsion, this was not done in those places on the strength of the geonic enactment. [We would conclude that it was done on the strength of the geonic enactment if,] for example, at the time that the *geonim* enacted the *takkanah,* they communicated it to those places and they [the people in those places] then accepted it. If that had been done, the matter would be known through tradition handed down through the generations revealing how they came to accept it on the authority of the *geonim;* a fundamental *takkanah* such as this would not likely be forgotten in subsequent generations had it been accepted by the people.
>
> For example, there was a halakhic authority in our land whose name was Rabbenu Gershom. He enacted beneficial *takkanot* in the area of divorce, and he lived in the days of the *geonim.* His enactments are firm and anchored as if given at Sinai, because they were accepted and transmitted from generation to generation. However, I observe that in those lands [where divorces are compelled before the expiration of the twelve-month waiting period], they primarily rely on the books of Alfasi, because they noted that such compulsion was authorized in his [book of] laws;[83] this was the basis of the custom in some places to engage in this practice.

82. According to Asheri, the legal basis for the enactment by the *geonim* to compel a husband to grant an immediate divorce and to permit his wife to remarry on the strength of such a divorce was not that the *geonim* validated a legally invalid divorce. It was rather that the marriage had been originally conditioned on the consent of the halakhic authorities and was retroactively annulled by them. This was also how the Babylonian *amoraim* explained Rabban Gamaliel the Elder's enactment that the cancellation of a bill of divorcement in the absence of the wife is ineffective. *See supra* pp. 631–633.

83. Alfasi to Ketubbot 63a (printed eds., p. 27a of Alfasi), where the geonic enactment is quoted.

Asheri's first reason for rejecting the geonic enactment was that it was not accepted by a majority of the people,[84] in contrast to Rabbenu Gershom's enactments, which were accepted by a majority of the people and are firm and solid as if given at Sinai.[85]

Asheri then stated his second reason, which involves a change that had occurred in the socio-moral climate:

> In addition, I say that the *geonim* who enacted this *takkanah* did so for that [*i.e.*, their own] generation, as they deemed necessary to meet the needs of Jewish women of that time. Present-day conditions, however, call for a directly contrary approach. Jewish women in this generation are brazen. If a wife could free herself from her husband by declaring, "I do not want him," there will not remain a daughter of our Father Abraham living with her husband. They will become attracted to someone else and reject their husbands. It is therefore wise to be careful to avoid the use of compulsion to force a husband to grant a divorce to a *moredet.*

Asheri's second reason for not following the geonic enactment stems from the complete change in circumstances between the time of the enactment and his own time. When adopted, the enactment was necessary to obviate the problem of illegally coerced divorces and to prevent Jewish women from leaving the community and falling into "evil ways."[86] However, at the time of Asheri these concerns had disappeared. The problem lay in the opposite direction—the moral climate was such that women would wrongfully exploit the ability to compel a divorce for the asking. The availability of a divorce solely on the basis that a wife was no longer willing to live with her husband would raise serious concern that she would leave her husband simply because she is attracted to some other man and "there will not remain a daughter of our Father Abraham living with her husband."

Asheri's detailed response related to an actual case submitted to him in which a woman rejected her husband and demanded a divorce. In his conclusion, after setting forth his view of the underlying principles, Asheri gave this answer to the specific question put to him:

84. Those who did follow it did so, according to Asheri, because it is recorded in Alfasi's code and not because they accepted the enactment. Rashba, too, stated that the enactment had not been accepted in most countries and added, "Perhaps they enacted it only for their own generation," *i.e.*, the *geonim* had originally intended it for their own time only; *Resp. Rashba Attributed to Naḥmanides* #134. *See also Resp. Rashba*, I, #573, #1192, #1235; II, #276; V, #95.

85. Actually, a significant portion of the people did not accept even Rabbenu Gershom's enactments, but his enactments were more widely accepted than the geonic enactment on the *moredet*. *See infra* pp. 674–675.

86. The reference to "evil ways" may possibly be to apostasy. *See supra* n. 69.

> However, in this case, her brothers [*i.e.*, the brothers of the woman who demanded a divorce] have given me reasons that brought about her rejection [and it is possible that her reasons are justified]; and you, the judge [who sought advice on how to decide the case], should investigate the matter to determine if there is truth to her claims, and if his purpose is to keep her "chained" [*i.e.*, if you come to the conclusion that the intent of the husband is to leave his wife as an *agunah* (married, but not cohabiting)], it is appropriate for you to rely on your custom in this case to compel him to give a divorce after a time.

Asheri thus did not doubt that the *geonim* were authorized to adopt the enactment on the basis of the principle that "all who marry do so subject to the conditions laid down by the Rabbis." However, he held that in his time the enactment should not be followed for two reasons: first, it had not become generally accepted by the Jewish people;[87] and second, the enactment was adopted on the basis of particular circumstances that had fundamentally changed.

It is interesting that Asheri's decision in the actual case submitted to him was that the enactment should be followed if it had customarily been followed in the particular locality and if the circumstances of the case justified following it, *e.g.*, if the judge concluded that the wife's request was well-founded, and that failure to compel the husband to give the divorce might have resulted in the wife's becoming an *agunah*. One may deduce from this decision that Asheri placed primary emphasis on his second reason, and he therefore permitted the enactment to be applied, when appropriate under the circumstances, in those places that had been following it.

Most halakhic authorities have accepted the view and the rationale of Naḥmanides and Asheri as to the law of the *moredet*. The majority view is that the legislative power of the *geonim* was not limited to monetary matters (as Rabbenu Tam held it was), but was fully effective even with regard to marriage and divorce. However, this question of legislative authority arose again later in regard to post-geonic legislation, at which time the question was resolved differently. The background and the reasons that account for this difference are discussed in a subsequent chapter.[88]

87. An enactment that is not accepted by the majority of the people is void. *See supra* pp. 538–541.

88. *Infra* pp. 846–879.

Chapter 18
POST-GEONIC LEGISLATION: INTRODUCTION

I. THE DIFFUSION OF SPIRITUAL HEGEMONY AND THE RISE OF THE *KEHILLAH* (LOCAL JEWISH COMMUNITY)

Toward the end of the geonic period, a substantial change occurred in the situation of the Jewish people. Up to that time, there had generally been one single center exercising spiritual hegemony over the entire Jewish diaspora. At first, when the Jewish people had an independent sovereign state, and for some time thereafter, this center was in the Land of Israel. Its decisions and legislation were addressed to and binding upon the entire Jewish people. After a time, the Jewish community of Babylonia became an autonomous center; and with the decline of the settlement in the Land of Israel in the wake of the oppressive political conditions there, the Babylonian center succeeded to spiritual hegemony over the entire Jewish diaspora.

By the end of the geonic period, this situation had fundamentally changed. For various reasons, external and internal, the Babylonian center lost its preeminence; thereafter, there was no longer a single Jewish center exercising spiritual hegemony over all the others. The major portion of the Jewish people migrated to the countries of Europe, where there was never a preeminent single center but rather a group of parallel centers, none of which was acknowledged as possessing authority over the others. In addition to Jewish communities in North Africa, other Jewish settlements were established over the course of time in such places as Germany, Spain, France, Italy, the Land of Israel, Turkey, the Balkans, Poland, and Lithuania. Although, from time to time, spiritual giants arose whose authority spanned various settlements, each autonomous center, in the main, turned to its own halakhic authorities in most legal matters, and no single center any longer made binding law for the entire diaspora.[1]

This fundamental change in the Jewish diaspora also produced a change in the character and status of the *kehillah* (local Jewish community). According to Yitzhak Baer,[2] "the foundations of the *kehillah,* which endured until the modern Enlightenment (*Haskalah*), were laid mainly in the first generations of the Second Temple period," and many of the tannaitic sources setting forth laws with regard to "the town residents" and "the townspeople" are attributable to this early period.[3] Thereafter, local autonomy continued to exist in varying degrees both in the Land of Israel and in Babylonia.[4]

The autonomous Jewish community has been well characterized as follows:

> [It is] an inherent and abiding creation in our people's history. The diaspora did not give birth to it; its organizational form was suitable anywhere, whether in the Land of Israel or in the diaspora. This organizational form fitted every social and economic class: farmers, tradesmen, and even merchants—subject to the obvious proviso that the external structure of the *kehillah* should be appropriate for the socio-religious objectives that brought it into being and that it seeks to realize.[5]

However, for the entire time until the end of the geonic period, there are no extant records indicating any noteworthy autonomous authority of the community in regard to local government and judicial administration.[6] Only from the middle of the tenth century C.E. is there evidence of a substantial increase in the power and prestige of the community:

> The Jewish *kehillah* now appears as a living organism that unites all the community members alike in all areas of public life, religious and "secular" (insofar as any such distinction is possible). . . . The *kehillah* enacts legislation on religious, political, administrative, and economic matters and enforces public discipline against individuals by means of the ban [*e.g.,* ostracism] and fines.

1. For further details, *see supra* p. 43 and references cited *id.* n. 128.
2. Y. Baer, "Ha-Yesodot ve-ha-Hatḥalot Shel Irgun ha-Kehillah ha-Yehudit bi-Mei ha-Beinayim" [The Foundations and Beginnings of Jewish Communal Organization in the Middle Ages], *Zion,* XV (1950), p. 1.
3. *See, e.g., Tosefeta* Bava Meẓi'a 11:23; TB Bava Batra 8b. *See also supra* pp. 487–488 and *infra* pp. 679–681.
4. *See* Baer, *supra* n. 2 at 7 and n. 17, for G. Alon's views.
5. Baer, *supra* n. 2 at 3.
6. *See infra* p. 681 n. 12.

These communities increasingly appeared in many different European cities. In the course of time, associations of a number of communities were also formed, and at times even countrywide bodies that consolidated a large, autonomous, and independent center.[7]

II. CONTRACTION OF THE TERRITORIAL SCOPE OF LEGISLATIVE JURISDICTION

The historical changes discussed above had a far-reaching influence on various areas of Jewish law,[8] including the nature and methodology of legislation. The single great change in this area related to the territorial scope of legislative jurisdiction. The legislation of the Sages until the end of the Talmudic period was intended for the entire nation; "their decrees, enactments, and customs were recognized by the entire Jewish people wherever they lived."[9] To a great extent, this situation continued in the geonic period, although some halakhic authorities maintained that geonic legislation did not have the same universal quality as the enactments of the Talmudic period;[10] and some geonic enactments were not accepted in all Jewish communities or by all halakhic authorities.[11]

However, during most of the geonic period, the rulings and enactments of the Babylonian *geonim* were complied with; they were recognized as authoritative and, by most halakhic authorities, as binding on the entire Jewish people[12] to the same extent as legislation had been in the previous

7. The organization of the Jewish community preceded that of the Christian city, which began in the twelfth century C.E.; *see* Baer, *supra* n. 2 at 28–29.

8. *See infra* this chapter and p. 936.

9. Maimonides, *MT,* Introduction. *See supra* p. 645 and n. 6.

10. Maimonides particularly emphasized this difference in his Introduction to the *Mishneh Torah; see supra* n. 9. Asheri was also explicit in this regard: "Moreover, I cannot understand how the *geonim* could issue new decrees after R. Ashi completed the Talmud" (*Piskei ha-Rosh,* Shabbat, ch. 2, #15); *see also Piskei ha-Rosh,* Berakhot, ch. 1, #16 (at end). Apparently these statements of Asheri are connected with his basic view on the question of the right of subsequent authorities to disagree with the *geonim; see Piskei ha-Rosh,* Sanhedrin, ch. 4, #6. For fuller discussion of this question, *see supra* pp. 268–271 and *infra* pp. 983–986, 1226–1229 *See also Resp. Ribash* #271.

11. *E.g.*, the enactments concerning four cubits in the Land of Israel (*supra* pp. 650–651) and the divorce of a *moredet* (*supra* pp. 658–665), etc.

12. *See infra* pp. 1460–1461, and *Resp. Rashba,* III, #411:

> The same is true with regard to enactments by leading halakhic authorities when they deem it necessary to legislate for the public welfare. Thus, the *geonim* enacted a number of *takkanot* to which all Israel conformed because they [the *geonim*] were the Jewish people's tribunal . . . and the entire Jewish people follows them in all their enactments.

Rashba's views are quoted at greater length *infra* pp. 669–671. Rashba perceived the geonic enactments as being intended for the entire Jewish people, although he too was of the

periods.[13] Toward the end of the geonic period, this situation substantially changed. From then on, the enactments of the halakhic authorities in each center were directed from the outset to the people of that center alone: "A rabbi may not issue decrees directed to another country outside his jurisdiction that prohibit what Talmudic law permits."[14]

A major cause of the local character of legislation was the substantial increase in the number of enactments by the public and its leaders since the geonic period. This public legislation, known from this period onward as "communal enactments" (*takkanot ha-kahal*) or "communal agreements" (*haskamot ha-kahal*), was limited by its very nature to the territory of the community or the association of communities by which it was adopted.

The local character of such legislation is discussed in a responsum by Rashba dealing with the question of whether legislation enacted in the city of Barcelona bound the inhabitants of the surrounding villages whose consent had not been sought.[15] After pointing out that Barcelona and the surrounding villages comprised a single unit for the payment of taxes to the general government, Rashba said:

> We never adopt legislation affecting them [the surrounding communities], even though we are the majority and the leading province for all matters. If

---

opinion that not all those enactments were universally accepted; *see, e.g.*, regarding the enactment concerning the divorce of a *moredet*, *Resp. Rashba Attributed to Naḥmanides* #134. *See also supra* p. 664 n. 84.

13. *See further Maggid Mishneh* to *MT*, Ḥameẓ u-Maẓẓah 5:20: "But I say that we may not issue decrees on our own authority after the time of the *geonim*, of blessed memory." *See also* Moses Sofer, *Resp. Ḥatam Sofer*, ḤM #41, discussed *infra* n. 14.

14. *Resp. Ribash* #271, and *see Resp. Ḥatam Sofer*, ḤM #41, which quotes the remarks of Mordecai Banet:

> With regard to matters that are not required by existing law, no rabbi or halakhic authority has the right to enact in his own country legislation that applies to another country, as Ribash wrote in a responsum.

The reference is to the responsum of Ribash cited *supra*, and *see* the later statement of Moses Sofer that he did not know to which responsum Banet was referring; *see also Resp. Kol Mevasser*, I, #13. Regarding the actual question discussed, Sofer also agreed that generally no authority exists to adopt enactments for another country, but he viewed the enactment prohibiting interference with another's trade or business as an exception; *see infra* n. 30. In his responsum cited *supra*, Ribash added that even in Talmudic times, when legislation was intended for the entire Jewish people, enactments were adopted by a quorum of Sages; an individual Sage legislated only for his own town and its satellite communities. *See id.* for details. However, the difference between the two periods is that in the Talmudic period local enactments were the exception and generally legislation was intended for all Jews, whereas from the tenth century C.E. on, the legislation in each center was almost always intended for that center only.

15. *Resp. Rashba*, III, #411. The question involved the customary practice in Rashba's locality as to legislation concerning various types of taxes. The ensuing discussion, however, deals with legislation in general.

we were to act without their counsel, they would not obey us. Sometimes we send people to them, and sometimes representatives (*berurim*) come from them to us with their consent. . . .

There are, however, other places where the main *kehillah* legislates for its satellite villages and directs them regardless of their consent, for in these matters, different places have different customs. Our practice has always been as I have stated; this is the custom that we follow, and it certainly is the law.

The differences in customs revolved around whether the consent of the small satellite villages was necessary for legislation to be binding on them. However, no one disputed that the legislation of one community cannot bind another. Rashba went on to say:

For what right or authority does one community have over another, or even one over many,[16] in matters of civil law, customs, or enactments, except in certain well-known instances? These instances include: when the High Court [in Jerusalem] agreed to institute a certain practice or prohibit a particular act, and their decree was one to which the community could conform, such as the decrees concerning bread, wine, and cooked food, and other enactments of the court;[17] or when the king issued a decree, such as the decree of King Saul whereby Jonathan incurred the death penalty[18] (even though he did not know or hear of the decree; whatever the king decrees with the concurrence of the Jewish people is valid and applicable to all, as it is written:[19] "Anyone who does not come in three days . . . will have his property confiscated").

Another instance is a decree of the *nasi* (patriarch) or the exilarch . . . since he is the ruler.

Also, where the majority of a community issues decrees or adopts enactments for communal needs, inasmuch as the majority has acted, it [the majority's legislation] is binding on the minority even against its will—what is done is done. However, it must be the act of the majority, and such that a majority of the public is able to conform to it, as is stated in Chapter *Ein Ma'amidin*,[20] for in every community the minority is subject to the authority of the majority. The minority must conduct themselves in all their affairs according to the will of the majority, and the minority stand in relation to the people of their town as the entire Jewish people stands in relation to the High Court or the king. . . .

The same is true with regard to enactments by leading halakhic authorities when they deem it necessary to legislate for the public welfare. Thus, the

16. A small part of *Resp. Rashba,* III, #411 is also found in *Resp. Rashba,* I, #781, where the text reads: "or even many over one"—which seems to be more correct.

17. For these enactments, *see* M Avodah Zarah 2:6; TB Avodah Zarah 35b *et seq.*

18. I Samuel 14:24–45.

19. Ezra 10:8; *see also supra* p. 508.

20. TB Avodah Zarah 36a.

> *geonim* enacted a number of *takkanot* to which all Israel conformed because they [the *geonim*] were the Jewish people's tribunal. [For example], the *geonim* enacted that the personal property of an heir is subject to a creditor's lien to the same extent as land,[21] they decreed the "ordinary" ban,[22] and they also adopted many other enactments; and the entire Jewish people follows them in all their enactments. . . .
>
> The foregoing are the instances where I perceive it possible to compel others to conform. However, in other instances, I do not see how the people of one town have the authority to impose their will on the people of a different town in the absence of consent, nor may they [the people of one town] put them [the people of a different town] under a ban.

The High Court, the king, the *nasi,* the exilarch, and even the *geonim* could all enact legislation binding on the entire Jewish people because their authority, whether viewed as spiritual-halakhic or political-governmental, extended over the entire nation. This, however, was no longer true after the geonic period. Although the majority in a particular place could adopt an enactment binding the minority there (inasmuch as "the minority stand in relation to the people of their town as the entire Jewish people stands in relation to the High Court or the king"), nevertheless, the inhabitants of one locality are not subject to the authority of the inhabitants of a different locality. Consequently, it was established that the territorial scope of every enactment, whether based on halakhic or communal authority, is ordinarily limited to the locale of enactment unless it is shown that it was also voluntarily accepted elsewhere as binding. As Jacob Moellin stated: "Although Rashi and Rabbenu Tam promulgated their enactments in France, I have not found or heard that the enactments have spread to these countries [Germany, Austria, and Bohemia], and they mention only France in their enactment."[23]

The following excerpt from a responsum well expresses the point that one community cannot legislate for the inhabitants of another:

> All of you from these three regions who have signed [the request for a ruling] and all those associated with you have no obligation whatsoever to accept or obey these enactments. This is a point that needs no elaboration, for how can penalties be imposed on you for violating legislation enacted without your authorization?[24]

21. *See supra* pp. 646–648.

22. *See supra* p. 653 n. 44.

23. *Resp. Maharil* #121; *see,* to the same effect, *Resp. Mahari Weil* #66, #101. However, in those localities where the enactment is in force, it is assumed that all legal transactions are entered into conformably with it even if not explicitly so stated; *see* Rema to Sh. Ar. ḤM 42:15.

24. Israel Isserlein, *Terumat ha-Deshen,* Pesakim u-Khetavim, #252, and *see* #253. *See also infra* pp. 793–794. The language referring to the infliction of penalties (*lehassi'a al*

Similarly, the members of one community, even though it includes many greater halakhic authorities than another community, may not nullify an enactment that has been adopted by the members of the other community:

> Because the community selected its authorized representatives (*ne'emanim*) and enacted a *takkanah* under the guidance of its experts and decreed a *gezerah* with their consent, no other community has the power to nullify or cancel it, either on the basis of greater wisdom or on the basis of greater numbers. . . . For the halakhic authorities have authorized and empowered every community to legislate for itself, and no other community has any right to nullify such legislation.[25]

The perimeters of "locality" varied from place to place and from time to time, and ranged from communities whose entire adult population numbered only ten[26] to major Jewish population centers. There were instances when one city contained more than one community; sometimes there would be as many as thirty "communities" in a single city. Each community was autonomous and was known by name of the city or country from which its members had migrated, and each one adopted enactments binding only on its own members.[27] Some enactments, however, applied not only to a single community but to a group of many communities and even to entire countries.[28]

---

kiẓatkhem) is from TB Bava Batra 8b, where it is used in connection with legislation by the townspeople; *see also* Rashi, *ad loc.*, s.v. Lehassi'a al kiẓatam, and *see infra* p. 679.

25. A responsum of Joseph Tov Elem, printed in *Resp. Maharam of Rothenburg*, ed. Lemberg, #423; *see also infra* pp. 688–690 for a discussion of this responsum. However, the halakhic authorities had the power to nullify communal enactments that deviated from the principles of justice and equity in Jewish law. Thus, the responsum continues (*id.*): "The court in every community may issue decrees binding on the members of the community as they deem necessary for the needs of the time, and no one else may cancel any such enactment so long as it does not transgress basic concepts of the Torah." For detailed discussion, *see infra* pp. 760–777.

26. *See Resp. Rashba*, V, #253:

> You have also asked, What constitutes an established community? If a village contains three or four [Jewish] households but, together with their servants, there are ten people, will it be considered an established community or not? Response: I do not know the purpose of your question, and furthermore, to my knowledge, the term "established community" is not mentioned anywhere. Any group of ten [male] adults is called an *edah* (congregation), whether they all belong to one household or to many. Therefore I cannot answer you on this without knowing the purpose of your question.

See further Judah al-Bargeloni, *Sefer ha-Shetarot*, p. 132, *ketav takkanta* (document of enactment). *See also infra* p. 728 and n. 195.

27. *E.g.*, as to North Africa, *see supra* p. 456 n. 32; as to Salonika, *see infra* p. 865 n. 301.

28. *See infra* pp. 798–804, 838 as to the enactments of "Shum" (Speyer, Worms, and Mainz) and Valladolid, and other legislation governing more than a single community. En-

There were also enactments which were progressively accepted in a large number of communities in different countries, until it became settled that they were to be generally assumed to be universally applicable.[29] However, the expansion of the territory in which some enactments were applicable did not change the essentially local nature and quality of the legislative process after the geonic period. It was only on rare occasions, when no other alternative appeared to be available to rectify a particular situation, that the halakhic authorities endowed such legislation with binding authority over the entire Jewish people.[30]

---

actments intended for many communities are also called *takkanot medinah* (regional enactments); they dealt with problems common to the whole population, such as taxation, or were to be used as models for the various communities. Regional enactments occasionally contained a provision that each community was to follow its own local enactments. *See, e.g.*, I. Halpern, *Takkanot Medinat Mehrin* [Enactments of Moravia], #176, p. 57. *See also id.*, Introduction, as to the legislative process for regional enactments. A regional committee, made up of representatives of the various communities, appointed a smaller body to prepare the substance and language of proposed enactments; *see id.* at 13–15. *See also infra* pp. 819–820.

29. *See, e.g., infra* p. 739 n. 230, as to the enactment that the testimony of relatives or interested parties is admissible, which became the operative law in many communities in various countries.

30. At times, limiting the applicability of legislation to the locality where it was adopted defeated the entire purpose of the enactment. In these situations, a way was found to vest authority in the legislator to enact legislation applicable to the entire Jewish people. Moses Sofer's opinion, issued at a time when Jewish judicial autonomy was coming to an end, offers an interesting example (*Resp. Ḥatam Sofer*, ḤM #41, #79; *id.*, Likkutim #57).

The case concerned a dispute between printing firms in Vilna and Horodna, on one side, and in Salavita, on the other, over the right to print the Talmud. The dispute gave rise to a difference of opinion between Mordecai Banet and Moses Sofer on the law relating to interference with another's trade or business (*hassagat gevul*, lit. "moving a landmark," *see supra* pp. 394–397). Mordecai Banet held, *inter alia*, that the halakhic authorities have no power to bind the residents of a country other than their own to an enactment prohibiting such competition, since after the completion of the Talmud all legislation is local in character. Moses Sofer agreed in principle but felt that legal protection against competition in this situation should be made an exception to the rule because its purpose was to benefit the entire Jewish people; otherwise, no one would be willing to undertake the printing of halakhic works, and the study of the *Halakhah* would be seriously impeded:

> Since printing was invented, scribal copyists have ceased to exist; and if, Heaven forfend, there will be no printing, the Torah will disappear, may God save us from such an eventuality! It is impossible to publish except at great expense; and no one can undertake to publish unless he is assured of the market in all Jewish centers, for as a consequence of our great sins we Jews are scattered throughout the whole world, a few here and a few there. As a result, the publisher needs a great deal of time and a clear field to bring his venture to a successful conclusion, and if we do not close the door to other publishers, who will be so foolish as to risk many thousands? Thus, publication will come to an end, Heaven forfend, and Torah will disappear!
>
> Therefore, for the good of all Jews and for the exaltation of the Torah, our predecessors enacted a ban (*guda*, lit. a wall) on anyone who trespasses on what the rabbis of the time define as the territory of the one who publishes first . . . not for the benefit of the scribe [*i.e.*, the publisher] but in order to exalt the Torah. . . . Therefore,

This historical and halakhic reality explains why various enactments—some of them fundamental and substantial—were accepted from the tenth century C.E. onward in only part of the Jewish diaspora, and not in all Jewish centers. An outstanding example is the well-known enactment of Rabbenu Gershom prohibiting polygamy.[31] This fundamental enactment, which introduced decisive changes in Jewish family law, was not accepted until relatively recently in some large and important Sephardic Jewish communities, and it has been similarly stressed that many other significant enactments have been accepted only in certain places.[32]

Notwithstanding the local character and applicability of post-geonic legislation, such legislation constitutes an integral and essential part of the overall Jewish legal system, as is demonstrated by the enactments of Rabbenu Gershom. Those enactments, in spite of their local character, not only became an integral part of Jewish law, but "his enactments are firm and anchored as if given at Sinai."[33] Even if an enactment was not universally accepted, "in the places where it was accepted, it is established, as we find in regard to the enactments of Rabbenu Gershom; they were not accepted

---

> when any rabbi, at the time of any publication, finds it necessary, in view of the time, place, and book involved, to fix a period of time in which competition is to be proscribed, his ban will fall on all Jews wherever they may be, and in pronouncing the ban that rabbi is acting as an agent of the earlier authorities (*id.*, Likkutim #57).

Moses Sofer thus offered two rationales for his ruling. First, the ruling meets the need of the entire Jewish people, and second, this was an early enactment, similar to the enactment against the breaking of engagements to be married (*ḥerem ha-shiddukhim*) and the enactment prohibiting settlement in a town without the townspeople's consent (*ḥerem ha-yishuv*). The second rationale was highly novel. The enactments concerning engagements and settlement in a town are attributed to Rabbenu Gershom (*see infra* p. 784 n. 13), whereas the enactment against unfair competition originated with Rema, whose formulation is quoted by Sofer (*id.* #41). According to Sofer, this latter enactment applied to all Jews because "the enactment is early and was adopted by all the *geonim* and applied to all persons, even in the depths of the sea." However, there is no source indicating that the enactment against unfair competition was adopted by all the halakhic authorities in all their localities so as to apply to all Jews. Even the enactments of Rabbenu Gershom were "local" and were not accepted by all Jewish communities (*see infra*).

We must therefore conclude that Sofer's opinion rests mainly on the first rationale, *i.e.*, that this is an essential matter affecting all Jews and therefore even today an enactment can be adopted that will apply to and bind every Jewish person. *See further* the comprehensive responsum of Meshullam Rath in *Resp. Kol Mevasser*, I, #13, regarding a proposal made at a rabbinical conference to proclaim a ban against any Jew treading on the soil of Germany subsequent to the horrors of the Holocaust. Rath discusses, *inter alia*, the aspect of the proposal that involves the possibility of adopting an enactment to apply to all Jews wherever located, and rejects this possibility.

31. As to this enactment, *see infra* pp. 784–785. *See also infra* n. 34.

32. *See, e.g.*, the sources cited *supra* n. 24.

33. *Resp. Asheri* 43:8; as to this responsum, *see* in detail *supra* pp. 662–665.

throughout the Jewish world, but even so, in the area where they were accepted, they are as binding as the laws of the Talmud."[34]

There is another conclusion to be drawn from this phenomenon of local legislation. As previously noted,[35] all the various types of legislation are a reaction to needs arising from social, economic, and moral changes. This reaction is most clearly reflected in local legislation, precisely because of the very fact that sometimes a given enactment was found necessary in one place but not elsewhere. Again, the enactment of Rabbenu Gershom prohibiting polygamy is an instructive illustration of this point. The adoption of this enactment was influenced by the economic and social conditions in Europe in Rabbenu Gershom's time and by the fact that the general law there prohibited marrying multiple wives. Consequently, this legislation was not enacted or accepted by the Jews in the Moslem countries of the East, where the economic conditions and social outlook were entirely different, and where polygamy was a valid and widespread practice. Local legislation, therefore, especially underscores the sensitivity of Jewish law to constantly changing economic and social conditions and illustrates how Jewish law characteristically related to these conditions.[36]

34. *Resp. Radbaz* #1165. *See* Radbaz' comment, *id.*, that in his own time, the enactments of Rabbenu Gershom "had become accepted in most areas of Germany, France, and Catalonia." Radbaz (*id.*) discussed an enactment in Egypt that the cantor in the synagogue should recite the *Amidah* prayer once aloud and the congregation should accompany him in an undertone (as opposed to the usual practice whereby the congregation first recites the prayer quietly and then the cantor repeats it aloud). Radbaz opposed the enactment on two grounds: "This enactment has been accepted only in this country, and even here it does not have the same force as other enactments." Nevertheless, Radbaz concluded: "If they can be persuaded without arousing controversy to return to the law of the Talmud and repeat the prayer, it is fitting to do so, but if it is impossible to change their practice without controversy, then do nothing about it." *See also infra* p. 810 and n. 112.

35. *See supra* p. 495.

36. Another limitation on legislation during the period under discussion is connected with the special circumstances of the Jewish community in the diaspora. Occasionally, it was impossible to legislate directly in the normal manner because the particular matter affected both Jews and non-Jews and the enactment could obviously be binding only on Jews. For example, one of the early enactments attributed to Rabbenu Gershom—and subsequently reenacted numerous times in various periods and with various additions—concerned unfair competition for rental housing. The purpose of the enactment was to protect the tenant's right to remain in his dwelling even when someone else was willing to offer a higher rental. The simple way to achieve this purpose would have been to restrict the landlord's right to evict the tenant, in line with the approach taken in current tenant-protection laws. However, this straightforward approach could not be used, because the landlords were not always Jews and the enactment would in such cases be ineffective. Therefore, the enactment provided that a Jew is forbidden to obtain living quarters by offering to pay a higher rental than that paid by the tenant. *See infra* p. 784 n. 13 and pp. 811–813.

Another example is the prohibition of competition in publishing books. This prohibition ideally should have been directed at those who print books already published, and

III. CONTRACTION OF THE SUBSTANTIVE SCOPE OF LEGISLATIVE AUTHORITY

Another substantial change in Jewish legislation following the geonic period was the trend (which ultimately prevailed) not to use legislation as a source of law to affect the validity of a marriage or divorce.

As described in the previous chapters,[37] in the area of family law there was always a very high level of legislative activity, which included enactments affecting the validity of marriages and divorces. This activity spanned the various historical periods up to and including the geonic period. Even in the time of the *amoraim,* when it became an accepted principle that a court may not mandate the performance of an act forbidden by Biblical law, the primary exception to this rule involved matters relating to the validity of marriages and divorces.[38] After the geonic period, and especially from the twelfth century C.E. on, distinguished halakhic authorities declared that the rabbis in their time were not authorized to annul a marriage valid under then-existing law;[39] and some were of the opinion that even the *geonim* did not have such authority.[40] After a time, most halakhic authorities stated that although, as a matter of law, an enactment with regard to marriage is fully binding, and the marriage of one who violates the provisions of the enactment should be annulled, nevertheless, in practice such legislation should be avoided. Indeed, legislation that in any way affected the validity of marriages or divorces gradually diminished to the point that it virtually ceased.[41]

This contraction of legislative activity is likewise essentially related to the new situation that came about after the geonic period. The fact that legislation became local gave rise to the justified concern about the possible proliferation of contradictory enactments in the area of family law. The local character of legislation carried with it a serious threat to the uniformity of the law on one of the most sensitive questions of the *Halakhah, i.e.,* whether a person is considered to be married and therefore forbidden to marry anyone else. The validity of a marriage could very well depend on

---

should have been part of the law of unfair competition (very much along the lines of contemporary copyright laws). However, such an enactment could bind Jewish but not non-Jewish publishers. For this reason, the prohibition was addressed to prospective purchasers, who were forbidden to buy a book published in violation of a "copyright." This made the enactment effective and meaningful. *See Resp. Ḥatam Sofer,* ḤM #41, #79; *id.,* Likkutim #57.

37. *Supra* pp. 521–530, 564–566, 631–642, 656–665.

38. *See supra* pp. 521–530, 634–636.

39. *See infra* pp. 846–856.

40. This is the opinion of Rabbenu Tam; *see supra* pp. 661–662.

41. *See infra* pp. 856–879.

whether the couple were members of a community that had adopted an enactment nullifying such a marriage or were members of a community that had not adopted such an enactment.[42] Abstention from this type of legislation avoided that undesirable result but, at the same time, left unresolved problems that required solution.[43]

IV. LOCAL LEGISLATION AND CONFLICT OF LAWS

Although the local character of legislation constrained some legislative activity, as discussed above, it was a major stimulus to creativity in a different legal area, namely, conflict of laws. In the Talmudic period, conflict of laws was a subject of very modest scope,[44] primarily because Jewish law is personal law applicable to every Jew wherever situated—even outside the territorial boundaries of Jewish sovereignty or autonomy. Consequently, there is no legal significance to the fact that a contract between two Jews was entered into in state A and is to be performed in state B—a fact that gives rise to many problems in the area of conflict of laws in other legal systems.[45]

The emergence of local legislation brought about the adoption of different local enactments that were often inconsistent with one another. As a result, problems of choice of law arose, for example, when one part of a legal transaction occurred in place A and another part in place B. The choice was not between Jewish law and the law of another legal system, but between laws contained in different enactments within the Jewish legal system. An additional significant factor in the increase of problems of conflict of laws was the multiplicity of local customs. Such customs had already existed to a certain extent in the Talmudic period, but they progressively increased, especially in the post-geonic period, when there was no single predominant center. Local legislation and local custom were extremely important factors in the growth of the field of conflict of laws in Jewish law. This subject has been treated in some detail elsewhere.[46]

42. *See infra* pp. 867–869.

43. *See infra* pp. 878–879.

44. For details, *see* M. Elon, EJ, V, pp. 882–890, s.v. Conflict of laws (reprinted in *Principles*, pp. 715–724). *See id.* for the rules of conflict of laws in Jewish law that apply in cases involving both Jews and non-Jews and the rules that apply as a consequence of the doctrine of *dina de-malkhuta dina* ("the law of the land is law"). *See also supra* pp. 78–79.

45. *See* Elon, *supra* n. 44.

46. *See id.*, and *infra* p. 936.

Chapter 19
COMMUNAL ENACTMENTS

I. LEGISLATION BY THE TOWNSPEOPLE AND THE COMMUNITY

Legislation stemming from communal action[1] first appears in early laws concerning "the townspeople." The *Tosefta* states:[2]

> The townspeople may obligate each other to build a synagogue and to buy scrolls of the Torah and of the Prophets.
>
> The townspeople may fix market prices [of wheat and wine], weights and measures, and laborers' wages, and they may enforce[3] their regulations.[4]

1. The earliest legislative source other than the halakhic authorities was the king or government, whose legislative authority antedated that of the community. *See supra* pp. 55–57, 486–487; *infra* p. 714 n. 145.

2. *Tosefta* Bava Meẓi'a 11:23. Part of this section of the *Tosefta* is quoted in TB Bava Batra 8b. *See infra* n. 3.

3. The Hebrew phrase in the *Tosefta* meaning "enforce their regulations" is *le'assot kiẓatan; le'assot,* as distinguished from *la'asot* ("to do"), means "to impose" or "to compel" as in the following examples: *get me'usseh*—a compelled or coerced divorce (TB Gittin 88b); "an admonition to the court *she-ye'assukha*—that they should force you" (TB Rosh ha-Shanah 6a); "*Ha-me'asseh* (the person who causes another to do) [a good deed] is greater [*i.e.,* is more meritorious] than the one who actually does the deed" (TB Bava Batra 9a); "Compel (*ussu*) one another [to do good deeds]" (TB Bava Batra, *id.*); *see* J.N. Epstein, *Mevo'ot le-Sifrut ha-Amoraim* [Introduction to Amoraic Literature] (hereinafter, *Amoraim*), p. 218 n. 82.

TB Bava Batra 8b reads: "*u-lehassi'a al kiẓatan,*" which *Yad Ramah* (*ad loc.,* par. 91, s.v. Tashlum baraita) interprets: "To help in the fixing of their stipulations [*i.e.,* enactments], to provide that any person who changes the fixed amounts will be liable to a monetary fine, a ban, or flogging, as it is written, 'Anyone who does not come in three days . . . [Ezra 10:8].'" The same interpretation is given by Rabbenu Gershom (*ad loc.,* s.v. U-lehassi'a al kiẓatan).

Ritba, Novellae, *ad loc.,* also bases the legislative authority of the townspeople on the principle of *hefker bet din hefker* (the court has power to expropriate property) by analogy to the rationale given for communal enactments in his own day; *see infra* n. 88. Rashi (*ad loc.,* s.v. Lehassi'a al kiẓatam) explains: "[They have the authority] to fine any person who violates their regulations, even if the regulations diverge from laws of the Torah." This is also the interpretation given by Ritba, *supra,* and *Nimmukei Yosef* to Alfasi (*ad loc.,* s.v. U-lehassi'a al kiẓatan, printed eds. of Alfasi, p. 6b.)

The sense of the Hebrew term *lehassi'a* is similar to *lehassiaḥ, i.e.,* "to remove" or "divert," M Eruvin 8:5 (*see* H. Albeck, *ad loc.,* and *Arukh ha-Shalem,* III, p. 227; V, p. 355), or "to uproot," *cf.* Psalms 80:9. *See also* Epstein, *Amoraim,* p. 218 n. 82; *Tosafot,* Bava Kamma 116b, s.v. Ve-rasha'im ha-ḥamarim lehatnot beineihem. The original reading is probably that of the *Tosefta. See also Resp. Maharik* #181 (= #179), noting the difference between the text of the *Tosefta* and TB and asserting that the meaning is identical (s.v. Ve-hi hi, p. 105a, end of column).

4. The literal meaning of the Hebrew term *kiẓah,* translated here as "regulations," connotes a fixed and specified thing or amount; *see Tosefta* Ketubbot 4:7; TJ Ketubbot 6:4, 40a/b (6:4, 30d); TB Nedarim 86a; Bava Meẓi'a 67b.

> The townspeople may declare: "Whoever shows [another's property] to a third party [*i.e.*, thieves, so that it can be stolen] or informs [lit. "appears before"] the government [so that the property can be confiscated] shall be penalized in a specified amount;[5] and whoever permits his cow to graze among the vegetation shall be penalized in a specified amount"; and they may enforce their regulations.

The townspeople may thus legislate on various matters that are essentially municipal and economic, and they may enforce compliance with their legislation.[6]

Subsequently, the *Tosefta*[7] discusses internal regulations, legislative in nature, adopted by various occupational groups:

> The wool dealers and the dyers may declare: "We shall all be partners in all merchandise that comes into the town."
>
> The bakers may enter into an agreement (*regi'ah*)[8] among themselves.
>
> The donkey drivers may declare: "We will provide another donkey to anyone whose donkey dies."[9] If the death occurs as the result of [the owner's]

5. As to the Hebrew terms *yar'eh eẓel peloni* ("shows [another's property] to a third party") and *yero'eh eẓel malkhut* ("appears before the government"), *see* S. Lieberman, *Tosefet Rishonim*, II, pp. 132–133. The Hebrew term *ve-her'ah mamon ḥavero* ("shows another's property") and the Aramaic parallel, *aḥavei*, in the sense of "inform on," or "betray," appear in TB Bava Kamma 117a.

6. The notion of compulsion or enforcement is expressed in the *Tosefta* by the term *le'assot* and in TB by the term *lehassi'a* as interpreted by Rashi and *Nimmukei Yosef; see supra* n. 3. Neither the *Tosefta* nor TB (according to interpretations such as that of *Arukh ha-Shalem*) explicitly states that legislation by the townspeople may be inconsistent with the law of the Torah; and it is possible that the interpretations of Rashi and *Nimmukei Yosef* reflect the situation of their own times, when communal enactments could be inconsistent with a law of the Torah; *see infra* p. 736. For the scope of legislation by the townspeople, *see infra* n. 12.

7. *Tosefta* Bava Meẓi'a 11:24–26; parts of this section of the *Tosefta* are quoted in TB Bava Kamma 116b.

8. *Sefer ha-Shetarot* [Book of Legal Instruments] of Judah al-Bargeloni, pp. 89–90 (quoted in A. Gulak, *Oẓar ha-Shetarot*, p. 359), contains the text of a *regi'ah*, which was the name given to an agreement among the bakers. Naḥmanides, Novellae to Bava Batra 9a, s.v. Ha de-amrinan be-hanhu, explained the term as follows: "The meaning of *regi'ah* is the allocation of time [*rega* = minute, *i.e.*, time]: 'You will not sell during my allotted time and I will not sell during yours.' The term *regi'ah* is found in geonic literature in the *Sefer ha-Shetarot* of Judah al-Bargeloni." *Maggid Mishneh* to *MT*, Mekhirah 14:10, comments: "*Regi'ah* has been defined as the division of time, *i.e.*, [the agreement is], 'You will work at a given time and I will work at a given time.' However, I believe that the derivation is from the word *margo'a*, which connotes rest, *i.e.*, [the agreement is], 'You will rest [*i.e.*, abstain from work] on a given day, and I [will rest] on a given day.'" *See* Levy, *Wörterbuch*, IV, p. 426, s.v. Regi'ah, defining *regi'ah* as "a mutual agreement," parallel to a similar term in Arabic.

9. *See* v.l. in *Tosefta* Bava Meẓi'a 11:24–26. TB Bava Kamma 116b reads: "who loses his donkey."

> negligence,[10] they need not replace it; but if it is not the result of [such] negligence, they must replace it. If the owner states, "Give me the money and I will buy one for myself," they need not comply with his request, but they may purchase one and give it to him.
>
> The boatmen may declare: "We will provide another boat whenever anyone's boat is lost." If the loss is the result of [the owner's] negligence, they need not replace it; but if the loss is not the result of [such] negligence, they must replace it. If he [the owner] took it to a place where people do not ordinarily take their boats, they need not give him another boat.

This is detailed legislation on a number of topics: the establishment of a type of partnership by the members of the wool dealers' and dyers' association; a division of labor among the bakers; a plan of mutual insurance by the members of the donkey drivers' and boatmen's associations.[11] Under these internal regulations, there was no right to indemnification if the damage resulted from an insured's negligence. It is also noteworthy that an insured was entitled only to replacement of the item necessary to conduct his business—the donkey or the boat—but not the value of the item in money. The reason, apparently, was to ensure that he would not use the money for some purpose other than the purchase of a replacement for what was lost. This type of legislative activity appears to have continued in all later periods to cover matters such as these, although it is difficult to identify with any certainty what laws originated in legislation by local autonomous groups.[12]

A substantial and decisive change came at the end of the tenth century

10. Aramaic: *be-vusya.* TB Bava Kamma 116b reads: *be-khusya,* which is also given in v.l. of the *Tosefta.* Ms. Munich reads, *be-visiya,* and *see Dikdukei Soferim, ad loc.* The meaning of *be-khusya* is "as the result of negligence." *See Targum Jonathan b. Uzziel* to Exodus 22:8 and Rashi, Bava Kamma 116b, s.v. Be-khusya.

11. As to the existence of guilds of craftsmen, *see Tosefta* Sukkah 4:6 and TB Sukkah 51b in regard to the special sections in the great synagogue in Alexandria for members of the various guilds. *See also* S. Lieberman, *Tosefta ki-Feshutah,* Sukkah, pp. 889–892, for commentary on the *Tosefta, ad loc.*; M Bikkurim 3:3.

12. *See, e.g.,* Y. Baer, "Ha-Yesodot ha-Historiyyim Shel ha-Halakhah" [The Historical Foundations of the *Halakhah*], *Zion,* XVII, pp. 24–27, expressing the view that the various provisions governing relations between neighbors set forth in M Bava Batra chs. 1 and 2 "are not the creations of academies, courts, legislative authorities, or later Sages, but are rather taken from a living historical and social reality. Such provisions were adopted by the residents of towns and villages who at some time decided to establish regulations for the mutual benefit of all the townspeople." If this is correct, as it may well be, then these are examples of legislation by the townspeople, in addition to the list in the *Tosefta.* However, it is equally possible that these laws originated as enactments by the courts and the halakhic authorities. In any event, explicit evidence of early legislation by townspeople exists only regarding the fixing of food prices, weights and measures, wages, and municipal services and administration. For an example of legislation by a tradesmen's association, *see* TB Bava Batra 9a as to butchers; *see infra* pp. 752–753. *See also infra* p. 1074 n. 151.

C.E. with the rise in the power of the Jewish community (*kehillah*).[13] The community was a social unit with authority to regulate all areas of its members' activities, and it shaped the social patterns and spiritual character of its members. It had a very large measure of autonomy. It had internal governmental agencies composed of elected and appointed representatives; it provided for the educational and social needs of its members; its court had jurisdiction over matters of civil and administrative law as well as, to a certain extent, criminal law;[14] and it also levied and collected taxes from its members in order to pay the tax imposed by the general government on the community and to finance the community's services to its members.

Often, a number of communities acted jointly to carry out a substantial part of these tasks, such as maintaining governmental institutions and enforcing the levy and collection of taxes. The organization and regulation of these many functions was to a considerable extent accomplished by enactments[15] adopted by the community and its representatives, the representatives of associations of communities, and provincial and national councils.

The legislative activity of the public, starting with the tenth century C.E., extended over a very large part of the areas of *mishpat ivri*—all branches of civil law, substantial portions of public law (*e.g.*, taxation, elections, the relation of the public authority to its citizens and employees, and the legal status of the public authority), and various matters in the area of criminal law.

These far-reaching changes in the scope of the subject matter of public legislation presented the halakhic authorities with many fundamental legal problems for which the existing law had no explicit response. Thus, for example, the Talmud contains no discussion of the source of authority of the public to legislate, and therefore provides no guidance as to the breadth or scope of that authority. The Talmud is similarly silent with regard to many fundamental questions concerning the legislative process itself as well as the extent of legislative jurisdiction. For example, must a communal enactment be adopted by all the people and in their presence, or can it be adopted in the name of the public by the public's delegated representatives? Can a majority of the people impose their view on the minority, or must an

13. *See supra* pp. 666–668.

14. Communities frequently had a lay tribunal made up of communal leaders, householders, and the like, which had jurisdiction in various legal areas, particularly public, commercial, and criminal law. Such tribunals in particular based their judgments on, *inter alia*, communal enactments. For further discussion, *see supra* pp. 20–29.

15. In Ashkenaz, *i.e.*, Germany and Northern France, these were known as *takkanot ha-kahal* or *takkanot ha-kehillot*. In Spain, Italy, North Africa, and the eastern countries, they were called *haskamot* ("agreements") of the public or the communities. The corresponding verb forms of these various appellations are *tikkenu* (or *hitkinu*) and *hiskimu*.

enactment be adopted unanimously, obligating only those who accept it from the outset? How and on what basis can an enactment obligate someone who at the time of its adoption is not a member of the community but joins it only later, or someone who is born after the enactment was adopted? For the solution to these and similar questions that are discussed below, one would ordinarily look to the field of public-constitutional law; but the Talmud did not deal with these questions at all,[16] and it is impossible to find answers by analogy from similar situations in the area of private law.[17]

Furthermore, the increase in the power of the local Jewish community came at the same time as the momentous transformation at the end of the tenth and the beginning of the eleventh centuries C.E., *i.e.*, the decline and

16. A.H. Freimann, "Rov u-Mi'ut ba-Ẓibbur" [Majority and Minority in the Community], *Yavneh*, II, Tishri 1948, p. 1, sought to deduce the principle that the majority can impose their will on the minority from the rule that "no legislation should be imposed on the public unless the majority can conform to it" (TB Avodah Zarah 36a). That conclusion is, however, unjustified because the rule refers to enactments by halakhic authorities who are obligated to take into account the degree of acceptability of their legislation to the majority of the people. The rule in no way addresses the question of whether the decision of the majority is binding on the minority; *see supra* pp. 538–541.

It was only in later periods that sources such as TB Avodah Zarah 36a were perceived as providing a basis for the principle that an enactment adopted by the majority can bind the dissenting minority (*see, e.g., Resp. Rashba Attributed to Naḥmanides* #280; *Resp. Rashba*, V, #125), but this was only a supportive device (*asmakhta*) at best and was by no means the plain meaning of the sources. Exodus 23:2, "*aḥarei rabbim le-hattot*" ("follow the majority") was understood in the Talmud as referring to a decision by the majority of the judges of a court, not as giving the majority of the public the right to impose their opinion or enactment on the minority (*see* TB Sanhedrin 2a–3b). It was also understood as providing the basis for an inference drawn from the preponderance of probabilities (TB Ḥullin 11a.)

See infra pp. 715–727 in regard to majority and minority in communal enactments, and pp. 762–763 as to the rule that no legislation should be enacted unless the majority of the public can conform to it. *See also* Y. Baer, "Ha-Yesodot ve-ha-Hatḥalot Shel Irgun ha-Kehillah ha-Yehudit bi-Mei ha-Beinayim" [The Foundations and Beginnings of Jewish Communal Organization in the Middle Ages], *Zion*, XVI, p. 7 n. 18.

17. If the private law of partnership between individuals were to be applied to the public, the majority could not bind the minority; *see, e.g.*, TB Bava Batra 21b and *Piskei ha-Rosh, ad loc.*, ch. 2, #11: "If two persons occupy one courtyard, each can preclude [any activity by] the other; and one partner can also preclude [any activity by] his other partners, however many. The same rule applies to a person who owns a house in a courtyard that is owned in common."

This rule is also codified as law in Sh. Ar. ḤM 156:1. *See also Sema, ad loc.*, subpar. 6, distinguishing the law of partnership in this respect from the rule applicable to communal enactments: ". . . but with regard to enactments adopted by the community, Rosh [Asheri], principle 6, rule 4 [the correct reference is *Resp. Asheri* 6:5] has written that an individual cannot nullify them, because the verse 'follow the majority' applies to them." *See also infra* pp. 717–718. By the same token, if ordinary partnership law were to govern communal affairs, it would, for example, be impossible to create rights or obligations in a person not yet born. *See further* M. Elon, EJ, XV, pp. 844–847, s.v. Taxation (reprinted in *Principles*, pp. 667–671).

disappearance of a single center—the Babylonian center—that had exercised spiritual hegemony over the entire diaspora, and the emergence of many centers, concomitant and successive, throughout the dispersion.[18] This decisive shift gave rise to important changes in the economic and social conditions of the various Jewish centers, and it was imperative to regulate these changes in the interest of the public life of the autonomous community.

To a considerable extent, the community accomplished this adjustment through the adoption of enactments that were often inconsistent with accepted Talmudic law. This situation necessarily gave rise to questions as to the extent of the community's right to adopt enactments inconsistent with existing law, and the degree of control vested in the halakhic authorities over the legislative activity of the public. Although a certain measure of control already existed in Talmudic law, this control, to the extent that it was necessary, involved only a narrow and limited review.[19]

Consequently, the task facing the halakhic authorities in this period was to fashion a standard of halakhic judicial review—based on general principles designed to protect the fundamental and essential character of Jewish law—that would be applicable even when legislation enacted to meet an immediately pressing need conflicts with an existing rule of law. Here again, the halakhic authorities were faced with the need to formulate principles of judicial review testing the fairness, rationality, justice, and equity of public legislation.

In addition to the question of the source of authority for communal legislation and, as a corollary, the definition of the areas in which such legislation would be effective, two topics were central to the Jewish law of communal legislation during this period:

a. The nature and legal effect of communal legislation as a norm of public law. The grappling with this question resulted in exempting communal legislation from the requirements that private agreements had to meet—and the limitations with which private agreements had to comply—in order to be legally effective.[20]

18. *See supra* pp. 666–667.

19. A regulation of a tradesmen's group required approval by a "distinguished person"; *see infra* pp. 752–753. According to the plain meaning of the Talmudic passage, such approval was required only for a regulation adopted by a tradesmen's group, but not for an enactment of the townspeople. Also, such approval was necessary only if at the time the regulation was adopted such a "distinguished person" was present in the locality; for detailed discussion, *see infra* pp. 753–754, 759.

20. This period saw the beginning of intensive creativity in public law with regard to the economic and fiscal relationships within the community, the status and prerogatives of communal authority, and the legal relationships between the public authority, its employees, and the public. For detailed discussion of all these matters, *see* M. Elon, EJ, VIII, pp. 279–

b. The relationship between communal legislation and the halakhic system. One aspect of this relationship involves the power of the community to resolve various legal problems by legislation prescribing rules contrary to the *Halakhah,* and a second aspect concerns the extent to which the halakhic authorities were entitled to participate in determining the objectives and substantive provisions of communal legislation.

The essential points of each of these topics are examined in the sections of this chapter that follow.[21]

II. THE SOURCE OF THE AUTHORITY AND LEGAL EFFECTIVENESS OF COMMUNAL ENACTMENTS

A. Civil Law

Beginning in the tenth century C.E., the halakhic authorities devoted much attention to the question of the legal basis for a community's power to enact legislation.

A responsum written in the middle of the tenth century C.E. by Hananiah b. Judah Gaon, the father of Sherira Gaon, states:[22]

> Whenever a community enacts legislation that meets a need, promotes the public welfare, and applies equally to everyone, the legislation is enforceable; the agreement[23] of the elders governs, and all the townspeople are bound by it, as Scripture states:[24] "[A proclamation was issued that] anyone who does not come in three days, as required by the officers and elders, will have his property confiscated and himself excluded from the congregation of the re-

---

287, s.v. Hekdesh (reprinted in *Principles,* pp. 645–654); XV, pp. 840–873, s.v. Taxation (reprinted in *Principles,* pp. 662–701). *See also infra* pp. 699–707 as to parallels between the status of the community and that of the court with respect to legislative authority.

21. Several of these issues are discussed in the articles of Freimann and Baer, *supra* n. 16; S. Albeck, "Yaḥaso Shel Rabbenu Tam le-Va'ayot Zemano" [Rabbenu Tam's Attitude Toward the Problems of His Time], *Zion,* XIX (1954), pp. 128–136; *id.,* "Yesodot Mishtar ha-Kehillot bi-Sefarad ad ha-Ramah" [The Foundations of Communal Government in Spain until Ramah], *Zion,* XXV (1960), pp. 85–121; I.A. Agus, "Ha-Shilton ha-Aẓma'i Shel ha-Kehillah ha-Yehudit bi-Mei ha-Beinayim" [The Autonomy of the Jewish Community in the Middle Ages], *Talpiot,* V, pp. 176–195, 637–648; VI, pp. 305–320.

The major part of the discussion in this chapter is based on M. Elon, "Le-Mahutan Shel Takkanot ha-Kahal ba-Mishpat ha-Ivri" [On the Nature of Communal Enactments in Jewish Law], *Meḥkerei Mishpat le-Zekher Avraham Rosenthal* [Legal Studies in Memory of Abraham Rosenthal], Magnes Press, 1964, pp. 1–54.

22. *Teshuvot ha-Geonim Sha'arei Ẓedek,* IV, Sha'ar 4, #16 (ed. Jerusalem, 1966, pp. 126–127).

23. *I.e.,* enactment; Hebrew *ve-haskamat ha-zekenim; see supra* n. 15.

24. Ezra 10:8.

> turning exiles"; and our Rabbis have declared:[25] "The townspeople may fix market prices, weights and measures, and laborers' wages, and they may enforce their regulations"—and this is all by vote of the elders. We learn from this verse and statement that the elders of the town have the authority to adopt enactments for, and to enforce compliance by, their townspeople.

This responsum cites as the source of authority for communal enactments the Talmudic passage with regard to legislation by the townspeople as well as the verse in the Book of Ezra upon which the Sages based the legislative power of the halakhic authorities to expropriate property pursuant to the principle of *hefker bet din hefker.*[26] The reliance on the verse from the Book of Ezra is discussed in greater detail in another responsum from the end of the tenth century C.E. A question asked of Rabbenu Gershom told of the sinking of a ship whose passengers succeeded in saving themselves as well as a number of valuable articles. Under the circumstances, it was feared that some people would acquire rights in property that did not belong to them. The responsum states:[27]

> The communities that gathered there and grieved[28] over the loss of their brethren issued a decree providing, on penalty of a solemn imprecation, that anyone who obtains anything that was lost on the ship must restore it to its owner according to the custom practiced in most Jewish communities, *i.e.*, an enactment was adopted for the benefit of anyone who loses anything either by theft or in any other manner, requiring anyone who obtains any lost article to restore it to its owner.
>
> Thirty days later, when Reuben was still searching for his lost property, a certain non-Jew sold to Simeon the gold of Reuben that had been lost on the ship and he [Simeon] refused to return it to Reuben, declaring, "I have become its owner because an article carried away by the sea is free to all."

Simeon thus admitted that the gold had belonged to Reuben, but he argued that property lost under circumstances where it is reasonable to assume that the owner had abandoned (lit. "despaired of") it—as where it was swept away by the sea—legally belongs to its finder; and indeed this is

25. TB Bava Batra 8b.

26. *See supra* pp. 507–508.

27. *Resp. Rabbenu Gershom Me'or ha-Golah* #67 (ed. Eidelberg, pp. 154–158).

28. The word "grieved" follows Eidelberg's text, in which he changes the Hebrew *nit'aẓmu* to *nit'aẓvu*. However, there is no need to make this change, as was correctly pointed out by A. Grossman in "Yaḥasam Shel Ḥakhmei Ashkenaz ha-Rishonim el Shilton ha-Kahal" [The Relationship of the Early Ashkenazic Halakhic Authorities to Communal Government], *Shenaton,* II (1975), p. 179 n. 10, explaining *nit'aẓmu* as meaning "struggled vigorously." Grossman's point is apt, as the term *nit'aẓmu* reflects halakhic terminology; *see, e.g.*, TB Sanhedrin 31b: "Two who struggled vigorously over the law" ("*nit'aẓmu be-din*"), and *see* Rashi, *ad loc.*; Maimonides, *MT,* Sanhedrin 6:6; *Resp. Ḥakhmei Ẓarfat ve-Lutir* #29.

the law in the Talmud.[29] Therefore, Simeon refused to obey the communal enactment, which prescribed that even in such circumstances the lost property must be restored to its owner.

After discussing the question whether in fact Reuben (the owner) had abandoned the lost property, Rabbenu Gershom stated:

> Even if Reuben did abandon hope of recovering his property, since a communal enactment was adopted there providing that anyone who obtains anything that was lost must restore it to its owner, Simeon must return the article to Reuben even though the Torah gave it to Simeon [*i.e.*, even though, under Biblical law, a lost article in such circumstances belongs to Simeon as the finder], because *hefker bet din hefker* [the court has the power to expropriate an individual's property]. . . .
>
> As R. Isaac said:[30] "What is the source of [the principle of] *hefker bet din hefker?* It is written, 'Anyone who does not come in three days, as required by the officers and elders, will have his property confiscated.'"
>
> R. Eleazar said: "[The deduction is made] from the following [verse]: 'These are the portions assigned by the priest Eleazar, Joshua the son of Nun, and the heads of the ancestral houses [lit. "the heads of the fathers"] of the tribes of the children of Israel [before the Lord at Shiloh, at the entrance of the Tent of Meeting . . . they . . . finished dividing the land].'[31] Why is the connection made between 'heads' and 'fathers'? To tell us that just as fathers bequeath to their children whatever they wish, so, too, the 'heads' [*i.e.*, the leaders] assign whatever portions they wish to the people."[32]

After Rabbenu Gershom cited this legislative principle of Jewish law, he continued:

> An objection that we apply *hefker bet din hefker* only to a distinguished court such as that of Shammai or Hillel, but not today, is not a valid objection, as the Rabbis taught:[33] "Scripture states 'and the Lord sent Jerubaal, Bedan, Jephthah, and Samuel . . .'[34] [to teach] that even if the most insignificant person is chosen as a leader of the community, he should be considered the equal of the mightiest." Therefore, all the communal decrees and acts are valid, and Simeon may not violate them; he must return the property to Reuben, and should not covet property that does not belong to him.

Rabbenu Gershom thus based the legal authority of the community to enact legislation, even though inconsistent with a halakhic rule, on the

29. TB Bava Meẓi'a 22b.

30. TB Yevamot 89b *et al.*; *see supra* pp. 508–509.

31. Joshua 19:51; 20:1.

32. For detailed discussion of the principle of *hefker bet din hefker* and for the derivations by R. Isaac and R. Eleazar, *see supra* pp. 508–510.

33. TB Rosh ha-Shanah 25a/b *et al. See also supra* p. 266.

34. I Samuel 12:11.

principle of *hefker bet din hefker,* which is to be interpreted as applying to "the most insignificant person [who] is chosen as a leader of the community"; and consequently, Rabbenu Gershom determined that the communal enactment was valid and binding, and Simeon was obligated to return the property he had obtained.[35]

B. Criminal Law

A responsum by Joseph b. Samuel Tov Elem, a leading French halakhic authority in the middle of the eleventh century C.E., cites an additional legislative principle as a basis for the legal effectiveness of communal legislation:[36]

> The people of Tiberias agreed among themselves on the method of collecting taxes to be transmitted to the king; each complained of the other saying, "You

35. The same provision described in Rabbenu Gershom's responsum as a communal enactment is cited as a *minhag* (custom) in a responsum by Sherira Gaon. *Teshuvot ha-Geonim Sha'arei Ẓedek,* IV, Sha'ar 1, #20 (ed. Jerusalem, 1966, p. 75):

> Regarding the statement in your letter that there is a custom in your locality that if a person buys something from bandits or thieves, he must return it to its owner and is reimbursed for the purchase price, if that is definitely your custom, no one may deviate from it. For we say, "What is the basis for the binding force of custom? It is the verse, 'You shall not move your neighbor's landmarks, set up by previous generations'" [Deuteronomy 19:14]. This certainly applies in a matter that significantly promotes the public welfare and prevents disastrous strife. Therefore, act according to your custom and neither change nor depart from what your fathers and forebears have done. There can be no complaint against those who so act in this matter [*i.e.,* those who act according to the custom].

As to this responsum, *see infra* p. 894 n. 61. *See also* B.Z. Dinur, *Yisra'el ba-Golah* [Israel in Diaspora], I(3), p. 331 n. 76, maintaining that the principal innovation in this enactment was Rabbenu Gershom's transformation of a custom into a legislative enactment binding on everyone and not subject to change by any individual. This enactment is also quoted by Raban in his commentary on Bava Meẓi'a, ch. 2 (beginning), and in *Resp. Maharam of Rothenburg,* ed. Prague, #770. The following rationale is given by *Resp. Maharam of Rothenburg:*

> He must restore it [to its original owner] because of the communal enactment that is for his own benefit and advantage, since if the same thing happens to him the same rule will also be applied to him. This is similar to the enactment [concerning lost property] about which Rava said (TB Bava Meẓi'a 27b): "If you assert that [the return of a lost object on the basis of] identification marks is not [required under] Biblical law, why did they [the Sages] say that a found article must be returned to its owner on the basis of identification marks? So that if he [the finder] loses something, it will also be returned to him on the basis of identification marks."

This is a "utilitarian" rationale for the enactment. *See also* Rema to Sh. Ar. ḤM 356:7, where the rule is grounded on *dina de-malkhuta dina* ("the law of the land is law"); and *Shakh, ad loc.,* subpar. 10, ascribing to the rule a legislative origin.

36. The responsum can be found in *Resp. Maharam of Rothenburg,* ed. Lemberg, #423. A part of this responsum was quoted *supra* p. 672 in connection with a community's lack of power to interfere with another community's enactments.

> are easy on yourself, but hard on me" [*i.e.*, the tax is being imposed in a discriminatory fashion].[37] They thereupon selected as authorized representatives (*ne'emanim*) from among the leaders of the town the most knowledgeable and trustworthy members of the community to hear their complaints. They all agreed that they would pay to the tax collectors whatever was assessed and that whoever refused to do so would be fined a *litra* [a certain sum of money] and subjected to a ban so long as he persisted in his refusal.
>
> The community, for fear of God and respect for the decree [*i.e.*, the communal enactment], was in full agreement to pay the tax as directed, except for two individuals who refused to obey and ignored the decree. These two went to Sepphoris,[38] where they described the entire incident. Residents of Sepphoris invited them to their homes, ate and drank with them, and discussed the matter with them. They [the townspeople of Sepphoris] then wrote out a document exempting them [the two individuals from Tiberias] from any obligation under the decree of their community of Tiberias.
>
> When they returned to Tiberias, they arrogantly boasted of their accomplishment [of having been exempted from the communal enactment]. When the people of Tiberias heard this, they became angry and considered informing the king so that he would order the police to seize the apportioned shares of the recalcitrants, since the community's regulations would be ineffective if others could annul what the community had enacted.
>
> Afterward, they decided to determine first whether their decree remained valid and whether the exemption given by the townspeople of Sepphoris had any validity, and to look generally into the entire matter.

Thus, before turning to the general government, the leaders of the community of Tiberias decided to submit to Joseph Tov Elem the question whether the enactment legally obligated all of the townspeople, and whether another community was empowered to interfere.

Joseph Tov Elem's discussion includes a general treatment of communal enactments, as follows:

> Certainly, they [the people of Tiberias] adopted their enactment properly, like other communities, and selected authorized representatives according to the enactment, as they agreed. For the halakhic authorities have authorized and empowered every community to legislate for itself, and no other community has any right to nullify such legislation, as we have learned:[39] "The townspeople may fix weights and measures, market prices, and laborers' wages, and they may enforce their regulations"; and R. Isaac said,[40] "What is the source of [the principle of] *hefker bet din hefker?* . . ."

37. "Tiberias" is a fictitious name given by the author of the responsum to the Jewish community involved. *See infra* p. 1512–1515.

38. This is also a fictitious name; *see supra* n. 37.

39. TB Bava Batra 8b; *see supra* p. 679.

40. TB Yevamot 89b *et al.*

> It also was taught:[41] R. Eliezer said: "I have heard that the court may impose flogging and punishment not prescribed in the Torah—not to transgress the law of the Torah but in order to make a fence around the Torah."[42] Thus we learn that the court in every community may issue decrees binding on the members of the community as they deem necessary for the needs of the time, and no one else may annul any such enactment so long as it does not transgress the basic concepts of the Torah.[43] We see here no such transgression, inasmuch as no individual may exempt himself from paying taxes or other communal assessments. . . .
>
> Whenever the people adopt an enactment or issue a decree to govern themselves, how can anyone overturn and nullify it? This would remove all restraints! If this were permissible, everyone could exempt himself from the tax and from all court enactments. It is impossible to coerce evildoers nowadays except by means of bans and fines, and whoever nullifies these sanctions increases licentiousness among the Jewish people.

Like Rabbenu Gershom, Joseph Tov Elem also saw in *hefker bet din hefker* a basis for the legislative authority of the public. As an additional basis for the binding force of communal enactments, he relied on the legislative principle that a court may decree punishment not prescribed by strict law, which he applied not only to enactments by a court (*i.e.*, legislation by the halakhic authorities), but also to communal enactments.

Indeed, the public has authority to legislate not only in civil law matters but also in the field of criminal law: "The public has authority to fine and to punish for every improper act according to one's station in life."[44] In connection with an incident where "Simeon took hold of another's throat and drew out his knife against him and said, 'I will crush your skull,'" Maharam of Rothenburg wrote:

> It is clear that he committed an extremely wicked act. . . . In every community it is customary to enact essential *takkanot* and safeguards according to the circumstances, and if the village where this wicked deed was done is attached to a community that provides for a fine, he should be fined in accordance with the custom of that community.[45]

As stated, this authority was based on the extension to communal enactments of the principle that a court may decree punishment not prescribed by strict law; and, as a consequence, the community was vested

41. *Id.* 90b; *see also* TB Sanhedrin 46a.

42. As to the principle that the court may impose punishment not prescribed in the Torah, *see supra* pp. 515–519.

43. *I.e.*, that it does not violate the basic principles of equity and justice of Jewish law; for a detailed discussion, *see infra* pp. 760–777.

44. *Resp. Maharam of Rothenburg*, ed. Berlin, #220 (p. 37).

45. *Resp. Maharam of Rothenburg*, ed. Prague, #383.

with authority to adopt enactments when necessary in the field of criminal law, even if the enactments conflicted with a halakhic rule. A responsum of Rashba[46] thoroughly discusses this point. The question posed was:

> The community agreed to choose us as *berurim* to eradicate crime [*i.e.*, to be judges for criminal matters], and we took an oath to do this. The enactment[47] states that we have authority from the general government to enforce discipline, inflict corporal punishment, and impose monetary penalties at our discretion.
>
> If witnesses who are credible but are next of kin [to each other] testify that Reuben violated his oath, or if this is disclosed to us by a woman or a minor, please inform us whether we may punish Reuben. Or, if one or more of the witnesses are Reuben's relatives and we have reasonable ground to believe that these witnesses are telling the truth, do we have authority to take action on the basis of their testimony even though we do not have testimony that is technically sufficient?

Rashba's response was clear and unequivocal:

> It is clear to me that you may act at your discretion. Those rules cited by you [that witnesses who are next of kin, etc., are incompetent] apply only to a court that judges according to the laws of the Torah, such as the Sanhedrin or a similar body.
>
> But whoever is appointed on the basis of a communal enactment does not judge directly according to the laws set down in the Torah itself; he may do whatever is necessary to satisfy the needs of the time, with the consent of the government. Otherwise, . . . no one could be flogged or punished on the basis of his own confession, since under strict law one may not incriminate oneself,[48] and even if there are competent witnesses, he could not be flogged unless he had been forewarned, since a court may not flog unless the defendant commits the offense after first having been explicitly admonished not to do so.[49]
>
> However, all those rules apply only to a court that acts according to the Torah. . . . It has also been said that punishment not prescribed by strict law may be imposed—not to transgress the Torah but in order to make a fence around the Torah. . . . All the more does this apply to you, for the major

46. *Resp. Rashba*, IV, #311. This responsum is also found in an abbreviated form in *Resp. Rashba Attributed to Naḥmanides* #279.

47. Hebrew: *tikkunei ha-haskamah*. *See supra* n. 15.

48. Under strict law, the admission of an accused is not accepted if it involves self-incrimination; TB Yevamot 25b; Maimonides, *MT*, Sanhedrin 18:6. For detailed discussions, *see* A. Kirschenbaum, *Self-Incrimination in Jewish Law*, New York, 1970; A. Enker, "Self-Incrimination in Jewish Law, A Review Essay," *Dine Israel*, 1973, p. cvii (English section).

49. *I.e.*, the defendant had to be warned that what he was about to do constituted a crime; *see* M Sanhedrin 5:1; TB Sanhedrin 40a/b; Ketubbot 32b; Maimonides, *MT*, Sanhedrin 16:4.

> purpose of the enactment was to permit you to act at your discretion, as is stated in the text of the enactment that you quoted. This is clearly the case among us and in any place where there is an enactment on these matters.[50]

Communal legislation has brought about an interesting development in the law of criminal procedure and evidence. Such legislation was adopted because of the need to punish offenders shown to be guilty of criminal acts even though the evidence against them is insufficient under strict Biblical law. This development has been extensively discussed in the decisions of the Israeli Supreme Court; the opinion in *Nagar v. State of Israel*[51] contains the following detailed description:

> In *Ḥaliḥal v. State of Israel,*[52] the late Justice Silberg quotes the words of R. Tarfon and R. Akiva: "Had we been members of the Sanhedrin, no person would ever have been put to death."[53] The Talmud explained as follows:[54]
>
> > What would they [as judges] have done? Both R. Johanan and R. Eleazar said [that they would have asked the witnesses questions such as]: "Did you note whether the [murder] victim was suffering from some fatal condition or was in good health?" R. Ashi said: "Even if the reply is that he was in good health, there may have been a lesion where the sword cut [from which he would have died in any event]."
>
> Justice Silberg contrasts this view of R. Tarfon and R. Akiva—that a defendant should be acquitted on the basis of the most far-fetched and remote possibility that his act may not have caused the death—with the accepted view of modern law that—
>
> > . . . since there is *a need* for judicial action to punish offenders, it is *essential* to disregard "remote possibilities," *i.e.,* unusual and aberrant occurrences, even though this may possibly cause a miscarriage of justice. In other words, the legislature realized the risk, but found it to be necessary, since otherwise the need for adjudication would never be satisfied, and necessity may not be gainsaid.

50. *See also Resp. Asheri* 101:1: "If it can be ascertained that the town has adopted enactments regarding [the punishment to be imposed for] insult, these enactments, rather than Talmudic law, should be followed." *See further* Meiri, *Bet ha-Beḥirah,* Bava Kamma 84b (ed. Schlesinger, pp. 246–247), in regard to jurisdiction in capital cases: "I say that in those places where they are authorized by their government to judge according to Jewish law and all the people [*i.e.,* all the Jews] agree to it, it is to be assumed that the parties have agreed to apply Jewish law. On the basis of that agreement, they adjudicate even capital cases as the times require." *See also Resp. Rashba,* III, #318; *Resp. Ritba* #131. For several communal enactments dealing with criminal law, *see* Assaf, *Onshin, passim;* Elon, *Ma'asar,* pp. 171–201.

51. 35(i) *P.D.* 113, 163 (1980). The quotation is from the opinion of Elon, J.

52. 23(i) *P.D.* 733, 741 (1969) (emphasis throughout in original).

53. M Makkot 1:10.

54. TB Makkot 7a.

Indeed, this extreme approach of R. Tarfon and R. Akiva was controversial even in their own time. Rabban Simeon b. Gamaliel the Patriarch responded sharply: "They would also have multiplied murderers in Israel!"[55] Rashi explains: "If they had done so [*i.e.*, judged as they would have liked], they would have increased the number of murderers, because the people would not fear the court."[56] At the same time, it is correct to state that as to the proof of the occurrence, namely, whether or not A pierced B with a sword, basic Jewish law insisted on direct evidence. This requirement and its rationale are explained by Maimonides as follows:[57]

> We are forbidden to punish on the basis of strong or even virtually conclusive circumstantial evidence. Thus, if A pursues B with intent to kill and B takes refuge in a house into which the pursuer follows, and we enter after them and find B in his last gasp and his pursuing enemy, A, standing over him with a knife in his hand, and both of them are covered with blood, the Sanhedrin may not find A liable to capital punishment, since there are no eyewitnesses to the actual murder. . . .
>
> Do not let this puzzle you and do not think this law unjust. For among events within the bounds of possibility, some are very probable, some highly improbable, and some fall between the two extremes. The bounds of possibility are very wide. If the Torah had permitted us to punish on the basis of a very strong probability that might seem absolutely convincing, as in the example we have given, we would soon be punishing on the basis of a lesser probability and then on a still lesser probability, until we would be punishing and executing people on the basis of a judge's speculative evaluation of the evidence.
>
> The Almighty has therefore foreclosed this possibility, ordaining that no punishment may be imposed unless there are witnesses who testify that they have clear and indubitable knowledge of the occurrence and it is impossible to explain the occurrence in any other way. If we do not impose punishment even on the basis of a very strong probability, the worst that can happen is that a transgressor will go free; but if we punish on the strength of probabilities and suppositions, it may be that one day we shall put an innocent person to death; and it is better and more desirable that a thousand guilty persons go free than that a single innocent person be put to death. . . .

Maimonides' reasoning is interesting. The fear is that if circumstantial evidence is accepted as sufficient, we might go too far, to the point where "we would be punishing and executing people on the basis of a judge's speculative evaluation of the evidence." It is, therefore, preferable to insist on direct evidence, even if, as a consequence, we may free a guilty person, for it is "better

55. M Makkot 1:10.

56. Rashi, Makkot 7a, s.v. Af; *see also* Tosafot, *ad loc.*, s.v. Dilma.

57. *Sefer ha-Mizvot* (ed. Kafaḥ, Mosad ha-Rav Kook, Jerusalem, 1958), Negative Commandment #290.

. . . that a thousand guilty persons go free than that a single innocent person be put to death."[58]

Close to the end of the tannaitic period, a principle was formulated which had been previously applied in practice for many years. . . .[59] This principle represented a substantial change in Jewish criminal law with regard not only to sanctions but also to evidence and procedure:

> It was taught: R. Eliezer b. Jacob said: "I have heard that the court may impose flogging and punishment not prescribed in the Torah—not to transgress the law of the Torah but in order to make a fence around the Torah."[60]

According to this principle, the court may apply other law than that of the Torah in all matters of criminal law and procedure if the needs of the time so require in order to protect society against criminals. For this purpose, the courts and the communal leaders exercised their legislative authority to create a wide-ranging and extensive body of enactments, adopted throughout the generations, against a background of diverse religious, social, economic, and moral circumstances. . . .

There has been a remarkable development in Jewish law as to the required proof in a criminal case, . . . and we will discuss some of the main precedents. . . .

At the end of the thirteenth century, Rashba accepted the testimony of the defendant's relatives, of women, and of minors; and he affirmed convictions based on the defendant's own confession. . . . [61]

A responsum of Ribash . . . at the end of the fourteenth century—which he sent to Menahem ha-Arokh, who was a judge first in Salamanca and later in Zamora—reviewed a murder conviction. Ribash ruled that when there is no doubt as to the circumstances of the victim's death a conviction may be based on circumstantial evidence that provides "convincing proofs and valid grounds." Ribash wrote:[62]

> You know that the law applicable to criminal cases in these times when the government has granted criminal jurisdiction to Jewish courts is not the strict law [*i.e.*, Biblical law], for jurisdiction over criminal cases [under the law of the Torah] has been abrogated.[63] However, in order to

58. As to the origin and history of this well-known maxim, *see* G. Williams, *The Proof of Guilt,* London, 3rd ed., 1963, pp. 186ff. Maimonides is entitled to particular credit for his use of this maxim.

59. *See, e.g.,* the incident attributed to Simeon b. Shataḥ in *Sifrei,* Deuteronomy, Ki Teẓe, #221 (ed. Finkelstein, p. 253). For detailed discussion of the legislative principle that the court may impose punishment not prescribed in the Torah, *see supra* pp. 515–519.

60. TB Yevamot 90b; Sanhedrin 46a. TJ Ḥagigah 2:2 reads: "I have heard that they may impose punishment not prescribed in the *Halakhah* and that they may impose punishment not prescribed in the Torah." *See supra* p. 515 n. 94.

61. *Resp. Rashba,* IV, #311, quoted *supra* pp. 691–692. *See also Resp. Rashba,* III, #393.

62. *Resp. Ribash* #251.

63. As to when, in relation to the destruction of the Temple, jurisdiction over capital cases was terminated, *see supra* pp. 6–7 and n. 10.

> "create a safeguard," the courts, when the exigencies of the time demand, impose flogging and punishment not prescribed in the Torah. . . .
>
> If the death penalty—although not prescribed by the Torah—was carried out for other offenses because of the exigency of the time, then it goes without saying that it may be carried out in cases of murder, concerning which our Sages were most stringent. . . . In any event, in order to "create a safeguard," since someone from among you has died, if you decide that the death penalty is called for because a crime has been committed heinously, violently, and deliberately (as it appears that they lay in wait for him [the victim] at night and during the day, and they openly brandished weapons against him in the presence of the communal leaders), then you may [impose the death penalty], as Maimonides has written,[64] even when there are no eyewitnesses, if there are convincing proofs and valid grounds.

As stated in the responsum of Rashba, referred to above,[65]. . . Jewish law, at this new stage, permitted a conviction on the basis of the defendant's own confession. This was a departure from the original position of Jewish law, according to which the defendant's confession may not be used against him, pursuant to the principle that ". . . no one may incriminate himself." . . .[66] The background of this significant innovation in the Jewish law of evidence is revealed by the responsum of Ribash to the *mukademin* (the communal leaders, who often carried out judicial tasks) in the town of Teruel, in the district of Aragon in Spain—where there was a large Jewish community with judicial autonomy even in many areas of criminal law—in regard to a Jew accused of being an informer and slanderer, who was tried by a Jewish court in Teruel.[67] Ribash's responsum states:

> At present, the Jewish court has jurisdiction over criminal cases only by virtue of the Royal Warrant; and we must justify our decisions also to the non-Jewish judges of the land, so that they do not accuse us of deciding unjustly or illegally. Moreover, in our times we judge criminal cases according to the needs of the time, since jurisdiction over criminal cases [under the law of the Torah] has been abrogated.
>
> Jewish courts [at the present time] impose flogging and punishment not prescribed by the strict law, but according to the needs of the time, and even without uncontroverted testimony, so long as there are clear grounds to show that he [the accused] committed the offense. In such a case, it is the practice to accept the defendant's confession even in a capital case where there is no clear proof, in order that what he says, together with some measure of corroboration, may clarify what occurred.

64. *MT,* Roẓe'aḥ u-Shemirat ha-Nefesh 2:4–5.
65. *Resp. Rashba,* IV, #311.
66. TB Yevamot 25b; *see also* Maimonides, *MT,* Sanhedrin 18:6.
67. *Resp. Ribash* #234.

When there is no clear proof, a defendant's confession is admissible against him but is not sufficient to convict: there must be added to it, in the words of Ribash, "some measure of corroboration"—an idea that reminds us, interestingly, of the requirement of "something in addition" to the defendant's confession, which this Court has introduced in its opinions.

The halakhic authorities attached importance to the fact that the non-Jewish government granted them jurisdiction over criminal cases as a vital means of maintaining good public order in the Jewish community; and, in furtherance of this purpose, they adopted far-reaching legislation in criminal procedure and evidence.

Judah b. Asher, the son of Asheri, wrote in the first half of the fourteenth century in Spain:[68]

> It is well known that from the day the Sanhedrin was exiled from the Chamber of Hewn Stone, jurisdiction over criminal cases [under the law of the Torah] has been abrogated for the Jews, and the only purpose of the law today is to protect the current generation against wrongdoing. Blessed be the Almighty, Who has inclined the hearts of the rulers of the land to give to the Jews the authority to judge and to sweep out evildoers. Without this, the Jews could not survive in this country. Moreover, many Jews who would have been executed by the non-Jewish judges have been saved by the Jewish judges. And the law which we apply in criminal matters is not in full conformity with the Torah. . . .

What is the law applied in criminal cases? This question is dealt with by Judah b. Asher in another responsum, which was sent to the judges of Cordoba, in connection with a defendant who was accused of assaulting and severely wounding one of the judges:[69]

> It is well known that the cases that constantly arise are innumerable; it is impossible to copy them into a book and to explain all the rules by which they are to be decided. For this reason, our Sages formulated a general principle encompassing many specific aspects. They gave the court power to "create a fence" at all times to meet contemporary needs, as stated in chapter *Nigmar ha-Din*. . . .[70]
>
> Even though there are no eyewitnesses that he struck him, it is nevertheless notorious in the town and incessantly repeated that he struck him; there are also corroborations and [other] proofs, as well as hearsay testimony and witnesses who saw him wait in ambush with his eyes covered by his clothes to prevent him from being recognized, at the place where the judge was struck. In addition, after the judge was struck, he [the defendant] fled and was not seen any more in the town. . . .

68. *Resp. Zikhron Yehudah* #58.
69. *Id.* #79.
70. TB Sanhedrin 46a, quoted *supra* in text accompanying n. 60.

> It seems to me that he should be punished just as if there had been witnesses who saw him strike [the judge], since the purpose of the punishment is to prevent such things from happening again, so that every judge will be able to decide in accordance with the truth without fear of the litigants. . . .
>
> Whenever a criminal sentence is imposed by a court to satisfy the needs of the time, in a case in which the charge has proved to be well grounded, the court may impose the punishment it thinks proper, provided that the sole intention is to pursue justice and truth, and there is no other motive.

Not every part of the Jewish diaspora enjoyed such wide autonomous criminal jurisdiction, and even in any given location, the extent of juridical authority fluctuated over time.[71] As we have seen, the Spanish Jewish center enjoyed wide criminal jurisdiction—even including the power to inflict capital punishment—over a long period; and for a limited time such jurisdiction existed also in Poland, where, as a result, there were changes in the Jewish law of evidence in criminal cases. Thus, for example, a responsum of Maharam of Lublin, a Polish halakhic authority of the sixteenth century, states:[72]

> I have received your decision concerning the repulsive and outrageous act—the murder committed by one of our own criminals, as recorded in the testimonies Your Honor sent to me. Even though the testimony of the second witness is hearsay, it appears that the crime is well-known. . . .
>
> The foundation for the ruling of the codifiers that in our time, too, the court has power to impose corporal and capital punishment is the passage in chapter *Nigmar ha-Din*[73] and in chapter *Ha-Ishah Rabbah*. . . . [74] Rabbenu Jeroham . . . has written: "All of this applies even outside the Land of Israel, even if the defendant did not receive a forewarning, etc., and even without clear testimony; whatever the judge sees fit to do he may do. . . ."[75]

These principles have been succinctly set forth in the later codificatory literature. Jacob b. Asher, who in the *Sefer ha-Turim* devoted an entire chapter[76] and a small part of another[77] to criminal jurisdiction after the destruction of the Temple, wrote:[78]

> If the court sees that the need has arisen, inasmuch as crime is rampant among the people, it may impose the death penalty, monetary fines, or

71. *See supra* pp. 10–11 and nn. 23–25; p. 39 and n. 112.

72. *Resp. Maharam of Lublin* #138.

73. TB Sanhedrin 46a, quoted *supra* in text accompanying n. 60.

74. TB Yevamot 90b.

75. *See also Resp. Eitan ha-Ezraḥi* #43-#44, by Abraham ha-Kohen Rappaport, a halakhic authority in Poland at the beginning of the seventeenth century, and responsum #45, by Meir b. Abraham Zack, of Poland in the sixteenth century.

76. Tur ḤM ch. 2.

77. *Id.* ch. 425.

78. *Id.* ch. 2.

> other punishments . . . and even if there is no absolute proof, which would have been necessary for a finding of guilt when criminal cases were decided under the strict law, but there is a rational basis for a finding [of guilt] and the facts are common knowledge, then if the judge concludes that the exigencies of the time demand that he so rule, he has such authority. . . . But in all matters he should act for the sake of Heaven, and he should not esteem human dignity lightly.

Joseph Caro, in the *Shulḥan Arukh*, is even more succinct:[79]

> Every court . . . if it sees that crime is rampant among the people [Rema adds in a gloss: "and it is an exigency of the times"] can impose the death penalty, monetary fines, or other punishments, even if there is no absolute proof . . . , and all their [the judges'] acts should be for the sake of Heaven.

What is striking is the extreme brevity of the *Turim* and the *Shulḥan Arukh* in their exposition of Jewish criminal law, both substantive and procedural, in contrast to the great detail in which these two codes set forth the substantive and procedural rules of the civil law. It is reasonable to assume that to a certain extent this was due to the limited criminal jurisdiction of the Jewish communities at that time as compared to their extensive civil and administrative jurisdiction. An additional factor may be that criminal activity was not widespread in the Jewish communities, although—as indicated above—here, too, there were periods of "high" and "low."

To summarize: With the passage of time and the changes in circumstances, Jewish law could not keep to the rule that "no punishment may be imposed unless there are witnesses who testify that they have clear and indubitable knowledge of the occurrence and it is impossible to explain the occurrence in any other way."[80] It became necessary, due to the exigencies of the times, to be able to base convictions on circumstantial evidence and on the strength of probable inferences; and, in order to protect against the danger of convictions "on the basis of a judge's speculative evaluation of the evidence," it was constantly emphasized that although clear and direct testimony may not always be necessary, the evidence must be such that the judges "believe it to be the truth";[81] that the charge is "proved to be well grounded"; and that "the sole intention is to pursue justice and truth, and there is no other motive."[82] As a consequence, when there was no doubt as to the death of the victim, Jewish law came to the view that a conviction of murder may be based on the testimony of relatives or others incompetent under Biblical law to testify, or on the defendant's own confession together with "some measure of corroboration," or on circumstantial evidence.[83]

79. Sh. Ar. ḤM ch. 2; and *see* Rema's gloss to *id.* 425:1.

80. Maimonides, *Sefer ha-Miẓvot, supra* n. 57, quoted *supra* p. 693.

81. *Resp. Rashba Attributed to Naḥmanides #279.*

82. *Resp. Zikhron Yehudah #79.*

83. *See also* Al Baḥiri v. State of Israel, 37(iii) *P.D.* 169, 184 (1983). In that case, the majority of the Supreme Court of Israel accepted the view of M. Elon, J., that the failure of a defendant to testify in court should not be considered as the "something in addition" to

C. Equating the Standing of the Community with That of the Court

The halakhic authorities based the authority for communal legislation on the same foundation that supports the legislative competence of the halakhic authorities themselves.[84] The use of the same principles as the basis for the legislative competence of both the halakhic authorities and the lay community reached its full expression when these two bodies were fully equated in regard to their legislative competence. In the words of Rashba:[85]

> Each community as to its own locality has the same status as the *geonim* had with respect to all Jewry; and they [the *geonim*] adopted many enactments directed to and binding upon the entire Jewish people, *e.g.*, [the enactment] that personal property in the possession of heirs, which under strict law is not subject to execution to pay the decedent's debts, is nevertheless subject to be taken to satisfy such debts. . . .[86]

It is not only to the authority of the *geonim* but even to the authority of the Sanhedrin itself that Rashba compared the authority of the public in each locality:

> The agreement [*i.e.*, legislation] of the inhabitants of a locality has the full force of law; whenever a majority adopt an enactment upon which they have agreed, the views of the minority are disregarded because the majority [of the

---

an extrajudicial confession that is needed in order to convict the defendant. The rationale for this result was stated to be:

> A defendant should not be convicted on the basis of his extrajudicial confession alone, even if the confession was made in a proper manner and was not produced by any external pressure. The main reason for this is the concern that there may have been "internal pressure" on the defendant, who may blame himself for a crime that someone else has committed. . . . This concern was expressed by Maimonides in the following terms: "Perhaps he is among the melancholy and depressed who wish to die, [and] who thrust swords into their bellies or throw themselves down from rooftops; perhaps such a person will come and confess to something he did not do, in order that he may be killed" (Maimonides, *MT*, Sanhedrin 18:6).

84. *See Be'ur ha-Gra* to Sh. Ar. YD 228:33, applying to communal enactments the Biblical source from which the Sages deduced the authority of a court to legislate, namely: "You shall keep My charge" (Leviticus 18:30)—"Make a safeguard for My charge" (TB Yevamot 21a; *see supra* p. 483). Sh. Ar. YD 228:33 lays down the rule that "whoever takes an oath not to be bound by a communal enactment has taken a vain oath, and the enactment applies to him notwithstanding his objection," which *Be'ur ha-Gra* (*ad loc.*, subpar. 93) explains: "This is because he is vowing to violate a commandment (*mizvah*), as stated in TB Yevamot ch. 2 (21a), 'You shall keep My charge'—'Make a safeguard for My charge,' and the Torah has authorized every generation to adopt enactments and erect safeguards." This rule, as has been pointed out, refers to communal enactments. *See also infra* n. 114. For another rationale for the authority of communal enactments, *see infra* n. 117.

85. *Resp. Rashba*, I, #729.

86. As to this geonic enactment, *see supra* pp. 646–648.

> residents] of every town have the same relation to the minority as the High Court has to all of Israel. Any enactment they adopt is valid, and whoever violates it is subject to sanctions. . . .[87]
>
> In every community, the [residents in the] minority are subject to the will of the majority; they must conduct all their affairs under the majority's rules. The relation of the minority to the general population of their town is the same as that of all Israel to the High Court or to the king; and this is so whether or not they [*i.e.*, those in the minority] are actually present [when the enactment was adopted].[88]

In fact, the halakhic authorities went further than simply drawing a parallel between the court and the community: they asserted that the community functions as a court, and every member of the community acts as a judge. To quote Elijah Mizraḥi, a leading halakhic authority in Turkey in the latter half of the fifteenth and early part of the sixteenth centuries:[89]

87. *Resp. Rashba,* V, #126.

88. *Resp. Rashba,* III, #411. *See also Resp. Rashba,* III, #417 (I, #769; VII, #490):

> No one can free himself from [the obligations imposed by] communal legislation, because individuals are subject to the community; just as all the communities are subject to the High Court or the patriarch, so too is each and every individual subject to his local community.

See further Resp. Rashba, I, #1206; II, #360, and *see* Rema to Sh. Ar. ḤM 2:1. *Resp. Rashba,* IV, #142 already contains the expression *hefker ẓibbur hefker* ("the community has the power to expropriate property") parallel to *hefker bet din hefker* ("the court has the power to expropriate property"). *See also* Ritba, Novellae to Bava Batra 8b, s.v. Lehassi'a al kiẓatan (ed. Blau, 1954, p. 18 and n. 28 xxxx); *Resp. Ribash* #399: "Any established court in a town may expropriate property, and certainly the community may do so"; *Resp. Tashbeẓ,* I, #133 and II, #5; *Resp. Maharashdam,* ḤM, #447; and *infra* p. 865 n. 303. *Yad Ramah,* Bava Batra 8b, par. 91, s.v. Tashlum baraita, cites Ezra 10:8 as a source for the rule that "the townspeople may obligate each other . . . ," *i.e.*, may adopt communal enactments.

In this context, the interpretation that one of the leading halakhic scholars of recent times, Abraham Duber Cahana Shapiro, gave to Ezra 10:8, from which the principle of *hefker bet din hefker* is derived, is of great interest. He pointed out that there is a view that the doctrine of *dina de-malkhuta dina* ("the law of the land is law") is based on the principle of *hefker bet din hefker.* He reasoned as follows:

> The conclusion reached in TB Gittin (36b) that a court has the authority to expropriate property applies not only to a Jewish court but also to a non-Jewish court, by the law of the land. It also seems that the authority of a Jewish court to expropriate does not rest on its role as a court but rather on governmental prerogatives ("the law of the land"). [This conclusion arises] from the fact that the authority to expropriate is derived from the verse (Ezra 10:8), "[Then a proclamation was issued . . . that] anyone who does not come in three days, as required by the officers and elders, will have his property confiscated"; and "officers and elders" exemplify "the law of the land." For these reasons, the rule that "the law of the land is law" stems from the authority to expropriate property. (*Devar Avraham,* Warsaw, 1906, I, #11, par. 7, p. 59).

"Officers and elders" is thus interpreted as referring not to judicial but to general governmental authority, which is vested in the community.

89. *Resp. Elijah Mizraḥi* #53 (Jerusalem, ed. Darom, 1938, pp. 145–146).

> The community as a body is denominated a court in these [communal] matters. Its members are like judges at a session of court, who may not shirk their judicial responsibilities notwithstanding a difference of opinion as to whether something should be declared pure or impure, or whether the defendant should be found innocent or guilty. They must cast their vote; and the decision of the majority governs, in accordance with the instruction of our holy Torah to "follow the majority." Hence, one who refuses to follow the majority is considered a sinner. It makes no difference whether the majority consists of the wealthy, the poor, the scholarly, or the unlettered, because the entire community is denominated a court in dealing with matters of communal interest.

Putting the community on a par with the court was both revolutionary and far-reaching. Extensive research in Talmudic literature has revealed no precedent for such an equation. The idea was apparently first conceived in the tenth century C.E.: the halakhic authorities at first simply declared that the power of the majority of a community is equivalent to that of a court, but they did not state any legal-halakhic rationale to support this conclusion. Only later did they advance any such rationales, two of which are discussed here.

Elijah Mizraḥi, quoted above, justified the equation on the basis that both the court and the communal leaders derive their power and authority from the same source—the community as a whole. He stated:[90]

> The power conferred upon the High Court in Jerusalem [the Sanhedrin] and upon every court in every generation—as our Sages expounded on the basis of [the verse[91] "If a case is too baffling for you to decide] . . . you shall . . . appear before the priests [the Levites, and the judge] . . .": Jephthah in his generation had the same authority as Samuel in his, although the two were hardly on the same level—rests on the fact that the members of every generation agree to accept the decrees, enactments, and customs of the highest court in each generation. It is for this reason that that court is vested with greater authority than the other courts of the generation to issue decrees, promulgate enactments, and institute customs. Although that court was not elected [by the community as the supreme authority], and there was no explicit agreement [establishing it as such], it is known that everyone recognizes its decisions as conclusive; even if someone does object, he is reckoned as if he had explicitly consented and then reneged.
>
> This being so, whenever a court has these attributes, it clearly has the same authority as the High Court in Jerusalem because the same rationale applies. The same is therefore true of the communal leaders, for all the townspeople look to them [for guidance] in all matters relating to the welfare of

90. *Id.* #57 (p. 186).
91. Deuteronomy 17:8–9.

> the community and agree to accept their determinations. Consequently, it is as if the townspeople have chosen the communal leaders on the express condition that their decisions are conclusive. Even if the townspeople's agreement was not fully explicit, it is known that everyone recognizes their [the communal leaders'] decisions as conclusive. And [here, too,] although some may object to those [communal] enactments, they [the objectors] are reckoned as if they had explicitly consented and then reneged.[92]

Another interesting rationale was offered by one of the leading halakhic authorities of our time, Abraham Isaiah Karelitz, the author of *Ḥazon Ish*. It was his opinion that "the grant to the townspeople of the power of a court may have been the result of a *takkanah*," *i.e.*, the halakhic authorities adopted an enactment specifically designed to confer upon the communal leaders the status and authority of a court, in order to establish Jewish governmental autonomy.[93]

92. *Cf.* Meiri, *Bet ha-Beḥirah*, Bava Batra 9a, expressing the view that the approval of a "distinguished person" was required only for an enactment by a tradesmen's association, but "the community as a whole . . . may legislate without his approval, as they have the power to revoke his appointment." *See also infra* n. 283.

An interesting rationale as to why a communal agreement has greater force than an agreement between individuals is given by Joseph Colon (*Resp. Maharik* #179—1st resp., ed. Lemberg; ed. Warsaw #181):

> A communal agreement partakes of "God's ways are pleasant ways and all God's paths, peaceful" [Proverbs 3:17]. Therefore, such an agreement, when all were of one mind and united together, is effective, and none of them may renege and undermine the prevalence of truth and peace.

Maharik's quotation of the verse from Proverbs was poetic license: The verse, speaking of wisdom, says "Her ways are pleasant ways." Maharik quotes the verse as saying "God's ways are pleasant ways."

(The letters in the Hebrew spelling for "her ways" and "the ways of God" are the same, but the Hebrew for "her ways" is one word, and for "the ways of God" is two words.) Maharik's "reading" was not a printer's error, as this is the text in the first edition of *Resp. Maharik*, ed. Venice, 1519. As to the rationale of Maharik, *cf. Resp. Rashbash* #566; *see also* Elon, *Samkhut ve-Oẓmah*, p. 18.

Maharik's rationale is based on legal reasoning, since it is the reasoning of the respondent that determines what are pleasant ways. *See, e.g., Resp. Maharashdam*, OḤ, #37; ḤM, #421, quoted *infra* p. 724, taking the view that the vote of a wealthy person should have greater weight than the vote of a poor person, and arguing that a different practice would not reflect "pleasant ways." Other halakhic authorities, however, take a contrary view, as discussed *infra*. They thus disagree in their judgment as to what constitutes "pleasant ways."

93. *Ḥazon Ish*, Bava Batra, 4:8. *Ḥazon Ish* used the same rationale to justify the authority of tradesmen's associations over their members:

> A tradesmen's association has the same power as a community. Just as the townspeople have the same authority as a court, so do tradesmen's associations have the same authority as a court over their members. Their enactments are as valid as those of a court and can confer a lien upon property for the recovery of debts. There is no need for a *kinyan* [formal act of acquisition]; the court's enactment fulfills the requirement of a *kinyan*. A tradesmen's association thus has the same type of authority as a

Equating the legislative competence of the community to that of the court had many implications for the authority of the public and its leaders in a number of additional substantive matters. In a fifteenth century case in Germany,[94] an individual swore falsely in a tax declaration submitted by him. He was fined by the governmental authorities and reached a settlement with the community in regard to the amount of his taxes. After a time, he sought appointment as a member of the community's governing council, and Israel Isserlein was asked whether "he could participate as one of the communal leaders when they sit to legislate for the public needs . . . and to oversee the affairs of the public and of individuals," it being clear that he had previously sworn falsely. Isserlein's response was that the individual could not be a communal official. He had sworn falsely out of greed; therefore, he was comparable to a thief or robber and consequently incompetent to be a judge. "Communal leaders who sit to oversee the affairs of the public and of individuals stand in place of the court"; consequently, the aspirant was not eligible to be a communal leader.

The guideline accepted as governing law for the requisite qualifications of those exercising public authority[95] was the principle: "The communal leaders selected to deal with the needs of the public or of individuals are like judges, and it is forbidden to seat among them anyone who on account of moral turpitude is ineligible to act as a judge."[96] Of course, it goes without saying that the equation of communal leaders with judges is applicable only to the extent of the authority bestowed upon them as communal leaders and no further.[97]

> community. This grant of the authority of a court to the townspeople and to the members of each particular trade was possibly the result of legislation by the Sages.

In subpar. 10, *Ḥazon Ish* states:

> If all the tradesmen agree, their decision has the same force as a communal enactment, which, in turn, has the same force as an enactment by the halakhic authorities of the generation for the entire Jewish people.

As to equating the standing of the community with that of the court with respect to legislation, *see* Elon, *Samkhut ve-Oẓmah,* pp. 13–17. *See also id.,* comparing communal enactments with the king's law and the law of the patriarch.

94. *Terumat ha-Deshen,* Pesakim u-Khetavim, #214.

95. *See, e.g., Terumat ha-Deshen* #344; *see also* M. Elon, EJ, XV, pp. 843ff., s.v. Taxation (reprinted in *Principles,* pp. 666ff.)

96. Rema to Sh. Ar. ḤM 37:22. Another rationale offered for equating communal leaders with judges is that a major portion of the communal leaders' function is to provide for the social needs of the people, and support and relief of the needy is in the nature of a judicial function in Jewish law; *see* TB Bava Batra 8b and Rashi, *ad loc.,* s.v. Mipenei she-hu ke-dinei mamonot; Sh. Ar. YD 256:3; *Mishpetei Uzzi'el,* ḤM, ch. 4.

97. For example, when communal leaders are given authority to select the body that is to oversee communal affairs, they cannot delegate that authority, because delegation

Equating the position of the community to that of the court made it possible for Jewish law to solve various problems involving the legal relationship between the community and its individual members. Jewish law generally requires an act of *kinyan* (formal juristic act of acquisition) to make a legal transaction binding.[98] This requirement could have interfered with the establishment of legal relations between the community as a public body and anyone seeking to transact business with it, since such formalism would be exceedingly burdensome in view of the many and varied transactions to which the public authority is a party.

In the thirteenth century, a new legal doctrine emerged: every legal transaction entered into by the community is valid even without a *kinyan*. It appears that this doctrine was first enunciated by Maharam of Rothenburg in a case where a particular community had hired a teacher. Under the law, if no *kinyan* had been made and the teacher had not yet begun to work, his appointment could have been revoked. However, Maharam of Rothenburg ruled that revocation was not permitted since "whatever is done by the public does not require a *kinyan* even if it is something for which a *kinyan* is necessary in the case of an individual."[99] He also ruled

---

would exceed their authority. A court, however, can appoint an agent to perform certain of its functions (*Resp. Ribash* #228). It is worthy of note that the Supreme Court of Israel has adopted the principle of equating the status of communal leaders with that of judges (*dayyanim*) and has based decisions on that principle in a number of cases involving issues of administrative law. *See* Altegar v. Mayor and Local Council of Ramat Gan, 20(i) *P.D.* 29 (1966); Fadel Salem v. Minister of the Interior, 21(i) *P.D.* 59 (1967); Yehudah Malkah v. Oved Seri Levi, 20(i) *P.D.* 651 (1966); Katebi v. Libby, Chairman of the Kiryat Ekron Council, 20(ii) *P.D.* 102 (1966). *See also* M. Elon, EJ, XIII, pp. 1351–1359, s.v. Public authority (reprinted in *Principles*, pp. 645–654).

98. *See supra* pp. 580–584.

99. Responsum of Maharam of Rothenburg, quoted in *Mordekhai*, Bava Meẓi'a, #457–458. Although Maharam based this innovation, by way of expansive interpretation, on various laws in the Talmud that suggest a different attitude to the community than to the individual (*e.g.*, TB Megillah 26a; Gittin 36a, 46a), those sources say no more than that an act performed by the community is not comparable to an act of an individual, as indeed Maharam himself emphasized. Those sources give no indication that a transaction by the community does not require a *kinyan*. This is also true of the proof adduced from TJ Megillah 3:2 (cited erroneously as ch. 2).

The proof from TB Nedarim (also cited erroneously as ch. "Ha-Shutafin" instead of ch. "Arba'ah Nedarim," 27a/b) is irrelevant to the subject under discussion (although Maharam's intention possibly was to allude to the equation of the status of the community with that of the court, and the passage in TB Nedarim states that the rule as to *asmakhta* does not apply to a court; *see infra* p. 706 and n. 107).

The proof from the butchers' agreement (TB Bava Batra 9a) must also be rejected, since there is no indication that there was no *kinyan* there. In addition, Maharam compared a transaction by the community to a "small gift" (which does not require a *kinyan*); but this comparison, too, is problematic, since in that case reneging on the gift is only a moral delict

that a *kinyan* was not required to validate a guaranty of the performance of the obligations under the employment contract, even though as a general rule such a guaranty requires an act of *kinyan* to make it binding.[100] Similarly, a gift given by the community is fully valid even without any formal *kinyan*,[101] as are other legal transactions involving the community.[102]

The principle gradually became so rooted in the various communities that "it is generally accepted that what the communal leaders agree to do is completely valid without a *kinyan*."[103] In the sixteenth century in Constantinople it was stated: "The law practiced among the Jewish people is that all public matters and things done in the presence of the public are valid without a *kinyan*, and the laws relating to the modes of acquisition do not apply to such transactions."[104] Similarly, Rema ruled: "Communal undertakings do not require a *kinyan*."[105] In addition, a number of other basic requirements of the laws of acquisition were drastically relaxed for public authorities. Thus, it was settled that the community may acquire and trans-

---

exhibiting a lack of trustworthiness and is not a violation of a fully binding legal rule (TB Bava Meẓi'a 49a; Maimonides, *MT*, Mekhirah 7:9; Sh. Ar. ḤM 204:8).

The same objection applies to the proof adduced later in Maharam's responsum: "And at the end of Tractate *Shevu'ot* it is stated that it becomes a vow, and the Sages are displeased with one who retracts it." Here, too, the reference appears to be erroneous and may perhaps be to the last *mishnah* in Tractate *Shevi'it* (10:9): "All chattels may be acquired by *meshikhah* ("pulling"), but the Sages are pleased with whoever keeps his word"; and to TJ Shevi'it 10:4: "Sometimes the Sages are displeased with one who enters into transactions by oral agreement," and the incident concerning Rav described there. However, these sources, too, are concerned with acts of piety and not legal rules; *see further* in TJ, *ad loc.*

The main reason for the innovation is undoubtedly the fact that the community's status was equated with the court's, as is demonstrated *infra*. *Cf. also* Maharam's comments, *infra* n. 100 (*Resp. Maharam of Rothenburg*, ed. Prague, #38). That responsum is most instructive with respect to the process of decision making by the leading halakhic authorities and to their method of creating new legal principles by means of purposeful and expansive interpretation as well as analogies to various Talmudic laws, in order to provide a basis and rationale for existing customs. *See also* Maharam's statement quoted in *Mordekhai*, Bava Meẓi'a #457–458: "Therefore, they have followed the custom (*nahagu*) that no communal transaction requires a *kinyan*, [even] where a *kinyan* would be required for the same transaction by an individual."

100. Maharam of Rothenburg, quoted in *Mordekhai*, *supra* n. 99. *See also Resp. Maharam of Rothenburg*, ed. Prague, #38, also quoted in *Mordekhai*, Bava Meẓi'a, #334: "A guaranty by a community is like [a guaranty by] a guarantor approved by a court and does not require a *kinyan*." *See* M. Elon, EJ, XV, pp. 524–529, s.v. Suretyship (reprinted in *Principles*, pp. 281–287).

101. Sh. Ar. ḤM 204:9; the source is Maharam of Rothenburg, cited *supra* n. 99; *see also Be'ur ha-Gra, ad loc.*, subpar. 11.

102. *See, e.g., Resp. Ribash* #476; Rema to Sh. Ar. ḤM 81:1 (where the reference is erroneously given as *Resp. Ribash* #376).

103. *Resp. Asheri* 6:19; 6:21.

104. Elijah b. Ḥayyim, *Resp. Mayim Amukkim* #63, p. 67c, sec. Responsa of Ranaḥ.

105. Sh. Ar. ḤM 163:6.

fer an object that has not yet come into existence;[106] and, contrary to the rule of Jewish law that "an agreement affected by an *asmakhta* is not valid," it was established that there is no defect in such an agreement when the community is involved.[107]

This important innovation was sometimes grounded on the theory that in every transaction involving the community there is a deliberate and final intention to be bound (*gemirut da'at*) even without an act of *kinyan* and even in the case of an *asmakhta* and the like.[108] However, the main rationale was that the public authority had the same status as the court: "It was based on *hefker bet din*—the power of the court to expropriate. . . . The relation of the community to its members is the same as that of the court to all Jews."[109] Consequently, the community may not argue that it did not seriously intend to enter into a particular transaction or that it was mistaken and did not understand it:[110]

106. *Resp. Mayim Amukkim, supra* n. 104. In regard to transfer or acquisition of an object that does not yet exist, *see supra* p. 392 and M. Elon, EJ, V, pp. 923–933, s.v. Contract (reprinted in *Principles,* pp. 246–256); XII, pp. 1310–1316, s.v. Obligations, law of (reprinted in *Principles,* pp. 241–246).

107. *Resp. Mabit,* III, #228; *see also* M. Elon, EJ, s.v. Contract, *supra* n. 106. As to *asmakhta, see supra* p. 120 n. 118.

108. *See, e.g., Resp. Ribash* #476; Rema to Sh. Ar. ḤM 81:1; *Sema,* Sh. Ar. ḤM 204:9, subpar. 14.

109. *Resp. Rashbash* #566 and #112.

110. *Resp. Rashbash* #566. From this point of view, a community's acts are more binding than those of a court, since if a court errs in its appraisal, a judicial sale is void. This point is emphasized in *Resp. Mayim Amukkim, supra* n. 104 at 67d. The case there involved a community that reached agreement with a taxpayer on the sum to be paid as an inheritance tax on the estate of the taxpayer's father. After some time, the community sought to rescind the agreement on the ground, *inter alia,* that it had erred in valuing the estate. Ranaḥ rejected the claim:

> This is no argument. Since they valued the property at that amount, even if it turns out that they undervalued it, he pays only the amount assessed, because they made the valuation. [This is so] notwithstanding that the communal leaders may seem to be no more than agents of the community, and if an agent errs, the transaction is voidable because the principal may claim, "I sent you for my benefit and not to damage me" [TB Ketubbot 99b].
>
> The result holds even against the argument that the communal leaders have the same status as a court, as indeed Mahari [Israel] Isserlein ruled they have [*Terumat ha-Deshen, supra* n. 94]. [With regard to a court] we are told, "If the appraisal by the judges either undervalues or overvalues the property by one-sixth, the judicial sale is void; Rabban Simeon b. Gamaliel said: 'If so, of what value is the authority of the court?'" R. Naḥman ruled that the law does not follow the view of Rabban Simeon b. Gamaliel because the argument "If so, of what value is the authority of the court?" applies only when the court has not erred, but not when it has erred [TB Ketubbot 99b *et seq.*].
>
> Nevertheless, Maharam has already written in a responsum that every act of the communal leaders, even if in error, is irrevocable, even though [the general rule is that] a judgment that is the result of a mistake is invalid. This principle applies to the case before us: every act of the communal leaders to whom the affairs of the com-

> If you examine the conduct of all of the communities in such a matter, you will see that they never revoke or rescind [an agreement] either on account of a transaction concerning an object not yet in existence or on account of overreaching . . . , as it is unseemly for the community to say, "We have made a mistake. . . ."[111] The authority of the community is as strong as that of the court, and if we set aside sales made by communal authority, of what value is the authority of the court?[112]

D. Communal Legislation and Matters of *Issur* ("Religious" Law)

The doctrine that the community has the same power as the court does not apply to matters of *issur*—"religious" law. Legislative authority in such matters to permit what is otherwise prohibited is vested exclusively in the halakhic authorities. "How can the public agree to permit what is [religiously] prohibited? Whoever agrees to such a dispensation is like one who agrees to join a wicked gang to commit a wrongdoing; the greater the number of parties to the agreement, the greater the sinfulness of the agreement and the greater the calamity."[113] Every enactment that is "contrary to one of the Torah's commandments . . . requires atonement, as one may not take an

---

> munity have been entrusted is valid; and the community cannot retract, even if it is evident that the communal leaders erred in the matter.

Ranaḥ's responsum is an indication of the far-reaching extent of the power of the halakhic authorities to interpret and prescribe the rules of public administrative law governing the relationship between the community and the individual. *Cf. also infra* p. 865 n. 303.

111. The exemption that the community enjoyed in its legal transactions from the requirement of formal acts of acquisition, and from the taint of *asmakhta*, etc., also applied, of course, to the individual who dealt with the community; he, too, could not retract even where there had been no act of *kinyan*, etc. *See Resp. Rashbash* #112; *Resp. Sha'ot de-Rabbanan* #14; *Resp. Ba'ei Ḥayyei*, ḤM, ch. 81.

112. The District Rabbinical Court and the Rabbinical Court of Appeals of Israel recently used the legal principles discussed here, which were established to govern communal affairs, in deciding a case in the field of administrative law brought before them as an arbitration tribunal. The case involved an agreement between political parties with respect to an election. *See* Agudat Yisra'el v. Mafdal, Reḥovot Branch, 6 *P.D.R.* 166, 178ff. (1966). The principles of Jewish administrative law, which are based on communal enactments, have also been discussed by the Supreme Court of Israel. *See, e.g.*, Goldberg v. Chairman of the Council of Ramat ha-Sharon, 34(iv) *P.D.* 85, 89–90 (1979); Lugasi v. Minister of Communications, 36(ii) *P.D.* 449, 467–470 (1981). For detailed discussions, *see also* M. Elon, EJ, XIII, pp. 1351–1359, s.v. Public authority (reprinted in *Principles*, pp. 645–654); *id.*, "Darkhei ha-Yeẓirah ha-Hilkhatit be-Fitronan shel Ba'ayot Ḥevrah u-Mishpat ba-Kehillah" [The Methodology of Halakhic Creativity in Solving Social and Legal Problems in the Jewish Community], *Yitzhak Baer Memorial Volume* (*Zion*, XLIV[1979], pp. 241, 245–249.

113. *Resp. Tashbeẓ*, II, #132, quoting a responsum of Rashba. The responsum originally appeared in *Resp. Rashba*, VII, #244. It is also quoted in *Resp. Ribash* #467 and in *Resp. Tashbeẓ*, II, #239. *See also Resp. Ribash* #178, #185.

oath to nullify a commandment, and if one does so, he is guilty of having taken an oath in vain."[114] In the area of *issur,* the rule applicable to the community is the same as that applicable to an individual; and just as an individual may contract out of a law contained in the Torah only in a civil law matter but not on a matter of *issur,*[115] so the community may not legislate contrary to Biblical law on a matter of *issur.* This distinction is explained by Ribash:[116]

> If a community enacted that legal documents accepted in non-Jewish courts are as fully valid for us as they are for non-Jews under their law, and that every transaction recorded in a legal document is effective to transfer property between Jews just as it is effective between non-Jews under their law, the community certainly may legislate on such matters, as these are conditions involving civil law and it is as if every single individual in the community so stipulated and undertook for himself. . . . Nevertheless, the community may not enact legislation that involves condoning usury, since usury is prohibited by the Torah even when the debtor pays it voluntarily, and no stipulation is effective in this matter. . . . Consequently, since the debtor himself cannot consent to usury, legislation by the community is also ineffective to permit usury.[117]

The area of *issur,* as to which the community has no authority to legislate, includes a considerable portion of those matters within the compass of the principles of justice and equity in Jewish law that communal enactments may not contravene,[118] because, under Jewish law, violation of the requirements of justice and equity is *ipso facto* a violation of the laws of *issur.*

114. *Resp. Rashba,* III, #411. The adoption of an enactment was accompanied by the pronouncement of a ban or oath; an oath taken in connection with an enactment to permit what the Torah prohibited was like an oath to abrogate a commandment, *i.e.,* it was a vain oath, and the swearer was still required to keep the commandment (M Nedarim 2:2; M Shevu'ot 3:8). *See infra* p. 713 as to an oath not to abide by a communal enactment.

115. *See supra* pp. 123–127.

116. *Resp. Ribash* #305 (p. 84d).

117. Ribash provides an additional rationale for the validity of communal enactments concerning civil law. A communal enactment is comparable to an agreement of all the people of the community with regard to a particular matter. Just as two individuals may reach an agreement to govern their legal relationship in a certain manner in the area of civil law even if the relationship they agree on is contrary to what the law would otherwise prescribe, the community may likewise so agree. For an additional example of the invalidation of a communal enactment dealing with a matter of *issur, see Resp. Tashbeẓ,* II, #63. A communal enactment providing that witnesses who are relatives of a party are competent to testify is valid for civil and criminal cases (*see supra* pp. 691–692 and *infra* pp. 737–739) but not for questions of marriage and divorce, which are matters of *issur. See also Resp. Rashbash* #211.

118. *See infra* pp. 760–777.

For example, Jewish law placed great emphasis on the protection of the personal freedom and elementary necessities of life of a debtor; and one of the specific consequences of this attitude is that a debtor may not be imprisoned for nonpayment of debt.[119] The developments in commercial and economic life and the changes in the socio-moral climate over the course of time necessitated more effective methods of collecting debts;[120] and in the fourteenth century a communal enactment in Saragossa, Spain, permitted imprisonment of the debtor, as indicated in a responsum of Ribash.[121] At the beginning of his discussion, Ribash fully explained the position of Jewish law that a debtor may not be imprisoned for failing to pay his debt. He then continued:

> In truth, in our town the judges, pursuant to a communal enactment, customarily imprison a debtor who has agreed to this sanction.[122] The community also enacted legislation providing that even without prior consent[123] one may be imprisoned for any claim against him unless he provides a guarantee for the claim, known as *kiyyum bet din* ("confirmation by the court"). I desired to object to this enactment, since it is contrary to the law of our Torah, but I was told that this was an enactment needed to promote commerce, to protect against chicanery, and to prevent the closing of doors to borrowers; and I acquiesced in their practice.

The communal enactment[124] thus permitted the imprisonment of the debtor, and Ribash sought to object to this enactment and to set it aside as invalid "since it is contrary to the law of our Torah" in that it permits what the Torah prohibits. However, Ribash did not press the objection; and to the extent that it was possible to reconcile the enactment with the prohibition of the Torah, he ruled the enactment valid, inasmuch as it satisfied an emergent need to promote commerce, protect the marketplace against fraud, and prevent the closing of doors to borrowers.

Ribash accomplished this reconciliation by an interpretation of the law to the effect that when a debtor has money with which to pay but conceals his assets he may be imprisoned; "however, if the debtor is indigent and unable to pay, it is clearly forbidden to imprison or oppress him."[125] When

119. For detailed discussion, *see* Elon, *Ḥerut,* pp. 111ff., and *supra* p. 652 and n. 35.

120. *See* Elon, *Ḥerut,* pp. 118ff.

121. *Resp. Ribash* #484.

122. *I.e.,* at the time of the loan; *see* the question put to Ribash, *id.*

123. *I.e.,* even though he did not consent in the promissory note. The imprisonment was to be imposed as a matter of law.

124. Ribash's language indicates that there were two communal enactments regarding imprisonment for a debt; *see* Elon, *Ḥerut,* p. 143.

125. *Resp. Ribash* #484. For a detailed discussion as to how Ribash arrived at this innovative conclusion, *see* Elon, *Ḥerut,* pp. 144ff.

the debtor evades the payment of his debt, imprisonment is a means of compulsion to enforce payment and is therefore permitted; but if the debtor is unable to pay, imprisonment is a means of vindictive punishment and is therefore prohibited.

From the seventeenth century C.E. onward, with the worsening of the economic situation in the Polish and Lithuanian communities and with the increase of business failures, some of these communities adopted enactments under which even a debtor who was unable to pay his debt could be imprisoned for a certain period of time.[126] However, Joel Sirkes invalidated these enactments, stating:[127]

> Surely, the practice under the communal enactment of imprisoning even someone unable to pay has no foundation on which to rest; Ribash wrote similarly[128] that it is forbidden to imprison him. And the community does not have the power to enact this law, which violates a [religious] prohibition (*issur*).[129]

The line between a "religious" matter (*issur*) and a monetary or civil law matter (*mamon*) cannot be clearly and definitively drawn.[130] Consequently, the community was sometimes deprived of its authority to legislate on a particular matter that at first glance appears to be a civil law matter,[131] and at other times the halakhic authorities were of the opinion that a particular matter that at first blush seemed to be a matter of *issur* was in reality properly within the community's authority to enact legislation even though contrary to the existing law.[132] The halakhic authorities drew the line in each instance in light of the nature and circumstances of the particular matter and the needs of the time.[133]

126. *See* Elon, *Ḥerut,* pp. 172ff.

127. *Bayit Ḥadash* to *Tur* ḤM 97:28.

128. *Resp. Ribash* #484.

129. Elon, *Ḥerut,* pp. 189ff. Jonathan Eybeschütz reached the same conclusion with regard to these communal enactments; *Urim ve-Thummim* to Sh. Ar. ḤM 97, subpar. 13. *See* Elon, *Ḥerut,* pp. 223ff.

130. *See supra* pp. 111–122.

131. *See, e.g., Resp. Tashbeẓ,* II, #132, where dice-playing and informing are included, together with damaging another person by offering a higher rental, as matters concerning which the community may not legislate contrary to existing law.

132. *See* Yom Tov Lipmann Heller, *Pilpula Ḥarifta* to *Piskei ha-Rosh,* Bava Meẓi'a, ch. 5, #38, subpar. 2, justifying the communal enactments that provided for the imprisonment of even an impecunious debtor where there was reasonable apprehension that otherwise people would refrain from lending; *see* Elon, *Ḥerut,* pp. 191ff.

133. *See supra* n. 132 for Yom Tov Lipmann Heller's opinion upholding a communal enactment that seems to relate to a matter of *issur,* on the ground that otherwise people would refrain from lending. Another striking example of this contextual approach relating to a matter of *issur* is the novel distinction made by Ribash between a poor debtor, who may not be imprisoned, and a rich debtor fraudulently secreting his assets, who may be impris-

The legislative authority of the community sometimes extended even to matters that affect questions of *issur.* For example, many communities in different centers adopted enactments providing that Maimonides' opinions were to be followed in deciding all halakhic questions except for particular matters specifically listed in the enactments.[134] Such a communal enactment had an indirect influence on decision making in matters of *issur.*

It was also possible for a communal enactment to influence directly what is clearly a matter of *issur.* An obvious example is the communal legislation to prevent mock marriages and marriages effected by fraud. This legislation provided that in order for a marriage to be valid at least ten

---

oned, and the resulting validation of communal enactments to the extent that they reflect this distinction.

134. *See, e.g.,* the Tudela enactment of 1305 (the date is recorded at the end of the enactment—"the year 5065 according to our chronology [*i.e.,* the reckoning according to the Jewish calendar]"):

> The community, may God preserve it, has agreed that all questions in any matter whatsoever that shall arise in this town shall be decided according to the opinion of our master, Rabbenu Moses, of blessed memory [*i.e.,* Maimonides], wherever it is possible to ascertain his opinion, except for two subjects on which the community has agreed not to accept his view, namely, cancellation of debt [in the sabbatical year] and abatement of mortgages on houses. . . .

The enactment is quoted by Y. Baer, *Die Juden im Christlichen Spanien* [The Jews in Christian Spain], Part I, Urkunden und Regesten, I (1929), p. 949; *see also id.* at 955, par. 12. A similar enactment is referred to in *Resp. Ran* #62:

> The community in which she lives . . . agreed and enacted that in all their laws and legal controversies they will follow the books of Maimonides, of blessed memory, in regard to everything that is written in them concerning matters of religious law (*issur*), civil law (*mamon*), marriage, *ketubbah,* and divorce.

All legal rules generally applicable to communal enactments governed this enactment as well. In the case decided by Ran, it was argued that the enactment did not apply to the particular situation since the husband was not bound by it, first, because he was not a member of the community that had adopted the enactment and, second, because his marriage predated the enactment:

> The above-mentioned Reuben [the husband] argues that he is neither a resident of the above-mentioned town nor included in its enactments, and that the townspeople there have no authority to compel him to comply with the enactment, especially since the enactment was adopted after his marriage. Leah [the wife] responds that since she is a resident of that place, the marriage was entered into on the understanding that all of the present and future customs and enactments of the town would apply to it, and that since he has no permanent residence and she resides in her town, he should be treated as if he were resident there and should be bound by its enactments.

Ran accepted Reuben's argument. As to communal enactments requiring Maimonides' opinions to be followed in deciding halakhic questions, *see further Resp. Tashbeẓ,* II, #196 and #256; *Resp. Ribash* #21, #105, #345, #478, #493; and many other sources. *See* I.Z. Kahane, "Ha-Pulmus mi-Saviv Kevi'at ha-Hakhra'ah ke-ha-Rambam" [The Polemic Concerning the Determination of the Law in Accordance with Maimonides' Opinions], *Sinai,* XXXVI (1956), pp. 402ff., and continued in vols. XXXVII and XXXVIII. *See also infra* pp. 1222–1223.

people and a rabbi or similar personage must be present, and that a marriage entered into in violation of the enactment is void. This legislation had the full force of law, and a marriage entered into in violation of its provisions was invalid. The rationale generally accepted by the *rishonim* for this result is that the community has the authority to expropriate the item of value (customarily a ring) given to the bride to effect the marriage, in which case the violator of the enactment is considered to have effected the marriage by means of an asset that did not belong to him, and thus the marriage is void. Another suggested rationale is that the marriage is invalid because "'all who marry do so subject to the conditions laid down by the community in its enactments,' since all who marry . . . do so in accordance with the customs of the town . . . ; any marriage that contravenes a communal enactment is invalid, and no divorce is necessary."[135]

Here, the communal enactment is able to affect a matter of religious law—the prohibition of forbidden sexual unions—either because the validity of a marriage depends upon a monetary factor, namely, the money or other item of value given to the bride, which the community has the authority to expropriate, or because the marriage is entered into subject to the condition of the community's consent, which the community may withhold.[136]

Various factors led over the course of time to more limited use of communal authority to enact legislation affecting matters of *issur.* The authority to adopt enactments nullifying marriages had become restricted by the middle of the period of the *rishonim,* and in the course of time the communities completely abstained from the exercise of this authority.[137] Similarly, Joseph ibn Lev (Maharibal), in the sixteenth century, ruled that although the community had previously had authority to adopt an enactment that all decisions with regard to any halakhic matter—whether involving *mamon* or *issur*—should be in accordance with the opinions of a specified halakhic authority, "in these times" the community's authority is limited, in that "only as to civil law matters (*mamon*) may they enact such a *takkanah;* in matters of religious law (*issur*), divorce, and marriage, such a *takkanah* is not within the power of the townspeople to enact."[138]

135. *Resp. Rashba,* I, #551; *Resp. Ribash* #399; and many other sources. *See infra* pp. 850–859.

136. For detailed discussion, *see infra* pp. 858–859. A similar instance of a communal enactment affecting a matter of *issur* was noted *supra* pp. 511–514 in regard to the use of the principle of *hefker bet din hefker* for a matter of *issur* that turns on the question of who is the owner of property.

137. As to this, *see infra* pp. 846–879. For the same reasons, the halakhic authorities also refrained from legislating to annul marriages.

138. *Resp. Maharibal,* I, 12:75(73), ed. Jerusalem, 1959, p. 183. Maharibal established that in the Talmudic period the townspeople had the power to adopt such an enactment. Rashba reached the same conclusion in upholding the practice of some communities to

E. Binding Force of Communal Enactments

The halakhic authorities accorded the same binding force to a law based on a communal enactment as they did to a law of the Torah. Consequently, "whoever takes an oath not to be bound by a communal enactment" in effect swears to violate a religious commandment (*mizvah*).[139] A responsum states:

> If someone, hearing that a community was about to adopt an enactment, hurriedly takes an oath not to obey their enactment, and afterward they make the enactment applicable to him, he must obey their enactment . . . since whoever takes an oath to violate a law adopted by the community has taken a vain oath. . . . He is not exempt from the communal enactment if it has been adopted lawfully, even if he took his oath prior to the enactment, for he has taken an oath to violate a religious commandment.[140]

---

follow Alfasi's opinions and of other communities to follow Maimonides' opinions. *Resp. Rashba,* I, #253. To the query why in his own time the community did not have such authority in matters of *issur,* Maharibal answered:

> [This could be done] only in those times when every town had one rabbi who taught them, as it is stated, "Babylon and all its neighboring towns follow Rav; Nehardea and all its neighboring towns follow Samuel," and each town was obligated to give its rabbi [lit. "teacher"] the proper respect. However, nowadays all the authorities and rabbis on whose works we draw are our teachers, and we are obliged in matters of Biblical law to follow the more stringent view. I have several proofs for this.

We have noted this contraction in the creative and decision-making authority in Jewish law, which came about in the wake of the disappearance of the spiritual hegemony of a single center after the geonic period. *See, e.g., supra* pp. 668–675. Maharibal similarly limited the power to adopt an enactment providing that all decisions should follow the opinions of a specified halakhic authority. It should be pointed out that other halakhic authorities did not adopt this approach; Joseph Caro, a contemporary of Maharibal, explicitly ruled that a communal enactment providing that all of Maimonides' rulings—both leniencies and stringencies—must be followed was valid and must be complied with; *see Resp. Avkat Rokhel* #32.

139. This view had been transmitted in the name of Yehudai Gaon; *see Ozar ha-Geonim,* Nedarim, Responsa, p. 15. With regard to an oath not to perform a *mizvah,* the rule is: "Whoever takes an oath not to perform a *mizvah, e.g.,* that he would not build a *sukkah* [for the festival of *Sukkot* (Tabernacles)], or take a *lulav* [the palm branch used on the *Sukkot* festival], or put on phylacteries, has taken a vain oath, which, if willful, is punishable by flogging but, if not taken with the intent to transgress, is not punishable" (M Shevu'ot 3:8).

140. *Resp. Ḥakhmei Ẓarfat ve-Lutir* #24 (ed. Müller, p. 13). Part of the responsum is quoted by *Mordekhai,* Shevu'ot, ch. 3 (beginning), #755, in the name of Rashi. The law is codified accordingly in Sh. Ar. YD 228:33: "Whoever takes an oath not to be bound by a communal enactment has taken a vain oath, and the enactment applies to him notwithstanding his objection; if he does not conduct himself like them [*i.e.,* the other townspeople], he is subject to the ban [which accompanied] their enactment." *See Be'ur ha-Gra, ad loc.,* subpar. 94, where the Gaon of Vilna expressed his surprise: "Is a communal enactment superior to an enactment of the Sages?" *See also* B. Lipkin, "Samkhut ha-Ḥakikah Shel ha-Ẓibbur" [The Legislative Authority of the Public], *Sinai,* XXV, pp. 249ff., where the query of *Be'ur ha-Gra* is discussed. As to a person who takes an oath not to accept an appointment by the community, *see Resp. Tashbez,* II, #98 and #153. *See also supra* n. 84.

In order to give full recognition and effectiveness to laws based on communal enactments, the halakhic authorities continually emphasized that a communal enactment was as obligatory as a law of the Torah:

> It is clear that the public may erect safeguards and enact *takkanot* as they deem appropriate. These have the same status as a law of the Torah, and they may impose penal sanctions upon anyone who violates their enactments.[141]

Rashbash (Simeon b. Solomon Duran, the grandson of Rashbeẓ [Simeon b. Ẓemaḥ Duran]), a fifteenth-century halakhic authority of North Africa, summarized the authority and efficacy of communal enactments:[142]

> Concerning your letter about your enactment . . . , you should be aware that a court may adopt enactments and erect safeguards as it deems appropriate and may expropriate an individual's property, since it has the power to transfer any property that could not otherwise be transferred under strict law. . . . Not only may a duly ordained court do this, but the courts of every generation may expropriate private property, because Jephthah in his generation is equal to Samuel in his generation. . . .
>
> Do not think that only a court, because of its great power, has the authority to expropriate private property and that the community may not expropriate in the same way as the court. For just as a court may expropriate, adopt enactments, and vest ownership of property otherwise than according to the strict law, so may the community expropriate, as is stated in the first chapter of Tractate *Bava Batra:*[143] "It was taught: The townspeople may, etc.". . . .
>
> We learn from this that the community, like a court, may punish and expropriate, provided that it does so with the approval of a "distinguished person" (*adam ḥashuv*),[144] *i.e.,* a halakhic authority whom the community has accepted. Thus, the law is that the community is equal to the court and also has the authority to punish and to expropriate property.[145]

141. *Resp. Rashba,* IV, #185. *See also Resp. Tashbeẓ,* II, #63, in the name of Maharam of Rothenburg: "A custom of the community is [like a law of the] Torah, and in all such cases custom overrides the law" (in regard to the admissibility of testimony by witnesses who are related to a party); *Resp. Tashbeẓ,* I, #159. Israel Isserlein similarly deduced from the legal rule that whoever takes an oath not to be bound by a communal enactment has taken an oath as vain as an oath not to eat *maẓẓah* (unleavened bread) on Passover or as an oath not to dwell in a *sukkah* on the *Sukkot* festival, that "it follows that a communal enactment also has the force of a law of the Torah" (*Terumat ha-Deshen* #281).

142. *Resp. Yakhin u-Voaz,* II, #20. For more about this responsum, *see infra* pp. 862–863.

143. TB Bava Batra 8b, quoted *supra* p. 679.

144. For the requirement of the approval by a "distinguished person," *see infra* pp. 751–759.

145. Communal enactments, both generally speaking and with specific respect to the source of their authority, can be viewed as a continuation of the legislative authority vested in the king and, later, in the Jewish governmental authorities; *see* the discussion *supra* pp. 55–61. However, such an explanation is more historical than legal. The halakhic authorities

III. MAJORITY AND MINORITY IN COMMUNAL ENACTMENTS

A. The Principle of Majority Rule

Communal enactments were legislated by the majority; once they were enacted, they obligated the dissenting minority as well. Apparently, this was the accepted rule, although in the early stages of communal legislation no legal-halakhic rationale for the rule appears to have been developed. Thus, Isaac Alfasi in the eleventh century C.E. stated in a responsum:[146] "The basic requirement for [effective] legislation[147] is that the majority of the community, with the advice of the elders of the community, enact whatever *takkanah* they wish, and they [all] abide by it; this is legislation."[148]

In the twelfth century C.E., Jacob b. Meir (Rabbenu Tam) declared his opposition to the principle of majority rule. According to Rabbenu Tam, the majority has no power to impose its enactment on a dissenting minority; only the explicit or implicit consent to the enactment by the minority entitles the majority, through fines or other punishments, to compel compliance by anyone who initially consented but later refuses to abide by the enactment. However, if an individual from the outset refuses to accept the burden of the enactment, the majority has no power to compel him to do so:

> The rule that the townspeople may impose penalties for violation of their enactments[149] applies when the enactment has been adopted and agreed upon unanimously, one who originally agreed to the enactment now violates it, and the enactment has been approved by the town's halakhic authority (*ḥaver ir*).[150] [The rule is] similar to that of the case of the two butchers who entered into an agreement, and one of them repudiated it.[151]

---

generally grounded the legislative power of the community primarily on the equation of communal authority with the authority of a court. However, the king's law was also regarded as a source for communal legislative authority. *See Resp. Ḥatam Sofer,* OḤ, #208, discussed *supra* p. 61 n. 37.

146. *Resp. Alfasi,* ed. Leiter, #13, ed. Byednowitz, #85. The same conclusion can be inferred from the responsum of Joseph Tov Elem, quoted *supra* pp. 688–690.

147. Alfasi used the term *minhag,* which usually means custom, although at times it is used, as here, to mean legislation. *See supra* p. 492 and *infra* pp. 885–886.

148. The principle of majority rule also appears in one of the enactments attributed to Rabbenu Gershom. *See infra* p. 784 n. 13; Finkelstein, *Self-Government,* pp. 49ff.

149. TB Bava Batra 8b. *See supra* pp. 679–680.

150. By *ḥaver ir* Rabbenu Tam meant the scholar or rabbi of the town. *See also* Rashi, Megillah 27b, s.v. Ḥaver ir ("A halakhic scholar who occupies himself with the town's needs"); *Tur* YD 256:10 ("an important person [*adam gadol*] under whose supervision all [charity money] is collected and who determines how it is to be distributed to the needy"); Ritba, Novellae to Avodah Zarah 36b, s.v. Katuv be-shem ("Any enactment to which the

> Since there is no *kinyan* and the situation is analogous to a transfer of something not yet in existence, it requires the approval of the town's halakhic authority. . . . However, expropriating property against the will of its owner is prohibited unless done pursuant to a *takkanah* unanimously adopted by the community or adopted by the court.[152]

Thus, Rabbenu Tam interpreted the *baraita* in Tractate *Bava Batra* (to the effect that the townspeople may agree on particular legislation) as meaning only that if they all do so a *kinyan* is unnecessary, and that legal flaws, such as the fact that the property affected does not yet exist, do not vitiate such legislation; since the legislation agreed upon involves the public, it is not subject to requirements that apply in the law of private agreements.[153]

It is difficult to determine conclusively the meaning intended by the text of the *baraita* concerning enactments of the townspeople. In any case, Rabbenu Tam's opinion[154] remained a minority view;[155] the majority of leading halakhic authorities disagreed. Eleazar b. Joel ha-Levi (Raviah), one of the leading halakhic authorities in Germany at the end of the twelfth century C.E., held that the majority may enact legislation binding on a dissenting minority, and the majority of the halakhic authorities[156] concurred.[157]

---

majority of the community . . . agreed . . . and if there is in the town a *ḥaver ir,* they must obtain his approval, and if not, their act is ineffectual, as is stated in Bava Kamma ch. 1"—the reference is, thus, to a "distinguished person," as in TB Bava Batra 9a; *see infra* pp. 752–753). The original meaning of *ḥaver ir* still requires investigation; it is possible that it meant a single individual, as described. However, it may have meant a representative body, such as a municipal council. For a detailed discussion, *see* L. Ginzberg, *Perushim,* III, pp. 410–428 and bibliographical references cited there; S. Lieberman, *Tosefta ki-Feshutah,* Pe'ah, p. 190, and Megillah, p. 1211.

151. TB Bava Batra 9a.

152. *Mordekhai,* Bava Kamma, #179, Bava Batra, #480; *Resp. Maharam of Rothenburg,* ed. Cremona, #230; *Resp. Maimuniyyot,* Shofetim, #10.

153. Concerning the exemption of a public body from the requirement of a *kinyan* and other formal procedures of the Jewish law of acquisitions, *see supra* pp. 704–707.

154. Baer, *supra* n. 16 at 39, remarks that in this period, *i.e.,* the twelfth century, the view still prevailed in Europe that in order to be valid, a communal decision had to be unanimous and that the majority had to obtain—by force or by negotiations—the agreement of the minority. This view differed from the Roman law, which recognized the right of the majority to impose its will on the minority.

155. For other halakhic authorities who followed Rabbenu Tam's view, *see Resp. Maharam of Rothenburg,* ed. Prague, #968; *Mordekhai,* Bava Batra, #481. *But see* the responsum of Maharam of Rothenburg quoted in *Resp. Maimuniyyot,* Kinyan, #27, and *Resp. Maharam of Rothenburg,* ed. Berlin, #865. As to the uncertainty regarding Maharam's position on the question, *see* his other responsa discussed by Agus, *supra* n. 21 at VI, pp. 305–320.

156. *Resp. Maharaḥ Or Zaru'a* #222; *Mordekhai,* Bava Batra, #482; *Resp. Ribash* #249 ("Sometimes it has been the practice that a few individuals exclude themselves from their

What is the legal-halakhic basis for the power of the majority?[158] The rationale of Asheri is interesting:[159]

> Your question is whether two or three ordinary inhabitants of the town may exclude themselves from enactments agreed to by the community or from a decree enforced by a ban concerning any matter. Know that as to matters involving the public, the Torah states:[160] "Follow the majority." The majority governs in all matters of public enactment; and the minority must abide by all that is agreed to by the majority, because otherwise, if a few individuals could veto the enactment, the community would never be able to legislate. Therefore, the Torah declared: "Follow the majority" with reference to all communal enactments.

This is an example of the development of a legal doctrine through expansive interpretation. The verse containing the expression "Follow the majority" is interpreted in the Talmud as referring to the rule that the decision of the majority of the judges hearing a case constitutes the judgment of the court, and to the rule concerning the legal effect of the preponderance

---

enactments . . . and the community permits them to do so. . . . Since this practice has the sanction of custom, they may do so"); *see also* the responsa cited *supra* as to the binding force of communal enactments, and *see Resp. Rashba*, II, #279; V, #242, #270, and *Resp. Rashba Attributed to Naḥmanides* #65 and #280.

Resp. Rashba, IV, #185 seems to imply that unanimity of the community is required, but even this responsum may be interpreted consistently with the view Rashba stated clearly and unequivocally in a long series of responsa, namely, that the decision of the majority binds the minority. It should be pointed out that Rashba noted that there were communities "that pretentiously provided" that their enactments had to be unanimous, but this went beyond what the law required (*Resp. Rashba*, V, #126 and III, #394). *See* Baer, *supra* n. 16 at 38–40; Freimann, *supra* n. 16 at 1–6; S. Albeck, *supra* n. 21 at 128ff.; B. Lipkin, "Shittot ha-Rishonim be-Takkanot ha-Kahal" [The Approach of the *Rishonim* to Communal Enactments], *Ha-Torah ve-ha-Medinah* [Torah and State], II (1950), pp. 41–54. *See also* the comprehensive material on the subject in *Resp. Elijah Mizraḥi* #57; *Resp. Binyamin Ze'ev* #290, #296, #298–300; *Resp. Mahari Minz* #7, quoted *supra* pp. 418–421.

157. Some halakhic authorities distinguished between communal enactments, which could be adopted by a majority, and regulations by a tradesmen's association or craftsmen's guild, which they held had to be unanimous. The rationale is that a group such as a guild is usually a small body and does not have the same responsibilities as a community; a regulation by a guild involves the very serious possibility of harming the occupational interests of the minority. *See* Naḥmanides, Novellae to Bava Batra 9a, s.v. Ha de-amrinan be-hanhu bei trei tabḥei; *Nimmukei Yosef* to Alfasi, *ad loc.* (in printed eds. of Alfasi, fol. 6b, s.v. Aval heikha de-ikka adam ḥashuv); *Bet Yosef* to *Tur* ḤM 231:30, s.v. U-m"sh, and Rema to Sh. Ar. ḤM 231:28. *Resp. Leḥem Rav* #216, by Abraham di Boton, the author of *Leḥem Mishneh* to *MT*, presents an instructive example of this tendency in a case where the majority of tailors adopted a regulation aimed at a particular tailor who opposed the regulation.

158. This question is not discussed in the Talmud; *see supra* n. 16.

159. *Resp. Asheri* 6:5.

160. Exodus 23:2.

of probabilities.[161] On its face, the verse provides no basis for any conclusion one way or another with regard to the problem here involved. However, Asheri interpreted the principle contained in this verse as applicable to any matter "involving the public" and not just to judicial decisions and legal presumptions. The underlying rationale for Asheri's interpretation is undoubtedly the practical consideration that "otherwise, if a few individuals could veto the enactment, the community would never be able to legislate." Or, as he put it in another responsum: "For if you do not say this, there could never be a communal enactment, for when would a community ever agree unanimously on anything?"[162]

By the end of the thirteenth century, there were those who saw in this fundamental principle of public democracy a rule of law that "no one would ever think of" contesting.[163] Thus, a responsum evidently written at the end of the thirteenth century[164] states:

> It is our opinion that all Jews have an obligation to compel and constrain one another to maintain truth, justice, and God's laws and teachings. . . . Therefore, when the community agrees to erect a safeguard or "fence" around the Torah, no individual may exclude himself from the community and thus nullify the actions of the majority by saying, "I did not agree to this enactment." The view of the individuals in the minority is unavailing; the majority may impose an oath or issue a decree or redeem or expropriate his [a dissenter's] property and create any kind of safeguard. We have found a basis for this in a number of places in the Torah. . . .
>
> Therefore, no individual may exclude himself from the general community. This is true not only with respect to matters as to which it is required to erect a safeguard and "fence" around the Torah, but even with respect to matters of discretionary authority, such as taxes or other *takkanot* the community enacts for itself. An individual may not nullify and exclude himself from their enactment, as was taught: "The townspeople may fix weights and

161. *See supra* n. 16.

162. *Resp. Asheri* 6:7. As to the view that Asheri used Exodus 23:2 as only a support (*asmakhta be-alma; see supra* p. 300 n. 50) for the principle of the binding power of majority decision, *see* Samuel de Medina, *Resp. Maharashdam,* YD, #117, quoted in Elon, *Samkhut ve-Oẓmah,* pp. 7, 25 n. 52. *But cf.* the discussion of Asheri's position by Isaac Adarbi, a colleague and fellow-countryman of de Medina: "Indeed, he [Asheri] wrote explicitly that it is an affirmative commandment of the Torah to follow the majority." *Divrei Rivot* #68, p. 29, col. 3.

163. However, not all halakhic authorities, even in this period, agreed that the majority of the community may bind the minority.

164. *See* Baer, *supra* n. 16 at 38 n. 31; E.E. Urbach, *Ba'alei ha-Tosafot, Toledoteihem, Ḥibbureihem ve-Shittatam* [The Tosafists: Their History, Writings, and Methodology], Jerusalem, 1956 (hereinafter, *Tosafot*), p. 410 and n. 25. *See also* Agus's reconsideration of the date of this responsum, *supra* n. 21 at V, pp. 192–193.

measures, market prices, and laborers' wages, and they may enforce their regulations." Therefore, this idea should never occur to anyone.[165]

The relationship between majority and minority also raised many other questions. Thus, for example, the problem arose as to whether legislation by the majority binds only those members of the minority present at the time an enactment is adopted or also binds those not then present. As has been noted, the power of the majority to impose its will on the minority was based on the principle of majority rule applicable in the context of judicial decisions. Since full attendance of all members of the Sanhedrin was required for deliberation and decision,[166] it might be concluded that just as the decision of the majority of a court is not valid unless the full court is in attendance, legislation adopted by the majority of a community should not be valid unless the dissenters are present at the time of its enactment. However, if this were indeed to be the case, the right of the majority to impose its will on the minority would become meaningless, since the members of the minority could prevent the adoption of any enactment through the simple expedient of absenting themselves from the discussion.

This problem was much discussed in halakhic literature and was resolved in various ways.[167] Some halakhic authorities found legal support in the proposition that those who absented themselves "are in the position of having yielded their own views in favor of the views of those present"[168]—a theory of implied consent. Others relied on the force of custom: "It has been the settled practice in all places to enact legislation which is valid though some are absent."[169] Other authorities declared:

> For the enactment of a *takkanah* by the community concerning a matter as to which the public welfare requires legislation, it is not necessary that everyone

165. *Kol Bo* #142; *see also id.* #116.

166. M Sanhedrin 5:5: "They debate with one another," *i.e.*, those for conviction try to persuade those for acquittal and vice versa.

167. *Resp. Rashba*, III, #304; *Bet Yosef* to *Tur* ḤM 13:9 and YD ch. 228 (toward the end, after s.v. U-m"sh ve-yesh lahem hattarah); *Resp. Maharik* #177, #179; *Resp. Maharit*, I, #58, #68, #95; *Resp. Mabit*, I, #264; *Resp. Maharashdam*, YD, #117, #151, ḤM, #398, #406; *Naḥalat Shiv'ah* #27; *see also* Shalom Mordekhai Schwadron, *Mishpat Shalom* #231, Kunteres Tikkun Olam; I.M. Ginzburg, *Mishpatim le-Yisra'el*, pp. 60–63. Some halakhic authorities required that the minority be present at the vote. *See*, particularly, *Resp. Maharibal*, I, #115, #122, #126; *Resp. Maharashdam*, YD, #82; *Resp. Maharshakh*, II, #109; and the various sources cited by them. *See also* Ḥayyim Benveniste, *Keneset ha-Gedolah, Haggahot Bet Yosef*, ḤM, #13, from Letter *kaf* on.

168. *Mishpat Shalom*, *supra* n. 167, on the basis of *Resp. Ḥatam Sofer*, ḤM, #116, for details of which *see infra* pp. 720–723.

169. *Resp. Mabit*, I, #264; similarly in *Resp. Mishpat Ẓedek*, II, #4 and #35: "Even if the [individuals in the] minority were not in the town [when the enactment was adopted], they are bound by the majority's decision, and that is the custom."

> be present, but legislation for which there is no such necessity (*she-eino le-migdar milta*) and which adversely affects anyone requires full attendance.[170]

The reason given by Abraham Alegre, the rabbi of Constantinople in the first part of the seventeenth century and one of the leading authorities of Turkish Jewry, for the binding force of an enactment on those who absented themselves is instructive:

> They [the minority] caused their own loss, and of necessity they must bend their shoulders and bear the yoke of the enactment; for the majority will never govern if the dissenters could succeed in becoming exempt by not joining with the others and not conferring together or being counted. It is clear beyond argument that such a possibility is repugnant to reason.[171]

The socio-communal practicalities thus brought about a complete solution empowering the majority to reach a binding decision through the removal of all arbitrary and meritless obstructions on the part of the minority.

An apt conclusion to this discussion of the problem of majority and minority in communal enactments is provided by a responsum written some hundreds of years later at the beginning of the nineteenth century by Moses Sofer (Ḥatam Sofer) in connection with an occurrence that was then common in the Jewish community. As will be discussed, by that time Jewish juridical autonomy had considerably declined.[172] In light of this decline, Moses Sofer's approach to the legal analysis of this important problem of majority and minority is ironic as well as instructive.

He was asked the following question:[173]

> The government levied a new tax on the community, and the communal administrators sought to collect the money from the residents. The administrators publicly announced a number of times that they would hold a public hearing to determine the procedure for collecting the amount levied; and all

170. *Keneset ha-Gedolah, Haggahot Bet Yosef,* ḤM 13:39; *Massa Melekh,* V, gate 1, law 3. *See also Resp. Maharik* #177, #179.

171. Abraham Alegre, *Resp. Lev Same'aḥ,* ḤM, #5. At the end of the responsum, Alegre states:

> And besides this, in our case, where the majority sent for the minority and its leader to take part in the case and present their arguments to the court but they did not come . . . , their guilt is on their own heads. As to this, everyone would agree; and there is no judge or judgment [that would not rule that] the act of the majority is the work of God, and what they agreed upon and arranged must be upheld. This argument is irrefutable.

The entire responsum extensively discusses the question of whether communal enactments adopted by a majority require the presence of all the townspeople.

172. *See infra* pp. 1578–1584.

173. *Resp. Ḥatam Sofer,* ḤM, #116.

> residents were requested to attend. Nevertheless, only about thirty householders attended; and they agreed to choose nine householders—three wealthy, three of average means, and three poor—who were to confer with the administrators to determine the procedure.
>
> The nine individuals and the administrators all agreed to impose a tax on a certain business transaction, for reasons known to them, with a specified amount to be paid from the proceeds of that transaction. The decision became known to all members of the community, and no one protested except one of the nine above-mentioned individuals, who was in the wealthy group and was also personally involved in that type of transaction. He therefore protested and, together with another individual who is one of the communal administrators, is in opposition to the community. They are engaged in a dispute and request that you reach a decision for them on the basis of the law of our Holy Torah as to whether the community may impose the tax on them against their will.

Sofer began his responsum with an exposition of the different opinions with regard to whether unanimity is required to adopt a communal enactment or whether a majority of the community is sufficient. He concluded that on a superficial view the enactment in this particular case appeared to be invalid:

> In this case, no community members were validly chosen for this purpose from the outset, as we note that they announced a meeting of all residents yet only approximately thirty householders—and no more—came, and the overwhelming majority, a much greater number, were absent. Those thirty chose nine individuals and gave them authority to act, but those nine did not all agree. Rather, only eight of them agreed, and the ninth is the complainant. In such a case, a majority is insufficient, and unanimity is required, as stated by Rashba in a responsum[174] cited by *Bet Yosef* in *Ḥoshen Mishpat* at the end of chapter 13, paragraph 9; and here all nine did not agree. From all the above, it would seem at first glance that the individual should prevail.

However, Sofer subsequently held the enactment to be fully valid, reaching this conclusion through an interesting legal interpretation:

> Nonetheless, my decision is that the community should prevail. Even though only approximately thirty householders came to the meeting, it seems clear that since it had been publicly announced on a day when the entire community was present in the city that they should come to consider the matter, anyone who did not come to the communal meeting implicitly gave his proxy to those that did come.

174. *Resp. Rashba*, II, #104. In that case, there was a requirement that a particular matter had to be determined by a fixed number of persons. It was, therefore, insufficient for the matter to be determined by only a majority of that number.

> There is clear authority for this in the statement in chapter *Mi she-Hayah Nasuy:*[175] "If one of the brothers or one of the partners litigates with a third party, he [another brother or partner] may not say [to the third party]: 'I am not bound by the decision [in your favor],'" and the conclusion is reached there that if he is in the city he must appear in court, *i.e.,* he must accept the judgment; since he did not appear, he impliedly accepted the result, and this is the ruling of all authorities. . . . [176]
>
> This applies even more to our case, since they [the absentees] never objected to the choice of the nine individuals by the thirty householders. On the contrary, this was acceptable to all community members, and even the individual who now objects was satisfied with that choice. It therefore appears that those nine individuals were specifically chosen from all community members to oversee this matter, and all their acts in the matter are equivalent to the acts of the communal leaders in the presence of the entire town. This is so because the entire town became aware of what occurred and failed to object, except for the above complainants, and all the [other] residents, or a majority of them, are satisfied.

Subsequently, Sofer discussed the difference of opinion between Rabbenu Tam and the opposing halakhic authorities as to whether unanimity of the community is necessary or a majority is sufficient. Later in his responsum, he demonstrated that in the case submitted to him a majority was clearly sufficient and, moreover, on the strength of custom and practical necessity, majority approval is sufficient for every communal enactment:

> Even without this reasoning, it has become the custom in all these areas to follow the majority on all such matters; if we wait for unanimity, no matter

175. TB Ketubbot 94a.

176. This analogy, drawn from the law relating to a claim by a partner, constitutes a purposeful development of a new legal theory. The law in TB Ketubbot upon which Ḥatam Sofer relied provides as follows (in Maimonides' formulation, *MT,* Sheluḥin ve-Shutafin 3:3):

> If one of the brothers who have not yet divided [the estate] or one of the partners brings a lawsuit, he sues for all; since he is a joint owner of the property, he does not need a power of attorney from the other partners. Nor can another partner say to the partner who brought the suit, "If I had been there, I would have made different arguments and the other side would have been held liable," because the latter can reply, "Why did you not also participate in the litigation?" Therefore, if he [the other partner] had been in another country [when the case was tried], he may seek out the adverse party and bring suit against him, saying, "I do not agree with any of my partner's arguments."

In any claim made by a partner, the presumption is that that partner [the plaintiff] represents all the partners, but this presumption is not made in the Talmud with regard to the community and its enactments. Ḥatam Sofer, however, applied the same theory to communal enactments by way of analogy. The *rishonim* had already analogized from the laws of partnership to communal enactments; *see* M. Elon, EJ, XV, p. 844, s.v. Taxation (reprinted in *Principles,* p. 668).

> will be concluded, and that would be to the detriment of all. For this reason, it seems to me that even according to Rabbenu Tam, who takes the view that the townspeople may not impose penalties for violation of their enactments unless there was prior unanimity, that is so [only] under strict law; even he would admit that on the strength of custom the majority may compel the minority to follow their laws.
>
> These are the words of Rema in the *Shulḥan Arukh* [*Ḥoshen Mishpat*] chapter 2: "It is the custom in all places that the communal leaders in their community have the same status as the High Court. . . . Even if there are those who disagree, . . . nevertheless the custom of the town is followed. . . ." His intent is to point out that Rabbenu Tam would also concur that the custom of the town is followed. It appears to me that in terms of both theory and practice, the community must prevail.[177]

These clear and unambiguous words, completely justifying the legislative power of the majority of the community on a basis on which all halakhic authorities agreed, provide an important foundation for the governmental procedures and internal autonomy of the Jewish community. It is indeed a cruel irony that at that very time, as a result of various external and internal factors, Jewish autonomy had already begun to disappear.

B. What Constitutes a Majority

After the principle of majority rule was established, the fundamental question that next arose was, On what basis is the majority to be determined? For example, should every person have an equal vote? Should votes be weighted on the basis of wealth, intelligence, learning, or a combination of these factors? These problems have been extensively dealt with in many legal systems, and various standards have been adopted at different times and under different forms of government. It is reasonable to conclude that there was reciprocal influence—both positive and negative—between the Jewish communities and the surrounding non-Jewish environment. The halakhic discussions on this subject evince a grappling with the problem

177. Ḥatam Sofer continued:
Although in another responsum I have followed the responsum of Rema [*Resp. Rema*] #73, to the effect that the community may not impose a tax on a particular transaction [singled out for the purpose] and so discriminate against an individual; nevertheless, in this case, they have a good reason to do so, since such a transaction is appropriate as the subject of a new tax. Furthermore, the meeting of the nine was originally convened to decide on which transactions to impose a tax, and they also taxed [the sale of] meat, wine, fowl, and the like. Even the objector agreed to these taxes; he objects only to what concerns him personally. Therefore, his claim cannot be accepted, and any examination will demonstrate that the distinction [we have drawn] is clear[ly sound].

that yielded a variegated array of responses shaped by, and in turn affecting, the realities of life.

At one end of the spectrum, for example, is the above-mentioned opinion of Elijah Mizraḥi, who was the foremost halakhic authority of Constantinople in the latter half of the fifteenth and the early part of the sixteenth centuries:

> It makes no difference whether the majority consists of the wealthy, the poor, the scholarly, or the unlettered, because the entire community is denominated a court in dealing with matters of communal interest.[178]

A dramatically opposite view was expressed by Samuel de Medina (Maharashdam), one of the leading halakhic authorities of Salonika in the sixteenth century:

> The Torah speaks of following the majority only when the participants in the dispute are of equal standing; only in that case is the numerical majority decisive. But when there is a disparity between the contestants, [the opinion of] a single individual may have as much weight as that of a thousand others.
>
> Thus, when the parties are equal, the majority is determined by number; when the parties are not equal, ["the majority" is determined] by the preponderance of quality. The heart of the matter is that majority rule by shifting alignments of ignorant men will tear the fabric of the law; for if there are a hundred people in a town—ten honorable, distinguished, and wealthy, and ninety of a poor and low class—and the ninety wish to install a leader who suits them, would the ten distinguished citizens be bound to accept his leadership no matter who he happened to be? Heaven forbid! This would not be a "pleasant way."[179]

Absolute equality, without regard to wealth or wisdom, is, in de Medina's view, contrary to law and the opposite of a "pleasant way"; therefore, when the members of the community are not of the same quality, the "majority" is determined not by number, but by the preponderance of quality, *i.e.*, by appropriate weighting of individual votes.

Between these polar positions there is a broad spectrum of views. For example, Isaac Adarbi, a halakhic authority in Salonika during the sixteenth century, held that in financial matters the majority should be determined by the preponderance of wealth, but that in all other matters, the majority should be defined as the greater number of individuals, with the vote of every individual being given equal weight.[180] And Abraham di Boton, another halakhic authority in Salonika during the sixteenth century,

178. *Resp. Elijah Mizraḥi, supra* n. 89.

179. *Resp. Maharashdam,* OḤ, #37; ḤM, #421. The allusion is to Proverbs 3:17.

180. *Resp. Divrei Rivot* #68, #244.

gave a very broad interpretation to the term "financial matters," which left only matters completely unrelated to money (such as enactments "to safeguard the matter" in the area of *issur*) to be determined by a numerical majority.[181]

Earlier, in discussing the relation between *Halakhah* and *Aggadah*,[182] we considered a responsum by Menahem Mendel Krochmal, who was one of the leading halakhic authorities in Germany in the mid-seventeenth century. The issue submitted to him arose when a number of distinguished citizens of the town sought to establish a rule that not all taxpayers should have the right to vote, but only those who "have the distinction of paying a substantial tax, or the distinction of being learned in the Torah. . . . Since the greater part of the community's business involves the expenditure of money, how can the opinion of a poor man be of equal weight with that of a rich man? Likewise, how can the opinion of an ignorant man who does not have the merit of wealth be of equal weight with that of a scholar?" Against these distinguished citizens, "the poor, who are the mass of the people, protest: Since they are taxpayers and give their share, why should their rights be curtailed? Although the rich pay more, it is a greater burden for the poor to pay their small sum than it is for the rich to pay their larger amount."[183]

Krochmal held that the majority should be determined on the basis of a combination of both factors—wealth and number, or, as he put it, a majority in quality and number (*rov binyan ve-rov minyan*).

On the basis of his innovative interpretation of various aggadic texts,[184] Krochmal reasoned that the contribution of the poor may rank even higher than that of the wealthy "since a poor person must labor strenuously to earn enough to bring [his contribution] . . . , [whereas] a rich person . . . brings what he already has, and does not exert himself [to obtain it for the specific purpose of offering it]." He concluded that "the argument of the poor is valid, since the little that they give is as difficult for them as the substantial amount is for the rich."[185]

181. *Resp. Leḥem Rav* #2. *Accord, Resp. Maharshakh,* II, #95; III, #76. Apparently, it was generally accepted that only those who paid some tax had the right to vote. *See Resp. Maharam of Rothenburg,* ed. Berlin, #865, and the responsum of Maharam quoted in *Resp. Mahari Minz* #7, *supra* pp. 418–421.

182. *See supra* pp. 94–104.

183. *Resp. Ẓemaḥ Ẓedek* #2.

184. *See supra* pp. 96–99.

185. *Cf. Resp. Maharit,* I, #69: ". . . all those who pay taxes are equal—the rich who give of their wealth and the poor who give of the little they have . . . ; for the poor are as concerned with their pennies as the rich are with their *denarii,* because payment depends on the amount of money each possesses."

In the course of his argument, Krochmal had difficulty in reconciling his conclusion with the *dictum* of Asheri (*Resp. Asheri* 7:3) that "if a community imposes a ban relating to

No less original was Krochmal's refutation of the argument that there should be a difference in the weight given to a vote on the basis of whether the individual involved was learned or unlettered. As authority, he quoted the following Talmudic passage:[186]

> R. Papa said: "On whose authority do we accept today the testimony of the unlettered [which is contrary to the opinion in the *baraita* in TB Pesaḥim 49b that the testimony of the unlettered is not competent evidence]? This is the opinion of R. Yose [who held that 'everyone may testify to the ritual purity of wine and oil throughout the year, so that people should not go off and build their own altar and burn their own red heifer']."

From this Krochmal concluded:

> It is thus clear that even the testimony of ignorant men is accepted as competent so as to prevent animosity; if they see that they are set apart, they will build their own altar [*i.e.*, leave the community]. This is even more of a concern in regard to the question before us. If we reject the unlettered to the

---

fiscal matters, the 'economic majority' rules. . . . It cannot be that a majority composed of those who pay only a small portion of the taxes may impose a ban on the wealthy." In order to reconcile his own conclusion with Asheri's *dictum*, Krochmal interpreted Asheri restrictively, following, in this regard, Joshua Falk (*Sema*, Sh. Ar. ḤM 163, subpar. 13), who said:

> It can be said that Asheri's *dictum* that the "economic majority" rules means only that the numerical majority cannot legislate over the dissent of the wealthy minority, but it does not mean the wealthy minority can legislate over the objection of the numerical majority. Asheri's view can thus be said to be that both groups have equal weight in such matters and that action may be taken only if the two groups agree on a compromise. The matter requires further consideration.

Krochmal concluded on this basis that the correct criterion gives weight to both numbers and wealth. *See also supra* p. 98 n. 27.

The opinion of Abraham Isaiah Karelitz (*Ḥazon Ish*, Bava Batra 5:1, p. 154) is instructive. He believed that a numerical majority alone should rule and expressed surprise at Asheri's *dictum:*

> If the matter concerns assessment of taxes and it was agreed that "seven communal leaders" should be selected [for this purpose], it would seem that the choice of the numerical majority governs even if the wealthy townspeople choose others. There can be no distinction between the poor and the wealthy, for they are all taxpayers. . . . Asheri's *dictum* that the poor cannot enact legislation binding on the wealthy is not correct, because the poor do not act to advance their personal desires but rather make their decision on the basis of truth and justice for the sake of Heaven. If we were to suspect the poor of acting [unfairly] to increase the burden of the wealthy and decrease the burden on themselves, we should also suspect the wealthy of doing the opposite if they had the power! It follows, therefore, that Asheri's *dictum* cannot refer to assessment of taxes. [The ascertainment of] his actual intent requires further investigation.

See also the statement of *Ḥazon Ish*, *id.*, explaining the view of Israel Isserlein quoted in *Terumat ha-Deshen* #344; *see* Elon, *Samkhut ve-Oẓmah*, pp. 21, 24.

186. TB Ḥagigah 22a.

point of not making them a part of the process of communal legislation, they will certainly resent it and separate themselves from the community, with the result that dissension, Heaven forbid, will be multiplied. This, therefore, is certainly to be avoided.

IV. COMMUNAL ENACTMENTS BY COMMUNAL REPRESENTATIVES

At the head of the community stood the appointed or elected representatives of the people, known by various titles.[187] The composition of the representative body and the personal qualifications of its members varied from place to place. The halakhic authorities extensively discussed the composition of this body, and also the fundamental question of whether the communal representatives were authorized to legislate in the name of the community or whether legislative authority was vested only in the public, *i.e.*, in the assembly of all the members of the entire community.

Rashba wrote concerning the personal qualities and prerogatives of the communal leaders:[188]

> The communal leaders [*shiv'ah tovei ha-ir*, lit. "the seven good citizens of the town"],[189] who are frequently mentioned, are not seven people who excel in wisdom, wealth, or honor,[190] but seven people chosen by the people and authorized generally to be the administrators and trustees of the town affairs. . . .

187. *Tovei ha-ir* [lit. "the good citizens of the town"], "*parnasim*," and the like; *see further supra* p. 27 and n. 84. They were frequently called "the seven *tovei ha-ir*," a term in use as early as the Talmudic period; *see* TB Megillah 26a; TJ Megillah 3:2, 24a (3:2, 74a). Josephus (*Antiquities*, IV, 8:14) wrote: "Every town shall be ruled by seven men who, even before their appointment, have been distinguished by their pious ways and zeal for justice. In each town two men of the tribe of Levi shall be appointed to help in the administration of municipal affairs." *See* the further discussion *infra*.

188. *Resp. Rashba*, I, #617.

189. *See supra* n. 187.

190. *See* the statement of Elijah Mizraḥi (*Resp. Elijah Mizraḥi* #53, p. 149):

> The term *tovei ha-ir*, wherever used, does not mean the wisest, oldest, or wealthiest persons but rather those who are most active in communal affairs, who deal with all the needs of the community, and upon whom the community depends to take care of its requirements. . . . They are therefore denominated as the leaders of the community because they make all the decisions with regard to communal needs. . . . It is more fitting to give the title "communal leader" to one who, although not a scholar, is active in communal affairs, than to a scholar who is not at all active in communal affairs but devotes himself exclusively to his studies. The needy persons of the community—indeed the whole community—depend exclusively on those who occupy themselves with communal needs and not on those who engage only in scholarly pursuits.

See further id. #57. For a different attitude, *see Resp. Mabit*, I, #84; *see also infra* n. 205.

> You may ask: If the leaders are recognized, why is there a need for seven? This was asked by the Jerusalem Talmud[191] . . . and it was explained that it refers to an appointment conferring general authority, *i.e.*, the community chose seven leaders and conferred upon them general power to administer the town's affairs. Therefore, when there are seven, they have full authority to act on all matters without further specific authorization, [and their acts are] as if done by all the townspeople. However, if there are less than seven, they do not have general authority to act for the townspeople but are limited to the performance of those acts the townspeople specifically authorize. There is a hint of this in the seven advisers of the king.[192]

The seven (and sometimes there were more than seven) communal leaders were thus the political and economic heads of the community, in the nature of trustees for the public; and when seven[193] or more were chosen by the community, the legal effect of their acts was the same as if the acts had been done by all the townspeople. An enactment adopted by the communal leaders thus had the same status as if adopted by the entire community. In another responsum, Rashba clearly affirmed this point:[194]

> Communal affairs are entrusted to leaders and to a number of members of the community who act as trustees for the rest of their brethren in their locality. Sometimes a large community will number a thousand,[195] and only thirty or forty, constituting the group authorized to perform such duties, will meet and legislate and pronounce a ban; the others are not notified, nor do they object.
>
> Otherwise, no community could carry on its business, make any expenditures, or enact general legislation until the entire community of taxpayers—both the women and the men—assemble to consider and unanimously agree on an item of expenditure, since who may issue a decree concerning

191. TJ Megillah 3:2, 24a (3:2, 74a).
192. Esther 1:14.
193. *See also Resp. Maharaḥ Or Zaru'a* #65:

> It also seems to me . . . that the Sages determined that when seven persons discuss a matter they will be able to arrive at a true evaluation of what is needed for the improvement and safeguarding of the town, since with regard to intercalation of the year we find that seven persons were required to complete the process, as is stated in the first chapter of Sanhedrin [M Sanhedrin 1:2; TB Sanhedrin 10b].

194. *Resp. Rashba*, III, #443.
195. *Cf.* Ḥayyim Or Zaru'a's contrasting description of Ashkenazi communities in the thirteenth century (*Resp. Maharaḥ Or Zaru'a* #65). In a responsum to "the illustrious community, praises to it, our rabbis in Regensburg, a major Jewish city" he wrote, *inter alia:*

> It is my humble opinion that even our communities are like the villages of tannaitic and amoraic times, because we are very few in number; for from the many only a few have survived, and a village in their days contained more Jews than a large community today.

In Spain, there were also very small communities consisting of "three or four households"; *see Resp. Rashba*, V, #253, and *supra* p. 672.

their property without their consent? The conclusion is, therefore, that the largest taxpayers and some other members of the community are delegated to act as trustees for the rest of the community.[196]

The question of the authority of communal representatives to legislate in the name of the community continued to be a subject of extensive discussion in the halakhic literature for hundreds of years. One reason was that the statements of some of the outstanding halakhic authorities seem to indicate that the communal leaders had the power to legislate only during an assembly of the community's members.[197] A detailed summary of this discussion is found in the writings of Moses b. Joseph Trani (Mabit), in the sixteenth century in Safed:[198]

> It is clear that inhabitants of a town do not have the power to enact *takkanot* for the entire town without the consent of all or a majority of the townspeople, since as to matters involving the public, the Torah states: "Follow the majority"[199] . . . , as Rashba has specifically written. . . . And if a minority proclaims a ban or adopts an enactment without the majority's consent, the enactment or ban is a nullity, since a majority is necessary. . . .
>
> But the matter needs further clarification: Is the entire community obligated to follow a decree or enactment that the communal leaders have adopted? It would seem that the majority of a community can impose its will on the minority but not *vice versa*—not even if the minority consists of the town's communal leaders. Naḥmanides in *Mishpat ha-Ḥerem*[200] and Ribash[201] . . . wrote: "If all or a majority of the townspeople agreed in the presence of the town's communal leaders, all are obligated to follow, etc.," which implies that even the communal leaders require the agreement of a majority of the

196. *See Resp. Maharaḥ Or Zaru'a* #65:

> But certainly, even when there are a number of communal leaders, if seven of them conclude a transaction (*osin ma'aseh*) for the improvement and safeguarding of the community, even though the other townspeople become aware of the transaction only afterward and seek to reverse it, they cannot.

The same point is also made further on in the responsum.

197. *See, e.g., Mordekhai,* Bava Batra, #480, and Naḥmanides and Ribash, quoted in *Resp. Mabit, infra.*

198. *Resp. Mabit,* I, #84.

199. These are the words of Asheri in *Resp. Asheri* 6:5; *see supra* p. 717.

200. Naḥmanides, *Mishpat ha-Ḥerem,* at the end of *Sefer Kol Bo* (fol. 16c/d, Fyorda, 1782):

> The same applies to the townspeople; if all or a majority of them agreed in the presence of the communal leaders and adopted an enactment that they may impose penalties for violation of their regulations and may put under a ban [anyone who does not comply], their ban applies to all those who are bound by their enactment. Thus, any member of the community who does not comply violates the enactment and breaks the oath . . . and is under a ban in his town.

201. *Resp. Ribash* #249 (beginning).

townspeople; yet the responsum by Rashba[202] indicates that the communal leaders have the authority on all matters as if their enactments had been adopted by all the townspeople.[203]

This can be resolved by saying that a majority is always necessary and that the basis of the authority of the communal leaders on all matters is that they are considered the equivalent of the majority; they represent the majority who selected and empowered them generally to administer all public affairs, as Rashba proved from the Jerusalem Talmud.[204] However, unless so selected and empowered, they have no authority even though they are the communal leaders.

What Naḥmanides and Ribash meant when they referred to a majority of the townspeople in the presence of the communal leaders is that such a majority must have the concurrence of the communal leaders. Even if there is a majority, the concurrence of the communal leaders is also required because they are the leaders of the town in wisdom and fear of sin,[205] and they are therefore best able to determine that their enactment will make things better and not worse. And even if the communal leaders are present, the presence of a majority of the townspeople is also necessary unless, as stated, the authority to administer all public affairs has been delegated to those leaders.

If the public designates representatives to administer all its affairs, the representatives' power is equal to that of the public that selected them. This is not inconsistent with the principle that at least a majority of the townspeople is required. The people's representatives are the equivalent of the majority of the townspeople, inasmuch as the majority selected them and the power of the majority has been delegated to them. However, if the public did not constitute the representatives as agents authorized to administer all public affairs, it cannot be said that they always represent the majority, and the townspeople must be present when the communal leaders adopt communal enactments.

202. The reference is to *Resp. Rashba*, V, #125; the same idea is expressed explicitly in a number of Rashba's other responsa, as demonstrated *supra*.

203. *I.e.*, Mabit saw a contradiction between Naḥmanides and Ribash on the one hand, and Rashba on the other. Both Naḥmanides and Ribash implied that a decision of the communal leaders is legally valid only if reached at a meeting of all or at least a majority of the townspeople. Rashba, however, indicated that whatever the communal leaders decide obligates the community as though it had been enacted by all the townspeople, even if fewer than a majority of the whole community are present when the enactment is adopted.

204. *See supra* p. 728 and n. 191.

205. This is a different qualification for the communal leaders than was required by Rashba and Elijah Mizraḥi, *supra* nn. 188–190. Various other sources also present these differing approaches to the qualifications required for communal leadership.

V. THE APPLICABILITY OF COMMUNAL ENACTMENTS TO MINORS, PERSONS YET UNBORN, AND PERSONS JOINING THE COMMUNITY SUBSEQUENT TO THE ADOPTION OF THE ENACTMENT

As stated, the halakhic authorities had to go beyond the rules of private law in order to fashion norms of public law governing communal legislation. They accomplished this to a large extent by the acceptance of the principle that legislation by the majority is binding on a dissenting minority; this principle, as we have seen, was based on an expansive interpretation of the principle of majority rule applicable to judicial decision making. An even more difficult problem was, How could communal enactments be made binding on those who, under the basic principles of private law, lacked capacity to assume a legal obligation—*e.g.*, minors, and, even more so, those not yet born at the time of the adoption of the enactment? Obviously, an enactment would have no practical value if it applied only to those who at the time of its adoption had legal capacity to consent to be bound by it.

This fundamental problem, too, was solved with the assistance of analogies from the "religious" part of Jewish law involving the laws of oaths, vows, and festivals, and even from the very acceptance of the Torah itself; the basic impetus for the search was, once again, the practical necessity for a fully sound and effective system of communal legislation.

In a responsum in which Rashba discussed many problems concerning communal enactments,[206] he also stated his position with regard to the problem of the binding force of a communal enactment upon future generations not yet born when the enactment was adopted:

> Even those born later, in future generations, are obligated to follow what was agreed to and enacted by their ancestors; all such enactments were adopted for themselves and their descendants; for this was the way the Torah—as well as the rabbinic enactments, such as the reading [on *Purim*] of the *Megillah* [the Book of Esther] and the observance of *Hanukkah*—was accepted.
>
> Even if the ancestors practiced a fixed custom as a result of an oath, without a specific enactment, the descendants after them must follow their custom. As the Jerusalem Talmud states:[207] "Do not change the custom of your deceased ancestors." . . . Whoever breaches this rule is like one who breaks the fence of the Torah, since the ancestors are the roots of their descendants.

206. *Resp. Rashba,* III, #411. This responsum has already been discussed in a number of connections *supra.*

207. TJ Pesaḥim 4:1.

Giving communal enactments binding effect on future generations was accomplished by an analogy from the principle of "acceptance" applicable to the holidays of *Purim* and *Hanukkah*, and to the Torah itself, and from the binding force of custom, even upon future generations.[208] In all of these instances, the general principle is that "the ancestors are the roots of their descendants"; and this is also the law with respect to communal enactments.

This principle was cited by Rashba in conjunction with a general description of communal enactments. In other responsa, this problem was discussed in the context of a halakhic exposition specifically addressing the question, How can an enactment obligate anyone who has no capacity to assume a legal obligation?

Ribash was asked about a communal enactment that expropriated the money given to effect a marriage that took place in the absence of the communal leaders and without a quorum of ten people.[209] One of the issues was put as follows by Ribash:

> You are in doubt whether the community has the power to expropriate . . . money even from minors, who have no capacity to validate or to agree to a *takkanah*, and even more so from those who are born later or who come from outside the town to live there.

Ribash responded:

> Under the law of the Torah, the townspeople may adopt enactments, regulations, and agreements, and may penalize violators, as stated in Tractate *Bava Batra*:[210] "The townspeople may fix weights and measures, market prices, and laborers' wages, and they may enforce their regulations". . . . Their power is not restricted to these matters alone; rather, they have the same authority with regard to any matter concerning which they see fit to legislate and penalize the violator. . . . Minors are also included within their *takkanah* when they become of age; otherwise, when the townspeople fix market prices, weights and measures, and laborers' wages, and they impose penalties for violations, they would be required to reenact their *takkanah* daily, because of

208. *See infra* pp. 880ff. It should be pointed out that communal enactments were also generally accompanied by the declaration of a ban or oath, which strengthened the analogy from the oath of Joshua and the incident of the concubine at Gibeah (*see infra* p. 733) as to the binding force of the enactment upon future generations. However, all the responsa emphasize that an enactment is binding on future generations, like a custom or any other tradition, because "the ancestors are the roots of their descendants." *See further infra* n. 217.

209. *Resp. Ribash* #399. This enactment answered the need to prevent secret and fraudulent marriages. *See infra* pp. 856–859.

210. TB Bava Batra 8b.

the minors who daily become of age, and this would make no sense. Rather, all the townspeople are included within their *takkanah*.

Also included are those who are born later; for the public may enact a *takkanah* to bind themselves and their descendants, as we have seen in connection with the incident of the concubine in Gibeah. They swore: "None of us will give his daughter in marriage to a Benjaminite,"[211] so future generations as well as that generation were prohibited, until they interpreted [the vow, as meaning] "None of us—'us' but not our sons," as was explained in chapter *Yesh Noḥalin*.[212] If they had said: "None of us or our children," or they had simply made a general declaration, the ban would also have applied to future generations.

Naḥmanides wrote in *Mishpat ha-Ḥerem*[213] that every public undertaking obligates the people and their descendants, as shown by the acceptance of the Torah, as well as the reading of the *Megillah* or the institution of fast days. In addition, even with regard to matters not adopted by enactment of the townspeople but engaged in as a customary practice to create a fence and safeguard for the Torah, the descendants are also obligated to follow that practice.

Tractate *Pesaḥim*, chapter *Makom she-Nahagu*, states:[214]

> The residents of Beisan [Bet-Shean] were accustomed not to take the trip from Tyre to Sidon [for market day] on the eve of the sabbath. Their children came to R. Johanan and said to him: "Our fathers were able to observe this. What is the law for us, who are unable to do so?" [*I.e.*, our fathers were rich and did not need to attend the market on the eve of the sabbath, but we are poor and need to do so]. He said to them: "Your fathers accepted it [the custom] upon themselves, and it is written,[215] 'My son, heed the discipline of your father and do not forsake the instruction of your mother.'"

If the fathers could not obligate the children, why were the children forbidden from doing what the fathers forbade to themselves? For even if they had deliberately and explicitly erected that safeguard, they could not have joined their children with them! The conclusion, therefore, must be that the townspeople may bind themselves and their descendants; and since they can bind them, they may also establish penalties for violations of their enactments.

The same applies to those who come from outside the town to live there. They are like the townspeople and are obligated to obey their [the townspeople's] enactments, as they implicitly undertook to obey all the town's enactments when they came. . . . This is especially true in regard to matters involving money, such as the fines provided for in the enactments;

211. Judges 21:1.
212. TB Bava Batra 121a.
213. *See supra* n. 200.
214. TB Pesaḥim 50b.
215. Proverbs 1:8.

> for it is reasonable to say that they accepted the enactments when they came to live in the town, and they are in the same position as the townspeople and subject to their enactments.
>
> Thus, we have concluded that the community may prescribe penalties in their enactments, as they see fit.[216]

Ribash produced no halakhic proof for the application of the enactment to minors, but only a simple and persuasive practical reason that "otherwise, . . . the townspeople . . . would be required to reenact their *takkanah* daily, because of the minors who daily become of age, and this would make no sense. . . ." With regard to the unborn, Ribash solved the problem in the same way that Rashba had already solved it: by analogy to an oath (which also obligates future generations), and to the Jewish people's acceptance of the Torah and the festivals, and by invoking the efficacy of custom practiced by ancestors, which likewise obligates not only the ancestors but also their descendants. It is certainly possible to find flaws in these analogies, but they illustrate the method of Jewish law, which finds various supporting arguments drawn from different subjects and legal fields to solve current halakhic problems.[217]

216. *See also* Ribash's discussion, in the continuation of that responsum, of the degree to which communal enactments are binding. Ribash first raised the query:

> In TB Gittin, ch. "Ha-Shole'aḥ" [36b], it is stated regarding the *prosbul* that "perhaps when Hillel instituted the *prosbul* for all generations, he intended it to be issued by a court like that of R. Ammi and R. Assi, which is strong enough to expropriate property, but not by an ordinary court." Would this not indicate that not every court has the power to expropriate?

Ribash then gave two answers:

> Even if we concede the point, it presents no difficulty with regard to the matter under discussion. The *prosbul* involves the expropriation of money contrary to [Biblical] law; but when the townspeople act in their own town by means of legislation, they are like the court of R. Ammi and R. Assi and are even stronger. [*I.e.*, the difference is that Hillel's enactment was universal, with no territorial limitations, but communal enactments bind only the residents of the community that adopts them. This distinction is explicitly made in *Resp. Maharaḥ Or Zaru'a* #222.] Furthermore, as Rabbenu Tam has already explained, the Talmud does not refer to the court of R. Ammi and R. Assi exclusively, but to every court that is distinguished [*i.e.*, authoritative] in its locality, for Jephthah in his generation is equal to [*i.e.*, has the same authority as] Samuel in his . . . . Any permanently established court can expropriate property in its town, and the community even more so has this power. Furthermore, the court, even in criminal cases, can impose flogging and punishment not provided for in the Torah, in order to create a fence around the Torah and a "safeguard for the matter." . . . Similar power certainly exists in monetary matters, which are less consequential.

217. *Resp. Maharam Alashkar* #49 reached the same conclusion on the basis of similar arguments. So, too, did Rashbeẓ (Simeon b. Ẓemaḥ Duran) in a case involving a community that sought to ignore communal enactments adopted there by earlier generations. The responsum (*Resp. Tashbeẓ*, II, #132) states:

As a result of the establishment of the rule that a communal enactment is binding even on minors and those not yet born at the time of the enactment's adoption—regardless of their lack of legal capacity to consent—communal enactments received the full and unqualified status of norms of public law. The validity of these enactments was no longer measured by the yardsticks and requirements applicable to legal transactions in private law. This development not only resolved the problem of communal legislation but was also an important contribution to the development of public law as a field of Jewish law—a field which at that very time was showing tremendous creativity over a broad range of subject matter.[218]

> A community enacted that no member would exempt himself from communal service or from paying [his share of] the taxes and assessments levied on the community; that no member would inform [on another to the general authorities]; and that no member would offer a higher rental for a dwelling [than that paid by the current tenant]. The earlier generations adhered to this tradition, as is fitting; and when anyone violated it, they [*i.e.*, the community] informed him that he had disobeyed the enactment that their ancestors had accepted under sanction of a ban. Now they seek to abrogate the enactment; and they argue that although their ancestors had adopted it for themselves, they, the descendants, do not wish to adhere to it and that their ancestors bound only themselves and not their descendants. You have asked whether there is any merit to their argument.
>
> Response: The argument that their ancestors did not adopt the enactment both for themselves and for their descendants is not valid, because the ancestors' acceptance binds the descendants. Naḥmanides so wrote in *Iggeret Mishpat ha-Ḥerem*, and he brought proof from Joshua's ban that bound Hiel the Bethelite and his descendants [I Kings 16:34], as it is written [Joshua 6:26]: "At that time Joshua pronounced this oath: Cursed of the Lord be the man who shall undertake to fortify this city of Jericho . . . ," and this decree was enforced after several generations. There is also proof from the incident of the concubine . . . [in Gibeah. *See* text accompanying nn. 211–212 for the same proof in *Resp. Ribash* #399.] A responsum of Rashba is to the same effect. . . .
>
> [Furthermore], even if there had been no formal enactment but it was only a custom the ancestors had practiced and the descendants now find difficult to keep, they are still forbidden to abrogate that custom, as is stated in ch. "Makom she-Nahagu" [TB Pesaḥim 50b, quoted *supra* in text accompanying n. 214].

This is the same rationale as that of Rashba and Ribash.

218. A significant portion of the law governing the legal standing of the community and legal relationships with the community became part of Jewish public law as a result of equating the status of the community with that of a court. Thus, for instance, the fact that the subject of a transaction was not yet in existence did not invalidate the transaction if the community was one of the parties; *see supra* pp. 705–706. For a detailed discussion, *see* M. Elon, EJ, XIII, pp. 1351–1359, s.v. Public authority (reprinted in *Principles*, pp. 645–654). *See also supra* n. 20.

VI. THE RELATION BETWEEN THE SUBSTANTIVE CONTENT OF COMMUNAL ENACTMENTS AND THE PROVISIONS OF THE *HALAKHAH*

The discussion so far has pointed out the varied ways in which the halakhic authorities provided a firm legal basis for communal legislation by giving it the full validity and efficacy possessed by an enactment promulgated directly by the halakhic authorities themselves.[219] This gives rise to the obvious question, involving another central theme of the law of communal enactments: What is the relation of the *Halakhah* and halakhic authority to the substantive content of communal enactments?

As the previous discussion indicates, not only was the substantive content of communal enactments not required to be based on the provisions of the *Halakhah,* but those enactments could include provisions inconsistent with existing law. As previously noted, Rabbenu Gershom emphasized that an enactment could properly provide that a lost article does not belong to its finder but to its previous owner, notwithstanding the contrary rule of the Torah, which does not require the finder to return the article under the particular circumstances.[220] Many additional halakhic sources in both civil and criminal law have also been noted as being explicitly to the same effect.[221] Examination of the halakhic sources, and especially the responsa literature, reveals a very broad range of substantive rules in Jewish law that have been prescribed and adopted in communal enactments but are in substance diametrically opposite to the provisions of the *Halakhah* covering the same subject. A number of additional illustrations merit examination.

219. At times, it seems that the Sages gave more force to communal enactments than they did to their own; *see, e.g., supra* n. 140, for the surprise expressed by the Gaon of Vilna in connection with the law concerning an oath not to be bound by a communal enactment.

220. *See supra* pp. 686–688.

221. *See* the responsa quoted *supra* pp. 685–698. *See further Resp. Tashbeẓ,* I, #159:

> The townspeople—or even some of them, such as those engaged in the same occupation—may agree among themselves and adopt enactments even if the enactments are inconsistent with the law of the Torah. Whatever they agree to has the full force of law. . . . They do not require a *kinyan* or a legal instrument (*shetar*), because in this respect the many are stronger than the individual since they can impose their will on the dissenting minority . . . and the individual may not exclude himself from the community. Furthermore, the enactments bind those who come later, so long as the enactments do not specify any time limit.

See also supra pp. 714, 731–735. On the basis of the *baraita* stating that the townspeople may fix market prices, etc. (*see supra* p. 679), the responsum drew a number of conclusions, including the existence of the far-reaching authority in the community to appoint judges and require that all residents appear exclusively before those judges, with no party having the right to argue that more expert and learned judges are available. The judges referred to in the responsum were not even experts in the law.

A. Competence of Testimony in Communal Matters by Witnesses Halakhically Incompetent to Testify

The *Halakhah* has strict requirements for competency of witnesses. Consanguinity[222] and interest[223] disqualify a witness. Under these rules, testimony by members of a Jewish community concerning any matter involving the community's assets would be inadmissible, since the witnesses have a pecuniary interest in the matter[224] like that of a citizen of a town whom the Talmud ruled incompetent to testify concerning that town's property unless he waives all rights to any benefit from that property.[225] Also, since marriages frequently occurred between members of different families within a community, witnesses were often related to each other or to the parties. With the great expansion of Jewish communal life in the Middle Ages, the halakhic requirements of testimonial competency presented intolerable difficulties because witnesses possessing knowledge of facts pertaining to communal affairs were generally members of the community concerned. Consequently, many localities adopted communal enactments providing that members of the community were competent to testify notwithstanding these halakhic disqualifications. A responsum of Rashba[226] recorded the contentions of the parties as follows:

> [One party contended:] "Even if witnesses appear, there is no substance to their testimony, since they are related to the members of the community." The opposing party contended: "It is the practice of all communities, through their enactments and decrees, that community members do testify and that foreign witnesses [nonmembers of that community] are not needed to testify with regard to their enactments."

Asked to decide which side was correct, Rashba responded clearly and unequivocally:

> The argument that it is the practice of the communities that local residents may testify with regard to their enactments is a valid argument, since the effect of a contrary ruling would be to nullify all communal legislation. The

222. *See Tur* and Sh. Ar. ḤM ch. 33 and the Talmudic sources referred to by the commentators, *ad loc.*

223. *See Tur* and Sh. Ar. ḤM ch. 37 and the Talmudic sources referred to by the commentators, *ad loc.*

224. *E.g.*, in the matter of taxation, if one person is exempted, the burden of the others is correspondingly increased.

225. TB Bava Batra 43a; Sh. Ar. ḤM 37:18 *et seq.*

226. *Resp. Rashba*, V, #286. This responsum is quoted in *Resp. Tashbeẓ*, II, #63 and #191, where the ruling is attributed to both Maharam of Rothenburg and Rashba; the authorship of the responsum requires further investigation.

> customary practice of the communities is law; and in all questions such as this the rule is: custom overrides the law.[227]

A similar argument was made to Asheri:

> There are those who say that townspeople may not testify concerning one another or those similarly situated, since they are interested parties and they have many relatives in the town.

Asheri responded:

227. Rashba made the same ruling in *Resp. Rashba,* V, #184, where he added: "No community ever objected to this practice." In that responsum, he also stated an additional rationale:

> Furthermore, this practice conforms to the strict law, because it is no more a deviation than [the stipulation given effect in the case recorded in TB Sanhedrin 24a] where a party says, "My father is acceptable to me [as a judge]" or, "Your father is acceptable to me [as a judge]." In our case, the whole community had already agreed to accept all the witnesses in question in regard to all the enactments that they adopt, whether in the nature of a safeguard or in matters of taxes and *corvée.* It is unnecessary for each party to [declare that he] accept[s] the witnesses in every case, since such acceptance is presumed.

This is an example of a legal rationale designed to support an already existing practice. The rationale is based on the premise that the entire community has agreed to accept the testimony of witnesses related to the parties, and therefore there is no need for the agreement to be reaffirmed in individual cases.

Rashba's reasoning is less than compelling. If the rationale is that everyone has agreed to accept relatives as witnesses, why is it impossible for each individual to reconsider and retract that agreement for the future, as in the case of any other agreement? Indeed, Rashba himself raised this very query in a different responsum (*Resp. Rashba Attributed to Naḥmanides* #65, quoted *infra* in connection with the substitution of the signature of the town scribe in place of subscribing witnesses), and he reverted to the rationale that a communal enactment has binding effect because "no individual can nullify it, for . . . the majority may impose its view on the minority." In fact, the presumption itself is only the response to a particular social situation, and not the cause or factor that produced that situation. For more on this enactment, *see Resp. Rashba,* II, #107; V, #273; I, #680.

In the case under discussion in this last-mentioned responsum, one of the witnesses to an indemnification agreement (*shetar hazzalah*) on a loan to a community was related to a member of the communal council (*berurim*). The question was whether the agreement was valid in spite of the kinship of the witness on the ground that "the rule that a relative is an incompetent witness does not apply to communal matters." Rashba replied:

> We have already discussed this question several times, and we have concluded that it would be impossible to manage communal affairs for the public good if we require the community to bring in witnesses from the outside who are not related to any resident. Such a search will succeed only in one case out of a thousand! This explains our regular practice in all communal affairs, even as to charities.

See further Resp. Rashba, I, #811 (supporting the practice on the basis of TJ's statement, "Whenever you are uncertain about a law and do not know its nature, go out and see how the public is accustomed to act and do likewise"); VI, #7. As to this enactment, *see also Resp. Ritba* #131; *Resp. Rashbash* #211; *Bet Yosef* to *Tur* ḤM 37:12 and *Keneset ha-Gedolah,* Mahadura Kamma and Mahadura Batra, *ad loc.*; *Resp. Ribash* #475–#477 (toward end of #476).

> It is a widespread practice among all Jews that witnesses are not brought from outside the town to testify with regard to their enactments and decrees, but local witnesses may testify on all their matters and are competent even with respect to their relatives, since the townspeople have accepted that they may testify.[228]

Communal enactments providing that the testimony of halakhically incompetent witnesses is both admissible and competent became so widespread that Joseph Caro in the *Shulḥan Arukh*[229] declared the legislative rule to be settled law and accepted practice:

> It is the current practice to accept witnesses from the community with regard to their enactments and decrees, charitable endowments, and all other matters; and they are competent to testify even as to their relatives, since it has become accepted that they may testify.[230]

B. Competence of Judges Related to the Litigants or Having a Personal Interest in the Case to Sit in Communal Matters

The same question and the same arguments noted above in connection with related and interested witnesses also arose with regard to judges resid-

228. *Resp. Asheri* 5:4. *See id.* 6:21, where Asheri states that, in principle, witnesses who are members of the community are not competent to testify, and does not mention any enactment. In *id.* 58:3, Asheri ruled that *silluk* [*i.e.*, renunciation of interest in the particular matter], if done in the correct manner, is effective; in *id.* 6:15, he ruled that *silluk* is not effective in tax matters, because "it is impossible to disassociate oneself to the degree that one will never obtain any benefit from the tax that the assessed party will pay," and that only an enactment can correct the situation. *See further id.* 13:20 and *Tur* ḤM 37:12.

229. Sh. Ar. ḤM 37:22.

230. *See also Resp. Ḥikrei Lev,* ḤM, #23; after a lengthy discussion of the views of the halakhic authorities on the subject, the responsum concludes:

> The totality of rabbinic opinion provides sufficient evidence that this is the practice in all places of Jewish settlement. The testimony of the *Shulḥan Arukh* [*i.e.*, Joseph Caro, sixteenth century] suffices for all the Land of Israel; the testimony of Re'em [Elijah Mizraḥi, end of the fifteenth, beginning of the sixteenth centuries] is adequate for Constantinople; the evidence of *Massa Melekh* [*i.e.*, Joseph ibn Ezra, sixteenth century] and those who followed him is sufficient for Salonika; the testimony of the author of the *Mappah* [Moses Isserles, sixteenth century] is good for the whole land of Ashkenaz [Germany, Poland, etc.]; and the testimony of Radbaz [sixteenth century] and *Darkhei No'am* [*i.e.*, Mordecai ha-Levi, seventeenth century] covers Egypt and adjoining areas. Thus, these cover all places where one needs to validate [the testimony of such witnesses].

See also Pitḥei Teshuvah to Sh. Ar. ḤM 37, subpar. 14, which, after referring to the views of various halakhic authorities to the effect that there was no such practice in their localities, asserts: "However, in my humble opinion, all this does not constitute proof, because all these authorities lived before the *Shulḥan Arukh* was accepted throughout the world. Nowadays [middle of the nineteenth century], since the practice has been established in the *Shulḥan Arukh,* it has become a fixed and lasting custom."

ing in a community, who consequently had a personal interest in every case that concerned communal property or other communal matters such as taxes, charitable endowments, etc., and who were sometimes also related to each other or to the litigants. Here, too, Rashba was asked whether an enactment could validly permit such judges to sit:[231]

> When a community has enacted that two relatives may sit as judges so long as a third judge who is not related to either one also sits, is there ground for objection to this once there has been a communal enactment or not?

Rashba responded:

> This, too, is clear—the communal enactment is conclusive; and the practice in all the communities with regard to taxes is that local people may be judges and witnesses even though they are related to the judges and the parties and, in addition, the court and the witnesses have a personal interest. Notwithstanding [these disabilities], the testimony is competent, all as a result of the communal enactments.

Here, too, the law was thus laid down in the *Shulḥan Arukh:*[232]

> Whenever a judge has any interest whatsoever in a matter, he cannot sit in judgment on it. . . . Therefore, local judges cannot sit in any case involving taxes of their town, because they or their relatives have a share in it. But if they enacted a *takkanah* or if there is a custom in the town that local judges may sit even on tax matters, such judges may properly adjudicate these matters.

Jehiel Michal Epstein at the end of the nineteenth century ruled:[233]

> If a *takkanah* was enacted or if it is the custom of the town that local judges may sit on matters that concern the town, they may properly adjudicate these matters, and this practice has spread. We have neither seen nor heard that local judges do not sit on any matter that concerns the town; and since this is the custom, it is as if they [the townspeople] have expressly consented, and local judges may sit on any communal matter.

231. *Resp. Rashba,* VI, #7. As to this enactment, *see also Resp. Ribash* #475-#477, toward the end of #476. It seems that the enactment in question applied to matters involving the general community, such as taxes and charities. *See Resp. Ribash* #311; *Oẓar ha-Geonim to Tractate Sanhedrin,* ed. Taubes, p. 171, #358.

232. Sh. Ar. ḤM 7:12. *See also* Rema to Sh. Ar. ḤM 37:22 and *Darkhei Moshe* to *Tur,* ḤM 7, subpar. 7, to the effect that communal legislation may change the rule that the testimony of two witnesses has the same weight as the testimony of a hundred (*trei ke-me'ah*).

233. *Arukh ha-Shulḥan* ḤM 7:22. *See also Keneset ha-Gedolah,* ḤM 7:53; *Tur* ḤM 7:18 and *Bet Yosef, ad loc.*; *Pitḥei Teshuvah* to Sh. Ar. ḤM 7, subpars. 26–29.

C. Signature of the Town Scribe Instead of Signatures of Witnesses

Many sources indicate that in various communities in Spain enactments were adopted pursuant to which the signature of the town scribe had the same validity as the signatures of two competent witnesses. The following responsum of Rashba discusses the background and validity of such an enactment:[234]

> Question: Sometimes one person makes a sale to another in the presence of witnesses [and the transaction is] to be recorded in a document; but before the document is prepared and signed, the witnesses die or travel abroad, resulting in a loss to the purchaser. The community, desiring to prevent these difficulties, wishes to enact a *takkanah* that the town scribe should write the terms and conditions of the sale in his record book and that the record book should be considered as reliable as two witnesses, as is the practice with regard to the records of the non-Jewish courts. Advise us whether or not such a *takkanah* is valid.

The purpose of the enactment was to obviate the difficulties caused if witnesses die or travel abroad, and the enactment proposed a legal procedure accepted in non-Jewish law—"as is the practice with regard to the records of the non-Jewish courts." Rashba responded:

> The public has authority to agree on any enactments [it desires] on civil matters, and these are approved and accepted as absolute law; such enactments become the law so long as they are adopted with the consent of the people. . . .
>
> > It is taught in the *Tosefta:*[235]
> >
> > The townspeople may declare: "Whoever shows [another's property] to a third party [*i.e.*, thieves, so that it can be stolen] or informs the government [so that the property can be confiscated] shall be penalized in a specified amount," and they may enforce their regulations. The wool dealers and the dyers may declare: "We shall all be partners in all merchandise that comes into the town"; the donkey drivers may declare: "We will provide another donkey to anyone whose donkey dies"; and the boatmen may declare: "We will provide another boat whenever anyone's boat is lost."
>
> We deduce from this that tradesmen, such as butchers, dyers, donkey drivers, and boatmen—and certainly all the people of the town [collectively]—may enforce any condition and regulation that they agree upon with regard to a monetary matter.

234. *Resp. Rashba Attributed to Naḥmanides* #65.

235. *Tosefta* Bava Meẓi'a 11:23–25. *See supra* pp. 680–681.

> In addition, we have learned:[236] "[If a party declares]: 'My father is acceptable to me [as a judge],' or 'your father is acceptable to me [as a judge],' the Sages rule that he may not withdraw [his acceptance]." Under the strict law, his father is not competent; nevertheless, he cannot withdraw his acceptance [after judgment].[237] Although in that case [where the waiver is voluntary] he may withdraw his acceptance before final judgment, there is not even that route of escape from a communal enactment. No individual can nullify it, for even at the very outset, the majority may impose its view on the minority.

Enactments "become the law" by virtue of the absolute authority of the community to legislate. Although the rule relating to "my father is acceptable to me" (*i.e.*, a waiver of disqualification in private litigation) provides some support for the rule regarding enactments, this analogy can easily be shown not to hold, for the Talmudic rule is that a party may withdraw his acceptance before the judgment, whereas the procedure provided by the communal enactment is authorized from the very outset and is not subject to challenge at any stage. Moreover, a communal enactment has special force, since the majority may impose its view on the minority, so that the minority, unlike the litigant in a private law case, has no power whatever to insist on the halakhic disqualification.[238]

236. M Sanhedrin 3:2.

237. TB Sanhedrin 24b.

238. Similarly, *see Resp. Rashba*, III, #438 (I, #729):

> You have asked: "Reuben was appointed communal scribe, and he has occasionally asked witnesses [to sign documents with him]—either Simeon or Levi, or others. It has happened that before the scribe managed to write and sign the document, the other witness died. When the community realized the damage caused to them by the death of the second witness, they agreed upon and adopted an enactment, carrying the sanction of a ban and a substantial fine [payable] to the king, that if the second witness should die before signing, the signature of the scribe would be sufficient and equal to that of two witnesses, and that anyone who objects to a document executed in that manner would be subject to a ban and a fine. . . . I have been commissioned by the community to write to you [and ask] whether what they have done is legally valid or not."

Rashba responded:

> The community had the right to adopt this enactment, because in civil matters the public can undertake to establish either more or less stringent [requirements than the law demands], for we read in ch. "Zeh Borer" [M Sanhedrin 3:2]: "If [one party] said [to the other], 'Your father is acceptable to me [as a judge],' R. Meir says, 'He may withdraw [his acceptance],' but the Sages say, 'He may not [withdraw his acceptance].'" The only dispute is whether he can retract; if he does not in fact retract before the judgment, all agree that his consent is valid—and this most certainly applies to a community [whose members have] agreed to and adopted enactments acceptable to them. Each community as to its own locality has the same status as the *geonim* had with respect to all Jewry; and they [the *geonim*] adopted many enactments directed to and binding upon the entire Jewish people, *e.g.*, [the enactment] that personal prop-

Other communal enactments provided that the town scribe could sign the name of a witness at the witness's request. This enactment was necessary because there were witnesses who could not sign their names. With regard to such an enactment in Lucena, Spain, Rashba stated:[239]

> You have asked: The practice in our town, Lucena,[240] is that the two witnesses themselves sign, but sometimes one of them signs and the scribe signs the other's name and writes: "So-and-so requested that I sign." There are instances when the scribe signs for both of them and writes: "They requested me to sign." We consider these documents valid, and they are used for collection purposes and for execution of a judgment against property in the hands of purchasers from the debtor.
>
> Shemtov is a resident of our town Lucena, grew up there, married a woman in Pupa, and owned houses in Lucena. Shemtov and Miriam, his wife, sold their houses in Lucena to Leah the wife of Joseph, and the deed was written in Lucena. One witness signed in his own handwriting and the second witness was away and did not sign. The scribe signed for him and wrote: "So-and-so requested that I sign."
>
> Soon afterward, Shemtov sued Joseph, Leah's husband, . . . who claimed that the deed was ineffective since the witness did not sign in his own handwriting. The court in our town ruled that it was valid because it was written in our town according to our custom and the houses are located in our town.[241] Our judgment is now being attacked.[242] Instruct us whether or not our ruling is correct.

Rashba responded:

> The first deed is valid, even though the second witness did not sign in his own handwriting, since this conforms to the enactment and custom of the town.

---

erty in the possession of heirs, which under strict law is not subject to execution to pay the decedent's debts, is nevertheless subject to be taken to satisfy such debts.

As to this last comment, *see supra* pp. 646–648.

239. *Resp. Rashba,* II, #111.

240. The original Hebrew text refers to *Alisana,* the accepted Hebrew name of Lucena.

241. The case also constitutes an interesting decision in the field of conflict of laws. Lucena had a communal enactment that the scribe could sign for one of the witnesses, but Pupa had no such enactment. The other parties to the transaction—Leah and her husband Joseph—were apparently residents of Pupa, and they therefore claimed that the signature of the scribe was invalid. The court in Lucena ruled that the Lucena enactment was applicable even though it was inconsistent with Talmudic law and even though it would not ordinarily be binding on the other party. The crucial considerations were that the disputed property was located in Lucena and that the deed was written there.

242. *I.e.,* Shemtov appealed from the decision of the Lucena court to Rashba. *See* Assaf, *Battei ha-Din,* p. 76 on *dayyanei ha-sillukin* ("appellate judges"). *See also infra* p. 825 and n. 171.

> It is not less valid than a deed accepted in non-Jewish courts, which is valid, as we presume it memorializes a valid transaction [lit. "they would not take the risk of injuring their reputation"].
>
> This is certainly true in the case of the town scribe who was appointed for this purpose, and whom the enactment designates to do just what he did, on account of illiterates who do not know how to sign. The sum and substance of the matter is that the law relating to all civil matters follows the enactments and customs of the locality.[243]

D. Enactment of a Limitation Period for Asserting Claims of Ownership

Another significant enactment provided that the court was to proclaim a specified period within which claims could be made to any asset about to be sold. Upon the expiration of the prescribed period, all claims to the property not timely made were extinguished. This enactment was the subject of a question put to Rashba:[244]

> It is the custom in this locality, pursuant to a communal enactment, that a proclamation is made in the synagogue with regard to every sale or seizure of property in execution carried out in the locality, that whoever has any right in that property or lien against it must produce his evidence in court within fifteen days; and the rights of anyone who does not do so within that time are extinguished.

Rashba ruled that although this enactment was contrary to the strict law, inasmuch as there is no basis in Jewish law for an individual to lose his rights because he does not claim them within a particular period,[245] nevertheless, "a communal enactment overrides the law, since the townspeople may stipulate among themselves as they see fit." This type of enact-

243. *See further Resp. Rashba,* II, #107; IV, #199.

244. *Resp. Rashba,* VI, #7.

245. *See* Ritba, Novellae to Ketubbot 100a:

> We learn from here that if a court has sold property after having issued a proclamation calling for the assertion of all claims to the property, no one's right is extinguished even if he does not assert his claim. This is as the law should be, for why should he lose his right? Perhaps [he did not make the claim] because the second person [*i.e.,* the purchaser] is an easier person for him to claim against than the first [*see* TB Bava Batra 30b]. And even if the proclamation specified that whoever does not make a claim will lose [his rights], it is of no effect.

See the further remarks of Ritba quoted *infra* n. 246. *See also* M. Elon, "Ha-Hityashenut ba-Din ha-Ivri" [Limitations in Jewish Law], *Ha-Praklit,* VII (1958), pp. 179–189, 243–279.

ment, with various differences in detail, was adopted in many communities.[246]

E. Enactments in Tax Law

As a result of two major factors, one internal and the other external, tax law developed into a vast field of Jewish law beginning with the tenth century C.E.[247] Internally, this period witnessed the rise in power and standing of the Jewish community.[248] The community was the chief agency for providing social services, and maintaining governmental and educational institutions and a judicial system; and various taxes had to be imposed to finance these activities. Externally, the non-Jewish government imposed heavy taxes on the Jews as "toleration money" for permission to live in its territory. The governmental practice in this period was to impose taxes on

246. *See Resp. Rashba,* IV, #142: ". . . In accordance with the practice of the town, they proclaimed in the synagogue that anyone having a claim must assert it within a certain time. . . ." This enactment was valid, because "if there is an enactment among you that the rights of any person who does not assert his claim within the time specified in the proclamation will be extinguished, [such an enactment is valid] because the community has the power to enact such legislation since it has the power to expropriate property, as is stated (TB Bava Batra 8b), 'The townspeople may . . . enforce their regulations. . . .'"

As to such an enactment in Lerida, *see Resp. Rashba,* I, #893 (for the text of the enactment, *see id.* #894). *Resp. Rashba,* III, #431 contains a detailed description of the Lerida enactment and its text. The question there was whether the claimant of property had to offer some proof of his claim within the time specified, such as by producing a deed, or whether it was sufficient for him merely to assert that he had a right to the property. After a detailed analysis of the text of the enactment, Rashba concluded that the bare assertion of the claim was sufficient. *See also Resp. Rashba Attributed to Naḥmanides* #59, and *Resp. Maharam of Rothenburg,* ed. Berlin, #238 (p. 239).

Ritba, Novellae to Ketubbot 100a (*see supra* n. 245), contains the following important limitation: "But there are some places where the townspeople have adopted the practice that their proclamation is effective [to extinguish the rights of those who fail to assert their claims]. The agreement to adopt this practice is effective with respect to local residents and their dependents who are of age, but they have no power to affect the rights of minors and nonresidents. This I have from my teacher." *See further* as to this enactment and its text, *Resp. Ribash* #388, which indicates that there was a similar enactment in Saragossa ("Ninety years ago, . . . the leaders (*berurim*) and the entire community adopted those enactments with the advice of Aaron ha-Levi b. Joseph ha-Levi"), and in Osca (or Huesca) and Tudela.

The question Ribash raised was whether the proclamation should be forbidden on the sabbath on the ground that discourse on the sabbath should not be secular (lit. "Your conversation on the sabbath should not be like your conversation on weekdays"). *See also* the detailed responsum of Rabbenu Nissim set forth in *Resp. Ribash* #390. For a similar law, on the basis of *dina de-malkhuta dina* ("the law of the land is law"), *see Resp. Asheri* 18:16; Sh. Ar. ḤM 104:2.

247. For tax law in the Bible and the Talmudic period, *see* M. Elon, EJ, XV, pp. 840–843, s.v. Taxation (reprinted in *Principles,* pp. 663–666).

248. *See supra* pp. 666–668.

the various autonomous groups living within the territory of the country. The halakhic authorities emphasized this particular circumstance as it affected the Jewish community:

> All of the different taxes are for protection, since they guard us among the nations; for what reason would the nations have to protect us and to allow us to live among them if not for the benefit they receive from the Jews in collecting taxes from them?[249]

The taxes of the non-Jewish government were imposed not directly on each individual but on a particular community or group of communities of the region; and the communal leaders were responsible to the government to produce the full amount of the tax. "In matters of taxes and forced labor, it became necessary for the members of each community to become partners with one another . . . because the king makes his demands on the collective and not on the individual."[250] Tax collection by the community, whether to finance the various communal services or to raise the tax payable to the non-Jewish government, brought with it the development of a comprehensive legal system governing such matters as: the method of determining tax rates; the types of taxes; the procedure for their assessment, adjudication, and collection; and the establishment of exemptions.[251]

This comprehensive system of tax law was based in part on directly relevant legal principles established in the Talmudic period,[252] and also on an analogy drawn between the legal relations among members of the community and the legal relations among partners.[253] However, these sources were not sufficient to solve all of the many problems in the area of tax law that faced the halakhic authorities and the communal leaders. These problems, by their very nature, are part of public law and could not be resolved by applying laws of partnership taken from private law. Not only could the solution of most tax law problems not be derived from partnership law, but the legal ordering of the relationship between two or three partners was often inappropriate for the legal arrangement needed to govern the relationships among the multitude of individuals who made up the community. Consequently, most of the tax laws were developed by means of communal enactments and custom, and the laws derived from these sources were fully valid even if they were inconsistent with the rules of the *Halakhah*. Because

249. *Resp. Ran* #2; *see Piskei ha-Rosh,* Bava Batra, ch. 1, #29.

250. *Resp. Rashba,* V, #270; *see further supra* p. 37.

251. For detailed discussion, *see* M. Elon, EJ, XV, pp. 843–872, s.v. Taxation (reprinted in *Principles,* pp. 666–699).

252. Such as various laws laid down in the Talmud in matters of taxation, and the application of the doctrine *dina de-malkhuta dina* ("The law of the land is law"); for details, *see id.* at 843–847 (reprinted in *Principles,* pp. 666–671).

253. *See id.*

we have elsewhere extensively discussed this aspect of tax law in the Jewish legal system,[254] only a few illustrations are discussed here.

In a responsum dealing with a controversy between a community and one of its members with regard to the extent of the member's tax obligation, Rashba stated:[255]

> Nowhere is tax law based on . . . the Talmud, and in every place you will find laws that vary according to custom and according to the enactments of leading authorities who earlier established the framework. The townspeople may enact fixed *takkanot* and establish well-recognized practices, as they see fit, which do not accord with the *Halakhah,* as this is a monetary matter. If, therefore, there is a known custom on the matter, it must be followed, since custom overrides the law in such matters. But if you ask me for a decision based on halakhic law for a place that has no known custom, in such case the law is clearly on the side of the individual.

Thus, if there was a communal enactment in a particular place—and the community could adopt such an enactment as it wished—the enactment governed, and the community prevailed. However, if there was no specific enactment, Talmudic law governed, and in that case, the individual prevailed.

Another interesting example of legislation contrary to existing law is an enactment concerning an individual's appeal of his tax assessment. Under strict law, the principle that the burden of proof is on the claimant applies to a dispute between an individual and the community, as well as to a dispute between two individuals. This was explicitly laid down by Rashba in a dispute involving the obligation to pay taxes: "The claimant [*i.e.,* the community] wishes to extract money from Reuben, and in that posture it has the burden of proof on any question where there is evidence on both sides."[256]

However, the community may adopt legislation reversing this basic rule, as we learn from the following responsum.[257] In a case submitted to Rashba, the tax collectors claimed that Reuben owed a particular sum as his tax, whereas Reuben contended that he was liable only for a smaller amount. Rashba was asked whether Reuben was required first to pay the full amount assessed against him and to obtain a refund only after judgment in his favor, or whether he could initially pay only the amount admittedly owed, with any balance due on the disputed amount to be collected from him only after judgment against him.

254. *See id.* at 845ff. (reprinted in *Principles,* pp. 668ff.)
255. *Resp. Rashba,* IV, #260.
256. *Resp. Rashba,* III, #406.
257. *Resp. Rashba,* III, #398.

Rashba responded:

I have already written that all these questions are not governed by the laws of the Torah but by custom and legislation in each place according to its practice. Indeed, it has been enacted everywhere that no one may declare, "I will not pay until there is an adjudication on my claim of nonliability," as otherwise everyone will make such a declaration, and the tax will never be collected, to the profit of the swindlers. We here [in Barcelona] also have enacted such legislation to the effect that whoever claims nonliability must first pay and only afterwards may he submit his claim for adjudication.[258]

Maharam of Rothenburg, in his discussion of this question, wrote:[259]

Tax matters depend neither on reasoning nor on the law set forth in the Talmud, but on the custom of the locality. It seems to me that the practice in all communities with which I have become acquainted is that whenever an individual has a dispute with his community concerning a tax matter, the community first collects the tax. Afterward, if he so desires, they will submit to adjudication the issue of whether they took more from him than is lawful; and, if so, the judges will order them to return it.

The community wishes to be considered as the party in possession—as defendant and not plaintiff. Thus, even when the taxpayer has retained possession [of the amount in dispute], the burden of proof nevertheless is on the taxpayer and not the community; and if under the law the matter involves the taking of an oath, the community will have the election to take an oath or require it to be taken by the adverse party, because they [the community] are always preferred suitors [lit. "at all times they have the upper hand"].

At first, I thought that there was no reason for this, other than the practice instituted by the localities, and that the custom provides no precedent for a new town that does not yet have a custom. On further consideration, I have concluded that it [the privileged position of the community] accords with the law of the Torah and is well-founded. Chapter *Eizehu Neshekh* states:[260]

> R. Papa said [to Rava]: "Observe those who pay the *karga* tax[261] [owed by other people] and thereby obtain the right to their service [*i.e.*, the service of those whose taxes are paid]!" R. Sheshet said: "Their guarantees are kept in the king's records and the king has declared that

258. This enactment was attributed to Rabbenu Gershom; *see Resp. Maharik* #17; *Resp. Binyamin Ze'ev* #295. *See also* M. Elon, EJ, XV, pp. 863–865, s.v. Taxation (reprinted in *Principles*, pp. 691–693).

259. *Resp. Maharam of Rothenburg*, ed. Prague, #106, #915, ed. Lemberg, #371; *Mordekhai*, Bava Batra, #522.

260. TB Bava Mezi'a 73b.

261. *Karga* was the name of a head tax common in Babylonia during the Persian period. *See further* TB Bava Batra 55a.

whoever does not pay the *karga* tax must serve those who pay it for him."[262]

Thus, the king is considered to be in possession of everyone's tax, and whenever there is doubt or someone makes a claim of exemption that is not clearly valid, we apply the doctrine of *dina de-malkhuta dina,* and their guarantees are kept in the king's records until it becomes clear that they are not liable.

There is another important reason. If this were not the law, everyone would declare to the community: "I am exempt according to the law" or "I have paid my tax, and if you wish to take it from me, I will take an oath that I paid it, or you will [have to] swear [that I did not pay it]." Then, rather than have every member of the community take an oath concerning his small share [of the disputed tax], the community would choose to relinquish its claim, and as a result the community will suffer loss!

We find in many instances that the Rabbis were very much concerned with preventing damage to the public. One example is the rule that "a path that is habitually used by the public may not be destroyed,"[263] *e.g.,* by the owner of the field where the path is located, who removes it and gives the public another one at the edge.[264] The reason [for the rule] is that whenever there is a claim against the public, the public is presumed to be in possession, as otherwise the public would have no remedy: everyone could act wrongfully, thinking that no one would sue, since some people will be pacified and others will do nothing because "a shared pot is neither hot nor cold."[265] The public should therefore be presumed to be in possession. . . .

To summarize, this is the law: An individual must pay tax on all his property unless it is absolutely clear that he is exempt;[266] however, in a doubtful case where the community disagrees with him and claims that he is obligated [to pay], he must pay [the tax] and then litigate the matter with them . . . and if he wishes to avoid liability, he must prove that he is not liable.[267]

262. For further discussion of this subject, *see* Elon, *Ḥerut,* pp. 15–16 and nn., *ad loc.*

263. TB Bava Batra 100a.

264. M Bava Batra 6:7 (and discussion in TB Bava Batra 99b–100a).

265. TB Bava Batra 24b.

266. When it is clear that the community is not justified in collecting the tax, the tax is not required to be paid until the objection is determined. For this aspect of Maharam of Rothenburg's responsum, *see infra* p. 769.

267. *See further Resp. Maharam of Rothenburg,* ed. Prague, #995, and the statement of Avigdor Kohen Ẓedek (Katz) cited in *Mordekhai,* Bava Batra, #477. *See also Terumat ha-Deshen* #342:

> [Concerning] taxes imposed on a community . . . , it seems to me that these matters depend more on custom than on Torah law. Similarly, I have seen a responsum that quotes the responsum of a leading authority, Ramam [the reference is to Menahem of Merseburg], which clearly states that most tax matters are governed by custom. Similarly, *Mordekhai* in ch. 1 of Bava Batra cites Avigdor Kohen Ẓedek to the effect that in tax matters custom overrides the law and supplants the rules of the Talmudic Sages even when they [the Talmudic rules] are supported by Scripture. . . . All actions taken

The discussion by Maharam of Rothenburg teaches that the main rationale for the rule in tax matters that the community is considered to be in possession and the burden of proof is shifted to the taxpayer is based on the socio-economic factors which he listed, and does not rest on the quotation from the Talmud dealing with tax law. That quotation is not at all compelling, because the discussion there does not deal with the question of payment in a doubtful case, but rather with the right of those who pay a tax for someone else to obtain the services of those who were obligated to pay it and for whose benefit the payments to the king's treasury were made.[268]

The same approach was taken by Maharam of Rothenburg with regard to communal legislation prohibiting an individual from settling in a town without the townspeople's consent (*ḥezkat ha-yishuv*).[269] In a responsum[270] discussing such legislation (which his teacher, Judah ha-Kohen, had already ruled on), he attempted to find support from Talmudic sources for his teacher's ruling. When he failed to find such support, he stated:

> It is possible that my teacher ruled in this way elsewhere not on the strength of clear proof [based on the Talmud] but on the basis of communal law that depends on communal practice. Every river has its tributaries; and there are many customs on this matter that have no strong foundation, like mountains hanging by a thread, and when he found even slight support he "constructed a peg and drove in some nails," and it is sufficient to follow this practice on the basis of his view and to continue it in that place as he determined; and even in the places where this is not practiced, it perhaps should be.

> by the public collectively are governed by the customs and arrangements they institute to meet their needs and circumstances. If you require them to follow the law of the Torah in all matters, there will always be strife among them; therefore, from the outset they have agreed to waive their rights under the law of the Torah and to be governed by their customary practices.

In subsequent comments, *Terumat ha-Deshen* distinguishes between tax and other monetary matters and indicates that even as to tax questions it is desirable to find some support in existing law; *see infra* p. 778 and n. 363. *See also Terumat ha-Deshen* #345, #346.

268. *See* Elon, *Ḥerut,* pp. 15–16. The privileged status enjoyed by communal bodies vis-à-vis the individual carried with it the danger of infringing the individual's rights, particularly in view of the rationale given for the community's privileged status: "[Otherwise,] everyone could act wrongfully, thinking that no one would sue." This rationale could be applied not only to tax matters but to all transactions between the community and the individual, as indeed was the case in the Talmudic sources (TB Bava Batra 24b, 99b), which provided the analogies for the law of taxes. In order to prevent injury to the rights of the "weak" individual in his dealing with the "strong" community, the privileged position of the community was hedged about by substantial qualifications; for details, *see* Elon, EJ, XV, pp. 864–865, s.v. Taxation (reprinted in *Principles,* pp. 692–693). *See also Darkhei Moshe* to *Tur* ḤM 4, subpar. 3.

269. As to this, *see infra* p. 784 n. 13.

270. *Resp. Maharam of Rothenburg,* ed. Lemberg, #213.

From the examples cited, and from many other similar examples that can be added,[271] it is apparent that the community was authorized and empowered to adopt civil and criminal legislation to regulate communal life according to substantive rules that it deemed necessary and appropriate for the particular time and place. Moreover, it could do so even if the rules it enacted were contrary to the substantive law contained in the *Halakhah*, since communal enactments, like custom, override the law.

VII. THE INTEGRATION OF COMMUNAL ENACTMENTS INTO THE HALAKHIC SYSTEM

The great latitude in enacting communal legislation that in substance did not accord with the rules of the *Halakhah* could very well have severed communal enactments from the living body of Jewish law. Legal precepts having their original source in communal enactments could have developed into a legal system parallel to that of the *Halakhah*, which would necessarily have meant that these legal precepts would not have been incorporated into the halakhic legal system. To prevent such a development, Jewish law created a number of connecting and bridging mechanisms between communal enactments and halakhic authority. On the one hand, these mechanisms did not affect the independence of communal legislation, but on the other, they were able to tie communal enactments in spirit and objectives to the system of Jewish law. There were three such mechanisms: one operated before the adoption of an enactment, and the other two afterward.

A. Approval of Communal Enactments by a "Distinguished Person"

The mechanism (accepted by most halakhic authorities) that operated before the adoption of a communal enactment was the requirement that the proposed enactment first be approved by a "distinguished person" residing in the community. The purpose of requiring this approval was to ensure a measure of prior (even if limited) review by halakhic authorities over communal enactments.[272]

271. For further such examples in the laws relating to the status of the communal governing body, its composition, appointment, and relationship with its employees and members of the community, *see* M. Elon, EJ, XIII, pp. 1351–1359, s.v. Public authority (reprinted in *Principles*, pp. 645–654). For laws relating to the administration of public property and property set aside for charitable purposes, *see id.*, EJ, VIII, pp. 279–287, s.v. Hekdesh (reprinted in *Principles*, pp. 701–708).

272. A very broad analogy may assist in clarifying the nature of the requirement of the approval of communal enactments by a "distinguished person." That requirement may

Support for the requirement of approval by a "distinguished person" is found in the Talmud in connection with a regulation adopted by a tradesmen's association. As shown by the *Tosefta* previously quoted at the beginning of this chapter,[273] legislative authority was vested not only in the townspeople as a whole, but also in more limited groups such as those engaged in the same occupation or in a particular commercial activity, *i.e.*, tradesmen and merchants. Of course, the regulations adopted by such an association bound only its members.

The Talmud discusses a specific incident concerning a regulation of a tradesmen's association:[274]

> Certain butchers[275] regulated their affairs together [the Munich manuscript has "agreed among themselves"] to the effect that whoever worked on another's day would have the hide of his animal torn up [*i.e.*, the butchers agreed on a division of the work days so that two of them would not work on the same day; the penalty for one who worked on another's day was that the hide of the animal he slaughtered was to be torn]. One of them worked on another's day, and they tore the hide of his animal. They came before Rava, and Rava ordered them to compensate him for his damage.
>
> R. Yeimar b. Shalmai queried Rava: "[Does it not say] 'They may en-

---

be loosely compared to the requirement of current Israeli law that the by-laws adopted by municipal councils and local authorities must be approved by the Minister of the Interior. The approval by the Minister of the Interior also contains an element of supervision of the by-laws, although it in no way detracts from the legislative initiative of the local authority. The character and scope of the Jewish community (*kehillah*) as a social unit may be compared to a present-day local authority in Israel. On the other hand, the scope of current Israeli municipal legislation is much narrower than the scope of Jewish communal enactments.

273. *Supra* pp. 680–681.

274. TB Bava Batra 9a.

275. This is the reading in ms. Munich, Alfasi, *Yad Ramah*, Asheri, and the glosses of *Bayit Ḥadash*. Current printed versions, however, read "A certain two butchers . . . ." "Certain butchers" is more likely correct, since an agreement between two butchers can hardly be called a regulation adopted by an association and cannot be compared, as the Talmud compares the agreement there, to communal enactments or regulations of associations of tradesmen. Similarly, the language "they tore the hide of his animal," "they came before Rava," and "Rava ordered them to compensate"—all in the plural—indicate that our reading is correct. Had there been only two butchers involved in the agreement, the reading should have been "Rava ordered him . . . ," since only the other butcher would have caused the damage. Several other *rishonim* also omit the number "two"; *see infra* nn. 286, 292, 293 and *Dikdukei Soferim, ad loc.*, and *id.* nn. 3, 4.

Some *rishonim* who hold that the reading "two butchers" is correct point to it as teaching that approval of a "distinguished person" is necessary only if some, but not all, of the occupational group involved are parties to the agreement; *see* Meiri, *Bet ha-Beḥirah*, Bava Batra 8b, s.v. Rasha'in benei ha-ir lehatnot (ed. Sofer, pp. 59–60). *Cf.* Naḥmanides, Novellae to Bava Batra 9a, s.v. Ha de-amrinan be-hanhu bei trei tabḥei. *See also Resp. Maharik* #181 (=#179) noting the v.l. and drawing a different legal conclusion from each (p. 105d).

force their regulations'?" [*I.e.*, have we not learned that townspeople may agree among themselves and impose penalties against anyone who violates their regulations? This being so, why did Rava order that payment should be made for the damage by the butchers?][276] He [Rava] did not respond to him.

R. Papa said: "Rava acted correctly in not responding [as there was no need for a response]; this rule [cited by R. Yeimar] applies where there is no distinguished person [in the town], but where there is a distinguished person, they may not enter into agreements [without his approval]."

The regulation by the butchers' association was thus not recognized as binding because there was a "distinguished person"[277] in the locality and the regulation was adopted without having obtained his approval. The purpose of such approval is twofold: (a) to ensure that members of any particular association would not adopt a regulation that would adversely affect the townspeople,[278] and (b) to symbolize and emphasize the link between the regulation and halakhic authority.[279]

Is approval by a "distinguished person" also required for an enactment adopted by all of the townspeople? No conclusion on this issue is compelled

276. It is possible that R. Yeimar's question was based on the passage in *Tosefta* Bava Meẓi'a 11:23–26 concerning the wool dealers, bakers, donkey drivers, and boatmen, *i.e.*, an agreement within a tradesmen's association. According to our passage, the question concerning the butchers was raised on the basis of the law applicable to the townspeople, but there are grounds to distinguish legislation by the townspeople from regulations of trade associations. *See* the commentators, *ad loc.*, and *Shakh*, Sh. Ar. ḤM 231, subpar. 4. *See also infra* and Epstein, *Amoraim*, p. 218.

277. The definition of a "distinguished person" is discussed *infra*.

278. *See* Naḥmanides, Novellae to Bava Batra, *ad loc.* ("Perhaps the customers will lose because the price will rise"); *Resp. Ribash* #399 ("The regulation [of the occupational group] may cause a loss to the townspeople"). Ran, Novellae to Bava Batra (ed. Sofer, p. 49), made the same point: "The reason is that their agreement causes loss to others because the price will go up and the consumer will lose. They do not, therefore, have the power to make such an agreement unless they receive permission from the person who is appointed over public affairs. But where there is no loss to others or, even if there is a loss but there is no distinguished person available, their agreement is valid." *See also* Sofer's nn., *ad loc.*; Sh. Ar. ḤM 231:28, Rema's gloss, and commentators, *ad loc.*; Ritba, quoted *infra* n. 279.

279. Ritba, Novellae to Bava Batra 9a, s.v. Hanhu (bei trei) tabḥei, states:

> The conclusion is that this applies when there is no "distinguished person" available, but if there is, they are not permitted to make agreements without him, either because of the respect due to him or to enable him to ensure that they have done it properly and that there is no loss to the townspeople. If there is a "distinguished person" in the locality but he was not consulted, their regulation is invalid even if it does not cause a loss to the townspeople; if the distinguished person was consulted, their regulation is valid even if it does cause a loss to the townspeople.

The first reason, the respect and honor due to the "distinguished person" who is the halakhic authority, is separate from the issue of loss to the townspeople and leads to the conclusion, contrary to Ran, *supra* n. 278, that the enactment is invalid even if it does not adversely affect the public interest.

by the text of the Talmud;[280] only after the passage of considerable time did a difference of opinion develop on the issue among the halakhic authorities.

Isaac b. Sheshet Perfet (Ribash), in fourteenth-century Spain, interpreted the Talmud according to the plain import of the text:[281]

> The statement in the Talmud with regard to the butchers—that [their regulation is valid] only when there is no distinguished person in that place but that where there is such a distinguished person they are not empowered to adopt such a regulation unless he also approves—apparently applies only to tradesmen. Where there is a distinguished person and they act without his approval, they are not equivalent to the townspeople, and they may not agree among themselves unless they act as individuals and with a *kinyan;* but the townspeople may always agree among themselves and do not require the approval of a distinguished person of the town.[282]

A number of other halakhic authorities agreed with Ribash.[283] Most halakhic authorities, however, held that approval by a "distinguished person" was required for the enactments of an entire community as well. A detailed exposition of this view appears in a responsum of Rashba:[284]

> It is clear that the community may institute safeguards, enact *takkanot,* and enter into agreements as they deem appropriate, and [when they do so] the

280. The requirement of approval by a "distinguished person" is mentioned only in connection with the agreement among the butchers, as is shown by *Resp. Ribash* #399, quoted *infra* at n. 281. It seems probable that the early law did not have this requirement even for a regulation of a tradesmen's association, since the requirement is not mentioned in the *Tosefta* or any other tannaitic source. Apparently, a distinguished person's approval was first required in Rava's time, and then only in the case of a tradesmen's association, which did not include the entire body of the townspeople.

281. *Resp. Ribash* #399.

282. The rationale for the distinction is that "the rule concerning a 'distinguished person' applies only to an occupational group, because their regulation may cause loss to the townspeople, but the townspeople themselves may legislate as they see fit." *Resp. Ribash* #399.

283. Ribash demonstrated that Maimonides and Naḥmanides shared his view. *See also Kesef Mishneh* to *MT,* Mekhirah 14:11. This was also the opinion of *Resp. Maharam Alashkar* #49, and *see Sema,* Sh. Ar. ḤM 231, subpar. 45. Meiri, *Bet ha-Beḥirah,* Bava Batra, *ad loc.* (ed. Sofer, pp. 59–60), also agreed and stated an additional reason: "The community as a whole . . . may legislate without his [the distinguished person's] approval, as they have the power to revoke his appointment." This is an interesting rationale, which requires clarification.

Haggahot Maimuniyyot to *MT,* Mekhirah 14, subpar. 3, quotes an even more limiting opinion in the name of Raban: "This [requirement of approval by a "distinguished person"] applies only when they legislate on municipal affairs, as in the case of the butchers, or when they fix weights and measures and prices, in which case they have no authority [without the distinguished person]. However, they can agree on matters having no public interest [lit. "transactions between a man and his fellow"] without the approval of a 'distinguished person,' if they so desire." This view is also expressed by Rema to Sh. Ar. ḤM 231:28.

284. *Resp. Rashba,* IV, #185.

result is as valid as a law of the Torah. They may fine and punish those who violate their enactments, so long as the entire community agrees to this without objection.[285] The same applies when all those in the same occupation in the town, such as butchers, dyers, boatmen, etc., enter into an agreement with regard to their work; for every group having a common interest is similar to a separate community, even if their agreement has not been approved by the other townspeople.

However, these agreements must be approved by a halakhic scholar (*talmid ḥakham*), if there is one in the town, or by a distinguished person who was chosen as a communal leader. If there is such a scholar or such a leader, and they acted without his consent, their agreement is invalid.

As we read in the first chapter of *Bava Batra:*[286] "Certain butchers agreed among themselves. . . . This rule applies where there is no distinguished person; but where there is a distinguished person, they may not enter into agreements [without his approval]." And it was taught in the *Tosefta* in Tractate *Bava Meẓi'a:*[287] "The townspeople may fix market prices, weights and measures, and laborers' wages, and they may enforce their regulations. . . ."

In short, all members of a single group have the same status as the inhabitants of a single autonomous community for all these matters, and every community may do this and exact fines and impose punishments that are not prescribed in the Torah, as we have written, and as mentioned in the Talmud in the first chapter of *Bava Batra* and in the *Tosefta* of *Bava Meẓi'a.* All the communities have so conducted themselves and no one has ever doubted this.

Rashba thus required the approval of a "distinguished person" for both types of legislation—the enactments of the entire community and the regulations of an association of tradesmen.[288]

This is also the view of Asheri:[289]

All tradesmen may stipulate [*i.e.*, enact binding regulations] among themselves, and they are considered as "townspeople" in matters that concern their occupation. A "distinguished person" means specifically a man like Rava, who was the head and leader of his town; and even the entire popu-

285. *See supra* n. 156.

286. TB Bava Batra 9a; Rashba's reading, "certain butchers . . ." (without the word "two"), follows ms. Munich, Alfasi, and Asheri; *see supra* n. 275. Rashba's reading, "agreed among themselves," also follows ms. Munich, as opposed to the current printed editions, which read "regulated their affairs together."

287. *Tosefta* Bava Meẓi'a 11:23.

288. This view is also expressed in *Resp. Rashba,* I, #1206:

It seems clear to me that the law is that the townspeople may do so, provided that they agree to it; but if there is a halakhic scholar there and he does not agree with them, they may not do so. . . . However, if there is a halakhic scholar there, it can be done only with his approval. . . .

289. *Piskei ha-Rosh,* Bava Batra, ch. 1, #33.

> lation of the town do not have the power to stipulate [*i.e.,* enact legislation] without the approval of such a "distinguished person."

As stated, most halakhic authorities accepted this view and required the approval of a "distinguished person" even for communal enactments.[290] It is a reasonable assumption that the Jewish communities actually followed this practice, and the text of compilations of enactments sometimes includes a specific requirement for such approval.[291] However, there is evidence that sometimes certain communities,[292] and even such a representa-

290. *See Resp. Maharaḥ Or Zaru'a* #222; *Tur* ḤM 231:30; Ritba, Novellae to Avodah Zarah 36b, s.v. Katuv be-shem ha-rav Rabbenu Yonah; Rema to Sh. Ar. ḤM 231:28; *Sema, ad loc.*, subpar. 45; *Shakh, ad loc.*, subpar. 4 and sources cited there. *See also Resp. Maharam Mintz* #6, and *Resp. Ve-Shav ha-Kohen* #92, comprehensively discussing the problem generally and Ribash's opinion in particular. *See also Mishpat Shalom* #231, and the sources cited in nn. *infra.*

291. The Moravian enactments included explicit provisions that approval of communal legislation by the local "*ḥaver ir*" or rabbi, or by the rabbi of the country, was necessary. *See* Halpern, *Takkanot Medinat Mehren* [The Enactments of Moravia], p. 96, for the enactment of the Council of Gai (1650), which provided: "All communal enactments adopted by the legislators or the townspeople shall be as worthless as a broken shard unless signed by the local *ḥaver ir* or rabbi, or, in the absence of a local rabbi, the district rabbi" (Enactment #286). Similar provisions were included in Enactment #176 of the Council of Gai of the same year (*id.*, p. 57) and in Enactment #335 of the Council of Dreznitz of 1659 (*id.*, pp. 110–111). These provisions are more strict than the otherwise applicable law, according to which, if there is no distinguished person in the locality, the enactment is valid without such approval. As to the meaning of *ḥaver ir, see supra* n. 150.

292. *See,* for instance, Levi ibn Ḥabib, *Resp. Maharalbaḥ* #99, to "the officers and leaders of the communities in Terikala, may the Almighty preserve them":

> First of all, there is something I must tell you. In all the enactments and general agreements that you adopt for the welfare of the communities, you should make an effort to get the approval of that true scholar, Rabbi Benjamin, because without his approval it can almost be said that they [the enactments] are valueless, even though they were adopted by the elected representatives (*berurei*) of all the communities, may the Almighty preserve them. Proof for this is in ch. 1 of Bava Batra (9a) in the case of certain butchers [following ms. Munich; *see supra* n. 275] who agreed among themselves, etc. The conclusion there is that the agreement is valid "where there is no distinguished person [in the town], but where there is a distinguished person, they [the butchers] may not enter into agreements [without his approval]. . . ."

Subsequently, Ibn Ḥabib cited Ribash, who had ruled that such approval is required only for an enactment by an occupational group (*see supra* text accompanying n. 281), and he also referred to Maimonides, whose position on this matter he found to be unclear. However, he continued, most authorities, such as Asheri, *Semag,* and the *Turim,* rejected Ribash's view and, therefore:

> From all this, it follows, as we have written, that in order to validate your enactments and agreements the above-mentioned scholar must concur with you, because he is a distinguished person. . . . He is a sage and a leader, and he must approve of your enactments, for otherwise they are not valid. . . .

The enactments included in the collection of the legislation of Cracow, 1595, are another example of legislation not signed by the rabbi. *See also* J. Katz, *Tradition and Crisis,* pp. 92ff.

tive body as the Council of the Four Lands (*Va'ad Arba ha-Araẓot*),[293] did not always take care to obtain the approval of a "distinguished person." Halakhic authorities reprimanded the communal leaders for this;[294] but, at the beginning of the nineteenth century, one of the leading halakhic au-

293. *See Resp. Baḥ ha-Ḥadashot* #43. The author, Joel Sirkes, addressed "the nobles of the land, those who erect safeguards and step into the breach so that catastrophe does not befall—the heads and leaders of the land—assembled at the fair in Lublin, to strengthen and maintain the House of Israel. . . ." He was directing his remarks to the leaders of the Council of the Four Lands at their general assembly in Lublin. He complained of the *ḥerem* (ban) they had imposed as a sanction against the violators of certain of their enactments. He charged that neither the wrongdoers nor the general community had abided by the terms of the punishment of *niddui* (semi-ostracism) in the manner prescribed by the *Halakhah,* and this had caused serious difficulties. He suggested that other sanctions be adopted, such as monetary fines, banishment, and the like, because the enactments themselves, "dealing with the matter of currency alteration which, because of our many sins, has emerged in this generation," are very important and desirable. The responsum states:

> In considering the sanction of bans in the enactments, the thought arises: Who gave you permission to impose bans on the general public without the approval of the leading halakhic authorities? Even though you are elected representatives from all the communities in the kingdom, it is entirely possible that all your bans are almost completely without legal effect. A clear proof for this is in ch. 1 of Bava Batra (9a), in the case of certain butchers [following ms. Munich; *see supra* n. 275] who agreed among themselves, etc. The conclusion of the Talmud is that the agreement is valid "where there is no distinguished person [in the town], but where there is a distinguished person, they [the butchers] may not enter into agreements [without his approval]." Rashi [*ad loc.*, s.v. Lav kol ke-minaihu de-matnu] adds the comment, "unless he [the distinguished person] is present [and approves]."
>
> Although some hold that the rule requiring the approval of a "distinguished person" applies only to tradesmen's associations and that a communal enactment does not require the approval of a "distinguished person" even if one is available, most commentators have disagreed with this interpretation. The conclusion is that a tradesmen's association has the same status as a community, and neither the association nor the community may validly legislate without the approval of a "distinguished person." This has been codified in ḤM at the end of ch. 231 [Sh. Ar. ḤM 231:28].
>
> Our master, Levi ibn Ḥabib [*Resp. Maharalbaḥ* #99, *see supra* n. 292], has explained that a "distinguished person" is one who is known as a leading halakhic authority of his generation and is also a communal leader. Now you have among you one of the great authorities of the generation, Rabbi Samuel Segal, the head of the court and of the *yeshivah* of Lublin; you should have consulted and been advised by him with regard to the serious ban that you proclaimed. Furthermore, since such a ban encompasses all the communities in the kingdom, it is, in my humble opinion, invalid unless all the leading halakhic authorities of the generation, or at least those of the major communities, approve. . . .

This responsum makes clear that even the leaders of the Council of the Four Lands did not always seek the approval of the halakhic authorities for their enactments, for which failure Sirkes roundly castigated them. Also of interest is Sirkes' view that since the enactments were intended to apply to a much wider public, the approval had to come from the halakhic authorities—who are also communal leaders—of that public, or at least from halakhic authorities of the leading communities within the geographical area to which an enactment is to apply. *See also supra* pp. 672–673.

294. *See supra* nn. 292, 293.

thorities, Moses Sofer, held that such approval was unnecessary under strict law and was required only as a result of the customary practice of the communities.[295]

What are the attributes of the "distinguished person" whose approval is necessary for communal enactments? A number of responsa by Rashba indicate that a "distinguished person" may be either a halakhic scholar (*talmid ḥakham*) or an official chosen to lead the community; and if either one is present in the town, his approval is required to validate a communal enactment.[296] In contrast to this view, it was the opinion of Joseph ibn

295. *Resp. Ḥatam Sofer,* ḤM, #116 (the essence of this responsum was quoted *supra* pp. 720–723):

> In any event, it appears from Tractate *Bava Batra* [*see* text accompanying nn. 274–276] that they cannot impose penalties without the approval of the local *ḥaver ir.* . . . *Mordekhai, ad loc.*, cites a difference of opinion between R. Joel [Sirkes], who held that such approval is required only for the imposition of sanctions, and the author of *She'arim* [*Sha'arei Shevu'ot* by David b. Saadiah], who held that no enactment is valid without such approval; Sh. Ar. ḤM ch. 231 (end) made no clear decision on this question. *Sema, ad loc.*, cites Maharam Alashkar to the effect that such approval is required only for a regulation of a trademen's association but not for a communal enactment; *Shakh* disagrees, although his objection is easily refuted.
>
> In any event, in the case before us, the enactment was not unanimously adopted; and, according to Rabbenu Tam, unanimity is required for an enactment to be valid. The result is that the enactment here in question is valid only on the basis of [the legal force of] custom, and we see that it is in fact the custom for most enactments to be signed by the rabbi of the town. . . .

Moses Sofer did not, therefore, agree to approve the communal enactment discussed in this responsum until the community—although it could legally impose its will on the minority—"agreed . . . to reach some kind of compromise with the above-mentioned individuals because of the requirement to do what is right and good." Sofer was thus inclined to rule that the law does not require a communal enactment to be approved by a "distinguished person," and that it is only by communal custom that legislative enactments were to be signed also by the town rabbi.

296. *Resp. Rashba,* IV, #185: "These agreements must be approved by a halakhic scholar, if there is one in the town, or by a distinguished person who was chosen as a communal leader. If there is such a scholar or such a leader, and they acted without his consent, their agreement is invalid." *Resp. Rashba,* I, #1206 makes the same point: "[T]he townspeople may do so . . . but if there is a halakhic scholar there and he does not agree with them, they may not do so. . . . However, if there is a halakhic scholar there, it can be done only with his approval . . . ," which implies that even if the scholar holds no communal office, his approval is required.

Similarly, *Resp. Rashba Attributed to Naḥmanides* #280 ("The community can impose penalties . . . and can certainly do so with the approval of a halakhic scholar, *i.e.*, a 'distinguished person'"); *Resp. Rashba,* VII, #108 (V, #245) ("But if they [*i.e.*, those who adopted the enactment] were not appointed heads of the community, they have no power to impose a ban unless the majority of the community and the halakhic scholars in the town agree"); *Resp. Rashba,* V, #125 ("But if there is a person distinguished in Torah, their enactment is invalid unless he agrees with them." Rashba then cites the opinion of Ibn Migash, discussed *infra*).

Migash[297] that a "distinguished person" must be a "halakhic scholar who has been chosen to lead the community,"[298] *i.e.*, a person who possesses both qualities: wisdom in Torah and acceptance as a communal leader.

The great majority of halakhic authorities agreed with Ibn Migash in requiring that the "distinguished person" be "a distinguished scholar (*ḥakham*) able to enhance the sound administration of the affairs of the locality and to promote the prosperity of its inhabitants"[299]—a "scholar *and* leader"[300] who has the responsibility to attend to the needs of the community. The requirement exists only if, in the place where the enactment is adopted, there is a person who possesses both qualities: "However, in the case of a leader who is not a halakhic scholar, or a halakhic scholar who is not a leader, an enactment adopted without his approval is binding";[301] such a communal enactment has full validity without the approval of a "distinguished person."

From these responsa, it is clear that according to Rashba a communal enactment requires the approval of a halakhic scholar—if there is one—even if he does not hold a communal appointment. Strangely, however, *Resp. Rashba Attributed to Naḥmanides* #65 expressed a contrary view: "The community may legislate as it pleases in civil matters . . . and if there is a halakhic scholar who holds a communal office, he must be in agreement with them, and they may act [only] with his approval and permission, as is stated in ch. 'Ha-Shutafin' [Bava Batra 9a], 'Certain butchers. . . .'" In this responsum, Rashba followed the view of Ibn Migash that both qualifications are required: he must be a halakhic authority and also hold a communal office. The issue requires clarification.

297. Joseph ibn Migash lived before Rashba, in Spain, in the first half of the twelfth century.

298. Quoted in: *Shittah Mekubbeẓet*, Bava Batra 9a, s.v. Heikha de-ikka adam ḥashuv; *Maggid Mishneh* to *MT*, Mekhirah 14:11; *Resp. Rashba*, V, #125; Ran, Novellae to Bava Batra 9a (ed. Sofer, p. 49); and other sources.

299. Maimonides, *MT*, Mekhirah 14:11.

300. *Tur* ḤM 231:30. *See also Piskei ha-Rosh*, Bava Batra, ch. 1, #33: "A 'distinguished person' means specifically a man like Rava, who was the head and leader of his town." The definition in Sh. Ar. ḤM 231:28 is: "A distinguished sage, appointed over the community." *See also Resp. Maharalbaḥ* #99, quoted *supra* n. 292:

> According to all opinions, a distinguished person is one who is a scholar, and we have ourselves seen and heard the wisdom, erudition, and depth of analysis of the abovementioned sage [Rabbi Benjamin, *see supra* n. 292]. . . . The authorities have also written in the name of Rabbi Ibn Migash ha-Levi that he must be a leader of the town. . . . We know that you took the consummate scholar, Rabbi Benjamin, from the outset to be a leader over all of you. . . . With respect to the administration of town affairs, the weight of leadership rests on him, for there is no other like him.

Resp. Radbaz, I, #65 also takes the view that a "distinguished person" must be both scholar and communal leader.

301. *Yad Ramah*, Bava Batra 9b, s.v. Hanhu tabḥei de-atnu be-hadi hadadi, #103. *See also* Ritba, Novellae to Bava Batra 9a, s.v. Va-asikna de-hani mili. Similarly, in *Maggid Mishneh* to *MT*, Mekhirah 14:11: "But if he was not appointed [to communal office], the enactment is valid even without him."

B. Consonance of Communal Enactments with the Principles of Justice and Equity Embodied in Jewish Law

The critical and determinative mechanism for integrating communal enactments into the overall system of Jewish law was the vesting of jurisdiction in the halakhic authorities to review such enactments in order to ensure that they would not—as current Israeli legal terminology would express it—violate the general principles of justice and equity embodied in Jewish law. It is true, as we have seen, that a communal enactment may conflict with the substance of a particular halakhic rule, and the halakhic authorities accepted that result. However, communal enactments could not violate the basic principles underlying the entire Jewish legal system, *e.g.*, equality before the law, the protection of minority rights and the rights of the disadvantaged, and the aspiration to improve social discipline and the social order. These principles were the common ground upon which both the halakhic system and communal enactments were based, and it was this common basis that established communal enactments as an integral part of the general system of Jewish law.

Of course, terms like "general principles of justice and equity" are by their very nature extremely flexible; they cannot be defined abstractly but only through examples of their application and through study of the legal system as it actually operates. We therefore examine a number of concrete illustrations in order to focus on the nature and content of these principles as established by the halakhic authorities in the course of their review of the validity of communal enactments.[302]

1. AN ENACTMENT MUST "BUILD FENCES AND TEND TO IMPROVE" AND NOT "BREACH FENCES AND SPOIL WHAT IS GOOD"

The general purpose of communal enactments must be to improve—not to impair or breach—social morality and discipline. This principle is expressed in various responsa dealing with the validity of communal enactments. The responsum of Joseph Tov Elem discussed at the beginning of this chapter has shown that the residents of a community may adopt legislation as they see fit to meet the needs of the time "so long as it does not transgress the basic concepts of the Torah."[303]

Rashba in his responsa repeatedly emphasized the nature of this principle. One responsum[304] dealt with a number of basic problems involving communal enactments; and one of the rules enunciated was that the com-

302. One example relating to the freedom of the individual has already been discussed *supra* pp. 709–710.

303. *Resp. Maharam of Rothenburg,* ed. Lemberg, #423, quoted *supra* pp. 688–690.

304. *Resp. Rashba,* VII, #108.

munal representatives may not legislate unless delegated to do so, and that even when there is such delegation, their enactment has no validity "if it is contrary to law and does not tend to improve, since if it does not build a fence and tend to improve, then even though it may have been enacted by the leaders and the most prominent members of the community, the people are not obligated to follow their wishes." Another responsum,[305] to be discussed more fully later, in construing an enactment, rejected a particular interpretation on the ground that "if that were correct, it would not build fences and tend to improve, but would breach fences and spoil what is good." Still another responsum[306] made the same point in a positive form:

> It is my opinion that the public may compel an individual to follow its enactment on any matter that involves the improvement of the community, even if he strenuously objects.

An enactment thus must "build fences and tend to improve." It must "improve the community," *i.e.*, be a safeguard against lawbreakers, and advance public morality; and it may not "breach fences and spoil what is good." Legislation that does not fulfill these conditions is invalid and need not be obeyed by the community.

An example of the nullification of an enactment that did not establish safeguards and bring about improvement is set forth in Rashba's response to the following question submitted to him:[307]

> Reuben [a fictitious name] attempted within the community to eradicate lawbreaking and to have violators punished. He had sufficient influence in the royal court to enable him to obtain the king's authorization to do this. Thereupon, some of the communal leaders imposed a ban enjoining him from obtaining authorization from the king, their intent being to prevent this meritorious act. . . . Please instruct us whether Reuben must desist on account of the ban, in view of the fact that it prevents the performance of a meritorious act and promotes license.[308]

Rashba's responsum explained why in his view the enactment was invalid:

> Although it was enacted by those who administer the bulk of communal affairs, they are empowered to adopt only enactments that tend to improve, but not enactments that constitute breaches; they may not breach the fences

305. *Resp. Rashba*, V, #287.
306. *Resp. Rashba*, VII, #340.
307. *Resp. Rashba*, II, #279.
308. The query emphasized that "some persons wiser and more worthy than they" objected at the time the ban was adopted, but they were not the men "through whom the community acts." As to fictitious names in reponsa, *see infra* pp. 1512–1515.

> of the Torah.[309] They may direct that the task should not be done by A but by B if it might be better done by B than by A; but if this is not so [if B would not better accomplish the task than A] and, even more so, if it is done by neither one [*i.e.,* if the purpose is that no one should supervise the enforcement of the law], it is invalid. Their enactment is a nullity.

Rashba thus invalidated the enactment, not because it was inconsistent with a particular rule of the Torah, but because it involved a breach in the "fences of the Torah"—because it was contrary to the general principles favoring the eradication of unlawfulness and the punishment of transgressors.

2. A MAJORITY OF THE PUBLIC MUST BE ABLE TO CONFORM TO THE ENACTMENT

Just as an enactment must not have the effect of encouraging lawbreaking, it must not be overly oppressive, even if it produces some benefits and is well motivated; for it is necessary that a majority of the public should be able to comply with it. This principle that no enactment should be imposed on the public unless the majority can conform to it was established in Talmudic law in connection with enactments by the halakhic authorities[310] and was subsequently applied to communal enactments. Rashba stated:[311]

> Certainly if it is a decree to which a majority of the public cannot conform, they are not obligated by it even if it was enacted as a fence and a safeguard. Who is as great as Daniel, who prohibited the use of [the] oil [of non-Jews], yet R. Judah Ha-Nasi nullified the decree because it had not been accepted by a majority of the Jews.[312] The same applies to any other prohibition: if the majority have not accepted it, they are not obligated to follow it.

In another responsum, Rashba again emphasized the point.[313]

309. *Cf.* the statement in *Sefer Ve-Hizhir,* Mishpatim, 38:1:

The Holy One instructed us to appoint judges who render "a true judgment to its very truth" [*i.e.,* a judgment that is completely and truly correct, *see supra* pp. 159, 179–181] and who respond to the needs of the people by mending the breaches and correcting what has gone wrong. When they render "a true judgment to its very truth" they put the world to right, and there is peace in the world. . . . When the judges of Israel and the great men and leaders of the generation act with uprightness and integrity and distance themselves from sin and repulsive acts, all Israel acts likewise in uprightness and integrity, because the body follows the head.

310. *See supra* pp. 538–541.

311. *Resp. Rashba,* VII, #108.

312. TB Avodah Zarah 35b *et seq.*

313. *Resp. Rashba,* II, #279.

> Even if they adopt an enactment and issue a decree for a meritorious purpose, so long as it is not accepted by the majority, the rest of the community may treat it as not binding, as we read in Tractate *Avodah Zarah* chapter *Ein Ma'amidin*[314] . . . where they relied on the statements of Rabban Simeon b. Gamaliel and R. Eleazar b. Ẓadok that no enactment should be imposed on the public unless the majority can conform to it.[315]

3. AN ENACTMENT MUST NOT ARBITRARILY PREJUDICE MINORITY RIGHTS

A fundamental principle that the halakhic authorities were particularly vigilant to maintain was the protection of the right of a minority group and of each individual not to be prejudiced unfairly and arbitrarily by the majority. This principle was expressed, at times in the most pointed manner, in a long series of responsa.

In one such responsum, three of the leading halakhic authorities of Mainz in the beginning of the thirteenth century were asked to decide the following case:[316]

> Reuben instituted litigation against the community, which chose an attorney to represent it. Reuben argued: "The community demanded that I pay a tax, inasmuch as a large sum of money had been given by them to the king. I responded to them: 'I will take an oath that I have no money to give you.' They refused to accept my oath and said: 'You must give such-and-such an amount of money, and we will neither take less nor accept an oath.' I had in my possession a bond issued by the government for a small amount belonging to my son. The community instructed the government officer to seize the bond, and he entered my home and took other bonds together with that bond."
>
> The community's attorney responded: "The community had enacted a *takkanah* that no one would be permitted to take an oath, since most would swear [if given the opportunity], but the amount due currently was to be based on what was paid the previous year, because it is not useful to permit

314. TB Avodah Zarah 36a.

315. To the same effect are *Resp. Rashba,* III, #411; a responsum of Joseph b. Samuel Tov Elem in Agus, *Teshuvot Ba'alei ha-Tosafot,* pp. 39–42; and many other responsa (*see supra* n. 16). The Sages derived support for the principle that no enactment should be imposed on the public unless a majority can conform to it from Malachi 3:9, "You are suffering from a curse, yet you go on defrauding Me—the whole nation of you"; *see* TB Avodah Zarah 36a/b, Horayot 3b. The responsum of Joseph Tov Elem cites as a source Job 37:23: "Shaddai—we cannot attain to Him; He is great in power. . . ." However, it is not clear what connection there is between the principle and this verse, nor is it clear whether there is a Talmudic source for this attribution.

316. The responsum is quoted in *Resp. Maharaḥ Or Zaru'a* #222. The three halakhic authorities of Mainz are identified *infra* p. 766.

> householders to take an oath. Thereupon, the communal leaders met and chose three people to exercise their discretion, pursuant to the decree, to notify each householder to pay a particular amount. The townspeople may legislate to meet the needs of the time by providing that no one should be able to take an oath . . . and I need say no more, as the townspeople may include in their legislation whatever they wish."[317]
>
> Reuben responded: "I wanted to take an oath that I have nothing and I am still prepared to do so.". . . He produced witnesses that the community was willing to accept an oath from some in the community, but these individuals were induced to pay what was assessed against them; and now Reuben cries out: "Why did they not accept my oath? I am still prepared to swear to those matters."

The central question under dispute between Reuben and the attorney was thus whether a communal enactment is valid if it provides that everyone must pay the tax assessed against him and no one may take an oath to prove that he has no money to pay the tax. The halakhic authorities of Mainz categorically declared this enactment to be invalid:

> It seems to us that Reuben is right. The principle of *hefker bet din hefker*[318] applies when there is a decree against an individual that he is able to carry out; and if because of recalcitrance or fraudulent purpose he refuses, his property is expropriated . . . after the manner of [the Scriptural verse], "Anyone who does not come in three days, as required by the officers and elders, will have his property confiscated. . . ."[319]
>
> But if *force majeure* intervenes, God forbid that his property be expropriated, as the Torah has exempted anyone acting under duress.[320] This is certainly so in this case, where their enactment obligates an individual to pay what he does not have. Does the fact that they are many give them a license to be robbers? God forbid! As [rhetorically] asked in Tractate *Bava Batra*, chapter *Ha-Mokher Perot:* "According to R. Eliezer, does the fact that they are many give them a license to be robbers?"[321]

317. The community's attorney made an additional argument, namely, that Reuben had admitted that he had money. Reuben vehemently denied this assertion, and the argument was rejected by the three halakhic authorities who decided the case.

318. The principle of *hefker bet din hefker* ("the court has the power to expropriate property") also served as a legislative principle for communal enactments, where it was transformed into *hefker ẓibbur hefker* ("the community has the power to expropriate property"). *See supra* pp. 699–707 and n. 88.

319. Ezra 10:8 (quoted in the responsum with slight variations; the quotation here is from the text in Ezra, not as quoted in the responsum). This is the verse from which the principle of *hefker bet din hefker* was derived; *see supra* p. 508.

320. TB Bava Kamma 28b *et al.*

321. TB Bava Batra 100a states:

R. Judah said in the name of R. Eliezer: "If the public chose a path for themselves, what they have chosen is chosen [*i.e.*, they have a right to use it]." [The Talmud then

From your arguments, we understand that the community decreed that each one is to pay what belongs to him and not what belongs to someone else. If so, how can we obligate Reuben to pay what he does not have? The statement in chapter *Ha-Shutafin*[322] that the townspeople may enforce their regulations refers to the situation where there is a communal enactment and the people are able to carry it out . . . for it is of no benefit to require someone to pay what he does not have.

The principle that no enactment should be imposed on the public unless the majority is able to conform to it[323]—which implies that if the majority is able to comply, the enactment is binding even on the minority that cannot—does not hold when the enactment purports to take money from someone. To extract money as in this case is improper. In addition, he cries out against them, saying: "I am unable to do what their enactment requires." Also, so far as the case before us is concerned, there is no one who can comply with a requirement that he pay what he does not have.

Certainly, if Reuben were a wealthy man, and the community, in order to promote the public interest, enacted a *takkanah* against accepting oaths, the enactment could be enforced against Reuben. But if he cannot pay, why should he be harassed in a futile attempt to punish him in order to make him pay what he does not have? In view of the fact that they must support him and his children [*i.e.,* the community has a legal duty to support a person who is impecunious, in an amount sufficient to provide the necessities of life for himself and his family], how can they take from him? If he is not suspected of swearing falsely, why should he not take an oath and be absolved from payment, in view of his never-ending cries? In addition, the community agreed to accept oaths from others, so why should he be treated worse than they?

---

raises the query:] According to R. Eliezer, does the fact that they are many give them a license to be robbers? ["May they steal another's land?"—Rashbam, *ad loc.*, s.v. U-metamhinan atu rabbim gazlanin ninhu.]

R. Giddal said in the name of Rav: "It refers to a case where they lost [knowledge of the exact location of] their path through that field." ["They had had a right of way through it; and the public has a greater power than the individual, in that an individual who loses his path through another's field cannot choose (another path) for himself except through court action or with the agreement of the field's owner, whereas the public is on a par with a court, because whom among them can (the owner) summon to court?"—Rashbam, *ad loc.*, s.v. Ki-she-avdah lahen derekh be-otah sadeh.]

The halakhic authorities of Mainz, in the course of ruling that the community may not arbitrarily infringe an individual's rights, adapted to the subject of communal enactments the expression "Does the fact that they are many give them a license to be robbers?" Rashbam's statement that "the public is on a par with a court" accords with the equation of the status of the community to that of a court, discussed *supra* pp. 699–707.

322. TB Bava Batra 8b.

323. TB Avodah Zarah 36a.

A communal enactment must be for the public benefit, and compliance with it must be possible. Consequently, an enactment that imposes the payment of a tax on someone and does not permit him to prove his poverty is completely invalid. "Compliance with it must be possible" means that even the minority must be able to comply with it; and whether it is possible for the minority to do so is to be assessed by determining whether, if a member of the majority were in the situation of the minority, he would be able to obey the enactment and fulfill the obligations it imposes.

Also instructive, as bearing on the reciprocal relationship between law and morals in Jewish law, is the conclusion of the responsum of the halakhic authorities of Mainz:

> Even if Reuben is wrong as a matter of strict law,[324] [the fact is that] he is needy,[325] and therefore the community should act toward him *lifnim mi-shurat ha-din* [more generously than the law requires]; concerning this, it was written,[326] "So follow the way of the good and keep to the paths of the just," as stated at the end of chapter *Ha-Sokher et ha-Umanin* with regard to such a case.[327]
>
> May you have peace tenfold: [signed] Judah b. Kalonymus, Moses b. Mordecai, Baruch b. Samuel.[328]

A responsum of Rashba[329] provides another illustration. The communal leaders sought to collect a tax from Reuben, who resided in the community but whose property was located neither in that community nor within the territorial jurisdiction of the governor who imposed the tax. Reuben refused to pay the tax, contending that the tax was a property tax, and his property was not located in that community. The communal leaders argued that the tax was assessed *per capita,* as a tax on the person and not on property, and therefore Reuben was obligated to pay the amount of his assessment inasmuch as he and his family resided in that community. Moreover, added the communal leaders, even if the tax were considered a

324. This is apparently a reference to the argument that Reuben had admitted that he had money, *see supra* n. 317.

325. The Hebrew term used is *daḥuk,* which can mean "hard-pressed." The reference, therefore, may be to the fact that Reuben was in financial difficulty. *Daḥuk* also means "strained," so that the meaning may be that the claim that Reuben had admitted he had assets was far-fetched and not believable.

326. Proverbs 2:20.

327. TB Bava Meẓi'a 83a, and *see supra* pp. 141–189 in regard to the relationship between law and morals in Jewish law and for comments on the discussion in TB Bava Meẓi'a.

328. As to these three halakhic authorities, *see* Urbach, *Tosafot,* under their names in the name index.

329. *Resp. Rashba,* V, #178; I, #788; *see also Ginzei Schechter,* II, p. 128.

tax on property, Reuben would still be obligated to pay because "the community may enact legislation to prevent an individual from being exempt, as it was stated:[330] 'The townspeople . . . may enforce their regulations.'"

Rashba first responded to the question whether the tax was a tax on the person or on property:

> Under the strict law, no locality may require that a tax be paid on real property that a person owns elsewhere, even if he resides here [in the locality seeking payment of the tax] with his wife and family . . . ; the *karga* tax[331] is paid where an individual resides because it is assessed *per capita*, but the *taska*[332] [the tax involved in the question submitted] is assessed against property, and property is at the disposal of the owner of the land, *i.e.*, the ruler of the country in which the property is located. . . . Unless otherwise specified, he imposes the tax on the basis of property, and we pay the tax on that basis.

After deciding this initial question, Rashba proceeded to discuss the alternative argument of the communal leaders concerning their authority to obligate Reuben to make payment on the basis of the particular enactment contrary to the strict law:

> As to your argument that the community may legislate on this matter, it appears to me that this amounts to nothing more than robbery, and no legislation can validate robbery. In any case, if all the townspeople agreed to this and accepted it as binding, it would be binding for those who agreed to it and their successors. But if there was an individual in the town who opposed that agreement, he is not bound by it, as the community has no right to steal his money and appropriate it to communal use.

The community has no right to exploit the legislative authority vested in it by adopting an enactment imposing on an individual an obligation that violates justice and law and amounts to robbery, and this is true notwithstanding that the enactment expresses the wishes of the majority. The enactment in that case was actually aimed only at Reuben, from whom the community sought to collect the tax because he was extremely wealthy; the enactment subjected his property to double taxation.[333] Rashba there-

330. TB Bava Batra 8b.

331. This was the name of a head tax in the Talmudic period; *see supra* p. 748 n. 261.

332. This was the name of a tax on land in the Talmudic period, *see* TB Bava Meẓi'a 73b; Bava Batra 55a.

333. For detailed discussion of questions of double taxation and taxation on the basis of place of residence, situs of property, and place of business, *see* M. Elon, EJ, XV, pp. 847–854, s.v. Taxation (reprinted in *Principles*, pp. 671–680).

fore invalidated the enactment, since a community has no authority to enact legislation that amounts to robbery of an individual.[334]

Meir ha-Levi Abulafia (Ramah) strongly condemned communities that adopted arbitrary enactments prejudicial to individual rights. Ramah was asked:[335]

> A community adopted an enactment providing that the bread of anyone who does not pay his tax assessment is [to be treated] like the bread of a gentile, and his wine is to be considered as if used for idolatrous libations [*i.e.,* his bread and wine may not be used or purchased by other Jews]. An individual has violated that enactment. Is it permitted to buy his wine?

Ramah responded:

> We have observed that every enactment adopted by the majority of a community with the approval of a "distinguished person" who resides there will contain nothing unlawful. If a penalty is imposed against one who does not do or pay what he is obligated by law [to do or pay], the community must follow the enactment. If they do not do so, Scripture states concerning them: "You are suffering from a curse, etc."[336]
>
> However, it is clear that if they enact legislation requiring an individual to pay when he has no obligation at all, or that he must pay more than he is obligated to pay, we do not obey their mandate, and Scripture states concerning them: "You must not call 'agreement' all that this people call an agreement. . . ."[337] Moreover, it [*i.e.,* the sanction prescribed by the enactment] is but a feckless curse.

334. It should be pointed out that the text of this enactment did not single out Reuben as an individual, but formally applied in general terms to all the townspeople. This is clear from *Resp. Ribash* #477, which cites the responsum of Rashba quoted in our text:

> Rashba gave the same answer when he was asked about a similar case where the community sought to adopt an enactment providing that the town residents would be taxed on all their property, whether located within the town or elsewhere. The objective was to obligate a particular individual who resided in the town but had property elsewhere.

This indicates that the enactment did not in terms discriminate against that individual, but that in the particular circumstances it was clear that the enactment was directed against him. Therefore, notwithstanding the formally correct text, Rashba ruled that the enactment was arbitrary and invalid. *See infra* in regard to the requirement of equality of treatment in enactments.

335. The responsum is quoted at the end of *Resp. Zikhron Yehudah,* by Judah b. Asher, the son of Asheri.

336. Malachi 3:9; *see also* TB Avodah Zarah 36a/b.

337. Isaiah 8:12. The actual meaning of the Scriptural verse in its context is "You must not call conspiracy all that which people call conspiracy." *See* Rashi, *ad loc.*: "'You must not call conspiracy'—you, of Hezekiah's faction, even though you are smaller than Shevna's faction, should not say that one must follow the majority in everything Shevna's people say, because that is a conspiracy of wicked men and does not count." The Hebrew

Not every agreement by the public is valid; only those agreements are valid that do not arbitrarily prejudice the rights of the individual.[338]

Maharam of Rothenburg reiterated the principle forbidding the majority to prejudice arbitrarily the rights of individuals and expressed it in the same idiom that the rabbis of Mainz had taken from the Talmudic discussion of a different issue.[339] The responsum of Maraham of Rothenburg concerning the case of an individual who claimed that he was not liable for the tax assessed has already been discussed.[340] Maharam ruled in that case that although the individual's liability was doubtful, the case was an exception to the halakhic principle that the burden of proof is on the claimant, and the taxpayer must pay first and only afterward litigate his right to a refund.

After Maraham presented his rationale for this ruling, he added an important qualification:

> [This ruling does not apply] when it is clear that their [the community's] claim has no basis, for just because they are the majority they do not on that account have the right to victimize any individual. Does the fact that they are many give them a license to be robbers?
>
> To summarize, this is the law: An individual must pay tax on all his property unless it is absolutely clear that he is exempt; however, in a doubtful case, where the community disagrees with him and claims that he is obligated [to pay], he must pay [the tax] and then litigate the matter with them, as even barley in the pitcher is subject to tax,[341] and if he wishes to avoid liability, he must prove that he is not liable.

However, if it is clear that the majority is incorrect, their desire is not sufficient to justify prejudicing individual rights. As the Talmud put it, "Does the fact that they are many give them a license to be robbers?" Being in the majority is not a license to steal.

This idea was strongly expressed by Moses Isserles (Rema) in the sixteenth century in Poland. A responsum by Rema[342] dealt with a case where residents of town A were engaged in business in town B. To prevent busi-

---

word for "conspiracy," *kesher,* also means "agreement," and it is this latter meaning that enables Ramah to use the verse to support his ruling. *See also Mezudat David, ad loc.*

338. *See further Yad Ramah,* Bava Batra 35b, s.v. U-mi-de-kametamhinan mi metakkenei rabbanan milta de-ati bah li-dei peseida, #67:

> It follows that every communal enactment must be examined carefully to ensure that no one will be able to use it fraudulently to injure his fellow. If that is impossible, it must not be adopted.

339. *See Resp. Maharaḥ Or Zaru'a* #222, quoted *supra* pp. 763–766.

340. *Supra* pp. 748–750. The responsum is found in *Resp. Maharam of Rothenburg,* ed. Prague, #106.

341. TB Bava Batra 55a.

342. *Resp. Rema* #73.

ness in town B by residents of town A, the townspeople of B adopted an enactment prohibiting any resident of B from doing business with anyone from A. They argued that even if they had previously agreed to permit residents of A to do business in their town—and under the *Halakhah* they had no power to prevent the residents of A from doing business in B—"we have the power to adopt enactments and to legislate as we see fit, particularly to forbid our own residents from doing business with you. . . . Townspeople have authority to legislate as they wish, and no one may prevent them from doing so."

Rema responded to the position of the residents of B as follows:

> It is clear that the communal leaders do not have the power to legislate except in accordance with law and justice; and they may not abuse individuals, nor may the majority rob individuals! This is what Maharik wrote in *Resp. Maharik* #1 in connection with a similar case; and Rashba wrote to the same effect, in a responsum cited by Ribash in Responsum #477 concerning a community that sought to adopt an enactment to collect taxes on all property there or elsewhere, their purpose being to impose liability on a particular individual who resided among them: "As to your argument that the community may legislate on this matter, it appears to me that this amounts to nothing more than robbery, and no legislation can validate robbery . . . ," and the responsum expanded on this point. It is therefore clear that the townspeople do not have the power to legislate as they please, but have only the power conferred on them by law. This [unlimited power they have claimed for themselves] never was and never will be!

Rema relied in his ruling on Rashba's responsum previously discussed,[343] and his highly significant declaration is worthy of being the

343. *Supra* pp. 766–768. *See also* Katz, *supra* n. 292 at 93. Ezekiel Landau, *Resp. Noda bi-Yehudah*, Mahadura Tinyana, ḤM, #40, contains another interesting example of what may be classified as an enactment violative of the principles of justice and equity. There were two methods of assessment of an individual's property for purposes of taxation: (1) an independent assessment and (2) a declaration under oath by the taxpayer. A community sought to use both methods and to levy the tax on the basis of whichever yielded the higher valuation. Ezekiel Landau sharply objected to this practice:

> In his community they wish to do something new, which we have never heard of before; to follow the stringencies of both [methods], to assess [the property independently] and to impose a ban [to ensure the truth of the taxpayer's declaration]. They do not reduce the amount of their own assessment, but if he [the taxpayer] knows that he has more than they have assessed him for, he must pay the difference. That is robbery and oppression. You cannot kill a man by two methods of execution. One may not invent new stringencies; and once they have assessed his property, they cannot force him to take an oath. The arguments of those who insist on using whichever method produces the larger tax in any given case are baseless.

See also M. Elon, EJ, XV, pp. 858–863, s.v. Taxation (reprinted in *Principles*, pp. 685–690).

guideline for communal legislative authority: "The townspeople do not have the power to legislate as they please, but have only the power conferred on them by law. This [unlimited power they have claimed for themselves] never was and never will be!"

4. AN ENACTMENT MUST APPLY EQUALLY TO ALL MEMBERS OF THE COMMUNITY

Another principle, which is a corollary of the principle prohibiting robbery of individuals, is the principle of equality, *i.e.,* that a communal enactment must apply equally to all, and not only to certain individuals singled out for special treatment.

This principle of equality was set forth in a responsum by Hananiah b. Judah Gaon, the father of Sherira Gaon:

> Whenever a community enacts legislation that meets a need, promotes the public welfare, and applies equally to everyone, the legislation is enforceable; the agreement of the elders governs, and all the townspeople are bound by it.[344]

This requirement of equal treatment—not only in form but also in substance and purpose—was also reflected in Rashba's responsum[345] invalidating a communal enactment because the purpose of the enactment was to require a particular individual to pay taxes even though his property was located outside the town. As previously noted, that enactment on its face appeared to be "legal" in that it apparently applied to all residents of the town and did not name any particular individual; but Rashba disregarded the outward form, searched out the essence of the enactment, examined its true objectives, and accordingly invalidated it.

Ritba expressed the principle of equality as follows:[346]

> My teacher and master, of blessed memory, said: "Every enactment agreed to by a majority of the community, *i.e.,* [a majority] in both number and wisdom, must be followed by the minority, even when the minority has vociferously opposed it, provided that it appears to that majority that the enactment is for the public good, and provided also that it applies to all equally."

An enactment agreed to by the majority thus obligates the entire community if two conditions are fulfilled: first, it must promote rather than

344. *Teshuvot ha-Geonim Sha'arei Ẓedek,* IV, Sha'ar 4, #16 (ed. Jerusalem, 1966, p. 126); the responsum is discussed more fully *supra* pp. 685–686.

345. *Resp. Rashba,* V, #178; *see supra* pp. 766–768.

346. Ritba, Novellae to Avodah Zarah 36b, s.v. Katuv be-shem ha-Rav Rabbenu Yonah.

subvert the public good; and second, it must have general application and must not unfairly discriminate.[347]

The principle of equality does not mean, of course, that every enactment will always apply to and affect every single member of the community. Often, some part of the community will not be at all affected by a particular law. The term "equality" must therefore be interpreted reasonably according to the particular circumstances of each case. An instructive statement in this regard was made by Jair Ḥayyim Bacharach in an extensive responsum concerning tax law and communal enactments.[348] Bacharach pointed out that although in most communal enactments the matter concerns a few individuals and does not concern the rest of the people, this does not mean that the law denies equal treatment:

> The purpose of those enactments is to advance the interests of the public and the community, and therefore all are treated equally. For example, if an enactment is adopted that a tax must be paid from foreign funds or from money outside the town, although it is known at the time who possesses foreign funds or money outside the town, nevertheless, the wheel always comes full circle; sometimes one householder has such transactions, sometimes another. In addition, to counterbalance those enactments, there are other enactments that impose liabilities on others; none are exactly the same. It was therefore decided to adopt and validate them all, and they constitute a single structure in which all the elements reinforce one another.[349]

5. AN ENACTMENT MUST APPLY PROSPECTIVELY AND NOT RETROACTIVELY

The requirement that legislation satisfy the principles of justice and equity led to an additional principle, namely, that the provisions of an enactment may not create obligations retroactively but may apply only pro-

347. Equality of treatment is an absolute prerequisite for any law. The applicability of non-Jewish law—through the doctrine of *dina de-malkhuta dina* ("the law of the land is law")—is also conditional on the law's being nondiscriminatory. *See* Maimonides, *MT,* Gezelah va-Avedah 5:14, and *supra* p. 72.

348. *Resp. Ḥavvot Ya'ir* #81.

349. The contributions of members of the community toward communal taxes and expenditures for services were required to be determined according to uniformly applied standards, even if not everyone benefited from the communal services thereby financed. *See, e.g., Resp. Mahari Minz* #7:

> The majority may compel the minority to participate in the purchase, construction, or renovation of a wedding hall, even though this may mean overruling many objections, such as: "I have no children yet," or "They are not yet adults," or "All my sons and daughters are already married," or "I may not have the wedding here," or "The expense is great." We reject arguments even as strong as these, and we build the wedding hall. . . . Similarly, the claims of some old women that they are past the age of needing the water of the ritual bath to purify them are mere excuses. . . .

This view is codified as law in Rema to Sh. Ar. ḤM 163:3. *See also supra* pp. 418–421.

spectively. For example, the law is that whoever joins a community after a tax has been imposed but before it is to be collected is not liable to pay, since the basis of liability for the tax antedated his joining the community.[350] The rule laid down was that not even legislation can enable a community to require any of its members to pay a tax for a period prior to residence in that community. Since such a resident came to the town only after the occurrence of the event giving rise to the tax, *i.e.*, after the non-Jewish ruler had imposed the tax on the community, he is not liable for payment of this tax; and even an explicit enactment cannot impose such a liability.[351]

The principle of prospective application was given expression in connection with a discussion of the following problem: A community had borrowed to cover expenditures for communal needs. A long period of time elapsed, and when the loan fell due and had to be paid, a tax was imposed on the residents of the community to finance the repayment. In the meantime, the financial condition of some members of the community had changed. The question was: Must a member of the community pay his share of the tax according to his financial condition in the past when the obligation was created, or according to his current financial condition at the time of the collection and repayment? The question was posed to Rashba as follows:[352]

> Ten years ago the community undertook the obligation of a debt, which must now be paid. In the meantime, assessments have changed. Some contend that payment should now be made on the basis of the first assessment; and some argue that payment should be made on the basis of the present assessment. Who is correct?

Rashba's response was as follows:

> I observe that all tax matters are everywhere governed by custom and not by strict law. Therefore, whenever there is a known custom, it must be followed; but if they wish to adjudicate under strict law, the law clearly requires that they use the first assessment. It is analogous to partners who borrow money to pay a debt; each partner must now pay according to his obligation for that debt at the time the loan was taken or when it was charged to his account. Even if he had been wealthy and is now poor, he must pay, even from the shirt on his back. However, I have noted that some communities pay according to the second assessment; this is also our custom here and in communities of which we have knowledge.

350. *Resp. Rashba*, V, #179; *Mordekhai*, Bava Batra, #656; *see also Resp. Rashba*, IV, #260.

351. *Resp. Rashba*, III, #412, quoted in *Resp. Ribash* #477 (toward the end). Rashba's responsum is discussed in detail immediately *infra*.

352. *Resp. Rashba*, III, #412, as it appears in *Resp. Ribash* #477.

Under the strict law, a communal debt is like every other debt resulting from a loan taken by a partnership; and just as a partnership debt must be paid in proportion to the partners' interest in the partnership at the time of the loan, a communal debt should also be paid according to the financial situation of each member of the community at the time the loan was obtained. However, the community may adopt an enactment pursuant to which each resident is to pay his share of the loan according to his situation at the time of payment, even though such legislation enacts a rule contrary to the strict law. If, indeed, such an enactment is adopted, it must be followed, so that if, in the interim, the financial condition of members of the community has changed, the payment will accord with their present and not their past condition. This enactment is explained on the basis of the difference between private law with regard to a loan obtained by a partnership of individuals and public law concerning a loan made to a community:

> A community that borrows for public needs differs from those who borrow for themselves; for it borrows for the communal treasury[353] on the assumption that it will pay the debt out of what is found in the treasury at the time of payment. This is the custom everywhere. Those who were poor and became wealthy or were wealthy and became poor . . . pay only according to the assessment made against each at the time of payment. This is our practice and it would be impossible to function otherwise.[354]

However, the power of the community to determine that the crucial date is the time of the payment of the tax and not the time the obligation was created exists only with respect to the *amount* of the tax and not with respect to the basic liability for the tax:

> In any case, neither we nor the surrounding communities have instituted this practice except in regard to taxpayers who resided here at the time the community borrowed the funds and became obligated to pay that debt . . . ; [the enactments apply to all such taxpayers even if] it happened that some who were affluent lost their wealth, or some who were poor and had very little have now become wealthy. However, a stranger who came to live here in the interim [between the time the debt was incurred and the time for its payment] does not pay any part of the debt that antedated his arrival, since we apply strict law to the newcomers.
>
> According to our practice, those people to whom you refer that moved into your community in the interim should pay no part of the antecedent debt, even if the practice is to pay according to the present assessment. This

353. Lit. "communal box," a term that appears frequently in responsa; *see, e.g., Resp. Rashba,* III, #410, #411; IV, #309. The concept here is one of a separate legal entity—a communal treasury that is different from partnership funds.

354. *Resp. Rashba,* III, #412.

> is both law and good sense, for why should he pay what he has not borrowed, and how can he return what he has not stolen? However, those who did reside in the town make their payments according to the customary practice.[355]

Rashba thus laid down the following rules:

a. Under strict law, a ten-year-old communal debt should not be paid according to the present assessment of the taxpayers, but on the basis of the assessment as of ten years previously when the loan was obtained and the debt was incurred. Therefore, whoever has become wealthy in the interim is liable to pay only that share for which he was liable when the debt arose; and whoever has become poor must similarly pay the share for which he was liable at the time the debt was incurred.
b. The community may provide by legislation that each taxpayer's proportion of the tax levied to provide funds to pay the debt should be based on the taxpayer's assessment as of the time of payment rather than the assessment as of the time the debt giving rise to the tax is incurred. This would move communal action out of the area of private partnership law and into the area of public law.
c. Legislative power is limited to imposing liability on those who were citizens and residents of the town at the time the debt arose. The community may not, even by legislation, impose upon someone who moved into town in the interim the duty of paying part of the tax occasioned by something that occurred previously; for "why should he pay what he has not borrowed, and how can he return what he has not stolen?" Such legislation is invalid because it is contrary to justice and equity; it unlawfully prejudices such an individual.

The principle prohibiting retroactive liability for payment of taxes was also stated in a responsum by Ribash, who added another rule to supplement the basic principle. This responsum[356] concerned a cantor who moved into a community that owed debts from prior years. The question was whether the cantor was required to participate with the other residents in paying the tax to be used to repay those loans. This question has two aspects: first, whether the cantor, as a scholar and a teacher of children, was completely exempt from taxation; and second, whether, even if not exempt, he nevertheless escaped liability for payment of this tax because he

355. Rashba's responsum (III, #412) as it appears in *Resp. Ribash* #477. Apparently not all halakhic authorities agreed with this view; *see, e.g., Resp. Maharaḥ Or Zaru'a* #226. However, it is possible that in the latter case the individual knew of the debt and waived his rights, as in Ribash's responsum *infra. See further* M. Elon, EJ, XV, pp. 852–854, s.v. Taxation (reprinted in *Principles*, pp. 677–680).

356. *Resp. Ribash* #477.

became a resident of the town after the debt that gave rise to the tax had already been incurred.

Ribash's response to the first question was that in his opinion, on the facts of this particular case, the cantor was entirely exempt from all liability for taxes.[357] However, since others might dispute this ruling and take the position that the law is to the contrary, Ribash proceeded to address the second question:

> You should be aware that under strict law those who move into a community are never liable for debts assumed by the community prior to their coming, nor for any associated expense. The question asked by the Sages[358] as to how long one should reside in a community in order to be considered a resident [for purposes of taxation] refers to the expenditures that the community incurs after his arrival to protect or improve the town, as was said:[359] "The Mishnah refers to payments for repair of the town walls." But why should he pay for debts that the community incurred for expenditures that were made in the past before his arrival?

Ribash here reiterated the principle stated by Rashba, namely, that one is not legally required to pay anything to cover expenditures incurred before he became a resident.

Ribash continued:

> It is true that every community may legislate for itself with regard to taxes and debts; and whatever the community agrees on must be followed, since they have so agreed and it concerns a monetary matter. However, the community may not legislate to the prejudice of any of its members; and any such legislation is unlawful as to any individual thus prejudiced who does not consent to being included within its ambit. The governing principle is that the community may not legislate to steal from anyone.

These comments also echo those of Rashba in both aspects:

a. The community has broad power to adopt enactments with regard to taxes, including enactments that are contrary to the strict law.
b. An enactment may not be arbitrarily aimed against a particular individual in the community, nor may it retroactively require the payment of a tax. Such an arbitrary enactment is like robbery and is therefore invalid.

Ribash completed his treatment of this subject by adding a novel rule:

357. *See id.* #475, #476. As to tax exemptions, *see* M. Elon, EJ, XV, pp. 854–858, s.v. Taxation (reprinted in *Principles,* pp. 680–685).

358. M Bava Batra 1:5.

359. TB Bava Batra 8a.

> Whenever there is in a town a duly enacted law agreed upon by the community to the effect that all those who come from outside the town to take up residence there are responsible for previous communal debts, it can be argued that anyone who moves there accepts the community's agreements and enactments and waives any right not to be bound by them, so long as the court is convinced that the new resident had notice of the enactment [*i.e.*, that the resident knew or should have known of the existence of this enactment].
>
> However, if the new resident did not have notice of the enactment and desired to leave the town when he became aware of it, it would seem that the community does not have the power to hold him liable, because he is not liable under the strict law, and the only possible basis for liability is the enactment. Thus, so long as he was not aware of the enactment, he may not be made liable, since he did not knowingly waive his rights.

Ribash thus determined that legislation cannot validly require the payment of a tax by an individual who was not a resident of the town when the event occurred that occasioned the tax; but if such legislation had been enacted and was in effect before that individual moved into the town, and he had notice of the enactment, it can be assumed that he impliedly consented to pay the tax. If, however, he did not have notice of the enactment and, when he learns of it, wishes to leave the town, he is to be permitted to leave and cannot be compelled to pay the tax. The question of whether the new resident had notice of the enactment when he moved into the town is a question of fact to be determined in each case by the court.

There was thus developed a finely wrought doctrine in regard to retroactive legislation—a doctrine that retained the basic principle against retroactive imposition of liabilities yet found a way to facilitate effective administration of the financial affairs of the community.[360]

C. Interpretation of Communal Enactments by the Halakhic Authorities

An additional significant factor bringing about the integration of communal enactments into the Jewish legal system was the fact that the authoritative interpreters of communal enactments were generally the same persons who interpreted the entire *corpus juris* of Jewish law, namely, the halakhic authorities. In performing their task of interpreting communal enactments, the halakhic authorities relied on various rules of interpretation applicable in Jewish law; their responsa analyzed the substance and the text of each

360. Regarding retroactive legislation, *see further Resp. Zikhron Yehudah* #78; *Resp. Tashbeẓ*, II, #292, *tikkun* 9 and 11. *See also infra* p. 806 and n. 95.

enactment in issue by using Talmudic and codificatory literature as sources for analogies. In this way, communal enactments were incorporated into Jewish law through the responsa literature, which has preserved a substantial portion of these enactments and made them an integral part of the halakhic system.

The approach of the halakhic authorities to the interpretation of communal enactments has been extensively discussed earlier in this work as part of the general treatment of exegesis and interpretation in Jewish law.[361]

VIII. SUMMARY

Our exposition of the attitude of the halakhic authorities toward communal enactments has shown that, on the one hand, the community was given full authority in matters of civil, criminal, and public law[362] to legislate as necessary in light of the economic and social trends of the time, even to the point that the content of such legislation could be contrary to a halakhic rule. On the other hand, this legislation itself became an integral part of the halakhic system through three mechanisms of supervision by the halakhic authorities: (a) the requirement, to a certain extent, of the prior approval of a "distinguished person"; (b) review by the halakhic authorities to ensure that such legislation reflected the halakhic principles of equity and justice; and (c) interpretation of the legislation by the halakhic authorities.

While practices based on communal customs and enactments superseded the rules of the *Halakhah* in broad areas of Jewish law, it was emphasized that "it is always appropriate and correct to consider carefully whether it is possible to reconcile all customs with the law of the Torah. Even if this cannot be done completely, it is highly desirable to find reinforcement and support in the words of the halakhic authorities and buttress them [the practices] with good reason and logic."[363]

361. *See supra* ch. 12, which also contains many examples of communal enactments in various fields of Jewish law.

362. This authority extended even to enactments with far-reaching effects on religious laws. *See supra* pp. 711–712.

363. *Terumat ha-Deshen* #342. This statement of Israel Isserlein was made in a discussion of tax law and concerned the principle that custom overrides the law. However, the statement also applies to communal enactments, which had at least as great an effect as custom in the field of taxation and indeed in all other areas of the law in which custom and communal enactments were both operative and would override the preexisting law—*i.e.*, in all areas of civil, penal, and public law.

Recent literature on various aspects of communal enactments includes: A. Naḥlon, "Samkhut ha-Ẓibbur le-Hatkin Takkanot Lefi ha-Tashbeẓ: Ha-Guf ha-Matkin Takkanot" [The View of Tashbeẓ on the Authority of the Community to Enact Legislation: The Legislative Body], *Shenaton*, I (1974), pp. 142–178; *id.*, "Samkhut ha-Ẓibbur le-Hatkin Takkanot

The dual aspect of communal legislation, whereby it conflicts with the *Halakhah* in respect to the substance of the governing rules yet is integrated as a constituent part of the halakhic system, is understandable and even natural, considering the character of Jewish society until the onset of the Emancipation at the end of the eighteenth century. The entire Jewish community recognized the same supreme and ultimate guiding values—the primacy of the Torah and the authority of the *Halakhah.* The communal leaders did not view their enactments as a method of undermining or evading the authority of the *Halakhah.* The opposite was true—they saw in the enactments that they adopted a unique way, taking account of the needs of the place and the time, to base both public and private life in their community on the principles, objectives, and spirit of Jewish law.

Communal enactments constitute one of the great achievements of Jewish law during its long and variegated history. These enactments did more than create a mechanism for regulating within the wider framework of the Jewish legal system all of the particular legal problems that arose out of the social and economic conditions over the course of time in the various centers of the diaspora. These enactments also created basic legal principles for the legislative process of the Jewish community; and they developed and crystallized the principles of equity and justice, the protection of minority rights, equality, and other similar principles, to which communal enactments were required to conform.

Lefi ha-Tashbeẓ: Mahutan ha-Mishpatit Shel Takkanot ha-Kahal" [The View of Tashbeẓ on the Authority of the Community to Enact Legislation: The Legal Nature of Communal Enactments], *Shenaton,* III-IV (1976–1977), pp. 271–326; A. Grossman, *supra* n. 28 at 175–199; Elon, *Samkhut ve-Oẓmah,* pp. 28–34 (discussing legal creativity in the Jewish community and the significance of that creativity for our time); *id.,* "Darkhei ha-Yeẓirah," *supra* n. 112 at 241–264.

Chapter 20

SURVEY OF LEGISLATION FROM THE TENTH CENTURY C.E. TO THE PRESENT

I. Introduction
II. Legislation in the Various Centers: Personages and Legislative Bodies and the Scope of Their Legislative Activity
  A. Germany and France
    1. Enactments of Rabbenu Gershom Me'or Ha-Golah ("Light of the Exile"): Prohibitions against Polygamy, and against Divorce without the Wife's Consent
    2. Enactments of Rashi
    3. Enactments of Rabbenu Tam and of the Community of Troyes
      a. Enactments Concerning the Relation Between Jews and Non-Jews
      b. Enactment Limiting a Husband's Right to Inherit
      c. Enactment Prohibiting Challenge to the Validity of a Divorce after Its Delivery
      d. Enactment Prohibiting Prolonged Separation by a Husband from His Wife
    4. Enactments of David b. Kalonymus
    5. Enactments of "Shum" (Speyer, Worms, and Mainz)
    6. Enactments of Maharam of Rothenburg and Rabbenu Pereẓ of Corbeil
    7. Enactment of Ḥayyim Or Zaru'a against *Ex Parte* Decisions
    8. Enactments of Mainz at the End of the Fourteenth Century
    9. Enactments in the Fifteenth and Sixteenth Centuries
      a. Enactment of the Synod of Nuremberg on the Language to Be Used in Court Proceedings
      b. Enactments of Bingen
      c. Enactments of Frankfurt
  B. Spain and North Africa
    1. Legislation by Local Communities: Toledo and Molina
    2. Countrywide Legislation
    3. Enactments of the Aragonian Communities, 1354
    4. Enactments of the Castilian Communities at Valladolid, 1432
      a. The Educational System: Organization and Financing
      b. Appointment of Judges and Other Public Officials; Judicial Authority; Civil and Criminal Procedure
      c. Enactments Concerning Informers and the Relation between the Government and the Jews
      d. Enactments Concerning Tax Law
      e. Enactments Outlawing Extravagance in Dress and Festive Banquets
    5. Enactments of the North African Center
      a. Algerian Enactments, 1394
      b. Enactments of Fez
  C. The Mediterranean Countries and Italy
    1. Enactments of Maimonides in Egypt
    2. Enactments of Candia (Crete); Enactment for the Protection of Tenants

- 3. Italy
  - a. Enactments of Forli, 1418
    - (1) Enactments Concerning Taxes
    - (2) Prohibition of Games of Chance
    - (3) Limits on Luxuries and Extravagant Festive Banquets
    - (4) Sumptuary Legislation
  - b. Enactments of Florence
  - c. Enactments of Ferrara
- 4. Enactments of Corfu

D. Enactments of the National and Regional Councils of Poland, Lithuania, and Moravia in the Seventeenth and Eighteenth Centuries
- 1. Enactments of the Council of the Four Lands (*Va'ad Arba Araẓot*)
- 2. Enactments of the Council of the Principal Communities of Lithuania
- 3. Enactments of Moravia

E. Enactments of Individual Communities in the Seventeenth and Eighteenth Centuries
- 1. The Book of Enactments of the Community of Cracow
  - a. Jails and Imprisonment
  - b. Imprisonment for Gambling
- 2. Other Compilations

F. Legislation after the Onset of Emancipation

G. Enactments of the Chief Rabbinate of the Land of Israel
- 1. Establishment of a Rabbinical Court of Appeals
- 2. Procedural Enactments for the Rabbinical Courts of the Land of Israel, 1943
  - a. Procedure for Litigation and the Payment of Court Costs
  - b. Adoption
  - c. Equalization of Daughters with Sons, and Wives with Husbands, in Regard to Inheritance
- 3. Enactments of 1944
  - a. The Minimum Amount of the *Ketubbah*
  - b. Support by a *Levir* of His Brother's Widow
  - c. Support of Children up to the Age of Fifteen
- 4. Enactments of 1950
- 5. Termination of Legislative Activity

III. The Special Legislative Trend in Regard to Some Aspects of Family Law and the Law of Succession

A. Exercise of Full Legislative Authority over Financial Aspects of Family Law and the Law of Succession
- 1. Restriction on the Husband's Right of Inheritance
  - a. Enactment of Rabbenu Tam; Enactments of "Shum"
  - b. Enactments in Spain; Enactments of Toledo, Molina, Algeria, and Fez
- 2. Right of a Mother to Inherit
- 3. Restriction on a Widow's Right to Recover the Amount of Her *Ketubbah*
- 4. Equal Rights of Inheritance for Sons and Daughters in Certain Circumstances

B. Decline in Legislation Directly Affecting the Validity of Marriage and Divorce
- 1. Controversy Between the Authorities of Mainz and the Authorities of Worms and Speyer in the Twelfth Century
- 2. Annulment of Marriage on the Strength of an Explicit Enactment; the Views of Asheri, Rashba, and Rabbenu Jeroham
- 3. The Demand for "The Approval of All the Halakhic Authorities of the Region"; the View of Ribash
- 4. Basic Distinction Between Theory and Practice in Regard to Legislative Authority; the Views of Rashbeẓ (Simeon b. Ẓemah Duran) and Rashbash (Simeon b. Solomon Duran)

I. INTRODUCTION

As we have seen,[1] there were two principal modes of legislation during and after the tenth century C.E.: (1) legislation by the halakhic authorities, *i.e.*, the courts or the authoritative halakhic scholars in the different centers, and (2) legislation by the public, *i.e.*, communal enactments adopted by a single community or by associations of communities. These two legislative agencies—the halakhic authorities and the communities—often cooperated closely; and many enactments were adopted jointly by them.[2] This cooperation was natural and predictable, since the whole of Jewish society—the general community as well as the halakhic authorities—was imbued with a strong sense of tradition that viewed the *Halakhah* as the supreme value in its way of life, and everyone in that society sought, each in his own way, to further this common value. For that very reason, even when the two legislative agencies acted separately, the legislation enacted by each one merged into the overall Jewish legal system.[3]

The legislation enacted by these agencies is vast and impressive. The two preceding chapters contain various examples, and a considerable amount of such legislation is discussed in the works of scholars[4] and histo-

1. *Supra* pp. 666ff.

2. For examples, *see infra* p. 784 n. 12, p. 791 (enactment of Ḥayyim Or Zaru'a), pp. 832–833.

3. *See supra* pp. 751–779.

4. *See* Finkelstein, *Self-Government,* which includes a comprehensive survey of the various personalities and councils and the legislation they adopted; I. Schepansky, "Takkanot Rabbenu Gershom Me'or ha-Golah" [The Enactments of Rabbenu Gershom, the Light of the Exile], *Ha-Darom,* XXII (1966), pp. 103–120; *id.,* "Takkanot Shum" [The Enactments of "Shum"], *Ha-Darom,* XXVI (1968), pp. 173–197; *id.,* "Takkanot ha-Rishonim" [Enactments of the *Rishonim*], *Ha-Darom,* XXVIII (1969), pp. 145–159.

rians.[5] The bulk of this rich legislative material is found in the responsa and other post-Talmudic halakhic literature, in the collections of enactments adopted by councils and communities,[6] and in the vast array of historical records and documents. This material still awaits full collection and analysis.[7] This chapter surveys the major legislative personages and bodies active from the tenth century C.E. to the present and also the scope of their legislative activity, with particular emphasis on legislation in the areas of family law and the law of succession. In the course of this period, legislative authority was substantially curtailed in all matters affecting the validity of marriages and divorces;[8] and this development will be extensively examined, particularly in view of the substantial effects it has had on the problems emerging in Jewish law today.

II. LEGISLATION IN THE VARIOUS CENTERS: PERSONAGES AND LEGISLATIVE BODIES AND THE SCOPE OF THEIR LEGISLATIVE ACTIVITY

A. Germany and France

1. ENACTMENTS OF RABBENU GERSHOM ME'OR HA-GOLAH ("LIGHT OF THE EXILE"): PROHIBITIONS AGAINST POLYGAMY, AND AGAINST DIVORCE WITHOUT THE WIFE'S CONSENT

Among the earliest legislative enactments were those of Rabbenu Gershom b. Judah, who lived in Germany at the end of the tenth and the beginning of the eleventh centuries C.E. and was the recognized leader of German Jewry and the neighboring Jewish centers. He is described by

5. For some of these works, *see supra* p. 37 and n. 108. *See also* bibliography, *infra* vol. IV.

6. Some of these collections of enactments will be discussed in this chapter. *See also infra* pp. 1531–1532.

7. The digests of the responsa published by The Institute for Research in Jewish Law of the Hebrew University of Jerusalem contain entries under the titles "Contents of Enactments of Associations" and "Contents of Communal Enactments," which summarize all the enactments recorded in the responsa literature. This is in addition to the entries "The Community," "Communal Enactments," "Associations," and "Artisans," each of which deals with the law relevant to its subject. The enactments contained in the responsa written in Spain and North Africa from the eleventh to the fifteenth centuries are published in the *Digest of the Responsa Literature of Spain and North Africa, Legal Digest,* Jerusalem, II (1986), pp. 580–581 ("Contents of Enactments of Associations"), pp. 581–591 ("Contents of Communal Enactments"). *See also id.* at 565–580 ("Contents of Customs"). A similar compilation of communal enactments and customs is contained in the *Historical Digest,* ch. II, "The Community," supplemental chapter, "Institutions and Procedures"; ch. V, "Behavior and Life-style," supplemental chapter, "Customs." *See also* vol. I (1981), pp. 6–7, 13–14, 51, 53, 64–65, 112–113, 116, 145–157, 179–184; vol. II (1987), pp. 40–64, 109–123.

8. *See supra* pp. 676–677 and *infra* pp. 846–879.

Rashi as "Rabbenu Gershom, the light of the exile, whose words sustain us all [lit. "from whose mouth we all live"], and all the inhabitants of the diasporas of Germany and Kutim [France and Italy] are the disciples of his disciples."[9] The appellation "light of the exile" seems especially connected with Rabbenu Gershom's legislative activity, as indicated by reference to him as "the great luminary, Rabbenu Gershom, may his memory be for a blessing, [who] legislated for the entire diaspora,"[10] and "Rabbenu Gershom b. Judah, the light of the exile, who enlightened the eyes of the exile with his enactments."[11] Early traditions attribute to Rabbenu Gershom[12] a long series of enactments in various fields of law: civil, criminal, and public law, rules of procedure, execution of judgments, and the regulation of religious, moral, and social life.[13]

Two of the well-known enactments of Rabbenu Gershom[14] are in the

9. *Resp. Rashi* #70 (ed. Elfenbein, p. 83). For the term *Kutim* as referring to France and Italy, *see* Elfenbein's notes, *ad loc. See also* Rashi, Shabbat 85b, s.v. Be-noteh shurah le-khan ve-shurah le-khan: "Rabbenu Gershom, the father of the diaspora."

10. Rabbenu Simḥah, a disciple of Rashi, in *Maḥzor Vitry* #380 (p. 442).

11. *Sefer Hazkarat Neshamot* [Memorial Book] of the Community of Worms, in *Koveẓ al Yad,* III, p.1.

12. Rabbenu Gershom's enactments are sometimes called "the enactments of the communities"; *see, e.g., Resp. Maharam of Rothenburg,* ed. Prague, end of collection, p. 159c; *Resp. Maharam Mintz* #102. This is an early example of the interrelation between legislation by the halakhic authorities and communal legislation.

13. For details of these enactments and their variant texts as preserved in various sources, *see* Finkelstein, *Self-Government,* pp. 111ff.; B.Z. Dinur, *Yisra'el ba-Golah* [Israel in Diaspora], I(3), pp. 269–275; Schepansky, "Takkanot Rabbenu Gershom Me'or ha-Golah," *supra* n. 4. Some of the matters dealt with in the enactments are: establishment of local jurisdiction over nonresidents temporarily present in the community; prohibition against resort to non-Jewish courts; return of lost property (*see supra* pp. 686–688); binding effect of majority enactments on a dissenting minority (*see supra* pp. 715–723); methods of tax collection; deposit of security on an appeal of a tax assessment (*see Resp. Maharik* #17; *Resp. Binyamin Ze'ev* #295; M. Elon, EJ, XV, pp. 863–865, s.v. Taxation [reprinted in *Principles,* pp. 690–693]); procedure for service of process; limitation of the right to settle in a town; prohibition against the rental of a dwelling from a non-Jew without the agreement of the current Jewish tenant (*see infra* pp. 811–813); breach of engagement to be married; prohibition against humiliating an apostate or Marrano who returned to the faith; prohibition against reading correspondence addressed to another; synagogues; interrupting the prayer service; and maintaining the *minyan* (prayer quorum).

14. Some scholars have recently cast doubt on the attribution of a significant number of these enactments to Rabbenu Gershom. *See* Finkelstein, *Self-Government,* pp. 111ff.; Y. Baer's critique of Finkelstein in *MGWJ,* LXXI (1927), pp. 392–397, LXXIV (1930), pp. 31–34; Y. Baer, "Ha-Yesodot ve-ha-Hatḥalot Shel Irgun ha-Kehillah ha-Yehudit bi-Mei ha-Beinayim" [The Foundations and Beginnings of Jewish Communal Organization in the Middle Ages], *Zion,* XV (1950), pp. 30–31 and n. 9. Most extreme is the opinion of P. Tishbi ("Ha-im ha-Takkanah she-Lo Laset Shetei Nashim mi-Rabbenu Gershom Hi?" [Is the Enactment Prohibiting Polygamy That of Rabbenu Gershom?], *Tarbiẓ,* XXXIV (1965), pp. 49–55), that even the enactment prohibiting polygamy is not Rabbenu Gershom's (*see* S. Eidelberg's comments on Tishbi's article, *Tarbiẓ,* XXXIV (1965), pp. 287–288).

area of family law. One prohibits any Jewish man from entering into a bigamous or polygamous marriage. As early as the Talmudic period, there were Sages who ruled that "whoever marries an additional wife must divorce his first wife and pay her *ketubbah*";[15] and it was customary in the post-Talmudic period for a husband to promise in the *ketubbah* that he would not take an additional wife.[16] However, in the absence of such a promise, polygamy was permitted and was practiced in Jewish family life in many places. Rabbenu Gershom prohibited polygamy and subjected those who practiced it to excommunication (the enactment is known as "the ban [*ḥerem*] of Rabbenu Gershom"); the prohibition could be lifted only in certain circumstances and with the consent of one hundred rabbis from three different countries.[17]

The second enactment, which complemented the first,[18] placed a ban against anyone who divorced his wife without her consent. Under Biblical law, a man could divorce his wife against her will, although it was considered improper to do so unless he "has found something obnoxious about her."[19] Rabbenu Gershom enacted legislation "prohibiting the divorcing of

---

However, the doubts and reservations expressed by these scholars do not provide a sufficient basis to challenge the clear tradition of the *rishonim* that attributes the enactments to Rabbenu Gershom. Dinur convincingly demonstrated "the truth of the historical tradition that attributes many enactments to Rabbenu Gershom and sees in them the principal element of his greatness" (*Yisra'el ba-Golah,* I(3), p. 330 n. 71, and nn. 69–72). *See also* Schepansky, "Takkanot Rabbenu Gershom Me'or ha-Golah," *supra* n. 4.

15. TB Yevamot 65a.

16. *See* Gulak, *Oẓar ha-Shetarot,* document 30, p. 35; document 32, p. 37; document 34, p. 39; document 46, p. 52; and *see also id.* p. 23.

17. *Resp. Maharam of Rothenburg,* ed. Prague, #153; *Kol Bo* #116; *Resp. Maharam Mintz* #102; *Resp. Maharam of Padua* #14. On the various sources, *see* Finkelstein, *Self-Government,* pp. 23–29, 139ff.; Dinur, *supra* n. 13 at n. 88; and *see id.* as to the period in which the rule regarding the consent of one hundred rabbis was instituted.

Resp. Maharik #101 (end) quotes Rashba as having said, "We have heard that his [Rabbenu Gershom's] enactment was to be effective only until the end of the fifth millennium [*i.e.*, 1240 C.E.]"; Finkelstein (p. 142 n. 2) is extremely skeptical of the authenticity of this report, which has no support in the responsa of Rashba or in any other source. *But see* S.Z. Havlin, "Teshuvot Ḥadashot le-Rashba' [New Responsa of Rashba], *Moriah,* 1st annual, III–IV, pp. 58ff., which contains the same responsum quoted by Maharik, as taken from the responsa of Rashba in ms. Jerusalem. *See also id.* at 62 for a question addressed to Rashba by a rabbi of Provence: ". . . for we have a tradition that the time he specified for the effectiveness of his enactment has passed."

For the various opinions on the existence of a time limit on the continued effectiveness of this enactment, *see id.* at 59, 66. *See also* Havlin, "Takkanot Rabbenu Gershom Me'or ha-Golah be-Inyanei Ishut bi-Teḥumei Sefarad u-Provenẓ" [The Enactments of Rabbenu Gershom Concerning Marital Status in the Regions of Spain and Provence], *Shenaton,* II (1975), pp. 200–257.

18. *See Resp. Ḥatam Sofer,* EH, #1.

19. Deuteronomy 24:1–2; M Yevamot 14:1; M Gittin 9:10. *See supra* pp. 292–295.

a wife against her will, such a divorce being a nullity,"[20] and in this way he "legislated to equate the power of the woman with that of the man; just as a man divorces only if he is willing to do so, so a woman can be divorced only if she is willing to be divorced."[21]

2. ENACTMENTS OF RASHI

Later in the eleventh century C.E., enactments were promulgated by Rashi in the areas of tax law[22] and marriage ceremonies.[23]

3. ENACTMENTS OF RABBENU TAM AND OF THE COMMUNITY OF TROYES

a. ENACTMENTS CONCERNING THE RELATION BETWEEN JEWS AND NON-JEWS

At the end of the eleventh and the beginning of the twelfth centuries C.E., as a consequence of the Crusades, it became necessary to legislate in a number of subject areas. In the middle of the twelfth century, Jacob b. Meir (Rabbenu Tam) and his older brother Samuel b. Meir (Rashbam) presided over a synod in Troyes attended by leading halakhic authorities and by representatives of communities in Germany and France. This synod adopted a number of major enactments.

These enactments deal in part with such subjects as informers, the prohibition against bringing a controversy between Jews before a non-Jewish court, and the prohibition against attempting to obtain a public office in the Jewish community with the help of non-Jews.[24]

20. Enactments of Rabbenu Gershom, quoted in *Resp. Maharam of Rothenburg,* ed. Prague, end of collection (p. 159c *et seq.*); *Resp. Maharam Mintz* #102. The language used implies that the enactment is not simply a prohibition *ex ante,* but that a divorce given against the will of the wife is invalid, notwithstanding its validity under Biblical law. However, most commentators interpreted even this language as meaning that the divorce, once given, is valid, in accordance with Biblical law. *See* Rema to Sh. Ar. EH 119:6; *Keneset ha-Gedolah,* EH, #119, comments on *Tur,* subpar. 9; *Resp. Noda bi-Yehudah,* Mahadura Tinyana, EH #129. For further information on these two enactments of Rabbenu Gershom, *see* Silberg, *Ha-Ma'amad,* pp. 158–170, 429–432; B.Z. Schereschewsky, *Dinei Mishpaḥah* [Family Law], pp. 67–80, 273–274, 323–326; Z. Falk, *Nissu'in ve-Gerushin* [Marriage and Divorce], pp. 4–31, 96–120; Elon, *Ḥakikah,* pp. 104–116. On the nature and geographical reach of Rabbenu Gershom's enactments, *see supra* pp. 663–664, 674–675.

21. *Resp. Asheri* 42:1.

22. *Resp. Rashi* #248 (ed. Elfenbein, pp. 290–291); *Terumat ha-Deshen* #342.

23. *Sefer ha-Yashar le-Rabbenu Tam* #45, par. 5 (ed. Rosenthal, p. 82).

24. The enactments are quoted in *Resp. Maharam of Rothenburg,* ed. Cremona, #78. *See also* Finkelstein, *Self-Government,* pp. 42, 150ff. These enactments were in part intended to supplement and strengthen laws that originated in the Talmud (*e.g.,* the prohibition against resort to non-Jewish courts) or that were enacted by Rabbenu Gershom; *see supra* n. 13.

b. ENACTMENT LIMITING A HUSBAND'S RIGHT TO INHERIT

A short time later, another synod was held in Troyes, where an important enactment previously adopted for the residents of Narbonne was expanded to cover other cities. It restricted the right of a husband in the estate of his wife by requiring the return of the wife's dowry to her heirs if she died shortly after the marriage.[25] This enactment went so far as to contravene the Biblical law on the husband's rights of inheritance.[26] Toward the end of his life, Rabbenu Tam changed his mind about this enactment,[27] but it was later readopted, with some additional details, as an enactment of the communities of "Shum" (the acronym for the Hebrew names of the communities of Speyer, Worms, and Mainz).[28]

c. ENACTMENT PROHIBITING CHALLENGE TO THE VALIDITY OF A DIVORCE AFTER ITS DELIVERY

There were other enactments reported to have been promulgated by Rabbenu Tam, particularly in family law. One such enactment provided:

> In an assembly in the market of Troyes, under the penalty of a severe ban and as a firm proscription, [it is declared] that no one may challenge any divorce after it is delivered—not even immediately thereafter. If there is to be any challenge, it must be made before the divorce is delivered.[29]

This enactment was adopted to prevent challenges to the validity of a divorce, with all of the serious consequences such a challenge might have when a woman has remarried in reliance on a divorce that had been delivered to her.[30]

d. ENACTMENT PROHIBITING PROLONGED SEPARATION BY A HUSBAND FROM HIS WIFE

Another enactment forbade a husband to leave his wife for more than eighteen months (in other versions: twelve months) without the permis-

25. For the text of the enactment, *see Sefer ha-Yashar le-Rabbenu Tam,* Novellae, #788 (ed. Schlesinger, p. 465); *Resp. Maharam of Rothenburg,* ed. Prague, #934, and ed. Cremona, #72; Finkelstein, *Self-Government,* pp. 163–165; S. Assaf, "Ha-Takkanot ve-ha-Minhagim ha-Shonim bi-Yerushat ha-Ba'al et Ishto" [The Various Enactments and Customs in Regard to the Husband's Right to Inherit from His Wife], *Madda'ei ha-Yahadut,* I (1926), p. 91.

26. For detailed discussion, *see infra* pp. 836–838.

27. *Tosafot,* Ketubbot 47a, s.v. Katav lah perot kesut ve-khelim (in the continuation thereof at 47b); *Yam Shel Shelomo,* Ketubbot 4:14.

28. *Yam Shel Shelomo,* Ketubbot 4:14. *See also infra* pp. 788–789, 836–838, concerning the enactments of "Shum."

29. *Sefer ha-Yashar le-Rabbenu Tam,* Novellae, #140 (at the conclusion), ed. Schlesinger, p. 105.

30. *Tur* EH ch. 154; Sh. Ar. EH 154:22. *See also* Finkelstein, *Self-Government,* pp. 44–46; Schepansky, "Takkanot ha-Rishonim," *supra* n. 4 at 150–152.

sion of the court, unless she consented in the presence of credible witnesses. Moreover, the husband was not permitted to leave even for the time specified in the enactment, except when necessary to earn a livelihood or to study Torah, and, even then, only if the relations between him and his wife were harmonious. After the husband's return, he was required to remain with his wife for at least six months.[31]

A collection of enactments by Rabbenu Tam is extant, which in part repeats and supplements earlier legislation, especially that of Rabbenu Gershom.[32]

4. ENACTMENTS OF DAVID b. KALONYMUS

An important enactment dating from the end of the twelfth century C.E. relates to the division of a decedent's estate between the decedent's widow and his brother, the *levir,* who performed the rite of *ḥaliẓah* (release of the widow from the requirement of levirate marriage). It is attributed to David b. Kalonymus of Minzburg. This enactment was later the subject of discussion in the framework of the enactments of "Shum," and its provisions were disputed for a long time. Since the details of its provisions were insufficiently clarified, it was subsequently ruled that in practice an attempt should be made to effect a compromise between the *levir* and the widow.[33]

5. ENACTMENTS OF "SHUM" (SPEYER, WORMS, AND MAINZ)

At the beginning of the thirteenth century, a number of synods took place in Germany at which many diverse enactments were adopted in every area of Jewish law. Among the rabbinical leaders who participated in those synods were Eliezer b. Joel ha-Levi (Raviah), Simḥah b. Samuel of Speyer, and Baruch b. Samuel of Mainz (author of *Sefer ha-Ḥokhmah* [The Book of Wisdom], which is not extant). The enactments adopted at these synods, known as the "*Takkanot* of Shum," contained various rules relating to

31. *See* the text of the enactment in *Resp. Binyamin Ze'ev* #64 and Finkelstein, *Self-Government,* pp. 44, 168–169. Apparently, this enactment antedated Rabbenu Tam and was reaffirmed by him. *See* the conclusion of the enactment: "And Rabbenu Tam wrote: 'This is a fitting and an early enactment and we have always followed it in accordance with our rabbis in France because peace is paramount.'"

32. *See Resp. Maharam of Rothenburg,* ed. Prague, #153, #1022; for detailed discussion, *see* Finkelstein, *Self-Government,* pp. 48ff., 171–215. *See also* Schepansky, "Takkanot ha-Rishonim," *supra* n. 4 at 153–154.

33. *See Terumat ha-Deshen* #220; *id.,* Pesakim u-Khetavim #262–264; Sh. Ar. EH 163:2 (and *see* Rema's gloss, *ad loc.*), 165:4; *Yam Shel Shelomo,* Yevamot 4:18. This enactment was not accepted by Sephardic Jews because they held that the fulfillment of the commandment of levirate marriage takes precedence over *ḥaliẓah.* For detailed discussion, *see* Finkelstein, *Self-Government,* pp. 56–59; Schepansky, "Takkanot Shum," *supra* n. 4 at 192–197; M. Elon, EJ, XI, pp. 122–131, s.v. Levirate marriage and *ḥaliẓah* (reprinted in *Principles,* pp. 403–409).

Jewish-gentile relations, laws governing loans, taxes, informers, prohibition of gambling, restrictions on expenditures for meals at festive occasions, adjudication before Jewish judges, the division of a decedent's estate between the widow and the *levir,* the prohibition of slander ("no one may call another a *mamzer* or mention any other flaw in lineage"), restriction of a husband's right to inherit from his wife when she dies shortly after the marriage, and many other enactments concerning prayer, education, tithes, and charitable contributions for public needs, etc.[34]

The enactments of "Shum" were accepted in all the French and German communities and later also in the communities of Poland and the other Eastern European Jewish centers. As stated, the enactment restricting the husband's right to inherit from his wife was included in the enactments of "Shum" and is known in halakhic literature as the "*Takkanah* of Shum" even though it originated in an enactment of Rabbenu Tam.[35] This is one of the most significant enactments in post-geonic legislation because it reversed the pre-existing law on a highly important subject. This enactment is discussed in detail later.[36]

6. ENACTMENTS OF MAHARAM OF ROTHENBURG AND RABBENU PEREẒ OF CORBEIL

At the initiative of Maharam of Rothenburg in Germany and of Rabbenu Pereẓ b. Elijah of Corbeil in France, various enactments[37] were

34. For these enactments, *see Resp. Maharam of Rothenburg,* ed. Prague, #1022 (p. 158b *et seq.*). For the variant texts and their contents, *see* Finkelstein, *Self-Government,* pp. 59–63, 218ff. Among these enactments, too, many were designed to affirm and strengthen existing legislation.

35. *See supra* p. 787.

36. *See infra* pp. 836–838.

37. *E.g.,* the enactment that the *moredet* (*see supra* pp. 658–665) loses not only her *ketubbah* but also the property she brought to the marriage. This enactment was adopted because of the increase in the number of wives deserting their husbands; *see Resp. Maharaḥ Or Zaru'a* #126:

> Our master, Rabbenu Meir [Maharam of Rothenburg], of blessed memory, . . . when the number of "rebellious" wives increased, sent [a message] to our master, Rabbi Jedidiah of Speyer, and to the group of communities to convene and to adopt an enactment that a *moredet* should also lose what she had brought to the marriage and go forth empty-handed; however, I do not know if that enactment has been accepted.

See also id. #69, #191, and the responsum of Maharam of Rothenburg quoted in *Haggahot Maimuniyyot* to Maimonides, *MT,* Ishut 14, subpar. 30 (". . . the communities enacted when they convened in Nuremberg that whenever a wife rebels [against her husband] because her relatives incite and persuade her to rebel, the husband shall take everything and have the right to all of the property"). This responsum also describes the background of the increased incidence of desertion by wives. *See also Haggahot Asheri,* Kiddushin, ch. 3, #16; Finkelstein, *Self-Government,* pp. 66–69. For another enactment, *see Resp. Maharam of Rothenburg,* ed. Berlin, #290 (p. 42): "There is at present a communal enactment that wherever there is a proper local court, no party may reject [that court] and say, 'Let us go to the Place of Assembly [a superior court].'"

adopted, especially in the area of family law, in the second half of the thirteenth century.

An enactment known to us from Rabbenu Perez̤ is specifically directed against wife-beating. There is an early responsum dating from the geonic period to the effect that a husband who strikes his wife is subject to a fine;[38] and in the thirteenth century, Maharam of Rothenburg vehemently admonished against wife-beating:

> A stranger, who is not commanded to honor her, is prohibited from striking her [*i.e.,* the striking of any person is prohibited].[39] Should not a husband all the more so be prohibited from striking his wife, whom he is bidden to honor? Indeed, he is required to honor her more than himself.[40] . . . It is not the way of our men to strike their wives, as men of the other nations are wont to do. God forbid that any Jew do such a thing, and if a case should come before us where a woman complains that her husband has struck her, we would take more severe action against him than if he had struck a stranger.[41]

Rabbenu Perez̤ placed a ban against a husband who strikes his wife, and his enactment provided that a woman who leaves the home of her husband because of his wrongful behavior toward her is entitled to support in accordance with her station and the custom of the women of her town.[42] The text of the enactment reads:[43]

> The cry of the daughters of our people has been heard from afar concerning Jews who raise their arms to strike their wives. Who has given a husband the authority to strike his wife? Has he not been warned that it is forbidden to strike any Jewish person? . . . Behold, we have heard that there are Jewish women who complain that they have been battered, but no action is taken in their communities on their behalf.
>
> We have therefore ordained, by decree and oath, that on the application

38. *See Oz̤ar ha-Geonim,* Ketubbot, Responsa, p. 191, #477; *see also* #476.

39. *See* Maimonides, *MT,* Sanhedrin 16:12; *Sefer ha-Miz̤vot,* Negative Commandments, #300.

40. TB Yevamot 62b; Maimonides, *MT,* Ishut 15:19.

41. *Resp. Maharam of Rothenburg,* ed. Cremona, #291.

42. Generally, the law is that a woman who deserts her husband and lives separate and apart from him has no right to support. This enactment recognized the wife's right to support even though she refuses to live with her husband if his wrongful behavior toward her was the reason for the separation; in that event, he is deemed to have deserted her and gone abroad. *See* Rema to Sh. Ar. EH 70:12; and Schereschewsky, *supra* n. 20 at 137ff. *Cf.* the doctrine of "constructive desertion" in Anglo-American domestic relations law, which "construes" a wife's separation from her husband under similar circumstances as desertion by the husband; *see Black's Law Dictionary* (5th ed. 1979), pp. 284, 401, s.v. Constructive desertion.

43. Finkelstein, *Self-Government,* p. 216.

of the wife of any Jew or any of her near relatives, the husband shall undertake, under penalty of a ban, not to strike his wife—whether in anger, or out of cruelty, or in a degrading manner—for these things may not be done among Jews.

If, God forbid, there will be a "root that brings forth poison and wormwood," [a husband] who will disobey our words and will not heed this edict, we instruct the court in which the wife or her relatives bring their complaint to order that she be supported in accordance with her station and the custom of the place where she resides; they shall fix her support as though her husband had left her to go on a distant journey.

Signed, Pereẓ b. Rabbi Elijah.[44]

7. ENACTMENT OF ḤAYYIM OR ZARU'A AGAINST *EX PARTE* DECISIONS

An important enactment dating from the end of the thirteenth century requires that no decision of any case should be rendered without first hearing both parties.

This enactment is set forth in a responsum of Moses Isserles:[45]

> Under a communal enactment promulgated by Rabbi Ḥayyim of Vienna[46] and the communal leaders, any judge who decides a case without hearing both parties, but instead writes [a decision] after the appearance of only one party who asks, "Hear me and then write as you deem appropriate," shall not sit in any other case.

This enactment is especially significant with regard to the rendering of a decision by means of a written responsum. The halakhic authorities took care to respond to a request for a ruling on any litigated matter only if the local judge submitted the matter to them after it had first been brought before him, or if the parties submitted the matter jointly.[47]

44. Rabbenu Pereẓ of Corbeil's enactment is composed of two elements: (1) at the request of the wife or her relatives, the husband is required to swear, under penalty of a ban, not to strike his wife; and (2) if the husband refuses to subject himself to the ban, the wife is entitled to support as if the husband had gone abroad. It should be pointed out that Rabbenu Pereẓ sent his proposed enactment to other halakhic authorities in an effort to have them join in its adoption; *see* the conclusion of the enactment in Finkelstein, *supra* n. 43, and *see also id.* at 69–71. *See also Resp. Maharam of Rothenburg,* ed. Prague, #81, #927; *Sefer Meisharim* of Rabbenu Jeroham, *nativ* (path) 23:5, in the name of Meir ha-Levi Abulafia; *Terumat ha-Deshen* #218; Rema to Sh. Ar. EH 154:3.

45. *Resp. Rema* #57; *see* Finkelstein, *Self-Government,* pp. 72–73.

46. The reference is to Ḥayyim Eliezer (the son of Rabbi Isaac of Vienna, Austria), the author of *Or Zaru'a,* who is therefore also known as Ḥayyim Or Zaru'a and whose responsa are known as *Resp. Maharaḥ Or Zaru'a.*

47. *See, e.g., Resp. Ribash* #5; *Terumat ha-Deshen,* Pesakim u-Khetavim, #62, #214; *Resp. Rama of Fano* #89. For a detailed discussion, *see infra* pp. 1501–1506.

8. ENACTMENTS OF MAINZ AT THE END OF THE FOURTEENTH CENTURY

The fourteenth century was a difficult and "black" period for the Jews of France and Germany. Very early on, in the year 1306, the Jews of France were expelled from that country; and many of them emigrated to Germany. In the middle of the century, in the years 1348–1351, the plague of the Black Death spread throughout Europe and claimed many victims among the Jews, as among the rest of the population. In addition, the Jews of Europe suffered from harsh pogroms and were accused of causing the plague by poisoning the wells to kill Christians. The first pogroms took place in Spain, from which they spread to Western Europe; and they were especially harsh and frightful in various German communities. In this situation, it was impossible to convene synods to enact legislation.

However, at the end of the fourteenth century, "communal enactments . . . [were] adopted at the assembly of the people and in the presence of rabbis and leaders . . . in the community of Mainz"[48] with regard to two significant matters. Among the initiators of the synod whose signatures appeared on the enactments was Moses b. Jekuthiel ha-Levi Moellin, the Rabbi of Mainz and the father of Jacob Moellin (Maharil). One enactment supplemented previous legislation, adopted at the end of the twelfth century, concerning the method of dividing a decedent's estate between the *levir* and the widow.[49] The second enactment conformed to the economic conditions of that period the amount that the husband undertook in the *ketubbah* to pay his wife.[50] The enactment stated:

> Prior to this time, payment of the *ketubbah* in this area was to be made in the coinage of the city of Cologne. Such coinage is no longer available [*i.e.*, the currency of Cologne was previously stable and could be used to compute the amount of the *ketubbah*, but it can no longer perform such a function]. We have agreed that a virgin is entitled to no more and no less than 600 gold florins and a widow to 300 gold florins, unless the husband wrote otherwise [in the *ketubbah*] or the wife has waived her rights.

48. *See* the text of the enactment in Finkelstein, *Self-Government*, pp. 252–253, as contained in various sources; *Yam Shel Shelomo*, Yevamot 4:18; *Resp. Maharam Mintz* #10.

49. *See supra* p. 788. As to how the legislation was changed, *see* Finkelstein, *Self-Government*, pp. 74–75, 245–255.

50. In the absence of legislation, the amount of the *ketubbah* is 200 *zuz* for a virgin and 100 *zuz* (a *maneh*) for a widow or divorcee. M Ketubbot 1:2; *see supra* p. 215. As to this enactment, *see Minhagei Maharil*, Laws of Marriage, ed. Cremona, #318, p. 87b; *Resp. Maharam Mintz* #10.

9. ENACTMENTS IN THE FIFTEENTH AND SIXTEENTH CENTURIES

a. ENACTMENT OF THE SYNOD OF NUREMBERG ON THE LANGUAGE TO BE USED IN COURT PROCEEDINGS

In the fifteenth century, a number of synods convened with the purpose, among others, of enacting legislation to meet the needs of the time. A responsum of Jacob Weil, one of the leaders of German Jewry in this period, discusses a synod held in Nuremberg and an interesting enactment of that synod involving court procedure. This responsum[51] takes us into the courtroom of that time:

> Concerning the dispute between Tuvia and Friedel, in which Tuvia sought to present his case in German and Friedel responded that his attorney could not write German.
>
> When we were at the Nuremberg synod, we adopted many enactments. One of them was as follows: If one party wishes to present his case in German, his opponent must also present his case in German. If our enactment has been accepted in your locality,[52] Tuvia is correct, so long as Friedel himself understands German.
>
> If Friedel's attorney cannot write German, he should hire another attorney who can. Otherwise, our enactment becomes a nullity, since everyone will hire an attorney who cannot write German and make the same argument. How much more so is Tuvia in the right if the fact is as Tuvia has written, namely, that Friedel's attorney can write German. However, if Friedel does not understand German, he is right. This does not require any careful analysis.
>
> Signed, Jacob Weil.

b. ENACTMENTS OF BINGEN

In the middle of the fifteenth century, at the initiative of Seligmann Oppenheim, a synod of various communities took place in Bingen and adopted a number of enactments. These enactments are not extant, but the halakhic literature contains an extensive discussion of the opposition by other communities, led by Moses Mintz, to these enactments. The matter was brought before Israel Isserlein, who ruled[53] that the enactments did not bind the communities that refused to accept them:

> I conclude that all of you from these three regions who have signed [the request for a ruling], and all those associated with you, have no obligation

51. *Resp. Mahari Weil* #101.

52. *I.e.,* the place from which the query was sent. The enactments were local in nature and applied only where they were specifically accepted. *See supra* pp. 668–675.

53. *Terumat ha-Deshen,* Pesakim u-Khetavim, #252; *see also id.* #253.

> whatsoever to accept or obey these enactments. This is a point that needs no elaboration, for how can penalties to be imposed on you for violating legislation enacted without your authorization?[54] How much more so is this true when, as I have written, the majority of [the members of] your communities are not able to comply with those enactments.[55]
>
> I have already written to Rabbi Seligmann and supplied him with sufficient proofs that he does not have the power to compel compliance even by those communities that are adjacent to him, except for the upper region of the Rhein, since Rabbis Nathan and Moses Mintz and the other scholars and householders refuse to accept the *takkanot* and since they were adopted without your consent.[56]

There are reports of additional synods convened from time to time at the end of the fifteenth century and during the sixteenth century, but we do not have any records of legislation in this period on subjects relating to *mishpat ivri.* The persecutions and pogroms that crushed the economic and social life of German Jewry necessarily resulted in a diminution of legislative activity.

c. ENACTMENTS OF FRANKFURT

An important synod convened in the year 1603 in Frankfurt-Am-Main and adopted many enactments in many areas of *mishpat ivri.*[57] One enactment deals extensively with the prohibition against instituting actions in non-Jewish courts and imposes a severe ban as a penalty for violation. Since it was not always possible for the local Jewish courts to compel "men of power and influence" to appear before them, five regional courts were established by this legislation;[58] if a local court certified that it was powerless to compel a particular person to appear before it, the case was transferred to one of the regional courts.

Numerous enactments dealt with assessment of taxes, methods of tax collection, and safeguarding the proceeds of such collections. Other enactments prescribed severe punishments for offenders in commercial matters,

54. The Hebrew translated here as "penalties . . . imposed on you" is *lehassi'a al kiẓatkhem. Cf.* TB Bava Batra 8b, which uses the same expression in regard to enactments of the townspeople. *See supra* p. 679.

55. *Cf.* TB Avodah Zarah 36a. *See supra* pp. 762–763.

56. *See Leket Yosher,* YD, pp. 77–79, where this responsum is quoted with certain v.l. *See also Resp. Maharam Mintz* #63; Finkelstein, *Self-Government,* p. 77.

57. The original text of these enactments was published in 1897 in M. Horovitz, *Die Frankfurter Rabbinerversammlung von Jahre 1603* [The Frankfurt Rabbinical Synod of 1603]; Finkelstein, *Self-Government,* pp. 257–264, contains a summary of the enactments; and a small portion of them was printed in Assaf, *Battei ha-Din,* pp. 109–110. *See also* M. Horovitz, *Rabbanei Frankfurt* [Frankfurt's Rabbis], Heb. trans., Jerusalem, 1972, pp. 29ff.

58. Regional courts were established in Frankfurt, Worms, Fulda, Friedburg, and Ginzburg.

e.g., counterfeiters, forgers, receivers of stolen property, purchasers of merchandise who did not pay the correct price, and usurers. A special enactment prohibited a rabbi or the head of a court (*av bet din*) from exercising jurisdiction over communities within the jurisdiction of a different rabbi or court. Another series of enactments regulated the slaughter of animals by authorized slaughterers, precluded the appointment of a rabbi without the consent of the heads of three *yeshivot* (academies), prohibited extravagant dress and the wearing of ritually prohibited clothing (*sha'atnez, i.e.*, mixture of linen and wool), etc. This is a comprehensive collection of laws reminiscent of the wide-ranging legislation by Rabbenu Gershom and the legislation during the twelfth and thirteenth centuries in Germany.

The degree of halakhic authority and the commanding leadership exercised by this synod is evidenced by the drastic sanctions for violation of the enactments. The sanction against one who violates the provisions as to payment of taxes is typical:

> All sums determined by us shall be collected each year, and each person shall pay the sum assessed against him. The name of any Jew who fails to pay his share and who disobeys the community's agent shall be publicized in every community in Germany.
>
> The announcement shall take this form: "The following who are mentioned by name have been separated from the rest of the community of this diaspora. Neither they nor their children may mingle or intermarry with us. No person may conduct a marriage ceremony for them. If anyone transgresses this directive and does enter into a marriage with them, whether willingly or under compulsion, that marriage is null and void."

This far-reaching provision nullifying marriages entered into in violation of the provisions of the enactment evidences recognition of the strength of the position and authority of those who enacted this legislation.[59] However, this was the last great synod held within the original boundaries of Germany. Since that time, although there were enactments by halakhic authorities in various communities, there is no longer evidence

59. *See infra* pp. 846–879. *But see*, for a view that the enactment was less far-reaching, Freimann, *Kiddushin ve-Nissu'in*, p. 217 (following Horovitz, *supra* n. 57 at 28–29):

> At the conclusion of the enactments, they noted: "The word *le-ḥuppah* [nuptial ceremony] is inserted between the lines, and the word *le-kiddushin* [marriage, technically "betrothal"] is crossed out." The reason why *le-kiddushin* was crossed out is clearly so that it should not be mistakenly thought that a wife in such a case is permitted to marry another man without first obtaining a divorce. The correction reveals that the halakhic authorities of that time were not prepared to annul the marriage, but they did create a new sanction: "the invalidation of the nuptial ceremony," *i.e.*, the children of those who disobeyed the enactment would carry the stigma of being "children of fornication" [in that the nuptial ceremony was not valid]. However, the validity of the marriage and the personal status of the couple would not be affected.

of any collection of laws or legislative synods in Germany similar to the synod of Frankfurt of 1603. The Jewish center in Germany gradually declined and was replaced by the center in Poland and adjacent areas.

B. Spain and North Africa

1. LEGISLATION BY LOCAL COMMUNITIES: TOLEDO AND MOLINA

As a result of various external and internal factors, legislation by countrywide councils occurred later in Spain than in Germany. From the eleventh to the thirteenth centuries, there were countrywide legislative synods in Germany, but there is no evidence of anything comparable from that period in Spain.[60]

On the other hand, the Jewish communities in Spain developed during this period a broad and comprehensive autonomy that resulted in the creation of an extremely elaborate body of local legislation in all areas of Jewish law. This legislation included not only enactments by the halakhic authorities but also a considerable amount of legislation by the public in the form of communal enactments. The preceding chapter contains many examples of such communal legislation in the Spanish center, and additional illustrations are discussed below. This communal legislation often had an influence far beyond the boundaries of the enacting community; and enactments were often accepted by nearby[61] and even by distant communities.

An example of the influence of legislation beyond the boundaries of the enacting community is provided by the enactments adopted in the thirteenth century[62] in Toledo, the capital of Castile, and in Molina.[63] These enactments include important provisions limiting a husband's rights of inheritance in his wife's property,[64] similar to the *takkanot* of "Shum"; their contents will be discussed below. These enactments were first adopted only for the community of Toledo and its environs[65] and were afterward accepted

60. *See* Baer, *Spain,* I, pp. 213–215; Finkelstein, *Self-Government,* pp. 99–101.

61. In various localities, the smaller communities were subject to the authority of major communities nearby; *see, e.g., Resp. Rashba,* III, #411. *See also supra* pp. 669–670; Baer, *Spain,* I, pp. 216–217.

62. *See infra* p. 839 and n. 217.

63. In *Resp. Asheri* 55:1–3 and 55:5, the enactments are called "the enactments of Toledo," and in *id.* 55:7–8, "the enactments of Molina." It is possible that they were first adopted in Toledo and later followed in Molina with certain changes.

64. *Resp. Asheri* 55:1–3, 5, 7–8; *Tur* EH ch. 118.

65. *See Tum'at Yesharim* #173 in the name of Joseph Taitazak; quoted in *Keneset ha-Gedolah,* EH, Haggahot ha-Tur, 118, subpar. 47:

> The enactment of Toledo applies to Toledo and its environs. If it is followed in another town where the enactment was not adopted, that is a mistaken practice. But it is not

in many, although not all, Spanish communities.[66] In the wake of the Toledo enactments, similar legislation was adopted, with certain changes, in many Jewish communities in Greece, Algeria and other areas of North Africa, Syria, and the Land of Israel.[67]

2. COUNTRYWIDE LEGISLATION

In the fourteenth century, Spanish Jewry, led by the communities in the kingdom of Castile, organized inter-communal associations. Although there is little evidence from this period itself of this type of inter-communal organization, there is substantial information from the fifteenth century that establishes that these associations existed as early as the fourteenth century.[68] In the aftermath of the difficult times European Jews lived through in the middle of the fourteenth century as a result of the plague of the Black Death and the ensuing pogroms against the Jews, an inter-communal synod was also convened in the kingdom of Aragon. One of the major objectives of such countrywide bodies and synods was to adopt legislation necessitated by the changing times and circumstances. The enactments of two countrywide synods, one in Aragon in 1354 and the other in Castile in 1432, are two significant examples.

3. ENACTMENTS OF THE ARAGONIAN COMMUNITIES, 1354

The severe pogroms against the Jews of Spain following the plague of the Black Death broke out first in Aragon. In 1354, in an effort to create an organization to represent all of the Jews in the kingdom of Aragon, representatives of all of the communities in Catalonia and the region of Valencia gathered in Barcelona. This assembly produced a broad range of enactments. The introduction to the legislation[69] describes the difficult situation of the Jewish communities and the need for organizing to defend against attack:

> a mistaken practice if they wrote [*i.e.*, if the custom of the community was to write, *e.g.*, in a *ketubbah*] that the practice of Toledo should govern the matter and they [the community] in fact apply that practice to their cases. However, even if they wrote that the practice of Toledo should govern, if they do not in fact apply it to their cases, then their own practice will govern.

See further id., subpar. 48.

66. In Valencia, for example, a century later, in the days of Ribash, the Toledo enactment was not followed. *See Resp. Ribash* #105.

67. *See infra* pp. 838–840. Another example is the series of enactments adopted in 1327 in Barcelona, which were later accepted in Valencia (1364) and Heusca (1374). *See Resp. Ribash* #214, #228; Baer, *Spain* (Heb. ed.), pp. 240–241.

68. *See* Baer, *Spain*, I, pp. 314–315.

69. *See* text of enactments in Finkelstein, *Self-Government*, pp. 328–347; Baer, *Spain*, I, pp. 24–28, and sources cited in n. 30 at p. 522 of the Hebrew edition of *Spain*.

> We have seen the weakness of the communities and that each acting alone cannot achieve what is essential for it or succeed in sustaining itself. If the communities will not help one another to heal the sick of their wounds, then we fear that we shall become defenseless. . . .
>
> We have agreed to unite as one and to act jointly with respect to all of the agreements, enactments, and safeguards that are written in this book, from the day that we receive the authority and permission from our Master, the King.[70]

Part of the legislation concerned the relations between the Jewish communities and the central government. Some of the enactments dealt with the consequences of the pogroms against the Jews, matters concerning the Inquisition, and the return of stolen Jewish property. Other enactments placed a severe ban on informers. There was legislation to establish a common fund for all the communities to help pay taxes, and another series of enactments formulated various proposals to be brought before the central government with regard to such matters as the payment of taxes and the procedure to be adopted in prosecutions against Jews.

Another part of the legislation, dealing with the establishment of internal rules governing the administration of communal affairs, has been lost, and details of its provisions are unknown.[71]

4. ENACTMENTS OF THE CASTILIAN COMMUNITIES AT VALLADOLID, 1432

In 1432, Don Abraham Benveniste, who was rabbi of all the Castilian communities and who had been appointed Court Rabbi (*Rab de la Corte*) and Chief Justice as well as tax superintendent for the Castilian Jewish communities, convened the representatives and halakhic authorities of these communities in the city of Valladolid, where the king's court was then located. This synod adopted a full array of enactments covering all areas of legal and religious life; it is the most comprehensive known collection of legislation up to that time. The collection has been preserved in its entirety in a language that combines Hebrew and Castilian.[72] It is divided into five parts, and the major portion of the legislation deals with legal subjects.

70. Finkelstein, *Self-Government,* pp. 329–330.

71. *Id.* at 101–102.

72. The original text of the enactments is found in Y. Baer, *Die Juden im Christlichen Spanien, Urkunden und Regesten* [The Jews in Christian Spain: Documents and Government Records], Part I, vol. II, pp. 280–298; *see also supra* pp. 8–9, 25–26. For an English translation, *see* Finkelstein, *Self-Government,* pp. 348–375. Our quotations *infra* are a free translation. For a description of this collection, *see* Baer, *Spain,* I, pp. 315ff., 444; II, pp. 260–270.

a. THE EDUCATIONAL SYSTEM: ORGANIZATION AND FINANCING

The first part of the Valladolid enactments concerns the study of Torah. It contains extensive provisions for indirect taxes from the slaughter of animals, from the sale of wine and other items, and from weddings and other festive occasions. The proceeds of the taxes were to be set aside to support teachers of young children and scholars ("teachers of Torah") who would teach "Talmud, *halakhot,* and *aggadot.*" Each one of these scholars was to maintain "a permanent academy to study with anyone desirous of learning *Halakhah* from him." It was forbidden to divert the funds raised by these taxes to any use other than the study and dissemination of Torah.

There are also provisions concerning the relation between the size of the community and the number of students, teachers of young children, and heads of academies (*roshei ha-yeshivah*), and the determination of reasonable compensation for the teachers of young children and the teachers of Torah.

b. APPOINTMENT OF JUDGES AND OTHER PUBLIC OFFICIALS; JUDICIAL AUTHORITY; CIVIL AND CRIMINAL PROCEDURE

The second part of the Valladolid legislation deals mainly with the judicial system. Judges were required to be appointed in every community "to adjudicate claims, contentions, and complaints, and to punish transgressions."[73] The legislation governs such matters as the method of appointing judges, their terms of office and jurisdiction, the times of regular court sessions, and the power to issue process to compel appearance by the parties. This second part also deals with the methods of appointing other public officials of the community.

There are special provisions regarding suits against judges. Such suits were to be heard by other judges from the same community or from nearby communities. In every case, a community could request the Court Rabbi to convene a special court when "the community feels that it does not want to entrust the differences arising among them to their own judges." A duty is imposed on the community scribe to hear and record the evidence given against a judge.

Detailed provisions deal with civil and criminal procedure and representation by an attorney. The following are some examples.

The provision concerning written pleadings states:

73. The enactments emphasized that although the judges often were not versed in Jewish law, nevertheless the most fitting and honest men in the community should be chosen and the case should be submitted to them rather than to non-Jewish courts; *see supra* pp. 25–26.

> If we permit any party to put his claim in writing and submit the document to the court, he would probably write more than is necessary, and perhaps even vilify his opponent. This would prolong litigation and increase costs. Since those who instruct others to plead in ways well-known are included among those to whom the saying applies that "he who teaches another how to plead injures the community," and "he who teaches them to plead falsely is a sinner,"[74] we have agreed and ordered that no party shall submit written pleadings unless he receives permission from the local judge.
>
> Even when a local judge grants such permission, the pleading must be properly worded, without insults or injurious expressions against anyone, and must be signed by the person who drafted it; and the person submitting it shall state under oath that it was drafted by the person who signed it and that no one else drafted it for him. Any pleading that does not conform to these rules will not be accepted by the judge.

Concerning representation by an attorney:

> We ordain that without written permission from the court no one shall advise a litigant how to present his arguments. Whoever does so without the court's permission, unless he is a relative of a party,[75] shall no longer receive any stipend from the Talmud Torah Fund if he is a scholar; and if the pleadings suggested by him are false, he shall be proclaimed "a counselor of evil." If he does not receive any such stipend, he shall be fined such amount as appears to the court and to the rabbi to be just.

This enactment thus laid down two procedural rules:

a. No written pleading was to be submitted unless permission to do so had been obtained from the court. If permission was given, the written pleading had to be worded with propriety, and signed by the person who drafted it. As a general rule, claims were to be made and argued orally.
b. Special written permission of the court had to be obtained for giving legal advice and for the right to act as an attorney.

The objective of these provisions was to eliminate the provocative language and false claims that had been proliferating in written pleadings; such practices can be more effectively curbed if only oral pleadings are permitted. Attorneys played a prominent role in the events leading to this enactment; hence the limitation on their activity.

The following is representative of the enactment concerning the right of appeal:

74. *See* M Avot 1:8 and Maimonides' commentary, *ad loc.*
75. *See* TB Ketubbot 52b, 86a.

> On request of a party, every judge must allow an appeal from his decision to the Court Rabbi to be filed within a reasonable time. The appellant shall give security guaranteeing that he will pay the costs of the litigation, and he shall take an oath that he is appealing because he believes the judgment was in error and that the appeal is not taken to delay enforcement of the judgment.[76]

Another rule, in the area of criminal procedure, provided:

> We ordain that no judge may order the arrest of any Jew or Jewess except by written warrant signed by the judge and by two witnesses. Except in cases involving an accusation of having been an informer (*malshinut*) [see the discussion immediately following] or of a capital offense, the judge shall state the specific grounds for the issuance of the warrant.

c. ENACTMENTS CONCERNING INFORMERS AND THE RELATION BETWEEN THE GOVERNMENT AND THE JEWS

The third part of the enactments of Valladolid begins with an introduction describing the broad judicial autonomy conferred upon the Jewish communities in matters of civil, criminal, and public law.[77] This introduction leads into and explains the succeeding enactments, which prohibit resort to a non-Jewish court and which vest broad jurisdiction in the Jewish court, even to the extent of passing a death sentence against informers.

The first enactment strictly forbids resort to "any other judge, ecclesiastic or secular, who is not of our faith," even if the case is to be decided under Jewish law, unless the defendant has a violent disposition and has three times refused to appear before the Jewish court, in which case the plaintiff may obtain an order permitting suit to be filed in a non-Jewish court. The ban on anyone who wrongfully resorts to a non-Jewish court entails the prohibition of any commercial dealings with him, the barring of his burial among Jews, etc.

Other enactments include various provisions with regard to marriage, such as the prohibition of marriages resulting from fraud or duress;[78] the requirement that a marriage must take place "in the presence of ten adult Jewish males, one of whom is a relative of the bride, and if the father or brother of the bride is in the locality, one of them must be present and give consent; and the cantor must also be present and recite the betrothal ben-

76. Appellate review of lower court decisions developed in the diaspora in the post-Talmudic period. *See* Assaf, *Battei ha-Din,* pp. 74ff., and *supra* p. 743 and n. 242. Appeals were first incorporated as an integral part of the Jewish legal system in 1921, through legislation by the Chief Rabbinate of the Land of Israel. *See infra* pp. 824–826 and n. 171; pp. 1809–1818.

77. *See supra* p. 8.

78. *See infra* pp. 847–856.

edictions." Various criminal sanctions were imposed on violators of these provisions.

Another section forbids resorting to the government in order to obtain a particular office in the Jewish community or to attempt to compel someone to perform a particular act. Other sections deal with commerce in wine.

The provision that confers judicial authority to punish informers is particularly noteworthy. Enactments against informers are frequently found in post-Talmudic legislation.[79] In a substantial part of the diaspora, courts were even authorized to impose the death penalty on informers, as is evidenced by a responsum of Asheri written some 150 years before the legislation of Valladolid:

> It is the practice throughout the diaspora that when there is a confirmed informer who has three times betrayed Jews or their property to a non-Jew, ways and means are sought to execute him [lit. "remove him from the world"] as a protective measure and to deter others so as to prevent the proliferation of informers among the Jews and to save all the Jews who would be persecuted because of him.
>
> Therefore, in this case where witnesses testified that he is a confirmed informer and slanderer and they were also present at the time he in fact informed and slandered, the decision to sentence him to death by hanging is a correct one. So shall all the enemies of God be destroyed. . . .[80]

The enactments of Valladolid confirmed this kind of authority for passing the death sentence at a time when the yoke of the gentile government over the Jewish people of Spain was becoming increasingly heavy:

> A Jew or Jewess who slanders another Jew or Jewess in a manner that is likely to cause harm if heard by the Christians shall be fined one hundred gold pieces and shall be imprisoned for ten days for each act of slander, even though no Christian was present at the time of the slander and no harm was

79. *See supra* pp. 11, 531.

80. *Resp. Asheri* 17:1. Our text follows ed. Constantinople, 1517, which is the same as ed. Venice, 1552, ed. Venice, 1607, and ed. Zolkiew, 1803. In the two latter editions, instead of the word "non-Jew" (*goy*), the Hebrew abbreviation for "idol worshipper" is used. In ed. Vilna, 1885, the text is significantly different. In place of "non-Jew" the reading is "extorters"; instead of "remove him from the world," the text states, "punish him"; in place of "to sentence him to death by hanging," the reading is, "to sentence him to be punished." These changes were made in order to satisfy the censor.

The text of the query submitted to Asheri states: "Now the Jews have been secretly given permission by the king to judge him [the informer], and if he is found guilty [ed. Venice, 1607, and ed. Zolkiew state: "liable for the death penalty"], to execute him." This passage was retained even in ed. Vilna, 1885, and also demonstrates that the matter under discussion was the death penalty; however, the part of the response which indicated that infliction of the death penalty on informers was a widespread practice approved by Asheri was changed.

in fact caused. If any harm has been caused to a fellow Jew, the slanderer must pay damages to compensate for all the harm caused by him.

If any Jew betrays the person or property of a Jew or Jewess to a Christian man or woman, and his guilt is not clearly established by witnesses but appears only by circumstantial evidence, the local judges, with the counsel of the town rabbi, shall order his apprehension and shall punish him as deemed appropriate by the greatest halakhic scholars that can be found [*i.e.*, even if there is no clear testimony that the alleged informer is guilty, but only circumstantial evidence against him, he must be punished if in the opinion of the local halakhic authorities the suspicion is well grounded].

If the guilt of the informer is proved by two witnesses, he shall receive one hundred lashes for the first offense and be banished from the place of the offense, in accordance with the decision of the rabbi, the judges, and the communal leaders; for a third offense, the Court Rabbi may order him to be put to death, in accordance with Jewish law, through the legal officials of the king [*i.e.*, for commission of the offense three times, the Jewish Chief Justice may impose the death penalty, which is to be carried out by the king's officers].

d. ENACTMENTS CONCERNING TAX LAW

The fourth part of the legislation of Valladolid includes various enactments concerning tax law. It contains provisions prohibiting tax exemptions from being obtained without the consent of the Court Rabbi; prescribing the procedure for the appeal of tax assessments; specifying the categories of those for whom the tax burden should be lightened (*e.g.*, orphans and widows); prescribing regulations to enable all members of the community to participate in communal meetings at which rules governing tax assessments and distribution of tax proceeds are adopted; and providing that "any enactment or agreement not adopted either by the entire community or by or with the consent of a majority is void."

e. ENACTMENTS OUTLAWING EXTRAVAGANCE IN DRESS AND FESTIVE BANQUETS

The fifth part of the legislation of Valladolid includes enactments, similar to the enactments found in most Jewish centers in the diaspora, aimed against extravagant dress and festive banquets.[81] One enactment prohibits the wearing of extravagant clothing made of silk and fine dyed linen (*argaman*), as well as the wearing of gold and silver jewelry, and it lists in great detail the types of prohibited dress and jewelry. The prohibition does not apply to single women or to women during their first year of marriage.

81. *See infra* pp. 809, 814–815, 820.

Another enactment prohibits the wearing of extravagant clothing by men. This prohibition does not apply to times of joyous celebration or similar occasions.

Another enactment requires every community to enact detailed regulations within thirty days to limit the amount spent on festive banquets and similar affairs to sums consistent with the financial condition of the community's members. The purpose of this legislation, as therein stated, was to prevent the people from becoming mired in debt and to forestall jealousy and hatred on the part of non-Jews.

We have described in some detail this instructive collection of communal enactments of the Jews of Castile in the mid-fifteenth century since these enactments not only reflect the condition of the life of this Jewish community in this period, but "a good deal could doubtless be learned from them regarding not only the conditions prevailing at the time of their adoption, but also the organization of the Castilian communities in the days of their past glory—especially in the fourteenth century."[82]

5. ENACTMENTS OF THE NORTH AFRICAN CENTER

One of the oldest Jewish centers is that in North Africa.[83] Its halakhic authorities and leaders also asserted administrative as well as spiritual influence over Spanish Jewry in the tenth and eleventh centuries.[84] While it may be assumed that there was communal legislation in this center at that time, such material in the halakhic and historical literature remains to be researched. We here examine two collections extant from a later period: the first is from the end of the fourteenth century, and the second includes a series of enactments beginning at the end of the fifteenth century.

a. ALGERIAN ENACTMENTS, 1394

In 1391, the Jews of Spain suffered "severe persecution . . . in which Jews were attacked and murdered . . . and the year was identified as the year of 'the jealous God.'"[85] This was the harsh beginning that foreshadowed the complete destruction of the Spanish Jewish center one hundred years later, in 1492.[86] As a result of the events of 1391, two of Spain's lead-

82. Baer, *Spain,* II, p. 261.

83. *See* H.Z. Hirschberg, *Toledot ha-Yehudim be-Afrikah ha-Ẓefonit* [History of the Jews of North Africa], Jerusalem, 1962.

84. *See* Baer, *Spain,* I, pp. 27ff.; Hirschberg, *supra* n. 83 at I, 235, 241ff., 260ff; *infra* pp. 1476–1479.

85. *Sefer Yuḥasin ha-Shalem,* p. 225. The word "jealous" (*kana*) indicates the date—1391: the numerical value of the letters of the Hebrew word *kana* signifies the Hebrew year 5151 A.M. which corresponds to 1391 C.E.

86. For the events of 1391, *see* Baer, *Spain,* II, pp. 95ff.

ing halakhic authorities migrated to Algeria: Isaac b. Sheshet Perfet (Ribash) and Simeon b. Ẓemaḥ Duran (Rashbeẓ), the younger of the two, who was the author of *Resp. Tashbeẓ.* In 1394, twelve enactments were adopted in the community of Algiers, dealing mainly with family law and the law of succession.[87] Among the enactors of the legislation were the two above-mentioned authorities, together with a third, Isaac Bonstrok:[88]

> After they adopted them [the enactments] with the agreement of the said community leaders and the counsel of the rabbis, the cantor proclaimed them in the synagogue in the presence of the entire community on the sabbath before taking the scroll of the Torah out of the ark, and not a single person objected. . . . This took place here in the city of Algiers.[89]

Almost thirty years later, Rashbeẓ again recorded the enactments, adding a detailed commentary. He explained his reason for doing so—of all the scholars who participated in the adoption of the enactments, he alone was still alive:

> I was the youngest of them all, and they authorized me to draft them as I thought best; and I did so and they agreed with me. I conferred with them on all that is written above as to each enactment. I have therefore written all of this to clarify and elucidate the intended meaning of the enactments and their basis in the Talmud, in order to remove doubts and uncertainties on the part of the judges who will make decisions on the basis of these enactments, since some questions brought to me by the other communities that accepted them indicate some disagreement as to their meaning.[90]

The enactments established, *inter alia:* the minimum sum for the optional increment to the prescribed amount of the *ketubbah;* the law relating to the increment and also to the additional "special gift" contained in the *ketubbah* in the event of divorce or the husband's death;[91] a limitation on

87. *Resp. Tashbeẓ,* II, #292, *tikkun* 12.

88. *Resp. Tashbeẓ,* II, #103.

89. *Resp. Tashbeẓ, supra* n. 87.

90. *Id.* The responsum concludes: "I wrote this entire document in Algiers in Iyyar, 5181 A.M. [1421 C.E.], after I had become sixty years of age." As stated, the drafting of the enactments was entrusted to Rashbeẓ. *See also Resp. Tashbeẓ,* II, #103: "They turned to me to put those enactments into proper form . . . and my whole aim was to keep the legislation close to Talmudic law, with only narrow deviations in regard to the law of inheritance, and to maintain the rights of the husband and his heirs." *See infra.*

91. As to the "deed of special gift," *see* J.N. Epstein, "Shetar Mattanah le-Ḥud ve-ha-Ẓedak" [The Deed of Special Gift and the *Ẓedak*], *Ha-Mishpat Ha-Ivri,* IV, pp. 125–134. As to the meaning of the document called *Ẓedak, see id.* at 131 n. 26.

the husband's right to inherit his wife's estate;[92] and an authorization to the heirs to pay a widow the amount of her *ketubbah* after the expiration of three months from the death of her husband, thus precluding any claim for her maintenance from that time forward, unless her husband had directed that she was to be maintained from the assets of the estate.[93] The enactments provided that no dispute between a husband and wife may be brought before a non-Jewish court,[94] and also that the provisions of the legislation apply prospectively to those who marry after the adoption of the enactments but not retroactively to those who married before the enactments were adopted.[95] The right was reserved to a husband and wife to agree on terms contrary to those provided in the legislation. Soon afterward, the Algerian enactments were accepted in Tunis and other African communities.[96]

b. ENACTMENTS OF FEZ

There is extant a large and comprehensive compilation of about 250 enactments that were adopted, starting at the end of the fifteenth century,

92. For detailed discussion, *see infra* pp. 838–840.

93. *Cf. supra* pp. 573–574, the difference of opinion between the Judeans and Galileans as to whether the husband's heirs may compel his widow to accept the amount of her *ketubbah* in full satisfaction of all her claims against his estate. *See Resp. Tashbeẓ,* II, #292, *tikkun* 7, which (echoing the comment in TJ that the Judeans held that the heirs can force the widow to accept payment of her *ketubbah* and thus free themselves from the obligation to support her, because "they were concerned about their money and not about their honor") concludes that "in this enactment they [the enactors] have revealed that they are concerned about their money." *See also,* on this Algerian enactment, *Resp. Ribash* #107. There had already been an attempt in Spain to limit the widow's rights in a similar manner, but Judah b. Asher (the son of Asheri) had vehemently opposed it; *see Resp. Zikhron Yehudah* #78. *See also* Assaf, *supra* n. 25 at 86–87 and n. 7.

94. *See Resp. Tashbeẓ,* II, #292, *tikkun* 8, explaining the need for this particular enactment notwithstanding the general rule that no dispute between Jews may be brought before non-Jewish courts:

> There is no doubt that resort to non-Jewish courts, even if their laws are the same as ours, is a transgression for which one is punished by being placed under a ban. Such resort is forbidden even if both parties agree to the application of non-Jewish law; and they must be stopped, as indeed the *rishonim* have written. However, this enactment states this explicitly because, as is well known, a husband is in a stronger position than his wife; and she may, therefore, ally herself with non-Jews who will want the matter litigated in their courts. Therefore, this enactment comes to place a ban on such behavior.

95. *Id., tikkun* 9 and 11. *Tikkun* 9 provided that these enactments were to be in effect for twenty years and "thereafter for so long as there was no agreement to repeal them"; not only were they not repealed after that time, but they were even accepted by many other communities.

96. *See, e.g., Resp. Ribash* #110; *Resp. Tashbeẓ,* II, #265, III, #73, #303; *Resp. Rashbash* #78; *Resp. Yakhin u-Vo'az,* II, #12. *See also* Assaf, *supra* n. 25 at 87 nn. 4 and 5; I. Epstein, *The Responsa of Rabbi Simon b. Zemah Duran,* 1930 (Jews' College Publications, No. 13), pp. 84–87.

in Morocco. With the massive and final expulsion of the Jews from Spain at the end of the fifteenth century, the Spanish Jews turned in different directions, eastward and westward, to build new settlements. Once again, one of these places of asylum was North Africa—particularly, Morocco.[97] Here too, the result was the same as in all other places where the Spanish exiles struck new roots: a conflict between the customs, lifestyles, and traditions of the "new immigrants," *i.e.*, the Spanish exiles, and the long-time residents of the locality.[98] The newcomers, who excelled the local Jewish inhabitants in general and cultural attainments, within a short time left their imprint on the character of the entire Jewish community of Morocco.

One of the outstanding illustrations of this development is the legislation enacted by the rabbis and leaders of the communities of the exiles in Fez, Morocco, acting in conjunction with the local halakhic authorities, that was ultimately accepted as binding on all the Jews of Morocco:

> After the settlement of the exiled rabbis in Fez, as soon as they recovered from the travails of their wanderings and hardships, they turned their attention to the regulation of the affairs of their community, which became a unique and outstanding community, possessing great influence and power. They set forth in a special book, as a permanent record, all of the enactments of the exiled rabbis that were adopted to strengthen the faith and promote the public welfare. This was "The Book of the *Takkanot* of the Holy Community of the Exiles and Their Leaders in Fez," which afterward became the cornerstone of Jewish life in Morocco as a whole, and the code of law on which everyone relied.
>
> This book of enactments includes all of the legislation adopted by the leaders of a number of successive generations over approximately two hundred years (1494–1700), and was the basis for the decisions in most of the disputes and religious controversies among the Jews of Morocco, notwithstanding possible disagreement by some of the more famous authorities with [rulings contained in] it. In most situations, the rabbis of the exiles tended in their book of *takkanot* to be extremely lenient. . . . [99]

We owe our knowledge of the contents of this book of *takkanot* to Abraham Ankawa, one of the outstanding judges of Moroccan Jewry in the middle of the nineteenth century.[100] The enactments cover wide areas of

97. *See* I.M. Toledano, *Ner ha-Ma'arav, Toledot Yisra'el be-Marokko* [The Light of the West: A History of the Jews in Morocco], pp. 49–71 (which presents a detailed description of the early absorption of the Spanish exiles in Morocco); Hirschberg, *supra* n. 83 at 298ff.

98. The same conflict had also occurred when the Spanish emigrants arrived in Algiers in 1391; *see* Epstein, *supra* n. 96 at 14ff.

99. Toledano, *supra* n. 97 at 69 n. 21 and 77–78. *See* #142 (p. 26a/b) of the enactments (*infra*) as to their wide acceptance in various communities.

100. The Book of *Takkanot* was published in Ankawa's *Kerem Ḥemer,* II, pp. 2–43. The enactments were first transcribed by Jacob ibn Ẓur of North Africa, the author of *Resp. Mishpat u-Ẓedakah be-Ya'akov* in the middle of the eighteenth century; *see Kerem Ḥemer,* II, p. 2.

family law: the marriage ceremony (the required presence of ten people, etc., with violators subject to imprisonment); the amount, the writing, and the collection of the *ketubbah;* the *moredet;* spousal and child support (support for a divorcee until her *ketubbah* has been paid);[101] polygamy (various limitations on polygamy);[102] levirate marriages; engagements; and the *agunah.*

A large number of enactments deal with questions of inheritance: the right of a widow in her husband's estate,[103] restriction of the right of a husband to inherit his wife's property,[104] equalization of sons and daughters in regard to the right of inheritance under particular circumstances,[105] many details concerning the drafting of wills, and a specification of assets that are and are not subject to testamentary disposition. Other enactments regulate the laws of guardianship of minors. A substantial portion of the legislation deals with various aspects of the laws of acquisition and obligations: leases, pledges, commercial transactions, rights of adjoining property owners, loans, measures against those who fraudulently conceal assets, imprisonment for debt, etc.

A particularly noteworthy enactment outlaws the formation of cartels and monopolies:[106]

> Associations have been organized under the laws of partnership consisting of three or four people. . . . Their entire aspiration and desire is to "cast up a mound and to build a bulwark" to consume the poor and the needy, and the plague has become "streaky green or red,"[107] persecuting the unfortunate poor and depriving them of their livelihood. For they [the monopolists] have taken counsel and conspired against them [the poor], and there is not enough

On pp. 33d–36a, there is a brief compilation of enactments by Raphael Berdugo, a leading North African halakhic authority of the latter half of the eighteenth century, which contains a short summary of the main points of some of the enactments. For a detailed discussion, *see* Elon, *Yiḥudah Shel Halakhah,* p. 19. *See further* Elon, *Ḥerut,* Index. *Kerem Ḥemer* (pp. 43c–63d) also contains a complete collection of forms of various legal instruments, called *Et Sofer. See infra* p. 1539.

101. *E.g.,* #65 (p. 10d), #98 (p. 19c).

102. *E.g.,* #36, #37, #39 (pp. 6c–7b).

103. *E.g.,* #4, #5 (p. 2b/c). Here, the widow does not collect the amount of her *ketubbah. See also infra* pp. 835–836, 841–842.

104. #2, #3, #4 (p. 2b/c) and #19 (p. 3d). These enactments follow those of Toledo and Algiers (*see supra* pp. 796–797, 805–806 and *infra* pp. 835–840) with certain changes for the benefit of the wife.

105. *E.g.,* #8 (p. 2c/d). For further discussion, *see infra* pp. 842–846.

106. #173 (p. 31b).

107. The allusion is to Leviticus 13:49: "if the infection . . . is streaky green (*yerakrak*) or red (*adamdam*)," the Hebrew of which is given a metaphorical interpretation: "And the green (*yerak*) will be desolate (*rak*) [or empty (*reik*)] and humankind (*adam*) will be blood (*dam*)."

> room to record the devices of oppression. The cries of the poor for help have ascended to God, and we have adopted an enactment that is recorded herein. . . . They [the monopolists] will surely be punished in the manner agreed upon by the court and the communal leaders, may the Lord protect them.

These enactments, like those of other centers, contain much detail on tax law. Many of the enactments deal with the prohibition against resorting to non-Jewish courts, although one enactment provides that "every lien or sale transcribed by a Jewish scribe must also be recorded in the non-Jewish courts. . . . The same applies to joint ownership of land . . . and to leases of land."[108] This conformed to the practice in many centers that in matters involving land, the requirements of the laws of the general government as well as of Jewish law had to be complied with.[109] In these enactments, too, there is a continual emphasis on the prohibition against extravagant festive banquets, jewelry, etc.

The social background of these enactments, described in the following quotation,[110] reflects a condition common to various centers:

> WHEREAS the demands of our neighbors in tax matters have enormously increased, and the "gates of influence" are very hard to open, and we have noted that people, hard-pressed and lacking in influence as they are, feel obligated to make extravagant expenditures for festive banquets—whether they are poor or rich—and they borrow on interest in order to limit the immediate outlay, because they see others who preen themselves and spend without limit; and
>
> WHEREAS the result has been that even those who are pressed for a livelihood suffer losses and make extravagant expenditures in order to appear equal to those who are more well-to-do;
>
> NOW THEREFORE, in order to limit extravagance and to benefit the entire community, we have seen fit to enact. . . .

This enactment and others[111] prescribe many details concerning the number of guests, the size of the festive meals, the wearing of jewelry, etc.

C. The Mediterranean Countries and Italy

1. ENACTMENTS OF MAIMONIDES IN EGYPT

From various literary sources, especially the different types of halakhic literature, some conclusions may be drawn about legislative activity in the

108. #52 (p. 9b).
109. *See supra* p. 17.
110. #45 (p. 8a/b).
111. *E.g.*, #81 (p. 14a/b), #92 (p. 17c/d), #94 (p. 18a/b). As to the Fez enactments generally, *see* Elon, *Ḥerut*, pp. 164–167, 216, 218, 225; *id.*, *Yiḥudah Shel Halakhah*, pp. 19ff.

Jewish centers of the Mediterranean countries, among which were the earliest and most ancient Jewish centers. One example is the various enactments of Maimonides, revealed by his responsa and other halakhic literature. Maimonides' enactments concerned prayer,[112] the use of the ritual bath,[113] etc.[114] Two of his enactments relate to the law of marriage. The first provides:[115]

> No woman may be married anywhere in Egypt to a foreigner [*i.e.*, a foreign Jew who came to Egypt from a different country] until he brings proof or takes an oath on the Pentateuch that he is unmarried;[116] and if he has a wife, he must divorce her and he may then marry here. A foreigner who marries here may not leave to go to another country even if his wife agrees,[117] until he writes and delivers a divorce to her to be effective at a time agreed on between them—one, two, or three years, but not longer.

The second enactment[118] forbade the men of certain villages "to marry and divorce in those villages except through the offices of the rabbis of the Egyptian villages . . . and we have enacted that anyone who vests authority in an individual who is not competent in the laws of divorce and marriage shall be placed under a ban."[119]

112. Maimonides promulgated an enactment providing that the congregation should not recite the *amidah* prayer in an undertone before the cantor's recitation, but the cantor should say it aloud and the congregation should follow him, in an undertone, word by word. The reason was that otherwise, during the cantor's recitation, the congregation, having finished reciting the *amidah* prayer first, would engage in idle conversation, or otherwise conduct themselves in a manner disrespectful of the sanctity of the synagogue, and it would also be a desecration of God's name before the gentiles. *See Resp. Maimonides*, ed. Blau, #258; *Resp. Radbaz* #1165. *See also supra* p. 675 n. 34.

113. The enactment provided that after menstruation, a woman should perform ritual ablution according to the *Halakhah* and not according to Karaite law. *See Resp. Maimonides*, ed. Blau, #242; *Resp. Radbaz* #796 (ed. Warsaw, 1882, omitted this responsum from its proper place and published it at the end of the second part of *Resp. Radbaz*).

114. *See* Schepansky, "Takkanot ha-Rishonim," *supra* n. 4 at 154–159.

115. *Resp. Maimonides* #347.

116. *See* TB Yoma 18b and Yevamot 37b:

> R. Eliezer b. Jacob said: "A man should not marry one woman in one country and another woman in another country, lest [the children] marry one another, resulting in a marriage between brother and sister."

This law is codified in Maimonides, *MT*, Issurei Bi'ah 21:29. Maimonides' motive in adopting the enactment was to protect the woman. It should be remembered that in Maimonides' time polygamy was permitted in Egypt.

117. *Cf.* TB Ketubbot 61b *et seq.*; Maimonides, *MT*, Ishut 14:2. *See supra* pp. 787–788.

118. *Resp. Maimonides* #348.

119. *See also Resp. Avraham b. ha-Rambam* #106 (pp. 182–183), quoting this enactment by Maimonides, which was also adopted later in Alexandria, Egypt. For further information about such enactments, *see* Freimann, *Kiddushin ve-Nissu'in*, *passim*, and *infra* pp. 856–860, 869, 874.

2. ENACTMENTS OF CANDIA (CRETE); ENACTMENT FOR THE PROTECTION OF TENANTS

Beginning in the thirteenth century, legislation was adopted by the Jewish community of Candia, the capital of the island of Crete. The island of Crete served as a way station between the European countries and the Land of Israel. From the thirteenth century on, the number of Jews who left France and Germany because of persecutions and set out for the Land of Israel progressively increased;[120] some of them tarried on the way and settled in Crete. As a result, the Jewish community there grew and its legislative activity increased.

The enactments of Candia, contained in a recently published compilation,[121] deal with various matters of *issur* (religious law): sabbath, prayer, kosher food, ritual slaughter, ritual immersion, burial, etc., and with matters of *mishpat ivri:* civil and criminal law, family law, commercial law, public law (laws concerning elections), etc.

The legislation protecting the rights of tenants is illustrative. The first such legislation has been attributed to Rabbenu Gershom[122] and had its background in the living conditions of the Jews in the Middle Ages. Most of the Jews lived on streets and in areas inhabited mainly by Jews, but the houses in which they lived were owned by non-Jews. It often happened that the demand for dwellings in a Jewish neighborhood exceeded the supply and that a Jew would offer to pay the non-Jewish landlord an increase over the current rent in order to induce the landlord to rent the dwelling to him and evict the current tenant. Rabbenu Gershom forbade any Jew to live in a house from which a Jewish tenant had been evicted (except, of course, when the eviction was for nonpayment of rent) for a period of one year after the eviction.

The simplest method would, of course, have been to provide, as current tenant protection laws do, that the landlord may not evict the tenant. However, since the landlord was a non-Jew, the enactment could not prohibit him from evicting the Jew; that objective was achieved indirectly by prohibiting any other Jew from renting the dwelling. From that time on, this enactment reappears in many Jewish centers against the background

120. At the beginning of the thirteenth century, Samson of Sens settled in the Land of Israel at the head of a large group of French and English rabbis; they were followed shortly afterwards by Baruch b. Isaac Ashkenazi, the author of *Sefer ha-Terumah.* In the second half of the thirteenth century, Jehiel of Paris and Naḥmanides moved to the Holy Land; and at the end of that century, Maharam of Rothenburg also set out for the Land of Israel but was captured en route and imprisoned. *See also infra* pp. 1239–1240.

121. Artom-Cassuto, *Takkanot Candia ve-Zikhronotehah* [The Enactments and Annals of Candia], Jerusalem, 1943. *See also* Finkelstein, *Self-Government,* pp. 82–85, 265–280.

122. *See supra* n. 13.

of the same causes and needs. The legislation of Candia is clear and explicit:[123]

> We have agreed and enacted:
>
> From this day forward, no person who bears the name of Jacob and has issued from the waters of Judah[124] shall be permitted for any reason to offer a higher rental to any landlord for any dwelling rented to another, unless the current tenant desires to move and to leave it voluntarily. In addition, if the owner himself, *i.e.*, the landlord, through pretext and cunning, demands that the tenant leave his dwelling, or asks for an increase in the rental to match the amount offered to him by the instigator and forces him to leave his dwelling on the assumption that after a day or two he will rent it to the evildoer who instigated him to evict the man from his home, then in such case our entire community has agreed to, accepted, and enacted under pain of a ban,[125] that for a full year after the eviction, no member of our community may rent the dwelling from which the first tenant was evicted, unless the instigator informs the first tenant of the deceit and the trickery [*i.e.*, unless the new tenant informs the prior tenant that he intends to offer the landlord a greater rental] and compensates him in some way so that the misdeed is expiated and the evicted tenant will be appeased. In such case, he [the new tenant] may remain peacefully in that dwelling.

The punishment of violators of the enactment is then stated:

> However, if, God forbid, there will be a man of evil deeds who delights in wickedness and insolence and violates this enactment in his stubbornness and his contemptible evil-heartedness, we ordain and require the leader of the community[126] or his surrogate among the officers present on that day to gather the entire community together in one of the synagogues, and there reveal his [*i.e.*, the wrongdoer's] wickedness and his evil deed to the entire community. He shall be declared "a breaker of the fence" in Israel; and everyone will thereupon become duty-bound to separate from him, neither participate in his joyous occasions, nor approach him in his mourning, and may Israel have peace.

This enactment is set forth in greater detail and with a more elaborate exposition than the earlier one on the same subject. No Jew is allowed to

123. Artom-Cassuto, *supra* n. 121 at 7–8, and *see also id.* at 6. This enactment is set out in an abridged form among the first ten enactments adopted by Baruch b. Isaac Ashkenazi (*see supra* n. 120) together with the rabbis of Candia; some time later they were reenacted, and this time "Rabbi Ẓedakah, may he live long, restored them to our community."

124. *Cf.* Isaiah 48:1.

125. The Hebrew term used is *berakhah*, lit. "a blessing," here a euphemism for a curse, *i.e.*, a ban.

126. *Kondostavlo*, the title of the head of the community; *see* Artom-Cassuto, *supra* n. 121 at Introduction, p. 11.

offer a higher rental for a dwelling to a landlord if it is occupied by someone else, unless the prior tenant consents to leave voluntarily. If the landlord evicts the tenant against the tenant's will, then for one year after the eviction no Jew is permitted to rent that dwelling. However, if the offeror compensates the prior tenant and the prior tenant leaves of his own free will, the offeror may occupy the dwelling. The end of the enactment sets forth the sanction against Jews who violate its provisions; it is a severe ban—the most effective enforcement measure available to the Jewish community, which lacked external sovereignty and power.[127]

An interesting development occurred in connection with this enactment over three hundred years later in Italy. Among the enactments adopted in Ferrara in 1554 was the following:[128]

> In view of the fact that there are some who transgress the enactment of Rabbenu Gershom concerning the protection of tenants, on the assumption that whenever the owner of the dwelling sells it, the rights of the Jew who lives there are extinguished, we therefore decree that even though the non-Jewish owner sells the dwelling, the rights of the original Jewish tenant are not extinguished but remain as before, and whoever violates this provision transgresses not only this enactment, but also the ban of Rabbenu Gershom.

The objective of this enactment was to expand the rights of the original tenant so that he would not be evicted even if ownership of the dwelling had been transferred. In other words, the right of the tenant was no longer merely personal against a particular landlord, but was a right in the dwelling. It was therefore forbidden for any other Jew to become a tenant in that dwelling until one year had passed from the date of the eviction. It appears that the enactment in its original form was interpreted as being inapplicable if the ownership of the dwelling changed, and landlords (together with the Jews who offered a higher rental) attempted to evade the original enactment by arranging a sale. Consequently, an additional enactment was adopted in Ferrara to close this loophole.

3. ITALY

The legislative activities of the Jewish center in Italy are disclosed by the halakhic and historical literature of Italian Jewry. Beginning with the fifteenth century, enactments were adopted in countrywide synods.

a. ENACTMENTS OF FORLI, 1418

(1) Enactments Concerning Taxes. In 1418, a synod of halakhic authorities and of leaders from various communities of Italy took place in

127. *See supra* pp. 11–12.
128. Finkelstein, *Self-Government,* p. 302.

Forli. One of its major purposes was to regulate the collection of taxes. These taxes were needed for two purposes, as explained in the preamble to the legislation:[129]

> We have realized that we must in any case send to our master, the Pope, the King of the Nations, may he live and his majesty be exalted, a request that he treat our people favorably, issue for our people new privileges and rights, and reaffirm the old rights in accordance with Papal custom; and this should not be delayed, for it was in regard to such things that it has been said "better sooner than later." For this purpose, great expenditures are necessary, as is known to all who are wise. To cover the expenses necessary for this task and for other expenditures needed to improve the condition of the communities mentioned, may God protect them and redeem them, we have decided to levy the following taxes. . . .

The purposes were thus twofold, as was the case for all taxes collected by the Jewish community: first, to pay for obligations to the non-Jewish government, *i.e.*, the Pope, and, second, to defray the costs of the internal services provided by the Jewish community. The enactments covered in detail the methods of the assessment and collection of the taxes.

(2) Prohibition of Games of Chance. Another part of the legislation prohibited "the playing of any game of dice or cards or any other game," with two exceptions involving only small sums of money. Also "on fast days or if, God forbid, a person is sick, it is permitted to play cards to ease the pain, provided that only one *quattrino* is wagered for each person per game." A fine was assessed against any violator of this provision in the amount of "one ducat to be given to the communal treasury for each transgression."[130]

(3) Limits on Luxuries and Extravagant Festive Banquets. Other enactments established limits for ostentatious dress of women and men, imposed a monetary fine on violators, and provided that "men shall be held responsible for their wives." Here, too, there were special provisions against extravagant festive banquets:

> WHEREAS we have seen that those who make weddings and other festive banquets have become haughty and spend more than they can afford and

129. *See* Finkelstein, *Self-Government*, p. 283. The text of the enactments is quoted in *id.* at 282–288; parts of some of these enactments are quoted *infra*.

130. For further details of the Italian enactments prohibiting extravagant festive banquets and games of chance, and limiting luxuries, *see Resp. Ziknei Yehudah*, ed. Simonson, #78 and nn. *ad loc.*

> more than the wealthy of the non-Jews among whom we live, and this causes a loss of money,
>
> WE HAVE THEREFORE ENACTED that from the end of this month of Sivan in the year 5178 A.M. [1418 C.E.] until the end of the year 5186 A.M. [1426 C.E.] . . . no Jew living in the above-mentioned communities may invite to a wedding feast more than twenty men, ten women, and five girls, whether visitors or local residents; but relatives up to and including those of the third generation may be invited without limit, in addition to the above number.

Similar enactments were adopted in connection with other festive occasions, such as circumcision feasts. The sanction prescribed for violation of these directives was:

> Whoever violates any one of the above enactments, and invites more men or women to a wedding or circumcision feast than is permitted, must pay to the community treasury one ducat for each man or woman whom he shall invite beyond the number provided for according to the regulation above set forth.

(4) Sumptuary Legislation. These enactments of Forli are, so far as we know, the first to legislate against vice:

> WHEREAS we have observed that the people are open to sinfulness, swearing vain oaths, engaging in immoral sexual acts even with married women, and paying no heed to the seriousness of the transgression . . . and they believe non-Jewish women to be permitted to them . . . ,
>
> WE HAVE THEREFORE ENACTED that local officials in every town and province shall investigate and search out those guilty of transgressions, vain oaths, or sexual immorality and forewarn them and urge them to repent their sins and resolve to sin no longer. . . . The above officials shall have the power and authority to adopt appropriate regulations to punish the transgressors and return them from their evil ways, whether by monetary penalties or a ban, as they deem necessary for the needs of the time; and the entire population of that town should assist the officials and encourage them and perform whatever they are requested to do.
>
> If the sinner refuses to repent . . . , he shall be removed from his community until he does repent. If he persists, he shall also be removed from the adjoining communities, and thereafter from the distant ones, until he repents or until it becomes clear that [there has been a mistake and] the individual is not a sinner, at which time he shall be brought back among the people and restored to good standing.

At the end of this compilation of enactments, authority is given to every community to enact additional legislation to meet local needs. It is also prescribed that every community must make a copy of the enactments "and place them in the synagogue or in the Ark so that everyone may read them and follow them and no one will be able to say, 'I did not know of it.'"

b. ENACTMENTS OF FLORENCE

Ten years after the enactments of Forli, another synod was held, this time in Florence. Here, too, while the major task was to regulate the collection of taxes to pay the Pope, additional enactments were also adopted in other legal areas. Of these enactments, only one is extant; it deals with the prohibition against usury and spells out the circumstances in which, and the legal transactions to which, this prohibition does not apply.[131]

c. ENACTMENTS OF FERRARA

More than one hundred years later, in 1554, a "general synod" took place in Ferrara,[132] among whose prime movers was Meir Katzenellenbogen (Maharam of Padua). This synod adopted various enactments, some of which are noted in the following discussion.

The invention of printing—and the censorship existing at that time—brought about legislation on these subjects. The first enactment forbids the printing of a previously unpublished book without the consent of three rabbis and communal leaders, whose names were required to appear on the title page of the book.

Another rather unusual enactment deals with the question of suing in non-Jewish courts:

> When anyone in the first instance violates the [Israelite] covenant and sues his fellow Jew in a non-Jewish court without the consent of his community or his community's rabbi and thereafter regrets his act and seeks to sue his fellow under Jewish law, no rabbi or community shall heed his request to require his opponent to appear before the Jewish court.

This enactment is extremely mild in comparison to other enactments prohibiting recourse to non-Jewish courts. As a general rule, the prohibition was absolute, although suits in non-Jewish courts were sometimes permitted if both parties agreed.[133] According to this enactment, if one party sues another in a non-Jewish court, he may no longer change his mind and bring his case before a Jewish judge without the consent of his opponent.[134] This provision can be explained on the basis of the general situation in that

131. Finkelstein, *Self-Government,* pp. 90–92, 295–300.
132. *Id.* at 92–95; the text of the enactments is set forth in *id.* at 300–306.
133. *See supra* pp. 13–18.
134. The enactment does not even limit its applicability to cases where the adverse party has been prejudiced.

period among Italian Jews, who were not so scrupulous about the prohibition against litigating in non-Jewish courts.[135]

Other enactments provide that a decision should not be reached in a contested case until both parties have been heard,[136] and that a rabbi may not rule in a matter beyond his jurisdiction. Still other enactments deal with protection of tenants,[137] the procedures for the marriage ceremony, etc.[138]

4. ENACTMENTS OF CORFU

A compilation of enactments of the Jewish community on the island of Corfu has been recently discovered.[139] These enactments were adopted in 1642. Their major emphasis is on family law; they provided, *inter alia,* that the *kiddushin* (the betrothal) and the *ḥuppah* (the nuptial ceremony) should take place consecutively and without interruption:

> The *kiddushin* must take place immediately prior to the recital of the seven [marriage] benedictions, so that the betrothal will be simultaneous with the *ḥuppah* and not some time beforehand.[140]

Other enactments require that the marriage ceremony take place in public,[141] establish the rights of orphans in their mother's dowry and their father's property, etc. Various enactments deal with the laws of the sabbath, kosher food, etc.

D. Enactments of the National and Regional Councils of Poland, Lithuania, and Moravia in the Seventeenth and Eighteenth Centuries

In the seventeenth and eighteenth centuries, when Jewish juridical autonomy in the diaspora was ending, countrywide legislative activity reached one of its highest peaks. This activity took place in the major centers of Jewish life in this period—Poland and Lithuania.

135. *See supra* pp. 50–51.

136. *See supra* p. 791 for the similar enactment of Ḥayyim Or Zaru'a.

137. *See supra* pp. 811–813.

138. *See further infra* p. 872. For additional enactments in Italy, *see* Finkelstein, *Self-Government,* pp. 306–315.

139. The enactments were discovered by A. Marx in the manuscript of the Corfu *Maḥzor* (festival prayer book). *See further* Finkelstein, *Self-Government,* pp. 96–98. The text of the enactments, which is difficult to decipher because of the poor condition of the manuscript, appears in Finkelstein at 316–327.

140. Similar legislation had been previously adopted soon after the completion of the Talmud; *see supra* pp. 656–658 and *infra* p. 974.

141. *See supra* pp. 656–658 and *infra* pp. 847–878.

1. ENACTMENTS OF THE COUNCIL OF THE FOUR LANDS (*VA'AD ARBA ARAZOT*)

Polish Jewry had a central institution, known as the "Council of the Four Lands," one of whose major tasks was to legislate. The earliest document extant attributed to the Council of the Four Lands is from 1580; historians differ as to when this central institution was organized.[142] The large communities in Poland sent representatives to the council of the region (also referred to as the "land" or the "province"), such as the Council of the Province of Greater Poland or of the Province of Little Poland. Each province sent its representatives to the transregional council, thus creating the Council of the Four Lands. This institution, in which rabbis and communal leaders met together, existed in Poland for over two hundred years; and it, together with its associated branches, was the highest legislative and judicial institution of Polish Jewry.

The enactments of the Council of the Four Lands were recorded in the record books of "the leaders of the province" and "the judges of the province," and became established law, to be used as a basis for decision making and for regulating the conduct of the social and legal affairs of the Jews of Poland. These books have been lost. Early in the twentieth century, a few pages from these books were discovered, but these too were lost during the Holocaust.[143] In 1945, Israel Halpern published *Pinkas Va'ad Arba Arazot* ("The Record Book of the Council of the Four Lands") in which he compiled from various sources the enactments of the Council; the sources include the codificatory and responsa literature of that period, record books of communities, government archives, etc. Even the fragments that remain give some idea of the multifaceted countrywide legislation of the large Jewish center in Poland in the areas of civil, criminal, and public law.[144]

2. ENACTMENTS OF THE COUNCIL OF THE PRINCIPAL COMMUNITIES OF LITHUANIA

At that time, Poland was a confederation of the Kingdom of Poland and the important principality of Lithuania. The Jews of Lithuania had their own council, "The Council of the Principal Communities of Lithuania," which was the highest judicial and legislative institution of all the Jewish communities in Lithuania. We have no knowledge of the activities of the Council of Lithuania prior to 1623, although there is evidence clearly indicating that the Council functioned before that time. There is extant a complete compilation of "*Takkanot* of the Council of Lithuania" for the period

142. *See* I. Halpern, *Pinkas Va'ad Arba Arazot* [The Record Book of the Council of the Four Lands], Introduction, pp. 17–24.

143. *See id.,* Preface.

144. *See infra* n. 152.

1623–1761.[145] This compilation of Jewish legislation enacted by a representative body of a thriving, learned, and populous Jewish settlement is the largest such compilation known to have survived intact.

Throughout Jewish history there has been much creative legislation, most of which was lost during times of persecution and affliction. It is ironic that this compilation that has survived—a substantial, comprehensive, and excellent exemplar of Jewish parliamentary legislation in the conditions of exile under the rule of a non-Jewish government—dates from the very time when Jewish autonomy in the diaspora was coming to an end. The historian Simon Dubnow, who published this book of enactments, justifiably stated: "A complete book, among the finest of statutory compilations enacted by parliaments throughout the world, is open before us in manuscript form, with variant texts, and it calls out, 'Study me.'"[146] This book still awaits comprehensive and thorough researach and analysis.[147]

This compilation of enactments contains a wealth of material concerning all the areas of *mishpat ivri:* the delineation of the legal authority of communal agencies, the relationship between the individual and the community, the relationship among the communities *inter se,* the relationship between the Council of the Four Lands and the Council of Lithuania, the relationship between this latter Council and the general government, taxes, elections, the composition of elected and appointed bodies, the court system and its different levels, family law, the law of succession, guardians, property transfers, obligations, torts, franchises, partnerships, criminal law, and procedure. The compilation also contains many enactments on matters of religion and morality, many detailed provisions with regard to the educational system at all levels, and legislation against all forms of excessive luxury and ostentation.[148]

3. ENACTMENTS OF MORAVIA

Another association of autonomous communities functioning in this period, but smaller in scope than the Council of the Four Lands and the Council of Lithuania, was the League of Communities in the Province of

145. S. Dubnow, *Pinkas ha-Medinah o Pinkas Va'ad ha-Kehillot ha-Rashiyyot bi-Medinat Lita* [The Record Book of the Land or the Record Book of the Council of the Principal Communities of Lithuania], Berlin, 1925; Introduction, p. XI; and *see also id.* at XI–XXIX for a detailed discussion of the composition, authority, meetings, and activities of the Council of Lithuania, and a brief description of the enactments.

146. *Id.* at XI.

147. At the end of the record book (pp. 337–338), there are some halakhic-legal notes of Abraham Elijah Kaplan on some of the provisions. Kaplan had intended to write an extensive halakhic-legal introduction to the whole compilation, but did not manage to do so before his untimely death. *See* Dubnow, *supra* n. 145, Introduction.

148. *See infra* n. 152.

Moravia in Austria. This association also engaged in multifaceted legislative activity, and the enactments it adopted from 1650 to 1748 were recently compiled and published.[149]

The General Assembly (called "the Council of the Province") consisted of the representatives of the communities of Moravia and met once every three years. Fifteen of its members were selected to constitute a special body, one of whose functions was legislative. There was also an additional body consisting of nine members, known as "the Masters of *Takkanot,*" specially charged with the sole function of enacting legislation. The enactments were recorded in the record book of the province, which was kept in the provincial archives.[150] The compilation covers various broad areas of *mishpat ivri:* the structure of the judicial system, marriage, the *ketubbah, ḥaliẓah,* inheritance, guardianship, taxes, property acquisition, secured transactions, partnership, criminal law, rules of trial and appellate procedure, relationship to non-Jewish courts, enactments against excessive luxury, etc. Other enactments deal with the laws of kosher food and the ritual slaughter of animals, charity, burial, etc.

As stated, the compilations of enactments of these three groups of communities in Poland, Lithuania, and Moravia[151] include abundant and wide-ranging material in the various areas of *mishpat ivri.* This material is being increasingly used by historians of these periods to shed light on the social, economic, and moral conditions reflected in the legislation. It has also been used to some extent in various research projects in Jewish law but still awaits detailed and thorough legal research that could greatly enrich our knowledge of the legal aspects of this important period of Jewish juridical autonomy.[152]

E. Enactments of Individual Communities in the Seventeenth and Eighteenth Centuries

Books of enactments adopted by individual communities in the seventeenth and eighteenth centuries are extant. These books contain rich and comprehensive material in the various areas of *mishpat ivri.*

149. I. Halpern, *Takkanot Medinat Mehrin* [Enactments of Moravia], Jerusalem, 1952.

150. *See id.,* Introduction, at 13–15, which also discusses the respective functions of these two legislative bodies.

151. Additional compilations can be added to the list: *e.g.,* the enactments of Posen. *See* L. Lewin, *Die Landessynode der Grosspolnischen Judenschaft* [The National Synod of Greater Polish Jewry], Frankfurt-am-Main, 1926.

152. We have not quoted excerpts from these compilations at this point, because they are voluminous. An index at the end of each compilation facilitates study and research. Various excerpts are quoted throughout this present work where relevant to the subject matter under discussion; *see* Index, under specific items.

1. THE BOOK OF ENACTMENTS OF THE COMMUNITY OF CRACOW

The earliest extant book of this type is the *Book of Enactments of the Jewish Community of Cracow,* the major part of which was compiled in 1595, with supplements in 1604, 1605, and 1615–1616.[153] These enactments cover wide areas of civil and criminal law, tax law, etc.

a. JAILS AND IMPRISONMENT

These enactments reveal the existence of jails maintained by the Jewish community: one jail was called "dudik"; another "the new dudik," which, it appears, was used for women; another jail was called "stock," and it seems to have been used for short-term imprisonment for less serious offenses.[154] These enactments also preserve the names and salaries of two jailers.[155]

b. IMPRISONMENT FOR GAMBLING

The following is an example of criminal legislation enacted in Cracow in 1595, providing for imprisonment for gambling:[156]

> Everyone—including householders, young men and boys, residents, and visitors—is prohibited from gambling in the street, whether in Cracow, Kazmir, Stradum, or in any part of the city, and particularly in saloons.

The enactment is especially severe with regard to women who gamble:

> Women may not engage in any gambling whatsoever, even if deceit or cunning is not involved, and even if only for pleasure and not for money—except on the intermediate days of Passover and *Sukkot,* and on *Hanukkah.*
>
> Any woman who violates this enactment by playing cards shall be punished by imprisonment in the new jail ("the new dudik") from the end of the morning prayer until the end of the evening prayer [it was forbidden to keep a woman in jail at night, and she returned at night to her husband's or her parents' home]. She shall be proclaimed in all the synagogues as a transgressor and her name shall be announced; the communal leaders shall not make any exception for reasons of pity, and it shall make no difference that she is an important woman or is pregnant or nursing, since it is she herself who failed to have proper regard for her own dignity.

153. This book of enactments was originally published in Yiddish, with a small admixture of Hebrew words, by M. Balaban in *Jahrbuch d. Jüdisch Literarischen Gesellschaft* [Jewish Literary Society Annual], X, pp. 296–360, XI, pp. 88–114. For additional publications of these enactments, *see* Elon, *Ḥerut,* p. 174 n. 241.

154. *See* Elon, *Ma'asar,* pp. 183–184; *see also id.* as to Jewish prisons in other communities.

155. *See id.* at 183 n. 7.

156. Balaban, *supra* n. 153 at XI, 88–89.

Nevertheless, a woman guilty of this transgression could free herself from jail by paying a fine of three *adummim* (coins).

The enactment further provides that not only the card-player but also the householder who permits card-playing in his home is subject to punishment.

It is interesting to note the greater severity with which this offense was dealt with in the subsequent enactment of the Province of Moravia in 1650:[157]

> Everyone, whoever he may be, is prohibited from playing cards; and not only cards and dice but all types of gambling, whatever the mouth can speak and the heart can contrive. [The prohibition applies] even on *Rosh Ḥodesh* [the New Moon (a semi-holiday)], *Hanukkah, Purim,* the intermediate days [of Passover and *Sukkot*], and the other festive days on which supplicatory prayers are not recited, and even to women in childbirth[158] and men when they let blood. In short, all manner of gambling is prohibited. Everyone, no matter who—householder, young man or young woman, servant or maid—will be fined according to his ability to pay if any such person, God forbid, transgresses and gambles.
>
> This is the punishment for the transgressor: if he is wealthy, he must pay two *hagars* for each violation, with no remissions—half to be dedicated for the study of Torah and the other half for the poor of Jerusalem. Those who have no financial resources and cannot pay a fine will be punished by imprisonment and suffer being placed in metal shackles as is appropriate for such a transgressor. It all depends on the status of the one causing the indignity and of the one who is disgraced, and on the needs of the time. In any event, his disgrace shall be proclaimed publicly, there shall be no forbearance on account of his honor, and it shall be announced that the transgressor violated this enactment. . . .
>
> The leaders in every community must see to it that this is carried out. If they do not see to this, and if any of the leaders attempt, God forbid, to look the other way, they will be included in the ban and subject to the fine of two *adummim* as above, without any remission whatsoever. Any householder who permits gambling in his home will be fined two *adummim* of full weight, without any remission or forgiveness whatsoever, and there shall also be a proclamation concerning him in the manner set forth above.[159]

157. Halpern, *supra* n. 149, Enactment #280 (p. 92).

158. As previously stated, the Cracow enactments permitted women to play cards on the intermediate days of Passover and *Sukkot* and on *Hanukkah.* The Cracow enactments (Balaban, *supra* n. 153 at XI, pp. 88–89) also allowed designated persons to play games of chance with women during childbirth in order to distract their attention from labor pains.

159. Enactments against gambling were adopted in many Jewish communities, apparently because gambling was widespread; the communities attempted to deter it by fines and imprisonment. For examples of additional enactments, *see supra* p. 814 and n. 130; *see also* Halpern, *supra* n. 149 at 92 n.6.

2. OTHER COMPILATIONS

Compilations of enactments of other communities are extant, such as the collections from the communities of Nikolsburg,[160] Kremzir, Tribich, Helishuh, Boskowitz, Tiktin,[161] Lvov,[162] etc.,[163] which are comparable to the enactments of Cracow. There are also compilations of enactments by associations of various types of craftsmen.[164] The collections do not always have the same legal significance; one may have more material on civil law, while the major part of another may concern ritual law, the administration of the community, and similar matters.

A considerable amount of material on enactments adopted in various communities in all areas of Jewish law is also contained in the different types of halakhic literature, especially in the responsa literature, as well as in the extensive historical literature. This enormous body of material in halakhic and historical literature and in the compilations of communal enactments awaits study and research that will surely enrich the Jewish legal system.[165]

160. *Sefer Takkanot Nikolsburg* [The Book of the Enactments of Nikolsburg], ed. Roth, 1962.

161. *See* the bibliography on Tiktin in *id.*, Introduction, pp. 1–2; Elon, *Ḥerut*, pp. 196, 218–219.

162. The enactments are quoted by Solomon Buber, *Anshei Shem* [Men of Renown], Cracow, 1895, pp. 222–225.

163. *See Pinkas Hekhsherim Shel Kehillat Pozna* [The Record Book of Kosher Food Certification of Posen], ed. D. Evron, Jerusalem, 1967. *See also infra* pp. 1531–1532.

164. The enactments of such associations also are of importance for *mishpat ivri*, like those of the bakers, donkey drivers, boatmen, butchers, etc., that are recorded in the *Tosefta* and TB. *See supra* pp. 680–681, 752–753. In Poland, for example, Jewish artisans organized themselves into guilds, along the lines of the Christian artisan guilds, which were not subject to the authority of the community. Balaban compares the relationship between the Jewish artisan guild and the Jewish community to that of the Christian guild and the municipal authorities.

The Jewish guilds were governed pursuant to an *iggeret kelaf* (lit. "a document on parchment"), *i.e.*, the guild by-laws, which were generally recognized by the Christian guilds. There were guilds for various crafts, such as tailors, furriers, and hat-makers; *see* Balaban, *Bet Yisra'el be-Folin* [The Jews in Poland], ed. Halpern, I, pp. 56–57. One of the earliest sets of by-laws was that of the Cracow furriers' guild of 1613, the full text of which appears in Balaban at II, pp. 244–245. These by-laws established the various officers of the guild, namely: five directors (*gabba'im*), three auditors, and three judges. The judges were given "the rod, the strap, and the license to judge [disputes] between members of our society, may the Almighty preserve them, *i.e.*, [to decide] what one member owes another on account of the sale of goods on credit . . . and also matters of unfair competition—all will be judged according to their sound judgment." The judges were even given jurisdiction over cases where one member insulted or assaulted another. Any member who refused to abide by the judges' decision could be punished "by fine, imprisonment, or other punishment."

165. The digests of the responsa literature published by the Institute for Research in Jewish Law of the Hebrew University of Jerusalem contain a section devoted to the enactments dealt with in the responsa literature.

F. Legislation after the Onset of Emancipation

With the onset of the Emancipation, the output of legislation in Jewish law markedly and progressively decreased. The decline of juridical autonomy to the point of virtual extinction necessarily resulted in a similar fate for legislation, since legislation and autonomy are correlated. The purpose of legislation is to respond to pressing new problems that arise in real life. When a legal system ceases to be functional, legal problems become merely theoretical, and legislation serves no purpose.

G. Enactments of the Chief Rabbinate of the Land of Israel

A turning point can be discerned early in the twentieth century with the establishment in 1921 of the Chief Rabbinate of the Land of Israel as the highest and central halakhic institution for the Jewish community in the Land of Israel and the diaspora. When this important halakhic body was established, its first head, Chief Rabbi Abraham Isaac ha-Kohen Kook, was desirous that it continue in the path of the halakhic and public bodies of all previous eras, which adopted legislation to meet the needs of the *Halakhah* and the times:

> In our new national life in the Land of Israel, there will sometimes surely be a great need to enact important *takkanot,* which, as long as they are approved by the majority of the generally recognized halakhic authorities of Israel and then accepted by the community, will have the same force as a law of the Torah.[166]

To a certain extent, this hope was realized by the adoption of a number of enactments in the area of family law as well as some related procedural changes in connection with the vesting of jurisdiction over these matters in the rabbinical courts.

1. ESTABLISHMENT OF A RABBINICAL COURT OF APPEALS

One important and indeed fundamental procedural enactment adopted in the very same year that the Chief Rabbinate was organized was the establishment of a Rabbinical Court of Appeals. One of the major problems on the agenda of the first conference to inaugurate the Chief Rabbinate[167] was the question of the establishment of an appellate court to hear appeals from decisions of district and local rabbinical courts. There is

166. From the remarks of Chief Rabbi Kook at the discussions on the establishment of a Chief Rabbinate in the Land of Israel; for a fuller quotation, *see infra* pp. 1596–1598.

167. *See Ha-Tor,* 1921, from issue XV of 12th Shevat onward; for a detailed report of these discussions, *see* issue XXI–XXII of 24th Adar I.

no provision for an appellate court in Talmudic law, but there were situations when a party could request that his case be tried before the High Court.[168] Nevertheless, prior to the conferring of jurisdiction on the rabbinical courts, various governmental and communal groups urged that it was imperative to establish an appellate court—analogous to such courts in other contemporary legal systems—in order to maintain a degree of internal control within the court system and to gain public confidence that additional and final review would be available for any case.[169] The question gave rise to a serious difference of opinion among the participants in the conference. The Rabbinical Office of Jaffa, for example, proposed a resolution stating:

> There is no place in the law of the Torah for an appellate court, except that if a High Court is established, the parties have the right to appear before this High Court instead of submitting their case to a court of three judges; and even more so, if a case has already been brought before a court to which the parties have formally agreed to submit their case and a decision has been rendered, none of the parties may reject the decision by filing an appeal to the Chief Rabbinate.[170]

Nevertheless, an appellate court was established, and thus an important new legal institution was purposefully introduced into Jewish law.[171]

A decision rendered by the Rabbinical Court of Appeals in Jerusalem in 1945 involved a matter of civil law, in a case—not within the regular jurisdiction of the rabbinical courts—which had been brought to a rabbinical court sitting as an arbitration tribunal. The losing party in the lower court sought to appeal to the Rabbinical Court of Appeals; but his opponent argued that the appeal was barred because the arbitration agreement did not contain a clause permitting an appeal. When this question was brought for decision to the Rabbinical Court of Appeals, that court ruled that a right of appeal did exist "because the matter of an appeal has been accepted as an enactment of the halakhic authorities that has the status of a law of our Holy Torah, and whoever appears as a party in a case does so on that ba-

168. TB Sanhedrin 31b; Sh. Ar. ḤM ch. 14; *see infra* pp. 1460–1461.

169. *See Ha-Tor, supra* n. 167.

170. *Id.*, issue XVIII.

171. Although Assaf, *Battei ha-Din*, pp. 74–86, 137–140, has demonstrated the existence of appellate courts throughout the diaspora in the rabbinic period (in Spain, Turkey, Poland, and elsewhere) and the availability of appeal has been noted *supra* pp. 800–801 (in the Valladolid enactments of 1432) and pp. 818–820 (in Lithuania and Moravia), these provisions for appeal arose out of specific historical circumstances and were hardly discussed, either positively or negatively, in halakhic literature. At any rate, the establishment of the Rabbinical Court of Appeals in Jerusalem was generally considered to be a legislative innovation.

sis."[172] Once the enactment has been adopted, the right of appeal in the rabbinical court system has the status of a law of the Torah even when the proceedings in the lower court are based on an agreement to arbitrate.[173] This result is in marked contrast to the rule in the general courts, where there is no right of appeal on the merits from an arbitration award unless the arbitration agreement specifically provides for an appeal.

2. PROCEDURAL ENACTMENTS FOR THE RABBINICAL COURTS OF THE LAND OF ISRAEL, 1943

In 1943, procedural enactments for the rabbinical courts in the Land of Israel were adopted by the Council of the Chief Rabbinate. As appears from the introduction to these enactments, their preparation had already begun in the days of Rabbi Kook and Rabbi Jacob Meir. The introduction also states that "most [of the enactments] have their basis in the *Shulḥan Arukh* and the other codes; and some were enacted by the Council of the Chief Rabbinate of the Land of Israel for the purpose of regulating procedure in the courts of the land and for the public good." The following discussion concerns three areas in which the enactments constituted a significantly creative innovation.

a. PROCEDURE FOR LITIGATION AND THE PAYMENT OF COURT COSTS

The enactments include detailed provisions concerning the method of commencing an action, trial procedure, evidence, filing an appeal, appellate hearings, and similar matters; and an appendix contains a series of forms for a complaint, a summons for a party, a subpoena for a witness, a notice of appeal, etc. The third part of the enactments contains detailed provisions as to liability for court costs (then called "taxes") for the litigation of various legal claims.

The preparatory discussions had considered the need to require the payment of court costs in litigated cases in order to provide financial support for the judicial system and perhaps also to curb litigation and forestall frivolous suits; and the rules of procedure as enacted contain detailed requirements, similar to those of other legal systems, for the payment of court costs. Under ideal conditions, every citizen would have the right to obtain a judicial determination without charge, and this was traditionally the po-

172. B. v. A. (1944), *Osef Piskei ha-Din Shel ha-Rabbanut ha-Rashit le-Ereẓ Yisra'el* [A Compilation of the Rulings of the Chief Rabbinate of the Land of Israel], ed. Warhaftig, 1950 (hereinafter, *Osef Piskei ha-Din*), p. 71.

173. This was established in Enactments #4 and #101 of the Procedural Enactments for the Rabbinical Courts of the Land of Israel (Jerusalem, 1943), discussed *infra*.

sition of Jewish law.[174] However, conditions then existing did not permit this; hence the adoption of the enactment under discussion, which is based on the legislative principle of *hefker bet din hefker* (the court has the power to expropriate property).[175]

b. ADOPTION

Another substantial innovation introduced by these enactments is the provision for adoption. Jewish law did not previously recognize adoption, although there was an accepted practice, considered a *mizvah* (good deed), of rearing children who were in need, for "whoever rears an orphan in his home is considered by Scripture as if he gave birth to him."[176] Legally, however, the child was not considered to be the child of the foster parents. Article 51 of the Palestine Order in Council included adoption as an aspect of personal status; and the need for adoption became much more pressing, especially after the Holocaust, when many children were placed in foster homes and the foster parents sought to become adoptive parents. The procedural enactments included a separate section[177] on the adoption of children, which served as the starting point for the legal treatment of this problem.[178]

174. M Bekhorot 4:6; TB Bekhorot 29a; Sh. Ar. ḤM 9:3–5. It should be pointed out that legislation and responsa in Germany, Poland, and Lithuania had already referred to "court costs;" *see* Assaf, *Battei ha-Din*, pp. 93ff.

175. *See supra* pp. 507–514, 685–688, 699–702.

176. TB Sanhedrin 19b; *see also* TB Ketubbot 50a.

177. Enactment #189.

178. This legislation and the judicial decisions to which it gave rise provide only for the establishment of a legal relationship between the adoptive parents and the child; the relationship between the child and the biological parents is not severed. Such a severance would be contrary to Jewish law, according to which the natural relationship to the biological parents cannot be changed or severed. For this reason, Jewish law has never stigmatized a child born out of wedlock as "illegitimate." Even a child born to parents who are not married to each other is "legitimate" and has the same legal status as any other child.

The term *mamzer*, often erroneously translated as "bastard," refers in Jewish law to the offspring of an incestuous relationship of the first degree of consanguinity—such as a brother and sister or son and mother—or the child of a married woman where it is absolutely certain that the father is a man other than her husband. A *mamzer* has the same relationship to his natural parents as any child has to its parents, and the parents must fulfill all parental obligations. Thus, a *mamzer* is not an "illegitimate child," although he does suffer from the severe disability of being drastically limited as to those whom he may marry.

In 1960, the Knesset passed the Adoption of Children Law, 1960 (*Laws of Israel*, 317, p. 96), which was a compromise between the approach of Jewish law and that of various other legal systems in regard to the severance of the adopted child's relationship with his natural parents. (The objective of severing a child's relationship with his natural parents is to prevent the natural parents from demanding the return of the child after the child has found a home with the adoptive parents.) The terms of the compromise were: on the one hand, adoption creates reciprocal rights between the adoptive parents and the child, and

c. EQUALIZATION OF DAUGHTERS WITH SONS, AND WIVES WITH HUSBANDS, IN REGARD TO INHERITANCE

Another significant innovation, which involved a far-reaching change in the halakhic method of distribution of decedents' estates, was adopted in these enactments.[179] Pursuant to this legislation, the rabbinical courts undertook to distribute an estate according to the provisions of the British Mandatory Succession Ordinance of 1923. Section 21 of that Ordinance provided that a will was ineffective with regard to *miri* property (which constituted most of the property in the country), and that such property was to be divided among the heirs in the manner stated in the supplement to that Ordinance; this provision was, as stated in Section 21, also binding on the religious courts. In the second supplement to the Ordinance, the order of distribution was set forth as follows in regard to spouse and children: surviving children receive three-fourths of the estate, and the surviving spouse (husband or wife) one-fourth. If there are no children, the spouse receives half, and the other half goes to the parents of the decedent or their descendants. If there are no children, parents, descendants of parents, or grandparents of the decedent, the spouse inherits the entire estate.

This order of succession puts daughters on a par with sons, and wives on a par with husbands. It is contrary to the rules of Jewish law under which (a) a daughter does not inherit unless there are no sons; and (b) a husband inherits from his wife, but a wife does not inherit from her husband, although she is entitled to full support from his estate until she remarries. Although enactments were adopted in different periods[180] giving daughters (even if there was a son) and wives a share in the estate, this legislation of the Chief Rabbinate marked the first time that Jewish law accepted the equality of daughters with sons, and of wives with hus-

---

terminates the prior reciprocal rights and obligations of the child and his natural parents and other natural relatives; on the other hand, the court in the adoption order may limit the legal effects of the adoption in these respects.

The legislation also provides that adoption in no way affects the religious laws governing marriage and divorce, *i.e.*, the adopted child still may not marry those natural relatives forbidden to him by Jewish law (sec. 13). The law also requires that a registry of adoptions be kept in the court, in which all the information concerning the natural parents is to be recorded (secs. 26–27). *See* Elon, *Ḥakikah,* pp. 45–46. In the Adoption of Children Law, 1981, the Knesset made some changes in the law but retained the basic compromise approach of the 1960 legislation.

179. Enactments #174, #182–183.

180. *See supra* pp. 575–580 and *infra* pp. 842–846. *See also* Chief Rabbi Herzog's remarks regarding the legislation with respect to inheritance proposed by him just after the State of Israel was established, *infra* p. 1494 n. 124, p. 1684.

bands.[181] Even with regard to other than *miri* property, the legislation provided[182] that the rabbinical court must comply with a request by any of the heirs that the estate be divided according to the general law.[183]

3. ENACTMENTS OF 1944

In the following year, 1944, the Chief Rabbinate of the Land of Israel continued to develop a number of important aspects of family law through legislative enactments. The introduction to these enactments states:[184]

> In accordance with the holy duty placed upon us, we have found it necessary to assemble our colleagues—the rabbis and outstanding scholars, the members of the Council of the Chief Rabbinate of the Land of Israel, and the Chief Rabbis of Tel Aviv-Jaffa, Haifa, and Petaḥ-Tikvah—to deliberate on the need to adopt necessary enactments for the protection of the women and children of Israel; and after study and consideration of the *Halakhah*, it was unanimously decided to adopt the following three enactments for the entire Land of Israel. . . .

181. The reason given in the enactments for this equality is "that the law of the existing government [*i.e.*, the Succession Ordinance] requires them to be divided in a fixed and definite manner, *i.e.*, only according to the provisions in the second supplement to the Succession Ordinance" (Enactment #182). It should be noted that these two paragraphs of the Procedural Enactments of 1943 (Enactments #182 and #183), accepting equality of daughters and sons and of wives and husbands in regard to inheritance, "disappeared" from the Procedural Enactments for the Rabbinical Courts of Israel published in 1960 by the Chief Rabbinate Council and the judges of the Rabbinical Court of Appeals. Although the rabbinical courts continue in fact to apply the same law of inheritance as they previously did, one wonders why this omission occurred.

182. Enactment #183.

183. This enactment was adopted as a consequence of the Succession Ordinance (sec. 8). The Succession Law, 1965, passed by the Knesset (*Laws of Israel*, 446, p. 63), did away with the distinction between *miri* property and *mulk* property with regard to succession (sec. 149), and provided that inheritance was thereafter to be governed solely by the new legislation (sec. 148). The 1965 law, too, puts wives on a par with husbands, and daughters on a par with sons, but provides for a slightly different division of the estate than the Succession Ordinance (secs. 10–16). According to the 1965 legislation, a rabbinical court may issue a decree as to inheritance "if all the parties who have rights under this statute so agree in writing," in which case the court may rule "according to the religious law it follows, provided that if one of the parties is a minor or has been declared incompetent, his rights of inheritance, whether by law or bequest, and his right to support from the estate shall not be less than the rights provided under this statute" (sec. 155, pars. [A] and [B]). *See* M. Elon, "The Sources and Nature of Jewish Law and Its Application in the State of Israel," 4 *Israel Law Review* 126ff. (1969).

184. For the text of these enactments, as well as of those of 1950 discussed *infra, see* Schereschewsky, *supra* n. 20. The 1944 enactments are in Appendix A, pp. 427–430, and the 1950 enactments are in Appendix B, pp. 431–433. *See also* A.H. Freimann, "Ha-Takkanot ha-Ḥadashot Shel ha-Rabbanut ha-Rashit le-Ereẓ Yisra'el be-Dinei Ishut" [The New Enactments of the Chief Rabbinate of Israel on Family Law], *Sinai*, XIV, p. 254.

a. THE MINIMUM AMOUNT OF THE *KETUBBAH*

One enactment concerned the minimum amount of the *ketubbah,* which at that time was ten *lirot* (Israeli pounds) for a virgin and five for a widow:

> Having considered the standard of living in the *yishuv* [the Jewish community in the Land of Israel] at this time, as well as economic factors, we have determined that the established and customary amount . . . does not suit the present situation and cannot achieve the goal that our halakhic authorities sought to attain in their [original] enactment, *i.e.,* to make it more difficult for a husband to divorce his wife, and to give dignity to a wife in the eyes of her husband, who must honor her more than himself, as our Rabbis, of blessed memory, have stated.[185]

It was therefore provided that the minimum amount of the *ketubbah* of a virgin shall be 50 *lirot* and of a widow 25 *lirot.*[186]

b. SUPPORT BY A *LEVIR* OF HIS BROTHER'S WIDOW

The second enactment requires a *levir* (deceased husband's brother) who refuses to give the widow *ḥaliẓah* (a release from levirate marriage) to support her until he gives her *ḥaliẓah.* The enactment sets forth the circumstances that led to its adoption: "There are occasions, to our sorrow, when Jewish women who are subject to a levirate marriage [*i.e.,* when the deceased left no children] are "anchored" (*agunot*) [to the *levir* and unable to remarry] because of [the *levir*'s] refusal to give *ḥaliẓah,* and the suffering and calamity are indeed great."

There is a halakhic dispute as to whether and under what circumstances a *levir* who refuses to release a widow may be obligated to support her as long as he does not release her. The enactment states that it is reasonable to decide in favor of the view that the *levir* may be required to support the widow—"as otherwise she may, God forbid, remain an *agunah* forever." However, in order not to rely solely on a decision as between the conflicting views, the law was established by specific legislation:

> To give greater support and increased validity [to these rules], we have decided to adopt the following *takkanah:* when a court orders a *levir* to give *ḥaliẓah* to his brother's widow [and thus release her], and he does not obey the order and the court rules that he is to be considered in contempt, he shall

185. TB Yevamot 62b.

186. These sums were increased by an enactment in 1953 to 200 and 100 Israel pounds (*lirot*). For similar enactments relating to the amount of the *ketubbah, see supra* pp. 792, 805.

be required from that day forward to support the widow until he releases her, as required by the Torah and the Commandment.[187]

c. SUPPORT OF CHILDREN UP TO THE AGE OF FIFTEEN

The most fundamental of the three enactments imposed a legal duty on a father to support his children up to the age of fifteen. Originally, Jewish law imposed no legal obligation to support children; the religious and moral obligation of a father to support his family was sufficient. However, when cracks in the Jewish family structure appeared after the Bar Kokhba rebellion and as a result of the Hadrianic decrees, the Sanhedrin sitting at Usha adopted legislation providing that a father must support his children when they are "small," the accepted interpretation of which was "under the age of six years." When it became necessary to require fathers to support their children over the age of six, this was accomplished on the strength of the principle that charitable contributions may be compelled.[188]

This was the halakhic situation until 1944. At that time, it became clear that compulsion pursuant to the law relating to charity was insufficient, as was explained by those who adopted the enactment. In describing the background for the enactment, they stated:

> Previously among the Jewish people, although under strict law a father was compelled [by the court] to support his minor children from his assets only up to the age of six, he would be shamed and publicly excoriated in order to compel him to support them until they became adults. However, in our times, the generation is deficient, to our sorrow, and such moral pressure is not at all effective. . . .
>
> There have been occasions when a father acted cruelly from hardness of heart to force his wife to accept a divorce from him, and the governmental courts [which are required to apply Jewish law in the matter] relieved him from any duty of child support on the basis that the children were over the age of six. To the argument on behalf of the children that, under Jewish law, the father can be compelled [to support his children] pursuant to the law relating to charity if he has sufficient resources, the counterargument was made that the law of the state could not give any weight to this contention.
>
> This is a matter for great shame and anger. Whoever looks at this fairly will conclude that the situation requires appropriate remedial legislation. In our time, even adolescent children (girls as well as boys) under the age of

187. The Rabbinical Courts Jurisdiction (Marriage and Divorce) Law, 1953 (*Laws of Israel,* 134, p. 165), further provides that if a rabbinical court issues a decree that a *levir* must grant *ḥalizah* so as to release the widow from levirate marriage and he refuses, he can be imprisoned until he complies (sec. 7). *See* Elon, *Ḥakikah,* p. 31.

188. For detailed discussion, *see supra* pp. 116–117, 567–568.

> fifteen face serious moral dangers if their support is not assured on a legal basis. There is no need to elaborate on a matter that is understood by anyone whose eyes are open to the present situation.

The possibility was then considered of finding a solution under the existing *Halakhah.* After making clear that existing law could not rectify the situation, the statement continued:

> There is only one way to overcome the confusion and complications, namely, to adopt an all-inclusive enactment that will apply universally; and after this enactment is adopted by the Chief Rabbinate of the Land of Israel and its expanded Council and by the rabbinical courts and the rabbis who function in the communities (under the sanction of the Chief Rabbinate) and with the approval of the communities through their councils and committees, this enactment will have full force and effect to the same extent as the enactments of "Shum," Toledo, the Council of the Four Lands, etc.
>
> It will be law in the full and strict sense of the term. It will be the basis of decision by the Jewish courts in the entire Holy Land. In a case of noncompliance, the governmental courts will necessarily rule in accordance with this enactment; and this enactment will apply both prospectively and retroactively, until the realization of the prayer, "I will restore your judges as of old, etc." May it be speedily in our days. Amen.

It is not superfluous to quote the rest of the explanatory statement, which expresses the keen sense of the great authority and responsibility that those who adopted the enactment assumed in legislating as they did:

> God forbid that we compare ourselves to our rabbis, the *geonim,* of blessed memory, . . . may their merit protect us and all Israel. However, Jephthah in his generation is equal to Samuel in his generation; and enactments were adopted in every generation to counteract wrongdoers, to promote the public welfare, and to maintain the rule of law. Why should we be deficient when the time requires such action, especially when this enactment will also be a communal enactment? . . .
>
> It is for this reason that we have adopted this general enactment for the entire Land of Israel. . . . Just as from ancient times until today a Jewish court has had the power to impose on a father the full legal obligation to support his children up to the age of six years and to enforce this obligation against his property and through all possible legal means, so from this time forward it will have the power to impose upon him the full legal obligation to support his sons and daughters up to the age of fifteen years and to enforce this obligation against his property and through all possible legal means.[189]

189. *See* the decision of the Rabbinical Court of Appeals, A. v. B. (1947), Warhaftig, *Osef Piskei ha-Din,* p. 148. It was argued in that case that even after the enactment by the Chief Rabbinate the duty to support one's children above the age of six years rested on the grounds of charity only, and was not a legal duty. The court held:

As the last two quoted excerpts indicate, the Chief Rabbinate in its legislative activity followed the same method employed during most of the post-Talmudic period, *i.e.,* the combination of halakhic authority and public administrative authority in the form of legislation by both the halakhic authorities and the communities.

4. ENACTMENTS OF 1950

In 1950, soon after the establishment of the State of Israel, in the wake of the heavy immigration from all parts of the diaspora—which brought to Israel immigrants with a variety of customs with regard to marriage, levirate marriage, and *ḥaliẓah*—the Chief Rabbinate adopted a number of enactments "to renew the *takkanot* of our rabbis of prior generations, of blessed memory, and to add such additional *takkanot* as the times require in order to promote peace and tranquillity, and family harmony in Israel." These enactments required that *kiddushin* (betrothal) be celebrated at the same time as the *ḥuppah* (the nuptial ceremony) and in the presence of at least ten people;[190] prohibited anyone not certified and appointed by the Chief Rabbis of the cities of Israel from performing a marriage ceremony;[191] prohibited bigamous marriage except with the permission of the Chief Rabbis of Israel, duly signed and certified by them;[192] and prohibited levirate marriage and mandated *ḥaliẓah.*[193] These provisions reflected what had already been long-standing practices in most Jewish communities, except for some Sephardic communities that had not accepted them. The enactments were made applicable to all Jews in the State of Israel, whatever their national origin, in order "to promote the ways of peace and unity in the Jewish state so that the Torah will not be as two separate Torahs."

> The assumption that the above-mentioned rabbinical enactment is based only on the moral duty to give charity is erroneous. That is simply not the fact; the enactment itself creates a completely independent legal duty, which does not rest on charity at all and is therefore not limited by the narrow scope of the rules relating to charitable obligations. The Chief Rabbinate's enactment raised the age until which a father has the duty to support his children, not on the basis of giving charity to the needy, but on the basis of the legal duty of a father to support his children.

(*Id.,* p. 150, par. 2.) This is also the view of *Resp. Mishpetei Uzziel,* EH, I, #92. *But see* A. v. B., 2 *P.D.R.* 65, 92 (1956); A. & B. v. C., 3 *P.D.R.* 170, 172 (1959); A. v. B., 4 *P.D.R.* 3, 7 (1959). And *cf.* Family Law Amendment (Maintenance) Law, 1959, sec. 3 (*Laws of Israel,* 276, p. 72).

190. For similar enactments, *see supra* pp. 656–658, 817 and *infra* pp. 857–877.

191. *See supra* p. 810 for similar legislation of Maimonides in Egypt.

192. Some of the new immigrants to Israel were Sephardic Jews who did not follow Rabbenu Gershom's enactment prohibiting polygamy.

193. The question whether the primary obligation is *ḥaliẓah* or levirate marriage was disputed from a very early period, and different customs developed. *See* M. Elon, EJ, XI, pp. 122–130, s.v. Levirate marriage and *ḥaliẓah* (reprinted in *Principles,* pp. 403–409).

A new enactment adopted on the same occasion responded to the practice among some immigrant groups whereby girls were married at a very young age. The enactment prohibited child marriages:

> It is forbidden for any Jewish man to take in marriage a girl who is below the age of sixteen years and one day, because the pregnancy of anyone younger puts the mother and the child in danger of death in our times when the generations have become weaker and strength has declined, and because such marriages result in difficulties and abandonment, as evidenced by many cases. This enactment prohibits a father from giving his daughter in marriage if she is below the aforesaid age.[194]

5. TERMINATION OF LEGISLATIVE ACTIVITY

After the enactments of 1950, legislative activity ceased[195]—but not because of any lack of real-life questions requiring and demanding legislative solutions. To the contrary, many problems in all the areas of Jewish law resulting from various economic and social changes that have occurred since the end of Jewish autonomy await solution through halakhic legislation. The civil and public law by which the State of Israel is presently governed is not Jewish law, but the need and the possibility exists to infuse the principles of Jewish law into the legal system of the Jewish State; such an undertaking would require a long series of enactments in the areas of Jewish civil and administrative law.[196] Especially pressing is the need for legislation in the area of family law, inasmuch as the law of the State of Israel makes Jewish law the governing law on that subject. There are a number of problems in family law that cannot be resolved except by legislation,[197] particularly with regard to the validity of marriage, such as questions of *agunot* and *ḥaliẓah*.

194. During the same year, the Knesset passed the Marriage Age Law, 1950 (*Laws of Israel*, 57, p. 286), which established seventeen as the minimum age for marriage. However, that statute also provided that if a younger girl either gave birth or became pregnant, the district court could allow her to marry the father (sec. 5). Some ten years later, the Knesset amended the law by adding a provision that the district court could give such permission even without a birth or pregnancy, "if the girl is over the age of sixteen and the court finds that special circumstances exist to justify such permission." Marriage Age Law (Amendment), 1960 (*Laws of Israel*, 313, p. 60).

195. In 1960, a new edition of the Procedural Enactments for the Rabbinical Courts of Israel was published. The 1960 edition made some stylistic changes in the 1943 rules and added some new provisions of only minor significance. *See supra* n. 181, as to the omission in the new edition of the two paragraphs of the 1943 edition that explicitly accepted the equality of daughters and sons, and of wives and husbands, in regard to inheritance. However, this omission does not indicate any legislative intent on the part of the halakhic authorities.

196. *See infra* pp. 1600–1606, 1608–1611.

197. For example, the question of rights in property acquired by one of the spouses after marriage.

Unfortunately, however, it is precisely in regard to issues concerning the validity of marriage that there has existed for quite some time a particular reluctance to legislate. The balance of this, our final chapter on the subject of legislation as a source of law, is devoted to a historical analysis of this particular trend. This analysis will acquaint us with the factors that produced this abstention from legislating. Knowledge of these factors leads to the conclusion that today, in the current situation of the Jewish people in the State of Israel, there is no longer any impediment to the renewal of legislative activity (even on the subject of the validity of marriage) similar to that which occurred during most of the periods of Jewish legal history.

III. THE SPECIAL LEGISLATIVE TREND IN REGARD TO SOME ASPECTS OF FAMILY LAW AND THE LAW OF SUCCESSION

Legislative activity embraced the different areas of civil, family, and administrative law, and the laws of succession, evidence, and procedure. There was also wide-ranging, although less extensive, legislative activity in the area of criminal law. Jewish law confers full authority to enact criminal legislation,[198] although the extent to which this authority was actually exercised depended on the degree of juridical autonomy in the area of criminal law granted by the general government to the particular Jewish center.

One area of legislation in Jewish law, namely, family law and the law of succession, developed in a manner markedly different from all other areas. On the one hand, the authority to legislate was fully exercised in regard to the financial relationships of family members and the financial aspects of the law of succession, even when a particular enactment overrode previously existing law. On the other hand, legislative enactments voiding otherwise valid marriages gradually disappeared. Each of these two types of legislative activity will be examined, and some of the enactments already referred to will be reviewed more closely.

A. Exercise of Full Legislative Authority over Financial Aspects of Family Law and the Law of Succession

1. RESTRICTION ON THE HUSBAND'S RIGHT OF INHERITANCE

In the absence of legislation, the halakhic rule is that a husband's right to his deceased wife's property has priority over the right of any other heir,

198. *See, e.g., supra* pp. 10–11, 23–24, 47, 515–519, 688–698, 801–803, 821–822. *See also* Maimonides, *MT,* Sanhedrin 24:4–10.

including the wife's children.[199] This rule gave rise to difficulties even in an early period, inasmuch as it was at cross purposes with the trend to give a daughter a share in her father's property.[200] In particular, when a wife died soon after her marriage and her husband inherited all the property that she brought to the marriage, the rule produced a result akin to one of the Biblical curses: the wife's father "buries his daughter and also loses his money."[201] In the Talmudic period, instances are mentioned where it was agreed at the time of the marriage that if the wife died without leaving children, her dowry would return to her father's house;[202] however, if there was no such agreement, the strict legal rule applied whereby the husband inherited everything.

a. ENACTMENT OF RABBENU TAM; ENACTMENTS OF "SHUM"

A substantial change in the law relating to the husband's right of inheritance was brought about by the enactment promulgated by Rabbenu Tam at the synod at Troyes.[203] The enactment states:[204]

> Following the precedent of the inhabitants of Narbonne, whom we know and recognize and from whose elders we may learn, we have declared: Let there be an oath between us, the inhabitants of France, Anjou, and Normandy,[205] similar to what the leaders of Narbonne and its vicinity have ordained as a severe decree. . . . If a man marries a woman and she dies within twelve months, leaving no child surviving at the expiration of one year following the marriage, he shall return the wife's entire dowry and jewels to her heirs or to the donors. He shall not deceitfully consume that part of the dowry remaining in his possession which has not yet been spent or consumed; whatever has not been spent or consumed shall be first used to pay for her burial in keeping

199. *See* the sources cited *supra* p. 573 n. 122.

200. As to the *ketubbah* clause concerning the wife's sons, *see supra* pp. 575–578.

201. *Sifra,* Leviticus, Beḥukkotai, 5:3, on Leviticus 26:20 states:

> "Your strength shall be spent to no purpose." . . . Another interpretation: This refers to a man who gives his daughter in marriage with a large sum of money [as dowry], and before the end of the seven days of the post-marriage festivities his daughter dies, with the result that he buries his daughter and also loses his money.

See also the text of Rabbenu Tam's enactment, quoted *infra.*

202. TJ Ketubbot 9:1, 53b (9:1, 33a), the statement of R. Yose. *See also supra* p. 126 n. 141.

203. *See supra* p. 787. The various enactments in Germany, Spain, and elsewhere on the husband's right of inheritance are fully discussed by Assaf, *supra* n. 25 at 79–94. Some of the enactments are also set forth in Schepansky, "Takkanot Shum," *supra* n. 4 at 177–192; apparently Schepansky was unaware of Assaf's article, which he did not mention.

204. *Sefer ha-Yashar le-Rabbenu Tam,* Novellae, #788 (ed. Schlesinger, pp. 465–466).

205. Later in the enactment, the inhabitants of Poitou are also referred to as being bound by the enactment. The text implies that the halakhic authorities of Narbonne adopted the enactment before Rabbenu Tam, but that it was not then widely accepted, and it was Rabbenu Tam who established it as binding.

with her dignity, and the balance shall be returned within thirty days upon demand. He is not subject to this decree until demand has been made upon him. . . .

We, the inhabitants of Troyes, have accepted this enactment . . . and we have sent [the enactment] to nearby villages within a day's journey and they were pleased with it; for, after a wife's death, who other than the donor should consume or enjoy[206] what a father or anyone else who gave the woman in marriage had given [lit. "jumped to give"][207] to the groom? Should the husband consume it and be joyful?[208] We have decided on a one-year limit because after one year what has been given is forgotten and will not increase the sorrow.[209]

The enactment thus provided that if a wife dies within one year after her marriage, the entire dowry is to be returned to her heirs or to the person who gave it to her. The rationale is that it is inequitable for a husband to have the use of money that belongs to someone else—in this case, to the father or whoever else furnished the dowry. Consequently, the enactment applies only if the wife dies during the first year of her marriage; after that time, the father or the donor of the dowry begins to forget what he gave.

This enactment is inconsistent with the halakhic rule that a husband is the heir of his wife irrespective of when she dies. In his statement, Rabbenu Tam emphasized that Talmudic law does indeed provide that the husband is the heir of his wife even in the case to which the enactment was directed, and he continued:

Afterward, I remembered what was written in Leviticus, and I thanked God that we succeeded in escaping from being worthy of the Biblical curses; for we read in that Biblical section, "Your strength shall be spent to no purpose," and there is a comment[210] to the effect that this refers to a man who gives his daughter in marriage with a large sum of money [as dowry], and before the end of the seven days of the post-marriage festivities his daughter dies, with the result that he buries his daughter and also loses his money.[211] Just as we have escaped from this [through the enactment], so shall we escape from all evil decrees, and may we hear only good tidings and let there be peace for Israel.

206. *Cf.* Ecclesiastes 2:25: "For who eats and who enjoys but myself?"

207. *Cf.* TB Ketubbot 52b: "To encourage a man [lit. "so that a man should jump"] to give to his daughter as much as he gives to his son." *See supra* p. 576.

208. *Cf.* TB Bava Batra 171b: "Shall he consume and be joyful [at spending someone else's money]?"

209. *Cf.* Proverbs 10:22, according to Schlesinger's comments, *supra* n. 204.

210. *See supra* n. 201.

211. This is the end of the comment of *Sifra; see supra* n. 201.

The Tosafists have informed us that toward the end of his life Rabbenu Tam changed his mind about the enactment.[212] However, the enactment became accepted, and was even extended at the beginning of the thirteenth century in the Enactments of "Shum":

> The enactment of "Shum" is as follows: If she dies leaving no child surviving, during the first year he shall return the entire amount, and during the second year he shall return half of all that remains from the dowry that has not been consumed. He shall not deceitfully consume anything, but he may pay [out of the dowry] the cost of the burial in accordance with the custom of the locality and according to her station and his.[213]

The enactments of "Shum" limited the right of a husband to inherit even when his wife dies within two years after her marriage, although during the second year the wife's heirs would be entitled to only half of the dowry. The enactments of "Shum" were followed in France and Germany, and afterward also in Poland, Lithuania, Russia, Hungary, Moravia, and Bohemia; and there is extensive and detailed halakhic literature dealing with the particulars of the enactments and the changes made in them in the various places in which they were in force.[214]

b. ENACTMENTS IN SPAIN; ENACTMENTS OF TOLEDO, MOLINA, ALGERIA, AND FEZ

In the very same period as the enactments of "Shum," legislation was adopted in the Spanish center that even further limited a husband's right of inheritance and applied even when there were surviving children, and without regard to the time of his wife's death. Such legislation was the subject of a responsum by Meir ha-Levi Abulafia (Ramah).[215] Ramah was asked for a ruling as to the division of the estate of a woman who had died leaving a husband, son, and father, and his responsum referred to various enactments in force in his time that were contrary to Talmudic law. Ramah stated:

> It is our view that if you have neither an agreement nor an enactment (*minhag*)[216] with regard to the husband's succession to his wife's property, but

212. *Tosafot,* Ketubbot 47a, s.v. Katav lah perot kesut ve-khelim (in the continuation thereof at 47b). *See also supra* p. 787.

213. *Yam Shel Shelomo,* Ketubbot 4:14. For v.l. in other sources, *see* Schepansky, "Takkanot Shum," *supra* n. 4 at 179ff.

214. *See* Assaf, *supra* n. 25 at 90–93. The Ashkenazic communities in Italy, the Balkans, and the Land of Israel also continued to follow the "Shum" enactments. *Id.*

215. *Resp. Ramah* #298.

216. The term *minhag* (which ordinarily means "custom") occasionally refers to an enactment, as it does here; *see infra* pp. 885–886.

> solely Talmudic law, Reuben [the husband] should inherit all of his wife's property, and neither her son, nor Simeon, her father, has any rights whatever. If you have an enactment that the son inherits everything, Reuben has no right to his wife's property during his son's lifetime. . . . If you have an enactment providing that the husband and son inherit equally, or that one of them receives more than the other, the law is that whatever Reuben inherits under the enactment, whether little or much, is to be given to him; he may use it as he wishes, and no one has any right to object to this. The portion distributable to the son pursuant to the enactment, whether little or much, is to be dealt with like any other property belonging to heirs.

This responsum indicates that, with regard to succession by the husband, different enactments were in force, varying from place to place: (a) the son inherited everything, and the husband received nothing; (b) the husband and son inherited equally; (c) the husband took a greater share than the son, or vice versa. These enactments cover the case of a woman survived by children and do not contain any limitations based on the time of the wife's death; in both these respects they are at variance with the enactments of "Shum."

In the middle of the thirteenth century, detailed enactments were adopted in Toledo and, after a short while, also in Molina and in other communities, on the subject of the husband's right of inheritance.[217] The enactments of Toledo and Molina provided that if a wife dies leaving children (whether male or female), her estate is to be divided equally between her husband and her children. If the wife dies without children, her estate is to be divided equally between her husband and her legal heirs. These enactments, which, with certain modifications, gradually spread to most of the Spanish communities and afterward to the Jewish centers in Morocco and Algeria,[218] made substantial changes in the Talmudic law concerning the husband's rights of inheritance. From this time on, it was prescribed that a husband never inherits the whole of his wife's estate (even though he is entitled to it under the strict law) but only half. The other half passes to the children, or, if there are none, to the wife's legal heirs.

217. The enactments are quoted in *Resp. Asheri* in various sections of *Kelal* 55, and in *Tur* EH ch. 118. Ramah (who died in 1244) did not know of these enactments, and Asheri (*Resp. Asheri* 55:9–10) refers to them as enactments that were adopted one or two generations previously. *See* Assaf, *supra* n. 25 at 85 n. 1.

218. *See* Assaf, *supra* n. 25 at 84–90. As to the enactments in Algeria, *see Resp. Tashbeẓ*, quoted *infra* (text accompanying n. 220). In various places, enactments described as "after the practice of Damascus" (*ke-minhag Damesek*) were adopted that were more similar to the "Shum" enactments in that if there were surviving children, the husband inherited all of his wife's property. The Damascus enactments were followed in Egypt, the Land of Israel, Turkey, and the Balkans.

As stated, these enactments were also adopted in Algeria, with certain changes in favor of the husband.[219] At the outset of his discussion of them, Simeon b. Ẓemaḥ Duran (Rashbeẓ) stated:[220]

> The enactment abrogates the husband's Biblical right of inheritance. There is authority to do this, for we find that the Sages of Israel enacted the *ketubbah* clause concerning the wife's sons to encourage a man to give to his daughter as much as he gives to his son.[221] Similarly, Rabbenu Tam enacted that if a wife dies during the first year of the marriage, her father should inherit her dowry so that the curse "Your strength shall be spent to no purpose," which was interpreted to apply to this situation,[222] should not be fulfilled. Since it has become the practice to give a large dowry, it was enacted that some of the husband's inheritance should be taken from him, and such an enactment is valid.[223]

These enactments were also adopted in the community of Fez, this time with changes in favor of the wife, and in many other communities.[224]

2. RIGHT OF A MOTHER TO INHERIT

An enactment of Toledo introduced an additional substantial change in the order of succession to an estate, in regard to a mother's right of inheritance.

219. The main change was that if there were no children, the wife's heirs received not one-half of the estate, as in the Toledo enactment, but only one-third; *see Resp. Tashbeẓ,* II, #292, *tikkun* 3. It was also provided that the wife could not by will deprive the children of their half of the estate; however, if there were no surviving children, she could bequeath the one-third as she wished.

220. *Resp. Tashbeẓ,* II, #292, *tikkun* 3. For the enactments referred to in this responsum, *see supra* pp. 805–806.

221. TB Ketubbot 52b.

222. *See supra* p. 836 and n. 201.

223. *See Resp. Asheri* 55:1: ". . . they took away the right of inheritance from the husband, who inherits under Biblical law, and gave it to her heirs." *See also* the further comments in *Resp. Tashbeẓ:*

> Although the *rishonim* wrote that an agreement between a man and his wife that he would not inherit from her is valid only if made while they were betrothed [*i.e.,* before the nuptial ceremony], as is clear from chapter "Ha-Kotev" [TB Ketubbot 83a] and chapter "Ḥezkat" [TB Bava Batra 43a—although the Talmud there does not refer to a husband and his betrothed], a communal enactment is not so limited. This is shown by the statement in chapter "Yesh Noḥalin" [TB Bava Batra 131a] in connection with the enactment relating to the *ketubbah* clause concerning the wife's sons that even though it [the clause] involves a transfer of ownership of something not yet in existence, the Sages said that a stipulation [*i.e.,* an enactment] of the court is different [from a private agreement]. The same rule and the same rationale apply to a communal enactment. . . . Rashba also wrote in a responsum that a communal enactment is like a stipulation of the court.

See the discussion, *supra* p. 706 n. 10 and pp. 713–714, on the nature of communal enactments.

224. *See supra* p. 808 and n. 104.

Under the strict law, the order of succession (except for a husband) is as follows: (1) surviving sons; (2) descendants of deceased sons; (3) surviving daughters; (4) descendants of deceased daughters; (5) father; (6) father's descendants, *i.e.*, brothers and sisters of the decedent; (7) grandfather; (8) descendants of grandfather, etc.[225] Under this order of succession, a decedent's mother does not inherit from him. Thus, under the enactment of Toledo, discussed above, if a mother gives a dowry to her daughter and the daughter dies childless, then half the dowry—*i.e.*, half of the daughter's property—passes to her heirs and not to her mother, as the mother does not inherit from her children, even though she provided the dowry. Therefore, an additional enactment was adopted in Toledo providing that if a wife dies childless and her estate consists of a dowry received from her mother, the mother receives half of the daughter's estate, to the exclusion of the other heirs;[226] the other half, as stated, is inherited by her husband. This enactment established for the first time, although in a limited form, the right of a mother to inherit from her children.

3. RESTRICTION ON A WIDOW'S RIGHT TO RECOVER THE AMOUNT OF HER *KETUBBAH*

Under the strict law, a widow recovers the entire amount of her *ketubbah* from her husband's estate, even if the entire estate is thereby depleted. At times, this law resulted in the widow's receiving the great bulk of the estate and the heirs receiving almost nothing, although they, no less than she, were often in need of a distributive share. The legislation of Molina and Toledo therefore enacted the following new rules:[227]

a. If there are surviving children and the widow seeks to recover not only what is legally hers under the "main" *ketubbah* together with the supplementary increment stated in the *ketubbah* (*tosefet ketubbah*), but also her dowry, she may recover only up to half the value of the estate. The heirs may elect either to pay the entire amount due to the widow (which they would do if this amount was less than half the value of the estate) or to give her half the estate (which they would do if the amount of her claim exceeded half the value of the estate).
b. If there are no surviving children, but only other heirs, the widow first receives what has remained in tangible form from the property that she

225. Numbers 27:8–11; M Bava Batra 8:1–2.

226. *Resp. Asheri* 55:1; *Tur* EH ch. 118. *See also* Gulak, *Yesodei*, III, p. 94.

227. *Resp. Asheri* 55:7–8; *Tur* EH ch. 118. In connection with these enactments, both these sources refer to "the community of Molina, [which] agreed . . ." and "the text of the enactment of the community of Molina. . . ." However, this enactment was also adopted in Toledo; *see Resp. Asheri* 55:7: "It also appears to me that this is the practice here in Toledo. . . ."

> brought with her from her father's house as a dowry; in addition, she is entitled to recover on her claim up to half the value of the estate, with the other half being divided among the other relatives. Here, too, the heirs were given an election: they could either give her the entire amount of her *ketubbah* and her dowry or they could give her half the estate.

The widow's rights were thus greater if the husband was not survived by children: if there were no surviving children, she could recover the property that she brought with her from her father's house (if the property remained in tangible form), and also whatever else she was entitled to up to half the value of the estate, whereas if there were surviving children, she could recover her property (including her dowry) only up to half the value of the estate.

As stated, particular circumstances made this enactment necessary to prevent the children and the other heirs from being deprived of a share of the estate. The purpose here, too, was to change the law: "The purpose of the enactment is to effect a different result from that prescribed by the law of the Torah, for that law provides that the widow may recover the entire amount of her *ketubbah*."[228]

4. EQUAL RIGHTS OF INHERITANCE FOR SONS AND DAUGHTERS IN CERTAIN CIRCUMSTANCES

At the beginning of the fourteenth century, there was legislation in effect in Valladolid (some of which was based on the enactments of Toledo) that provided for equality of inheritance rights under certain circumstances between sons and daughters.[229] These enactments are set forth in a responsum by Yom Tov b. Abraham Ishbili (Ritba):[230]

> The community of Valladolid and its leaders (*berurim*), chosen with the approval of Rabbenu Todros ha-Levi (may God protect and save him), have decided to adopt the following enactment concerning which they have decreed a full and severe ban, to be effective for a period of fifty years from the date of its enactment.
>
> If a woman dies during the lifetime of her husband, leaving a son or sons by him surviving, the sons shall inherit half of the estate, and the father shall inherit the other half.
>
> If the son has a sister born to the deceased mother, and the sister has never been married and is a virgin, she shall receive and inherit an equal share with the son in the half of the property that is to be received by him.

228. *Resp. Asheri* 55:7.
229. A tendency to give a daughter a share in her father's estate and also to make her an heir was already apparent in the Talmud; *see supra* pp. 575–580, 655–656.
230. *Resp. Ritba* #180.

If a man dies during the lifetime of his wife, leaving issue by her surviving him, such issue shall inherit two-thirds of all the property and the widow shall inherit one-third, with a son having priority over a daughter in all matters of inheritance, unless the daughter has never been married, as stated above, in which case she shall take her share among the sons in the manner above described.

If a man dies during the lifetime of his wife, leaving no issue by her surviving him, his wife shall take half of the estate for her *ketubbah* and her dowry, and the other half shall be inherited by his legal heirs.

If a woman dies during the lifetime of her husband, leaving no issue by him surviving her, the husband shall give to her legal heirs from her father's family one-third of all her property, and the husband shall receive the other two-thirds.

This enactment shall apply to all those who have not agreed otherwise with regard to the manner in which they will inherit each other's property. . . . The law of succession and rights of inheritance for men and women as stated shall apply to all those whose *ketubbah* was written in Valladolid, and to their descendants and their heirs after them even if they shall not live in that town; the law shall be the same for all of them.[231]

These enactments follow the model of Toledo and Molina in regard to the division of a wife's estate between her husband and her children and in regard to restricting a widow's right to recover the amount due her by allowing her only a portion of the estate, although the actual proportions are not the same as in the enactments of Toledo and Molina. The innovation in the Valladolid enactments is that if the wife dies leaving a son and a daughter, each one of them inherits an equal share in the half of the estate that goes to her children according to the enactment of Toledo.[232] It is true that the daughter's right of inheritance is conditional: it exists only for a daughter who has never married, and its purpose is to permit her to inherit property that will provide for the expenses of her marriage, just as in the case of the earlier enactment concerning one-tenth of the estate.[233] However, the

231. Subsequent sections of the enactments limit the husband's right to make bequests contrary to the legislative provisions.

232. The Toledo enactment (*Resp. Asheri* 55:1; *Tur* EH 118) states: "If a woman dies during the lifetime of her husband leaving issue by him surviving, a son or a daughter, . . . her entire estate . . . shall be divided equally between the husband and such issue." This can be interpreted as meaning that the son and daughter receive equal shares, although this is not stated explicitly. An alternative interpretation is that "a son or a daughter" is a description of surviving issue, and the provision that the husband shares equally with such issue means only that the husband takes one-half and the children one-half, but the enactment does not specify how the children are to divide their share *inter se*. Apparently, such specification was a later development, which appears in the Valladolid enactment.

233. *See supra* pp. 578–580 as to the enactment concerning one-tenth of the estate. *See further Resp. Ritba* #180, to the effect that the dowry promised by the girl's father or mother is to be included in the half she inherits.

essential difference between the two enactments is that, contrary to the earlier enactment that the daughter was to inherit one-tenth of the estate, the Valladolid enactment establishes a right of inheritance which, although its sole purpose is to finance marriage, is fully equal to the son's.

It is interesting to note how Ritba in his responsum explains the halakhic validity of the Valladolid enactment on the basis of the discussion in Tractate *Yevamot:*[234]

> The principle of *hefker bet din hefker* (the court has the power to expropriate property) is a sufficient basis to transfer the entire inheritance from a father, who is a Biblical heir, to a husband, who is a complete stranger under Biblical law [*i.e.,* where a husband inherits from his wife who is a minor, even though under Biblical law he is not married to her at all].[235]
>
> It is also stated in chapter *Yesh Noḥalin:*[236] "No one [not even a patriarch (*nasi*) of Israel] may rule that a decedent's daughter inherits together with the daughter of the decedent's son, because this is the view of Sadducees."[237] The most logical explanation by our rabbis of the reason why reference is made to the patriarch of Israel is that [ordinarily] he has the power to expropriate property, and the only reason that he may not do this in the case discussed is that such a ruling would reflect the view of the Sadducees; but, if not for that reason, the patriarch may legislate by the power of expropriation to transfer a portion of an inheritance from a son to a daughter.
>
> This is also shown by the stipulation that was made concerning the tribe of Benjamin.[238] On what basis can a distinction be made between those transfers and the transfer of part of an inheritance from a son to a daughter, inasmuch as both involve transfers that infringe a Biblical right?

Ritba's explanation is extremely enlightening. On the basis of the power of the court to expropriate property, the order of inheritance can be determined, if sufficient reason exists, by the needs of the time; and in this respect there is no difference between permitting a daugher to inherit even when there is a son—a result contrary to Biblical law—and conferring a right of inheritance on any other person contrary to Biblical law. It is true

234. TB Yevamot 89b.

235. *See supra* pp. 508–509.

236. TB Bava Batra 115b.

237. According to Biblical law, a daughter inherits only if there is no son. Similarly, if a son dies in his father's lifetime leaving issue, his issue—and not the decedent's daughter—inherit, since the son's issue succeed to his rights. Thus, a son's daughter, *i.e.,* the decedent's granddaughter, has priority over her aunt, the decedent's daughter. The Sadducees disputed this rule and deduced by means of an *a fortiori* inference that a daughter should inherit together with a granddaughter: "If the son's daughter, who succeeds to the rights of the son, inherits from the decedent, the decedent's own daughter, who directly succeeds to the rights of the decedent, should certainly inherit!" Rabban Johanan b. Zakkai demonstrated the invalidity of this inference. *See* the discussion in TB Bava Batra 115b–116a.

238. TB Bava Batra 116a.

that if in a particular case this would reflect the view of the Sadducees, the enactment would be prohibited because it would appear that the interpretation of a Biblical law by the Sadducees is being accepted, contrary to the acccepted traditional interpretation of the Sages, and "it would be thought that we do so as a matter of Biblical law and that we accept their [*i.e.*, the Sadducees'] view."[239] However, when this concern is absent, the halakhic authorities may adopt enactments—even if radically inconsistent with Biblical law—with regard to the division of an estate, to accord with the needs of the time and circumstance: "If not for the position of the Sadducees, that enactment may be adopted even if it is contrary to Biblical law."[240]

It may be conjectured that the Valladolid enactment was followed in practice in places other than Valladolid; but in any event, almost two hundred years later, an enactment providing for equality of rights of inheritance between daughters and sons, with certain limitations, was adopted by the Castilian exiles in Fez, Morocco.[241] The enactment provides:[242]

> If they [husband and wife] are survived by sons and daughters, the daughters shall inherit equally with the sons. This applies only before the daughters are married. If they were betrothed, the share that they will inherit shall be devoted to their marriage, because the purpose of their inheritance under this enactment is to enable them to marry if the amount of the inheritance is adequate for that purpose. If it is not adequate, the expenses of the marriage shall be made up from the remainder [of the estate]. If the amount of the inheritance of a betrothed girl is greater than the expense of the marriage, she shall receive the entire amount.

This enactment was undoubtedly influenced by the legislation of Valladolid, and both have the common purpose of enabling a daughter to marry. However, this enactment of Fez did not apply (as the enactment of Valladolid did) only to the one-half share that the wife's children receive from their mother's estate under legislation like that of Toledo. The Fez enactment deals with the children's general rights of inheritance, and applies even to their father's estate.[243] As to whether there is halakhic author-

239. Ritba, Novellae to Bava Batra 115b, s.v. Kol ha-omer tirash. *See* his interpretation there, which accords with his explanation quoted above with regard to the Valladolid enactment. Similarly, *see Tosafot, ad loc.*, s.v. Afillu nasi she-be-Yisra'el.

240. *Nimmukei Yosef* to Alfasi, Bava Batra 115b, s.v. Kol ha-omer tirash bat, where this conclusion is based on the Talmudic passage: "From here it may be concluded that if not for the position of the Sadducees. . . ."

241. As to these enactments, *see supra* p. 808.

242. *Kerem Ḥemer*, Enactment #8 (p. 2c/d).

243. Although the enactments set forth first in the compilation are patterned on the Toledo enactments—in the form in which they were accepted in Algeria—and provide that when a wife dies leaving children, the children inherit one-half of her estate, and that if there are no children, the wife's heirs inherit a one-third share (Enactments #2 and #3, p.

ity to enact such legislation, the explanation of Ritba, above noted, certainly establishes that such authority exists with respect to any estate.[244]

B. Decline in Legislation Directly Affecting the Validity of Marriage and Divorce

In contrast to the legislative activity concerning financial relationships in family law and the law of succession, there developed a reluctance—culminating in almost complete abstention—in regard to enacting legislation affecting the basic validity of marriage and divorce. As noted in previous chapters, the halakhic authorities in all earlier periods, including the geonic period, exercised to the full their legislative prerogative in the area of marriage and divorce. Although there was a difference of opinion between some of the Babylonian *amoraim* and the *amoraim* in the Land of Israel with regard to the authority of the Sages to annul a marriage that is valid under Biblical law, this disagreement transcended marriage and divorce; it concerned the basic general issue of whether a court has the power to "uproot a Biblical rule through an affirmative act," *i.e.*, to mandate or permit an act the Torah forbids.

Moreover, this disagreement, even according to the *amoraim* of Babylonia, did not impair the continuation of legislative activity with regard to the validity of a marriage. Such legislative activity rested on two bases: (a) the authority to annul a marriage that was "improperly effected," and (b) the authority to annul a marriage on the basis of the principle that "all who marry do so subject to the conditions laid down by the Rabbis, and the

---

2b), the enactments set forth later (#4, #5, #6, #7; p. 2b/c) refer to a husband's death or the death of either husband or wife. Enactment #143 (p. 26b/c) is explicit: ". . . If the husband dies first, his wife shall take one-half, and the other half shall be divided equally among all males and unmarried females . . ." (*id.*, p. 26c). Enactment #143 likewise emphasizes that a daughter inherits "only if she has never been married. But married females, widows, or divorcees take nothing when there are males" (*id.*, p. 26b). Enactment #143 contains an additional restriction on a daughter's right to inherit equally with a son, which is also present in #30 (p. 5d), #214 and #215 (p. 38d); *see* there for details. Apparently this restriction was not in Enactment #8 (p. 2c/d) as originally adopted in 1545.

244. The question of a daughter's right to a share in her father's estate was also widely discussed in Germany, Poland, and Lithuania; and it was largely resolved by the institution of what was called "a deed of half a male" (*shetar ḥazi zakhar*, also known as "a deed of inheritance"). *See, e.g.*, *Resp. Maharil* #88; *Resp. Maharam Mintz* #47; Rema to Sh. Ar. EH 90. For detailed discussion, *see* S. Assaf, "Li-She'elat ha-Yerushah Shel ha-Bat" [On the Question of Inheritance by a Daughter], *Jacob Freimann Jubilee Volume*, pp. 8–11. *See also supra* pp. 828–829 as to the equalization of daughters with sons (and of wives with husbands) with respect to inheritance, in the Procedural Enactments of the Chief Rabbinate of the Land of Israel, 1943 (Enactments #182, #183).

Rabbis annul this marriage."[245] This latter principle served as a foundation for the legislation by the *geonim* affecting the validity of a marriage or divorce.[246]

Starting with the twelfth century, there was a tendency to restrict such legislation. This trend began in Germany and after a while extended to Spain. Starting in the fourteenth century, statements were made in various Jewish centers that although the authority to adopt enactments annulling marriages has been conferred and still exists, this authority should not actually be exercised. This position was gradually accepted in the overwhelming majority of Jewish centers, although in certain Sephardic Jewish communities, such enactments were still being adopted in the eighteenth and nineteenth centuries. The following discussion examines certain aspects of this progressive attenuation of one of the important areas of Jewish legislation[247] and attempts to identify the causes that brought it about.

A major impetus for the debate concerning the authority to enact legislation annulling marriages was the problem created by fraudulent marriages, also called "abduction marriages," "secret marriages," and "deceitful marriages."[248] Under the strict law, a woman who, in the presence of two witnesses, is given a ring or any article of value for the purpose of marriage is married even without any additional ceremony or the recital of the marriage benedictions or any other formalities.

In all Jewish centers, in every era, there were incidents when a young man succeeded, by trickery, abduction, or other improper means, in giving a young woman a ring in the presence of two witnesses. The argument can, of course, be made that such a marriage is invalid *ab initio*—that there was no real consent on the part of the woman, that the witnesses were not competent, etc.; but the question was not entirely free from doubt, and the halakhic authorities required a divorce to permit the woman to remarry. This situation had the potential of making many women *agunot* and putting them in a desperate plight; it invited successful attempts at extortion by the "husband."

245. *See supra* pp. 506, 521–522, 564–566, 631–642. In this and the subsequent discussion, the Hebrew term *kiddushin*, which literally means "betrothal," is translated as "marriage," since the reference is to the marital relationship. *See supra* p. 506 n. 58.

246. *See supra* pp. 656–665. According to some halakhic authorities, the annulment of a marriage is also a consequence of Rabbenu Gershom's enactments. *See supra* p. 786 and n. 20.

247. This question is comprehensively discussed by A.H. Freimann, *Kiddushin ve-Nissu'in, passim*. Our discussion will attempt to discern from the responsa the causes for this attenuation.

248. A similar question had arisen as early as the geonic period; *see supra* p. 657. Marriage following a kidnapping had actually occurred and had already been a subject of discussion in the tannaitic and amoraic periods. *See supra* pp. 424–425, 638–639.

Consequently, many communities adopted enactments containing various requirements to assure that a marriage would be effected only in a public ceremony (*e.g.*, by requiring the presence of ten people, a rabbi, etc.) and providing for fines and other sanctions against anyone (including the witnesses to the proscribed marriage) violating the enactment. These sanctions, however, were inadequate. The only effective sanction was to render fraudulent marriages totally invalid. This had indeed been done under similar circumstances in one way or another in prior periods.[249] However, here the central question arose: Does the authority to annul an otherwise legally valid marriage also exist in the post-Talmudic period?

This question has been the subject of very extensive debate in halakhic literature, which the following discussion briefly reviews.

1. CONTROVERSY BETWEEN THE AUTHORITIES OF MAINZ AND THE AUTHORITIES OF WORMS AND SPEYER IN THE TWELFTH CENTURY

In the twelfth century, an incident occurred that involved a fraudulent marriage. No explicit enactment regulating the manner of effecting a marriage was applicable to the case, and the halakhic authorities disagreed as to whether it was possible to annul the marriage. Raban (Eliezer b. Nathan of Mainz) described the incident:[250]

> An incident occurred in Cologne in which a young man was in the midst of negotiating with the parents of a young woman of his acquaintance for her marriage when another man of wealth appeared on the scene and arranged to marry her. Her father instructed her to marry the second man; and the public was invited, as is customary for a marriage. When the second man was about to marry her, the first man's relatives deceitfully got to her first and the first man married her [*i.e.*, recited the marriage formula and gave her a ring] in the presence of witnesses who had been prepared in advance. When her parents realized what was happening, they told her, "Throw away the ring." She did so and married the second man on that occasion.
>
> The girl's father came to Mainz and gathered all of the scholars of the communities in the synagogue of Mainz. They all strongly condemned the act of the first man, for such deceit has no place among Jews. The scholars of the time—Jacob ha-Levi of Worms and his academy and Isaac ha-Levi of Speyer and the members of his academy—wanted to annul completely the marriage to the first man.
>
> They relied on the incident described in Tractate *Yevamot*, chapter *Bet*

249. *See supra* n. 248.
250. *Resp. Raban*, EH, III, p. 47b (ed. Jerusalem).

Shammai,[251] which took place in the city of Naresh. A girl had been betrothed while still a minor. When she became of age and while her father was preparing to finalize the marriage by means of the *ḥuppah* [the nuptial ceremony], another man appeared, abducted her, and married her. The court returned her to the first man and did not even require a divorce from the second. R. Ashi explained that the second man had acted improperly in abducting her from the first, whom she was supposed to marry.

> Even though the first man was not betrothed to her (since the betrothal of a minor is ineffective) and he had not yet married her when she became of age, the Sages annulled the marriage to the second man notwithstanding that the marriage ceremony had been correctly performed, because he [the second man] acted improperly. In this case too [*i.e.,* the incident in Cologne, the rabbis of Worms and Speyer argued that] we should annul the marriage of the first man who abducted her from the second man whom she was supposed to, and was about to, marry.

The authorities of Worms and Speyer were thus prepared to annul the marriage to the first man, as in the case in the Babylonian Talmud, because it was effected improperly; but this was not the view of the halakhic authorities of Mainz. Raban continued:

> My teacher and father-in-law, Rabbenu Elyakim, and my colleague, Jacob ha-Levi, and I, following them, said that even if the first marriage amounted to no more than a public rumor, yet inasmuch as a report did spread that she married the first man . . . we must be concerned about a rumor. . . . Since the first man did negotiate a marriage to her, perhaps the girl agreed to the marriage even though she later threw away the ring as directed by her mother; and, furthermore, even if the Rabbis [*i.e.,* the Talmudic Sages] had the power to annul a marriage, we do not have such a power of annulment, and it stands to reason that we do not have such power. . . .
>
> We did not follow their opinion [*i.e.,* the opinion of the rabbis of Worms and Speyer] to annul the first marriage, because she was from our area [she was our relative (?)], and we feared a scandal in our city; those who committed the deed were influential with the government, and we had no coercive power. We advised her relatives to pay the young man some money to free her, and this is what happened. The first man gave her a divorce and the second one betrothed and married her and the matter was accomplished legally. I record this to teach future generations.

According to the scholars of Mainz, post-Talmudic authorities, unlike the Talmudic Sages, do not have the power to annul such a marriage, but a way out was ultimately found in that case by arranging for the young man who had married the girl through trickery to consent to a divorce. This view

251. TB Yevamot 110a; *see supra* pp. 638–639.

of the halakhic authorities of Mainz was also held by Rabbenu Tam, who denied that even the *geonim* had authority to annul such marriages.[252]

2. ANNULMENT OF MARRIAGE ON THE STRENGTH OF AN EXPLICIT ENACTMENT; THE VIEWS OF ASHERI, RASHBA, AND RABBENU JEROHAM

In the thirteenth century, Asheri and Rashba made an important distinction in regard to annulment of marriages. According to this distinction, the post-Talmudic halakhic authorities do not have the power to annul a marriage on the ground that it was effected improperly or on the ground that the marriage was entered into "subject to the conditions laid down by the Rabbis"; but if an enactment explicitly states that a marriage in violation of its provisions is void, the provision is effective and the marriage is invalid. Asheri's view is indicated in two responsa.

The first responsum "involved a widow who was a member of a prominent family, and an elementary school teacher who was living in her house. It happened that he married her in the presence of two witnesses."[253] The responsum indicates that the teacher married the widow through all manner of schemes and trickery, and the widow declared that she "despises him and sooner than being married to him, she would rather be an *agunah* all her life. She is a member of a prominent family and the widow of a scholar."

In addition to the problem of a fraudulent marriage, the responsum presented a second issue: the teacher married the woman with a ring he borrowed from his brother, and the halakhic authorities disagree as to whether a borrowed ring can be used to effect a marriage. After a long discussion, Asheri concluded that the marriage can be valid even though the ring was borrowed, and "it is advisable to appease and satisfy him with money to induce him to divorce her." As to the question of fraudulent marriage, he continued:

> It may appear to you, being close to the matter, that the man is not worthy or fit to be married to a woman of good family and that he misled her through schemes and trickery, so that the matter is quite similar to the incident at Naresh described in Tractate *Yevamot,* chapter *Bet Shammai,*[254] where a marriage was annulled because a man acted improperly. If so, although we will not annul the marriage in our case, yet we may rely on the opinion of some of the Rabbis who ruled that a divorce may be compelled in a case involving a *moredet* (wife who refuses to cohabit with her husband). Nevertheless, the

252. *See supra* pp. 661–662.
253. *Resp. Asheri* 35:2.
254. TB Yevamot 110a.

> attempt should be made to appease him with money; if he is not willing, I will support you in compelling him to divorce her.

Asheri was thus of the opinion that in his time there was no authority, similar to that exercised in the case that occurred in Naresh, to annul the marriage involved in the incident giving rise to the responsum, and that only the Talmudic Sages had the authority to decree such an annulment. However, the husband could be forced to grant a divorce on the basis of the geonic enactment that, if the wife is a *moredet,* the husband can be compelled to divorce her; such divorce is not the product of improper coercion (*get me'usseh*).[255]

From the second responsum[256] by Asheri, we may conclude that he took the view that while the rationale that "he acted improperly" is insufficient to annul a marriage, nevertheless, if there was an explicit provision in an enactment that invalidates a marriage effected in violation of the enactment, the marriage is void.

The question submitted to Asheri was as follows:

> May a court adopt an enactment that provides that any marriage that takes place without the consent of the bride's father or mother is invalid, and that the court shall expropriate the money [*i.e.,* thing of value, customarily a ring] given by the groom to the bride to effect the marriage? The issue is whether the matter concerns religious law (*issur*), in which case the court may not enact a rule different from the law of the Torah, or whether it is a matter of monetary law (*mamon),* governed by the rule that any stipulation on a monetary matter is valid.

It is likely that this enactment requiring parental consent was adopted in reaction to the problem of fraudulent marriages. The question was whether the enactment involved a matter of *issur,* in which event the court could not abrogate a law of the Torah by annulling a marriage the Torah regards as valid, or a monetary matter, as to which all stipulations—even those that vary from a law of the Torah—are valid.

The following was Asheri's response:

> There is no room to argue here that it is a monetary stipulation; it is quite clear that this argument cannot sustain this enactment. But the enactment is valid for a different reason, as stated in chapter *Ha-Ishah Rabbah:*[257] "What is the source of the principle that the court may expropriate property (*hefker bet din hefker*)? It is written [Ezra 10:8]: 'Anyone who does not come in three

255. *See supra* pp. 658–660 and Asheri's view of the geonic enactment, *supra* pp. 662ff.
256. *Resp. Asheri* 35:1.
257. TB Yevamot 89b.

days, as required by the officers and elders, will have his property confiscated.'"

All who marry do so subject to the conditions laid down by the Rabbis, and in every generation all who marry do so subject to the enactments that the halakhic authorities of that generation have adopted as protective measures. A marriage is valid only if it conforms to their legislation; even if the marriage is effected by means of intercourse, they have declared the act to be fornication. This applies even more so if the marriage was effected by means of money, in view of the principle of *hefker bet din hefker;* the court has expropriated the money he gave her and there is no marriage here at all.

Asheri's responsum made two points: On the one hand, it is clear that an enactment concerning the validity of a marriage is not a stipulation on a monetary matter, and therefore cannot be validated as such a stipulation; there is no authority to enact legislation that uproots a law of the Torah on a matter of *issur.* On the other hand, this enactment can be validated on the basis of the combination of the principles that the court has power to expropriate property and that all who marry do so subject to the conditions laid down by the Rabbis, *i.e.,* subject to the consent of the contemporaneous halakhic authorities. Consequently, the marriage is void even if it was effected by means of intercourse, because these authorities have declared the act to be fornication. This applies all the more if the marriage was effected by means of money given by the groom to the bride, because the halakhic authorities expropriated the money, and thus the marriage is invalid because he used money that was not his.

Rashba, a contemporary of Asheri, reached the same result. Rashba explicitly expressed his view that after the completion of the Talmud, absent legislation, authority no longer exists to annul a marriage on the basis that the marriage was effected improperly or that "all who marry do so subject to the conditions laid down by the Rabbis." Such authority was vested only in the Talmudic Sages, beyond whose rulings subsequent halakhic authorities may not go:

> It is not universally true that an act prohibited by the Sages, if done, is legally ineffective; it is true only in those cases where they specifically stated that the act was ineffective. Otherwise, we too could say that whenever anyone effects a marriage by improper means, the marriage is void . . . , but we do not say this in every case. Where this sanction has been explicitly stated [in the Talmud], it is applicable; but, if not, we do not ourselves impose it.[258]

258. *Resp. Rashba,* I, #1185 (=*Resp. Rashba Attributed to Naḥmanides* #125). *See Resp. Rashba,* I, #1162 (=*Resp. Rashba Attributed to Naḥmanides* #142) taking the view that the annulment of the marriage in both the incident at Naresh recorded in TB Yevamot 110a and the case in TB Bava Batra 48a, where the woman had been coerced into consenting to

On the other hand, Rashba was of the opinion that if a court or community adopts a enactment explicitly stating that a marriage must be effected in a particular manner or else is void, this enactment is effective and is legally well founded, even though the marriage may be valid under the law of the Torah.

There are two comprehensive responsa by Rashba where he makes this point. In one,[259] the following question was put to him:

> Does a community have the power to adopt an enactment that provides, in order to punish scoundrels, that a marriage effected in the absence of ten persons is void?

Rashba responded:

> It is clear to me that under the strict law a community may lawfully do this, so long as the townspeople agree, but not if there is a halakhic scholar (*talmid ḥakham*) in the locality who does not agree. The reason [the community may do so] is that the community may expropriate the property belonging to an individual, in which case he is considered to have effected the marriage by means of money that is not his. As stated in the Talmud,[260] "The Rabbis annul his marriage."
>
> In [Tractate *Bava Batra,*] chapter *Ḥezkat ha-Battim,*[261] and in [Tractate] *Yevamot,* chapter *Bet Shammai,*[262] R. Ashi stated: "He acted improperly; therefore the Rabbis treat him 'improperly' and annul his marriage." The principle of *hefker bet din hefker* applies in every case; and the community, like the local court, may expropriate property if they believe the expropriation to be for the welfare of the inhabitants.
>
> *Hefker bet din hefker* is derived from the Torah itself, as stated in [Tractate] *Yevamot,* chapter *Ha-Ishah,*[263] and in [Tractate] *Gittin:*[264] "What is the source of the principle that the court may expropriate property (*hefker bet din hefker*)? . . ." And it was taught in the first chapter of Tractate *Bava Batra:*[265] "The townspeople may [obligate each other]. . . ."
>
> However, if a halakhic scholar resides there, his approval is required, as stated in the first chapter of [Tractate] *Bava Batra.*[266] . . . A case arose in our community and I so ruled in the presence of our rabbis, and my teacher,

---

marriage, was based on the principle that "all who marry do so subject to the conditions laid down by the Rabbis." *See also supra* pp. 636–639.

259. *Resp. Rashba,* I, #1206.

260. *E.g.,* TB Ketubbot 3a and Yevamot 90b.

261. TB Bava Batra 48b.

262. TB Yevamot 110a.

263. TB Yevamot 89b.

264. TB Gittin 36b.

265. TB Bava Batra 8b.

266. TB Bava Batra 9a.

> Rabbi Moses b. Naḥman [Naḥmanides], agreed with me. Nevertheless, the matter requires further consideration.

Authority is vested in both the court and the community to provide that a marriage in violation of a legislative enactment is invalid, on the basis of the principle of *hefker bet din hefker,* pursuant to which the money given to effect the marriage is expropriated, thus rendering the marriage void. Rashba also conveyed the important information that Naḥmanides shared his view.

In this responsum, Rashba concluded that the matter required further consideration; but in another responsum, apparently written later, he concluded categorically and without reservation that the power to legislate includes the power to annul marriages.[267] This was the question posed to Rashba:[268]

> Our Master, the king, may his majesty be exalted, has asked me to rule on an incident here that involves a widow whom an acquaintance [relative (?)] would visit at her home daily. One day he came from the synagogue carrying a prayer book, and went to the widow's home together with some witnesses. He gave the prayer book to her in the presence of the witnesses and said to her: "You are hereby betrothed to me." He then directed the town scribe to record a document containing the witnesses' testimony, and they [the witnesses] left the country.
>
> The widow complained to the king that this marriage was against her will and without her consent. I could not investigate the matter by interrogating the witnesses to the marriage, since they had gone away. Now the widow cries out to me, and I have decided to order the man to give her a divorce and to flog him with whips. I request your opinion on this matter.

The local judge asked Rashba for advice as to how to rule. The man had used a prayer book as the means of effecting the marriage to the widow, and such a marriage is legally valid because an object of value was given. Moreover, there was even proof by a document signed by two witnesses who were no longer present, and it was therefore impossible to examine them as to whether the widow consented to the marriage or was the victim of trickery. The question was whether the marriage was void *ab initio* on account of fraud or whether the marriage was nevertheless valid and could not be dissolved except by divorce. Rashba responded:

267. The dates the responsa were written are indicated in *Resp. Maharam Alashkar* #48: "Although he [Rashba] wrote in that responsum, 'Nevertheless, the matter requires further consideration,' in other responsa he gave the same ruling after such further consideration." *See also Keneset ha-Gedolah,* EH, #28; *Haggahot Bet Yosef* #36; *infra* p. 858 n. 277.

268. *Resp. Rashba,* I, #551.

> It is surely reasonable to conclude that he acted deceitfully toward her and that she is not married; but questions involving marriage, because of their seriousness [since they involve prohibited sexual relationships], cannot be dealt with solely on the basis of conjecture as to probabilities, and I see no way out for her except through a divorce that he consents to give.
>
> However, he should be fined in an amount to be decided by the judge appointed by the king, so that it will be a lesson to others and will deter them from following his example—and any competent court may legally do likewise. . . . A competent court may even impose corporal punishment as a protective measure . . . , for a court may impose punishment not provided for by the Torah.

In this particular case, there was no explicit enactment governing the manner of effecting a marriage; Rashba therefore stated that in view of the gravity of the legal issues relating to sexual matters, the marriage could not be annulled, but the wife should be set free by a divorce. At the same time, it is possible and even essential for a judge of competent jurisdiction to punish the wrongdoer. However, the law would be otherwise where there is an explicit enactment on the matter, as Rashba subsequently stated:

> If the communities, or each individual community, should wish to erect a legislative safeguard against these unfortunate occurrences, let them all jointly adopt an enactment fully expropriating, whether permanently or for a fixed period, any money given [to effect a marriage] to any woman of their communities, unless the woman willingly accepts it with the consent of her father or in the presence of whomever they wish. I have found that Sherira Gaon and his forebears followed this practice,[269] and he advised another community to do the same.
>
> A man should also teach this in his household and instruct his daughters to take a vow "with the assent of God and the community," without any possibility of release or withdrawal, to renounce all money given to them to effect a marriage, even if willingly accepted, unless it is given in the presence of certain designated persons; and I have so advised the women of our city a number of times.

Every enactment—whether by a particular community or a group of communities—that expropriates the money given to effect a marriage is thus fully valid; and consequently a marriage that does not fulfill the conditions set forth in the enactment is void.

Rabbenu Jeroham also so held:[270]

269. *See supra* pp. 656–658.

270. *Toledot Adam ve-Ḥavvah,* Part Ḥavvah, path 22, sec. 4; Rabbenu Jeroham based his ruling on Rashba.

> Every community has the power to adopt an enactment and to agree that a marriage effected in the presence of fewer than ten persons is invalid; and it may also establish similar conditions, because all who marry do so subject to the conditions established by the residents of the community.

3. THE DEMAND FOR "THE APPROVAL OF ALL THE HALAKHIC AUTHORITIES OF THE REGION"; THE VIEW OF RIBASH

In the fourteenth century, a substantial change occurred in the attitude of the halakhic authorities with regard to the exercise of legislative power to annul a marriage. We have already noted a certain hesitation by Rashba, who first decided that the matter required further consideration but later ruled definitively that an enactment annulling a marriage is a proper exercise of legislative authority. At a later date, Isaac b. Sheshet Perfet (Ribash) was even more doubtful; and he conditioned his consent to give full validity to such an enactment upon "the approval of all the halakhic authorities of the region," in order to divide the responsibility for the decision among as many authorities as possible. His concern is evident in a detailed responsum to a question posed to him by Abraham b. Alfual concerning an enactment adopted by the community of Tortosa:[271]

> Your question is: The community agreed to adopt an enactment providing that no one may marry any woman except with the knowledge and in the presence of the communal officials, and in the presence of ten persons; and that if anyone should violate the law and marry contrary to these requirements, the marriage is void. At the time a marriage is contracted [in violation of the enactment], the community expropriates the money or other property given to effect the marriage, and the property is considered to be ownerless and of no value. The marriage is annulled, and the woman may marry without any divorce and is not even required to obtain a divorce to remove any possible doubt.
>
> You are in doubt whether the community has the power to expropriate the property of another . . . [and] whether even if the rabbi and elder of the town approve the enactment, they have the power, on the basis of the principle that "all who marry do so subject to the conditions laid down by the Rabbis, and the Rabbis annul this marriage," to annul a marriage that the Torah regards as valid.
>
> [You are concerned] as to whether this formula applies only to conditions laid down by rabbis who were great in wisdom and number and who also had the power to declare property to be ownerless, to punish, and to expropriate. But nowadays, when the halakhic authorities are regarded as being on the same level as laymen, you question whether they have the

271. *Resp. Ribash* #399. This responsum also contains a basic discussion of the issue of the validity of communal enactments and of enactments of guilds of artisans. *See supra* pp. 732–734, 754.

power to expropriate property, much less to annul a marriage that meets the Torah's requirements for validity, and whether the statement "Jephthah in his generation is equal to Samuel in his generation" refers only to deciding in accordance with the Torah and [is] not [authority for] setting aside a rule of the Torah itself.

The heart of the question is whether a community and its halakhic authorities have the power to expropriate property and thereby to bring about the annulment of a marriage that is valid under the law of the Torah, and whether the principle "all who marry do so subject to the conditions laid down by the Rabbis" applies to contemporary rabbis and continues to justify annulment of marriages; or whether it is more accurate to say that the analogy "Jephthah in his generation is equal to Samuel in his generation" refers only to "deciding in accordance with the Torah and [is] not [authority for] setting aside a rule of the Torah itself."

In his thorough response, Ribash first established that the community has the authority to enact legislation concerning monetary matters, including legislation expropriating property:

> Under the law of the Torah, the townspeople may adopt enactments, regulations, and agreements, and may penalize violators. . . . Since the townspeople agree on them, it is as if each one of them took them upon himself and became obligated to carry them out.[272]

He then proceeded to discuss the question of the authority of the community and of the halakhic authorities to annul a marriage:

> Therefore, if they enacted that if anyone marries a woman without the knowledge and presence of the communal officials, the money given the bride is to be considered as stolen money (since the community transferred it to someone else before it was given to her), then the marriage is not valid because it is as if he married her with stolen property. The conclusion in chapter *Ha-Ish Mekaddesh*[273] is that she is not married. . . .
>
> Even more so is the enactment effective if it was adopted with the approval of the scholar and elder of the town, Rabbi Moses (may God protect him), so that two elements are present: the agreement of the community and of the court. . . .
>
> This being so, the money is not his [the groom's] and cannot be used by him to marry the woman, and therefore we need not resort to the principle that "all who marry do so subject to the conditions laid down by the Rabbis." This principle is necessary only where there was a completely valid marriage but, because of some defect in the divorce proceedings, the divorce would

272. For detailed discussion, *see supra* pp. 685–714.
273. TB Kiddushin 52a.

> have been invalid under the law of the Torah and yet the Sages determined to validate it, as in the case at the beginning of Tractate *Ketubbot*[274] . . . and in chapter *Ha-Shole'aḥ.*[275] . . . In those cases, we rule that even though the marriage was valid, the Sages later decided to annul it retroactively, since the marriage was subject to their consent and they can annul it any time they wish.
>
> In this case, however, when the community explicitly expropriated the money, the marriage was effected with stolen property and is invalid even if the man did not agree in the first instance that his marriage was subject to their consent.[276]

Later, Ribash pointed out that this was also the view of Rashba, as previously noted:[277]

> Although Rashba wrote in his responsum that the authority to annul marriages applies only in those cases that are expressly mentioned by the Talmudic Sages and not in every case where one acts improperly . . . , *i.e.*, we exercise this authority only where the Sages did so explicitly . . . , nevertheless, in this case we do not need to annul the marriage on the ground that "he acted improperly, and [therefore] the Rabbis annul his marriage." . . . [The marriage is a nullity] because the community explicitly fined him and expropriated the money; he lost his ownership of it, and it is as if he married her with stolen property.

Moreover, according to Ribash, the principle that "all who marry do so subject to the conditions laid down by the Rabbis" can be expanded and applied to conditions laid down by the community:

> In addition, even if we had to resort to the rationale of "all who marry do so subject to the conditions laid down by the Rabbis" to justify every annulment of marriage, we may also state that "all who marry do so subject to the conditions laid down by the community in its enactments," since all who marry without any express stipulations as to the terms of marriage do so in accord-

274. TB Ketubbot 3a; *see supra* p. 633 n. 49.

275. TB Gittin 33a; *see supra* pp. 631–633.

276. On the basis of this reasoning, the responsum went on to explain why the Talmud in TB Bava Batra 48b and Yevamot 110a does not mention the principle of "All who marry . . ." in connection with the discussion there of the annulment of marriages resulting from coercion or abduction. However, Ribash took the view that when the Talmud in these two places states in regard to marriage by sexual intercourse that the "Rabbis declared his act to be fornication," they did so on the basis of the principle that "all who marry do so subject to the conditions laid down by the Rabbis." *See id. See also supra* p. 639 n. 63.

277. Both Rabbenu Jeroham and Ribash believed that Rashba was of the opinion that a marriage can be annulled by an explicit enactment. It thus follows that they too understood that Rashba's statement that "the matter requires further consideration" antedated his other responsa that held that marriages can be annulled pursuant to legislation. *See supra* p. 854.

> ance with the customs of the town. . . . Thus, we reach the conclusion that the community may adopt this enactment, and a marriage that contravenes a communal enactment is invalid, and no divorce is necessary.

Here, Ribash expressed his view that this enactment is legally valid, and a community is authorized to adopt an enactment annulling a marriage effected in violation of its provisions. However, as to the application of his decision in practice, Ribash added the following qualification:

> This is my opinion on this matter in theory. However, as to its practical application I tend to view the matter strictly; and I would not rely on my own opinion, in view of the seriousness of declaring that she needs no divorce to be free [to marry], unless all the halakhic authorities of the region concurred, so that only a "chip of the beam" should reach me [*i.e.*, so that I do not take upon myself the full responsibility, but only part of it].[278]

This requirement that all the authorities of the region concur—later interpreted in an instructive manner by Maharam Alashkar[279]—marked a crucial turning point in a course that culminated in complete abstention from the exercise of any legislative power to annul a marriage.

4. BASIC DISTINCTION BETWEEN THEORY AND PRACTICE IN REGARD TO LEGISLATIVE AUTHORITY; THE VIEWS OF RASHBEẒ (SIMEON B. ẒEMAḤ DURAN) AND RASHBASH (SIMEON B. SOLOMON DURAN)

Ribash had not yet drawn an inflexible line between the authority, as a matter of theory, to enact legislation annulling a marriage, and the use of such authority in practice; the qualification that Ribash introduced was only that such legislation requires the concurrence of all the halakhic authorities of the region. However, his younger contemporary, Rashbeẓ (Simeon b. Ẓemaḥ Duran), expressed a much more unyielding view—that legislation nullifying a marriage should never be applied in practice. His view is set forth in his responsum to the following question by Joseph Sasportas of Tenes[280] with regard to an enactment on annulment of marriages adopted by that community:[281]

278. The source of this expression is TB Sanhedrin 7b. *See also Resp. Ribash* #377, #378.

279. *See infra* pp. 864–869.

280. In North Africa, there were two cities with similar names: Tenes in the kingdom of Tlemcen (*benei Zeiyan,* after the Zeiyanide dynasty) and Tunis in the kingdom of Tunis (*benei Ḥefeẓ,* after the Ḥafsid dynasty). *See Resp. Tashbeẓ,* II, #83, and also the map of Jewish settlement in Morocco in B.Z. Hirschberg, *Ha-Yehudim be-Afrika ha-Ẓefonit* [The Jews of North Africa], pp. 273, 286.

281. *Resp. Tashbeẓ,* II, #5.

The community enacted legislation providing that any marriage that does not have the consent of the town scholar (*ḥaver ir*) and the communal elders is invalid. Is this analogous to the Talmudic principle[282] "all who marry do so subject to the conditions laid down by the Rabbis," so that they have the power through their enactment to annul the marriage? In this enactment they have also placed a ban against any violator.

Rashbeẓ answered as follows:

The correct rationale for all Talmudic statements that "the Rabbis annul this marriage" is that the court has the authority to expropriate the money used to effect the marriage, since the law recognizes the principle of *hefker bet din hefker.* This being so, the money does not belong to him [the groom]—and thus he did not marry her with his money, and she is not married at all.

If so, we may expand this principle to cover a communal enactment, since the community may expropriate the property of any of its members, and all courts in every generation have the power to expropriate private property because "Jephthah in his generation is equal to Samuel in his generation." . . . Consequently, a community that adopts an enactment to the effect that any marriage not having the consent of the communal leaders is invalid has thereby taken the property away from the man and transferred it to the woman on condition that the man shall have no right to it. Since it did not belong to him, he gave her nothing of his own; what she obtained from him was ownerless property that had been taken away from him. She is [therefore] not married at all.

The community may do this as a protective measure to prevent an unworthy man from coming forward to entice a girl from a distinguished family and marry her in secret. If it is an earlier enactment [before the man moved into the town], then everyone implicitly consented to it, and the matter is even simpler.

This is what emerges from the essence of the *Halakhah.* However, because of the gravity of improper sexual unions, one should be apprehensive that perhaps what is needed is a court that has the same power to expropriate property as the court of R. Ammi and R. Assi. Even though in civil law matters we may rely on the authority of every court to expropriate property, we should be stricter on questions of marriage. As it is said . . . : "One should be lenient in civil law matters but strict on matters of religious law (*issur*)."[283] We cannot [necessarily] put into actual practice whatever we perceive the law to be.[284] Also, the communal enactment does not explicitly state that they are expropriating any property. In addition, we have heard that this has never been done in any actual case.

282. TB Gittin 33a *et al.*

283. TB Ketubbot 73b *et al.* *See supra* p. 132.

284. *See* TB Gittin 19a, 37a. *See also infra* p. 949.

Rashbeẓ had no doubts that the "essence" of the law is that authority does exist to annul a marriage on the basis of the principle of *hefker bet din hefker,* and he emphasized that such authority is vested in every competent court and every community in every generation. This, however, is only in theory: practice with regard to marriage must be stricter than theory because of the seriousness of sexual matters; hence, this authority should not be exercised.

To justify this distinction between theory and practice, Rashbeẓ added a new rationale—that the enactment involved in the case before him did not expressly state as the ground for annulment that the man's property has been expropriated; and since the annulment was based on the principle of *hefker bet din hefker,* the enactment should have expressly expropriated the property used to effect the marriage. This is a new and surprising rationale. Most, if not all, prior enactments contained no express provision for expropriation of property, and such an express provision had never been previously required.

Rashbeẓ also added another rationale—"we have heard that this has never been done in any actual case"—a kind of negative precedent. This rationale, however, is troublesome, in that Rashbeẓ himself cited Naḥmanides and Rashba to the effect that such an enactment may be applied in practice.[285] In the final analysis, the basic rationale is: "Because of the gravity of improper sexual unions, one should be apprehensive" about adopting an enactment annulling a marriage valid according to the Torah.

Rashbeẓ took the same position in another responsum in connection with an enactment adopted in Constantine, Tunisia, to the effect that the *kiddushin* (betrothal) must be celebrated simultaneously with the *nissu'in* (*ḥuppah,* the nuptial ceremony):[286]

> You have asked about a town that has an enactment to the effect that the *kiddushin* must be celebrated simultaneously with the *nissu'in;* the enactment expressly provides that violation of this requirement renders the *kiddushin* void. What should the law be if the *kiddushin* is celebrated at a time other than the *nissu'in?* Does a communal enactment have the power to annul the marriage? You have written that you found authority for such power in a responsum of the *geonim*[287] on the basis that all who marry do so subject to the conditions laid down by the Rabbis.
>
> This is my response. First, permit me to inform you that whatever I say on this matter is only theoretical, because this question has been raised often, and we have never found that the sanction [of annulment] has actually been applied. It has also come to our attention that Naḥmanides was asked a sim-

285. *See* Rashbeẓ's further comments in *Resp. Tashbeẓ,* II, #5.
286. *Resp. Tashbeẓ,* I, #133; *see also* the beginning of #131.
287. *See supra* pp. 656–658.

> ilar question, and he also responded that all who marry do so subject to the conditions laid down by the Rabbis, etc.
>
> It is clear that a marriage may be annulled in two situations: first, annulment at the very time of a marriage that—except for its invalidation by the Rabbis—would have been valid, as in the cases . . . where the marriage followed an abduction[288] . . . or was coerced.[289] . . . The second situation involves an annulment at the time of divorce, even though the marriage had taken place long before and children had been born. The Rabbis annulled the marriage at the time of the divorce in order to effectuate dissolution of the marriage, as in the cases of *force majeure* with regard to a conditional divorce[290] and where . . . a bill of divorcement was cancelled by the husband.[291] The legal basis in all of these cases is the annulment of the marriage by the Rabbis. . . . The Talmud clearly explains that a court may annul a marriage on such grounds, and this does not need any elaboration.
>
> However, what remains to be considered is whether this power has been expanded to include communal enactments. It would appear that the power of the Rabbis and the power of the community are equivalent, since the power of the community over an individual is the same as the power of the *nasi* (patriarch) over all of Israel, and any individual who marries does so subject to the conditions laid down by them, and they annul this marriage.

At the outset of this responsum, Rashbeẓ stated that his discussion was only theoretical and not to be applied in practice, even though here, too, he clearly stated that in theory the power to annul a marriage is vested not only in the court but also in the community when it legislates "since the power of the community over an individual is the same as the power of the *nasi* (patriarch) over all of Israel."[292]

This view and this rationale are echoed in a responsum by Rashbeẓ's grandson, the second Rashbash (Simeon b. Solomon Duran), at the end of the fifteenth and the beginning of the sixteenth centuries. There, the subject was an enactment adopted in the city of Tlemcen in North Africa, providing that *kiddushin* (betrothal) must take place simultaneously with the *ḥuppah* (nuptial ceremony). The purpose of the enactment was to prevent frivolous and mock marriages and to forestall disputes and litigation between the

288. TB Yevamot 110a.

289. TB Bava Batra 48b.

290. TB Ketubbot 3a; *see supra* p. 633 n. 49.

291. TB Gittin 33a; *see supra* pp. 564–566, 631–633.

292. *Cf. Resp. Tashbeẓ,* I, #154, for a thorough and instructive responsum on the annulment of marriage by communal legislation, which also throws interesting light on Jewish juridical autonomy: ". . . in an important community like yours, of which we have heard that you follow the paths of the Torah in all civil matters and certainly in matters of family law. . . ."

parties over the validity of the marriage. Rashbash was asked whether a marriage in violation of this enactment was void. He responded:[293]

> Concerning your letter about your enactment that *kiddushin* before the time of the *ḥuppah* is void, you should be aware that a court may adopt enactments and erect safeguards as it deems appropriate and may expropriate an individual's property. . . . The basis for this is the principle of *hefker bet din hefker.* . . . Not only may a duly ordained court do this, but the courts of every generation may expropriate private property, because Jephthah in his generation is equal to Samuel in his generation. . . . Just as a court may expropriate, adopt enactments, and vest ownership of property otherwise than according to the strict law, so may the community expropriate. . . . The community, like a court, may punish and expropriate, provided that it does so with the approval of a "distinguished person," *i.e.*, a halakhic authority whom the community has accepted.[294]

Rashbash further stated:

> It is necessary to consider further the question of the power of the community to enact legislation prohibiting *kiddushin* until the bride enters under the *ḥuppah* and declaring that if the enactment is not complied with, the marriage is void.

His conclusion was unequivocal:

> Clearly, a court may annul a marriage, as it is stated in the first chapter of Tractate *Ketubbot*[295] that "all who marry do so subject to the conditions laid down by the Rabbis, and the Rabbis annul this marriage." . . . Thus, it is explicitly stated in the Talmud that a court may annul a marriage, and this point requires no elaboration. The standing of a court and the community in this regard is the same, since the power of a community over an individual is the same as the power of the *nasi* (patriarch) over all of Israel, and anyone who marries does so subject to the conditions laid down by the community, and the community may annul the marriage.
>
> Consequently, a community, by adopting an enactment that *kiddushin* performed before the time of the *nissu'in* is invalid, has thereby expropriated the groom's money; and since it does not belong to him, he gave the bride nothing of his own. What he gave her was acquired by her as ownerless property, and she is not married at all.[296]

293. *Resp. Yakhin u-Vo'az,* II, #20 (p. 75a/b). As to this responsum, *see supra* p. 714.
294. For detailed discussion, *see supra* pp. 751–759.
295. TB Ketubbot 3a.
296. Later in his responsum, Rashbash added that this was also the opinion of the *geonim,* of Naḥmanides, and of Rashba. In many of his arguments, Rashbash repeated, even stylistically, the arguments of Rashbeẓ, discussed earlier.

The discussion up to this point was theoretical; for actual practice, the response was different:

> However, some commentators have written that all this is only theoretical but not for practical application. Rabbi Isaac b. Sheshet (Ribash) similarly wrote that in actual practice this reasoning should not be relied on,[297] and he wrote that Rashba agreed to this.[298] My grandfather, Rashbeẓ, also wrote: "We cannot put into actual practice" a communal enactment that annuls marriages; and "We have heard that this has never been done in any actual case." Consequently, the conclusion is that . . . the marriage of the individual in question is valid and is not to be annulled.[299]

5. EXPLANATION FOR ABSTENTION FROM EXERCISING LEGISLATIVE POWER TO ANNUL MARRIAGES; THE VIEW OF MAHARAM ALASHKAR

In this same period (the end of the fifteenth and beginning of the sixteenth centuries), the first detailed explanation was given for the growing inclination to abstain from exercising legislative power to annul marriages that are valid according to the Torah. Such an explanation was given in a responsum by Moses (Maharam) Alashkar,[300] who was active during this period in Egypt and in the Land of Israel. He first clearly pointed out that the halakhic authorities and the community have the power to provide by legislation that a marriage in violation of their enactment is void. However, he determined that in contrast to enactments in other legal areas, where there is no reason why each community may not fully exercise its legislative authority, the adoption of far-reaching enactments with regard to the annulment of marriage could not be sanctioned—mainly for reasons of general legal policy—unless the enactments are adopted by all or at least most of the communities in a particular country. Maharam Alashkar pointed out that in so holding he was following in the footsteps of Ribash, who also required that the enactment be adopted by all communities in the region. However, Maharam Alashkar explained this requirement in the particular context of marriage and divorce law.

297. As will be remembered, Ribash did not say that an enactment providing for the annulment of marriages should not be applied in practice. He went only so far as to require the concurrence of all the halakhic authorities of the region for such an enactment; *see supra* p. 859.

298. This statement, too, is surprising, since Ribash (in #399) explicitly distinguished between the case dealt with by Rashba's responsum holding that marriages are not to be annulled on account of the husband's improper behavior, and the case where legislation expropriates the money given to effect the marriage, thereby causing the marriage to be annulled. *See supra* p. 858.

299. *See further Resp. Yakhin u-Vo'az,* II, #46; Freimann, *Kiddushin ve-Nissu'in,* pp. 90–91.

300. *Resp. Maharam Alashkar* #48.

Maharam Alashkar stated the question submitted to him by the community of Salonika as follows:

> Your question concerns one of the communities in your locality[301] that, together with its halakhic authority, adopted an enactment to the effect that a marriage may take place only in the presence of ten Jews, including the halakhic authority; that any marriage in violation of this rule is forever null and void; that the money given to effect the marriage is expropriated; that the woman is in no way married; and that she may marry in the future without a divorce. You are now in doubt about this matter and wish to know my opinion whether they may do this; can they annul a marriage that is valid according to the Torah?

The response of Maharam Alashkar was specific and clear:

> Let not the matter surprise you; it is clear that in every generation the townspeople and their court may adopt enactments and protective measures even if these depart from the law as set forth in the Torah, as was stated in the first chapter of Tractate *Bava Batra:*[302] "The townspeople may fix weights and measures, market prices, and laborers' wages, and they may enforce their regulations." . . . The court may also expropriate property from its owner and declare it to be ownerless. . . .
>
> Therefore, since the court may declare property in the possession of its owner to be ownerless and expropriate it, an enactment by the townspeople may validly provide that the money given to the bride to effect a marriage in violation of their enactment is expropriated, no longer belongs to its owner, and is treated as stolen property in his and her possession. The marriage is void, since he is deemed to have married her through theft and wrongdoing; . . . and she is not married at all. . . .[303]

301. The reference is to Salonika; *see* beginning of the query. There were a large number of communities in Salonika; hence the reference in the responsum to "one of the communities in your locality." Each community was independent and was known by the name of the country or town of origin of its members, such as "the Community of Sicily," "the Community of Portugal," etc. Each community adopted enactments that were binding only on its own members (*see* Maharam Alashkar's statement, later in the responsum: "Although each community is independent . . ."). *See, e.g., Resp. Maharibal,* III, #72; *Resp. Maharashdam,* ḤM, #12; *Resp. Divrei Rivot* #56.

At the end of the sixteenth century, there were in Salonika some thirty communities established by immigrants from different places, such as Portugal, Italy, Sicily, Castille, Aragon, and Catalonia. *See* David Pipano, "Shalshelet Rabbanei Saloniki" [The Rabbinical Line of Salonika], at the end of his book, *Ḥagor ha-Efod,* p. 3a, par. 11, p. 4b, par. 15. *See also* M. Molkho, "Toledot Yehudei Saloniki" [A History of the Jews of Salonika], in *Saloniki, Ir va-Em be-Yisra'el* [Salonika, A Major Jewish City], 1967, pp. 5ff, 8ff. Several "autonomous" communities in a single city also existed in North Africa; *see Resp. Tashbeẓ,* II, #61; *supra* p. 456 n. 32.

302. TB Bava Batra 8b; *see supra* pp. 679–681.

303. Later in the responsum, Maharam Alashkar referred to an opinion (which was also mentioned in the responsa discussed *supra*) that only a court of the same standing as

> We thus conclude that every community may adopt a decree binding on its members and their descendants, expropriating the marriage money and rendering it ownerless; and anyone who enters into a marriage in violation of their enactment is deemed to have done so with stolen property and with money that does not belong to him. . . .
>
> It may also be argued that all who marry do so subject to the conditions laid down by the Rabbis, and, similarly, all who marry do so subject to the conditions laid down in communal enactments; and it is like the situation where one states, "You are betrothed to me on condition that my father consents," in which event there is no betrothal if he does not consent. Terms and conditions understood by all to be part of the transaction are regarded as incorporated in the agreement between the parties without any need to refer to them specifically. . . . Therefore, the townspeople may annul a marriage entered into in violation of their enactment, since all who marry do so subject to the conditions laid down by the townspeople, as we have stated.

There is thus authority to establish by legislation the manner of effecting marriages and to provide that any marriage effected in violation of the legislative requirements is void. Such authority is vested in the court, and certainly in the community, since they may expropriate the money given to effect the marriage. Similarly, all who marry do so subject to the condition that the marriage be consistent with communal enactments; and the community has expressly provided that any marriage not effected in a particular manner is void.

In his subsequent discussion, Maharam Alashkar relied on the responsa of Rashba[304] and Asheri, discussed above, and on other halakhic sources. The concluding source discussed by Maharam Alashkar is the responsum by Ribash, who, although also of the opinion that a community may adopt such an enactment, declined to rule on the basis of this opinion

---

the court of R. Ammi and R. Assi has the power to expropriate property (*see* TB Gittin 36b). Maharam Alashkar responded that even that opinion applies only where a court adopts an enactment on its own; "however, all the inhabitants of the town, acting in concert with the court, have greater power." This statement is interesting for its delineation of the community's authority and the legislative power that the community confers on the court. That the community has a greater power than the court is explicit throughout the rest of Maharam Alashkar's responsum:

> Therefore, the permanent court of the town that has the greatest power can expropriate property, and this is particularly true if it is accompanied by the concurrence of the entire community. . . . From this we learn that all courts, and certainly the community, have the power to expropriate property and to legislate.

Similarly, *see Resp. Ribash* #399 and *supra* p. 700 n. 88.

304. Maharam Alashkar established that the responsum in which Rashba wrote that "the matter requires further consideration" antedated a responsum in which Rashba held unequivocally that a marriage can be annulled pursuant to a legislative enactment. *See also supra* nn. 267, 277.

that a divorce was unnecessary; instead, Ribash required the concurrence of all of the halakhic authorities of the region to enable the woman to marry without first being divorced.

At first glance, this qualification by Ribash seems to be based on the theory that in view of the seriousness of the prohibition against sexual relations with a married woman, it is appropriate that the decision to permit her to marry without a divorce be given by the greatest possible number of authorities so that the responsibility for the decision will be shared among them.[305] However, Maharam Alashkar viewed this qualification by Ribash as being applicable to legislation concerning the validity of marriage only when the legislation is geographically limited. Maharam Alashkar stated:

> Therefore, if the entire country and its rabbis, with the concurrence of all or a majority of the communities, came to a decision, in reliance on those leading authorities, to adopt an enactment—to be effective forever or for such period as they see fit— to erect a safeguard, to punish all who marry in violation of their enactment, to annul the marriage, and to expropriate the money used to effect it—I will also follow in their footsteps and answer "amen" after them, and enter into the thickness of the beam rather than merely a chip of the beam.[306] However, I cannot concur in such an enactment by only a single community that acts without the agreement of the other communities of the region, since one may not deal so lightly with marriages valid according to the Torah.
>
> Although each community is independent, and the first chapter of Tractate *Bava Batra*[307] demonstrates that even those within a single occupation may agree among themselves and adopt enactments and can thus become the equivalent of a town if there is a "distinguished person" among them, as is stated there with regard to the butchers who adopted regulations to govern their activities, and although the *Tosefta*[308] states that the dyers may declare that they will be partners in all merchandise that comes into the town, and the bakers may agree among themselves that each of them may not sell during the time set aside for another, etc., nevertheless, these have no resemblance to an enactment of the type here under consideration.
>
> Moreover, even if this type of legislation could be enacted to annul a marriage that is valid under Biblical law, a community may expropriate only the property of its own members, but not the property [of members] of other communities. If a member of another community marries a woman [of the

305. *Resp. Ribash* #399: ". . . I would not rely on my own opinion, in view of the seriousness of declaring that she needs no divorce to be free [to marry], unless all the halakhic authorities of the region concurred, so that only a 'chip of the beam' should reach me [*i.e.*, so that I do not take upon myself the full responsibility, but only part of it].'" *See supra* p. 859.

306. An allusion to Ribash's figure of speech; *see supra* n. 305.

307. TB Bava Batra 9a.

308. *Tosefta* Bava Meẓi'a 11:24–25; *see supra* pp. 680–681.

community that adopted the enactment], his marriage is certainly valid and the woman would require a divorce, but their marriages [*i.e.*, between members of the community that adopted the enactment] would be invalid and she [the "bride"] would be free to marry without a divorce. Given this state of affairs, of what benefit is their enactment? On the contrary, it makes matters even worse, and the words and enactments of the rabbis become a laughingstock.

It cannot be said that one who marries does so subject to the conditions laid down by a particular community [where the marriage takes place], since one's intent is only to marry subject to the conditions laid down by all the communities of the country—and not merely individual communities. This is particularly true if there are courts in the country more distinguished than the courts of these communities [that have adopted such an enactment].

The conclusion of the matter is that such an enactment is not valid, and a divorce is necessary. This does not require further elaboration.

The fact that an enactment is adopted by a particular community and not by all the communities—or at least most of them—prevented Maharam Alashkar from declaring it valid. Although authority to legislate is also vested in the local community, and even in a tradesmen's association, it is not proper, on the basis of legislation by a single community, to "deal so lightly with marriages valid according to the Torah"; local legislation on marriage and divorce runs a serious risk of undermining the entire institution of marriage and turning it into "a laughingstock," because one community's enactment obviously does not bind members of any other community.

It follows, therefore, that if a member of another community marries a woman who belongs to the community that has adopted the enactment and the marriage is in violation of the enactment, the marriage is valid (since we apply the law of the husband's community); but if a member of the community that adopted the enactment marries a woman in violation of the enactment, the marriage is invalid, and the "bride" may marry someone else without a divorce. There is no situation worse than this for the stability of the institution of marriage and the family.[309]

Moreover, it is not reasonable to argue that the marriage was entered into subject to the conditions laid down by one community; the implicit conditions are those that are generally accepted by the people and the courts of the entire country. The conclusion is, therefore, that the principle

309. This rationale reappeared in the course of time, since enactments providing for annulment of marriage were adopted by many separate communities throughout a long period of time. This was emphasized in *Resp. Rashba*, I, #551: "If the communities, or each individual community, should wish to erect a legislative safeguard against these unfortunate occurrences, let them all jointly adopt an enactment fully expropriating . . . any money given [to effect a marriage] to any woman of their communities . . ."; *see also supra* p. 855.

that "all who marry do so subject to the conditions laid down in communal enactments" cannot justify annulment of a marriage on the basis of the legislation of a single community. Since the reason for the opposition to such legislation is that it is limited geographically, it follows that "if the entire country and its rabbis, with the concurrence of all or a majority of the communities, came to a decision . . . to erect a safeguard, to punish all who marry in violation of their enactment, [and] to annul the marriage . . . I will also follow in their footsteps and answer 'amen' after them, and enter into the thickness of the beam rather than merely a chip of the beam."

6. THE DIFFERENCE BETWEEN THE ENACTMENT OF FEZ, 1494, AND THE ENACTMENT OF FEZ, 1592

An interesting example of this significant change of direction in legislation relating to marriage is the difference between two enactments adopted approximately one hundred years apart in the very same place, the community of the Castilian exiles in Fez. The enactment adopted there in 1494 reads:[310]

> No Jewish man shall betroth any Jewish woman other than in the presence of ten persons among whom is either a scholar of the community (who receives his wages from the community treasury) or a local judge; the same applies to their entering under the *ḥuppah*. If it is done in any other manner, the marriage is void *ab initio*.

This enactment conformed to the views of Asheri and Rashba that an enactment may validly provide that a marriage in violation of its provisions is void. It is of interest that this enactment was adopted in North Africa more than one hundred years after the determination by Rashbeẓ, the Rabbi of Algiers, that such legislation should not be invoked in practice to annul a marriage.

One hundred years later, a new enactment was adopted in Fez, likewise requiring that a betrothal take place in the presence of ten persons. However, this enactment contains a substantial change in the sanction imposed on the violator—he is subject to punishment and fines, but the marriage itself is valid and is not annulled. Instead, the husband is compelled to give a divorce.

The later enactment, adopted in 1592, provides:[311]

> From this time forward, anyone wishing to betroth a woman may not do so except in the presence of a communal rabbi (*ḥakham me-ḥakhmei ha-*

310. *Kerem Ḥemer,* II, Enactment #1 (p. 2b); the enactment was adopted in 1494; *see id.,* Enactment #14 (p. 3a). For the Fez enactments, *see supra* pp. 806–809.

311. *Kerem Ḥemer,* II, Enactment #34 (p. 6b).

ma'amad) or the head of an academy (*rosh yeshivah*) together with ten Jewish persons. If anyone betroths a woman in a manner that does not conform to this enactment, any witness who is present and immediately notifies the court is blameless; but if he comes forward only later, in addition to being punished by flogging, afflictions, and imprisonment, he must pay [a specified sum][312] into the charity fund.

The groom must also pay into the charity fund an amount to be determined by the communal leader (*nagid*) and the judges sitting at that time. He shall remain imprisoned until he gives a valid divorce to the woman he has betrothed, and he shall not be released for sabbaths or festivals until he divorces her with a legally valid bill of divorcement. Even if her parents consent to her marrying him, he may not marry her until he first fully divorces her, after which, if they wish to enter into a new marriage, they may do so.

7. THE RULINGS OF JOSEPH CARO AND REMA (MOSES ISSERLES) CONCERNING ABSTENTION FROM THE EXERCISE OF LEGISLATIVE POWER TO ANNUL MARRIAGES

The view that legislation annulling a marriage should not be enacted became the accepted position of the *Halakhah* as set forth by Joseph Caro and Rema (Moses Isserles). In a responsum,[313] Joseph Caro stated the following question posed to him by the community of Ḥamah:

> Your question concerns a woman who, according to the testimony of witnesses, was married, yet a ruling was made that she is not married, because there is a local enactment that a marriage may be entered into only in the presence of the court or with its consent. This ruling was rendered in reliance on the responsum of Ribash; you have requested me to inform you whether or not this ruling is correct.

In his responsum, Caro distinguished between legislation providing that a marriage may be entered into only in the presence of a court or its equivalent, and legislation also providing that a marriage in violation of this requirement is void and that the money given to effect the marriage is expropriated. Where there is an enactment of the first type, as apparently was the case in the community of Ḥamah, a marriage in violation of the enactment is valid, and Caro strongly condemned the authority who ruled that the marriage was void:

312. The Hebrew text has the abbreviation *n.s.* (the Hebrew letters *nun* and *samekh*), which may mean fifty *sela'im*. Freimann, *Kiddushin ve-Nissu'in*, p. 103, gives a different reading, *n.m.*, which he takes to mean "fifty *metkal*," a local unit of currency (*see* his n. 2, *ad loc.*).

313. *Resp. Bet Yosef* #6.

> This ruling is perverse, and we are astonished that it is possible for anyone having even elementary knowledge of the Torah [lit. "even the aroma of Torah"] to conceive of rendering such a lenient ruling on this question.

Caro argued that the ruling had no basis in the responsum of Ribash[314] on which the ruling purportedly relied:

> For Ribash would recoil from ruling that the parties were free of the marriage bond in a case like the one before us. What impelled him in that responsum to rule the marriage invalid was that it involved a community that adopted an enactment that a marriage without the consent and presence of the communal officials and the presence of ten persons is void, and at the same time the community expropriated the money or the article used to effect the marriage. The money was to be considered ownerless and valueless, thus causing the marriage to be void. It was in such a case that he determined in that responsum to hold the marriage invalid, because the enactment expropriated the marriage money and because of the principle of *hefker bet din hefker.* However, if the enactment merely provides that a marriage must take place in the presence of the court, . . . it is clear that Ribash would agree that the enactment provides no basis for annulling the marriage.

Where an enactment provides that the marriage is annulled and that the money used to effect the marriage is expropriated, Caro was of the opinion, citing the responsa of Ribash and Rashbeẓ, that authority to annul does exist in theory but should not be exercised in practice.[315]

Rema similarly ruled, as follows:[316]

> If a community has agreed and enacted that a marriage may not take place except in the presence of ten persons or that some comparable requirement must be fulfilled, and an individual marries in violation of the enactment, we are apprehensive that the marriage may be valid; and, therefore, a divorce is

314. This is a reference to *Resp. Ribash* #399, discussed *supra* pp. 856–859.

315. *See further Bet Yosef* to *Tur* EH ch. 28 (end).

316. Rema to Sh. Ar. EH 28:21. After Rema's ruling, there were no further attempts in the Ashkenazic communities to adopt enactments that would nullify a marriage. *See* Freimann, *Kiddushin ve-Nissu'in,* pp. 238–239. Freimann (p. 239) deduces from *Be'ur ha-Gra* to EH 28, subpar. 57, that "the Gaon of Vilna was apparently doubtful about Rema's stringent ruling against even an enactment explicitly purporting to declare marriages void, since *Be'ur ha-Gra* remarked on this gloss: '. . . in any event, further consideration is required as to what should be done in practice.'"

However, it seems that Freimann's conclusion is not justified. The plain meaning of *Be'ur ha-Gra* is to the contrary, *i.e.,* the Gaon of Vilna sought to explain Rema's ruling that although there is legal authority to annul a marriage, as can be concluded from TB Yevamot 90b and 110a, this should not be done without further consideration, and actual practice should reflect the strict view—which is precisely what Rema held.

> required. Even if the community has expressly provided that the marriage is invalid and has expropriated his [the groom's] money, one must nevertheless be scrupulous in actual practice to comply with the strict view.

8. THE SIXTEENTH AND SEVENTEENTH CENTURIES IN ITALY AND THE MEDITERRANEAN COUNTRIES

In the sixteenth and even in the seventeenth century, enactments were still being adopted in various communities in Italy and elsewhere prohibiting marriages in the presence of less than ten persons and explicitly stating that a marriage in violation of the enactment is void *ab initio.*[317] However, the overwhelming majority of halakhic authorities held that in practice such marriages should not be annulled; and it appears that these enactments were not applied in practice.

For example, in an incident in Padua at the beginning of the seventeenth century, a girl was married in the presence of two witnesses without the consent of her parents. The case was submitted for decision to Jacob Heilprin, who dealt with it without even referring to these enactments of the Italian communities. The responsum by Jacob Heilprin is also extremely interesting for the light it throws on the mode of life and the general conditions of that Jewish community:[318]

> I will go down to see according to the outcry that has reached me,[319] the cries of a young woman[320] called Bonah. She is good and may she continue to be good;[321] but what is not good are the tales God's people spread about,[322] and their gossip and complaints against the young man, Naḥshon, concerning whom there are rumors spreading through the Jewish community that he married her in the dead of a dark night in the presence of two competent witnesses and with the consent of that young woman. In this matter, contention ensued among those who sit in judgment, as is to be expected when restraints are cast off in Israel;[323] one is lenient [lit. "permits"] and the other is strict [lit. "forbids"], and there is all manner of dispute and argument in Israel. Because of our many sins, there is no legal decision without flaw.

317. *See, e.g.,* the Casalli enactment of 1571; Corfu had a similar enactment as late as 1652. *See* Freimann, *Kiddushin ve-Nissu'in,* pp. 140–142, 202, 257–260; Finkelstein, *Self-Government,* pp. 307, 317.

318. *Resp. Naḥalat Ya'akov* #57. The responsum (as the conclusion indicates) was written in 1615.

319. *Cf.* Genesis 18:21 ("I will go down to see whether they have acted altogether according to the outcry that has reached Me").

320. *Cf.* TB Sanhedrin 109b.

321. This is a play on the Latin word *bona,* meaning "good."

322. *Cf.* I Samuel 2:23–24.

323. *Cf.* Judges 5:2,8,10. The connection between these verses and the passage of Heilprin's responsum with which comparison is suggested is more readily apparent from the Hebrew.

After a comprehensive legal analysis, Heilprin ruled that a divorce was necessary, especially in light of the fact that the young woman did not dispute that there was a marriage to which she consented:

> She herself stated to the court during her interrogation that, looking through the window, she saw two or three men with Naḥshon, the groom. . . . This being so, she was married in the presence of two witnesses. . . . Consequently, her contention that she was only jesting is not credible, because it is not a frivolous matter to lower down a crimson cord from the window[324] to get the ring,[325] considering the tenor of what they were saying at the time this was done.

In this entire discussion, there is not even a hint of the enactment pursuant to which a marriage in the presence of less than ten persons is void.

The advice with which Jacob Heilprin concluded the responsum is interesting. He addressed the girl's father and sought to convince him that the best solution would be to agree to the marriage of his daughter with Naḥshon and to stop searching for ways to break the girl's ties to him:

> Permit me to intercede for the young man, Naḥshon, for he is only a lad, and did not do any vile thing[326] in marrying the girl in secret and at night, because he did not do this out of rebellion or treachery. For love distorts judgment, and just as an opening in a wall invites a thief, so every beloved invites the adoration of her young lover. The girl's father should be persuaded to agree that this is a good match,[327] and this would be to his credit; so I and many others of greater stature have advised him not to sully in a courtroom his good name, nor the crown of God that he bears, nor the good name of his daughter, and not to make himself and his daughter the subject of ridicule and mockery of all the people. . . .
>
> Let him not seek greatness and magnificence, for there is nothing new under the sun. For the daughter of Calba Savua did the same with R. Akiva.[328] Whoever has a disposition that is pleasing to God and advises him [the father] in this manner, his resting place will be one of honor. Let there be peace in

324. *Cf.* Joshua 2:21 (". . . and she tied the crimson cord to the window").

325. The Hebrew term used is *shalshelet,* which literally means "a chain" but here seems to mean "a ring." Apparently the groom, Naḥshon, stood below, and the bride lowered a rope through the window; he attached the ring to the end of the rope, and she drew it up to herself, at which time Naḥshon in the presence of two or three witnesses recited the formula, "Behold, you are betrothed to me according to the law of Moses and Israel."

326. *Cf.* II Samuel 13:12–13 ("Such things are not done in Israel! Don't do such a vile thing!"); Genesis 34:7 ("He had done a vile thing in Israel").

327. Lit. "a good cleaving." *Cf.* TB Kiddushin 71b, following Genesis 2:24; Isaiah 41:7.

328. TB Ketubbot 62b; Nedarim 50a.

> Israel; let them not have quarrels and arguments brought to the court, and all will praise and acclaim him.

9. ENACTMENTS IN THE EASTERN COUNTRIES IN THE EIGHTEENTH AND NINETEENTH CENTURIES PROVIDING FOR ANNULMENT OF MARRIAGES

In various communities in the Jewish centers of the Eastern countries, legislation was enacted, even as late as in the eighteenth and nineteenth centuries, requiring marriages to be in the presence of ten persons and of the rabbi, and providing for annulment as a sanction for violation.

In the middle of the eighteenth century, such an enactment was adopted by the halakhic authorities together with the communal leaders, led by Mordecai Galante, in Damascus, Syria. The full text of the enactment has been preserved.[329] In order "to remove the stumbling blocks placed by deceivers" it was enacted that:

> No Jewish man may marry any woman, except in the presence of ten Jewish persons, including the rabbi who is then the communal judge and the teacher of Torah. . . . Two individuals from among the communal leaders and officials are also to be included among these ten persons. This, our enactment and decree, shall be in effect from this day forward until the day of the coming of the Righteous Teacher, the Messiah of the God of Jacob. . . .
>
> The marriage of anyone who intentionally marries a woman in the presence of two witnesses but in the absence of the above-mentioned ten persons shall be invalid, completely null and void, and shall be like the dust of the earth and like an object that has no reality. By the authority of the court's power that we possess, we hereby completely expropriate the money given to the woman to effect the marriage, and we completely annul the marriage, like the court of Ravina and R. Ashi, which had the power to expropriate private property.[330]

In the middle of the nineteenth century, the halakhic authorities and communal leaders of Damascus, led by Isaac Abulafia,[331] reenacted and strengthened this legislation:

> There is in our community an earlier enactment . . . that no man may marry in the presence of two witnesses unless the rabbi or his representative consents, and ten persons are present, two of whom must be communal leaders,

329. *Resp. Berekh Moshe* (by Moses Galante, the son of Mordecai Galante) #33 (p. 125a).

330. The enactment also imposed a ban on the groom and on the witnesses to the marriage.

331. *Resp. Penei Yiẕḥak* (by Isaac Abulafia), EH, #16 (p. 94d).

etc.; and that if any man shall intentionally marry in secret in the presence of two witnesses, etc., not only shall he be labeled a transgressor, but his marriage is annulled by the Rabbis and the money given to effect the marriage is completely expropriated under the principle of *hefker bet din hefker,* like the court of Ravina and R. Ashi, which had the power to expropriate property. . . . Inasmuch as such an incident occurred within the past three years, we have reenacted this legislation and proclaimed it publicly with full force and effect, with all transgressors being made subject to excommunication and ban, as is known.

A sharp dispute arose among the halakhic authorities as to the interpretation, validity, and applicability of this enactment.[332] Isaac Abulafia rendered a judgment annulling a particular marriage. The annulment rested on two grounds: (a) there were doubts about the competency of the witnesses to the marriage, and (b) the marriage was entered into without the presence of the ten persons required by the enactment. One of the questions in the case was, How was it possible to give effect to such an enactment in the face of the view of Joseph Caro—who had held that in actual practice such a marriage should not be annulled[333]—when Caro's rulings had been accepted as binding and determinative? To this question, Abulafia gave the following instructive answer:

The reason is that in this city of Damascus there is an explicit enactment that the marriage is to be completely null and void; this enactment was adopted during the time of the renowned Mordecai Galante, who, as is known, lived a long time after Joseph Caro. They, of course, knew of the view of Caro and others that even an enactment explicitly voiding a marriage is not to be put into effect and that a marriage that does not conform to the requirements of the enactment is nevertheless completely valid. In spite of this, they, in their wisdom, adopted an enactment to annul the marriage, notwithstanding the view of Caro and those who agree with him.

What could have been the purpose of the rabbis in taking the trouble to draft an enactment annulling a marriage when they were aware of the opinion of Caro and others that such an enactment has no effect? The only possible conclusion is that, despite Caro's view to the contrary, they intended to adopt such an enactment in order to completely annul the marriage and expropriate the money used to effect it. In a matter such as this, they may adopt an enactment and agree not to follow Caro's view in a particular respect, even to the point of leniency concerning a prohibition contained in the Torah, as a

332. *See* Freimann, *Kiddushin ve-Nissu'in,* pp. 286ff.

333. *Resp. Bet Yosef* #6; *see supra* pp. 870–871. Isaac Abulafia, *supra* n. 331, also cited the view that the undertaking to follow Caro's rulings applies only to his rulings in the *Shulḥan Arukh* and not to the rulings in Caro's responsa. *See Resp. Penei Yiẓḥak,* EH, #13 (p. 74c).

> protective measure, and even in these places, where we have generally accepted the view of Caro, as is known from the books of the codifiers.[334]

Shalom Moses Ḥai Gagin, of Jerusalem, took very sharp exception to this approach:

> This opinion in which the author states that he saw in the code books that it is permissible to adopt an enactment at variance with the rulings of Joseph Caro, even to the point of leniency concerning a prohibition contained in the Torah, is astounding; up to now, he has not disclosed to us the identity of this authority. This is nothing more than his own view, and it is completely unfounded. It cannot possibly be contended that the world's great scholars ever gathered together and agreed to rule contrary to the sainted Caro even in a single particular.[335]

According to Gagin, the enactment was intended to annul a marriage only in rare and exceptional cases.[336]

Abulafia strongly defended his position:

> What should I say in response to that author who is wise in his own eyes, . . . who compares those who studied and gained wisdom to ignorant reed cutters?[337] For the fundamental question, whether a court and a community may enact legislation to annul a marriage that is valid according to the Torah, has been extensively discussed by the *rishonim* Ribash and Rashbeẓ, and by other leading authorities. They proved directly from a number of Talmudic passages that enactments annulling a marriage regarded by the Torah as valid can be adopted on the basis of two sound and fully articulated reasons: (1) that "all who marry do so subject to the conditions laid down by the Rabbis, and the Rabbis annul this marriage"; and (2) that pursuant to the principle of *hefker bet din hefker,* the court has sufficient authority to exercise the power of expropriation. . . .[338]
>
> This being so, there is here an *a fortiori* inference: since they have the power to annul a marriage that is completely and clearly valid under the law of the Torah, as stated above, then *a fortiori,* in order to erect a safeguard, they may also adopt an enactment that is contrary to Caro on this particular point, and may instead follow the authorities who disagree with him. If they possess

334. *Resp. Penei Yiẓḥak,* EH, #13 (p. 74c). *Cf. supra* pp. 267–271 as to the principle that the law is decided according to the view of the later authorities.

335. *Resp. Yismaḥ Lev,* EH, #15 (p. 38d).

336. Such as when there were additional defects in the marriage or when, in particular circumstances, the wife was likely to become an *agunah.*

337. *See* TB Sanhedrin 33a.

338. Isaac Abulafia went on to state: "The rabbis and scholars of Jerusalem have already dealt with this at length . . . in their important responsum contained in *Resp. Nediv Lev,* II, EH, #8." For an abridged version, *see* Freimann, *Kiddushin ve-Nissu'in,* p. 289.

> the power to uproot, nullify, and dissolve a marriage that is valid according to the Torah, the conclusion must be that they may adopt an enactment contrary to the strict view of Caro, for otherwise, what have the halakhic authorities accomplished with their enactment? The matter is simple and clear and beyond all doubt.[339]

With regard to Gagin's statement that the Damascus enactment was intended to be limited to special circumstances, Abulafia stated:

> In my humble opinion, this is not so at all. There is no indication of this in the words of the enactment. Indeed, the rabbis and the community that enacted the legislation made it clear that they intended, solely by virtue of this enactment, to use their full power to completely uproot, expropriate, and render ownerless the money used to effect the marriage; and they needed no other support or anchor whatsoever, as is clear from the plain meaning of their words.[340]

These statements by Isaac Abulafia are certainly sound, for the leading *rishonim* emphasized and reemphasized that reluctance to legislate—especially reluctance to enact provisions explicitly annulling a marriage and expropriating the money given to effect it—is not due to lack of legal authority, but is rather based on practical considerations cautioning against the exercise of that authority. It is only because of such practical considerations that the halakhic authorities, even in the Jewish centers in the Eastern countries, refrained from annulling marriages on the basis of such enactments.

What brought about this abstention? The rationale undoubtedly is the one cited in almost all of the statements of every halakhic authority who has dealt with this subject—namely, the seriousness with which Jewish law regards marriage and forbidden sexual unions. However, this rationale alone is insufficient, because while these matters were always treated with the utmost seriousness in Jewish law, nevertheless, in most of the historical periods until well into the period of the *rishonim,* the halakhic authorities exercised their legislative power to annul marriages.

It is reasonable to conclude, as pointed out in the responsum of Maharam Alashkar,[341] that the rationale based on the seriousness with which Jewish law regards marriage and forbidden sexual unions acquired suffi-

339. These remarks are contained in a comprehensive responsum by Isaac Abulafia in *Resp. Lev Nishbar* #3 (p. 15a).

340. *Resp. Lev Nishbar* #3 (pp. 15b–16a). Later in the responsum, Abulafia pointed out that this was also the opinion of the rabbis of Jerusalem in their responsum in *Resp. Nediv Lev; see supra* n. 338.

341. *See supra* pp. 865–869.

cient force to bring about this legislative abstention in consequence of the new and unprecedented circumstances in which Jewish law operated after the geonic period. The fact that legislation in the post-geonic period was local led to the result that each Jewish center, and often each community,[342] enacted its own legislation in various areas of the law, so that conflicting laws proliferated on the same subject. Generally, this was not an unfortunate trend. Indeed, it even brought about considerable development in the Jewish law of conflict of laws.[343]

It was quite a different matter, however, when the legislation dealt with the validity of marriage and divorce. The possibility necessarily existed, in view of the local nature of legislation, that the validity of a marriage would depend on whether the couple were members of a community that had adopted an enactment voiding a marriage in violation of its provisions, or were members of a community that had no such enactment. This possibility constituted a serious threat to the existence of uniformity in one of the most sensitive areas of the *Halakhah*—the prohibition of sexual relations with a married woman by anyone except her husband. The only way to obviate this danger at that time was to limit legislative authority in this area.

10. CONTEMPORARY LEGISLATIVE AUTHORITY CONCERNING THE LAW OF MARRIAGE

From the foregoing discussion, it would appear that a number of conclusions may be drawn with regard to the authority to legislate on the subject of marriage in our own time. We currently face a number of problems in this area that cause pain and suffering, especially where the woman is an *agunah*, whether on account of the husband's mental illness or his malevolent behavior, or where there are similar circumstances or other difficulties with regard to *ḥaliẓah*. These and similar problems have always been solved in the Jewish legal system, either by way of interpretation or through legislation.

The *Halakhah* has always regarded itself as bound to provide solutions to such problems, not only because its appointed task is to safeguard the good and welfare of the people, but also because its interest is to make its constraints effective to the extent necessary to maintain the soundness, well-being, and sanctity of the family. The interest of the *Halakhah* is simply that a woman who is married to one man should not marry another and that a widow should undergo *ḥaliẓah* before she remarries; if there is a way

342. Occasionally, the various communities in the same city adopted different enactments; *see supra* p. 865 n. 301.

343. *See supra* p. 677. *See also* M. Elon, EJ, V, pp. 882–890, s.v. Conflict of laws (reprinted in *Principles*, pp. 715–723).

whereby a woman can be held to be unmarried, or a widow not to require *ḥaliẓah,* the *Halakhah* has the authority and the duty to find it.

The primary method for resolving such problems is to exercise, in the manner determined by the halakhic authorities, the legislative power to annul marriages.[344] It would seem that the great historic transformation of the condition of the Jewish people wrought by the restoration of Jewish sovereignty (a transformation seldom rivaled in magnitude during the entire course of Jewish history) should bring about a change in the existing reluctance to exercise the halakhic authority to legislate.

Just as the reasons for this abstention were the fragmentation and dispersal of the Jewish people, the local character of communal legislation, and the absence of a central authority, so the new circumstances—the ingathering, the unification, and the creation of a central authority for the Jewish people—are reasons for renewed exercise of legislative authority. The halakhic center in the State of Israel should be, and actually is, the main Jewish center, with halakhic hegemony over the entire Jewish diaspora. Consequently, it must do whatever is necessary to exercise the authority to adopt legislation, which, upon its enactment, will be, or in the course of time will become, the legacy of the Jewish people everywhere. The new historical situation should bring about a new halakhic situation in which the "crown" will be restored to its ancient glory. This new situation warrants the renewal of the full scope of creative legislative activity in all branches of Jewish law, including the law of marriage, in order to strive to perfect the *Halakhah* and promote the welfare of the Jewish people.

344. *See* Freimann, *Kiddushin ve-Nissu'in,* pp. 385ff., for various suggested enactments; E. Berkovitz, *Tenai be-Nissu'in u-ve-Get* [Contractual Conditions Regarding Marriage and Divorce], advocating a solution through contractual provisions agreed upon at the time of the marriage; Elon, *Ḥakikah,* pp. 182–184; I. Breitowitz, "The Plight of the *Agunah:* A study in *Halacha,* Contract, and the First Amendment," 51 *Md. L. Rev.* 312 (1992) (concluding that "technical devices such as prenuptial support agreements seem to present the fewest *halachic* dilemmas and offer significant and widespread potential for relief, at least for parties who have the foresight to utilize them").

Chapter 21

CUSTOM (*MINHAG*): ITS NATURE AND THE SOURCE OF ITS BINDING FORCE

I. INTRODUCTION

Before discussing custom as a source of law, it will be helpful to recall two of the three senses in which the term "source of law" is used.[1] In one sense, "source of law" means a historical source of law, *i.e.,* the source that in point of historical fact gave rise to a particular legal norm. A second meaning of "source of law" refers to a legal source of law, *i.e.,* the source that gives binding legal force to a particular rule and entitles the rule to recognition as part of the *corpus juris* of the legal system. An appreciation of this distinction is crucial to an understanding of the nature and function of custom, both in Jewish law and in legal systems generally. Sometimes custom functions as a historical source for a particular legal norm, sometimes it serves as a legal source, and sometimes it performs both functions.

II. CUSTOM AS A HISTORICAL SOURCE OF LAW

A study of the formative stages of any legal system reveals that some of the laws in the system were created by customs that evolved in the course of

1. *See supra* pp. 228–230.

practical experience. It was only at a later stage that legislation or judicial decision invested these customs with normative legal force. Jewish law is no exception. For example, there were practices in Israelite society before the Torah was given that the Torah explicitly confirmed and validated, as in the case of the law relating to the liability of bailees. There were other practices that the Torah retained, but with substantial modifications, as in the case of the laws relating to levirate marriage.[2] The historical source for these laws was custom practiced before the Torah was given; but their legal source was the Torah, which took cognizance of them and conferred upon them their legal force and effect. In every period of Jewish law, custom served as a historical source that developed particular norms to the point where the legal system was ready to receive them as legal norms.[3]

III. CUSTOM AS A LEGAL SOURCE OF LAW

As in all legal systems, custom plays an important role in Jewish law as a legal source of law. Custom becomes a legal source of law when, under particular circumstances and after certain conditions have been met, a legal system recognizes as an effective and binding legal norm some normative act previously followed only as a matter of custom and practice. When custom serves solely as a historical source of law, it merely develops the normative conduct to the point where it is ready to be accorded the force of law by virtue of legislation or some other legal source. However, when custom itself is a legal source of law, the normative conduct has the force of law solely by virtue of its being the practice, and there is no need for any other legal source such as legislation.

Custom as a legal source of law often serves the same purpose as legislation; both are resorted to when the need arises to solve new problems for which the existing law has no solution, or when existing law requires modification or reform. The formal distinction (which, as will be seen later, also has a substantive significance) between custom and legislation is that legislation operates openly under the direction of an authorized body, whereas custom operates anonymously and nondirectedly by the agency of the entire people or of some particular segment of the people. The study of a particular enactment is directed to the activities of the halakhic authorities, the courts, and the leaders of the people and the community; but if it is a custom that is the focus of inquiry, then, in the words of the Babylonian *amoraim*, one must "go and see what the people do,"[4] or, as the *amoraim* of

2. *See supra* pp. 196–199.
3. *See infra* n. 8.
4. TB Berakhot 45a, Pesaḥim 54a.

the Land of Israel put it, one must "go and see the practice of the people and follow it."[5]

It is true that normative rules based on custom are not established completely in isolation from the halakhic authorities; rules based on custom are subject to review and critique by the halakhic authorities, as is more fully explained later.[6] The relationship, however, is only indirect, and the public as a whole is the direct creative source of normative rules generated by custom.

The people are endowed with this decisive power and authority because there is a presumption that the people, who base their conduct on the *Halakhah,* intend their practices to be true to its spirit. As Hillel the Elder said in explaining why custom is given legal effect:[7] "Leave it to Israel; if they are not prophets, they are the descendants of prophets."[8]

5. TJ Pe'ah 7:5, 34b (7:6, 20c); TJ Ma'aser Sheni 5:2, 30a (5:3, 56b); TJ Yevamot 7:3, 40a (7:2, 8a).

6. *See infra* pp. 937–942. In several places, Maimonides used the three terms *gezerot, takkanot,* and *minhagot* interchangeably; *see MT,* Mamrim 1:2–3, 2:2, and his Introduction to the *Commentary on the Mishnah.* In *MT,* Mamrim 1:2–3 he wrote: ". . . and practices (*minhagot*) as to which they instruct the people . . . permitting the people to continue some customs and not others." This language implies that it is the Sages who teach the custom and guide the conduct of the people. However, it should be pointed out that the term *minhag* in Maimonides' writings sometimes means "enactment"; *see supra* p. 493 n. 78.

7. TB Pesaḥim 66a. *See further infra* pp. 901–902, 910 n. 54.

8. As stated, custom can simultaneously fulfill two functions: it can serve as a historical source of a particular norm that will later be given the force of law by a different legal source; and it can itself serve as a legal source that gives legal force to a particular practice.

The following are two examples of this dual function: First, according to the original law, a debt could be collected only from the realty of a deceased debtor's estate and not from the personalty (TB Ketubbot 51a, 69b). However, as early as in the Talmud, there is evidence that a certain type of debt was collected from the personalty of the estate because such was the local custom. TJ Gittin 5:3, 28b (5:3, 46d) states: ". . . I and our Rabbis permit collection from personalty according to local custom." *See also* TB Ketubbot 67a, and *Tosafot, ad loc.,* s.v. Gemalim shel aravya ishah govah parna mehem. In the geonic period, an enactment was adopted to permit various types of debts to be collected from the personalty of the estate (for details, *see supra* pp. 646–648). In this example, custom, in addition to its role as a legal source, was also a preparatory stage for the legislation.

The second example is from TB Sanhedrin 30a:

> R. Nehemiah said: "This was the custom of the scrupulously careful [judges] (*nekiyyei ha-da'at*) in Jerusalem: They would bring the parties [into the court] and hear what they had to say and then bring the witnesses [into court] and hear their testimony. They would then send them out [of the courtroom] and confer about the case."

The purpose of this practice was to prevent the parties from hearing the exchange of views among the judges, and from learning how the judges voted; if the deliberations were not private, the judges might be tempted to show partiality to one of the parties (*see* Maimonides, *Commentary on the Mishnah,* Sanhedrin 3:7). This custom is cited by the Talmud to explain the rule stated in M Sanhedrin 3:7: "When they [the judges] finished the matter, they would bring them in" (*i.e.,* after the conference on the case, they would bring the litigants back before the court). Maimonides states (*MT,* Sanhedrin 22:9) that this law was originally a custom of all the Jerusalemites, and not only of the scrupulously careful among them. *See*

IV. EXTENT AND RATIONALE OF THE EFFICACY OF CUSTOM AS A LEGAL SOURCE OF LAW

To what extent is custom a legal source of law? In the view of some Sages, the custom of the people cannot directly create law; the fact that the public follows a particular practice is, however, sufficient to prove the existence of a legal rule created in its time in some other manner. According to this view, every rule that presently appears to be based on custom came into existence and obtained its legal force through oral tradition, legislation, or some other legal source; but the original legal source was forgotten in the course of time, and custom is the only form in which the rule was preserved and transmitted to us.

This view has been expressed in various ways: "Any '*torah*' that does not have a definite source is no '*torah*.'"[9] Another formulation is: "A custom that has no Scriptural support is nothing more than mistaken reasoning."[10] This is also the view of some post-Talmudic authorities:

> The source of any practice customarily followed . . . is an enactment, . . . and even if in the course of time the source of the practice has been forgotten, nevertheless the practice has been generally accepted and retains its legal force.[11]

This theory as to the source of the binding force of custom necessarily limits the sphere in which custom operates: "Custom is considered to be

---

Radbaz, *ad loc.*, stating: "It is possible that he [Maimonides] omitted here 'the scrupulously careful,' since all judges should follow this practice." However, it appears that Maimonides' text is based on ms. Munich and other sources, according to which R. Nehemiah referred to "the Jerusalemites," and not "the scrupulously careful in Jerusalem." Maimonides (*MT*, Sanhedrin 22:10), in connection with the rule (based on TB Sanhedrin 23a) that a judge should not sit on a case until he knows who the other judges will be, refers to "the scrupulously careful in Jerusalem," since this is the language of the Talmudic source for that rule.

Tur ḤM 19:1 and Sh. Ar. ḤM 19:1 (*see also* Sh. Ar. ḤM 18:6) state the law as follows: "After they [the judges] finish discussing the case, they bring in the litigants"; but these authorities do not mention that the rule had its origin in a custom of the Jerusalemites.

A further example of transformation of custom into law, when both the custom and the law are post-Talmudic, appears in *Resp. Ḥatam Sofer*, ḤM, #21, regarding the protection of rabbinical incumbents against competition. *See also* M. Elon, EJ, VII, pp. 1463–1464, s.v. Hassagat gevul (reprinted in *Principles*, p. 344). Many more examples can be cited.

9. TJ Shabbat 19:1, 87a (9:1, 17a). The term *torah* here means "custom." The quotation refers to the *baraita* in TB Pesaḥim 66a, which reports that Hillel recalled that he had heard from Shemaiah and Avtalyon about the people's custom concerning the bringing of the paschal sacrifice on the sabbath. This *baraita* is discussed in detail *infra* pp. 901–902.

10. Tractate *Soferim*, ch. 14 (ed. Higger, p. 271). *See* editor's note, *ad loc.*, and Introduction, p. 23; *Mordekhai*, Bava Meẓi'a, #366.

11. *Resp. Alfasi*, ed. Leiter, #13. *See also* Naḥmanides' responsa in Assaf, *Sifran Shel Rishonim* #7 (pp. 61–62). Naḥmanides held the same view and relied on Alfasi's responsum (*see* Assaf, *loc. cit.* at n. 11). *See also infra* n. 12.

binding only when the townspeople or the communal leaders specifically and formally adopt it, but any custom not so adopted cannot override an existing legal rule unless the rule is doubtful."[12] In other words, custom does not have the power to override a legal rule unless the custom is incorporated in legislation; custom as such is not decisive unless the legal rule is unclear.

In addition, even when custom is used in matters of *issur* ("religious" law) for the limited purpose of determining the law when there is a dispute among the halakhic authorities, there are those who explain this power as being based on the fact that the existence of the custom indicates that there had been an earlier but now forgotten determination of the law of which all that remains is the customary practice.[13] This view, however, appears to be a minority view, and the extent to which custom is a legal source of Jewish law remains a subject of disagreement among halakhic authorities as well as recent scholars.[14]

What appears to be the majority view of the halakhic authorities is that the people can create law through custom, and that custom does more than merely prove the existence of a law created by some other means. These authorities agree that there are indeed customary practices the source of which is earlier law that did not itself originate through custom. This was the case with regard to the incident involving Hillel and the bringing of the paschal sacrifice on the sabbath,[15] and other examples.[16] However, such

12. Naḥmanides, Novellae to Bava Batra 144b, s.v. Ha de-amrinan. Naḥmanides cited this opinion as an *ikka de-amri* (lit. "there are some who say"), *i.e.*, a possible alternative ruling; but in fact he ruled in accordance with this opinion. This view would narrow the scope of every source that suggests that custom overrides the law: according to this view, "custom" in this context means legislation, *i.e.*, an agreement of the townspeople, or a communal enactment. (Here, too, the special relationship between legislation and custom is apparent). Custom in the usual sense of the term is effective, according to this view, only if there is a doubt as to the law; *see infra* text accompanying n. 13. And *see Resp. Ribash* #345, asserting that Naḥmanides' limitation does not apply to all customs and that there are matters as to which custom has legal force even without an enactment. *See further Resp. Ribash* #105, and Isaac Aboab's responsum in *Sheva Einayim*, Leghorn, 1735, particularly pp. 60ff.

13. *See Resp. Asheri* 55:10 (first part), concerning custom:

> And it is similarly stated in TJ that when the law is unclear, follow the custom—which means that if it is not clear to you which opinion has been accepted as law and you see how people are accustomed to act, follow the custom because it can be assumed that the authorities who instituted the custom knew that was the law.

14. *See* various opinions in *Pitḥei Teshuvah* to Sh. Ar. ḤM 163, subpar. 16. For a discussion of the problem, *see* Weiss, *Dor Dor ve-Doreshav*, II, ch. 7 (pp. 62–64); Ch. Tchernowitz, *Toledot ha-Halakhah* [History of the *Halakhah*], I, pp. 144–150.

15. TB Pesaḥim 66a, quoted in part *supra* p. 882 and discussed in greater detail *infra* pp. 901–902. It is regarding this incident that TJ states that "any '*torah*' that does not have a definite source is no '*torah*.'" *See supra* n. 9.

16. *See, e.g., Tosefta* Mo'ed 2:14–15, which indicates that the custom in Acre to refrain on the sabbath from sitting on a bench used by non-Jews (so as to avoid giving the impres-

instances reflect only a partial description of the character of custom and the source of its binding force generally.

The distinctiveness of custom as a legal source of law is not its probative power as evidence of the law but its embodiment of the creative power of the people both to determine the law when there is a conflict among the halakhic authorities, and to add to existing law. This distinctive quality is most clearly evident in matters of civil law, where custom may even supersede preexisting law on the basis of the general principle of Jewish law that the parties to a legal transaction—and even more so the public as a whole—may, by agreement, vary rules of law laid down by the Torah.[17] This principle thus reflects in striking form the creative force of custom.[18]

V. EXPLANATION OF TERMS; MEANINGS OF *MINHAG;* OTHER HEBREW TERMS FOR "CUSTOM"

The root of the term *minhag,* usually translated "custom," is the verb *nahog,* "to conduct oneself." *Minhag* refers to particular normative behavior that has been continuous and unquestioned.[19] At times, a particular halakhic rule based on custom is called *dat*[20] or *dat yehudit* (Jewish custom).[21] The halakhic authorities also sometimes use the term *minhag* in referring to a normative rule based on legislation; and the verb *hinhig* (causative form of *nahog,* "cause conduct to be practiced") is sometimes used to describe the act of promulgating an enactment.[22] The use of the same term for both

sion of engaging in business) originated in an earlier enactment that prohibited such conduct: "Originally they declared [*i.e.,* enacted] that on the sabbath one may not sit on a bench used by non-Jews." *See also* TB Pesaḥim 51a; TJ Pesaḥim 4:1, 25b (4:1, 30d); Alon, *Meḥkarim,* II, p. 242.

17. *See supra* pp. 123–127. This is the rationale accepted by most halakhic authorities for the rule that in matters of civil law, custom overrides the law. *See infra* p. 904.

18. Custom is also effective in areas other than the civil law—although to a very limited extent—not only to add strictures, but even to change a preexisting rule. *See infra* pp. 910–911.

19. *See infra* pp. 927–929 as to how frequent and common a practice must be before it qualifies as a custom, and as to how custom is proved.

20. TB Beẓah 25b and Rashi, *ad loc.,* s.v. Dateihen shel ellu. For the various terms, *see* A. Perls, "Der Minhag im Talmud" [Custom in the Talmud], *Tiferet Yisra'el* (*Israel Lewy Jubilee Volume*), German Section, p. 69. In the past, the primary meanings of *dat* were "decree" and "religion." In current Hebrew usage, *dat* generally means "religion."

21. M Ketubbot 7:6 and Rashi, Ketubbot 72a, s.v. Dat yehudit. *See also Tosefta* Ketubbot 7:7; S. Lieberman, *Tosefta ki-Feshutah,* Ketubbot, pp. 292–293; H. Albeck, Commentary on M Nashim, p. 352.

22. *See* sources quoted *supra* p. 493 n. 78, to which should be added *Midrash Mishlei* [Midrash on Proverbs] 22:28: "A *minhag* that your fathers made . . . Abraham enacted."

"enactment" and "custom"[23] is understandable in the light of the fact that in a broad sense each is a form of legislation—overt in the case of an enactment and covert in the case of a custom.

The term *minhag* is also used to describe a rule for which the Torah itself is the source. Thus, in the *Sifra*[24] the requirement of the Torah to dwell in a *sukkah* (booth, tabernacle) and to take the *lulav* (palm branch and other species: citron, willow, and myrtle) for seven days on the festival of *Sukkot* is termed *minhag le-dorot* (a *minhag*—prescribed practice—for all generations).[25]

The converse is also true. Sometimes, a normative rule for which the source is custom is termed *halakhah.* For example, the Torah states:[26]

> When you enter another man's vineyard, you may eat as many grapes as you want, until you are full, but you must not put any in your vessel.

This Biblical provision giving permission to eat fruit growing in another's vineyard was interpreted to apply only to a laborer in that vineyard, and only during a particular stage in the cultivation of the fruit.[27] To this limited class of persons entitled to eat fruit from the vineyard, the Mishnah adds:[28] "Those who guard the fruit may eat of it pursuant to the *halakhot* of the community, but not on the basis of the law of the Torah," *i.e.,* those who guard the fruit also have the right to eat the produce of the vineyard; however, the legal source of this rule is not the Torah but rather the custom of the community or the public, here termed *halakhah.*[29]

The use by the Sages of the term *halakhah* to refer to a rule having its source in custom led at the beginning of the amoraic period to a difference of opinion with regard to the legal source for the development of a rule of agricultural law. The Mishnah states:[30]

23. *See further supra* n. 6; *Resp. Rashba,* II, #268.
24. *Sifra,* Emor 17:5–8.
25. TB Sukkah 43a/b reads: *mizvah le-dorot,* "a commandment for all generations." *See also* TB Berakhot 11a, concerning R. Ishmael, who was reclining but stood up for the recitation of the *Shema,* "so that the disciples would not see [him reclining] and fix the law thus for all generations."
26. Deuteronomy 23:25.
27. M Bava Mezi'a 7:2 *et seq.*
28. *Id.* 7:8.
29. *See also* TJ Ma'aserot 2:4, 12a (4:7, 50a):

> R. Samuel said in the name of R. Hila . . . "R. Yose said: 'This is applicable only when one harvests and another transports, but if the same person both harvests and transports, at the beginning he may eat by virtue of the *halakhot* of the community and at the end he may eat by virtue of the law relating to a worker.'"

See further H. Albeck, Commentary on M Bava Mezi'a, p. 427.
30. M Kiddushin 1:9.

> Every precept directly relating to the land [*e.g.*, giving tithes and *terumah* (the priestly portion) from the produce of the land], is applicable only in the Land [*i.e.*, the Land of Israel and not in a foreign country]. If it does not directly relate to the land [*i.e.*, if it is not connected to the land, but is imposed on the individual personally, such as the commandment to observe the sabbath], it is applicable both in the Land [of Israel] and outside the Land [of Israel]. [This rule holds] except for the laws relating to *orlah*[31] and *kilayim*.[32] R. Eliezer said: "*Ḥadash*[33] also is excepted."

This passage establishes that, contrary to the general rule that a precept directly relating to the land is applicable only in the Land of Israel, the prohibition of *orlah*, *kilayim*, and *ḥadash*, even though they directly relate to the land, is applicable outside the Land of Israel as well. In another passage,[34] the Mishnah indicates the legal source by which these three exceptions were established: "*Ḥadash* is Biblically prohibited in all places;[35] *orlah* [is prohibited by] *halakhah*, *kilayim* [is prohibited] by declaration of the Scribes."

Thus, there are three distinct legal sources for the applicability of the prohibition of *ḥadash*, *orlah*, and *kilayim* outside the Land of Israel. The prohibition of *ḥadash* outside the Land of Israel is based on the Biblical text; and the legal source for the prohibition of *kilayim* outside the Land of Israel is a declaration of the Scribes, *i.e.*, an explicit enactment of the Sages.[36] But what is the meaning of the legal source, termed *halakhah*, for the prohibition of *orlah* outside the Land of Israel? On this question, there is a difference of opinion between the *amoraim* Samuel and R. Johanan.[37] According to Samuel, *halakhah* refers to a rule of the community, *i.e.*, a custom of the people; according to R. Johanan, *halakhah* means a law given orally to Moses at Sinai (*halakhah le-Moshe mi-Sinai*). Thus, it was the view of R. Johanan that the legal source for the prohibition of *orlah* outside the Land of Israel is the transmitted tradition;[38] on the other hand, according to Sam-

31. *Orlah* is fruit that grows on a tree during the first three years after the tree was planted. It may not be eaten, nor may any benefit be derived from it (Leviticus 19:23).

32. *Kilayim* is the result of planting two species of grain together, or grafting two kinds of trees, or planting grain and vegetables in a vineyard. Such hybridization is forbidden (Leviticus 19:19; Deuteronomy 22:9).

33. *Ḥadash* is new produce that may not be eaten before the *omer* offering is brought on the second day of Passover (Leviticus 23:14).

34. M Orlah 3:9.

35. With regard to *ḥadash*, Leviticus 23:14 states:

> Until that very day, until you have brought the offering of your God, you shall eat no bread or parched grain or fresh ears; it is a law for all time throughout the generations in all your settlements [*i.e.*, the prohibition also applies outside the Land of Israel].

36. *See supra* pp. 207, 478.

37. TB Kiddushin 38b; TJ Orlah 3:7, 20a (3:8, 63b).

38. *See supra* pp. 204–205.

uel, the legal source is custom, *i.e.*, a law conceived and created by the people, so that the term *halakhah* as used in this context in the Mishnah is synonymous with *minhag*, or "custom."

VI. DISTINCTIONS BETWEEN LAWS DERIVED FROM CUSTOM AND LAWS DERIVED FROM OTHER LEGAL SOURCES

The interchangeable use of the terms *minhag*, *takkanah*, and *halakhah* not only calls for the exercise of great care in identifying the true nature of each rule referred to by one of these terms but is also evidence of the efficacy and significance of those normative rules whose legal source is custom and of the status of those rules as an integral part of the overall Jewish legal system. Although the force of a rule based on custom is sometimes more limited than that of a rule whose source is legislation or one of the other legal sources of Jewish law, this distinction has only a limited significance, and applies only when the custom relates to religious law (*issur*). Even in the area of *issur*, where the scope of operation of custom is limited, sanctions may be applied against those who transgress rules based on custom: "Just as there is a fine for violating a *halakhah*, so there is a fine for violating a *minhag*";[39] and R. Abbahu even sought to punish by flogging one who transgressed a prohibition for which the source was custom.[40] As to civil law (*mamon*), a rule for which custom is the legal source generally has the same force as a rule for which the legal source is legislation.[41]

39. TJ Pesaḥim 4:3, 27a (4:3, 30d), concerning a person who sold small cattle to a non-Jew in a locality where custom forbade such sale.

40. TJ Kiddushin 4:6, 46a (4:6, 66a), concerning a *kohen* (priest) who married the daughter of a proselyte. According to R. Yose, she is eligible for marriage to a priest, but according to R. Eliezer b. Jacob, she is not. Although R. Yose's view became accepted as the law, "from the time that the Temple was destroyed, the priests, as a matter of custom, have been very fastidious and follow the opinion of R. Eliezer b. Jacob." *See* TB Kiddushin 78b.

41. *See infra* ch. 22 for many examples. Similarly, failure to follow a custom in civil law can deprive litigants of the right to present to the court even an intrinsically meritorious position. *Tosefta* Ketubbot 1:4 (TB Ketubbot 12a; TJ Ketubbot 1:1, 2b–3a (1:1, 25a)) states:

> In Judea, originally they used to have two attendants, one representing the groom's side and one representing the bride's side [to ensure that neither the groom nor the bride practices any deceit, *e.g.*, that the groom has not destroyed the evidence of the bride's virginity]. . . . Those who do not follow this custom can have no claim that the bride was not a virgin.

See Perles, *supra* n. 20 at 72. *See also* S. Lieberman, *Tosefta ki-Feshutah*, Ketubbot, pp. 193–194, on the various customs cited in this section of the *Tosefta*, parallel to TB and TJ. *Piskei ha-Rosh*, Ketubbot, ch. 1, #25 comments:

> Ribam [Isaac ben Mordecai] explained that he [the groom] does not benefit from the legal presumption that no man will go to the trouble of preparing a [wedding] feast

As has been seen, the Sages, particularly the *amoraim*, gave special attention to identifying the legal source of particular halakhic rules. This search for the source of legal rules was not merely academic or theoretical; it also influenced the legal conclusions reached with respect to those rules. The following are some examples.

The Talmudic discussion dealing with the legal source for the prohibition of *orlah* outside the Land of Israel,[42] which has just been noted, indicates that most *amoraim* were of the opinion that the source for that prohibition was custom; on this basis they found various ways to permit the eating of *orlah* of fruits grown outside the Land of Israel, which they would not have done had the source of this prohibition been a law given to Moses at Sinai.

Another example: The Talmud[43] discusses a dispute between R. Johanan and R. Joshua b. Levi with regard to the legal source for taking the willow branch (in addition to the willow bound with the *lulav*) on the festival of *Sukkot*—a custom observed today by taking and beating willow branches on *Hoshana Rabbah*, the seventh day of the festival. According to one view, the practice was introduced by the prophets, *i.e.*, the source of the law is an explicit enactment that the prophets promulgated. Another view is that the taking of the willow was merely "a custom of the prophets," *i.e.*, a customary practice that the prophets instituted.[44]

Subsequently, the Talmud concludes[45] that this distinction with regard to the legal source of the law has legal consequences. If the law of the willow branch is based on an enactment of the prophets acting as halakhic authorities, a benediction should be recited at the time of the beating of the willow branch, just as a benediction is to be recited when performing any religious obligation mandated by an enactment of the halakhic authorities,

---

> and then have it go to waste [*i.e.*, that a man will not prepare a wedding feast and then falsely allege that the bride was not a virgin]. Rabbenu Tam [the reading should be "Rabbenu Hananel," *see Tiferet Shemu'el*, subpar. 12, and *Korban Netanel*, subpar. 10, *ad loc.*] distinguished the case under discussion because the custom to have attendants was not followed, and we infer that it was not followed at his [*i.e.*, the groom's] instance and that he is deceitful, and therefore the presumption cannot be relied upon.

Thus, a custom prevails over a legal presumption, which is indeed the ruling of *Tur* EH ch. 68 and Sh. Ar. EH 68:2: "If it is the local custom to appoint witnesses to ensure that there is no deceit, and it happened that no witnesses were appointed, he [the groom] cannot claim that the bride was not a virgin." *See also* commentaries, *ad loc.*

42. TB Kiddushin 38b–39a; for details, *see supra* pp. 886–888.

43. TB Sukkah 44a.

44. *See* Rashi, Sukkah 44a, s.v. Minhag; Sherira Gaon, *Teshuvot ha-Geonim, Sha'arei Teshuvah*, #307.

45. TB Sukkah 44b.

such as the kindling of the *Hanukkah* lights. The reason for such a benediction is that the Torah has commanded obedience to the enactments of the halakhic authorities.[46] On the other hand, if the law of the willow branch is based on custom, its direct source is not the mandate of the halakhic authorities but "legislation" by the public, and therefore no benediction should be recited when the willow branch is beaten. Indeed, many halakhic authorities did not recite a benediction on the willow branch, on the ground that that ritual was based on custom and not formal legislation.[47]

With regard to determining the law when there are differing views, the *amoraim* were careful to ascertain whether the determination was explicit, or was implicit in a custom introduced by the Sages or in a spontaneous custom of anonymous origin.[48]

46. *See supra* pp. 481–483.

47. *See* TB Sukkah 44b:

> Aibu said: "I was once standing in the presence of R. Eleazar b. Ẓadok when a man brought a willow branch to him, and he took it and beat it without reciting any benediction; for he was of the opinion that it was a custom of the prophets." Aibu and Hezekiah, the sons of Rav's daughter, brought a willow branch to Rav; and he beat it without reciting a benediction, for he was of the opinion that it was a custom of the prophets.

See also Rashi, Sukkah 44a, s.v. Minhag, and 44b, s.v. Minhag nevi'im hu.

48. *See* TJ Shekalim 1:1, 2b (1:1, 46a) and TJ Megillah 1:5, 7b (1:7, 71a) in regard to the commandments that apply in the month of Adar I:

> R. Huna Rabbah of Sepphoris said: "R. Ḥanina instituted the custom in Sepphoris in accordance with the opinion of Rabban Simeon b. Gamaliel." He said no more than "instituted the custom," from which it follows that it does not have the force of law.

To the same effect is TJ Niddah 3:1, 9a (3:1, 50c), in connection with a dispute between the Sages and R. Judah:

> R. Jacob b. Aḥa [said] . . . "The law follows R. Judah's opinion." R. Lazar heard it and said, "I cannot accept that [because the law always follows the majority]." Samuel said, "The law follows R. Judah's opinion." R. Ze'eira said, "He did not say, 'The law follows R. Judah's opinion,' but he saw that some Sages conducted themselves according to R. Judah [and he said that the Sages instituted a custom in accordance with R. Judah's opinion]."

Similarly, in TJ Pesaḥim 4:6, 28b (4:6, 31a), after an opinion is stated to the effect that work before noon on the fourteenth day of the month of Nisan (the eve of Passover) is forbidden by law (apparently by an enactment for which support was found in a Biblical verse, *see id.*), R. Ze'eira said:

> We find here that three *tannaim* dispute this point. One says that it [work on the eve of Passover] is forbidden [by law, namely, the enactment]; one says that it is permitted; and one says that it is the custom [not to work].

TB makes a similar distinction between an explicit ruling that certain conduct is prohibited and a prohibition on the basis of custom. *See* TB Avodah Zarah 14b, concerning the custom not to sell small cattle to idol worshippers—"Are we to take it that there is no actual prohibition, but that it is only a matter of custom?" *See also* TB Yevamot 13b, concerning the prohibition *lo titgodedu* ("you shall not gash yourselves" [Deuteronomy 14:1], intepreted by the Rabbis in a play on words to mean "you shall not separate into factions [*agudot*]")—"I tell you that it is a prohibition . . . and you tell me that it is custom"; TB Niddah 66a,

In the latter half of the amoraic period, the Babylonian *amoraim* established an additional distinction that had practical consequences. In connection with the differences of opinion among the *tannaim* R. Meir, R. Judah, and R. Yose as to whether the priestly blessing should be given during the afternoon prayer on the Day of Atonement,[49] the *amoraim* stated:

> R. Judah said in the name of Rav: "The law (*halakhah*) is in accordance with the view of R. Meir"; Rava said: "The custom (*minhag*) is in accordance with the view of R. Meir"; R. Johanan said: "The practice of the people (*nahagu ha-am*) is in accordance with the view of R. Meir."[50]

As can be determined from various Talmudic sources, neither R. Johanan nor Rava attributed any legal significance to the difference between "custom" and "practice of the people."[51] However, the Babylonian Talmud

---

concerning one of the laws of menstruant women—"I tell you it is a prohibition and you [R. Ze'eira] say it is a custom."

It is noteworthy that the law in question concerning possibly menstruant women, which R. Ze'eira described as a custom, was called "a settled law" (*halakhah pesukah*) in TB Berakhot 31a: "What is the definition of a settled law? Abbaye said: 'One like the law of R. Zera [Ze'eira]; as R. Zera [Ze'eira] said: "The daughters of Israel are strict with themselves to the extent that if they see a blood stain even [as small] as a grain of mustard, they observe the waiting period of seven clean days. . . ."'" *See also* Rashi, *ad loc.*, s.v. Asur be-hana'ah u-mo'alin bah: ". . . these are settled laws, because they allow of no [complicated] questions or answers that require [extensive] thought." *See also* M. Ish-Shalom, Introduction to *Mekhilta;* E.E. Urbach, "Ha-Derashah ki-Yesod ha-Halakhah u-Va'ayat ha-Soferim" [Exegesis as the Foundation of the *Halakhah* and the Problem of the *Soferim*], *Tarbiẓ,* XXVII (1958), pp. 165ff., at p. 169; B. De Vries, *Toledot ha-Halakhah ha-Talmudit* [A History of Talmudic *Halakhah*], pp. 157–159.

49. TB Ta'anit 26b; as to the details of this dispute, *see infra* pp. 898–899.

50. Our quotation follows the order in which the opinions are stated in ms. Munich, which is the correct one, as shown by the parallel passage in TB Eruvin 62b, 72a, and the order in which the opinions are stated later in the same discussion: "According to the opinion that 'the custom is in accordance with . . .'; according to the opinion that 'the practice of the people is in accordance with. . . ." *See also Dikdukei Soferim, ad loc.* In ms. Munich, instead of "Rava said," the text reads, "R. Huna said."

51. *See* TJ Shevi'it 5:1, 13a (5:1, 35d) ("R. Johanan said: 'As to [the tithing of the fruit of] carob trees, the practice [of the people] is in accordance with the view of R. Nehemiah'"), as opposed to TB Rosh ha-Shanah 15b: ("Just because this was their practice, do we allow it?"). Similarly, TB Pesaḥim 103a (*see also* TB Berakhot 52a) ("R. Johanan said: The practice of the people is in accordance with the view of the School of Hillel as interpreted by R. Judah," and, on that basis, Rava first recited the benediction over spices and then the benediction over the light); TB Pesaḥim 104a ("As R. Johanan said: 'The son of holy ones [R. Menahem b. Sima'i, so called because he never even looked at money, TB Avodah Zarah 50a] recited one, but the practice of the people was to recite three'"). R. Menahem b. Sima'i was apparently considered to be a *tanna,* yet the custom prevailed against his opinion. *See further* TB Berakhot 50a as to Rafram b. Papa, when he came to a synagogue, and Rava's remarks, *ad loc. Cf.* TJ Berakhot 7:3, 55a (7:4, 10c).

drew specific conclusions from the use of the different terms "law," "custom," and "practice of the people":

> According to the opinion that "the law is in accordance with the view of R. Meir," it [the norm that accords with R. Meir's view] is to be publicly taught [in order to disseminate it]. According to the opinion that "the custom" [is in accordance with his view], it is not to be publicly taught, but [if anyone inquires] he is to be instructed [that this is the preferred practice to follow]. According to the opinion that "the practice of the people" [is in accordance with his view], we do not instruct [that this is the preferred practice to follow], but if it is done, we do not interfere.

The phrase "practice of the people" was thus interpreted by the Babylonian *amoraim* as referring to a practice that had not yet fully crystallized, and therefore possessed less legal force than a custom. Even when a custom has fully crystallized and the advice given upon inquiry is that it should preferably be followed, it is not on the same level as a ruling explicitly declared by the halakhic authorities and taught in public in order to disseminate it among the people.[52]

There were also occasions when opposition among the Babylonian *amoraim* to a particular custom was so great that the custom was ultimately nullified. This occurred when the *amoraim* were apprehensive that the custom might lead to a transgression; the custom was nullified even though during the tannaitic period the same custom had been given full legal force and there had been no concern about any possible adverse effects.[53]

52. *See also* parallels in TB Eruvin 62b, 71b–72a.

53. *E.g.*, *Tosefta* Pesaḥim 3:14 (ms. Erfurt 2:14): "In a locality where the practice has been to return the money used to effect betrothal, it should be returned. In a locality where it has been the practice not to return the money, it need not be returned." (In TB Bava Batra 145a this rule is attributed to R. Nathan and R. Judah Ha-Nasi.) This passage in the *Tosefta* (quoted also in TB Bava Batra 144b) establishes that in a case where betrothal does not eventuate in a full marriage, local custom will determine whether the betrothal money should be returned to the groom (*see* Rashbam, Bava Batra 144b, s.v. Makom she-nahagu le-haḥazir kiddushin, and the Talmudic discussion, *id.* at 145a). In TB the *amoraim* expressed various reservations concerning this rule. R. Joseph b. Abba in the name of Mar Akba stated that it was the view of Samuel that only if the bride dies before the marriage is the money to be returned; if the groom dies, the bride is not required to return the money because she can claim, "Give me my husband and I will be happy with him," *i.e.*, it is not her fault that there was no marriage. The conclusion of the passage (*id.* at 145a) states:

> R. Joseph b. Manyumi said in the name of R. Naḥman: "Wherever the practice has been to return [the betrothal money], it should be returned" [when the bride dies—Rashbam, *ad loc.*, s.v. Amar R. Joseph; this is Samuel's opinion, *see supra*]; and the reference is to Nehardea [where this was the practice].
>
> What is the law for the rest of Babylonia? Rabbah and R. Joseph [third generation of *amoraim*] both said: "Gifts [that the groom gave over and above the betrothal money] are returned; the betrothal money is not returned." [No reason is given for this distinction, but apparently this was the practice in the rest of Babylonia.]

The major application of these distinctions and limitations in regard to the scope of operation of custom is in the area of religious law (*issur*) and in situations where a custom involving civil law affects religious law.[54] However, in purely civil law matters, custom operates fully and effectively as a creative source of law, as is shown in the following chapter.

VII. SCRIPTURAL SUPPORT FOR THE BINDING FORCE OF CUSTOM

The halakhic authorities found various sources in Scripture to provide support for the binding force of custom. R. Simeon b. Yoḥai said: "Do not change the custom introduced by your ancestors"; support for this *dictum* is derived from a *midrash*[55] on the verse, "Do not remove the ancient bound-

---

> R. Papa [fifth generation of *amoraim*] said: "The law is that whether he died or she died, or he called off the marriage, the gifts are to be returned, but the betrothal money is not to be returned; if she called off the marriage, even the betrothal money is to be returned." [According to this view, the rule is independent of local practice.]
>
> Ameimar [sixth generation of *amoraim*] said: "The betrothal money is not returned, lest people be led to believe that he can marry her sister." [*I.e.*, the rule that the betrothal money is not returned is a safeguard to prevent people from thinking that no marriage relationship ever existed between the parties, in which case the groom would be able to marry the sister of the bride—a marriage the Torah forbids; Rashbam, *ad loc.*, s.v. Gezerah shemma yomru. This concern would be applicable where neither party has died and there was a refusal to enter into the marriage. According to Ameimar's opinion, too, the local practice carries no weight and the betrothal money is not to be returned.]
>
> R. Ashi said: "Her bill of divorcement is sufficient indication of her status." [R. Ashi would leave the matter to the local practice, because he believed that people would not misunderstand the situation—the woman will receive a *get* (bill of divorcement), whereby everyone will know that there had been a marriage relationship between them and that the groom may therefore not marry the bride's sister.]
>
> But R. Ashi's view is not correct, because it is possible that people will hear of one thing [the return of the betrothal money] without hearing of the other [the divorce]. [Apparently the conclusion of the passage—"But R. Ashi's view is not correct . . ."—is from a later period, perhaps the savoraic.]

This Talmudic passage illustrates how a tannaitic law, which gave the full force of a legal rule to a particular custom, was abrogated by the Babylonian *amoraim* because they believed that it could lead to untoward results. The same danger existed in tannaitic times, but the *tannaim* were not troubled by it. The conclusion of TB is codified as law by Maimonides, *MT*, Zekhiyyah u-Mattanah 6:18:

> If a man betroths a woman, even with the sum of 1000 dinars, whether she refuses or he refuses [to enter into a full marriage], whether he dies or she dies—the betrothal money is never to be returned, but constitutes an absolute gift that is not recoverable.

54. *E.g.*, as in the question of the return of betrothal money, lest people will say the groom may marry his ex-wife's sister, *see supra* n. 53.

55. *Midrash Mishlei*, ed. Buber, 22:28, and *see* editor's note, *ad loc.*

ary stone that your ancestors set up."[56] R. Johanan rested the binding force of custom on another verse in Proverbs:[57] "My son, heed the discipline of your father, and do not forsake the instruction of your mother."[58] Sherira Gaon refers[59] to a tradition not contained in the extant Talmudic texts:[60] "What is the basis for the binding force of custom? It is the verse: 'You shall not move your neighbor's landmarks, set up by previous generations.'"[61] The common teaching of all of these sources is that a norm that has been followed for a considerable time[62] acquires an established place in Jewish law and may not be abandoned or transgressed.[63]

56. Proverbs 22:28.

57. *Id.* 1:8.

58. TB Pesaḥim 50b; Ḥullin 93b. *See also She'iltot de-Rav Aḥai,* Va-Yakhel, *she'ilta* #67 (ed. N.Z.Y. Berlin, p. 431, where the text reads: "R. Johanan said in the name of Rav"; *see Ha'amek She'elah, ad loc.,* #5), and *she'ilta* #76 (ed. Mirsky, pp. 215–216; and commentaries and notes, *ad loc.*); *Halakhot Gedolot,* ed. Hildesheimer, Laws of Megillah (end), p. 198.

59. *Teshuvot ha-Geonim Sha'arei Ẓedek,* Part IV, Sha'ar 1, #20, ed. Jerusalem (1966), p. 75; *Tur* ḤM ch. 368. *See also Oẓar ha-Geonim,* Megillah, Responsa, p. 49.

60. A.A. Harkavy (*Ha-Peles,* year 2, 1902, p. 75) gives the source as *Midrash Mishlei,* cited *supra* n. 55; *see also* Mirsky, *supra* n. 58, editor's notes; Urbach, *The Sages,* p. 816 n. 24.

61. Deuteronomy 19:14. Sherira Gaon's statement was made with reference to a case involving an article stolen from its owner and sold to another person. According to the strict law, if the owner has abandoned hope of recovering his property, the purchaser need not restore it to him. Sherira Gaon ruled that since the custom was that the purchaser must restore it, the custom must be firmly obeyed and overrides the law. A similar rule, which in the responsum of Sherira Gaon is based on custom, is characterized in the responsa of Rabbenu Gershom as being based on a communal enactment. For details, *see supra* p. 688 and n. 35. *See also* Meiri, *Magen Avot* (ed. I. Last, 1909). Meiri's Introduction (p. 6) quotes a source from TJ that is not extant: "And that is what is stated by TJ: The verse 'Do not disdain your mother when she is old' (Proverbs 23:22) refers to customs" (*see* editor's note, *ad loc.* [n. 1]). Meiri adds: "Since that is so, it is fitting for every wise man and every discerning person to uphold the local customs, so as not to remove the landmarks of our early ancestors and Sages by changing a local custom without need or reason."

62. As to the length of time and the quantum of proof required, *see infra* pp. 927–929.

63. *Cf.* Philo's comments on Deuteronomy 19:14, *De Specialibus Legibus,* IV, 149. *See also* Y. Baer, "Ha-Yesodot ha-Historiyyim Shel ha-Halakhah" [The Historical Foundations of the *Halakhah*], *Zion,* XXVII, p. 126; Urbach, *The Sages,* pp. 291–292.

Chapter 22

CUSTOM: OPERATION AND CATEGORIES

I. INTRODUCTION

Anonymous legislation—*i.e.,* custom—like deliberate legislation, has operated as a creative force in all areas of Jewish law—the laws involving the relationship between people and God as well as the laws regulating human relationships, *issur* ("religious" law) as well as *mamon* (civil law). However, the authority of the covert legislation effected by custom is more limited in certain areas than the authority of the legislation overtly enacted by the halakhic authorities. The outstanding example of this difference is the general ineffectiveness of a custom that is contrary to a legal rule concerning a matter of *issur.* As has been noted,[1] the halakhic authorities are empowered to adopt enactments that are contrary to existing legal rules even in the area of *issur.* However, the rule that custom overrides the law (*minhag mevattel halakhah*) is fully effective only in the area of *mamon;* in the area of *issur,* only in specific and limited instances may custom permit what the law prohibits.[2]

A. Functions of Custom

Custom performs three functions in Jewish law:

1. Custom determines which view is to be accepted when the halakhic authorities disagree as to what the law is with regard to a particular matter. Custom plays this role even when, were it not for the custom, the accepted rules of decision making would dictate a different result.
2. Custom supplements existing law when new questions arise that existing law is unable to solve.
3. Custom establishes new norms that are contrary to existing law, *i.e.,* norms that modify or abrogate existing law.

B. Categories of Custom

In addition to this threefold classification of custom according to function, custom may also be classified according to whether it is legal ("custom"), conventional ("usage"), general, or local.

1. CUSTOM AND USAGE

Sometimes, custom operates as an independent force, precisely like a provision of an express enactment. In other instances, custom has an operative effect only because of a presumption that the parties in a particular

1. *See supra* pp. 505–533.

2. In several respects, the operation of custom (covert legislation by the public) is similar to communal legislation (overt legislation by the public). However, there is a significant difference between these two kinds of legislation in the area of religious law, where custom has operated much more frequently (to a certain extent even in the direction of leniency) than communal enactments, which are not directly operative in matters of religious law at all. *See supra* pp. 707–712.

matter act on the assumption that customary practice will govern their relationship. The same distinction also exists in other legal systems. In the common law, for example, the first category, *i.e.*, where custom operates independently, is termed "legal custom" or simply "custom"; and the second category, *i.e.*, where custom is given effect because the parties are presumed to have acted pursuant to it, is called "usage" or "conventional custom." In contemporary Hebrew legal terminology, a custom of the first type is ordinarily called *minhag*, and a custom of the second type is ordinarily called *nohag*.

2. GENERAL AND LOCAL CUSTOM

A custom may be general, obligating the nation or the entire people, or only local—as Roman law put it, *mores civitatis*—obligating only the inhabitants of the particular place where the custom is followed. Just as a custom can be limited geographically, it can also be limited to a certain segment of the population, such as a particular class or type of person. The fact that there are local customs, however, has no relationship to the social and historical factors that have caused legislation to become local in nature.[3] The essential character of legislation in Jewish law is its applicability to the entire Jewish people, except for certain municipal matters that are usually regulated by local legislation. The reason that, commencing with the tenth century C.E., legislation became largely local was that the historical circumstances of the Jewish people changed, in that there was no longer a single central authority for the entire nation. This development, however, did not affect the course of custom, which was sometimes general and sometimes local—as it has always been in the Jewish legal system.

The spontaneous and undirected way in which custom develops necessitates supervision and review to forestall the rise of custom based on error, to assure that custom develops reasonably and logically, and to make custom consonant with the fundamental general principles of Jewish law. There is similar supervision and review with regard to communal enactments, but the methods of control are even more comprehensive in the case of custom. As a general rule, the halakhic authorities attempt through various types of exegesis and textual support to integrate norms based on custom into the *Halakhah* as fully as possible.

The following sections discuss the functions of the various types of custom, the scope of creativity of custom in Jewish law in general and various areas of *mishpat ivri* in particular, and the methods employed by the halakhic authorities to supervise and control custom.

3. *See supra* pp. 666–675.

II. CUSTOM AS DETERMINING THE LAW

Custom is determinative in choosing between the conflicting views of halakhic authorities. Custom performs this function not only when, in a particular matter, there is no fixed rule for deciding whose view is to be accepted, but even when such a rule does exist but the custom is to the contrary.[4]

The Mishnah states:[5]

> If one drinks water to quench one's thirst, one recites the benediction "By Whose word all things exist (*she-ha-kol nihyeh bi-devaro*)"; R. Tarfon says, "Who creates many living things (*borei nefashot rabbot*)."

According to R. Tarfon, the benediction currently recited after drinking water, *i.e.*, "Who creates many living things . . . ," should be said before drinking. The Talmud in its discussion of this *mishnah* states:[6]

> Rava bar R. Ḥanan asked Abbaye, and according to some he asked R. Joseph, "What is the law?" He responded, "Go out and see what the people are doing."

In connection with a similar question with regard to the eating of *terumah* (the priestly tithe), R. Joshua b. Levi responded similarly.[7]

In another example, the Talmud states:[8]

> It has been taught: The *shaḥarit* (morning prayer), *musaf* (additional prayer), *minḥah* (afternoon prayer), and *ne'ilah* (closing prayer) all include the priestly

4. There are many such rules of decision making, such as the rule that in a dispute between R. Meir and R. Yose, R. Yose's view is to be followed. *See also infra* p. 1089.

5. M Berakhot 6:8.

6. TB Berakhot 45a; Eruvin 14b.

7. TJ Pe'ah 7:5, 34b (7:6, 20c); TJ Ma'aser Sheni 5:2, 30a (5:3, 56b); TJ Yevamot 7:3, 40a (7:2, 8a). Another example: M Eruvin 1:6—"The doorposts to which they referred must be ten handbreadths high, but their width and thickness may be any size. R. Yose says: 'They must be three handbreadths wide.'" In discussing this *mishnah*, TB Eruvin 14b states: "Rava bar R. Ḥanan said to Abbaye: 'What is the law?' He answered: 'Go out and see what the people are doing'" [and their practice was to require no minimum size for the width—Rashi, *ad loc.*, s.v. Ama devar], which follows the view of the first opinion in the *mishnah*, although according to the rules of decision making, the law should be in accordance with R. Yose, "whose reasoning is persuasive"; *see id.*

See also TB Pesaḥim 54a: "As R. Benjamin b. Yephet said . . . , 'and that is the practice of the people.'" Similarly in TJ Yevamot 7:3, 40a (7:2, 8a):

> A matter came before R. Joshua b. Levi. He said: "Go out and see what the people are doing." R. Avun [asked] in the name of R. Joshua b. Levi: "[But] is it not a matter of law?" [It is,] but whenever the law is unclear to the court and its true content is unknown, go out and see what the people are doing and do likewise. . . .

See also TJ Pe'ah 7:5, 34b (7:6, 20c); TJ Ma'aser Sheni 5:2, 30a (5:3, 56b), and *see supra* p. 884 n. 13, concerning Asheri's interpretation of TJ.

8. TB Ta'anit 26b.

blessing. This is the opinion of R. Meir; R. Judah says: "*Shaḥarit* and *musaf* include the priestly blessing, but *minḥah* and *ne'ilah* do not"; R. Yose says: "*Ne'ilah* includes the priestly blessing, but *minḥah* does not."

This *baraita* deals with the question as to which of the four prayer services on the Day of Atonement (*Yom Kippur*) include the priestly blessing. Routinely, the priests do not bless the people during the *minḥah* service, because this service comes after a meal when the priests may have drunk wine, and they might give the blessing while intoxicated. There is no such concern on the Day of Atonement, which is a day of fasting, and therefore R. Meir held that on that day the *minḥah* service includes the priestly blessing. On the other hand, R. Judah and R. Yose take the view that since the priestly blessing is not included in the *minḥah* service during the rest of the year, it should likewise not be included on the Day of Atonement; otherwise, people might erroneously conclude that the priestly blessing should be given during the *minḥah* service even on days other than the Day of Atonement.

A number of general rules for determining the law when the *tannaim* disagree, as in the *baraita* quoted above, were laid down by R. Johanan. Two of these rules are: (1) When R. Meir and R. Judah disagree, the law follows the view of R. Judah; and (2) when R. Judah and R. Yose disagree, the law follows the view of R. Yose. These two principles dictate that when R. Meir and R. Yose differ, R. Yose's view should be accepted.[9] Thus, according to these rules of decision making, R. Johanan should have decided the issue with regard to the priestly blessing in favor of R. Yose, who held that the *minḥah* service on the Day of Atonement does not include the priestly blessing. Nevertheless, he decided in favor of R. Meir because "the practice of the people is in accordance with the view of R. Meir."[10] Custom thus decided the law in favor of the lenient view, *i.e.*, that of R. Meir, who permitted the priestly blessing during the *minḥah* service on the Day of Atonement and was not concerned with the possibility that his ruling would lead to permitting the priestly blessing at the *minḥah* service during the rest of the year. R. Johanan, in so ruling, followed custom, although his own rules of decision making would have led him to decide in favor of the strict view of R. Yose.[11]

9. *See* TB Eruvin 46b.
10. TB Ta'anit 26b.
11. *See also Resp. Maharik* #171. *See further* TB Berakhot 22a: "R. Naḥman b. Isaac said: 'The practice of the world [*i.e.*, the public] is in accordance with the view of those three old men . . . ,'" which was a lenient ruling, contrary to the rules of decision making, according to which the stringent view should have been followed. *See* I.Z. Kahane, "Hala-khah u-Minhag" [Law and Custom], *Mazkeret le-Rav Herzog z.l.* [A Memorial to Rabbi Herzog], pp. 554ff., at p. 557 nn. 23, 24, and other examples, *id.* at 557–558.

According to some Babylonian *amoraim,* custom may not dictate the decision between conflicting authorities in a matter of *issur* when the accepted rule of decision making would dictate a result contrary to the custom. For example, when R. Johanan stated: "The practice of the people with regard to [the tithing of the fruit of] carob trees is in accordance with the view of R. Nehemiah"[12] (*i.e.,* the view of a single individual contrary to the majority of the Sages), the objection was raised in the Talmud: "When a matter of *issur* is involved, do we permit the custom to be followed?" However, the *amoraim* of the Land of Israel, led by R. Johanan, as well as some of the leading Babylonian *amoraim,* held that even in matters of *issur* custom determines which of the differing views of the *tannaim* was to be followed, even when the custom follows the view of a single individual against the majority,[13] and notwithstanding the principle that "when there is a conflict of opinion between a minority and a majority, the law is in accordance with the majority."[14]

12. TB Rosh ha-Shanah 15b.

13. TJ Shevi'it 5:1, 13a (5:1, 35d) quotes the passage in TB Rosh ha-Shanah 15b and states explicitly that R. Johanan ruled in accordance with the view of R. Nehemiah on the basis of the custom and not on the basis of the rules of decision making. TJ does not ask (as did TB): "When a matter of *issur* is involved, do we permit the custom to be followed?" A similar conclusion can be drawn from the passage in TB Ta'anit 26b regarding the priestly blessing on the Day of Atonement, which, too, is a matter of religious law. There Rava is quoted as saying: "The custom is in accordance with the view of R. Meir," which indicates that even Rava in Babylonia ruled according to R. Meir on the basis of custom, to the extent of ruling leniently even in religious matters, notwithstanding that according to the rules of decision making, the law should follow the view of R. Yose.

Ms. Munich has "R. Huna" in place of "Rava"; this seems to be the correct reading, as is evident from the parallels in TB Eruvin 62b and 72a and from the further discussion in TB Ta'anit 26b. *See supra* p. 891 n. 50. Rava held a similar opinion regarding the efficacy of custom; *see* TB Pesaḥim 103a and Berakhot 52b: "Rava recited the benediction on the spices first . . . and R. Johanan said: 'The practice of the people is in accordance with the view of the School of Hillel according to R. Judah's interpretation.'" Rava relied in the first instance on this custom, contrary to an anonymous *mishnah* reflecting the view of R. Meir, which, according to the rules of decision making, should be the law.

14. In the post-Talmudic period, the weight of custom in determining the law was given substantial attention by the halakhic authorities, and different Jewish centers apparently followed different views. *See* Z.H. Chajes, *Darkhei ha-Hora'ah* [Methodology of Decision Making], I, ch. 3 *et seq.*; Kahane, *supra* n. 11; J.L. Fishman (Maimon), "Ha-Minhag be-Sifrut ha-Geonim" [Custom in Geonic Literature], *B.M. Lewin Jubilee Volume,* 1940, pp. 132ff.; I. Dinari, "Ha-Minhag ve-ha-Halakhah bi-Teshuvot Ḥakhmei Ashkenaz be-Me'ah ha-Tet-Vav" [Custom and Law in the Responsa of the Halakhic Authorities of Germany in the Fifteenth Century], *B. De Vries Memorial Volume,* 1969, pp. 169–179.

The following are two examples from Ashkenazic authorities: In the thirteenth century, Maharam of Rothenburg stated: "In all matters on which the leading authorities differ, I rule according to the stringent opinion, except . . . when the lenient view has been accepted pursuant to earlier custom"; *Resp. Maharam of Rothenburg,* ed. Berlin, #386 (p. 294). In the fifteenth century, Jacob Moellin justified lending out orphans' money at fixed interest (*ribbit keẓuẓah,* defined *supra* p. 221 n. 149), despite the contrary opinion of most authori-

III. CUSTOM AS SUPPLEMENTING THE LAW

When custom determines the law in a conflict between halakhic authorities, no new rule is created; rather, a choice is made between two existing views. It is in the performance of the second function of custom—*i.e.*, establishing a rule in regard to a question newly arisen for which no solution is apparent under existing law—that the creative force of custom becomes manifest. Following are two examples of this function of custom.

The Torah states[15] that the paschal sacrifice is to be brought on the fourteenth day of the month of Nisan. The Mishnah states[16] that even if the fourteenth day falls on a sabbath, the paschal sacrifice should be brought on that day, because the paschal sacrifice has priority over the sabbath. According to a *baraita*,[17] "this rule was forgotten by the sons of Bathyra, and on one occasion the fourteenth day of Nisan fell on the sabbath and they forgot and did not know whether the paschal sacrifice has priority over the sabbath or not." They inquired of Hillel, who instructed that the paschal sacrifice does have priority over the sabbath. Subsequently, the *baraita* states:

> They asked him [Hillel]: "Master, what is the law if someone forgot and did not bring a knife on the eve of the sabbath?" [*I.e.*, the bringing of the sacrifice itself has priority over the sabbath, as its proper time is the fourteenth day of Nisan; but since it is possible to prepare the knife needed for the sacrifice in advance of the sabbath, carrying it to the place of the sacrifice should not take priority over the prohibition against carrying regularly applicable on the sabbath. This being so, is it permissible for one who forgot to prepare the knife on the day before the sabbath to do so on the sabbath?]
>
> He answered: "I have heard this law but I forgot it. However, leave it to

---

ties. *Resp. Maharil* #37. He relied on only one authority to support his conclusion, and in the particular circumstances even that minority opinion permitted lending out only charity money (*Or Zaru'a*, I, Laws of Charity, #30). Jacob Moellin, however, extended that minority view to include orphans' money—"and perhaps it was on this basis that the custom spread to lend out orphans' money at fixed interest, because all matters involving orphans are considered to be matters of *mizvah;* and indeed they are, because orphans are poor and have no one to care for them" (*Resp. Maharil* #37).

However, others differed with Jacob Moellin: "There are places where guardians are accustomed to lend out orphans' money at fixed interest, but it is a mistaken custom and should not be followed" (Rema to Sh. Ar. YD 160:18, and *see Shakh, ad loc.*, subpar. 27). *See further* Meiri, *Magen Avot*, Introduction, pp. 7–9; Caro, Introduction to *Bet Yosef* to *Tur* OḤ, quoted *infra* pp. 1317–1318 and nn. 25 and 27; Rema's comments in his Introduction to his glosses to the *Shulḥan Arukh*, quoted *infra* p. 1361 and n. 189, and *see* sources cited, *ad loc.*

15. Numbers 9:1 *et seq.*

16. M Pesaḥim 6:1.

17. TB Pesaḥim 66a; *see* v.l. in *Tosefta* Pesaḥim 4:13–14; TJ Pesaḥim 6:1, 39a/b (6:1, 32a).

> [the people of] Israel; if they are not prophets, they are the descendants of prophets" [*i.e.*, let us wait and see what the people do].[18]
>
> On the morrow,[19] whoever sacrificed a lamb stuck it [the knife] in its wool, and whoever sacrificed a goat [which has no wool] stuck it between its horns. He [Hillel] saw what was done, remembered the law, and said: "This is the tradition that I received from Shemaiah and Avtalyon" [*i.e.*, from his observation of what the people did, he recalled that that was what he had learned from Shemaiah and Avtalyon].

A question thus arose on the fourteenth day of the month of Nisan that fell on a sabbath as to whether those who forgot to bring the sacrificial knife on the eve of the sabbath may bring it on the sabbath. No one knew the answer, and Hillel taught that what the people did could be relied upon as expressing the law. As has been noted,[20] the source of a custom is sometimes an earlier law, as this incident illustrates. After Hillel saw what the people did, he recollected that this was what he had been taught by the Sages of the previous generation. The source of the custom was thus an ancient law of unknown origin, forgotten by the Sages but preserved in the customary practice of the people. In such circumstances, custom operates creatively, although the creativity is limited to restoring an earlier law that has been forgotten.

Another instance where custom supplements the law is recorded in the Jerusalem Talmud.[21] The question was asked whether tithes must be set aside from the fruit of trees in their fourth year (*neta reva'i*),[22] and the answer was that the applicable principle is: "Whenever the law is unclear to the court and its true character is unknown, go out and see what the people do, and do likewise; and we see that the people do not set aside these tithes." On the basis of this custom, the law was settled in accordance with

18. In *Tosefta* Pesaḥim 4:14 the reading is: "He said to them: 'Leave them alone, they are inspired with the heavenly spirit. If they are not prophets, they are the descendants of prophets.'"

19. The *Tosefta* does not have "On the morrow," but rather: "What did the Jews do at that time?"—which is the correct reading. *See also* S. Lieberman, *Tosefta ki-Feshutah*, Pesaḥim, pp. 567–568, noting *Tosafot Rid*'s question on the version in TB (Pesaḥim 66a, s.v. Lemaḥar), namely, "If they asked on Nisan 13 regarding the carrying of the knife, why did they not announce that they should bring the knives on that day [*i.e.*, before the sabbath]?" and *Tosafot Rid*'s answer, *i.e.*, that it was close to nightfall. It is actually implicit in the *Tosefta* itself that the question covered even the bringing of the paschal sacrifice on the sabbath (and not merely the carrying of the knife). *See Tosefta ki-Feshutah, loc. cit.*

20. *Supra* p. 884.

21. TJ Pe'ah 7:5, 34b (7:6, 20c); the same passage occurs in TJ Ma'aser Sheni 5:2, 30a (5:3, 56b).

22. The fruit a tree yields the fourth year after its planting, or the money for which it is redeemed, must be consumed in Jerusalem. *See* Leviticus 19:24, M Ma'aser Sheni 5:1 *et seq.* and 5:4.

the lenient view, *i.e.*, that tithes need not be set aside from the fruit of a tree in its fourth year.[23]

IV. CUSTOM AS CHANGING EXISTING LAW

As has been seen, custom is effective to settle conflicts of opinion among halakhic authorities as well as to establish new legal rules to solve problems for which existing law provides no solution. But does custom, like legislation, have sufficient creative force not only to prescribe new law but also to change or even abrogate preexisting law when circumstances require?

The extent to which custom has this latter power (termed in the Talmudic sources "custom overrides the law" [*minhag mevattel halakhah*])[24] is a question halakhic authorities and scholars have extensively debated.[25] It is a question that has occasioned differences of opinion also in other legal systems in which custom is a legal source. In Roman law, for example, there were different views as to whether it was within the power of custom (*consuetudo, mores*) to create a legal rule that was contrary to previously existing law (*contra legem*).[26]

A. Distinction Between Matters of *Mamon* (Civil Law) and Matters of *Issur* ("Religious" Law) in Regard to the Creative Power of Custom

With regard to the function of custom as a creative force for change in existing law, Jewish law as a general rule distinguishes between matters of civil law (*mamon*) and matters of "religious" law (*issur*).[27] Custom has the power to override legal rules in the area of *mamon;* but in the area of *issur,*

23. *See* Kahane, *supra* n. 11 at 560 nn. 51, 52. TJ Yevamot 7:3, 40a (7:2, 8a) cites this rule in connection with the function of custom as determining the law when there is a conflict between halakhic authorities; *see also Resp. Asheri* 55:10 and *supra* p. 884 n. 13 and p. 898 n. 7. For a further example of the creation of a legal rule on the basis of a custom when the existing law is inadequate to solve the problem, *see* TB Menaḥot 35b:

> R. Aḥa b. R. Joseph asked R. Ashi: "May it [a phylactery strap that is torn] be sewn on the inside ['so that the seam is not seen and the strap appears whole'—Rashi, *ad loc.*, s.v. Ve-ailah li-tefirah le-gev]?" He answered: "Go out and see what the people are doing" ["and since their practice is not to do this, do not do it"—Rashi, *ad loc.*, s.v. Mai ama devar].

24. *See infra* pp. 905–909.

25. *See* bibliography *infra* at end of this work.

26. *See* Salmond, pp. 189–212; C.K. Allen, *Law in the Making,* pp. 82–83.

27. As to this distinction, *see supra* pp. 122–141. Later, it will be seen that the principle "custom overrides the law" was used to establish various rules that relate neither to *mamon* nor to *issur,* such as laws relating to prayer and the public reading of the Torah.

while it may effectively prohibit what the law previously permitted, it is powerless to permit what the authorities unanimously agree the law prohibits. This distinction follows from one of the fundamental points of difference between *issur* and *mamon* already noted in earlier chapters, namely, the difference with respect to the principle of freedom of contract.

In matters of civil law, a person may "contract out of a law contained in the Torah." Biblical civil law rules have the character of *jus dispositivum;* they are binding only when the parties have not otherwise agreed. On the other hand, in matters of religious law the directives of the Torah are *jus cogens;* they are obligatory and not subject to change on the basis of the desire of the parties.[28] It follows logically, therefore, that just as Biblical laws relating to civil matters are subject to modification by the parties to a transaction, these laws can similarly be changed by the people as a whole through custom; the effect is the same as if everyone agreed in advance on a particular arrangement different from that set forth in the Torah.[29] Consequently, custom, as the expression of the collective will of the people, has the power to change rules of the civil law. This is not true, however, in regard to religious law, where the prohibitions are obligatory and cannot be changed either by the will of the immediate parties or the will of the people as a whole.

In regard to the power to change the law, there is an important difference between legislation and custom. The entire Torah was entrusted to the halakhic authorities;[30] and the Torah itself authorizes them to enact legislation—adding to or subtracting from the existing law—so long as they operate within the sphere of subordinate legislation and do not presume to add to or subtract from the Torah itself.[31] There is no similar authority with regard to custom. The people, pursuant to the power of custom, may decide disputes between halakhic authorities as to existing law, and may supplement existing law. However, they may not override a rule that is part of

28. For further details, *see supra* pp. 123–127.

29. *See, e.g.,* Asheri's statement about the custom not to cancel debts in the sabbatical year, which is contrary to the law: ". . . since the custom not to cancel has spread and all know of it, it is as though the creditor lent the money on condition that the debt should not be canceled in the sabbatical year" (*Resp. Asheri* 64:4). This ruling affects a religious law—the prohibition relating to the sabbatical year—which is based on a matter of civil law (*see supra* pp. 511–513). *Resp. Maharashdam,* ḤM, #380 explains as follows:

> Every monetary transaction may be effective on either of two bases: (1) the rules clearly set forth in our holy Torah, or enacted by the Sages in the Talmud, or (2) any stipulation agreed to by the parties. This is why the modes of acquisition practiced by merchants are effective although they are neither written in the Torah nor in accord with the strict law. When merchants follow a particular custom, it is as if all have agreed with one another that a transaction so entered into shall be effective, and transactions are entered into with that understanding.

30. *See supra* pp. 243–247.

31. *See supra* pp. 496–502.

existing law, except where the principle of freedom of contract is applicable, or, as explained below, where custom has special force because of the particular subject involved, or because of special circumstances.

B. The Maxim "Custom Overrides the Law"

The principle that custom has the power to override the law in civil law matters but not, generally speaking, in other legal areas, can be deduced from many different sources in the Talmudic and post-Talmudic literature. However, of the two Talmudic sources[32] in which the maxim "custom overrides the law" (*minhag mevattel halakhah*) is explicitly invoked, one at first blush may seem contrary to this basic distinction between civil law and other legal areas.

The first source is a *mishnah* clearly dealing with civil law:[33]

> One who engages laborers and instructs them to arise early and retire late [*i.e.,* to begin work in the early hours of the morning and to return to their homes in the evening] may not compel them [to do so] where the custom is not to begin early and work late.

We learn from this *mishnah* that there were two practices with regard to the working hours of a day laborer: one, that the laborer began his work early in the morning and returned from work when it was already evening, and the other, that he began his work later and finished earlier. The *mishnah* states that if the custom concerning hours of work in a particular locality was the one more favorable to the laborer, the employer may not compel the laborer to work during the longer hours. According to the Talmud,[34] under Biblical law,[35] work was to begin early and end late—as indicated by verses in the Book of Psalms:[36] "When the sun rises, they [the young lions and other animals of the forest] come home and couch in their dens. Man then [at the rising of the sun] goes out to his work, to his labor until the evening." The shorter hours of work under the custom more favorable to the laborer are thus different from the "legal" hours of work, and the *mishnah* establishes that the custom prevails over the law.

32. Both sources are in TJ. TB does not contain the maxim "custom overrides the law," although the basic idea that custom may supersede existing law in civil-law matters can be found in many passages in TB; *see infra.*

33. M Bava Meẓi'a 7:1.

34. TB Bava Meẓi'a 83a/b.

35. The term in TB Bava Meẓi'a 83b is *po'el de-oraita* (lit. "a laborer according to Biblical law"). *See supra* pp. 207–212 as to the terms *de-oraita* (Biblical) and *de-rabbanan* (rabbinic).

36. Psalms 104:22–23. It seems, however, that the verses from Psalms are only a support (*asmakhta*) for an existing rule.

Concerning this rule of the Mishnah, the Jerusalem Talmud states:[37] "R. Hoshaiah said: 'This tells us—custom overrides the law.'"[38] The Jerusalem Talmud then continues: "R. Immi said: 'The burden of proof is on the claimant except in this case.'" R. Immi's comment underscores the extent of the power of custom to override the law. It is a basic rule in Jewish law that one who seeks to obtain something in the possession of another must prove his entitlement. This rule that the burden of proof is on the claimant has even greater force than another important principle of Jewish law, namely, the principle that matters are determined according to the preponderance of probabilities (*kelal ha-rov*).

For example, suppose S Seller sells an ox to B Buyer, and the ox is found to be prone to gore and therefore impossible to keep on a farm and to use for plowing. B in such a case has no alternative but to slaughter the ox and to use it for food, which, of course, reduces the value of the ox to him. When B bought the ox from S, B did not stipulate that he was buying it for plowing and not for slaughter, but he now contends that that was his intent; and the evidence he adduces in support of his position is that most people who buy oxen intend to use them for plowing. The rule is that B may not rescind the sale, because in order to recover the money that S now possesses as a result of the sale of the ox, B must prove that *his* intent was to buy the ox for plowing; the evidence that this is the usual intent of most people is insufficient.[39]

R. Immi's comment shows that the force of custom is even greater than the rule that the burden of proof is on the claimant, since the conclusion from the *mishnah* is that the employer may not retain possession of the laborer's wages and say to the laborer: "You are seeking to take the wages from me, and the burden is on you to prove that your working hours follow the custom." The customary working hours are recognized as the legal

37. TJ Bava Meẓi'a 7:1, 27b (7:1, 11b).

38. The *mishnah* is to be understood as referring to a case where the employer did not stipulate the hours of work at the time of hiring but told the employees later that they were to work the number of hours prescribed by law, whereupon they claimed that they were to work only the number of hours required by custom. This is how the passage in TB Bava Meẓi'a 83a is explained by *Tosafot, ad loc.*, s.v. Ha-sokher et ha-po'alim ve-amar lahem le-hashkim u-le-ha'ariv, by Meiri, *Bet ha-Beḥirah, ad loc.* (ed. Schlesinger, pp. 321–322), and by *Shittah Mekubbeẓet, ad loc.*, s.v. Ha-sokher et ha-po'alim, in the name of Ramakh. Thus, this *mishnah* indicates that custom overrides the law, since the laborers work according to the custom and not the law, even though no stipulation was made at the time of hiring. *See also* B. De Vries, *Toledot ha-Halakhah ha-Talmudit* [A History of Talmudic *Halakhah*], pp. 164–165, which gives an unnecessarily strained interpretation.

39. TB Bava Kamma 46a/b; Bava Batra 92a/b. On the facts of the case discussed in these Talmudic passages, it is impossible to determine from the amount of the purchase price whether the purchaser bought the ox to slaughter or to use for plowing.

hours, and there is no need to prove that the intent of the parties was to act in accordance with the custom.

The other source in which the expression "custom overrides the law" is invoked seems at first glance to deal with a matter *par excellence* of *issur,* namely, one of the rules relating to the *ḥaliẓah* (release from levirate marriage) of a widow; however, on close examination we find that it does not involve a custom that conflicts with existing law.

The Mishnah states:

> If she [the widow] performed the *ḥaliẓah* with a *man'al* [a shoe made of leather], her *ḥaliẓah* is valid; if with *anpilin* [a shoe made of cloth or felt], it is invalid; if with a *sandal* [a shoe that has only a sole and straps but no leather covering the foot] to which a heel is attached, it is valid, but if it has no heel, it is invalid.[40]

This *mishnah* interprets the following Biblical verse concerning *ḥaliẓah:*[41] "His brother's widow shall go up to him [the *levir*] in the presence of the elders and pull his shoe (*na'al*) off his foot." The *mishnah* states that the term *na'al* in the Torah includes the *man'al* and the *sandal* but not the *anpilin.*

The Jerusalem Talmud states:[42]

> R. Ba [Abba] said [in the name of] R. Judah, [who said] in the name of Rav: "If Elijah [the prophet] should come[43] and say that *ḥaliẓah* may be performed with a *man'al,* he would be obeyed; [if he said] that *ḥaliẓah* may not be performed with a *sandal,* he would not be obeyed; for it has been the practice of the people to perform *ḥaliẓah* with a *sandal,* and custom overrides the law."[44]

40. M Yevamot 12:1. As to the meaning of *man'al, anpilin,* and *sandal, see* H. Albeck, *Commentary on the Mishnah, ad loc.*, and Hashlamot, *id.* at 341.

41. Deuteronomy 25:9. The 1985 JPS *Tanakh* translates: "pull the sandal off his foot." This rendering of *na'al* as "sandal" is inconsistent with the basis of the Talmudic discussion.

42. TJ Yevamot 12:1, 66a (12:1, 12c).

43. *Cf.* TB Avodah Zarah 36a: "In all matters, one court can annul the enactment [of another court] . . . for even were Elijah and his court to come [and declare them permitted], we do not obey him." *See also* TB Sotah 48b: "Like a man who says to his fellow, 'until the dead will come to life and the Messiah, the descendant of David, will come.'" *See also* Joseph Ergas, *Resp. Divrei Yosef* #27.

44. Another tradition in the name of Rav reads:

> R. Ze'eira said [in the name of] R. Jeremiah [who said] in the name of Rav: "If Elijah should come and say that *ḥaliẓah* may not be performed with a *man'al,* he would be obeyed; [if he said] that *ḥaliẓah* may not be performed with a *sandal,* he would not be obeyed; for it has been the practice of the people to perform *ḥaliẓah* with a *sandal,* and custom overrides the law."

TJ Yevamot 12:1, 66a (12:1, 12c).

At first glance, we might conclude from this passage that even in a matter of *issur* (the law of *ḥaliẓah* belongs to the area of "religious" law) custom has the power to override the law, since even if Elijah should come and say that *ḥaliẓah* may not be performed with a *sandal,* it would still be permissible to use the *sandal* because that was the practice of the people. However, this conclusion would be erroneous. The Mishnah states that *ḥaliẓah* may be performed with a *sandal,* and nowhere in the extant Talmudic literature is a view recorded that the use of a *sandal* for *ḥaliẓah* is prohibited.[45] The customary performance of *ḥaliẓah* with a *sandal* was therefore in conformity with existing law; and if Elijah should come and say that *ḥaliẓah* may not be performed with a *sandal,* he would be instituting a change in existing law. In such circumstances, custom certainly has the power to support the existing rule against a new and different rule even if this new rule comes from Elijah himself.[46] The reference here to "custom overrides the

45. There is a difference of opinion only with regard to whether *ḥaliẓah* may be performed with a *man'al; see Tosefta* Yevamot 12:11; TB Yevamot 102a; TJ Yevamot 12:1, 66a (12:1, 12c). Even if there were an opinion that *ḥaliẓah* may not be performed with a *sandal,* the custom to do so would determine which opinion prevails and would not be overriding the accepted law. *See also infra* n. 46.

46. *See* Meiri, *Bet ha-Beḥirah,* Yevamot 105a (ed. Dickman, p. 375, s.v. Zehu be'ur ha-mishnah):

> Any practice of the people that does not violate a prohibition or arouse [serious] concern that it will result in a transgression should not be revised even if there is a remote possibility that the practice will lead to transgression, and [even if] the revision is initiated by the most expert of authorities. This is the meaning of the statement of the Sages that even if Elijah were to come and purport . . . to issue a decree prohibiting [*ḥaliẓah* with] a *sandal* that has a heel, on the ground that some sandals do not have heels, he would not be obeyed, since the people are already accustomed to [perform *ḥaliẓah* with] a sandal; his decree, therefore, cannot stand.

According to tradition, Elijah will come and, in order to forestall untoward consequences, will promulgate new and more stringent rules contrary to the law existing up to that time. Joseph Ergas, a leading halakhic authority of Italy in the eighteenth century, who was the teacher of Malachi ha-Kohen, the author of *Yad Malakhi,* in a detailed responsum discussed in this context the power of custom (*Resp. Divrei Yosef* #27, ed. Leghorn, 1742, p. 48b/c):

> Even Rav did not say that custom can override a law involving a [religious] prohibition (*issur*). He stated that if Elijah were to come and say that *ḥaliẓah* may not be performed with a *sandal,* Elijah would not be obeyed because it is the established practice of the people to perform *ḥaliẓah* with a *sandal.* The reason [for not obeying Elijah] is that the custom in question in no wise contravenes even a rabbinic prohibition. To the contrary, it is universally agreed that the most common method of *ḥaliẓah* is with a *sandal;* it was on the question of whether a *man'al* should be used in the first instance (*le-khateḥillah*) that the *tannaim* and *amoraim* were divided, as is recorded in TB Yevamot 102a. The custom to perform *ḥaliẓah* with a *sandal* conforms to the *Halakhah.*

See also Alon, *Meḥkarim,* II, p. 242; Kahane, *supra* n. 11 at 557; De Vries, *supra* n. 38 at 162–164.

law" therefore is not to the power of custom to override existing law,[47] but to the power of custom to prevent a new rule from taking effect when contrary to existing law. In this respect, custom is decisive even in a matter of *issur,* since even in the area of *issur,* custom is determinative in the choice between conflicting views.[48]

C. Custom in Matters of *Issur* and in Other Areas of Jewish Law

The principle that in matters of *issur* custom may not permit what the law indisputably forbids is emphasized in the question asked by the Babylonian *amoraim* when they rejected the possibility that custom could override a religious prohibition: "Does the matter depend on custom?"[49] In the post-Talmudic period, this was again stressed:

> If some places have followed a custom that involves a transgression, the custom should be changed even if eminent authorities instituted the custom. . . . And it is not only a custom involving a transgression that should be changed, but even a custom instituted as a fence or safeguard should be abrogated if it may lead to untoward consequences.[50]

47. TB Menaḥot 31b–32a quotes Rav's statement, "If Elijah should come . . . ," in support of the power of custom to determine the law as to whether the Torah sections written in the phylacteries must be "closed," *i.e.,* separated from preceding sections by a space in the middle of a line, as opposed to being "open," *i.e.,* separated by beginning on a new line. The Sages and R. Simeon b. Eleazar disagreed on this question. The Talmud concludes that because the custom was to prepare the phylacteries according to the Sages' opinion, the law follows their view.

Here, too, the statement about Elijah is cited as authority not for abrogating a law but for deciding between conflicting opinions. As to the comment in Menaḥot, *loc. cit.,* "Now it is customary . . . ," *see Resp. Maharik* #54, discussing how we know that writing the sections in phylacteries "closed" had been the custom in Rav's time too. *See also Resp. Divrei Yosef* #27.

48. It is reasonable to assume that the maxim "custom overrides the law" was first stated with regard to the employment of laborers discussed in M Bava Meẓi'a 7:1, because there it can be interpreted according to its plain meaning, as has been discussed *supra* pp. 905–907. It was probably the redactor of the Talmud who applied it to *ḥaliẓah* with a *sandal.* This is a phenomenon frequently found in the Talmud.

49. TB Ḥullin 63a. This question was asked in response to Ameimar's statement, *ad loc.,* in regard to whether Biblical law prohibited eating certain kinds of fowl, that "where the custom is to eat them, they may be eaten." This question was also asked about R. Papa's statement in regard to the prohibition of interest, TB Bava Meẓi'a 69b–70a (according to the reading of Rashi, *id.* 70a, s.v. Attu be-minhaga talya milta; Meiri, *Bet ha-Beḥirah,* Bava Meẓi'a 69b, ed. Schlesinger, p. 262, and other *rishonim*).

50. *Resp. Asheri* 55:10, and *see* Ritba, Novellae to Pesaḥim 51a:

> It is clear that the Mishnah, the Talmud, and precedents follow custom only when it tends to stringency; but if a custom tends to leniency, it is never accorded any defer-

According to most halakhic authorities, custom may not override a religious prohibition even when the prohibition is rabbinic:[51]

> Obviously, if we may repeal a prohibition on the basis of custom, then all prohibitions may be repealed one by one; and the Torah, God forbid, will be abrogated.[52]

On the other hand, custom does have the power, even in matters of religious law, to prohibit something that has been permitted, since this does not repeal the law but makes the law more stringent: "Custom cannot repeal a prohibition, but it may prohibit what has been permitted."[53]

To a very limited extent, custom may override a law in some non–civil-law matters that do not involve religious prohibitions. According to various authorities, this is so with regard to the reading of the *Haftarah* portions from the prophets (the prophetic readings that supplement the weekly Torah portions read during the synagogue service on sabbaths and festivals) and with regard to the text of benedictions and prayers:

> The reading of the *Haftarah* is neither specifically forbidden nor specifically permitted, and whatever is customary should be followed, . . . and I have heard in the name of Rabbenu Isaac b. Judah that, when he was asked why the portion that begins "Now after the death of Moses" [Joshua 1:1] is customarily read as the *Haftarah* portion, he responded, "Whatever is customary should be followed, since custom overrides the law."[54]

---

ence—even though it was instituted by the greatest authorities—if a [contemporary] halakhic authority sees some reason to forbid it, because we can only follow "the judge who is in our own time." However, if no clear prohibition is involved and the custom is already established, . . . he [the halakhic authority] should so act as to avoid controversy until he can slowly wean them away [from the custom]. But if the case [against the custom] is clear, "no wisdom, no prudence, and no counsel can prevail against the Lord" [Proverbs 21:30] [*i.e.*, the custom must be extirpated even at the cost of controversy].

51. According to Rabad (Gloss to *MT,* Ma'aser Sheni ve-Neta Reva'i 1:3) custom does override the law where the prohibition is rabbinic. *See* Chajes, *supra* n. 14, and *see also id.* concerning the opinion of Joseph Colon, *Resp. Maharik* #8, #9, and #54.

52. *Resp. Rashbash* #419.

53. Maimonides, *MT,* Shevitat Asor 3:3; *see also Resp. Asheri* 55:10; Ritba, *supra* n. 50; *infra* pp. 933–934.

54. *Sefer ha-Pardes* of Rashi, ed. Ehrenreich, 1924, p. 353. *See Haggahot Maimuniyyot* to *MT,* Tefillah 13, subpar. 2, concerning the reading of the *Haftarah* on the New Moon of the month of Av when that day coincides with the sabbath; the accepted custom did not follow the law, "and Rabbenu Simḥah wrote, 'But what can we do, the custom uproots the law!'" *See also* the comprehensive discussion to similar effect in the correspondence between Rabbenu Tam and Rabbenu Meshullam of Melun, *Sefer ha-Yashar le-Rabbenu Tam,* Responsa, #43–50 (ed. Rosenthal, pp. 73–106, particularly pp. 97–99) and, as to the question of the priestly blessings, *Resp. Maharam of Rothenburg,* ed. Prague, #345.

In particular circumstances, customs responding to a "change in the natural order" or to changes in relationships with the non-Jewish environment, and customs changing various laws promulgated because of the apprehension of danger became accepted; and their validity was recognized even if they permitted what the law had theretofore prohibited.[55] However, these are exceptions to the rule that custom may not override a law in the area of *issur.*[56] Solomon b. Simeon Duran (Rashbash) summarized the matter as follows:

> The conclusion is that the principle that custom overrides the law is valid with regard to civil law matters, but is not valid to permit what the law has prohibited in the area of *issur,* because in matters of *issur* custom may only prohibit what has been permitted but may not permit what has been prohibited.[57]

V. CUSTOM AS A CREATIVE FORCE IN VARIOUS AREAS OF THE LAW

The power of custom to override rules of civil law endowed Jewish law with great flexibility in adapting to constantly changing economic and commercial conditions; and many laws—at times even entire fields of law—were based on custom as their legal source. This creativity existed in every period of Jewish law. The following are some examples in various areas of the law.

Other halakhic authorities are of the opinion that under no circumstance can a custom change a law. *See further* Chajes, *supra* n. 14, I, ch. 6; Urbach, *Tosafot,* pp. 62ff., 69–72; Kahana, *supra* n. 11 at 560–564; Dinari, *supra* n. 14 at 170–171; J. Katz, "Ma'ariv bi-Zemano ve-she-Lo bi-Zemano" [The Evening Prayer Within and Outside of Its Appointed Time], *Zion,* XXXV (1970), pp. 35–60, particularly pp. 45ff. Katz's research is instructive for its integration of halakhic explication with historical study of the conditions prevailing in the various Jewish centers—an integration of special significance to the subject of custom originated by the people, because "if they are not prophets, they are the descendants of prophets." *See also supra* p. 882.

55. For detailed discussion, *see* Chajes, *supra* n. 14 at I, ch. 4.

56. According to some halakhic authorities, even in civil-law matters custom cannot override the law unless the custom has been incorporated in a communal enactment. *See Nimmukei Yosef* to Alfasi, Bava Batra 144b (printed eds. of Alfasi, fol. 67b), s.v. Bi-mefaresh, quoting Ritba; Ritba, Novellae to Ketubbot 100a, quoting a responsum of Naḥmanides; *Shittah Mekubbeẓet,* Ketubbot 100a, s.vv. Ve-zeh leshon ha-Ritba and Ve-katav rabbenu ha-Ramban z.l. bi-teshuvat she'elah; *Bet Yosef, Tur* ḤM 368:6, explaining the view of Sherira Gaon. *See also supra* pp. 883–884.

However, this opinion seems contrary to the plain meaning of several Talmudic passages, and particularly to the passage regarding *sitomta* (*but see* Ritba, Novellae to Bava Meẓi'a 74a, s.v. Hai sitomta kanya, quoted *infra* n. 70, for a different interpretation); and it was not accepted by most halakhic authorities. *See also* the further discussion *infra.*

57. *Resp. Rashbash* #562.

A. Preparation and Certification of Documents; Recovery of Debts; Financial Relations Between Husband and Wife

Documents not drawn and executed in the manner required by law are valid if their preparation and execution conform to local custom.[58] In the tannaitic period, Rabban Simeon b. Gamaliel was the proponent of this view. In the amoraic period, the views of the other *tannaim* were interpreted as agreeing with his opinion that a document executed in conformity with local custom is valid even if its execution does not comply with the legal requirements.[59] Similarly, debts, which according to law can be recovered only from real property in the debtor's estate, can also be recovered from personal property if local custom with regard to the particular type of debt permits such recovery.[60] There are also many examples of custom overriding the law in matters involving financial relations between husband and wife.[61]

58. M Bava Batra 10:1.

59. TB Bava Batra 165a: "Doesn't the first *tanna* also hold [that a document executed in accordance] with local custom [is valid]? . . ."; similarly, TB Kiddushin 49a.

60. TJ Gittin 5:3, 28b (5:3, 46d): "I and my teachers collected [the one-tenth of the father's estate] for her [the daughter] from personalty, according to the local custom." According to the law, a daughter's maintenance, *i.e.,* one-tenth of her deceased father's estate, can be collected only from realty; *see* TB Ketubbot 51a, 69b: "Rava said: 'It is the law. . . .'" In the geonic period, an enactment was adopted to permit certain types of debts to be collected also from personalty of the estate, because by that time most people did not own land. *See also supra* pp. 646–648 and *Tosafot,* Ketubbot 51a, s.v. Mi-mekarke'ei ve-lo mi-metaltelei bein li-mezonot u-vein le-farnasah. Maimonides held that maintenance for a daughter could not be collected from personalty even after the geonic enactment; *see MT,* Ishut 20:5 and commentaries, *ad loc. See also supra* p. 882 n. 8.

61. *See* M Ketubbot 6:3–4:

> If the bride undertook to bring to the groom as a dowry [and has brought] one thousand *denarii,* he records [in the *ketubbah*] that he has received fifteen hundred *denarii.* If she has brought personal property [such as clothing and utensils], he records [in the *ketubbah*] the appraised value of the property, less twenty percent. [For the reasons for such valuations, *see* TJ Ketubbot 6:3, 39b–40a (6:3, 30c/d): the amount of money recorded in the *ketubbah* is greater than the actual dowry because the husband will make a profit from the money. The appraised value of property is discounted in the *ketubbah* because the appraisal is usually inflated for the honor of the bride.] . . . The bridegroom shall undertake to give her ten *denarii* for perfumes [lit. "for the basket"] for every one hundred *denarii* [she brings]. Rabban Simeon b. Gamaliel says: "In all things, the local custom governs."

Rabban Simeon b. Gamaliel's statement has reference to all the provisions of *mishnah* 3 and 4, as is explicitly stated in *Tosefta* Ketubbot 6:5–6:

> If she undertook to bring [as a dowry] two *selas* [a *sela* is worth four *denarii*], each *sela* is recorded as six *denarii.* . . . Rabban Simeon b. Gamaliel said: "That is so in a locality where the practice is not to change gold *denarii* into smaller coinage [in which case it is considered to be property and not money, and the appraised value is reduced by twenty percent]." . . . If she undertook to bring money, each *sela* is recorded as six *denarii.* The bridegroom shall undertake to give her ten *denarii* for perfumes for every one hundred *denarii* [she brings]. R. Yose said: "The same applies to the valuation of

From time to time, there were disputes as to the power of custom to change particular laws in various contexts. For example, the law requires documents to be certified by three persons; certification by only one individual, however expert, is ineffective.[62] However, a fifteenth century responsum states:

> It is the accepted custom among the scholars of the academies that one individual may certify documents, and this is apparently an application of the rule that custom overrides the law in matters of civil law.[63]

This custom was accepted by Moses Isserles,[64] although others differed with him.[65]

B. Custom in the Development of the Modes of Acquisition and the Creation of Obligations

Custom had a decisive influence on the development of the modes of acquisition and the creation of obligations in Jewish law; these areas are especially sensitive to the constantly changing flow of commercial life over the course of time. Jewish law prescribes fixed and well-defined methods for transferring ownership and creating obligations. As a general rule, these methods require a certain measure of formality, such as pulling or lifting the purchased article, as has been discussed.[66] This formality was at variance with the evolving needs of commercial life, which required more convenient and flexible modes of acquisition. A large part of the response to

---

> goods [she brings]." The *Halakhah* is that in a place where it is the custom not to deduct from the appraised value of property and not to add to the value of money [for the purpose of recording in the *ketubbah* the amount of the dowry], one may not deviate from the local custom.

Shittah Mekubbezet, Ketubbot 66b, s.v. Ve-zeh leshon ha-Re'ah z.l., comments:

> Rabban Simeon b. Gamaliel says: "In all things, the local custom governs." This applies to the whole *mishnah,* as is stated in the *Tosefta.* . . . The dispute is on this point: The first *tanna* holds that we follow the law, while Rabban Simeon b. Gamaliel holds that we follow the custom.

See also Meiri, *Bet ha-Beḥirah,* Ketubbot 66a (ed. Sofer, pp. 284–285); Rashba, Novellae to Ketubbot 66a, s.v. Ke-neged ha-shum; *Resp. Tashbeẓ,* II, #15.

62. TB Ketubbot 22a; for details on the authentication and certification of documents, *see supra* pp. 610–614.

63. *Terumat ha-Deshen* #332.

64. Rema to Sh. Ar. ḤM 46:4.

65. *Yam Shel Shelomo,* Bava Kamma 10:11; for detailed discussion, *see Shakh,* Sh. Ar. ḤM 46, subpar. 8.

66. *See supra* pp. 580–584. There were continual efforts to make the various modes of acquisition more efficient and convenient; *see id.* For further details, *see* M. Elon, EJ, V, pp. 923–933, s.v. Contract (reprinted in *Principles,* pp. 246–256).

this requirement to satisfy commercial needs came primarily by way of custom, *i.e.,* mercantile practice.

The Talmudic source for the power of custom in developing modes of acquisition is the following discussion:[67]

> R. Papi said in the name of Rava: "Affixing the *sitomta*[68] is a mode of acquisition." To what extent is it effective? R. Ḥaviva said: "It signifies complete transfer of ownership." The Rabbis said: "It merely subjects one to the imprecation 'He Who punished . . . (*mi she-para*).'"[69] The law is that it merely subjects one to the imprecation. . . . However, in places where it is the custom that it [the *sitomta*] transfers ownership, it is effective to do so.

In the fourth century C.E., in the days of Rava, it was the practice among the merchants in Babylonia to use a mode of acquisition called *sitomta.* A retail dealer in wine, for example, would buy a number of barrels of wine from a wholesaler. The retailer would have insufficient room in his shop to store all the barrels he purchased and, therefore, would take delivery of only one barrel at a time, leaving the rest with the wholesaler to be delivered as required. Since the barrels in the meantime remained with the seller, the buyer would affix a seal or a mark on the barrels that he had bought, and this act completed the sale. As a matter of strict law, these barrels did not become the property of the purchaser, since they remained with the seller and the purchaser had not yet "pulled" (taken possession of) them. R. Papi declared in the name of Rava that notwithstanding this rule, *sitomta* is nevertheless an effective method of completing the transfer.

As the quoted Talmudic passage shows, there was disagreement as to the degree of the efficacy of *sitomta* as a mode of acquisition. According to R. Ḥaviva, *sitomta* accomplishes a complete transfer of ownership to the same extent as any other mode of acquisition. Other Sages, however, held that *sitomta* does not accomplish a complete transfer; it puts the buyer under a moral and religious obligation not to retract (he becomes subject to the imprecation of "He Who punished . . ."), but the transaction is not legally enforceable. The Talmud declares the rule to be that *sitomta* does not have the full legal efficacy of the established modes of acquisition, but if the cus-

67. TB Bava Meẓi'a 74a.

68. The term *sitomta* means "a seal"; Rashi, Bava Meẓi'a, *ad loc.,* s.v. Sitomta. *See Targum Yonatan b. Uzziel* to Genesis 38:18, rendering the Hebrew *hotamekha* ("your seal") in Aramaic as *sitamtakh.* In the Talmud, the term is used in the sense of "a mark the shopkeepers make on barrels of wine. They buy many barrels at one time and leave them in the seller's warehouse; they transfer them one by one to sell in the shop, and mark them so as to indicate that all those inscribed have been sold"; Rashi, *ad loc.* For other interpretations of *sitomta, see infra* nn. 70, 71.

69. *I.e.,* it is not effective as a mode of acquisition in the full legal sense, but one who reneges on the transaction is subject to the ethico-religious imprecation, "He Who punished . . . ," as to which *see supra* p. 148.

tom in a particular place is that the act of marking the barrels fully effectuates transfer of legal ownership, then *sitomta* accomplishes this result to the same extent as any of the established modes of acquisition.

This is an illustration of custom overriding the law. Under the law, so long as the purchaser has not formally taken possession of the article by "pulling," the acquisition is not complete; both the seller and the buyer may rescind, and the article remains the property of the seller. However, the custom effects transfer of ownership; the transfer is complete, and neither the seller nor the buyer may rescind. This principle of *sitomta* paved the way for the development in Jewish law of various modes of acquisition having custom as their legal source, in order to meet the needs and accord with the practices of the different centers of the diaspora. Thus, Rashba concluded from the Talmudic discussion concerning *sitomta:*

> From this we learn that custom overrides the law in all similar situations [and] that custom determines the validity of acquisitions and transfers in all matters of civil law; therefore, merchants may acquire anything in any manner that conforms to their usual practice.[70]

Indeed, in the course of time, Jewish law recognized, on the basis of this principle, new modes of acquisition and of creation of obligations. For

70. Rashba, Novellae to Bava Meẓi'a (ed. Devoretz) 74a, s.v. Meshallem leih, and *see Nimmukei Yosef* to Alfasi, Bava Meẓi'a 74a, s.v. U-ve-atra de-kani, quoting Rashba; *Maggid Mishneh* to *MT,* Mekhirah 7:6, s.v. Ve-im minhag ha-medinah hu she-yikneh . . . ; *Sema,* Sh. Ar. ḤM 201, subpar. 2. Ritba, following his view that custom does not override law even in civil-law matters (*see supra* n. 56), interprets the passage in an entirely different manner:

> *Sitomta* is a kind of blank coin that a merchant gives as a means of identification when he takes an item, and it is not known whether he gives it as payment [which, in itself, does not transfer ownership] . . . and [therefore] the only sanction is the imprecation "He Who punished . . . ," or whether he gives it as barter (*ḥalifin*) [*i.e.,* a fully effective mode of acquisition], in which case he has acquired full ownership because the coin, being blank, can be used for barter [as distinguished from payment]. It is with respect to this that the *amoraim* are in dispute.
>
> We therefore say that in a place where the custom is that *sitomta* transfers ownership [we assume that] he certainly gave it for the purpose of barter. Thus, there is no need for an enactment to validate this practice; the custom itself is sufficient, because it does not run counter to any law (Ritba, quoted in *Shittah Mekubbeẓet,* Bava Meẓi'a 74a, s.v. Hai sitomta kanya).

Ritba's theory is that the custom merely clarifies that the purchaser gave the *sitomta* by way of barter and therefore his purchase is legally effective; the custom therefore need not be incorporated into a communal enactment.

Ritba's interpretation is very strained, since *sitomta* does not mean "coin" and it is extremely difficult to explain the dispute (and the custom) on the basis of whether the purchaser gave a coin as payment or as barter. For this reason, most commentators and authorities follow the plain meaning of the passage, *i.e.,* that custom overrides the law. Rabad, quoted in Ritba, Novellae to Bava Meẓi'a 74a, s.v. Satimta kanya, and in *Shittah Mekubbeẓet, ad loc.,* s.v. Ve-ha-Ra'avad peresh, agrees with Rashi's interpretation and adds a further example.

instance, a handshake,[71] the payment of a deposit, or the delivery of the key to the place where merchandise is stored is sufficient to give legal effect to the transaction if such is the practice of merchants. The law is summarized as follows in the *Shulḥan Arukh:*

> If there has been only a verbal agreement and the price was agreed upon, . . . whoever retracts . . . is subject to the imprecation "He Who punished. . . ." If it is the local custom that [affixing] a mark completes the acquisition, the article is acquired; neither party may rescind, and the purchase price must be paid. . . . The same applies to any mercantile practice engaged in as a mode of acquisition, such as a buyer's giving a coin to the seller, or a handshake by the parties, . . . or . . . delivery of the key to the buyer, . . . and all similar acts.[72]

The extent of the creative power of custom with regard to the modes of acquisition was the subject of extensive halakhic discussion that at times was based on economic considerations. For example, according to Joel Sirkes, custom may create new modes of acquisition only for transactions involving personalty. With regard to personalty, Sirkes explained:

> There are a substantial number of commercial transactions, . . . and there is no time to arrange for the witnesses necessary for acquisition by barter (*ḥalifin*); and, needless to say, the purchaser does not have the time to "pull" all the merchandise into his possession.[73]

Most halakhic authorities, however, took the view that custom may create new modes of acquisition even for transactions involving real prop-

71. *Piskei ha-Rosh,* Bava Meẓi'a, ch. 5, #72, citing Rabbenu Hananel as to the meaning of *sitomta:* "As merchants are accustomed to act at the closing of a sale: they shake hands and thus the sale is concluded." The plain meaning of the passage, however, appears to be that given by Rashi, Rabad, and others—that *sitomta* is a seal, which is the meaning of the word in Aramaic.

Furthermore, although the handshake is mentioned in the Bible as an act of acquisition (in connection with suretyship, for example; *see* Proverbs 6:1–5, 11:15, 17:18, 22:26–27; Job 17:3 and, perhaps, Ezra 10:19), there is no similar reference to the handshake in the Talmud. (In TB Bava Batra 173b, Proverbs 6:1–5 is quoted, but nothing connected with the handshake is derived from the verses).

It was only in the post-Talmudic period that the handshake reappeared as a mode of acquisition (or as part of the undertaking of a sworn obligation) by force of custom and under the influence of the general practice of merchants. *See, e.g.,* Sh. Ar. ḤM 207:19. Asheri cited Rabbenu Hananel ("R.H."—perhaps the reading should be Rabbenu Tam ["R.T."], a change which in the Hebrew would involve a scribal error of only a part of one letter) to the effect that a handshake was a mode of acquisition current in his time, and as interpreting the Talmudic *sitomta* to mean a handshake. *See further infra* pp. 1026–1027 and n. 35.

72. Sh. Ar. ḤM 201:1–2.

73. *Bayit Ḥadash* to *Tur* ḤM 201, subpar. 2.

erty.[74] Similarly, many authorities held that where it is customary to permit the transfer of something not yet in existence,[75] such a transfer has full legal effect.[76] Sometimes, custom operated in so far-reaching a manner that it not only added new modes of acquisition but also changed certain material features of modes of acquisition previously established by the halakhic authorities.[77]

In the thirteenth century, an extremely important question arose, the answer to which was to be of great significance for determining the extent of the creative power of custom. The question was, What is the law if the local practice is to finalize a transaction solely by oral agreement? The basic notion underlying the requirement of Jewish law that certain modes of acquisition must be used to complete a legal transaction is that the use of these modes demonstrates a clear and deliberate intention (*gemirut da'at*) on the part of both parties to carry out the transaction.[78] Those modes of acquisition validated by custom, such as *sitomta*, shaking hands, and similar acts, also manifested the same type of intention, using accepted mercantile practice designed for precisely that purpose.

However, it is a fundamental rule in Jewish law that spoken words alone are not sufficient to demonstrate the intention required for full legal validity to be given to a transaction.[79] Does custom have the power under

74. *Yam Shel Shelomo*, Bava Kamma 5:36; *Sema*, Sh. Ar. ḤM 201, subpar. 6; *Shakh*, *ad loc.*, subpar. 1; *Resp. Avkat Rokhel* #80, Mabit's remarks (p. 71b); *id.* #81, Joseph Caro's remarks (p. 73c).

75. According to the law, one cannot transfer ownership of something that does not yet exist; *see supra* p. 392. *See also* M. Elon, EJ, V, pp. 923–933, s.v. Contract (reprinted in *Principles*, pp. 246–256).

76. Maharam of Rothenburg, quoted by *Mordekhai*, Shabbat, #472–473; *Resp. Asheri* 13:20. Others disagree; *see* Rabbenu Jehiel's opinion in *Mordekhai*, Shabbat, #473; *Keẓot ha-Ḥoshen*, Sh. Ar. ḤM 201, subpar. 1; and *Netivot ha-Mishpat*, *ad loc.*, subpar. 5.

77. *See, e.g.*, *Resp. Ribash* #345. According to custom, the mode of acquisition of personalty incidental to a conveyance of land is valid even if the land is not specified, although this result is contrary to the opinion of Maimonides, whose authority was followed in that locality.

78. *See supra* p. 580; M. Elon, EJ, V, pp. 923–933, s.v. Contract (reprinted in *Principles*, pp. 246–256).

79. TB Bava Meẓi'a 48a ("oral agreements do not effect a transfer of ownership"); Maimonides, *MT*, Mekhirah 1:1 ("A purchase is not effected by an oral agreement even if witnesses testify to it"). Sh. Ar. ḤM 189:1 (following *MT*, Mekhirah 1:1–2) states:

> A purchase cannot be consummated by an oral agreement. If one person says to another, "How much do you want for this article?" and the other names a sum and they agree on a price, either one may retract, even if the conversation had been in the presence of witnesses and they had said to the witnesses, "Be witnesses for us that this person has sold and this person has bought." It is all ineffective unless the transaction is concluded in the proper manner—land according to its mode of acquisition, animals according to their mode, and personalty according to its mode. After a transaction has been concluded in a manner appropriate to the subject matter, neither party can retract, even if there were no witnesses.

Jewish law to override this rule? The leading *rishonim* differed on this question. Asheri held that the validation of custom in the case of *sitomta* extends only to instances where an affirmative act is performed, such as those mentioned above (handshake, etc.), "but not an oral agreement alone; even if it is the custom [to enter into transactions on the basis of an oral agreement], it is a 'bad custom' and we do not follow it."[80] This view held that regardless of custom, some act is required to manifest *gemirut da'at*. Custom may change the nature of the act, but if it seeks to eliminate altogether the need for any act, it is a "bad custom," not to be accorded legal effect.[81]

Most halakhic authorities, however, hold to the contrary: Where the custom is that an oral agreement alone consummates a legal transaction, such an agreement is sufficient to demonstrate the requisite intention on the part of the parties.[82] Radbaz was asked[83] concerning "one who promised his neighbor that the neighbor would be his *ba'al berit, i.e.,* would sit on the ceremonial chair to hold the baby during the circumcision ceremony. He now wishes to retract and give this honor to someone else."

Radbaz held, on the strength of custom, that the oral promise was fully enforceable:

> He may not give this honor to anyone else, since it has been the universal custom of the Jewish people that giving one's word is sufficient to confer a right to this honor; and it is well known that custom is an important factor in all such matters, as is shown by the statement in Tractate *Bava Meẓi'a* concerning the *sitomta*. . . . In that case, even though there was no transfer of ownership through one of the [established] modes of acquisition, the transfer was nevertheless effective because of custom. Similarly, here too, since it is the custom, one must keep one's word, for "the remnant of Israel shall do no wrong. . . ."[84] We also conclude from this that if the custom is to use a method that is not one of the [established] modes of acquisition, custom establishes that method as a [valid] mode of acquisition.

80. *Resp. Asheri* 12:3.

81. As to "bad custom," *see infra* pp. 941–942.

82. *Cf.* opinions of Maharam of Rothenburg and Rabbenu Jehiel in *Mordekhai*, Shabbat, #472–473.

83. *Resp. Radbaz*, I, #278.

84. Zephaniah 3:13; the entire verse reads: "The remnant of Israel shall do no wrong and speak no falsehood; a deceitful tongue shall not be in their mouths. Only such as these shall graze and lie down, with none to trouble them." Radbaz cites the verse only as an *asmakhta*, a Biblical support, because, although it contains the words "speak no falsehood," it does not necessarily follow that speech is legally effective and that the speaker cannot retract; and, indeed, nowhere in the Talmud is the verse used as a basis for concluding that oral statements alone are sufficient to create binding legal obligations. The basis on which verbal commitments may not be withdrawn is that such is the custom. *See further* TB Pesaḥim 91a.

According to Radbaz, as opposed to Asheri, the practice of conferring rights solely by means of the spoken word is not a "bad custom" undeserving of recognition. Therefore, since an oral designation is the customary method for conferring the honor of holding the baby at the time of the circumcision ceremony, an oral designation is sufficient to establish the right to this honor. The case of *sitomta* teaches that custom can transform into an effective mode of acquisition a method that does not meet the requirements of the law.

Radbaz expressed the same view in another context where the question involved the method of forming a partnership. According to the strict law, a partnership, like other legal transactions, becomes effective only upon the completion of an act of acquisition (*kinyan*):

> If individuals seek to become partners, the partnership is not effectively created by oral agreement. Even when they have said, "Come let us become partners," and have specified the terms, they may still retract. A partnership is formed only through an act of acquisition; and since it requires an act of acquisition, the partnership is formed as to each type of property by means of the mode of acquisition appropriate for that property. Therefore . . . each partner must bring his money, the money of both of them is to be put into a purse, and both of them must pick up the purse. . . . This is the rule: Whatever methods are used for a purchaser to acquire ownership are the very same methods by which partners acquire from each other ownership of the money they contribute to the partnership.[85]

Radbaz was asked[86] whether a certain partnership was legally formed. He responded in the negative, since the required act of acquisition was not performed and the parties purported to effect "acquisition by spoken words alone." However, he added:

> You should be aware that if there is a local custom to form a partnership by mere oral agreement, then the partnership is effective. We have such a custom in our locality: if an individual is about to purchase merchandise, his neighbor may come and say, "For both of us," and they share in the purchase. This is the decision we reach in every case, for custom is an important factor in civil law.

This view was accepted by the subsequent halakhic authorities, "for it is rational that if it is the custom to rely on oral agreement, it is like *si-*

85. Sh. Ar. ḤM 176:1–2, following M Ketubbot 10:4 *et al.*; *see* the commentaries, *ad loc.*, and Maimonides, *MT*, Sheluḥin ve-Shutafin 4:1 *et seq.*

86. *Resp. Radbaz*, I, #380.

tomta."[87] On this basis, Jewish law gave full effect to public sales,[88] sales through stock exchanges,[89] and similar transactions that by custom were effectuated solely by the spoken word.[90]

In decisions by the rabbinical courts of the State of Israel, there is strong reliance on custom,[91] especially in matters involving the modes of acquisition. A number of decisions recognize that a transfer of ownership is accomplished by registration in the land registry according to the law of the state; this is regarded as a mode of acquisition valid under Jewish law by virtue of custom.[92] In another leading decision, it was held that "in our times, a contract signed by the seller and the purchaser constitutes an act of acquisition on the basis of the rule of *sitomta*, both as to personal property and as to real property, since this is the mercantile custom."[93]

C. Custom in Tax Law

Custom, often at variance with Talmudic law, was to a great extent the legal source of tax law in the post-Talmudic period. In this period, internal conditions and external political factors produced a broad expansion of Jewish tax law. From the end of the geonic period, the various institutions of the Jewish community (*kehillah*) constituted the primary manifestations of Jewish autonomy. A single center, such as the Land of Israel or Babylonia, that had dominated the entire Jewish diaspora no longer existed. Instead, different centers arose and functioned, sometimes concurrently and sometimes successively.[94] The result was an increase in the power of the community and the development of communal institutions. The community rendered various social services, maintained educational institutions, operated a judicial system, and provided religious facilities, administrative agencies, etc.; and various types of taxes were required to finance these activities.

In addition, as was customary at that time with regard to different groups, the non-Jewish government imposed heavy taxes on the Jewish

87. *Kesef ha-Kodashim* to Sh. Ar. ḤM 201:1; the author is Abraham David of Buczacz, Galicia, who was one of the outstanding halakhic authorities of the first half of the nineteenth century.

88. *Mishpat u-Ẓedakah be-Ya'akov* #33; *Kesef ha-Kodashim, supra* n. 87.

89. *Resp. Maharsham*, III, #18.

90. *See* E.M. Horowitz, *Ohel Moshe*, II, 1970, #138.

91. *See infra* pp. 924–926.

92. *See, e.g.*, Kraka Ltd. v. Assaf Rothenburg and Partners, 4 *P.D.R.* 75, 81 (1961).

93. Histadrut Po'alei Agudat Yisra'el, Reḥovot Branch v. Histadrut Agudat Yisra'el, Reḥovot Branch, 6 *P.D.R.* 202, 203 (par. 12 (1)), 216 (1966); *see* the distinction there made with regard to the contractual language. *See also* A. v. B., 4 *P.D.R.* 346, 349 (1962).

94. *See supra* pp. 666–668.

community as "toleration money" in return for permission to reside within its territory.[95] These taxes were not imposed directly on individuals, but on all the communities in a given area or on some particular community; and the Jewish communal leaders were responsible to the government for the payment of the entire tax. "In matters of taxes and forced labor, it became necessary for the members of each community to become partners with one another . . . because the king makes his demands on the collective and not on the individual."[96]

The collection of taxes by the community for the purposes of financing communal services and paying the taxes levied by the non-Jewish government led to the development of an extensive body of tax law dealing with such questions as the method of determining the tax rates; the types of taxes and their assessment, adjudication, and collection; and the determination of exemptions. In part, the tax law of this period was based on legal principles different from those of the tax law of the Talmud and of Jewish law generally. Thus, reliance was placed on the doctrine that "the law of the land is law" (*dina de-malkhuta dina*), and that doctrine was expanded to meet new and changing conditions.[97] The communities also invoked the Talmudic principle that the townspeople must share the costs involved in maintaining their security, in rendering religious and social services, and in providing adequate sanitation.[98] In addition, the halakhic authorities applied the principles of partnership law to determine legal relationships among the members of the community, on the basis of which they established various rules of tax law.[99]

However, all this did not provide a sufficient legal basis for solving the large array of problems of tax law that confronted the halakhic authorities and the communal leaders. Tax law in the Talmudic literature is scant and limited, and the doctrine of *dina de-malkhuta dina* was applied only in a few special circumstances. In general, the variegated problems of tax law, which are essentially matters of public law, could not be solved by application of the principles of the law governing private partnerships. Often, the legal structuring of the relationship between a limited number of partners had nothing in common with the legal structuring of the relationships among all the members of the community. Consequently, the majority of tax law

95. *See Piskei ha-Rosh,* Bava Batra, ch. 1, #29; *Resp. Ran* #2.

96. *Resp. Rashba,* V, #270.

97. *See supra* pp. 64–74, 746 n. 252. For fuller treatment, *see* M. Elon, EJ, XV, p. 844, s.v. Taxation (reprinted in *Principles,* p. 667).

98. *See* M Bava Batra 1:5; *Tosefta* Bava Mezi'a 11:18, 23; TB Bava Batra 7b–8a. *See also* M. Elon, EJ, XV, pp. 841–844, s.v. Taxation (reprinted in *Principles,* pp. 664–667).

99. For detailed discussion, *see* M. Elon, EJ, XV, p. 844, s.v. Taxation (reprinted in *Principles,* p. 668).

problems were resolved by exercising the authority of the public to enact legislation[100] and by means of custom in its role as a legal source.

Although, at first, some authorities expressed a certain hesitation as to the extent that custom can be binding if contrary to the "established and known law" of the Talmud on tax matters,[101] the hesitation ultimately disappeared. In consequence of the obligatory force of both legislation and custom, many laws and practices relating to taxes were given full effect even though contrary to the *Halakhah*. The fact that legislation and custom were the means by which most of the rules of Jewish tax law in the post-Talmudic period were developed also explains the wide variety of Jewish tax laws as reflected in the different enactments and customs of the various Jewish centers of the diaspora.

This special circumstance has been emphasized by all the halakhic authorities in all the Jewish centers in every era. Thus, Rashba, the leader of Spanish Jewry in the thirteenth century, stated:

> Nowhere is tax law based on . . . the Talmud, and in every place you will find laws that vary according to custom and according to the enactments of leading authorities who earlier established the framework. The townspeople may enact fixed *takkanot* and establish well-recognized practices, as they see fit, which do not accord with the *Halakhah*, as this is a monetary matter. If, therefore, there is a known custom on the matter, it must be followed, since custom overrides the law in such matters.[102]

Rashba's contemporary, Maharam of Rothenburg, the leader of German Jewry, similarly held:

> Tax matters depend neither on reasoning nor on the law set forth in the Talmud, but on the custom of the locality,[103] . . . [because] tax law is part of local law; every river has its tributaries, and there are many differences in customs.[104]

Israel Isserlein, in the fifteenth century, emphasized that the flexibility of custom was preferable to halakhic law in the legal regulation of public affairs:

100. *See supra* pp. 679–685, 745–751.

101. *See* the statement of Baruch of Mainz, author of *Sefer ha-Ḥokhmah*, twelfth century, quoted in *Mordekhai*, Bava Batra, #477.

102. *Resp. Rashba*, I, #664; III, #398, #436; IV, #177, #260; V, #180, #263, #270; and others.

103. *Resp. Maharam of Rothenburg*, ed. Prague, #106.

104. *Id.* #995; *see also* the statement of Avigdor Kohen Ẓedek, quoted in *Mordekhai*, Bava Batra, #477.

> All actions taken by the public collectively are governed by the customs and arrangements they institute to meet their needs and circumstances. If you require them to follow the law of the Torah in all matters, there will always be strife among them; therefore, from the outset they have agreed to waive their rights under the law of the Torah and to be governed by their customary practices.[105]

This idea was reiterated by Benjamin Ze'ev in the sixteenth century in Arta, Greece, with the following addition:

> The custom of the townspeople overrides a court of the Sages even if the court finds Scriptural support [for its view]. Moreover, not only a custom of the halakhic authorities but even a custom of donkey drivers must be followed.[106]

At the same time, the halakhic authorities did all they could to integrate legal norms based on custom into the general tenor and spirit of the Jewish legal system. Israel Isserlein further stated:

> Even though . . . in tax matters custom overrides the law, it is always appropriate and correct to consider carefully whether it is possible to reconcile all customs with the law of the Torah. Even if this cannot be done completely, it is highly desirable to find reinforcement and support in the words of the halakhic authorities and buttress them [the practices] with good reason and logic.[107]

In this and other ways (such as the control exercised by the halakhic authorities to ensure that laws based on custom do not violate the principles of justice and equity of Jewish law), the rules of tax law, many of which, as has been stated, were based on custom,[108] became an integral part of the Jewish legal system.[109]

105. *Terumat ha-Deshen* #342.

106. *Resp. Binyamin Ze'ev* #293; *see also Resp. Maharashdam,* ḤM, #369 and #404; *Resp. Noda bi-Yehudah,* Mahadura Tinyana, ḤM, #40.

107. *Terumat ha-Deshen* #342.

108. For a general discussion of tax laws, including their various categories and sources, *see* M. Elon, EJ, XV, pp. 840–873, s.v. Taxation (reprinted in *Principles,* pp. 663–701). The close connection between the rules of tax law and the rules relating to custom led to an interesting juxtaposition in the book *Massa Melekh* by Joseph b. Isaac ibn Ezra, a sixteenth century halakhic authority in Salonika. Most of the book deals with tax law and constitutes a detailed code of that field as it had developed up to that time. A large chapter at the end, entitled "Ne'ilat She'arim" [The Closing of the Gates], is entirely devoted to the subject of custom in Jewish law. This chapter was added to a book dealing solely with tax law because a significant portion of tax law is based on custom. *See* the Introduction to the book, and also M. Elon, EJ, XV, p. 872, s.v. Taxation (reprinted in *Principles,* p. 700), and *infra* pp. 1445–1446.

109. For details, *see* M. Elon, EJ, XV, pp. 846–847, s.v. Taxation (reprinted in *Principles,* pp. 669–671), and *infra* pp. 937ff. Important general principles with regard to custom

D. Custom in Jewish Law in the State of Israel; Severance Pay

Custom operates extensively in the Jewish legal system even at present, as is particularly evident in the decisions of the rabbinical courts in the State of Israel. The reliance of the rabbinical courts on custom in regard to the modes of acquisition has previously been noted.[110] An additional interesting illustration involves severance pay for employees—a problem that has recently been the focus of much attention by the halakhic authorities.

The legal institution of employee severance pay is rooted in the law relating to the gratuity that the Hebrew slave is entitled to receive when he obtains his freedom after he has served for six years: "When you set him free, do not let him go empty-handed: Furnish him out of the flock, threshing floor, and vat, with which the Lord your God has blessed you."[111] The halakhic authorities found in this law the concept of giving a certain sum to an employee at the termination of his employment. Thus, this concept has practical application even after the institution of bond service, which gave rise to it, disappeared from Jewish law. The possibility of such application was noted in *Sefer ha-Ḥinnukh* as early as the end of the thirteenth century:

> This commandment [of furnishing a gratuity to a slave] was practiced when the Temple was in existence, since the law relating to the Hebrew slave applies only when the Jubilee Year is observed . . . ; but, in any case, even at the present time, the wise man should consider the implication: Whoever hires an individual who works for him for a long or even a short time, should pay him [the employee] a gratuity out of that which God has blessed him [the employer], when the employee departs from his work.[112]

As set forth by *Sefer ha-Ḥinnukh,* the obligation to give a certain sum to an employee at the termination of his employment is only a moral obligation. When the need arose, relatively recently, various halakhic authorities, particularly the rabbinical courts in Israel, made this obligation legally binding. Three methods were used to accomplish this result.

---

were established in connection with tax law, such as the establishment and incidence of a custom, proof of custom, the problem of "bad custom," and others. *See infra* pp. 928, 941–944.

110. *See supra* p. 920. Custom is an important legal source for the recognition and reception by the rabbinical courts of various laws of the general legal system of the State of Israel. *See* Wiloszni v. Rabbinical Court of Appeals, 36(ii) *P.D.* 733, 740 (1982), and *infra* p. 1822.

111. Deuteronomy 15:13–14. For details as to the gratuity, *see* M. Elon, EJ, VII, pp. 1003–1007, s.v. Ha'anakah (reprinted in *Principles,* pp. 315–319).

112. *Sefer ha-Ḥinnukh,* ed. Chavel, #450 (p. 577).

The first method is to follow *Sefer ha-Ḥinnukh* and rely on the principle of the slave's gratuity. Thus, a rabbinical court decision stated:

> The source for severance pay is the gratuity that had to be paid to the Hebrew slave. . . . We can see clearly that the intention of the Torah was to impose an obligation on the employer to be concerned about the future of the employee, so that when he [the employee] departs his employment, he should not be left empty-handed.[113]

The inference from the law of the Hebrew slave to the law of an employee was possible because under Jewish law the status of a Hebrew slave is comparable to the status of an employee;[114] and, in any event, "the laborer has all of the privileges of the Hebrew slave by inference *a fortiori.* The Torah dealt generously with the Hebrew slave even though he was a transgressor.[115] How much more so should a laborer, who is not a transgressor, be dealt with generously."[116]

However, reliance on the law of the slave's gratuity is not in itself sufficient to create a full legal obligation to give severance pay to an employee. Consequently, Chief Rabbi Ben-Zion Uziel based this obligation on a second ground, namely, the Talmud's exemption of laborers, in certain circumstances, from liability to the employer for damage caused by their negligence.[117] The exemption was based on the duty to act morally as expressed in the verse, "So follow the way of the good and keep to the paths of the just."[118] Although this Talmudic rule has only moral and not legal force, many authorities hold that a court has the discretion to enforce conduct more generous than the law requires (*lifnim mi-shurat ha-din*).[119] Therefore:

> A court has the authority to order the employer to make payments for the benefit of his employees whenever it sees that this will promote the goal of "follow[ing] the way of the good and keep[ing] to the paths of the just." In

113. Kaiserman v. Direnfeld, Director of Belz Talmud Torah, 3 *P.D.R.* 272, 286–287 (1959).

114. *See, e.g.,* Deuteronomy 15:18; Elon, *Ḥerut,* p. 2.

115. A person who sells himself as a slave transgresses the injunction in the Torah, "For it is to Me that the Israelites are servants" (Leviticus 25:55). From this verse the Sages deduced, "and not servants to servants," *i.e.,* a Jew should not be a bondman of another person, since everyone is God's servant, and one should not be a servant of a servant; *see* TB Kiddushin 22b; *Yam Shel Shelomo,* Kiddushin 1:22.

116. *Resp. Maharam of Rothenburg,* ed. Prague, #85. As to this comparison with the law of the slave's gratuity, *see* J.M. Toledano, *Yam Gadol,* #22. *See also infra* pp. 1633–1634 with regard to the debate in the Knesset on the Severance Pay Law, 1963, which was based on the slave's gratuity.

117. TB Bava Meẓi'a 83a.

118. Proverbs 2:20.

119. *Mordekhai,* Bava Meẓi'a #257; Rema to Sh. Ar. ḤM 12:2; *Bayit Ḥadash* to *Tur* ḤM 12:4. *See supra* pp. 155–167.

> exercising its discretion, it should take into account the manifest circumstances of the employer and employee, as well as the reasons why the employer dismissed the employee or why the employee stopped working for the employer.[120]

Since some authorities are of the opinion that a court does not have the power to enforce conduct more generous than the law requires,[121] a third line of authority prefers to base the law of severance pay on custom as the legal source; and the principle that "custom overrides the law" has been particularly applied to labor law.[122] Thus, it was determined that "since in our time this custom of awarding severance pay to employees has been widely accepted, . . . we must give it the same force as a law of the Torah, pursuant to the established principle of the employer-employee relationship that in all things the local custom governs."[123] Therefore, by virtue of the custom, the demand for severance pay "is not a request for magnanimity but is a claim founded on law." Even if the employer is a charitable institution, it must give severance pay.[124]

This third approach also establishes a link to the rule requiring a gratuity to be given to a slave. This link reinforces the custom because "we find that it [the custom] has support in the Torah and the *Halakhah*"; "this custom has a root in the Torah—the slave's gratuity"[125]—and is therefore "a suitable and proper custom."[126]

E. Local Custom as Overriding the Law

A custom need not be general to override the law in civil-law matters; a custom of a particular group has the same effect. For example, the *Tosefta* states:[127]

120. Responsum of B.Z. Uziel, quoted in M. Findling, *Teḥukat ha-Avodah* [Labor Law], p. 133.

121. *See* sources cited *supra* n. 119.

122. *See supra* pp. 905–907.

123. Nast v. Management Committee of Bet ha-Midrash ha-Merkazi, Haifa, 1 *P.D.R.* 330, 331 (1955).

124. *See* Kaiserman v. Direnfeld, *supra* n. 113.

125. A. v. Management of the General Old Age Home, Jerusalem, 4 *P.D.R.* 126, 129 (1960); *see* Toledano, *supra* n. 116.

126. Nast v. Management Committee, *supra* n. 123 at 331–332, and *cf. Terumat ha-Deshen* #342 in regard to finding reinforcement and support in the law of the Torah for a custom relating to taxes. *See further infra* p. 929. For additional examples of the rabbinical courts' reliance on custom, *see* A. v. B. (1945), Warhaftig, *Osef Piskei ha-Din*, pp. 110ff., at pp. 112–113.

127. *Tosefta* Bava Meẓi'a 7:13; *see also* parallels in TB Bava Kamma 116b; TJ Bava Meẓi'a 6:4, 27a (6:4, 11a).

> When a caravan traveling in the desert is attacked by a band of robbers and captured, the extent of each person's contribution [to the ransom] is proportional to the amount of money that he carries and is not determined on a *per capita* basis. If they wish to hire a guide, he is paid on a *per capita* basis as well; but the custom of caravan travelers is not to be departed from.

In other words, when a caravan is traveling in the desert and is attacked by bandits and held for ransom, the contribution to the ransom of each person in the caravan is not *per capita* but is proportional to the amount of property the person carries. If, however, it is necessary to hire a guide in a dangerous area, the contribution of each person to the compensation of the guide includes both a *per capita* and a proportionate charge. In any event, if it is the custom of caravan travelers that the contribution does not include a *per capita* charge but is solely proportionate, the custom must be followed.

Custom has similar force in the case of "a ship traveling on the ocean and battered by a storm; when cargo must be jettisoned, the choice [as to what cargo to jettison] is made on the basis of weight, not value; but maritime custom is not to be departed from."[128] This custom is not general but prevails only within a particular group, yet for the members of that group it has sufficient force to override a rule of law:

> In matters of civil law, custom is followed, even the custom of donkey drivers and boatmen, . . . for although the law of the Torah is to reckon [in some instances] according to value and [in other instances] according to weight, nevertheless the custom of donkey drivers or boatmen overrides the law. . . .[129]

VI. PROOF OF CUSTOM

In order for a custom to be binding, three conditions must be satisfied. First, the custom must have become generally accepted throughout the country or in the locality or within the group to which it is applicable. Maimonides, after listing the various customs with regard to the financial relationship between husband and wife, concluded:

128. TB Bava Kamma 116b, and *see* Rashi, *ad loc.*, s.v. Meḥashvin lefi masui: "If one jettisons one hundred pounds of gold, another must jettison one hundred pounds of iron." In *Tosefta* Bava Mezi'a 7:14, the text reads: "The choice is made on the basis of the weight and not *per capita.*" The *Tosefta*'s text is problematic. The text in TB is followed in Alfasi, *ad loc.*; Maimonides, *MT*, Gezelah va-Avedah 13:14; and Tur and Sh. Ar. ḤM 272:17.

129. *Resp. Maharik* #102; *see also Resp. Binyamin Ze'ev* #293, quoted *supra* p. 923.

> In all these and similar matters, the custom of the country is a fundamental consideration and must be followed, provided that the custom has spread throughout the country.[130]

If the custom exists in most parts of a particular region, it is assumed that it exists throughout that region.[131]

Second, the custom must be commonly and frequently practiced:

> It must be known that the custom is established and widespread, and that the townspeople have followed it at least three times, because the people often make *ad hoc* responses to some particular need without intending thereby to establish any general custom.[132]

The time necessary for a custom to come into being depends on the particular subject involved. Thus, in a responsum on the question whether a custom existed exempting a community's cantor from paying taxes, Ribash stated:

> This matter is not similar to a custom involving laborers, since many laborers are hired every day, and one can see what the custom is; but as to a cantor's tax exemption, since there is only one cantor in the town, how can the fact that there was no demand for tax payments from one or two cantors be called a custom unless it is known and recognized in the town that they were exempted pursuant to a custom of the town exempting cantors?[133]

The law was codified as follows:

> It is not considered a custom unless it is commonly and frequently practiced; if it was only done once or twice, it is not considered to be a custom.[134]

130. Maimonides, *MT,* Ishut 23:12, and *cf.* his statement of the law regarding enactments, *id.* 16:7–9. *See also supra* p. 645 n. 6 and pp. 668–675.

131. *Resp. Asheri* 79:4; *Bet Yosef* to *Tur* ḤM 42:21. Occasionally, there is a rebuttable presumption that a custom practiced in other places is also practiced in the place under discussion. For example, Menahem Mendel Krochmal ruled, on the basis of many sources among the *rishonim,* that it is customary to accept testimony from members of the community in cases involving taxation although they are relatives or personally interested and therefore not legally competent witnesses (*Resp. Ẓemaḥ Ẓedek* #37). As to this issue, *see supra* pp. 737–739. In this context, Krochmal added: "And if someone will disagree and argue that the custom may not have been accepted here in Vienna, tell him that since Vienna does not have a contrary enactment, we presume that the custom is also accepted here." Krochmal relied on the concluding section of *Resp. Ribash* #195. It would appear that this presumption does not apply to all customs, but only to those that have been very widespread for hundreds of years in many communities and are essential for orderly public administration and for the administration of justice "because otherwise it would never be possible to meet communal needs" (*Resp. Ẓemaḥ Ẓedek* #37).

132. *Terumat ha-Deshen* #342; *see Resp. Maharashdam,* ḤM, #436.

133. *Resp. Ribash* #475.

134. Rema to Sh. Ar. ḤM 331:1; *see also* Rema to Sh. Ar. ḤM 163:3.

Third, the custom must be well known and clear: "The custom must be clear in order to create an exemption."[135] Samuel de Medina held that the principle that "custom overrides the law" is applicable only if the custom is sufficiently clear:

> This case can be approached from two points of view: one, according to the law of our Holy Torah, and the second, according to mercantile custom; for there is no doubt that in such matters custom takes precedence, so long as the custom is widespread and unequivocal; but if there is any doubt as to the custom, we must turn to the law as set forth in the Torah.[136]

Jewish law dispenses with the formalities of the law of evidence to prove the existence of a custom, and it thus accords to custom a wide range of creativity. "Although it is necessary to prove the existence of a particular custom, one is not very strict with regard to [the manner of] such proof; hearsay evidence and the testimony of witnesses not generally competent to testify are admissible."[137]

The wide latitude Jewish law accords to the creative power of custom is illustrated by a rabbinical court decision in Israel with regard to severance pay for employees.[138] In 1945, Chief Rabbi Uziel had refused to base the law of severance pay on custom because of the rule that a custom is not binding unless it is widespread, commonly practiced, and well known—"and to the best of my knowledge, this custom [of giving severance pay] has not spread throughout the country, nor is it commonly practiced except in certain cases, and, for this reason, the court will not order the giving of severance pay on this basis."[139] Only ten years later, when the rabbinical court sought to find a legal basis on which severance pay could be fully grounded, it stated:

> Now that the custom has spread and is accepted throughout the country and is usual and common and practiced daily, this custom must be followed; and the statements [of Rabbi Uziel] mentioned above, made in 1945, are not at this time valid or applicable, since the custom is now established and has become widespread.

Such a recognition of change in the spread of a custom in only ten years indicates the special receptivity of Jewish law to the enrichment of its *corpus juris* through custom as a legal source.

135. *Resp. Ribash* #475.

136. *Resp. Maharashdam*, ḤM, #33.

137. *Terumat ha-Deshen* #342.

138. *See supra* p. 926 and n. 123.

139. Responsum of Rabbi Uziel, *supra* n. 120. The responsum based the right to severance pay on the ethical-legal principle "Follow the way of the good and keep to the paths of the just" (Proverbs 2:20). *See supra* pp. 925–926.

VII. CUSTOM AND USAGE

The examples discussed to this point belong for the most part to the category of "legal custom," *i.e.*, a norm that operates by virtue of its own force and is not dependent on the consent of the parties to a particular transaction. Thus, when custom creates a new mode of acquisition, the effectiveness of this mode does not depend on whether the parties to the particular transaction impliedly intended to give it legal validity. The new mode of acquisition is valid because custom has the power to create new legal norms that are *per se* effective in every case in which they apply. On the other hand, Jewish law recognizes many customs which, as in other legal systems, are effective not by virtue of their own binding force, but by virtue of a presumption that the parties to a particular transaction impliedly intend to include the practice as a part of their transaction. This type of custom is called "usage" or "conventional custom" (*nohag*).

The provisions that make up an agreement between the parties to a legal transaction are generally of two types: (a) express —stipulations expressly agreed upon, and (b) implied—terms not expressly discussed, but impliedly incorporated as part of the agreement. Implied terms can be inferred either by logical deduction and reasonable inference, or because they are customary and accepted. The theory is that the parties to the agreement intend to be logical and reasonable and also to follow accepted practices.[140]

There are many examples of usage in Jewish law. For instance, the Mishnah states:[141]

> If one rents a field from another [to work it as a sharecropper or under a rental][142] in a place where the practice is to reap [the crop with a scythe], he shall do so. If the practice is to uproot [*i.e.*, pull out by hand and not cut with a scythe], he shall do so. If the practice is to plow afterwards [after the reaping in order to pull out the grass], he shall do so. In all things the local practice governs.

The presumption is that a sharecropping arrangement or a land lease for a fixed measure of farm produce impliedly includes conditions concern-

140. *See* Salmond, pp. 193–197. The same rationale applies to legal custom, such as the creation of a new mode of acquisition. Such a custom has legal force because each member of the public is presumed to have stipulated *ab initio* that such mode of acquisition should be effective for various transactions; *see Resp. Maharashdam*, ḤM, #380, and *supra* p. 904 n. 29. However, as far as legal custom is concerned, this presumption is general and is applied *a priori* to the entire public, which is not so as regards usage. The question as regards usage concerns the parties in a specific concrete situation and is: What did they intend to be the terms of their transaction?

141. M Bava Meẓi'a 9:1.

142. In a sharecropping arrangement, the tenant farmer gives the owner of the land a stipulated portion of the crop; in a rental arrangement, the amount of produce to be paid as rent is fixed in advance and is independent of the actual yield.

ing the method of working the field in accordance with the practice in the locality. Neither the owner nor the tenant may contend, for example, that he intended that the field be reaped with a scythe, if the practice in the locality is that the crop should be pulled out by hand. According to the Talmud,[143] neither party may contend that he did not intend to abide by the local usage—even if his contention is supported by circumstantial evidence, such as a rental that is either higher or lower than usual.[144] Unless explicitly stipulated otherwise, both parties are held to have intended that local usage become a part of their agreement.

The Talmud records many examples, in most of the branches of civil law, where usage is an implied term of an agreement between the parties to a transaction. These examples involve such matters as joint ownership of property,[145] joint ventures,[146] pledges,[147] employer and employee,[148] and the

143. TB Bava Meẓi'a 103b.

144. *Id.*:

> It is necessary [to state the rule] in the case where everyone [*i.e.*, every landowner] gives [land for sharecropping] in return for [a] one-third [share of the crop] and he [the owner] gave for one-fourth . . . [and] in the case where everyone [*i.e.*, every sharecropper] takes [land for sharecropping] to give one-quarter [of the crop] and he [the sharecropper] agreed to give one-third.

However, the usage must be general and practiced by the majority of the people; the practice of a minority does not create a usage. *See id.*:

> R. Joseph said: "In Babylonia, it is the practice not to give straw to the sharecropper. What legal consequence [does that usage have]? That if there is a person who does give, he is merely being generous, and no conclusion should be drawn from his behavior."

See also Maimonides, *MT*, Sekhirut 8:6; Sh. Ar. ḤM 320:4–5. *But see supra* p. 928 and n. 131.

145. M Bava Batra 1:1–2:

> If two concurrent owners desire to make a partition in a courtyard, . . . in all things the local practice governs. So, too, in a garden, where the practice is to erect a fence [partitioning the area concurrently owned], there is a legal obligation to do so; but in a valley, where the practice is not to erect a fence, there is no obligation to do so.

See also v.l. in the text and H. Albeck's commentary, *ad loc.*; TJ Bava Batra 1:2, 1b (1:2, 12d): "A *baraita* teaches, 'In a garden—whether in a locality where it is customary to build a fence . . .'"; TB Bava Batra 4a: "In all things the local practice governs; 'All things'—to include what? . . ."

146. TB Bava Meẓi'a 68b: "The Rabbis taught: In a place where it is customary [in an agreement to raise cattle] to pay a fee for carrying [the animals] . . . ."; M Bava Meẓi'a 5:5, TB Bava Meẓi'a 69b: "Where the practice is to divide, . . . where the practice is [first] to rear them. . . ." Similarly, TJ Bava Meẓi'a 5:4, 21b (5:6, 10b); *Tosefta* Bava Meẓi'a 5:6–7. *See also* Maimonides, *MT*, Sheluḥin ve-Shutafin 5:1, 8:4.

147. TB Bava Meẓi'a 67b–68a, summarized in Maimonides, *MT*, Malveh ve-Loveh 7:2–3.

148. *Regarding working hours:* M Bava Meẓi'a 7:1 and TB Bava Meẓi'a 83a: "But surely that is obvious?! No! It is necessary in the case where he increased their wages. . . ." *Regarding the employer's responsibility to provide food for his workers:* M Bava Meẓi'a 7:1: "Rabban Simeon b. Gamaliel said: "It is not necessary [for the employer] to state [the extent of his obligation to provide meals for his workers]—in all things the local practice governs"; and

financial relationship between husband and wife.[149] Usage also plays an important role in the interpretation of deeds and other documents; various terms and conditions are interpreted in accordance with the relevant local usage.[150] Many halakhic authorities viewed the principle of *doreshin leshon hedyot*[151] in the interpretation of documents[152] as a recognition that a usage followed by the public has legal force even if the parties to the transaction did not explicitly include it in their legal document; the presumption is that the transaction was entered into subject to the usage.[153]

VIII. GENERAL AND LOCAL CUSTOM

Customs may also be classified as either general or local. A general custom is created by the people as a whole and therefore applies to the entire people; a local custom is created by the people of a certain place or group, and its applicability and binding effect are limited to the people of that place or the members of that group. Customs of different groups such as boatmen and caravan travelers have been previously mentioned;[154] and Talmudic sources cite various customs unique to such groups as priests,[155] women,[156] certain groups in Jerusalem,[157] and the "scrupulously careful" of Jerusa-

---

see TB Bava Meẓi'a 86a: "In all things the local practice governs. 'All things'—to include what? To include a locality where they are accustomed to eat bread. . . ." *Regarding wages:* TB Bava Meẓi'a 87a: "In all things the local practice governs. 'All things'—to include what? To include that which was taught: If a person hires a laborer and says to him, '[I will pay you] like one or two of the townspeople.' . . . "; *see* Rashi, *ad loc.*, s.v. Meshamnim beineihem.

149. *See supra* p. 912 n. 61.

150. TB Bava Batra 166b; Maimonides, *MT*, Malveh ve-Loveh 27:15; for further discussion, *see supra* pp. 432–443.

151. *See, e.g.*, *Tosefta* Ketubbot 4:9 *et seq.*; TJ Ketubbot 4:8, 29a/b (4:8, 28d–29a); TJ Yevamot 15:3, 78a (13:3, 14d); TB Bava Meẓi'a 104a.

152. For detailed discussion, *see supra* pp. 422–432.

153. This point is discussed in detail, *supra* pp. 429–432.

154. *See supra* pp. 926–927.

155. TB Kiddushin 78b ("From the time that the Temple was destroyed, the priests, as a matter of custom, have been very fastidious and follow the opinion of R. Eliezer b. Jacob"), quoted in TJ Bikkurim 1:5, 3b (1:5, 64a) and TJ Kiddushin 4:6, 46a (4:6, 66a). *See also supra* p. 888 n. 40 and A. Perls, "Der Minhag im Talmud" [Custom in the Talmud], *Tiferet Yisra'el* (Israel Lewy Jubilee Volume), German Section, p. 71, for various kinds of customs.

156. TB Pesaḥim 48b: "R. Joseph said: 'It is the custom of our women to . . .'"; TJ Pesaḥim 4:1, 25b (4:1, 30c/d): "Women are accustomed to refrain from work after the conclusion of the sabbath. . . . R. Ze'eira said: 'Women are accustomed to refrain from weaving from the beginning of [the month of] Av. . . .'" *See further infra* p. 940.

157. *Tosefta* Megillah 3:15 (ms. Erfurt, 4:15): "R. Leizar b. R. Ẓadok said: 'This was the custom of [certain] groups in Jerusalem.'"

lem.[158] Many customs are referred to as a "local custom" (*minhag ha-medinah*),[159] *i.e.*, a custom of a particular town or region. Customs have been cited as practices that were followed in Judea,[160] the Galilee,[161] or in particular towns such as Tiberias,[162] Acre,[163] Cabul,[164] Biro,[165] etc.[166] Such local or group customs relate to all the areas of Jewish law, both religious and civil.

There were many local customs whereby the inhabitants of a particular place prohibited conduct that the law permitted. A group of such strict customs, for example, is contained in Tractate *Pesaḥim*.[167] The following are two illustrations:

> Where it is the custom to work on the eve of Passover until midday, one may work; where it is the custom not to work, one may not work.

Under the law, work may be performed during the entire fourteenth day of the month of Nisan (the eve of Passover), but there was a general custom to refrain from work after midday, because from that time on the paschal sacrifice could be offered, and the afternoon was therefore treated as if it were a holiday. There were different local customs with regard to work on the eve of Passover before midday: in certain places work was done until midday, and in other places it was customary to refrain from work throughout the entire day before Passover so that the burning of the leaven and the other festival requirements would not be neglected. The

158. TB Sanhedrin 30a:

> R. Nehemiah said: "This was the custom of the scrupulously careful [judges] in Jerusalem: They would bring the parties [into the court] and hear what they had to say and then bring the witnesses [into court] and hear their testimony. They would then send them out [of the courtroom] and confer about the case."

See further supra p. 882 n. 8.

159. M Bava Meẓi'a 7:1, 9:1; M Bava Batra 1:1, 10:1; M Ketubbot 6:4; M Sukkah 3:11 (concerning the recitation of the *Hallel* prayer), *et al.*; *Tosefta* Bava Meẓi'a 5:6, 7, 23. In most instances, it is Rabban Simeon b. Gamaliel who says, "In all things the local practice governs."

160. M Ketubbot 1:5, 4:12; *Tosefta* Ketubbot 1:4; TB Ketubbot 12a; TB Bava Batra 100b.

161. *See supra* n. 160.

162. M Eruvin 10:10; TJ Pesaḥim 4:1, 25b–26a (4:1, 30d).

163. TJ Pesaḥim 4:1, 26a (4:1, 30d).

164. TJ Pesaḥim 4:1, 25b–26a (4:1, 30d).

165. TJ Pesaḥim 4:1, 26a (4:1, 30d).

166. Yavneh—*Tosefta* Rosh ha-Shanah 2:11 (ms. Erfurt, 4:11). Migdal Ẓabaya—TJ Pesaḥim 4:1, 25b (4:1, 30d); TJ Ta'anit 1:6, 6a (1:6, 64c). Benei Beishan—TJ Pesaḥim 4:1, 26b (4:1, 30d); TB Pesaḥim 50b. Sepphoris (Ẓippori)—TJ Pesaḥim 4:1, 26a (4:1, 30d). Benei Ḥozai—TB Pesaḥim 50b. *See further* M. Margaliot, *Ha-Ḥillukim she-bein Anshei Mizraḥ u-Venei Ereẓ Yisra'el* [The Differences between the People of the East and the Residents of the Land of Israel], 1938, Introduction, pp. 14ff.

167. M Pesaḥim 4:1–5.

Mishnah prescribes that each person should follow the custom accepted in his locality.

Similarly,

> Where it is the custom to do work on the ninth day of the month of Av [a fast day commemorating the destruction of the Temple], one may work [since under the law there is no prohibition against working on that day]; where it is the custom to refrain [in the manner of a mourner] from working, one may not work.

The halakhic authorities viewed customs that establish new prohibitions as a type of vow taken by the public, and, on that basis, explained their binding force. It was thus laid down that violating a prohibition based on custom is in the nature of breaking a vow. A *baraita* states:[168]

> When a custom prohibits what the law permits, one may not rule in the presence of those to whom the custom applies that the conduct is permissible; as it is stated:[169] "He shall not break his pledge."

The quoted verse is contained in the section of the Torah on vows, which, according to the interpretation of the Sages, deals with vows by which an individual undertakes to refrain from doing something that would otherwise be permissible.[170] The halakhic authorities analogized a custom establishing a new prohibition to a vow of self-abnegation undertaken by an individual, and the violation of such a custom to the violation of a vow by an individual. It appears that the Babylonian *amoraim* limited the rule stated in the *baraita* quoted above to cases in which there is reason for concern that when those to whom the custom applies hear that the conduct proscribed by the custom is permissible, they would make light even of prohibitions expressly based on the law.[171]

168. TB Nedarim 15a.

169. Numbers 30:3. The full text of the verse is: "If a man makes a vow to the Lord or takes an oath imposing an obligation on himself, he shall not break his pledge; he must carry out all that has crossed his lips."

170. *See* H. Albeck, Introduction to M Nedarim, p. 137.

171. In TB Pesaḥim 50b–51a, R. Joseph and R. Ḥisda interpret the rule that "when a custom prohibits what the law permits, one may not rule in the presence of those to whom the custom applies that the conduct is permissible" as applicable only to Samaritans. The fear was that if the conduct were permitted in the presence of a Samaritan, he would make light of other prohibitions, including those expressly based on the law. This was also R. Ashi's opinion, *id.* The passage (fol. 51a) adds: "This also applies to [Jews] overseas; because rabbis are not usually available there, they [these Jews] are like Samaritans."

This is a restrictive interpretation, inasmuch as all the *baraitot* cited plainly imply that the rule applies to all persons and is not grounded on the fear that legal prohibitions will come to be treated lightly.

The passage continues with an incident involving Rabbah bar bar Ḥana, who went to

These local customs were also considered from the perspective of the commandment "You shall not gash yourselves (*lo titgodedu*)."[172] This commandment was interpreted by the Sages, in a play on words, as a strict prohibition against the creation of separate factions (*agudot*) with regard to the halakhic laws; the Sages' purpose was to prevent the Torah from being fragmented into several Torahs. In the course of the discussion in the Jerusalem Talmud[173] concerning the *mishnah* in Tractate *Pesaḥim* quoted above, R. Simeon b. Lakish asked R. Johanan: "Is this [existence of local customs] not forbidden by the prohibition against the creation of separate factions?" R. Johanan responded: "[This prohibition applies] only if in one place the opinion of the School of Shammai is followed and in the other place the opinion of the School of Hillel is followed," since in that event the *Halakhah* itself would become fragmented. However, if there is unanimity as to the law, but part of the public undertakes to act more strictly than the law requires, there is no fragmentation of the *Halakhah* any more than in the case of individuals, who are free to take a vow to refrain from doing what the law permits.[174]

Despite this theoretical distinction, the halakhic authorities stressed that in practice the diversity of these customs might lead to controversy and schism, and therefore they established the following rules:[175]

> If one goes from a place where they [the people] work [on the eve of Passover before midday] to a place where they do not work, or from a place where they do not work to a place where they work, he is subject both to the restric-

---

Babylonia from the Land of Israel and ate fat *de-yitra* (fat that covers the curved section of an animal's stomach), which the Babylonian Jews treated as forbidden. When some Babylonian Sages entered the room, he covered the dish, on the basis of the rule, "When a custom prohibits what the law permits. . . ." When they told Rabbah bar bar Ḥana's father of the incident, he remarked, "He has likened you to Samaritans," since the restrictive Babylonian interpretation would not have required Rabbah bar bar Ḥana to cover the fat in the presence of the Babylonian Sages unless he considered them to be like Samaritans. However, Rabbah bar bar Ḥana certainly had no intention of insulting them; the original law, as practiced in the Land of Israel, forbade treating something as permissible in the presence of any Jew whose custom was to treat it as forbidden.

172. Deuteronomy 14:1.

173. TJ Pesaḥim 4:1, 26a (4:1, 30d).

174. *See Korban ha-Edah, ad loc.*, s.v. Amar leih be-sha'ah she-ellu osin ke-vet Shammai ve-ellu ke-vet Hillel, and *Penei Moshe, ad loc.*, s.v. Amar leih be-sha'ah . . . ; *see also* TB Yevamot 13b–14a for a more detailed and different discussion of *lo titgodedu.* For a different answer with regard to the prohibition of *lo titgodedu, see* Meiri, *Magen Avot,* Introduction, p. 10, and Meiri's final statement: "One should not have second thoughts and say, 'If this custom was properly instituted, how is it that in some other places they have a contrary practice?' In matters of wisdom, opinions may differ, but all are the words of the living God." *See further* Ginzberg, *Perushim,* Berakhot, I, pp. 152–160, and *infra* pp. 1061–1072.

175. M Pesaḥim 4:1.

> tions of the place from which he departed and to the restrictions of the place to which he went; but one must not act differently [from the local custom], lest this cause controversy.

The rule is thus that, generally, when an individual travels from one place to another, and the customs in the two places differ, he is obliged to follow the more stringent custom.[176] However, if this would mean being conspicuously different from others in the place where he is and this difference might lead to controversy, he must follow the custom of the place where he is, so as to avoid controversy.[177]

IX. CUSTOM AND THE CONFLICT OF LAWS

Custom, especially the different local customs, gave rise to proliferation of different laws on the same subject, so that sometimes the law in one place was contrary to the law on the same subject in another place. When a number of events giving rise to a particular legal obligation have occurred in different places, each with a different law applicable to that obligation, the question arises whether to apply the law of the place where the obligation was created, or the law of the place of performance, or some other law. Such questions of conflict of laws arose frequently in Jewish law against the background of different customs in many fields of law: marriage, divorce, labor, partnership, sharecropping, etc. As a result, elaborate principles governing the conflict of laws were developed. As previously explained,[178] the existence of local legislation from the tenth century C.E. on was also an important factor in the development of conflict of laws within the Jewish legal system. We have dealt elsewhere comprehensively with the rules of the conflict of laws in Jewish law and their development as a result of local custom and legislation.[179]

176. If he intends to return to his own place, he should follow the custom—whether stringent or lenient—of his own place; TB Pesaḥim 51a; Maimonides, *MT,* Yom Tov 8:20. However, even this rule is subject to the qualification that he should not act in a manner opposed to local custom if such action will lead to controversy.

177. *See further* TB Pesaḥim 51b for the interpretation of the end of the *mishnah;* Maimonides, *MT,* Yom Tov 8:20; *see also* H. Albeck, *Commentary on the Mishnah, ad loc.*, and Hashlamot, p. 447. For a more detailed discussion of these laws, *see Peri Ḥadash* to Sh. Ar. OḤ chs. 468 and 496.

178. *See supra* p. 677.

179. *See* M. Elon, EJ, V, pp. 882–890, s.v. Conflict of laws (reprinted in *Principles,* pp. 715–724). The contact between Jewish law and the general law of the countries in which Jews lived also brought about the creation of rules in the field of conflict of laws as a result of the doctrine "the law of the land is law" (*dina de-malkhuta dina*). *See* EJ, *loc. cit.*, and *supra* pp. 64–74.

X. CONTROL BY THE HALAKHIC AUTHORITIES OVER CUSTOM

The spontaneous and undirected development of custom understandably gave rise to many apprehensions. Customs were occasionally based on error, and they sometimes developed in an illogical and unreasonable direction. In addition, custom generated a large number of norms that were contrary to the law, yet valid nevertheless; and this substantial body of norms could well have become detached from the regular system of halakhic law. All of this induced the halakhic authorities to establish a system of review and control over customs. Sometimes, this review nullified or limited a particular custom that was unreasonable or based on error. Sometimes, it ensured that a custom would not contravene the essential and fundamental principles of Jewish law and thereby become impossible to assimilate into the *corpus juris* of Jewish law. A central purpose of this control was to integrate custom into the overall halakhic system by means of the many and variegated methods of interpretation and Scriptural support (*asmakhta*). The following discussion examines how the halakhic authorities exercised control over custom.

A. Custom Based on Error

The Mishnah[180] records a custom in Tiberias in connection with a certain type of bolt that was used to lock the door of the synagogue. The bolt had on its top a movable fastening contrivance. According to R. Eliezer, the people of Tiberias customarily used this bolt to lock the door on the sabbath "until Rabban Gamaliel and the elders came and forbade it to them." However, according to R. Yose, the custom forbade the use of this bolt on the sabbath until "Rabban Gamaliel and the elders came and permitted it to them." The Sages thus abolished the custom: according to one tradition, they permitted a practice previously forbidden; and according to the other, they forbade a practice previously permitted. Apparently, the reason for abrogating the custom was that the custom was based on an error.[181]

Another tannaitic source describes the background for the Sages' nullification of a different custom. The Talmud states:[182]

180. M Eruvin 10:10.

181. *See Tosafot,* Eruvin 101b, s.v. Rabbi Yose omer issur nahagu bo ve-hittiru lahem, which gives this reason for the abrogation of the custom. *See also* Weiss, *Dor Dor ve-Doreshav,* II, p. 63.

182. TB Ḥullin 6b–7a.

> R. Joshua b. Zeriz, the son of R. Meir's father-in-law, testified before R. Judah Ha-Nasi that R. Meir ate a leaf of a vegetable [without tithing it] in Bet-Shean, and R. Judah Ha-Nasi permitted [on the basis of this testimony] the entire territory of Bet-Shean [*i.e.*, its vegetables and fruit could be eaten without tithing].[183]
>
> Thereupon, his [R. Judah Ha-Nasi's] brothers and other members of his father's family joined in a protest to him, saying: "The place that your parents and ancestors used to regard as prohibited, will you now regard as permitted?"
>
> He [R. Judah Ha-Nasi] expounded to them the following verse: "He [Hezekiah] also broke into pieces the bronze serpent that Moses had made, for until that time the Israelites had been offering sacrifices to it; it was called Neḥushtan."[184] [R. Judah Ha-Nasi asked:] "Is it possible that Asa came and did not destroy it, that Jehoshaphat came and did not destroy it? Did not Asa and Jehoshaphat destroy every form of idolatry? It must be that his ancestors left room for him [Hezekiah] so that he could distinguish himself. In my case also, my ancestors left room for me to distinguish myself."
>
> From this is to be learned that whenever a Sage declares a legal rule, we should not try to make him recant.[185]

According to custom, it was forbidden to eat untithed fruit that grew in Bet-Shean. Apparently, R. Judah Ha-Nasi came to the conclusion that this custom was based on an error; produce grown outside the Land of Israel is not subject to tithing, but it had been mistakenly thought that Bet-Shean was part of the Land of Israel in that it had been taken and sanctified as part of the Land by those who returned from the Babylonian exile. He reached his conclusion on the basis of the testimony that R. Meir (of the fourth generation of *tannaim*) ate the fruit of Bet-Shean untithed. The other Sages, and even the members of R. Judah Ha-Nasi's family, opposed the abrogation of the ancient custom that had been followed by his ancestors,[186] but in spite of this opposition, R. Judah Ha-Nasi abolished the custom, since

183. R. Judah Ha-Nasi deduced from R. Joshua b. Zeriz's testimony that Bet-Shean had become part of the Holy Land when it was taken by those who came out of Egypt, but it was not included in the conquest by those who returned from Babylonia; therefore, there was no obligation to tithe produce grown there; *see* the discussion in TB Ḥullin and Rashi, *ad loc.* (fol. 6b), s.v. Et Bet She'an kullah.

184. II Kings 18:4.

185. *See* Rashi, Ḥullin 7a, s.vv. Mi-kan, and Ein mazihin: From the fact that R. Judah Ha-Nasi accepted the testimony and deduced a law from it, despite the surprising nature of the testimony (in Bet-Shean, the prohibition against eating untithed produce had always been observed), we learn that when a scholar declares a novel law no attempt should be made to impugn his tradition or treat it as an aberration by telling him, "Recant! You never heard this novel law."

186. *See also* TB Pesaḥim 50b, where R. Johanan ruled that the residents of Bet-Shean should continue to observe their ancestral custom although conditions had changed.

it was based on a factual error. He therefore permitted eating the untithed fruit of Bet-Shean.

In the third generation of *amoraim* of the Land of Israel, R. Abin laid down a clear general rule as to setting aside a custom based on mistake of fact:

> When one does not know that something is permitted, and mistakenly prohibits it, if he asks [a rabbi] it will be permitted to him; but when he knows that something is permitted, yet his custom is to prohibit it, then if he asks [a rabbi] it will not be permitted to him.[187]

If the prohibitory custom comes into being with the clear knowledge that what the custom forbids is legally permissible, it is a valid custom and may not be set aside; the prohibition stands. However, if based on an error, the custom should be nullified when the error is discovered, and the act prohibited by the custom should become permissible.[188]

In the post-Talmudic period, the halakhic authorities dealt extensively with the question of nullification of customs that were based on error. Rabbenu Tam rebuked those who permitted a minor when holding a Pentateuch to be counted as part of a religious quorum (*minyan*), contending that this was a "nonsensical custom. . . . Is the Pentateuch the same as a man?"[189] On another subject, Asheri investigated the source of a particular custom concerning the testamentary disposition of property by a woman and came to the conclusion that "it is certainly an erroneous custom" and

187. TJ Pesaḥim 4:1, 25b (4:1, 30d).

188. *See* Meiri, *Bet ha-Beḥirah,* Pesaḥim 51a, s.v. Hayu nohagim:

> This is what is meant in the Talmud of the West [*i.e.,* TJ] when it says that when one does not know that something is permitted and mistakenly prohibits it, if he asks [a rabbi] it will be permitted to him; but when he knows that something is permitted, yet his custom is to prohibit it, then if he asks [a rabbi], it will not be permitted to him. The statement that if one asks, it will be permitted [when it was prohibited as a result of error] does not mean that it is permitted only if he asks; rather, it is permitted even if he does not ask. The rule was formulated as it was, namely, "if he asks it will be permitted," because of the latter clause [when the custom was not the result of an error]. Since the latter clause states the rule that even if he asks it will not be permitted, the first clause was also formulated in terms of asking.

This interpretation is very plausible, because if the custom originates in an error, it is void without the necessity of a request to declare it invalid.

189. *Tosafot,* Berakhot 48a, s.v. Ve-leit hilkheta ke-khol hanei shematata ella ki ha katan ha-yode'a. In another matter, regarding the writing of a person's name in a bill of divorcement, Rabbenu Tam objected vehemently to a certain custom: "You have also written that the custom should not be changed because of the ridicule [the change will arouse]; the [Hebrew letters of the] word *minhag* read backwards spell *gehinnom* [Gehenna], and if idiots practice such a custom, the wise do not!" Rabbenu Tam's responsum is quoted in *Shiltei ha-Gibborim* to *Mordekhai,* Gittin, #444, and in Agus, *Teshuvot Ba'alei ha-Tosafot* [Responsa of the Tosafists], pp. 57–58. *See also* Urbach, *Tosafot,* pp. 70–71, 119–120.

that even if the custom was widespread, "it is not a custom that should be relied on for the disposition of property. . . . The custom is erroneous and must be invalidated."[190]

A similar investigation into the source of a custom was made by Mordecai Jaffe with regard to the custom of not reciting the grace after meals in the home of a non-Jew. Jaffe explained that "the spread of this nonsensical custom" is due to an error in the understanding of a Talmudic statement which had no connection whatsoever with this subject.[191] In another instance, a custom arose to take a stringent view that regarded a woman as being married although there was no disagreement that under the law there had been no marriage. Rashbeẓ did not mince words in setting aside this custom: "In circumstances where everyone holds that there is no marriage, but some people wish to impose a stringency on themselves, this is an ignorant custom that the public must not be compelled to follow."[192]

B. Unreasonable or Illogical Custom

At times, the halakhic authorities examined the nature of a custom in order to determine its reasonableness. Thus, it was established that the custom of women not to do any work during the entire evening following the sabbath was unreasonable, and the authorities set it aside except for the time required to recite the usual prayers on the evening after the sabbath.[193] Also, the custom of women not to do any work on Mondays and Thursdays was considered unreasonable and was set aside, but the custom not to do any work on a fast day or on the day of the New Moon (*Rosh Ḥodesh,* a half holiday) was considered reasonable and proper.[194]

Sometimes, customs were abrogated because they imposed hardships on the public and were contrary to the basic purpose of the law. The custom of those who prepared grits in Sepphoris and of the wheat crushers in Acre not to work on the intermediate days of festivals was considered a proper custom as it did not detract from the joy of the festivals; however, the Sages opposed the custom of the fishermen of Tiberias not to work on the intermediate days of festivals, because it was impossible prior to the festival to

190. *Resp. Asheri* 55:10.

191. *Levush ha-Tekhelet,* Laws of Birkat ha-Mazon, 193:6.

192. *Resp. Tashbeẓ,* I, #154; *see also Resp. Ribash* #146; *Resp. Avraham b. ha-Rambam* #89: "And these are new phenomena, and thus mistakes grow and become customs that are observed and defended by those of little wisdom."

193. TJ Pesaḥim 4:1, 25b (4:1, 30c/d); TJ Ta'nanit 1:6, 6a (1:6, 64c); *see* S. Lieberman, *Ha-Yerushalmi ki-Feshuto,* p. 429.

194. TJ Pesaḥim 4:1, 25b (4:1, 30d); TJ Tan'anit 1:6, 6a (1:6, 64c); *see* S. Lieberman, *Ha-Yerushalmi ki-Feshuto,* pp. 429–430.

prepare fresh fish for the entire festival, and the custom therefore detracted from the joy of the festival.[195]

C. "Bad Custom"

In the post-Talmudic period, the halakhic authorities disagreed as to the extent to which a custom in the area of civil law had to be accepted if it appeared to be a "bad custom" (*minhag garu'a*). For example, under the law, when two property owners share a courtyard between them "either one can compel the other to build a wall in the middle so that one will not see the other when he uses his portion, inasmuch as infringement of privacy [lit. "the injury caused by being seen"] is a real injury."[196] The width of the wall follows the local custom "even if the custom is to build a partition between them made of reeds and palm branches."[197]

What is the law if there is a local custom to build a partition made of material that is even weaker than reeds and palm branches? *Tosafot* states that according to Rabbenu Tam, anything less than reeds and palm branches—"even if it is a custom, is an ignorant custom; and he thus concludes that there are customs that should not be relied on, even where the Mishnaic rule is that 'in all things the local practice governs.'"[198] Many authorities agreed with Rabbenu Tam, but others held to the contrary in matters of civil law:

> I do not know of any custom that should not be relied on! It seems to me that if even a weaker partition is the custom, it is within the rule that in matters of civil law, custom is to be followed.[199]

Even those who held that a bad custom should not be followed made

195. TJ Pesaḥim 4:1, 26a (4:1, 30d).

196. Maimonides, *MT*, Shekhenim 2:14, following TB Bava Batra 2a–3a.

197. Maimonides, *MT*, Shekhenim 2:15, following the *mishnah* and the Talmudic discussion. M Bava Batra 1:1 states: "Where the custom is to build of unshaped stones, or of hewn stones, or of half bricks, or of whole bricks, that is the way they should build it; in all things local practice governs." The Talmud asks: "'All things'—to include what?" It responds: "To include a locality where the custom is to build with [only] reeds and palm branches" [TB Bava Batra 4a].

198. *Tosafot*, Bava Batra 2a, s.v. Ba-gevil zeh noten sheloshah tefaḥim; *Piskei ha-Rosh*, Bava Batra, ch. 1, #5, citing Rabbenu Tam, calls this custom an "idiotic custom" (*minhag shetut*); Naḥmanides, Novellae to Bava Batra 2a, s.v. Matnitin, calls it "a custom of fools" (*minhag shotim*).

199. Israel of Krems, *Haggahot Asheri* to *Piskei ha-Rosh, ad loc.*, as a reaction to Rabbenu Tam's opinion (*see also Haggahot ha-Baḥ, ad loc.*, #9). With regard to these conflicting opinions, *see* Naḥmanides, Novellae to Bava Batra 2a; Meiri, *Bet ha-Beḥirah*, Bava Batra 2a (ed. Sofer, p. 6); *Tur* ḤM 157:16; Rema to Sh. Ar. ḤM 157:4, and commentaries, *ad loc.*; *Haggahot Maimuniyyot* to *MT*, Shekhenim 2, subpar. 20; *Mordekhai*, Bava Meẓi'a, #366. *See also supra* p. 900 n. 14, regarding the dispute over the custom to lend orphans' money at interest, and p. 913, regarding certification of a document by only one individual.

exceptions in certain cases, such as in tax matters. Since public order depended on taxes, they ruled that any custom accepted by the public as binding on itself on that subject should be followed, even if it is a bad custom.[200]

D. Integration of Custom into Existing Law: Fundamental Principles of Equity and Justice in Jewish Law

The undirected creation of laws through custom had the potential that laws so created would develop separate and apart from the overall halakhic system. There was particular reason to be concerned that such a result might occur in the area of civil law, where custom could override the law; custom-generated norms contrary to the ordinary rules of Jewish law could become a separate legal system, parallel to but not an integral part of Jewish law. The halakhic authorities resorted to various methods to avert this possibility.

Mention has been made of the principle laid down by Israel Isserlein (with regard to law created by custom in the area of taxation) that an attempt should be made to find "reinforcement and support" for customs in the statements of the halakhic authorities and in reason and logic.[201] This approach was taken not only for tax matters, but for the entire vast body of laws based on custom. The halakhic authorities made every effort to find, as far as possible, "reinforcement and support" for customs in the rules of the *Halakhah*, and to integrate custom-based norms into the overall system of Jewish law.[202]

Moreover, the halakhic authorities carefully examined customs to ensure that they did not contravene fundamental general precepts or the principles of equity and justice in Jewish law; and they invalidated custom-based norms that did not fulfill these basic requirements.[203] Following are a number of examples.

As seen above, the authorities disagreed as to whether the custom of building in a shared courtyard a partition made of material weaker than reeds and palm branches was a bad custom, and hence invalid. What is the law if in a particular place there is a custom not to make any partition at

200. *Terumat ha-Deshen* #342; Rema to Sh. Ar. ḤM 163:3, and commentaries, *ad loc. See also* M. Elon, EJ, XV, p. 845, s.v. Taxation (reprinted in *Principles*, p. 669).

201. *Terumat ha-Deshen* #342, quoted *supra* p. 923. For a detailed discussion, *see* Moses Rothenburg (eighteenth century, Poland), *Resp. Moharam of Rothenburg ha-Aḥaronim* (ed. Lvov, 1857; and *see* the introduction thereto), ḤM, #20.

202. *See, e.g., supra* p. 926, concerning severance pay, which was based on custom but was also connected with the Biblical gratuity for slaves.

203. A similar power existed with respect to communal enactments (*see supra* pp. 760–777) and to the norms that flow from the king's authority and from the doctrine "the law of the land is law" (*dina de-malkhuta dina*), *see supra* pp. 57, 72–73.

all? To this question Rashba responded[204] that such a custom is invalid, and either owner may compel the other to build a partition:

> A custom to pay no attention to infringement of the privacy of houses and courtyards (*hezzek re'iyyah*) is an erroneous custom and no custom at all. One may waive a right only in matters of civil law, where one may give up what belongs to him or may consent to damage to his property; but one is not permitted to "breach the fences of Israel" or act immodestly so as to cause the Divine Presence (*Shekhinah*) to depart from Israel.
>
> For we have learned:[205] "No one shall open up windows facing a jointly owned courtyard," for Scripture states: "Balaam looked up and saw Israel encamped tribe by tribe."[206] What did he see? He saw that the entrances to their tents did not face each other, and this caused him to say, "These are worthy that the Divine Presence should abide with them."[207]

A custom denying the right to require a partition violates the basic principle of the right to privacy guaranteed to every individual in his personal domain, and is invalid because it is contrary to the essential character of Jewish law and "breaches the fences of Israel."[208]

Of course, it goes without saying that there may not always be unanimity of opinion as to whether a particular custom is contrary to a fundamental principle of Jewish law. An instructive illustration of such difference of opinion was discussed above in connection with the effect of custom on the modes of acquisition. As there noted, Asheri held that a custom whereby an oral agreement is effective to consummate a legal transaction conflicts with the basic principle that every legal transaction requires *gemirut da'at* (a clear and deliberate intention) and is therefore a bad custom that should not be followed.[209] However, most halakhic authorities have disagreed with Asheri and have held the custom valid. In the opinion of these authorities, since this is a mercantile custom, the basic requirement of *gemirut da'at* can be fulfilled by oral agreement.[210]

As stated, the halakhic authorities deny validity to customs that violate the principles of justice and equity in Jewish law. This basic requirement has been applied to every custom in every area of Jewish law. For example,

204. *Resp. Rashba,* II, #268.

205. M Bava Batra 3:7.

206. Numbers 24:2.

207. TB Bava Batra 60a; *see also Resp. Rashba,* II, #268, for an extensive discussion of the nature and force of custom in Jewish law.

208. *Cf.* the statement in *Resp. Rashba,* V, #287 and VII, #108, to the effect that communal enactments must "build fences and tend to improve" and not cause the "breaching of fences." *See also supra* pp. 760–762.

209. *Resp. Asheri* 12:3.

210. *See supra* pp. 918–920.

it has been seen that a custom accepted by the public relating to tax matters is valid even if it is a "bad custom";[211] however, the custom must not be so bad as to violate the principles of justice and equity of Jewish law. Consequently, a custom imposing a tax burden without adequately distinguishing between the wealthy and the poor is void:

> There is no validity to the contention of the rich, because it is certainly the law of the Torah that the tax burden should be shared on the basis of financial ability . . . and there is certainly no injustice greater than virtual equality between the rich and the poor in regard to bearing the tax burden. Even though this evil custom has existed for some years, it cannot be permanent and need not be followed in perpetuity.[212]

To summarize: Custom has operated to establish and develop Jewish law in every subject area. Through the medium of custom, the entire Jewish people, including its various groups and classes, have participated in the continued development and creation of the law. At the same time, the halakhic authorities, without constraining this public initiative and creativity, have guided custom into reasonable and logical channels and integrated it to the fullest possible extent with the overall halakhic system, and especially with the fundamental concepts and the principles of equity and justice in Jewish law.

The life of the people has been based on the foundations of the *Halakhah* and its processes. Even if the people are not prophets, they are the "descendants of prophets"; and it is thus to be presumed that their customs are in harmony with the spirit of the Torah. The covert legislation effected by custom operates with full force especially in the area of civil law, the essential corpus of *mishpat ivri.* The final product of this form of anonymous legislation is a faithful and complementary counterpart of the overt legislation of the halakhic authorities and the communal leaders of the people. The joint contributions of both kinds of legislation endow Jewish law with a flexibility and vitality that complement its stability and continuity.

211. *Terumat ha-Deshen* #342.

212. *Resp. Moharam of Rothenburg ha-Aḥaronim, supra* n. 201, ḤM, #20. *See also Pitḥei Teshuvah* to Sh. Ar. ḤM 163, subpar. 16, with slight variances.

Chapter 23
MA'ASEH AND PRECEDENT

I. *MA'ASEH* AS A LEGAL SOURCE

One of the important sources for the development of Jewish law is the *ma'aseh* ("act," "incident," or "event"), called *uvda* by the Babylonian *amo-*

raim,[1] and also *dilma* in the Jerusalem Talmud.[2] These terms as used in a legal context refer to a cluster of concrete factual circumstances with which some legal norm is connected. A norm based on interpretation, legislation, or custom is expressed as an abstract, self-contained legal proposition. By contrast, a norm deduced from a *ma'aseh*—a set of facts having legal significance—is interwoven with a specific situation; in order to apprehend the norm, one must extract it from the particular circumstances.

In other legal systems in which the law develops out of actual situations,[3] the legal source of norms developed in that manner is generally a judicial decision or "case"—an adjudication of a matter resulting from an occurrence in which different people have different interests. In Jewish law, however, the term *ma'aseh* includes not only a decision rendered by a court in an adversary proceeding but also a particular incident involving conduct by a person of acknowledged eminence as a halakhic authority. A particular act performed by such an authority, even if not in his capacity as a judge or decision maker, may, under certain conditions and with certain limitations, be a source for a legal norm in matters of civil as well as religious law.

Certainly, not every event or occurrence constitutes a source for the creation of a legal norm. It is possible, as the Talmud sometimes specifically points out, that the action or decision of a halakhic authority will not create a legal norm but will simply apply an already existing norm that originated in tradition, interpretation, legislation, or custom. In such a case, the *ma'aseh*—the event or occurrence—is not a legal source. It does not create or originate a norm but is merely declarative of an already established norm. However, even a declarative *ma'aseh* possesses special force. In the language of the Talmud, "*ma'aseh rav*"[4] (a *ma'aseh* is of great significance), or "*ma'aseh adif*"[5] (a *ma'aseh* is entitled to particular deference). As Maimonides put it, "Tradition and *ma'aseh* are important pillars of decision making, and should be relied on."[6] A legal norm that has been tested in the crucible of

1. *See, e.g.,* TB Bava Meẓi'a 70a: "What was the actual case (*gufa de-uvda*)?" and the various examples in this chapter, *infra.* There are many other instances of this usage in TB.

2. *See, e.g.,* TJ Berakhot 1:1, 4b (1:1, 2c): "It once happened (*dilma*) that R. Ḥiyya Rabba and R. Simeon b. Ḥalafta were walking in the Valley of Arbel. . . ." Similarly in TJ Pe'ah 3:9, 18a (3:9, 17d): "It once happened (*dilma*) that R. Huna, R. Phineas, and R. Hezekiah were leaving from a visit to R. Yose after three days. . . ." *See also* Jastrow's dictionary, s.v. Dilma (p. 300a), second meaning, and additional sources on this word in Levy, *Wörterbuch. Dilma* meaning *ma'aseh* is of Greek origin, and should be distinguished from *dilma* in TB, where it means "lest" or "perhaps."

3. *See infra* pp. 978–980.

4. TB Shabbat 21a.

5. TB Bava Batra 83a.

6. *MT,* Shemittah ve-Yovel 10:6. Maimonides made this statement in connection with the reckoning of the sabbatical year. In Maimonides' usage, tradition refers to the law as passed down from the *geonim* through an unbroken chain, *id.* 10:5; and *ma'aseh* refers to the custom and practice in the Land of Israel, *id. See likewise Resp. Rashba,* IV, #271.

real life is different from a norm with no record of ever actually having been applied in practice.

In considering the force of *ma'aseh* as a source of new legal norms or as strengthening existing norms, it is important to stress once again the fundamental principle of the entire *Halakhah*—that the Torah was entrusted to the halakhic authorities.[7] These authorities fulfill this responsibility through their judicial decisions and their conduct in daily life, so that even when it is not possible to point to an existing norm as the basis for the decision or conduct of an acknowledged halakhic authority, the very fact that he renders the decision or engages in the conduct verifies that the norm he applies is correct. The Torah was given to be subject to his authoritative opinion, and his decisions and his conduct are the ways in which that opinion is expressed. The judgments and the conduct of a recognized halakhic authority are understood to be the result of his profound understanding of the *Halakhah*, his ability to discern the similarities and distinctions between cases,[8] and his sound perception of the spirit and purpose of the Torah.

Moreover, while a halakhic authority's study and instruction express the *Halakhah*, his acts and conduct actually embody it in living form. "Application and service (*shimmush*) of the Torah rank higher than study of it,"[9] and one of the ways in which an understanding of the Torah is acquired is by "attending upon (*shimmush* [lit. "serving"]) halakhic scholars."[10] R. Meir said concerning the study of Torah, "If you have learned from one teacher, do not say 'That is sufficient,' but go to another scholar and learn Torah [from him as well]."[11] However, he urged even greater dedication to

7. *See supra* pp. 243–247.

8. *See* TB Bava Batra 130b: "All of Torah involves comparing things [*i.e.*, perceiving true relationships]," and TB Eruvin 21b: "He [King Solomon when teaching Torah] clarified a point by the use of a comparable example."

See also Yad Ramah, Bava Batra, *ad loc.*, #133:

> We do not analogize as to deformities that make an animal unfit for consumption . . . but in all the rest of the Torah we do make comparisons [*i.e.*, reason analogically]. Neither all the rules nor all the aspects of a prohibition are explicitly written, so if a matter not explicitly written occurs, one must rely on the aspect most closely analogous to those explicitly written in the Talmud. We also see that the Sages of the Talmud drew analogies in all their discussions and compared one matter with another.

9. TB Berakhot 7b. *See also* TB Temurah 16a:

> When Moses departed [this world] for the Garden of Eden, he said to Joshua: "Ask me concerning all the doubts you have!" He replied: "My Master, have I ever left you for even one hour and gone elsewhere? Did you not write concerning me [in the Torah]: 'But his attendant, Joshua son of Nun, a youth, would not stir out of the tent' [Exodus 33:11]?"

10. M Avot 6:5.

11. R. Meir went on to add an interesting reservation: "And do not go to all [teachers to learn] but to one for whom you have an affinity from the start, as it is said [Proverbs 5:15], 'Drink water from your own cistern, running water from your own well.'"

serving halakhic scholars in order to acquire an understanding of the Torah: "One should attend upon four scholars such as R. Eliezer, R. Joshua, R. Akiva, and R. Tarfon."[12] The knowledge of the *Halakhah* that can be obtained from study alone is on a level of bare abstraction, but attending upon halakhic authorities[13] and following closely their decision making and conduct in daily life leads to an understanding of the living law, which is the real guarantee of the correctness of the *Halakhah* and of the soundness of its creative force.[14]

Ma'aseh as a legal source of Jewish law refers to an event, occurrence, or incident *per se,* that is, to the facts as they occurred in an actual case, but not to a "case" in the sense of a binding precedent. It is not as authoritative precedent that *ma'aseh* is considered to be a legal source. As discussed later,[15] Jewish law, as a general rule, does not recognize the principle of binding precedent. *Ma'aseh* is considered a legal source because an action or an actual legal decision by a halakhic authority is viewed as a source from which to deduce principles that become part of the overall Jewish legal system.

It is indeed permissible to dispute a legal norm established by the decision or conduct of a halakhic authority. However, just as interpretation is concededly a legal source even though different halakhic authorities often deduced different and conflicting norms resulting from different interpretive approaches, so the legitimacy of dissent from the norm implicit in a *ma'aseh* does not diminish the status of the *ma'aseh* as a legal source of law. *Ma'aseh* is a source of Jewish law not because the conclusion derived from it is binding, but because Jewish law recognizes *ma'aseh* to be a method by which halakhic rules are created.[16]

12. *Avot de-R. Nathan,* 1st version, ch. 3 (ed. Schechter, p. 16).

13. Talmudic Sages also served apprenticeships under various craftsmen, even for protracted periods, in order to grasp thoroughly, from practical life, the pertinent factual background necessary to make sound decisions. *See, e.g.,* TB Sanhedrin 5b: "Rav said: 'For eighteen months I was an apprentice to a herdsman in order to learn what constitutes a permanent blemish [that would make a firstling unfit for sacred use] and what is merely a transitory defect [that would not preclude such use].'"

14. For an extreme expression of this sentiment, *see* TB Sotah 22a: "If one has studied Scripture and Mishnah but has not attended upon scholars, R. Eleazar says, 'He is an *am ha-areẓ* [*i.e.,* ignorant].' R. Samuel b. Naḥmani says, 'He is a boor.'" A *baraita, ad loc.,* states: "Who is an *am ha-areẓ?* . . . Others say: 'Even if he learned Scripture and Mishnah but did not attend upon scholars—he is an *am ha-areẓ.*" *See also* E.Z. Melamed, "Ha-Ma'aseh ba-Mishnah ki-Mekor le-Halakhah" [*Ma'aseh* in the Mishnah as a Source of *Halakhah*], *Sinai,* XLVI (1960), pp. 152–156.

15. *See infra* pp. 978–986.

16. The converse is true, according to Salmond (p. 145), in English law: "In other words, authoritative precedents are *legal* sources of law while persuasive precedents are merely *historical.*" (Emphasis in original.) This distinction is not consistent with the definition of "source of law" in the Jewish legal system. *See supra* pp. 229–230, 236–239.

II. THE CAUTION SHOWN BY THE HALAKHIC AUTHORITIES IN THEIR ACTIONS

The recognition by the halakhic authorities of the effect of *ma'aseh* made them extremely cautious and caused them to reflect thoroughly before rendering any ruling, and especially before invalidating a legal rule actually followed in practice. This caution is well expressed in the words of R. Johanan: "Because we perceive the law to be such and such, shall we put it into actual practice (*na'aseh ma'aseh*)?"[17] That is to say: Merely because "we perceive something to be so on the basis of our own reason and opinion," shall we establish that perception as the law to be followed in practice (*le-ma'aseh*) "when we have not heard it from our teachers"?[18]

The same caution is necessary in regard to personal conduct:

> It once happened that our Rabbis came upon Cuthean [Samaritan] towns near the highway [where the observance of the law of tithing was suspect]. Vegetables were brought to them [the Rabbis]. R. Akiva thereupon tithed them because he was sure they had not previously been tithed. This was contrary to the opinion of his colleagues.[19] Rabban Gamaliel the Patriarch turned to him and said: "What prompted you to contravene the views of your colleagues? Who gave you permission to tithe?"[20] R. Akiva responded: "Did I determine the law for Israel? . . . I tithed my own vegetables!" But Rabban Gamaliel retorted: "Know that you have determined the law for Israel in tithing your own vegetables."[21]

In another incident, R. Ishmael explained his great caution in regard to his conduct involving a particular halakhic rule[22] as being based on concern "lest the students see, and establish the law for generations."[23]

17. TB Gittin 19a, 37a.

18. From Rashi, Gittin 19a, s.v. Ve-khi mipenei she-anu medammin, and 37a, s.v. Medammin.

19. According to R. Akiva, it was certain that the Cutheans, *i.e.*, Samaritans, did not tithe their produce; therefore, a Jew eating their produce was required to tithe such produce himself. According to the other Sages, it was not certain that the Cutheans had failed to tithe; it was merely doubtful whether they had tithed, and therefore the rules applied to their produce were the same as for *demai* (produce as to which there is suspicion that no tithe has been taken).

20. The query "Who gave you permission to tithe?" was based on Rabban Gamaliel's assumption that R. Akiva had tithed all the vegetables offered them, including those that were for his colleagues.

21. *Tosefta* Demai 5:24, which reads: "'Did I determine the law for Israel?' He said to him (*amar lo*), 'I tithed my own vegetables.'" S. Lieberman, *Tosefta ki-Feshutah, ad loc.*, suggests that the correct reading is not *amar lo* but *ve-ha-lo* ("But wasn't it [my own vegetables that I tithed?"])

22. Relating to reciting the *Shema* in the evening, according to the School of Hillel; *see supra* pp. 320–321.

23. TB Berakhot 11a; *Tosefta* Berakhot 1:4 reads: ". . . so that the students not see and settle the law in accordance with your opinion."

Sometimes, a rule that has been applied in practice has a special force that precludes any change even if, at the time of its original application, it was understood that the rule had not yet crystallized. An interesting example is the law concerning the blowing of the shofar (ram's horn) when the holiday of *Rosh Ha-Shanah* falls on the sabbath. When the Temple was still standing, the rule was, "If the holiday of *Rosh Ha-Shanah* falls on the sabbath, the shofar was blown in the Temple, but not outside the Temple."[24] After the destruction of the Temple, Rabban Johanan b. Zakkai sought to endow Yavneh—the spiritual center of the people, where the Sanhedrin sat—with a special status in regard to the blowing of the shofar, similar to the previous status of Jerusalem. A *baraita* recounts:[25]

> Our Rabbis taught: Once, *Rosh Ha-Shanah* fell on the sabbath and all the [people of the] towns assembled [in Yavneh (just as they were accustomed, before the destruction of the Temple, to gather in Jerusalem) to hear the sound of the shofar even on the sabbath]. Rabban Johanan b. Zakkai said to the sons of Bathyra: "Let us blow." They said to him: "Let us discuss." [*I.e.*, let us discuss whether after the destruction the shofar should be blown on the sabbath in Yavneh just as it had been previously blown on the sabbath in Jerusalem]. He said to them: "Let us blow and afterwards discuss." After they had blown, they said to him: "Let us discuss." He said to them: "The shofar has already been heard in Yavneh, and the act having been done, debate is now pointless."

The law was thus established that the shofar should be sounded in Yavneh on a *Rosh Ha-Shanah* that falls on a sabbath; and in spite of the fact that the matter had not been fully discussed, the law would not be abrogated. The *ma'aseh* had already occurred and could not be undone.

III. *MA'ASEH* IN JUDICIAL DECISION MAKING

In the Jewish legal system, laws based on *ma'aseh* constitute a very significant portion of the *corpus juris*. Moreover, the nature of Jewish law and the way in which it has developed have made it *par excellence* a legal system based on cases that, taken together, form a comprehensive system of case law.[26] The Torah itself bears witness to this characteristic of Jewish law; many laws in the Torah are based on actual events, such as the law relating

24. M Rosh ha-Shanah 4:1.

25. TB Rosh ha-Shanah 29b.

26. The literature of Jewish law also bears the imprint of this characteristic of the Jewish legal system. *See infra* pp. 1072–1078, 1211–1214.

to a blasphemer,[27] a woodgatherer on the sabbath,[28] inheritance by daughters,[29] and the Second Passover.[30] In all these instances, Moses brought the matter before God, and the decision that came from Him established the law.

In Talmudic literature, a vast number of rules in all areas of the law are reported in the literary-legal form of *ma'aseh, i.e.,* either as a decision of a case or as a pronouncement of an abstract and self-contained rule of law accompanied by a report of some incident or occurrence. It is clear, as shown below, that the *ma'aseh* is not always the original legal source of the rule; sometimes the *ma'aseh* is cited to buttress an already existing rule or an opinion of one authority who differs with another on a particular issue.[31] Nevertheless, many Talmudic sources, from both the tannaitic and amoraic periods, indicate that the rule in question was deduced from the *ma'aseh, i.e.,* that the event was the source of the rule. Sometimes this is explicitly stated in the Talmud itself, sometimes it is implicit from the context, and sometimes it is apparent from a comparison of parallel Talmudic sources when one of the sources discloses the origin of the rule mentioned in the other. The following are several such instances.

A. The Tannaitic Period

1. PREPARATION AND SIGNING OF LEGAL INSTRUMENTS

The Mishnah in Tractate *Gittin* states:[32]

> A woman may write her own *get* (bill of divorcement) [and give it to her husband for the purpose of obtaining the witnesses' signatures and then delivering it to her]; and a man may write his own receipt [the receipt that the woman gives to her husband after the payment of her *ketubbah*], since the *get* is validated only by the signatures on it. [*I.e.,* what gives the document its validity is the signatures of the witnesses, and it is therefore immaterial whether it is actually written by the wife or the husband.]

This *mishnah* thus lays down the rule that when someone must deliver a legal instrument, he need not write it himself, so long as he obtains the signatures of the witnesses, inasmuch as it is not the act of writing but the attestation of the witnesses that validates the document.

27. Leviticus 24:10–23.
28. Numbers 15:32–36.
29. Numbers 27:1–11.
30. Numbers 9:6–14. *See also supra* p. 237 n. 34.
31. For examples, *see* Weiss, *Dor Dor ve-Doreshav,* III, p. 20 and n. 2; Melamed, *supra* n. 14 at 156ff., and his summary at 166.
32. M Gittin 2:5.

The text of this *mishnah* does not reveal whether the original source of this rule was interpretation, legislation, custom, or something else. However, the rule is also set forth elsewhere, and there its original source is clearly stated. Thus, the Mishnah in Tractate *Eduyyot* states:[33]

> He [R. Hananiah, the deputy High Priest] also testified concerning a small village in the vicinity of Jerusalem in which there was an old man who would lend money to all the people of the village. He would write [the promissory notes] in his own handwriting and others would sign [as witnesses].
>
> A case [involving this practice] was brought before the Sages, and they permitted it [in spite of the fact that the witnesses had not followed the practice common at the time, which was for them to write the instrument as well as to attest it by their signatures].[34] Hence, it may incidentally be deduced from this case that a wife may write her own *get* and the husband may write his own receipt, since the *get* is validated only by the signatures on it.

This *mishnah* explicitly states that the original source of the rule recorded in Tractate *Gittin* was the actual case involving the old man and the promissory notes that were signed but not written by the witnesses, and that the Sages nevertheless held to be valid and effective instruments.

2. GROUNDS FOR RELEASE FROM A VOW

In the example just discussed, the Mishnah explicitly states that the *ma'aseh* was the source of the law ("it may incidentally be deduced from this case"). Often, the Talmud does not explicitly state that a particular rule is based on a *ma'aseh,* but it appears that the source of the rule was a *ma'aseh* described in the immediate context. The following are two illustrations.

The Torah states in regard to vows[35] that a husband may annul the vows of his wife and that a father may annul the vows of his daughter. According to early Talmudic law, a Sage may annul a vow improvidently made by anyone. One who made such a vow would come to the Sage to be absolved from it, and the Sage would inquire into the motive for the vow in order to find an "opening" for absolution.[36] The Talmud lists a number of grounds that constitute a sufficient "opening." Concerning one of these grounds, the Mishnah states:[37]

> A wife's *ketubbah* [the payment of which must be made by the husband to the wife at the time of divorce] is a sufficient "opening" for a man [who vowed not to derive any benefit from his wife. The vow would preclude con-

33. M Eduyyot 2:3.
34. *See* H. Albeck's commentary, *ad loc.*
35. Numbers 30:2–17.
36. *See* H. Albeck, Introduction to M Nedarim, pp. 140–141.
37. M Nedarim 9:5.

jugal relations with her and he therefore would be obligated to divorce her and pay her the amount of her *ketubbah* unless he is absolved from his vow.]

It happened that a man vowed not to derive any benefit from his wife, and her *ketubbah* amounted to four hundred *denarii.* He came before R. Akiva, who ordered him to pay her *ketubbah.*

He [the husband] said to him [R. Akiva]: "Rabbi, my father left an estate of eight hundred *denarii,* of which amount my brother took four hundred and I took four hundred; is it not enough that she should receive two hundred and I two hundred?"

R. Akiva replied: "Even if you sell the hair of your head [even if you must sell the hair of your head for your sustenance, since you will be left with nothing], you must pay her *ketubbah.*"

He answered: "Had I known that this is so, I would not have vowed."

Thereupon, R. Akiva absolved him [from the vow, since it had become clear that the man had acted improvidently and did not foresee all of the consequences that would follow from his vow].

This *mishnah* first states the rule that a wife's *ketubbah* is a sufficient "opening" to absolve a man's vow and then recites the facts of the case brought before R. Akiva. However, it is probable that in point of historical fact the sequence was the opposite, *i.e.,* first came the case in which R. Akiva decided that the husband's ignorance of the fact that he would be obligated to pay the entire *ketubbah* to his wife though he would be left a pauper was a sufficient ground for absolution from the vow; and this decision by R. Akiva was the source of the rule establishing a new ground for release from a vow. Later, the editor of the Mishnah, following the style typical of a legal code, first set down the legal rule, and then set forth the case from which the rule was derived.

3. SURETYSHIP UNDERTAKEN AFTER CREATION OF THE PRINCIPAL DEBT

Concerning the laws of suretyship, the Mishnah states:[38]

If a surety signs after the signatures to a promissory note [*i.e.,* below the signatures of the witnesses], the creditor may recover from the [surety's] "free" property. [If the creditor cannot recover from the debtor, he may recover from the surety's "free" assets but not from his "encumbered" assets, *i.e.,* not from property that in the meantime had been sold to a third party, since there are no witnesses' signatures attesting to the surety's obligation, and recovery from the "encumbered" assets is possible only when an obligation is evidenced by an instrument signed by two witnesses.]

A case was brought before R. Ishmael, who declared: "The debt may be recovered from the [surety's] free property."

38. M Bava Batra 10:8.

> Ben Nanas said to him: "The debt may not be recovered either from encumbered property or from free property" [*i.e.*, the suretyship has no validity and the surety has no obligation at all].
>
> He asked him: "Why?" He replied: "It is as if he [the creditor] were strangling him [the debtor] in the marketplace [*i.e.*, the creditor was pressing the debtor to pay the debt] and his friend came upon him and said 'Leave him alone.' He [the surety] is not liable, because the money was not loaned on the strength of trust in him [*i.e.*, the loan was not given on the strength of the creditor's reliance on the surety, since the suretyship was not created until after the loan was made].
>
> "When, then, is a surety liable? 'Give him the loan and I will pay you' [*i.e.*, when the surety states to the creditor before the loan is made: 'Lend him the money and I will pay you']. [In such a case], he [the surety] is liable, since he [the creditor] lent him [the debtor] the money because of trust in him [the surety]."

This *mishnah* teaches a fundamental rule of the Jewish law of suretyship. According to the early halakhic rule, an individual is liable as surety only if the suretyship preceded the loan and was the basis on which the creditor agreed to lend.[39] R. Ishmael, in a case brought before him, decided that even one who becomes a surety after the loan has been made is liable if he signs below the signatures of the witnesses. However, Ben Nanas disagreed, maintaining that no surety can be liable unless his obligation was undertaken before the loan was made. The source of the rule that an enforceable suretyship obligation may arise even after a loan has been made is the case brought before R. Ishmael; however, the editor of the Mishnah first stated the rule deduced from the case, and then described the case itself.

B. The Amoraic Period

Ma'aseh in the form of judicial decision continued in the amoraic period to be a source for the creation and development of every field of Jewish law. The following are some examples.

1. LAWS CONCERNING CONVERSION TO JUDAISM

The Talmud states:[40]

> Rabbah said: "An incident (*uvda*) occurred in the academy of R. Ḥiyya b. Rabbi. R. Joseph taught [that] R. Oshaiah b. Rabbi [was also present], and

39. *See id.* 10:7: "If one lent his fellow money on the security of a surety . . . ," *i.e.*, if the loan was made on the strength of the guaranty.

40. TB Yevamot 46b.

> R. Safra taught [that] R. Oshaiah b. Ḥiyya [was also present—*i.e.*, a case came before these three *amoraim*].[41]
>
> "There came before him [them][42] a proselyte who had been circumcised [for the purpose of conversion] but who had not yet performed the ablution [in the ritual bath].
>
> "They said to him: 'Wait here until tomorrow and we shall arrange for your ablution' [in order to complete the conversion process].
>
> "From this incident, three rules may be derived: it may be deduced that conversion requires the presence of three [*i.e.*, since conversion is a judicial act, it must be carried out by three judges, like any other judicial proceeding that requires three judges];[43] it may be deduced that a man is not a proselyte until he has been circumcised and has also performed the ablution; and it may also be deduced that the ablution of a proselyte may not take place at night [since a judicial proceeding can take place only during the day, and for this reason they told the proselyte to wait until the next day for ablution in the ritual bath]."

The Talmud then raises the following question:

> Should we not say that it may also be deduced that experts are required [*i.e.*, why does Rabbah not deduce an additional rule from this case, namely, that conversion must take place before specially qualified judges, since the three mentioned were among the leading *amoraim*]?

The Talmud responds:

> Perhaps they came together only by chance [*i.e.*, it is possible that it was only by coincidence that these three leading scholars came together for that conversion; they may not have been deliberately convened as a court by reason of their particular qualifications].[44]

The *amoraim* thus deduced from an actual case three rules concerning conversion: one rule that conversion requires, in addition to circumcision, ablution in a ritual bath—an issue that had been a subject of dispute in the tannaitic period;[45] and two rules that originated in the amoraic period, namely, that conversion must be performed before three persons, and con-

41. *See* Rashi, *ad loc.*, s.vv. Uvda hava, and Ve-rav Safra matnei.

42. According to Asheri, the reading is not *lekammeih* (before him), but *lekammayhu* (before them). *See Piskei ha-Rosh*, *ad loc.*, end of #33.

43. *See* TB Yevamot 46b and *supra* pp. 346–347.

44. But that three are needed can properly be deduced: it is not assumed that they came together only by chance, for the *amoraim* who reported the case were careful to stress that there were three there. *See* Rashi, *ad loc.*, s.v. Dilma de-ikle'u, and *Tosafot*, *ad loc.*, s.v. Shema minah de-ger ẓarikh sheloshah.

45. *See* TB Yevamot 46a/b for the difference of opinion among R. Eliezer, R. Joshua, and the other Sages.

sequently cannot be performed at night. Finally, it is noteworthy that the *amoraim* were careful not to deduce any rules that did not necessarily follow from the circumstances; therefore, they did not draw any conclusion as to whether the judges had to have special qualifications.[46]

2. LAWS CONCERNING RETURN OF LOST PROPERTY

In the previous example, the Talmud specifically stated that the legal rule arose out of an actual incident. However, like the Mishnah during the tannaitic period, the Talmud during the amoraic period did not always explicitly so state; but even in such instances a comparison of parallel sources often makes clear that the origin of a particular rule was an actual incident. The following is an example.

The Mishnah establishes that the law requiring the return of lost property (Deuteronomy 22:1–3) applies only if the property has been found in a condition indicating that it was lost by its owner, and in that event the finder must take possession of it and publicly announce that he has found it. Thus, "if one finds fledglings tied together behind a fence or wall or on a trail through a field, he must not touch them,"[47] because the circumstances indicate that the owner of the fledgings deliberately left them in such a secluded place with the intention of returning and retaking possession of them; the property is not deemed to be lost and may not be removed.

The Babylonian Talmud states:[48]

> R. Abba b. Zavda said in Rav's name: "Whenever it is doubtful whether an item of property has been [deliberately] placed [*i.e.*, if the property is found in circumstances such that it is uncertain whether the owner left it there intentionally or whether it was lost], one should not remove it, but once it has been removed, one may not return it [to the place from which it was taken]."

This rule, which is quoted in the Babylonian Talmud as an abstract rule in the name of R. Abba b. Zavda, appears in the Jerusalem Talmud[49] in the form of an incident involving the same *amora:*

> R. Abba b. Zavda found a donkey covered by a leather blanket and took it. He went and asked Rav [what to do with it]. He [Rav] said to him [R. Abba b. Zavda]: "You did not act correctly" [because it is possible that the owner intentionally left the donkey in that place and it was not lost at all].
>
> He [R. Abba b. Zavda] asked him [Rav]: "Should I return it to its

46. *See infra* pp. 960–968 on distinguishing between the material and the immaterial parts of a *ma'aseh.*

47. M Bava Meẓi'a 2:3.

48. TB Bava Meẓi'a 25b.

49. TJ Bava Meẓi'a 2:4, 7a (2:4, 8c).

place?" He responded: "No, because it is possible that the owner returned to the place where he left the donkey, did not find it, and abandoned [lit. "despaired of"] it."[50]

The source of the rule is thus an actual incident (*ma'aseh*), in which Rav rendered a decision for R. Abba b. Zavda. In the Jerusalem Talmud, this rule is preserved in the form in which it originated,[51] *i.e.*, as a *ma'aseh;* but by the time it appeared in the Babylonian Talmud, it was in the form of an abstract rule of law stated in the name of the very same *amora.*

The Talmud also contains instances of abstract rules immediately followed by a description of a *ma'aseh* that the context indicates was the source of the rule. For example, a *baraita* states[52] that if the finder of a lost article is an old man and it would be beneath his dignity to take possession of it and to attempt to return it to its owner, he may ignore it. In the course of the discussion of this subject,[53] Rabbah said: "If he struck the animal, he is under an obligation to take it," *i.e.*, if the old man gave the lost animal a single blow so that it should go back to its owner, he is obligated to take it and return it to its owner; he may not leave it in its place. The Talmud then states:

> Abbaye was sitting before Rabbah [who was his teacher] when he saw some goats that were unattended. He took a clod of earth and threw it at them. He [Rabbah] said to him [Abbaye]: "You have obligated yourself with regard to them. Get up and return them to their owner."

Thus, in an actual incident, Rabbah ruled that inasmuch as Abbaye had begun in some form to deal with the lost goats, he was bound to continue to attend to their return to their owner, even though he could have ignored them altogether because it would have been beneath his dignity to deal with them. The legal rule emerged from this incident. Here, too, the Talmud sets out the abstract rule before describing the event out of which the rule developed.[54]

50. ". . . rather, announce it publicly and let the owner appear and retake his property"—*Penei Moshe, ad loc.* The indication from TJ is that the incident involved a chattel with a distinguishing mark. The implication of TB is that this was not the case. *See* Rashi, Bava Meẓi'a 25b, s.v. Safek hinu'aḥ; *Tosafot, ad loc.*, s.v. Ve-im natal lo yaḥazir; Rashi, Bava Meẓi'a 37b, s.v. Ve-ha amar R. Abba bar Zavda safek hinu'aḥ.

51. R. Abba b. Zavda was an *amora* of the Land of Israel who went to Babylonia to study and later returned to the Land of Israel.

52. TB Bava Meẓi'a 30a.

53. *Id.* 30b.

54. For many more examples of *ma'aseh* involving judicial decisions, *see* the bibliographical references in this chapter. *See also supra* pp. 402, 523–524 as to the difference of opinion between the schools of Shammai and Hillel recorded in M Yevamot 15:1–2 concerning the method of interpreting legal principles of which *ma'aseh* is the source.

IV. *MA'ASEH* IN THE CONDUCT OF HALAKHIC AUTHORITIES

As previously noted, not only a judicial decision but also the particular conduct of a recognized Sage can be a source of a halakhic rule. There are many such examples in Talmudic literature, some of which are next discussed.

A. The Tannaitic Period

1. LAWS CONCERNING THE SABBATH

The Mishnah states:[55]

> [On the sabbath,] one may block out the light [such as from a skylight through which the light enters a house] and measure a piece of cloth [in order to determine whether it is large enough to be considered an article of clothing, in which case it can become ritually impure and make other articles impure] or a ritual bath [in order to determine whether the ritual bath has the required minimum size].
>
> It happened in the time of R. Ẓadok's father and Abba Saul b. Batnit that they blocked out the light with a small earthenware bucket, and they tied a bowl [of earthenware] with reed grass to ascertain whether there was an opening of a handbreadth in a barrel [which was material to the question of a transfer of ritual impurity from one place to another]; and from what they did, we learn that one may block out the light and may measure and tie on the sabbath.

This *mishnah* illustrates two points discussed above: first, it explicitly informs us that the rule that one may block out the light and measure a piece of cloth or a ritual bath on the sabbath was derived from an actual incident. Second, although it specifically states that the rule was derived from the conduct of certain Sages, and the conduct thus preceded the rule, the Mishnah nevertheless sets forth the rule before describing the event that was the source of the rule. This is a frequent characteristic of Mishnaic and Talmudic style.[56] Thus, even though an incident may be recounted in the Mishnah after the rule itself has been stated, the incident may in fact be the true source of the rule.[57]

55. M Shabbat 24:5.

56. *See supra* p. 957 for an example of this in a passage in the Talmud (TB Bava Meẓi'a 30b).

57. *See also* H. Albeck, M Shabbat, Hashlamot, pp. 424–425.

2. LAWS CONCERNING THE *SUKKAH*

Sometimes, differences of opinion among the Sages as to what a particular Sage actually did led to disagreement with regard to the legal rule to be derived from his conduct.

The Mishnah states:[58]

> If one's head and most of one's body are in the *sukkah* and his table is in the house [*i.e.*, the *sukkah* is so small that it has no room for a table, but the head and most of the body of one who sits at the table is in the *sukkah*], the School of Shammai holds it invalid [*i.e.*, it is as if one who sits in it sits in the house and has not fulfilled the commandment to dwell in a *sukkah* on the festival of *Sukkot*]; but the School of Hillel holds it valid.
>
> The School of Hillel said to the School of Shammai: "Did it not once happen that the elders of the School of Shammai and the elders of the School of Hillel visited R. Johanan b. ha-Ḥorani and found him sitting with his head and most of his body in the *sukkah* and his table in the house, yet they did not criticize him?"
>
> The School of Shammai responded to them: "Does that incident prove your contention? [*I.e.*, that incident is indeed evidence of the basic law with regard to such a *sukkah*, but it is evidence against your view and supports our view.] They also told him: 'If this was always your practice, you have never fulfilled the commandment concerning the *sukkah* in your life.'"

The conduct of R. Johanan b. ha-Ḥorani and the reaction, or lack of reaction, by the elders of the Schools of Shammai and Hillel to his conduct was acknowledged by both schools to be the source for the rule concerning the minimum size required for a *sukkah*. However, since each one of the two schools had a different tradition as to what actually took place, each adopted the view of the law that was consistent with its version of what happened in the incident involving R. Johanan b. ha-Ḥorani.

B. The Amoraic Period: Assets of a Deceased Proselyte

During the amoraic period, many rules of Jewish law continued to be derived from the conduct of the Sages. Here, too, in some instances this process appears explicitly, and in others it appears from the context of the discussion.

The Talmud[59] discusses the case of a proselyte who died without leaving any heirs. The law is that since there are no heirs,[60] his assets may be

58. M Sukkah 2:7.

59. TB Bava Batra 53b–54a.

60. A proselyte, when admitted into the Jewish faith, is like a newborn infant, *i.e.*, his conversion makes him like a newborn child of the Jewish people. Hence, under Jewish

acquired by any person through the performance of any of the modes of acquisition. The Talmud quotes various rules which indicate that acts which are generally not considered sufficient as a mode of acquisition are sufficient to acquire assets of a proselyte who dies leaving no heirs. Such property is in effect ownerless; and, therefore, any act is sufficient if it indicates that the actor regards himself as responsible to care for, maintain, and improve the property. In this regard, the Talmud states:[61]

> Rav said: "If one draws a picture or design on the property [*e.g.*, on the walls of a house] of a proselyte, he acquires ownership"; and Rav acquired the garden adjacent to his study hall merely by making such a drawing. [Adjacent to Rav's study hall was a garden that had belonged to a proselyte who died without heirs, and Rav acquired this garden and made it a part of his study hall by decorating it with drawings.]

This illustration is like others already encountered a number of times: The Talmud states the law—that the drawing of a design is a sufficient mode of acquisition—as an abstract statement in the name of Rav, and then immediately indicates that Rav did not state the rule explicitly but that the rule stated in his name is derived from his conduct.[62]

V. DISTINGUISHING A *MA'ASEH*

A. The Process of Distinguishing in Jewish Law

As has been said, the fact that a *ma'aseh* has passed through the crucible of experience lends special force and significance to rules derived from that source. However, the very fact that a rule is enmeshed in a complex of particular facts and circumstances also means that there is always a risk of error in any attempt to derive a rule from such a legal source. Consequently, two critical distinctions must be kept in mind: first, one must distinguish carefully between the factual aspect and the legal aspect of the *ma'aseh;* and second (and more difficult), one must distinguish between the immaterial

---

law, his ties of blood and family become severed; he derives no rights from those who were his relatives prior to his conversion, and he owes them no obligation. Therefore, those who were his natural relatives before his conversion are not his heirs; only those who subsequently become blood relatives—*e.g.*, his children born after his conversion—can be his heirs. As a result, a proselyte may very possibly die leaving no heirs. *See generally* as to this subject TB Yevamot 22a; Maimonides, *MT*, Issurei Bi'ah 14:11–13; Sh. Ar. YD 269:10.

61. TB Bava Batra 54a.

62. *See also* Rashbam, *ad loc.*, s.v. De-rav lo kana le-ginta de-vei Rav: ". . . the statement attributed to Rav was deduced from this incident."

part of the *ma'aseh*—the part that has no bearing on the legal conclusion—and the part that is material to the legal conclusion. Any imprecision or error in making these distinctions is likely to result in an erroneous conclusion.

Sometimes, if the exigencies of a pending case so require, these distinctions will limit or modify a rule derived from a *ma'aseh*.[63] The usual formula used by the *tannaim* for the process of making distinctions is: "This is not the correct inference."[64] The *amoraim* employed the expression, "This was not stated explicitly but by implication," as well as other expressions discussed below. The problem of distinguishing a *ma'aseh* was much discussed in the halakhic literature, especially from the end of the tannaitic period on.

For example, the Mishnah states:[65]

> If A says, "B [who is not a child of A] shall be my heir," when A has a daughter [and certainly when A has a son], or if he says, "My daughter shall be my heir," when he has a son [under the law, if there is a son, a daughter is not an heir], he has said nothing [*i.e.*, his statement is ineffective], since he has stipulated out of a law contained in the Torah.[66]
>
> R. Johanan b. Berokah said: "If he designates someone who is entitled to be an heir [for example, he directs that one of his sons should inherit more than the other sons], his instructions are valid; but if he designates one who is not entitled to be an heir, his instructions are a nullity."[67]

The Talmud's discussion[68] of the disagreement recorded in this *mishnah* is extremely important for a proper understanding of the nature of *ma'aseh*, particularly in regard to the distinguishing of cases:

63. In the common law, which follows the system of case law and professes the principle of *stare decisis* (*see infra* pp. 978–980), the technique of "distinguishing" is highly developed. One of the principal functions of the jurist in this connection is to distinguish between the *ratio decidendi* (the ground of the decision), *i.e.*, the holding of a case, for which the case is binding authority, and the *dictum*, or *obiter dictum* (lit. "something said in passing"), *i.e.*, an incidental expression of opinion that is not essential to the decision and is not binding. The development and flexibility of the common law are in very substantial measure the result of this process of "distinguishing" cases. *See* Salmond, pp. 174ff.; R. Cross, *Precedent in English Law*, 1961, pp. 37ff. and 41ff.; Goodhart, "Determining the Ratio Decidendi of a Case," 40 *Yale L.J.* 161 (1930).

64. M Pesaḥim 1:6–7.

65. M Bava Batra 8:5.

66. *See supra* p. 124.

67. This is true only where the father uses testamentary language purporting to establish an order of succession contrary to that of Biblical law. If, however, he uses language of *inter vivos* gift, the authorities are unanimous that his wishes are effective, even though the result is to deprive his legal heirs of their inheritance. *See* M Bava Batra 8:5.

68. TB Bava Batra 130b.

> R. Zerika said in the name of R. Ammi [who said] in the name of R. Ḥanina [who said] in the name of Rabbi [Judah Ha-Nasi]: "The law is in accordance with the view of R. Johanan b. Berokah."
>
> R. Abba said to him: "He rendered such a decision" [*i.e.*, R. Judah Ha-Nasi did not state as an abstract proposition that the law follows the view of R. Johanan b. Berokah, but he rendered a decision to that effect in an actual case that came before him].
>
> What is the dispute? [Under both versions, did not R. Judah Ha-Nasi decide the law in favor of R. Johanan b. Berokah?]
>
> One Sage holds that a statement of the law is entitled to greater deference, and the other Sage holds that the decision of an actual case has greater weight. [The first opinion is that it is preferable if R. Johanan b. Berokah's view is ruled to be the law as a result of theoretical legal analysis, whereas the second opinion is that it is preferable if the decision was reached in a judgment on the facts of an actual case].

Rashbam commented on this passage of the Talmud as follows:

> [One Sage holds that] "a statement of the law is entitled to greater deference" because it sets forth [as a result of theoretical analysis] the law to be followed; but if the rule is derived from a judgment [*i.e.*, a decision in a concrete case], one may argue that the observer drew an erroneous conclusion. It is possible that the decision was not based on the view of R. Johanan b. Berokah, but rather that one of the sons was awarded all the property for other reasons, such as that the father coupled with his testamentary expression a declaration of gift, which all agree is effective.[69] As we also say, "This was not stated explicitly but by implication" . . . : the observer concludes that the decision was based on one ground, but the actual ground for decision is something else. But when a legal rule is explicitly declared, there is no need to delve any further.

Rashbam's comment points out that in a prescriptive statement of the law the intent is explicit, but the *ratio decidendi* of a case may not be what the observer believes it to be, and in that event the result will be the deduction of an incorrect legal principle from the case. For example, in the case under discussion, one may believe that the basis for the judgment was that the law is in accordance with the view of R. Johanan b. Berokah, whereas in fact the rationale may have been that in that particular case the testator also made a declaration of gift, which everyone agrees is valid because it does not purport to effect a result contrary to Biblical law (which relates only to inheritance and not to gifts).

Rashbam continued:

69. *See supra* n. 67.

"The other Sage holds that the decision of an actual case has greater weight": when a decision is rendered with the intent that it be carried out, it is to be relied on and followed; but when an abstract statement is made that the law is in accordance with a particular Sage, it should not be relied on as a basis for action unless it is specifically stated that it is intended to be applied in practice (*halakhah le-ma'aseh*). . . . For if he stated an abstract rule, it is possible to argue that he said this [as a matter of theory] in the course of study; but if an actual case came before him, he would consider his decision more carefully and thoroughly. As the Talmud goes on to state: "One may not derive a legal norm from academic study"; but when a decision is rendered with the intent that it be carried out, there is no need to delve any further.

According to the second view, a decision in an actual case is more authoritative, because there the law was tested in the crucible of an actual situation, and the decision was reached with greater deliberation and thoroughness than when a prescriptive statement of the law is framed in abstract terms.[70]

Subsequently, the Talmud quotes a *baraita* that sets out the basic guideline for retaining the advantage that comes from deriving legal principles from actual cases while at the same time avoiding the pitfall of drawing erroneous conclusions:

> Our Rabbis taught: One may not derive a legal norm [". . . as a guide for practical conduct"—Rashbam] from academic study (*talmud*)[71]
>
> > ["If a teacher is in the course of study and he declares that the view of Scholar X appears to be correct, his students should not conclude that this is the law, for if an actual case came before him, he would be more thorough and might be convinced by another point of view on the matter"—Rashbam.]
>
> or from an actual case (*ma'aseh*)
>
> > ["One who sees his teacher rendering judgment in a case should not determine the law from it, for it is possible that the ground for the decision in that case is erroneously perceived. This often occurs in the attempt to ascertain the *ratio decidendi*, as it is said, 'The rule was not stated explicitly but by implication,' and there was an error in the reasoning"—Rashbam.]
>
> unless they [the halakhic authorities involved] specifically state that the norm is intended to be applied in practice (*halakhah le-ma'aseh*).

70. For another explanation, *see Yad Ramah, ad loc.*, #132, and comm. of Ritba, *ad loc.*, s.vv. Mar savar and U-mar savar; *see also* Meiri, *Bet ha-Beḥirah, ad loc.*, s.v. Ein lemedin.

71. This reading is found in all the manuscripts, the works of the *rishonim*, and the old printed editions. In current editions of the Talmud, the reading, on account of censorship, has been emended to *limmud* (study). *See Dikdukei Soferim, ad loc.*

> ["Since the issue is posed by an actual case, and all they know about the matter is what he tells them, it cannot be said that they saw a reason of which he was not aware"—Rashbam.]
>
> If he [the student] asks and they tell him that the norm is intended to be applied in practice, he may go and apply it in practice.
>
> ["He may continue to do so in the future, and it is unnecessary to ask for guidance in each such case that comes before him"—Rashbam.]

Thus, to be able to derive a legal rule from a *ma'aseh,* one must be certain that he has full knowledge of all of the facts. In that event, it cannot be said that misapprehension as to the facts caused error in determining the *ratio decidendi.*[72]

This guideline for the method of deriving a legal rule from a *ma'aseh* does not detract from the use of *ma'aseh* as a legal source, which continued to be widespread throughout amoraic and post-Talmudic halakhic literature, as will be discussed below. Such a guideline simply ensures the optimum use of the technique of making appropriate distinctions when drawing legal conclusions from a *ma'aseh.* This result can be achieved only if one is fully apprised of the entire incident—the background, the factual details, the question at issue, and the ruling itself, with all of its practical consequences. Only after full consideration of all of this can one correctly distinguish between the factual and legal aspects of the *ma'aseh* and between the facts that are material and the facts that are not.

B. Distinguishing as a Technique in Drawing Conclusions from a Judicial Decision; An Example from the Law of Bailments

The Talmud states:[73]

> It has been said: If a bailee entrusts [a bailment] to another bailee [*i.e.,* if an individual accepts a bailment of personal property and delegates its care to another], Rav said he is not liable [*i.e.,* the transfer of the bailment to the care of another does not subject the first bailee to any greater liability than he would have had if he had kept the bailment himself, since he gave it to a second bailee who is himself an intelligent actor].

72. TB Bava Batra 130b goes on to discuss the methodology of deriving conclusions by analogical reasoning; *see supra* n. 8. *See also* the statements of R. Assi and R. Johanan, *id.;* TJ Pe'ah 2:4, 13a (2:6, 17a) ("R. Hananiah said in the name of Samuel: 'One does not derive a [practical] conclusion from *horayah* [a theoretical lesson] . . .'"); TJ Beẓah 2:1, 10a (2:1, 61b) ("He was propounding [it] to them [the students] as academic, but they took it to be applicable in practice"); TB Berakhot 24a; Shabbat 54a; Yevamot 77a; Bava Batra 109b.

73. TB Bava Mezi'a 36a.

R. Johanan said he is liable [for any damage to the bailment while it is in the possession of the second bailee, since the owner may say to the first bailee, "I entrusted the bailment to your personal care, and I did not want it to be in anyone else's possession"].

R. Ḥisda said that this ruling of Rav was not stated explicitly but was stated by implication[74] [from a decision given by Rav in an actual case, which R. Ḥisda proceeds to describe]. There were certain gardeners who were in the habit of depositing their spades every day [after completing their work] with a particular old woman; but one day they deposited them [not with her but] with one of themselves, who, hearing the sounds of a festive party, went out [to the party], entrusting the spades to that old woman. Between the time that he left and the time he returned, the spades were stolen.

He went before Rav, who declared him not liable. [The case came before Rav; the gardeners who had deposited their spades with this bailee demanded that he compensate them for the loss. They argued that although an unpaid bailee is not liable if the bailment is stolen from him without any negligence on his part, in this case the bailee should be liable because he had entrusted the bailment to the care of the old woman without the consent of the bailors; Rav, however, decided that the bailee was not liable.]

An observer [a student who was present when the decision was rendered] thought that it rested on the ground that the law is that a bailee who entrusts [the bailment] to another bailee is not liable.

But that is not so. [*I.e.*, that is an erroneous conclusion.] The situation there was different, inasmuch as every day they themselves would deposit their spades with that old woman [and therefore the bailee who left the spades with her was entitled to assume that the bailors would not object to entrusting her with the bailment].

By the technique of distinguishing, R. Ḥisda demonstrated that the attempt to regard this case as standing for the legal rule sought to be derived from it was erroneous. It is true that the case involved a bailee who entrusted the bailment to another bailee, and also that Rav decided that the first bailee was not liable; but the complete facts of that case indicate that the reason for the decision was not a general rule exempting from liability a bailee who entrusts the bailment to another bailee, but rather that the facts of the particular case precluded any contention that the bailor would have objected to the entrustment of the bailment to the second bailee.

This distinction, according to which Rav also could agree that as a general rule a bailee who entrusts the bailment to another bailee is liable, paved the way for the acceptance of that rule (as is shown by the contin-

74. Printed editions have *ella mi-kelala* ("but by implication"), but the correct reading is *ella mi-kelala itmar* ("but was stated by implication"); *see Dikdukei Soferim, ad loc.*

uation of the same Talmudic passage[75] and by other sources[76]), since the bailor may validly argue that the protection of the property is a matter of personal responsibility, and he does not wish his property to be in the possession of anyone other than the bailee whom he selected.

C. Distinguishing as a Technique in Drawing Conclusions from Incidents Involving Conduct of a Halakhic Authority; An Example from the Law of Interest

The Talmud states:[77]

> R. Anan said in the name of Samuel: "Money of orphans may be loaned out at interest."
>
> R. Naḥman said to him: "Because they are orphans, are we permitted to feed them with something forbidden? Let orphans who consume what is not theirs join those who left them this money."
>
> He [R. Naḥman] said to him [R. Anan]: "Tell me what actually happened." [R. Naḥman, who could not imagine that Samuel explicitly stated that it is permissible to lend at interest money belonging to orphans, assumed that the source of this rule lay in a *ma'aseh* involving Samuel, and he therefore sought to learn the details.]
>
> He [R. Anan] said to him [R. Naḥman]: "The children of Mar Ukva [the orphans] owned a copper kettle that was in Samuel's possession; he weighed it when he gave it, he weighed it when he took it back, he collected a rental, and he also collected for any diminution in weight. [*I.e.,* Samuel would rent the kettle to others; he would weigh the kettle at the time of the rental and reweigh it when it was returned to him, and he would collect a sum of money for the rental as well as an additional sum if he determined that in the course of its use the kettle had lost some of its weight; and in this way Samuel took care of providing income for the orphans.] If the charge is for rent, there should be no additional payment for loss of weight [since this is included in rent]. If the charge is for loss of weight, there should be no payment of rent in addition [since it is as if the additional payment for its use is made in exchange for delaying until the return of the kettle the demand for payment for the loss of weight; this would appear to be payment in exchange for delay in demanding a sum of money, which partakes of the nature of interest]."

75. TB Bava Meẓi'a 36b: "Rava said: 'The law is that if one bailee entrusts his bailment to another bailee, he [the first bailee] is liable. . . .'"

76. *See* TB Bava Kamma 11b.

77. TB Bava Meẓi'a 70a.

R. Anan thus deduced from this conduct by Samuel that it is permissible to lend orphans' money at interest. However, R. Naḥman responded that R. Anan had reached this conclusion in error:

> He [R. Naḥman] said to him [R. Anan]: "What was done is permitted even for those having full beards [*i.e.*, for anyone—not only orphans], because they absorb the loss of the copper; to the extent the copper is burned, the value [of the kettle] is diminished."[78] [*I.e.*, what Samuel did is permissible for everyone, because the orphans sustained a loss in value in addition to that caused by loss of weight, since burnt copper has less value than unburnt copper. The purpose of the rental payment is thus to compensate for the diminution in value caused by the burning of the copper and not to pay for delay in demanding payment for the loss of weight].

Through a more careful and detailed examination of the particulars of the conduct of Samuel (the disclosure of the fact relating to the additional loss caused by the burning of the copper), R. Naḥman distinguished between Samuel's conduct and the rule which R. Anan derived from it. In this way, R. Naḥman reconciled his view with Samuel's conduct, so that all would agree that it is prohibited even for orphans to lend their money at interest.

The Talmud frequently records distinctions made by the *amoraim* with regard to the conduct of the Sages.[79] Such distinctions often begin with one of the two expressions already mentioned: "This was not stated explicitly but by implication," or "Tell me what actually happened";[80] and generally, although not always, the conclusion resulting from the ensuing analysis is that the derivation of the legal rule from a particular incident was incorrect.

The fact that the Sages often looked for a *ma'aseh* as a source of a particular rule indicates how much they were aware of the function of *ma'aseh* and how highly they valued it as a source for the development and creation of the law.[81] This attitude motivated the Sages to be as careful and

78. These last words, "to the extent the copper is burned, the value [of the kettle] is diminished," are a *gaon*'s addition and were not in the original text of the Talmud. *See Dikdukei Soferim, ad loc.*

79. For many additional examples, *see* A. Weiss, *Le-Ḥeker ha-Talmud* [Researching the Talmud], pp. 111ff.; H. Albeck, *Mavo la-Talmudim* [Introduction to the Talmuds], pp. 452ff. Analogical reasoning and instances of distinguishing cases are also contained in TJ. *See, e.g.*, TJ Kilayim 2:8, beginning with "From the fact that R. Ze'eira raised an objection against [the *dictum* of] R. Johanan there . . ."; *see Penei Moshe* and Solomon Sirillo's commentary, *ad loc.*; TJ Orlah 1:1 (end), 1:3; TJ Shevu'ot 5:5. For further details, *see* Albeck, *supra* at 452–454, 500–504.

80. This latter expression, however, is not used exclusively in the context of the derivation of a halakhic principle from a *ma'aseh*. *See, e.g.*, TB Ketubbot 69a/b, 79a, 104b.

81. It should, of course, be borne in mind that a law may have originated in a *ma'aseh* without having been characterized as "not stated explicitly but by implication" or in some

deliberate as possible in drawing legal conclusions from *ma'aseh*. Abraham the son of Maimonides stressed this point:[82]

> The principle of the matter is this: I say that a judge whose decisions follow only what is explicitly written is weak and indecisive. Such a practice contravenes the [Talmudic] *dictum* that "a judge must be guided only by what his own eyes see." It [*i.e.*, to follow only what is explicitly written] is not correct. However, the written laws are of very great importance; and the judge or decisionmaker must weigh them according to the circumstances of each case that comes before him, analogize his case to those that are similar, and derive branches from those roots.
>
> The many cases recorded in the Talmud, which represent only a fraction of the law, were not written without a purpose. That purpose is not that one should decide the law on a particular matter exactly as written there, but rather to enable the decisionmaker familiar with them, through repeated study, to acquire the power of balanced judgment and the proper approach to deciding cases.

These words are helpful in understanding the nature of *ma'aseh* in Jewish law, the importance that must be ascribed to the technique of distinguishing when deriving a conclusion from a *ma'aseh*, and, finally, the relationship of *ma'aseh* to the doctrine of binding precedent—a question examined later in this chapter.

VI. *MA'ASEH* IN THE POST-TALMUDIC PERIOD

Ma'aseh, in both senses of the term, continued to be an important legal source in the post-Talmudic period, during which the halakhic authorities have derived legal conclusions not only from the decisions and the conduct of the Sages as recorded in Talmudic literature, but also from the decisions and conduct of the post-Talmudic halakhic authorities.

A. Deducing Legal Conclusions from an Incident Recorded in Talmudic Literature

Two examples, taken from Maimonides, illustrate the derivation of a legal principle by the halakhic authorities in post-Talmudic times from an incident recorded in the Talmud.

---

similar way. *See* Weiss, *supra* n. 79 at 130. Indeed, as has been pointed out, the legal source of a considerable number of laws cannot be determined.

82. *Resp. Avraham b. ha-Rambam* #97 (pp. 147–148).

1. LAW CONCERNING THE RECITING OF THE *SHEMA*

The *Mishneh Torah* states:[83]

> If one is engaged in the study of Torah and the time for reciting the *Shema* arrives, he should stop and recite the *Shema*,[84] as well as the benedictions that precede and follow it.[85] If one is engaged in ministering to some public need, he should not stop, but he should finish what he is doing and recite the *Shema* if there is still time to do so.

What is the source for this ruling by Maimonides that involvement in public matters is so important that it should not be interrupted in order to recite the *Shema?* It would appear that, as the Gaon of Vilna pointed out, the source is an incident described in the *Tosefta:*[86]

> R. Judah said: "I was once walking behind R. Akiva and R. Eleazar b. Azariah, and the time came to recite the *Shema*. It is my recollection that they refrained from reciting it, since they were engaged in matters of public concern."

R. Judah observed the conduct of R. Akiva and R. Eleazar b. Azariah, who did not interrupt their activities in order to recite the *Shema*, even though the time to recite it had arrived; and he concluded that the reason was that they were engaged in matters of public concern.[87] This, then, is a *ma'aseh*, in the form of the conduct of two Sages, from which Maimonides derived the rule that one who is engaged in ministering to a public need should not interrupt his activities even if the time arrives to recite the *Shema*.

2. ONE LIFE MAY NOT BE SACRIFICED TO SAVE ANOTHER

It is a fundamental principle of Judaism that one life may not be sacrificed to save another: "The blood of one person is not redder than the

83. Maimonides, *MT*, Keri'at Shema 2:5.

84. There is a fixed time for reciting the *Shema*, which therefore takes precedence over the study of Torah, since such study is not limited to a fixed time but is a commandment that can be fulfilled anytime during the day. *See* TB Berakhot 10b.

85. *I.e.*, the benedictions that are recited in the morning and evening prayers before and after reciting the *Shema*. *See MT*, Keri'at Shema 1:5 *et seq.*

86. *Tosefta* Berakhot 1:2; *see Be'ur ha-Gra* to Sh. Ar. OḤ 70:4.

87. For the meaning of this passage in the *Tosefta*, *see further* S. Lieberman, *Tosefta ki-Feshutah*, Berakhot, p. 3; *see also Tosefta* Berakhot 2:6:

> R. Eleazar b. R. Ẓadok said: "When Rabban Gamaliel and his court were in Yavneh and were engaged in matters of public concern, they did not interrupt [their work for the reading of the *Shema*] so as not to be distracted [from the important business being attended to].

blood of another."[88] This being conceded, the Sages were faced with the poignant question, May one life be sacrificed to save many lives?

The Mishnah states:[89]

> Similarly,[90] if gentiles say to a group of women, "Give us one of you that we may defile her, and if [you do] not [do so], we will defile all of you," let them all be defiled rather than hand over to them even a single Jewess.

The following additional rule is set forth in the *Tosefta:*[91]

> If there is a group of people to whom the gentiles say, "Give us one of you[92] that we may kill him, and if not, we will kill all of you," let them all be killed rather than hand over to them even a single Jew. However, if they specified one of them, as Sheba b. Bichri was specified,[93] he should be given to them, so that all will not be killed.
>
> R. Judah said: "To what situation does this rule [that they may not select a person to turn over to the gentiles when the gentiles have not designated a particular person whom they want] apply? When he is within and they are outside [when the individual who would be given up is within the walls of the city and the gentiles are outside the walls, in which case it is possible that the gentiles will not capture the city, so that even that individual will be saved]; but if he is within [the walls] and they are within [the walls], since he will be killed and all the others will also be killed, he should be handed over to them [even if he is not subject to the death penalty for anything he has done], so that all of them will not be killed.
>
> "Thus it is written: 'The woman came to all the people with her clever

88. *See* TB Sanhedrin 72b, 74a, and the codificatory literature. At the same time, there is a duty to attempt to rescue someone who is in danger. This is an express commandment: "Do not stand idly by the blood of your fellow" (Leviticus 19:16; *see* TB Sanhedrin 73a and the codificatory literature). (The 1985 JPS *Tanakh,* noting that the meaning of the Hebrew is uncertain, has "Do not profit by the blood of your fellow," which loses the sense of the halakhic point here made). *See also* M. Elon, "Ha-Halakhah ve-ha-Refu'ah ha-Ḥadishah" [The *Halakhah* and Modern Medicine], *Molad* (New Series), XXI (1971), pp. 228ff., and *infra* pp. 990–991. As to the complexities of the problems of translating Leviticus 19:16, *see* B. Levine, "On Translating a Key Passage," 1 *S'vara* 71 (1990).

89. M Terumot 8:12.

90. "Similarly" (*ve-khen*) is a transitional connective joining this *mishnah* to the one before it, which is not relevant to the subject here discussed.

91. *Tosefta* Terumot 7:20.

92. *See* S. Lieberman, *Tosefta ki-Feshutah, ad loc.*, in both his short and long commentaries (p. 420), showing that the meaning is: "Deliver to us the particular person of your group in whom the government is interested, but whose precise identity we do not know." In the case described in the *mishnah* where the demand was for a woman to be violated, the demand was not for any particular individual.

93. II Samuel 20. Sheba b. Bichri rebelled against King David. Joab and his army pursued him, and Sheba b. Bichri was killed by the residents of the besieged city, who surrendered him to Joab in order to save the whole city; *see id.*, vss. 21 and 22.

> plan. . . .'[94] She said to them: 'Since he will be killed and you will also be killed, hand him over to them and let not all of you be killed.'"
>
> R. Simeon said: "This is what she said to them: 'Whoever rebels against the kingdom of David is subject to the death penalty.'"

Thus, the rule is that just as one life may not be sacrificed to save another life, neither may one life be sacrificed to save many other lives. However, the Sages disagreed as to when there is an exception to this rule. According to R. Simeon and the *tanna* who stated the first ruling in the *Tosefta,*[95] an individual may not be handed over to save many lives unless he is designated by the gentiles and is subject to the death penalty under the law as a rebel against the kingdom. According to R. Judah, an individual may also be handed over if under the circumstances it appears that otherwise the gentiles will succeed in killing all of them.

Maimonides set forth the law on this question as follows:[96]

> If gentiles[97] say to a group of women, "Give us one of you that we may defile her, and if not, we will defile all of you," let them all be defiled rather than hand over to them even a single Jewess. Similarly, if gentiles say [to a group of men], "Give us one of you that we may kill him, and if not, we will kill all of you," let them all be killed rather than hand over to them even a single Jew.
>
> However, if they specified the individual and said: "Give us So-and-so or we will kill all of you," then if he was subject to the death penalty [for a crime], like Sheba b. Bichri, they may hand him over to them. But one should not instruct them *ex ante* that this is the law. If he is not liable to the death penalty, let them [the Jews] all be killed rather than hand over to them [the gentiles] even a single Jew.

Maimonides ruled, in accordance with the view of the first *tanna* and of R. Simeon as recorded in the *Tosefta,* that even many lives should not be saved at the expense of the life of a single individual unless the gentiles designate a particular individual who has committed a capital offense. Maimonides added that even in such a case one should not instruct *ex ante* that this is the law. The *Tosefta,* however, implies that the rule may be taught *ex*

94. II Samuel 20:22: "The woman came to all the people with her clever plan; and they cut off the head of Sheba son of Bichri and threw it down to Joab. He then sounded the horn; all the men dispersed to their homes, and Joab returned to the king in Jerusalem."

95. According to the first *tanna,* the meaning of "if they specified one of them" is that his identity is known and he is liable to the death penalty. But in TJ Terumot 8:10, 47a (8:10, 46b), R. Johanan and Resh Lakish differed as to whether it is permissible to surrender him only when, like Sheba b. Bichri, he is liable to the death penalty.

96. *MT,* Yesodei ha-Torah 5:5.

97. *Goyim* (gentiles) is the reading in ed. Rome, 1480. In the printed editions, the term is *akkum* (Hebrew acronym for "worshippers of stars and planets"), *i.e.,* idol worshippers.

ante as the law to govern action. What then is the source of Maimonides' qualification? Maimonides' source appears to have been an incident recorded in the Jerusalem Talmud:[98]

> Ulla b. Koshev was sought by the Roman government, [which had sentenced him to death]. He fled to Lydda, where R. Joshua b. Levi was, [and he hid there]. Government soldiers came and surrounded the town. They [the soldiers] said to them [the people of Lydda]: "If you do not turn him over to us, we will destroy the town." R. Joshua b. Levi went up to him [the person harboring Ulla] and persuaded him to give Ulla up, and he turned him [Ulla] over to the soldiers, [who executed him].
>
> Elijah, of blessed memory, used to appear to him [R. Joshua b. Levi] regularly, but did so no longer [after that incident]. He [R. Joshua] fasted a number of times, and he [Elijah] appeared to him.
>
> He [Elijah] said to him [R. Joshua]: "Do I appear to informers?"
>
> He [R. Joshua] said to him [Elijah]: "Did I not do what was stated in the Mishnah [*i.e.*, the *Tosefta*, that if a particular individual is demanded and he is subject to the death penalty, he may be handed over to save many lives]?"
>
> He [Elijah] said to him [R. Joshua]: "Is this the standard of the pious?"

Maimonides integrated the conclusion arising out of this story recorded in the Jerusalem Talmud with the law stated in the *Tosefta:* he ruled that even under such exceptional circumstances as when the particular individual is both specified and subject to the death penalty, the law stated in the *Tosefta* should not be taught as the law to govern action *ex ante;* it operates only to excuse the conduct after the fact.[99] The incident described in the Jerusalem Talmud thus served as an important factor in Maimonides' crystallization of the law on this significant question.[100]

98. TJ Terumot 8:10, 47a (8:10, 46b).

99. *See* Meiri, *Bet ha-Beḥirah,* Sanhedrin 72b, on the principle that "one life may not be sacrificed to save another" (ed. Sofer, p. 270), for Meiri's explanation of TJ's concept of *mishnat ḥasidim* ("standard of the pious"). *See* the detailed discussion in S. Lieberman, *Tosefta ki-Feshutah,* Terumot, p. 422 and n. 141.

100. The following instance, where a post-Talmudic halakhic authority explained an incident recorded in the Talmud differently than the Talmud itself explains it, is worthy of note. M Sanhedrin 7:2 states that "burning" as a method of capital punishment was not by actual burning, but by forcing a burning wick into the mouth of a condemned person. R. Mattnah explained (TB Sanhedrin 52a) that "burning wick" means a molten bar of lead. An incident is then related (*id.* 52b) about R. Ḥama b. Tobiah, a Babylonian *amora,* who condemned a priest's adulterous daughter to death by burning. The sentence was carried out by surrounding her with bundles of twigs and setting fire to them. The Talmud then comments:

> R. Joseph said, "He [R. Ḥama b. Tobiah] erred in two respects: (a) in not following R. Mattnah's statement of the law [according to which a molten bar of lead should have

B. *Ma'aseh* Occurring in the Post-Talmudic Period

Ma'aseh (in the sense both of judicial decision and the conduct of a halakhic authority) continued to function as a legal source in post-Talmudic times. Incidents involving the conduct of a halakhic authority are often recorded in post-Talmudic halakhic literature in the form of accounts by students reporting the conduct of their teachers in regard to numerous issues. Books were written that were largely based on the author's observations of the conduct of his teacher, from whom he learned not merely by precept but also by example while attending upon the teacher in his daily pursuits. An example of this type of book is *Sefer ha-Tashbaẓ* of Samson b. Ẓadok, a

---

> been used], and (b) in not following the tannaitic teaching on the verse 'You shall . . . appear before the priests the Levites and the judge of that time' [Deuteronomy 17:9], as meaning that when the priesthood functions, the judiciary [also] functions, but when the priesthood is not functioning, the judiciary [too] may not function. [*I.e.*, when there is no Temple and the priests perform no Temple service, the court has no power to impose capital punishment, because this criminal jurisdiction exists only when the Sanhedrin sits in the Chamber of Hewn Stone in the Temple.]"

Solomon Luria (Maharshal), *Ḥokhmat Shelomo, ad loc.*, s.v. Ta'ah bi-de-Rav Mattnah, commented:

> I am able to resolve it [*i.e.*, the strange ruling of R. Ḥama b. Tobiah] on the basis that he did not err and that the time was one of emergency; and, therefore, he ordered her to be burnt otherwise than with the molten bar of lead prescribed by Jewish law, so that it should not be said that the Biblical law of capital punishment still operates today. This sentence was a special emergency measure for his time only. . . . [As to the Talmud's comments], I am not setting myself up in opposition to the Talmud, as this has no practical effect on the law and is only for the Messiah [*i.e.*, a point of theoretical law having no operational significance until the Messiah comes].

Maharshal thus took the view that R. Ḥama b. Tobiah deliberately ordered the penalty of burning in a manner not authorized by law, because jurisdiction in capital cases since the destruction of the Temple is restricted to emergencies; and in order to distinguish between judgment pursuant to Biblical law, and criminal jurisdiction based on emergency powers, he deliberately changed the method of execution so that people should not fall into the error of believing that this criminal judgment was pursuant to Biblical law. Thus, Maharshal explained the two "errors" R. Joseph attributed to R. Ḥama b. Tobiah.

The principle of altering the method of execution in criminal cases since the destruction of the Temple for the purpose of avoiding confusion in such cases with criminal jurisdiction pursuant to Biblical law is extensively discussed in a responsum by Maharshal's contemporary, Meir b. Gedaliah of Lublin—*Resp. Maharam mi-Lublin* #138. (This responsum was deleted by the censor in the Warsaw edition but has been reprinted in a recent edition. *See She'elot u-Teshuvot Maharam mi-Lublin ve-Avodat ha-Gershuni*, Brooklyn, 1961, where the responsum is placed at the end of the volume after *Resp. Avodat ha-Gershuni*.)

This responsum points out that although Maharshal concluded that his explanation of the incident (which is contrary to the explanation in the Talmud itself) has no practical legal effect, the fact is that according to his interpretation of the Talmud, we deduce the principle that in order to distinguish the current administration of criminal justice from that of Temple times, a change should be made in the mode of execution. Maharshal's position therefore involves more than merely an academic point that is "only for the Messiah."

disciple of Maharam of Rothenburg.[101] This work deals mainly with the laws contained in the *Oraḥ Ḥayyim* and *Yoreh De'ah* parts of the *Shulḥan Arukh,* and to some extent also with matters of family and civil law; and its rules, to a considerable extent, are based on the conduct of the teacher as the disciple observed it.[102]

The following is an illustration of a *ma'aseh* involving a combination of both the conduct of a halakhic authority and a judicial decision. The issue concerned the law of marriage. The incident is attributed to Rashi, and is recorded by Rabbenu Simḥah, one of Rashi's disciples:[103]

> It once happened that an individual celebrated his betrothal (*erusin*) and marriage (*nissu'in*) on the same day.[104] [What happened was that] his *ketubbah* was written and brought to the elders who were assembling in the wedding-hall. After they arrived, the groom proceeded to betroth his bride; and competent witnesses, who were not related to the couple, were appointed to witness the betrothal. One of the witnesses signed the *ketubbah* for himself and for the other witness.
>
> My teacher [Rashi] was informed of this and took exception. My teacher said: "That witness made two errors. First, the witnesses to the betrothal may not sign the *ketubbah,* which should be signed by the witnesses to the delivery of the *ketubbah.* Second, he signed for the other witness; and one witness may not sign for his co-witness. Witnesses sign a document only for the 'public good': one of them may subsequently travel abroad and the court will show the document to the other witness to verify his signature and the signature of his co-witness, or if none of the witnesses are present, others will recognize their signatures.
>
> "Now [in this case] a document will be presented with the signatures in the handwriting of [only] one witness and no signature by the other witness, or the other witness will appear before us and be shown his signature on the

101. *Sefer Tashbaẓ min Rabbenu Shimshon b. R. Ẓadok Zaẓal, im Perush Shiv'at ha-Nerot le-Rabbi Moshe Beẓalel b. R. Shraga Feibush mi-Sochawlie* [*Sefer ha-Tashbaẓ* of R. Samson b. R. Ẓadok with Commentary "Seven Lights" by R. Moses Beẓalel b. R. Shraga Feibush of Sochawlie], Warsaw, 1901. The book has also been published in other editions. Care should be taken not to confuse it with another book with a similar name, *Resp. Tashbeẓ,* a book of responsa by Simeon b. Ẓemaḥ Duran (Rashbeẓ), of North Africa, in the fourteenth century.

102. The very first paragraph begins: "Maharam usually dined on sabbath eve at sunset and did not wait until it was actually night. . . ." For similar observations, *see* pars. 7, 18, 19, 20, 21, 22, 23, and many more.

103. *Maḥzor Vitry,* p. 588; *Sefer ha-Orah,* II, ch. 12. There are slight variations between the two versions.

104. According to Talmudic law, betrothal (*erusin* or *kiddushin,* effected by giving money or a ring to the bride) takes place some time before the nuptial ceremony (*ḥuppah* or *nissu'in,* the entrance under the nuptial canopy). *See Maḥzor Vitry* and *Sefer ha-Orah* for a discussion of the law on this subject before the incident described here took place. At the time of the incident, *i.e.,* the eleventh century C.E., there were some who had already begun to celebrate the betrothal and the nuptials together, as is the practice today.

document and asked whether it is his handwriting, and he will then not recognize his signature [since in fact it was not his]. Consequently, the document is invalid."

Thereupon, my teacher ordered that the witnesses' signatures be erased so that the *ketubbah* would not be invalid, since the [improper] signing did not validate it, but in fact rendered it invalid; witnesses' signatures to a *ketubbah* are the same as signatures to all other documents, since a *ketubbah* is like all other documents.

Since the signatures of witnesses to a *ketubbah,* as in the case of other documents, have only an evidentiary purpose and are not an integral part of the document, Rashi ordered that both signatures be erased, inasmuch as a *ketubbah* without the signature of any witnesses is substantively valid, whereas a *ketubbah* signed by witnesses in an improper manner, as occurred in this incident, is invalid.[105]

C. *Ma'aseh* and the Responsa Literature

With the development of the responsa literature as one of the main literary sources of Jewish law in the post-Talmudic period, *ma'aseh* played a highly important role as a legal source. The nature and unique features of the responsa literature will be discussed later;[106] at this point, a few observations about the responsa literature and its relation to *ma'aseh* will suffice.

Responsa literature is the "case law" of the Jewish legal system. Actual problems arising out of daily life—whether involving relationships in human society or the relationship between people and God, and whether pertaining to *mamon* (civil law) or *issur* ("religious" law)—were brought before the local judge or halakhic authority; and if he was in doubt or had difficulty in finding a solution to the problem, he would turn for guidance to the leading halakhic authorities of the generation. Certain matters, especially disputes between an individual, on the one hand, and the public and the communal government, on the other, were brought directly to the leading halakhic authorities. These authorities would examine and consider all

105. Rashi's *Sefer ha-Orah* and *Sefer ha-Pardes* contain further examples of laws that Rashi's students derived from their teacher's conduct. *See* A.M. Lifshitz, *Rashi,* p. 135, n. 27. For a *ma'aseh* involving conduct, *see also Resp. Ribash* #124, and for a *ma'aseh* involving a judicial decision, *see Resp. Rashba,* I, #1146.

An interesting example of the derivation of a legal rule from an actual case involves a matter submitted to Rabbenu Tam relating to delay of the burial of a debtor (*Or Zaru'a,* III, Piskei Bava Batra #199, p. 30a; *Haggahot Asheri,* Bava Batra, ch. 9, #32, codified as law by Rema to Sh. Ar. ḤM 107:2). For a detailed discussion, *see* Elon, *Ḥerut,* pp. 238–241. This rule was eventually eliminated from the Jewish legal system because it was in conflict with the basic principles of Jewish law. *See id.* at 241ff.

106. *See infra* pp. 1453–1528.

of the factual and legal particulars of the case, record their findings and conclusions in a written responsum, and send the responsum to whoever had sought their opinion.

The responsum is thus an obvious example of a *ma'aseh* in the sense of a judicial ruling as to the law applicable to an actual, concrete problem. The responsum fulfills all of the requirements for a *ma'aseh* to be considered a legal source: it meets the standard of the *baraita* quoted above:[107] "If he [the student] asks and they tell him that the norm is intended to be applied in practice, he may go and apply it in practice." This quality of living law, which is the essence of every responsum, has endowed the law derived from a responsum with a special standing and force exceeding that of the law based on commentaries or novellae.[108] Indeed, most halakhic authorities rank rules derived from responsa even higher than those based on the codificatory literature,[109] to the point of resolving an inconsistency between a code and a responsum in favor of the responsum.

The special force of a decision in a responsum has been extensively discussed and explained in the writings of the halakhic authorities. Two responsa are pertinent examples. The first is by Maharil (Jacob b. Moses ha-Levi Moellin, one of the leading halakhic authorities in Germany at the end of the fourteenth century):[110]

> As to what you wrote about not being able to rely on responsa, the contrary is true. Responsa embody decisions in actual cases, and we may learn more from them than from the statements of the codifiers, since they [the codifiers] did not write their conclusions in the process of determining the law for a concrete situation, as is stated in chapter *Yesh Noḥalin*.[111] For this reason, the Talmud in many places specifically states: "It is a law intended to be applied in practice"; and [the book] *Or Zaru'a*[112] also states this many times to make clear that the matter is beyond doubt or dispute. The responsa in actual cases constitute the law to be applied in practice. All of our rabbis after the com-

107. *See supra* pp. 963–964; TB Bava Batra 130b.

108. As to commentaries and novellae, *see infra* pp. 1104–1137. *See also* Meiri, *Bet ha-Behirah*, Introduction (ed. Dickman, Berakhot, 1960, p. 28):

> And I must tell you, as a general rule, . . . anyone who is not fully aware of how cases on the subject have actually been decided will often not understand the true meaning [of the text] . . . and as God lives, many a time in the study of a halakhic discussion in the Talmud, I have had the experience of thinking that I had found the correct interpretation, but when I researched the decisions of my predecessors in order to become familiar with the law as actually applied, . . . I realized that I had not really understood the passage correctly.

109. As to the codificatory literature, *see infra* pp. 1138ff.

110. *Resp. Maharil* #72.

111. The reference is to the *baraita* in TB Bava Batra 130b, quoted *supra* pp. 963–964.

112. As to *Or Zaru'a, see infra* p. 1241.

pletion of the Talmud cite [and rely on] prior responsa; and for us, who are like orphans of orphans, all the more so should this be the case.

The rationale given by Maharil for according greater weight to a rule derived from a responsum than to a rule based on a code (although the aim of both types of works is to ascertain the correct rule) is that the author of a responsum seeks and finds the rule in the course of deciding a concrete case that has actually arisen in real life, and he comes to his conclusion as part of the process of adjudication. The author of a codificatory work, on the other hand, arrives at his conclusion solely in the course of academic study.

Relatively recently, this fundamental question was again considered by one of the leading *aḥaronim*, Naftali Ẓevi Judah Berlin (Neẓiv), the head of the *yeshivah* of Volozhin. Neẓiv responded to Moses Aryeh Bamberger, the rabbi of Kitzingen, Germany, who had sought advice as to whether he should publish the responsa of his father, Isaac Dov Bamberger.[113] Neziv's responsum states:

> You have presented the view of your father, the distinguished scholar of blessed memory, that his responsa, in which he made halakhic rulings for practical application, should not be published, on the ground that little reliance should be placed on a responsum as compared to a conclusion reached through theoretical study. [His view is based on the premise] that theoretical study produces a clearer comprehension of the subject than that attained at a time when an actual problem is posed. . . .
>
> In my humble opinion, neither the conclusion nor the premise is correct. To the contrary, a more profound understanding of the subject is reached when responding for practical application than when engaging in theoretical study, and there is also greater divine guidance (*siyyata di-shemaya*) in an actual case . . . as stated in Tractate *Bava Batra*:[114] "One may not derive a legal norm from academic study or from an actual case unless they [the halakhic authorities involved] specifically state that the norm is intended to be applied in practice." See also the commentary of Rashbam [on this passage].
>
> The same is stated in Tractate *Sanhedrin*,[115] concerning the rebellious elder: "If he merely continues to teach in the same way that he previously taught, he is innocent, but if he instructs that his ruling be applied in actual practice, he is guilty."
>
> The conclusion is thus that there is greater force to a rule explicitly intended to be followed in practice. We see, therefore, that rulings arrived at in

113. *Resp. Meshiv Davar*, I, #24 (toward the end). *See also Resp. Yad ha-Levi* by Isaac Dov Bamberger, Jerusalem, 1965, at the beginning of the book, before the Introduction.

114. TB Bava Batra 130b.

115. M Sanhedrin 11:2.

> the course of a responsum in an actual case have greater force and are closer to the truth than conclusions reached as a result of theoretical study. Several great scholars who did not wish to publish their responsa based [their reluctance] on a different ground—that greater reliance is to be placed on responsa, and they did not wish their views to be relied on. They knew that the views they stated as a matter of theory would not be relied on; and they, therefore, did not hesitate to publish those writings.

The principle that the authority of a judicial decision is stronger and closer to the truth than an abstract rule contained in a code was one of the determinative factors that gave the vast responsa literature its primary and crucial role in creating and developing Jewish law in the post-Talmudic era.[116]

VII. PRECEDENT IN JEWISH LAW

It has been seen that *ma'aseh,* both as judicial decision and as conduct of a halakhic authority, is recognized in the Jewish legal system as a source for the derivation of halakhic norms. As previously stated, there is no necessary connection between this fact and the question of whether *ma'aseh* is also to be regarded as binding precedent for deciding future cases involving similar questions of law.[117] A brief examination of the approach of Jewish law to the question of precedent demonstrates this point.

A. "Case" and Precedent in Other Legal Systems

There is no unanimity among the various legal systems as to whether judicial decisions should be regarded as a legal source; and even where they

116. For further discussion concerning the greater deference accorded to a conclusion drawn in a responsum than to a proposition stated in the codificatory literature, *see infra* pp. 1457–1459. *See also* Hayyim Volozhiner in *Resp. Ḥut ha-Meshullash* #8 (beginning):

> With regard to the first part of your responsum transmitted to me by Rabbi H. Cohen concerning the *agunah* of Vilna [as to *agunah, see supra* pp. 522–530], I have examined every statement and word and have come to the conclusion that for the most part we are of the same mind. The only difference is that you incline toward stringency, since the responsibility for the matter is not yours. I, like you, did not turn to the more lenient aspects that emerge from the examination of the case until the yoke of decision was placed upon me. It seems that now, because of many sins, the generation has become bereft of scholars in these regions, and the yoke of judging the whole region has been imposed upon me to the extent that they will in no wise rule that anything is permissible without the concurrence of my humble opinion; hence, I wrestled with my conscience [lit. "my Creator"] and felt myself duty-bound to use my powers to the utmost to try to improve the plight of *agunot,* and may the One-Whose-Name-Is-To-Be-Blessed save me from errors.

117. *See supra* p. 948.

are so regarded, there is the additional question of whether the legal system should take on the burden of the doctrine of binding precedent, known as *stare decisis* (lit. "to stand by what has been decided").

The common law has gone further than any other legal system in recognizing case law as binding precedent. As J.W. Salmond has stated:[118]

> The importance of judicial precedents has always been a distinguishing characteristic of English law. The great body of the common or unwritten law is almost entirely the product of decided cases, accumulated in an immense series of reports extending backwards with scarcely a break to the reign of Edward the First at the close of the thirteenth century. . . . A judicial precedent speaks in England with authority; it is not merely evidence of the law but a source of it; and the courts are bound to follow the law that is so established.

Cases are thus a source of the common law and constitute precedents for the decision of later cases. To what extent are the courts bound by precedent? On this point, Salmond stated:[119]

> It is necessary to point out that the phrase "the doctrine of precedent" has two meanings. In the first, which may be called the loose meaning, the phrase means merely that precedents are reported, may be cited, and will probably be followed by the courts. This was the doctrine that prevailed in England until the nineteenth century, and it is still the only sense in which a doctrine of precedent prevails on the Continent. In the second, the strict meaning, the phrase means that precedents not only have great authority but must (in certain circumstances) be followed. This was the rule developed during the nineteenth century and completed in some respects during the twentieth.

The benefits of the doctrine of precedent in its strict sense have not gone unquestioned, and its soundness and utility have become subjects of extensive and increasing debate. Salmond has been especially helpful in getting to the heart of the issue:[120]

> The real issue is whether the doctrine of precedent should be maintained in its strict sense or whether we should revert to the loose sense. There is no dissatisfaction with the practice of citing cases and of attaching weight to them; the dissatisfaction is with the present practice of treating precedents as absolutely binding.

118. Salmond, p. 141.
119. *Id.* at 142.
120. *Id.* at 143.

Indeed, since these words were written, important changes in English law have occurred which have relaxed the doctrine of precedent and made precedents less binding.[121]

In contrast to the common law, Roman law assigned to decisions of actual cases an extremely modest rank in the hierarchy of legal sources, and certainly the doctrine of binding precedent had no place in Roman law at all. Justinian even expressly prescribed that judgments should be based not on precedent but on statutory law: "*Non exemplis sed legibus iudicandum est* [not according to precedents but according to statutes should judgment be rendered]."[122] Most European legal systems, following Roman law, are based on a legal code, and judicial judgments represent "jurisprudence"—material of a merely theoretical and persuasive nature, with no binding force.[123]

B. Similarities and Differences between *Ma'aseh* in Jewish Law and Precedent in the Common Law

A comparative study of case law and precedent in the Jewish and other legal systems reveals that at their origin Jewish law and the common law had considerable similarities, but the two systems followed very different paths in the course of their development.

121. The House of Lords overruled long-standing doctrine and announced that it is not bound by its own precedents but is permitted to deviate from them "when it appears right to do so." "Practice Statement (Judicial Precedent)," [1966] 1 *Weekly L.R.* 1234. *See* Leach, "Revisionism in the House of Lords: The Bastion of Rigid Stare Decisis Falls," 80 *Harv. L. Rev.* 797 (1967). *See also* Salmond, pp. IX–X. As to *stare decisis* in the State of Israel, *see* the Israeli Courts Law, 1957, sec. 33:

A. A court shall follow the ruling of a court superior to it.

B. A ruling by the Supreme Court is binding on all courts except the Supreme Court itself.

On the doctrine of precedent generally, *see* Barak, "Overruling Precedent," 21 *Israel L. Rev.* 269 (1986); Cross, *Precedent in English Law,* 3d ed., Oxford, 1977; Douglas, "Stare Decisis," 49 *Col. L. Rev.* 735 (1949); Goldstein, *Precedent in Law,* Oxford, Clarendon Press, 1988; Jackson, "Decisional Law and Stare Decisis," 30 *A.B.A.J.* 334 (1944); Kokourek and Koven, "Renovation of the Common Law Through Stare Decisis," 29 *Ill. L. Rev.* 971 (1935); Landes and Posner, "Legal Precedent: A Theoretical and Empirical Analysis," 19 *J. Law and Economics* 249 (1976); Annotation, "Prospective or Retroactive Operation of Overruling Decisions," 10 A.L.R. (3d) 1371 (1968); Schaefer, "Precedent and Policy," 34 *U. Chi. L. Rev.* 3 (1966); Shapiro, "Towards a Theory of Stare Decisis, 1 *J. Legal Studies* 125 (1972); Sprecher, "The Development of the Doctrine of Stare Decisis and the Extent to Which It Should Be Applied," 31 *A.B.A.J.* 501 (1945); "Status of the Rule of Judicial Precedent (Cincinnati Conference on Judicial Precedent)," 14 *U. Cinn. L. Rev.* 203 (1940); J. Stone, *Precedent and Law: Dynamics of Common Law Growth,* Sydney, Australia, Butterworth, 1985.

122. C. 7, 45, 13. *See also* Salmond, pp. 141–142; C.K. Allen, *Law in the Making,* pp. 172–173; A. Berger, *Encyclopedic Dictionary of Roman Law,* p. 678, s.v. Res judicata.

123. *See* Salmond, p. 141 note b, on the developments in this connection in several of the European countries. *See also infra* pp. 1140–1144.

Jewish law and common law are similar in that both legal systems regard "cases" as a legal source, and particular significance is accorded to the legal conclusion derived from a judicial decision. Both systems, in contrast to the Roman law systems, concentrate largely on case law. Jewish law continuously developed through practical decisions on issues arising in daily life; and even the basic material assembled and restated in the various codifications of Jewish law is the product of legal principles that emerged from day-to-day decision making.[124] The only difference in this respect between Jewish and common law is that in Jewish law the "immense series of reports"—the vast number of volumes of the responsa literature—began not at the end of the thirteenth century C.E., but as early as the middle of the eighth century.[125]

As against these similarities, Jewish law has not accepted the theory of binding precedent in the strict meaning of the term, *i.e.,* that a court is directed and required to follow prior decisions strictly. Judicial decisions in Jewish law have only the authority possessed by cases under the doctrine of precedent in its loose meaning; in Salmond's words, "precedents are reported, may be cited, and will probably be followed by the courts."

There is good reason why the theory of case law as a legal source did not develop in Jewish law into the theory of binding precedent, such as held sway in English law during the nineteenth and the first half of the twentieth centuries. Jewish law, both because of its view of the nature of a judgment rendered in adversary litigation and because of its method of determining the law generally, cannot accept a doctrine of precedent that binds and restricts a judge to the conclusion reached in prior decisions. The following sections of this chapter explain why this is so.

C. The Nature of a Judgment in Jewish Law and the Problem of Precedent

Jewish law contains many restrictions on the finality of a judgment, even as to the immediate parties to a case. In principle, a judgment in Jewish law is not absolute and final in the sense of *res judicata* in Roman law; it is final only to the extent that it is consistent with objective truth, both factually and legally. Consequently, when a party produces new evidence after judgment has been rendered on the basis of the evidence presented at trial, the judgment is set aside and the matter is retried.

Understandably, this was a serious obstacle to an effective legal order and an orderly economic life, both of which require that there be an end to litigation. This obstacle was overcome by having each party expressly de-

124. *See infra* pp. 1144–1148.
125. *See infra* pp. 1468–1473.

clare before the judgment is rendered: "I have no further witnesses, either here or elsewhere, nor any other evidence, either in my possession or in the possession of anyone else." In this fashion, the parties nullify in advance the validity of any evidence they might produce afterwards, and they thus become unable to overturn the judgment.[126]

The lack of finality of judgments was similarly mitigated where a judgment is shown to be the result of legal error. Only if the judgment conflicts with a clear and settled legal rule is the case reopened and the judgment set aside; error in the determination of a disputed point of law (*shikkul ha-da'at*) is not a ground for reopening a case.[127] Thus, even in cases of legal error, Jewish law found a way to give finality and stability to judgments.[128]

A judgment in Jewish law thus has a dual quality: theoretically it is not final, so long as the truth has not been fully determined. In practice, finality was achieved by means of undertakings by the parties that ultimately became virtually automatic; these undertakings ensured an end to litigation and an acceptance of the judgment as authoritatively settling the rights of the parties.

The hesitancy of Jewish law in regard to according finality to judgments even as between the immediate parties doubtless played a substantial part in leading to the conclusion that a judgment is not to be regarded as a binding precedent on future questions in other cases involving different parties. The following excerpt from the Talmud is an interesting expression of this point:[129]

> Rava said to R. Papa and to R. Huna b. R. Joshua: "When a judgment of mine comes before you and you think it is erroneous, do not reject it [lit. "tear it up"] before you come to see me. If I have a sound reason for my decision, I will tell it to you; and if not, I will retract my decision. After my death [if a judgment of mine comes before you, and you think it is erroneous], do not tear it up, but do not deduce the law from it. Do not tear it up, for had I been there I might have given you a sound reason for my decision [which would meet your objection]. Do not deduce the law from it, because "a judge must be guided only by what his own eyes see" ["Do not deduce the law from it for your own decision, but follow your own judgment, because a judge must

126. *See* TB Sanhedrin 31a; Maimonides, *MT,* Sanhedrin 7:6–8; Sh. Ar. ḤM ch. 20. For an interesting example of a retrial, *see* A. v. B., 1 *P.D.R.* 65, 68 (1954). At the second trial, new evidence was introduced, and the judgment was entirely different from that rendered at the first trial. It seems that in this case the parties did not make the declarations that would have made the first decision final.

127. TB Sanhedrin 33a; Maimonides, *MT,* Sanhedrin 6:1; Sh. Ar. ḤM 25:1–2. *See also Tur* ḤM 25 (at times a new trial is granted even when the error was in *shikkul ha-da'at*).

128. *See* Sh. Ar. ḤM 25:3 and Rema, *ad loc. See also* Gulak, *Yesodei,* IV, pp. 175–183, 201–202. The parties, prior to judgment, could undertake to accept the decision of the court as final even if erroneous.

129. TB Bava Batra 130b–131a.

be guided only by what his own eyes see . . . and in a matter that depends on reasoning, one must be guided only by his own understanding"—Rashbam].

The commentators clarify that these words, constituting the testament of Rava, one of the leading Babylonian *amoraim*, to his disciples, R. Papa and R. Huna b. R. Joshua, set forth the fundamentals of the doctrine of precedent in Jewish law. As Rabbenu Nissim Gerondi stated:[130]

> We learn from this that even under such circumstances [where there was an error with regard to a rule clearly stated in the Mishnah], a disciple must honor his teacher and not reject the teacher's ruling in that case itself, even though the law is that it should be set aside [even though under the law the judgment should be set aside, inasmuch as the teacher himself would have done so in his lifetime]. But this applies only to the particular case in which the judgment was given; if another case comes before him [the disciple], even if the facts are exactly the same, he may make his own decision, because a judge must be guided only by what his own eyes see; the same was written by Re'ah,[131] of blessed memory.[132]

D. The Approach to Decision Making in Jewish Law and the Problem of Precedent

As stated, the doctrine of binding precedent conflicts with the basic approach of Jewish law to decision making as developed over the course of

130. Ran, Novellae to Bava Batra 130b–131a, s.v. Ve-i la hadrana bei.

131. Re'ah is the acronym of Aaron ha-Levi of Barcelona, a contemporary of Rashba. The rule is also thus cited in Re'ah's name by Re'ah's student, Ritba: "'Do not tear it up'—this applies only to a disciple with regard to his teacher, and only in that same case; but in another case, though similar to it in all respects, he [the disciple] must be guided only by his own understanding. This I heard from my teacher." *See also* Meiri, *Bet ha-Beḥirah*, Bava Batra 130b–131a, s.v. Be-talmud ha-ma'arav.

132. *See also* the statement of Abraham son of Maimonides, quoted *supra* p. 968; *Yad Ramah*, Sanhedrin 33a, p. 34d, in which Meir Abulafia cites the opinion of Hai Gaon:

> As to the statement in M Eduyyot [1:5] that one court may not overturn the action of another court unless greater than the other both in wisdom and in number, Hai Gaon has written in his book *Musar ha-Dayyanim* [Proper Judicial Conduct] that a court may always overturn the action of another court even though it does not have more wisdom and a greater number of judges; and he adduced proof from what Rava said (TB Bava Batra 130b): "When a judgment of mine comes before you. . . ." He [Hai Gaon] considered the mishnaic rule that "one court may not overrule another court unless greater than the other in both wisdom and number" to be applicable only to legislative enactments. And this view seems reasonable.

See also supra pp. 541–543 to the effect that this rule is explained in the same manner by other halakhic authorities as well. Hai Gaon found support for his conclusion in the passage about Rava's statement to his disciples. As to the book *Musar ha-Dayyanim, see* S. Assaf, *Tarbiẓ*, VII (1936), p. 217.

time.[133] In the earlier period, a final judgment of the highest court of the nation, even when the court was not unanimous, was a binding precedent for a similar case in any other court. As a result of various internal and external factors, differences of opinion on halakhic questions increased; and over the course of time these differences of opinion became viewed as not only legitimate but also desirable. They evidenced the vitality of Jewish law and created the possibility of different approaches, based on generally accepted principles, to the solution of new problems.

The authoritative standard for determining which of the divergent opinions on a halakhic question is correct measures each view against "the Talmud as compiled by R. Ashi and Ravina,"[134] *i.e.*, against "the Babylonian Talmud when it speaks clearly to the point, and against the Jerusalem Talmud and the *Tosefta* when the Babylonian Talmud provides no clear-cut determination of the issue."[135]

For this reason, no code of Jewish law has ever been accepted which presents to the judge only a single opinion stated unqualifiedly as the law.[136] For the same reason, Jewish law accepted the principle, discussed more fully above,[137] that "the law is in accordance with the views of the later authorities" (*hilkheta ke-vatra'ei*). This principle is designed to ensure freedom of decision for later decisionmakers while still allowing for deference to earlier decisions, which are to be consulted and carefully considered.

A fitting conclusion to the discussion of this subject is the following statement of Asheri, which expresses the accepted approach of Jewish law to decision making:[138]

> Certainly, whoever has erred in failing to follow the decisions of the *geonim* as a result of ignorance of their views, and then has accepted the geonic decision as being correct when it was called to his attention, has committed the equivalent of an error on a law of the Mishnah [*i.e.*, he has erred on a matter of law that was clear and well settled, and it is as if his error concerned a law expressly set forth in the Mishnah]; and it goes without saying that this is true not only for such error in matters decided by the *geonim* but also in matters decided by the authorities in all succeeding generations, who, after all, are not simply reed-cutters in a bog [*i.e.*, they are not ignorant and untutored].[139] In all these cases, if an authority has rendered a decision contrary

133. This matter is discussed extensively in various places throughout the present work. *See, e.g., supra* pp. 240–272; *infra* pp. 1061–1072, 1223–1229, 1273–1275, 1277–1287, 1312–1322, 1345–1356, 1373–1385, 1451–1452.

134. *Piskei ha-Rosh,* Sanhedrin, ch. 4, #6.

135. *Yam Shel Shelomo,* Bava Kamma, Introduction.

136. *See supra* n. 133.

137. *See supra* pp. 267–271.

138. *Piskei ha-Rosh, supra* n. 134. *See also infra* pp. 1226–1229.

139. *See* TB Sanhedrin 33a.

> to earlier views and, upon being made aware of the earlier rulings, accepts those rulings as being correct and acknowledges that he has erred, it is as if his error concerns a matter stated in the Mishnah, and he must retract his decision.
>
> However, if he disagrees with the earlier opinions and brings proof for his own position acceptable to his contemporaries, then Jephthah in his generation has as much authority as Samuel in his generation—at any given time, there is only "the judge of that time," and he may choose not to follow the views of his predecessors. For as to all questions that were not definitively decided in the Talmud as compiled by R. Ashi and Ravina, one may "demolish and create" even to the point of disagreeing with the views of the *geonim* . . . just as the later *amoraim* sometimes disagreed with the earlier ones. Indeed, we consider the views of those later in time to have greater authority, since they were aware of the reasoning of the earlier authorities as well as their own, and they reached their decision on the basis of choice from among all views and after fully deliberating in order to get to the heart of the matter.[140]

Within this dynamic and flexible conception of law, there is, of course, no room for the doctrine that the *ratio decidendi* of a judicial decision can bind the judicial system to reach the same result in other cases. When a court considers the problem *sub judice,* it must carefully examine the matter and take into consideration all of the existing law, including, of course, the law derived from *ma'aseh.* Particular weight is to be given to a legal rule that has been accepted continuously in a series of decisions,[141] and sometimes even to a rule set forth in a single leading case.[142] However, after due consideration, "if he [the judge] disagrees with the earlier opinions and brings proof for his own position acceptable to his contemporaries" (*i.e.,* if

140. As to the method of decision making and establishing the law in the post-Talmudic era, *see further* the references cited *supra* n. 133. *See also* Ports Authority v. Ararat, Ltd., 31(i) *P.D.* 533 (1976), for the difference of opinion between Justice Haim Cohn (*id.* at 537) and Justice Yiẕḥak Kahan (*id.* at 545) as to the extent to which Asheri's statement can be applied to the question of binding precedent in Israeli law. On this question, *see also* Krauss v. State of Israel, 37(i) *P.D.* 365, 369 (1983).

141. "But surely [the law must be so because] cases are decided every day that . . ." TB Ketubbot 68b, 95b; Bava Batra 173b.

142. *See, e.g.,* TB Bava Batra 29a: "Abbaye said to him [Rava]: 'That being so, when the land is returned, it should be returned without the produce; why then did R. Naḥman rule that "the land is to be returned together with its produce?"'" R. Naḥman's statement was made in a judgment he rendered; *see* TB Bava Batra 33b: "One man said to another, 'What are you doing on [my] property?' . . . R. Naḥman ruled, 'The land is to be returned together with its produce. . . .'" The objection to Rava's view based on the opinion of R. Naḥman (both of them being *amoraim* and hence entitled to differ) apparently derives its force from the fact that R. Naḥman's authority as a judge entitled his view to special weight. *See* TB Ketubbot 13a, 94b; Kiddushin 59b; Bava Kamma 96b; Bava Mezi'a 66a, 110a; Bava Batra 65a; Sanhedrin 5a.

in a reasonable manner consonant with the principles of the halakhic system itself he reaches a conclusion different from that reached by the halakhic authorities who preceded him), it is not only his right but his duty to decide according to his own view. Indeed, his decision has more weight than a prior decision on a similar question, since he has had the benefit of the reasoning of the earlier authorities and yet, after full consideration, decided differently.

Ma'aseh is one of the significant legal sources in the Jewish legal system. Any rule derived from it becomes part of the overall corpus of Jewish law, which the judge must consider and by which he must be guided. Such a rule has a status and force no less than that of the rules generated by the other legal sources and contained in the works of the halakhic authorities and codifiers. All of the rules of Jewish law have one thing in common: the decisionmaker must weigh and examine each one on its merits and decide any matter brought before him according to his own knowledge and understanding, after thoroughly researching the relevant sources in the entire *corpus juris* of the Jewish legal system.

Chapter 24
LEGAL REASONING (*SEVARAH*)

I. DEFINITION OF LEGAL REASONING AS A LEGAL SOURCE

An important creative source of Jewish law is the legal reasoning (*sevarah*) employed by the halakhic authorities. Legal reasoning as a creative source of halakhic rules involves a deep and discerning probe into the essence of halakhic and legal principles, an appreciation of the characteristics of human beings in their social relationships, and a careful study of the real world and its manifestations.

In discussing legal reasoning as a legal source, it is necessary to review once again what "legal source" means. As previously defined,[1] a legal source of Jewish law is that channel recognized by the Jewish legal system as a route through which a rule becomes accepted as part of the system's *corpus juris.* A legal source is thus a direct source for the acceptance of a legal rule into the Jewish legal system, as distinguished from a historical source, which operates indirectly as the source of the rule in point of historical fact. It should therefore be noted that the discussion up to this point has already often dealt with legal reasoning as a historical source of Jewish

1. *See supra* pp. 229–230, 236–239.

law, since logic and reasoning in fact served indirectly as both source and impetus for all of the other legal sources previously discussed.

Clearly, any interpretation, whether explanatory, logical, or analogical, must be preceded by reasoning that leads and guides the interpreter. The same is true for legislation: legislative enactments are the result of certain needs dictated by logic and experience. Even custom, the covert legislation of the people as a whole, in the final analysis arises out of various logical and experiential needs perceived by the public or by some segment of the people. Certainly, *ma'aseh*—both as judicial decision and as conduct of a halakhic authority—is fashioned by the individual logic and reasoning of the authority involved.[2] The halakhic authorities stressed the importance of the role of logic and reasoning particularly in the civil-law areas of the *Halakhah.*[3]

In the case of all of these legal sources, however, logic and reasoning operate only indirectly and peripherally: the direct legal source through which the rule enters the halakhic system is not logic and reasoning but interpretation, legislation, custom, or *ma'aseh.* On the other hand, when legal reasoning is referred to as a legal source of Jewish law, the reference is to those instances where legal reasoning is the direct source for the particular rule, *i.e.,* the rule entered into the halakhic system directly by virtue of logic and reasoning alone, with no admixture of interpretation, legislation, custom, or *ma'aseh.* Here, legal reasoning itself is the instrument directly creating the legal rule.

Jewish law assigns to legal reasoning an important and honored place as a source for the creation of legal norms in all areas of the law, whether concerning the relationship between people and God or relationships in human society, and whether the issue is one of *issur* or *mamon.* Not only do a substantial number of laws have legal reasoning as their source, but these laws also have a special quality and status within the halakhic system. A rule for which the source is legislation or custom is classified as "rabbinic" (*de-rabbanan*), *i.e.,* created by the halakhic authorities,[4] whereas a law for which the source is the logic and reasoning of the halakhic authorities is

2. In this "factual" sense, legal reasoning is an indispensable prerequisite for studying and understanding the *Halakhah. See* TB Gittin 6b: "Does one's ignorance of this rule . . . mean that he cannot be considered a great scholar? If it [the rule] is dependent on *sevarah,* that would be so." *See also* TB Shabbat 63a; Sukkah 29a; Sotah 39b; Kiddushin 9b; and Rashi, Berakhot 47b, s.v. She-lo shimmesh talmid ḥakham, Sukkah 28a, s.v. Gemara (in ms. Munich and others the reading is "Talmud"; *see Dikdukei Soferim, ad loc.*), and Sukkah 28b, s.v. U-meshannen ba-sukkah.

3. For a more detailed discussion of legal reasoning as the major creative source of law in the civil-law areas of the *Halakhah, see supra* pp. 137–141.

4. *See supra* pp. 208–212, 477–478, 881–882.

generally classified as "Biblical" (*de-oraita*).[5] Rules based on legal reasoning have this special status by virtue of the principle underlying the entire structure of the legal sources of Jewish law, namely, that the Torah was entrusted to the halakhic authorities.[6]

When the halakhic authorities make use of their legislative prerogative on the basis of this fundamental principle, they must specifically declare, as was pointed out in the previous discussion of legislation,[7] that they are not operating in the area of primary legislation on the level of Biblical law but in the area of secondary legislation on the level of rabbinic law. There is no such declaration, however, when the halakhic authorities, on the basis of the very same principle, directly create rules by legal reasoning; every rule that has its origin in the legal reasoning of the halakhic authorities is considered to flow from the Torah itself and to be suffused by the Torah's spirit

5. As to inferences based on the preponderance of probabilities ("majority"), and as to legal presumptions and related subjects, as well as to the rule that "a half-measure is Biblically prohibited," *see infra* pp. 995–999. *See also* TB Bava Meẓi'a 47b: "R. Johanan said: 'According to Biblical law, the payment of money acquires'" [*i.e.*, passes ownership of chattels, and *meshikhah* ("pulling," or taking possession) is a requirement of rabbinic law]. The Talmud asks for the source of Resh Lakish's contrary opinion that Biblical law recognizes only *meshikhah* as an effective mode of acquisition, and a Scriptural verse is cited as the source; but the Talmud does not ask for the Biblical source of R. Johanan's rule that the payment of money transfers ownership of chattels. To explain this, *Shittah Mekubbeẓet, ad loc.*, s.v. Devar torah ma'ot konot, states:

> He [R. Johanan] said it on the basis of *sevarah*, because most acquisitions are effected with money, which is why the question is not raised here as to the basis of R. Johanan's view as it is with regard to the view of Resh Lakish; R. Johanan did not base his view on an *a fortiori* inference [from a verse] or on the exposition of a verse, but simply concluded [on the basis of legal reasoning] that an ordinary acquisition is effected with money.

Nimmukei Yosef to Alfasi, *ad loc.* (printed eds., fol. 28b), states:

> He [R. Johanan] did not derive it from Scripture but on the basis of *sevarah*, because it is logical that the payment of money should pass ownership, since most acquisitions are effected with money.

This explanation by *Shittah Mekubbeẓet* and *Nimmukei Yosef* for the failure of the Talmud to ask for the Biblical source for R. Johanan's view rests on the principle that the mere fact that the source for a rule is legal reasoning is sufficient to classify the rule as Biblical, and it is not necessary to base the rule on a Scriptural verse. *See also* Z.H. Chajes, *The Student's Guide through the Talmud*, p. 29:

> But there are still many cases in the unwritten law which belong to none of the . . . categories mentioned. Their basis is simply human reasoning. Yet such *halachoth* [*halakhot*] have the same authority as those which are supported by the written text. . . . Biblical texts and logical reasoning are of equal weight. . . . Any ruling which is based upon ordinary human reasoning is as authoritative as if it were deduced from Scripture, for the Talmud would not have questioned the necessity of Scriptural evidence . . . if reasoning alone did not suffice.

See also infra p. 992 n. 18 and accompanying text and pp. 998–1004..

6. *See supra* pp. 243–247.

7. *See supra* pp. 499–502.

and purpose. In this respect, legal reasoning has the same quality as interpretation—both of them extract from the Torah some hitherto unperceived content. The difference between interpretation and legal reasoning is that interpretation extracts this latent meaning by explaining and interpreting the Biblical text, whereas legal reasoning derives the latent content of the Torah without any ancillary aids; the legal reasoning of the halakhic authorities—directly reflecting the purpose, spirit, and true meaning of the Torah—merges, as it were, with the logic of the Torah.

The important role and value of legal reasoning as a legal source has been recognized by Jewish law throughout its history. The *amoraim* particularly emphasized the force and status of legal reasoning in the halakhic system. Sometimes legal reasoning operates to create new legal rules, and sometimes it creates general legal principles that underlie many different rules.

II. LEGAL REASONING AS THE CREATIVE SOURCE OF VARIOUS LEGAL RULES; THE RULE "BE KILLED RATHER THAN TRANSGRESS" IN THE LAW OF MURDER

The Talmud states:[8]

> R. Johanan said in the name of R. Simeon b. Jehoẓadak: "It was counted and resolved [a vote was taken and a decision reached] in [a room in] the upper story of the house of Nitzah in Lydda that if a man is commanded to 'transgress and you will not be killed,' he may transgress any prohibition of the Torah in order to escape death, except [the prohibitions against] idolatry, incest, and murder."

As a general rule, if a person is threatened with death unless he transgresses a prohibition, he should transgress the prohibition and save his life, because, as the Talmud states, a fundamental principle of the Torah is: "'By the pursuit of . . . [My laws] man shall live' [lit. 'One shall live by them'][9]—and not die because of them."[10] There are, however, three prohibitions that are exceptions to this rule: if a person is threatened with death unless he practices idolatry, commits incest, or murders another person, he must al-

8. TB Sanhedrin 74a; *see also infra* n. 11.

9. Leviticus 18:5.

10. *See, e.g.,* TB Yoma 85b as to the violation of the sabbath to save a life that may possibly be endangered. According to Maimonides (*MT,* Yesodei ha-Torah 5:1), "If a person dies rather than transgress, he himself bears the guilt for his death (*mitḥayyev be-nafsho*)." Other *rishonim* hold that the rule "transgress rather than be killed" is not mandatory but only permissive. *See Tosafot,* Avodah Zarah 27b, s.v. Yakhol afillu.

low himself to be killed rather than commit any of these transgressions.[11] The requirement that one "be killed rather than transgress" the prohibitions against idolatry and incest is derived in the Talmud[12] through interpretation of Biblical verses. But no interpretation was found as a source with regard to murder, and the Talmud asks in the same passage: "How do we know this with regard to murder?" The Talmud then answers:

> It stands to reason [lit. "It is *sevarah*"], as shown by the incident when someone came before Rava and said to him:[13] "Mari Dorai[14] [the non-Jewish ruler of the town[15]] has ordered me: 'Go and kill So-and-so; if not, I will kill you.'" He [Rava] answered him: "Let him kill you, and do not commit murder. Who can say that your blood is redder? Perhaps his blood is redder."[16]

This fundamental principle of Judaism, that one is forbidden to kill another human being even on pain of being killed himself, is based on *sevarah*—moral and intellectual reason and logic. Rashi explained the reasoning as follows:[17]

> It stands to reason that his fellow should not be killed, because two things are involved [in such homicide]—the loss of a life and the commission of a transgression. If only he is killed, only one thing is involved—loss of a life—but no transgression is committed [by him]. God commanded us to transgress the prohibitions [where life is in danger]; He commanded: "You shall live by them," because every Jewish person is precious to Him. In this case, with regard to murder, since there will inevitably be loss of a life, why should it be permitted to transgress? Who knows that his own soul is dearer to his Maker than the soul of his fellow man? Therefore, there is no basis for suspending God's command [prohibiting murder].

11. The application of "be killed rather than transgress" to murder is discussed in TB Sanhedrin 74a; in TB Pesaḥim 25b and in Yoma 82a it is also stated in a *baraita* in the name of R. Judah Ha-Nasi. With regard to idolatry, *see* TB Avodah Zarah 27b for the distinctions made by R. Ishmael. For details, *see* Maimonides, *MT*, Yesodei ha-Torah 5:2 *et seq.*

12. TB Sanhedrin 74a.

13. Our quotation to this point follows ms. Munich; *see Dikdukei Soferim, ad loc.*

14. "Dodai" in ms. Munich.

15. This is Rashi's explanation, *ad loc. See also* Levy, Wörterbuch, s.vv. Do'ar, Davvar, defines "Dorai" as the title of the head of the non-Jewish court.

16. Ms. Munich and Rashi, *ad loc.*, instead of "Who can say . . . ?" have "How can you perceive . . . ?"

17. Rashi, *ad loc.*, s.v. Sevara hu. *See also* Maimonides, *MT*, Yesodei ha-Torah 5:7. In connection with the use of legal reasoning to conclude that the principle "be killed rather than transgress" applies to murder, Z.H. Chajes (*supra* n. 5 at 125) stated:

> Both principles where based on common reason had the same authority as Biblical law, provided both had been voted on and decided regularly, for they were *halachah* which had been decided by a majority vote and could not be annulled.

See also infra n. 18.

III. LEGAL REASONING AS THE CREATIVE SOURCE OF GENERAL LEGAL PRINCIPLES

Legal reasoning operates as a legal source of law particularly in creating and developing general legal principles. In Jewish law, as in every legal system, there are a considerable number of general legal principles operating in and nurturing all areas of the system; without these principles, no part of the system could function. Among such general principles are: "the burden of proof is on the claimant" and "the majority governs," as well as certain legal presumptions. These principles operate in all areas of Jewish law: in civil and criminal law, in matters of *mamon* as well as *issur;* and their status in the hierarchy of legal norms is that of Biblical law. The source of these general principles is *sevarah*—legal reasoning that penetrates into the essence of things and reflects a profound understanding of human nature.[18] The halakhic authorities have explicitly identified legal reasoning as the source of some of these principles; this identification throws light not only on the particular principles but also on the entire category of such principles.

A. "The Burden of Proof Is on the Claimant"

The Talmud states:[19]

> R. Samuel b. Naḥmani said: "How do we know that the burden of proof is on the claimant? Scripture states: 'Let anyone who has a legal matter approach *(yiggash)* them'—*i.e.,* let him bring (*yaggish*) proof to them."[20]

18. *See* the instructive comments of Z.H. Chajes, *supra* n. 5 at 120–125:

> Many of the presumptions established by the Rabbis as basic principles in their legal decisions originated in the fact that they had observed the nature of man and his endeavours and habits in human society . . . and came to understand the laws of nature. . . . Also in connection with some other legal restrictions or relaxations the Rabbis relied on such presumptions, for, not having scriptural support for them, it was purely on the basis of their knowledge of the nature of things and the nature of men, of the circumstances of each . . . that they established such legal principles. . . . All these principles are rooted deeply in the ground of common reasoning alone; there is no basis for them either in Scripture or in oral tradition; but as we have already explained above, rulings derived from common reason are equal in authority to those derived directly from the Torah. . . . Although there was no Biblical support to be found for these assumptions of the "majority" and "presumption" rules, yet they were applied as recognized principles. It is true that the Rabbis sought a Biblical basis. . . . Yet although they found no Scriptural basis for such, they followed these fundamental guiding principles in their rulings, since they regarded a view based on factual experience as being equally authoritative with one derived from the hermeneutical rules.

See also supra nn. 3, 5, and 17.

19. TB Bava Kamma 46b.

20. Exodus 24:12–13 relates how Moses ascended the Mountain of the Lord in order to receive the tablets of stone, the Torah, and the commandments from God. Verse 14 states

> R. Ashi objected: "Why do we need Scripture [to tell us this]? It is common sense that if a man has a pain, he goes to a physician."

Why, R. Ashi asked, is there need to search for Biblical support for the principle that the burden of proof is on the claimant, when this principle can be deduced through logical reasoning? A person in pain goes to a doctor and tells the doctor his symptoms; the doctor does not run about looking for sick people. So, too, a person who has a claim against another must prove his claim, and the defendant need not prove nonliability.

R. Ashi thus based the principle that the burden of proof is on the claimant solely on logic and reasoning, and he saw no need to support this principle with a Biblical verse. Apparently, R. Samuel b. Naḥmani also believed that the source of the principle was logic, and his purpose in seeking to connect it with a Biblical verse was merely to give it additional support, by way of integrative, as distinguished from creative, interpretation.[21]

B. "The Mouth That Has Prohibited Is the Mouth That Has Permitted"

Among the principles of evidence in Jewish law is: "The mouth that has prohibited is the mouth that has permitted." Two examples will explain this principle.

The Mishnah states:[22]

> R. Joshua admits that if one [A] says to another [B], "This field belonged to your father and I bought it from him," he [A] is believed, for the mouth that has prohibited is the mouth that has permitted [*i.e.*, the same person who raised a doubt as to his right to the field has resolved the doubt in his own favor]; but if there are witnesses that it belonged to his [B's] father and he [A] says, "I bought it from him," he [A] is not believed.

This *mishnah* deals with a case where A tells B that the field now in A's possession was previously owned by B's father, but that he, A, bought it from B's father. At first glance, it appears plausible for B to argue that A

---

that before ascending the mountain Moses said to the elders: "Wait here for us until we return to you. You have Aaron and Hur with you; let anyone who has a legal matter approach them." Moses thus established that any legal matters that might arise while he was away should be brought before Aaron and Hur. R. Samuel b. Naḥmani interpreted this verse to support the principle that the claimant, who must "approach" the judges, Aaron and Hur, with his claim, must present proof of his claim to them.

21. As to creative and integrative interpretation, *see supra* pp. 283–286. *See also supra* pp. 384–387, noting the decline in the use of midrash—even of the integrative kind—in the amoraic period.

22. M Ketubbot 2:2.

should be believed only to the extent of his admission that the field belonged to B's father (because the admission by a party of a fact adverse to his own interest is "the equivalent of a hundred witnesses"), but A should not be believed in regard to the self-serving part of his statement that he bought the field from B's father. Thus, B's argument runs, inasmuch as the field clearly belonged to B's father, A cannot prevail unless he proves through witnesses or a deed that he really did buy the field from B's father.

At this point, however, the principle in the Mishnah—"the mouth that has prohibited is the mouth that has permitted"—comes into play and prescribes that A is to be believed when he says that he bought it from B's father, even if his statement is uncorroborated. The reason is that it was A's statement that originally established that the field belonged to B's father.

A is the one who "prohibited," *i.e.*, established a fact raising a doubt about his ownership of the field; except for A's statement, B would have no possible claim to the field, since he has no witnesses to prove that the field ever belonged to his father. Consequently, the same "mouth" (A) is believed when it "has permitted," *i.e.*, has made a statement that A bought the field from its previous owner. Understandably, if B's right did not depend on A's statement, but B had witnesses that the field belonged to his father, then A's bare statement that he bought the field from B's father would be insufficient to prove his entitlement to the field, and he would have to produce other proof (such as witnesses or a deed) of his purchase from B's father.

This principle that testimony is to be credited when "the mouth that has prohibited is the mouth that has permitted" applies not only in the civil law but also in matters of *issur*. Thus, the Mishnah further states:[23]

> A woman who says, "I was married but now I am divorced," is believed [as to the divorce even though she presently has no *get* (bill of divorcement) in her possession], as the mouth that has prohibited is the mouth that has permitted [there are no witnesses to her marriage nor was she known to have been married, but it is her own statement that prohibited her, as a married woman, from remarrying; and therefore she is believed when she declares that she was divorced, and she is thus free to remarry]; but if there are witnesses that she was married, and she says, "I am divorced," she is not believed [because when witnesses establish her marriage, the only way the effect of their testimony can be overcome is by other witnesses who testify that she was divorced, or by her producing a *get*].

The source for this principle is discussed in the Talmud:[24]

23. *Id.* 2:5.
24. TB Ketubbot 22a.

> R. Assi asked: "How do we know that [the principle that] 'the mouth that has prohibited is the mouth that has permitted' is from the Torah?"[25]

He responded by referring to a Biblical verse as a possible support,[26] but the question then was raised:

> Why is a Scriptural verse necessary? It stands to reason! He prohibited her [from marrying], and he permitted her [to marry].

The source of this principle lies in the logic of the matter, and there is no need to seek support for it in Scripture. It is logical that if the sole basis for concluding that a woman has been married or that a field was owned by someone else is an oral statement, the maker of that statement is believed when he adds that what had earlier been prohibited later became permissible or that the right that once existed in someone else now no longer exists.[27]

C. Legal Presumptions; Reliance on a Majority

The legal source of the two principles discussed above ("the burden of proof is on the claimant" and "the mouth that has prohibited is the mouth that has permitted") was specifically identified by the *amoraim* as being *sevarah*. Many other rules and principles, however, also appear to have their origin in the logic and legal reasoning of the halakhic authorities. One example is the concept of the legal presumption (*ḥazakah; praesumptio juris*). There are different types of such presumptions: the presumption of the continued existence of a fact or condition, such as the presumption that a person is still

25. This principle of credibility must have the force of Biblical law; otherwise, it could not be a basis for permitting the woman to remarry, since it is Biblical law that prohibits a woman, while married to one man, from marrying anyone else.

26. Deuteronomy 22:16: "'I gave my daughter to this man [in Hebrew the word order is reversed: "to man this"] to wife.' [When he said] 'to [a] man,' he prohibited her [to all, but when he specified] 'this,' he permitted her [to this man]." *See supra* pp. 385–387.

27. In the amoraic period, the principle "the mouth that has prohibited is the mouth that has permitted" was expanded into a principle called *migo* (Aramaic for "since"), which in TJ is called *me-aḥar* (Hebrew for "since"). The principle is also known as *mah lo leshakker* (why should he lie?) The theory is that "since" the party, if he wanted to lie, could have stated a better claim, which would have been accepted, the weaker claim that he actually made should also be believed. The principle applies even where the assertion of the right or prohibition is made by someone other than the party himself, so long as there are no witnesses to provide direct evidence as to the merits of the claim or the prohibition. The rules of *migo* constitute a significant portion of the Jewish law of evidence and pleading. *See* Gulak, *Yesodei*, IV, pp. 101–108.

alive;[28] the presumption of propriety (*ḥezkat kashrut*);[29] the presumptions relating to bodily condition;[30] etc. Sometimes, a presumption has a particular psychological-legal basis, such as the presumption that an agent carries out his charge,[31] the presumption that a *ḥaver* (person meticulous about tithing) does not allow anything untithed to leave his hands,[32] the presumption that a debtor does not pay his debt before the due date,[33] etc.

28. *See, e.g.,* M Gittin 3:3:

> If one [an agent] has brought a bill of divorcement, and he had left the husband aged or sick, he may deliver it to her [the wife] on the presumption that he [the husband] is still living. [We are not concerned that the husband may have died in the interim and that the divorce is therefore invalid, with the possible result that if he died without children the wife would be subject to the law of levirate marriage.] If the daughter of an Israelite was married to a priest and her husband went to a foreign country, she may eat of the *terumah* [which may not be consumed or enjoyed by anyone other than a priest or his family] on the presumption that he is still alive. If one sent his sin-offering from a foreign country, it is offered up as a sacrifice on the presumption that he is still living.

This *mishnah* thus presents three laws, all in the area of religious law, and all based on the presumption of the continuation of an existing state or condition. The husband, the priest, or the person who sent the sin-offering is presumed to be still alive until the opposite is proved, even though the sickness or advanced age of the divorcing husband and the great distance to the place where the priest or the donor of the sin-offering has traveled give grounds to believe that he may have died, and even though the actual facts are difficult to ascertain.

29. TB Bava Batra 31b. *Sifra,* Behar 8:8, presents an interesting derivation from Leviticus 25:53: "He [one who, because of poverty, sells himself into servitude] shall be under his [the master's] authority as a laborer hired by the year; he [the master] shall not rule ruthlessly over him [the bondman] in your sight."

The *Sifra* states:

> "He shall not rule ruthlessly over him." You might think that one may enter his [the master's] home to investigate how he [the master] is treating him [the bondman]; therefore, Scripture says, "in your sight": You are commanded [to intervene] only as to what is [done] in your sight.

A. Ehrlich, *Mikra ki-Feshuto,* I, p. 241, comments on this passage of *Sifra* as follows:

> . . . for this is the plain meaning of the verse. And if this rule applies to a [master who is a] resident alien [of whom the verse speaks], then how much more so does it apply to your brother [*i.e.,* a Hebrew master]. From here we can learn that every person is presumed to be acting properly until the contrary is established and that a person who snoops and eavesdrops to catch his fellow in misconduct is acting contrary to the Torah.

However, it appears that this presumption that a person is behaving correctly also originated in *sevarah* and was merely connected to the Biblical verse. *Cf.* the presumption of innocence in Anglo-American criminal law, and the Latin maxim *omnia praesumuntur rite et solemniter esse acta donec probetur in contrarium* [all things are presumed to have been rightly and duly performed until the contrary is proved].

30. M Ketubbot 7:8; TB Ketubbot 75b.

31. TB Eruvin 31b, 32a; Gittin 64a; Nazir 12a.

32. TB Avodah Zarah 41b; Eruvin 32a.

33. TB Bava Batra 5a/b.

Another example is the principle of reliance on a majority. The Torah states the rule that one should "follow the majority"[34] when there is an actual majority (in the Talmudic formulation, "a majority present before us"), such as the majority of the judges hearing a case.[35] But Jewish law also recognizes "a majority that is not before us," which is the kind of "majority" involved in a considerable portion of the law in which the concept of "majority" plays a role.[36] This latter type of "majority"—an inference on the basis of the probabilities in light of what occurs in "the majority" of instances—has the same effect as direct proof of a particular fact.

Although the halakhic authorities connected some presumptions[37] and rules concerning a "majority"[38] to various laws in the Torah, these presumptions and rules were originally established by the halakhic authorities on the basis of legal reasoning, taking into account their observations of the circumstances, conditions, and experiences of life. These presumptions and rules apply in all areas of the law, both civil and religious, and operate in every context, on matters of Biblical as well as rabbinic law, because "rulings derived from common reason are equal in authority to those derived directly from the Torah . . . since they [the halakhic authorities] regarded a

34. Exodus 23:2. The 1985 JPS *Tanakh* has "mighty," or, alternatively, "multitude" for *rabbim* ("majority") and gives a generally different meaning to the verse.

35. TB Ḥullin 11a.

36. *See id.* regarding the rule (M Yevamot 13:12) that if a *levir* who is a minor has sexual relations with the decedent's widow when she is also a minor, they may live together until they are of age, *i.e.*, neither has capacity to divorce while still a minor; and there is no concern that it may turn out later that one or both of them may be one of the relatively few people unable to have children (and having children is the purpose of levirate marriage), since the legal rule is fashioned to fit the majority of cases. The following law presents a further example:

> R. Taḥalifa of the West [*i.e.*, of the Land of Israel, which is west of Babylonia] taught in the presence of R. Abbahu: "Although a woman has committed adultery, her children are legitimate [*i.e.*, not *mamzerim*]; most acts of intercourse are with the husband" (TB Sotah 27a).

According to law, a child born of a married woman by a man other than her husband is a *mamzer;* R. Taḥalifa ruled that the child is presumed to be by the husband because of the probabilities, based on the perception that most ("the majority") of her acts of intercourse are with the husband, and thus the child is not a *mamzer. Tosefta* Yevamot 12:8 even prescribes that such children should perform levirate marriage (should the need arise), since they are in all respects legitimate brothers of their mother's husband's sons. "[Even] if a woman has acquired a bad reputation, her children are 'legitimate,' because they are presumed to be by her husband."

"A majority not present before us" is, in effect, a presumption; and the proposition that "most acts of intercourse are with the husband" is indeed explicitly labeled as a presumption in the *Tosefta. See further* Maimonides, *MT,* Issurei Bi'ah 15:20; Sh. Ar. EH 4:15; S. Lieberman, *Tosefta ki-Feshutah,* Yevamot, p. 129.

37. TB Ḥullin 10b.

38. *Id.* 11a–12a.

view based on factual experience as being equally authoritative with one derived from the hermeneutical rules."[39]

IV. LEGAL REASONING IN THE AMORAIC PERIOD

Many of the rules and principles created through legal reasoning originated in an early period of Jewish law; and it is a reasonable inference that a considerable portion (such as the principle that "the burden of proof is on the claimant," the rules relating to legal presumptions, and the rules relating to "majority") are very ancient, inasmuch as they are indispensable for determining and settling the law in most areas of the *Halakhah*. It also appears from Talmudic sources that *sevarah* was especially employed in the amoraic period as a recognized legal source of law. The general approach of the *amoraim* to laying down principles, based on reason, concerning the sources of the *Halakhah*, and to the way the *Halakhah* should be ascertained,[40] naturally resulted in attributing considerable importance to legal reasoning, in all of its aspects, as a legal source. As already pointed out, the *amoraim* often identified *sevarah* as the original source of various rules;[41] this becomes even clearer from an examination of some additional examples.

A. "A Half-Measure Is Biblically Prohibited"

The Talmud[42] records a disagreement between R. Johanan and Resh Lakish with regard to the prohibition of eating "a half-measure." When eating or drinking certain substances is forbidden, there is, as a general rule, a minimum amount that must be consumed before one can be considered to have

39. Chajes, *supra* n. 5 at 124–125, quoted *supra* n. 18. *See also id.* for additional examples of presumptions and rules relating to majority as well as for other rules, such as those relating to judicial discretion, which are also based on legal reasoning. *See also supra* p. 364, regarding proselytes from nations whose members it is forbidden to accept into the Jewish people but who are nevertheless permitted to be so accepted on the ground that those nations have been intermingled with all the other nations and "that which comes out, comes out of the majority." M Yadayim 4:4; *Tosefta* Yadayim 2:17–18; TB Berakhot 28a; Maimonides, *MT*, Issurei Bi'ah 12:25; Sh. Ar. EH 4:10. *See also* M. Elon, EJ, VII, pp. 1521–1522, s.v. Ḥazakah (reprinted in *Principles*, p. 595).

40. *See supra* pp. 505ff. and *infra* pp. 1090–1091.

41. *E.g.*, "the burden of proof is on the claimant" and "the mouth that has prohibited is the mouth that has permitted."

42. TB Yoma 74a.

43. As in regard to the eating of hard fat or suet, which is prohibited in Leviticus 7:23—"Speak to the Israelite people thus: You shall eat no fat of ox or sheep or goat"—*see* Maimonides, *MT*, Ma'akhalot Asurot 7:1.

eaten or drunk. This measure is often an olive-size,[43] but sometimes a different measure is established. Thus, with regard to fasting on the Day of Atonement, the measure for "eating" is a full-sized date with its pit, *i.e.*, a little less than the size of an egg; and the measure for "drinking" is a mouthful of liquid, *i.e.*, the full amount that a person takes into his mouth for a single swallow.[44]

Under the law, the divine punishment of *karet* (extirpation, lit. "being cut off" at the hands of Heaven) that is prescribed in the Torah applies only to one who has eaten at least the minimum amount. R. Johanan and Resh Lakish disagreed as to the law applicable to one who eats less than the specified measure:

> Concerning a half-measure [*i.e.*, less than the minimum that entails *karet*], R. Johanan said: "It is forbidden by the Torah" [*i.e.*, although there is no divine punishment of *karet* for consuming less than the specified measure, it is still forbidden by the Torah]. Resh Lakish said: "It is permitted by the Torah." [*I.e.*, Biblical law does not prohibit the consumption of less than the specified measure; such consumption is prohibited only by rabbinic law.]

The Talmud then explains the dispute between R. Johanan and Resh Lakish:

> R. Johanan said: "It is forbidden by the Torah," since they could be combined, and it is therefore forbidden food that is eaten [since one half-measure may combine with another half-measure to constitute a full measure]. Resh Lakish said: "It is permitted by the Torah," for the Torah speaks of "eating," and this is not eating. [*I.e.*, the Torah prohibited the act of eating, and the consumption of less than the specified measure is not considered eating.]

Both R. Johanan and Resh Lakish agreed that consumption of less than the amount that incurs *karet* is not in itself considered as eating, and therefore both agreed that there is no divine punishment for consuming less than that amount. Resh Lakish added that, in his opinion, since the consumption of less than the prescribed measure is not itself considered to be eating, it does not fall within the Torah's prohibition. However, R. Johanan took the view, relying on the logical reasoning of "they could be combined," that the Torah prohibits consuming even less than the amount that entails the punishment of *karet*. R. Johanan thus derived his view from this reasoning and, on that basis, ruled that the prohibition of "a half-measure" is Biblical.[45]

44. M Yoma 8:2; Maimonides, *MT*, Shevitat Asor 2:1; Sh. Ar. OḤ 612:9.

45. Later in the Talmudic discussion, a *baraita* is quoted in which the prohibition of a half-measure—as applied to prohibited animal fat—is derived from the Scriptural words "no fat" [*kol ḥelev*, lit. "all fat"; *see supra* n. 43], which implies that any amount of fat, even

B. Parallel Rationales: Biblical Verse and Legal Reasoning

The regard of the *amoraim* for *sevarah* as a legal source often motivated them to explain a particular halakhic norm—whether of *mamon* or *issur*—and to base it on two alternative sources, namely, Biblical exegesis and logical reasoning. This method of explanation is introduced by the formula: "If you wish, I will cite a Scriptural verse; if you wish, I will explain it on the basis of *sevarah.*" The following two examples are illustrative.

1. THE LAW PERTAINING TO WITNESSES

The Talmud quotes the following *baraita:*[46]

> It has been taught: Testimony [the *Tosefta* adds: "of witnesses"] cannot be combined [the *Tosefta* states: "cannot be admitted"] unless they have simultaneously seen [what they testify to—Rashi; the *Tosefta* states: "unless they saw each other"]. R. Joshua b. Korḥa says: "The testimony is valid even if they witnessed it consecutively" [the *Tosefta* states: "even if they did not see each other"].
>
> Their testimony is not admissible in court [to serve as the basis for a judgment—Rashi] unless they both testify together. R. Nathan says: "The testimony of one witness may be heard one day, and when the other witness appears on the next day, his testimony may be heard." [The *Tosefta* states: "The testimony of witnesses cannot be admitted unless they are together; R. Simeon says: 'The testimony of one witness may be heard one day, and when the other witness appears the next day, his testimony may be heard.'"]

The first part of the *baraita* lays down a rule with regard to the manner of witnessing the event about which the witnesses are to testify; the second part deals with the manner in which the witnesses testify in court.

The Talmud[47] asks, with regard to the two parts of the *baraita:* "On what do they differ?" *I.e.,* what is the basis of the dispute between the first *tanna* and R. Joshua b. Korḥa in the first part of the *baraita,* and of the

---

less than the minimum quantity, is prohibited. However, the Talmud prefers to explain R. Johanan's view concerning the prohibition of a half-measure as being based on *sevarah* rather than on Scriptural exegesis, just as it does with regard to the principles that "the burden of proof is on the claimant" and "the mouth that has prohibited is the mouth that has permitted," as previously noted and as will be further discussed *infra. See Tosafot,* Yoma 74a, s.v. Keivan de-ḥazei le-iẓtarufei issura ka akhil, asking why the rule is based on *sevarah* when the exegesis of the verse stating "no fat" is available. The answer given is that without the *sevarah,* the exegesis would be considered a mere *asmakhta,* and thus a half-measure would be forbidden by rabbinic law only; the *sevarah* strengthens the exegesis and renders a half-measure forbidden by Biblical law.

46. TB Sanhedrin 30a, and, similarly, *Tosefta* Sanhedrin 5:5.

47. TB Sanhedrin 30a.

dispute between the first *tanna* and R. Nathan (according to the *Tosefta,* R. Simeon) in the latter part?

With regard to the first part of the *baraita,* which deals with the witnessing of the event, the response in the Talmud is as follows:

> If you wish, I will cite a Scriptural verse; if you wish, I will explain it on the basis of *sevarah.*
>
> As a matter of *sevarah,* the *maneh* [a coin] to which the first witness testifies is not the one to which the second witness testifies; and the *maneh* to which the second witness testifies is not the *maneh* to which the first witness testifies [*i.e.,* the first *tanna* takes the view that if each witness sees an event at a different time, their testimony cannot be combined to form a single unit of testimony by two witnesses, since each witness testifies to a different *maneh*]; the other [R. Joshua b. Korḥa] takes the view that in any event both witnesses testify to a *maneh.*[48]
>
> And, if you wish, I will cite a Scriptural verse, as it is said: ". . . [he is] able to testify as one who has either seen or learned of the matter."[49]

The discussion continues by explaining that each *tanna* interprets this verse as proof of his own view.

The Talmud responds in the same vein in connection with the disagreement between the first *tanna* and R. Nathan in the latter part of the *baraita* with regard to the witnesses' testimony in court:

> If you wish, I will explain it on the basis of *sevarah;* if you wish, I will cite a Scriptural verse.
>
> As a matter of *sevarah,* one master [the first *tanna*] argues: "A single witness may impose an obligation to take an oath but may not establish liability." [*I.e.,* the Torah states:[50] "A single witness may not validate against a person any guilt or blame for any offense that may be committed; a case can be valid only on the testimony of two witnesses or more." Testimony of a single witness is thus not sufficient to impose liability to pay money; the only effect such testimony has is that the defendant is required to take an oath that his version of the facts is true, and upon doing so he is free of liability. The result is that when each witness testifies separately, there is no testimony that is sufficient to impose liability; while there are two witnesses testifying, each one merely requires the defendant to take an oath, and the combined effect of the witnesses is no greater than to require the oath.]
>
> The other master [R. Nathan] argues: "Even when they come together, do they testify with one mouth? Nevertheless, they are combined; so here, too, we may combine them." [*I.e.,* R. Nathan argues that we may view the

48. For a further explanation of this view, *see* Maimonides, *MT,* Edut 4:2–3; Sh. Ar. ḤM 30:6–8.

49. Leviticus 5:1.

50. Deuteronomy 19:15.

two separate acts of giving testimony by each of the witnesses as the combined testimony of two witnesses establishing liability, since, after all, even if two witnesses testify together, they do not testify with one mouth, but the judges hear one witness and then the second witness, and combine the two statements into a single unit of testimony. Just as this combination establishes the two statements of the witnesses as a single unit of testimony, so, too, joining the statements by two witnesses when each one testifies on a different day combines their testimony in the same way and with the same effect.][51]

And, if you wish, I will cite a Scriptural verse: ". . . he does not give information, so that he is subject to punishment."[52]

Here, too, each *tanna* interprets this verse as proof for his own view. The *amoraim* thus establish two possibilities, equal in status and weight, for the original source of two rules pertaining to witnesses: one that the rules were created by *sevarah,* and the other that the basis for the rules was Biblical exegesis.

2. THE LAW OF *ḤALIẒAH*

The amoraic approach of putting forward two alternative sources of equal weight for a particular rule was not confined to civil law; it was equally accepted in matters of *issur.*

The Talmud discusses the following situation:[53] A *levir* participated in the ceremony of *ḥaliẓah* (release from the obligation of levirate marriage) with the widow. Thereafter, it was discovered that she was pregnant by her husband at the time of the *ḥaliẓah,* but she later miscarried; and since she miscarried, her husband left no living children, so that either a levirate marriage or *ḥaliẓah* is required.[54] The question is whether the *ḥaliẓah* that took place while she was pregnant was valid and sufficient to render a second *ḥaliẓah* unnecessary to free her for remarriage to another, or was invalid because it was performed at a time when it was not mandated, since there was a possibility that the widow would give birth to a living child by her deceased husband. The Talmud states:

51. A closer examination of the dispute between R. Nathan and the first *tanna* produces this explanation: R. Nathan held that the testimony of even a single witness is legally sufficient to create liability in civil matters. However, the law provides that the defendant can avoid the liability by taking an oath. Thus, when two witnesses testify, even if separately, they establish liability; and in such a case the defendant's option of an oath is not available. The first *tanna,* however, held that a single witness creates no liability of payment at all, but only an obligation to take an oath. Thus, if two separate testimonies are combined, all they create is a twofold liability to take an oath, but no liability to pay.

52. Leviticus 5:1.

53. TB Yevamot 35b.

54. Deuteronomy 25:5–10.

> If a *levir* participated in *ḥaliẓah* with a pregnant woman who subsequently miscarried, R. Johanan said: "She need not undergo *ḥaliẓah* with the brothers." Resh Lakish said: "She must undergo *ḥaliẓah* with the brothers."
>
> R. Johanan said: "She need not undergo *ḥaliẓah* with the brothers; the *ḥaliẓah* of a pregnant woman is a proper *ḥaliẓah*, and [levirate] marriage with a pregnant woman is a proper [levirate] marriage."
>
> Resh Lakish said: "She must undergo *ḥaliẓah* with the brothers; *ḥaliẓah* with a pregnant woman is not a proper *ḥaliẓah*, nor do marital relations with a pregnant woman effect a proper [levirate] marriage."

Here, too, just as in regard to the issue of civil law discussed above, the Talmud continues:

> On what do they differ? If you wish, I will cite a Scriptural verse; if you wish, I will explain it on the basis of *sevarah*.
>
> As a matter of *sevarah*, R. Johanan's argument is as follows: If Elijah [the prophet] had appeared and declared that the woman would miscarry, would she not have been subject to *ḥaliẓah* or levirate marriage? In our case, too, the fact is established retrospectively. [*I.e.*, if we had known at the time of the *ḥaliẓah* that she would definitely miscarry, there is no doubt that the *ḥaliẓah* would be valid, since it would have been clear that there would be no living children, and the widow would require *ḥaliẓah*. This being so, even if at the time of the *ḥaliẓah* the facts are not known but it later becomes apparent that no living child was born from this pregnancy, we now say, after the miscarriage, that the facts have been established retrospectively: the pregnancy did not result in the birth of a living child, and therefore the *ḥaliẓah* was valid and effective.]
>
> Resh Lakish's argument is as follows: We do not accept that a fact can be established retrospectively. [*I.e.*, the circumstance that it was established retrospectively that the pregnancy would not result in the birth of a living child cannot validate the *ḥaliẓah*, since, at the time of the *ḥaliẓah*, the facts were not known; and it was possible that a living child would be born, so that the *ḥaliẓah* was not mandated when it was performed and it was therefore ineffective.]
>
> And, if you wish, I will cite a Scriptural verse. R. Johanan reasons: Scripture states: "[When brothers dwell together and one of them dies] and leaves no son" [lit. "and he has no son"], and in fact [in the present case] he has none. [*I.e.*, the Torah states that the requirement for levirate marriage or *ḥaliẓah* exists when the deceased "has no son," which is interpreted in the Talmud to mean "has no offspring"—male or female. R. Johanan interprets the verse to mean that if the husband has no child at the time of his death, the requirement of levirate marriage or *ḥaliẓah* then attaches; and even if the widow is pregnant, in fact she has no living children at the time of the husband's death, and in any event she subsequently had a miscarriage.][55]

55. *See Tosafot*, Yevamot 35b, s.v. Ve-ha leit leih.

> Resh Lakish reasons: ". . . and he has no son"—hold an inquiry concerning him. [The Talmudic text according to *Sefer he-Arukh* is: "Establish that there is no kind of child."][56] [*I.e.*, Resh Lakish interprets the verse to mean that only if no possibility of surviving children exists at the time of death is there a requirement for levirate marriage or *ḥaliẓah*. Therefore, if the widow is pregnant and may give birth to a living child, she need not then undergo levirate marriage or *ḥaliẓah*. Consequently, the *ḥaliẓah* that she did undergo is ineffective.]

This example demonstrates that even when the question was clearly a matter of *issur*—the release of a widow from levirate marriage by means of *ḥaliẓah*—the Babylonian *amoraim* explained the view of Resh Lakish, who held the *ḥaliẓah* invalid, and that of R. Johanan, who held that the *ḥaliẓah* is valid, in terms of both logical reasoning and Biblical exegesis. The logical force of the proposition that "the facts have been established retrospectively" is sufficient to create the rule that the *ḥaliẓah* of a pregnant woman who subsequently miscarries is valid and, consequently, no further *ḥaliẓah* is required after the miscarriage.[57]

V. LEGAL REASONING IN THE POST-TALMUDIC ERA

Legal reasoning contined to be a creative source of Jewish law in the teachings and decisions of the post-Talmudic halakhic authorities. This mode of creating law, like the other methods for the ongoing development of the *Halakhah*, is entrusted to the halakhic authorities of every generation, to whom the Torah was committed and who are chosen to oversee its interpretation and continued creativity. It is no simple matter to search out instances where legal reasoning was the legal source creating particular legal rules in the post-Talmudic period; the task requires comprehensive examination and research of the vast material in all the different types of post-Talmudic halakhic literature.[58]

56. For the text according to *Sefer he-Arukh, see Masoret ha-Shas,* Yevamot 22b.

57. Another example of parallel rationales based on legal reasoning and exegesis, respectively, may be found in TB Shevu'ot 22b. *See also Tosafot, ad loc.*, s.v. Iba'it eima kera:

> One may ask: "Since there is a *sevarah,* why is a Scriptural verse necessary?" This question is asked in ch. 2 of Ketubbot [22a] . . . : "How do we know that [the principle that] 'the mouth that has prohibited is the mouth that has permitted' is from the Torah?" [The Talmud responds:] "Why is a Scriptural verse necessary? It stands to reason! He prohibited her [from marrying], and he permitted her [to marry]!" However, one may draw a distinction, because not every *sevarah* is so obvious, and we need the verse to suggest the *sevarah* to us.

See also supra n. 45.

58. In certain cases, a particular principle may have become part of the corpus of Jewish law by way of legal reasoning but the halakhic authority did not emphasize that fact

Sometimes, a particular principle was established by means of one of the other sources of Jewish law, such as interpretation, but the logic of the circumstances and the nature of the matter were pointed to as the major impetus for the legal conclusion. For example, on the basis of Biblical interpretation, Asheri ruled that a majority of a community may adopt an enactment binding on a dissenting minority:[59]

> As to matters involving the public, the Torah states: "Follow the majority." The majority governs in all matters of public enactment; and the minority must abide by all that is agreed to by the majority. . . .[60]

However, the determining factor in the establishment of this principle was the force of necessity dictated by the logic of the circumstances. As Asheri stated later in his discussion: "Otherwise, if a few individuals could veto the enactment, the community would never be able to legislate." He emphasized the same point elsewhere:[61] "For if you do not say this, there could never be a communal enactment, for when would a community ever agree unanimously on anything?"[62] In this instance, legal reasoning was

---

in his commentary or responsum. Similarly, a particular principle may have been created by legal reasoning, but the halakhic authority did not explicitly use the term "*sevarah,*" preferring another term connoting the use of reason based on the objective facts and the logic of the circumstances. *See Resp. Ribash* #399, quoted *infra* p. 1006, for such an instance.

59. *Resp. Asheri* 6:5.

60. This constitutes an expansive interpretation of the verse, "Follow the majority." According to the interpretation in the Talmud, this verse means that the decision of a case by the majority of the judges is the decision of the court. The verse also refers to the making of an inference based on "majority"—the preponderance of probabilities. This verse was never used in the Talmud to support the principle that an enactment adopted by the majority of a community is binding on the minority. *See supra* p. 683 n. 16.

61. *Resp. Asheri* 6:7.

62. *See supra* p. 718. *Sevarah* also has been used in various other contexts. *See, e.g., Resp. Radbaz* #1052, holding that there is no legal obligation on anyone to allow one of his limbs to be amputated—even where the amputation poses no danger to life—in order to save another person from death (although there is no prohibition against such amputation). Radbaz stated:

> It is written: "Her ways are pleasant ways" [Proverbs 3:17. This means that] the laws of our Torah must accord with reason and logic, and how can we suggest that a person should allow his eye to be blinded or his arm or leg amputated in order that someone else not be killed? Therefore, I do not see such an act as a legal obligation, but as one of pious behavior (*middat ḥasidut*). Happy is the lot of anyone who can bring himself to do such a thing.

Halakhic authorities frequently make the point that a particular conclusion is "totally unthinkable" (*Resp. Tashbeẓ,* I, #61) or "unreasonable" (*id.* #81), or they make such comments as, "How can one even consider that the opinion of one individual should outweigh that of the community and compel the majority to obey enactments against their will? . . . . This would make the community subject to the individual and would prevent a majority from adopting an enactment that is contrary to the strict law. Such a proposition is simply

indeed the primary impetus for the creation of the principle of majority rule. However, legal reasoning was not the legal source of the principle; the direct legal source that made this principle part of the corpus of Jewish law was interpretation, *i.e.*, the interpretation of the verse "Follow the majority" as applying to "matters involving the public."

In other instances, legal reasoning is not only the primary impetus but also the direct legal source for the creation of a rule. For example, we have previously considered the problem of how to establish the binding force of communal enactments on minors, persons yet unborn, and others who, under the principles of private law, do not have the capacity to become party to a legal transaction.[63] With regard to minors, Ribash solved the problem by using legal reasoning as a legal source:[64]

> Minors are also included within their *takkanah* when they become of age; otherwise, when the townspeople fix market prices, weights and measures, and laborers' wages, and they impose penalties for violations, they would be required to reenact their *takkanah* daily, because of the minors who daily become of age, and this would make no sense. Rather, all the townspeople are included within their *takkanah*.

Ribash cited no halakhic source beyond the practical reason founded on the logic and circumstances of the matter, namely, that "otherwise . . . the townspeople . . . would be required to reenact their *takkanah* daily . . . , and this would make no sense." Thus, legal reasoning was the source for the creation of the rule that communal enactments apply to minors.[65]

---

amazing!" (*id.* #123). Similarly, Maimonides, *MT,* Malveh ve-Loveh 15:2 stated in connection with a determination as to which of two possible readings of a Talmud text is correct: "Furthermore, what I have said finds support in reason." This passage is more fully quoted *infra* p. 1189. *See also Resp. Tashbeẓ,* III, #106.

All these examples stress the role of legal reasoning in determining the law, even when it is not the legal source of the law. Thus *Resp. Maharashdam,* ḤM, #99 states:

> In my humble opinion, there is no doubt that even without the proofs I have adduced, [illegible]mpelled by the force of reason to hold these merchants liable to fulfill their sworn obligation, because otherwise who will ever be prepared to take the trouble to rescue valuable assets if he [the other party] can annul his vow and keep the fee he committed himself to pay? That being so, our ruling is valid in all respects.

See also Resp. Divrei Rivot #292.

63. *See supra* pp. 731–735.

64. *Resp. Ribash* #399.

65. As to the applicability of legislation to persons not yet born when the legislation was enacted, Ribash, following Rashba, relied on an analogy to such acts as vows, which bind even future generations, *see supra* pp. 732–734. However, with regard to minors, Ribash did not rely on any legal source except reason: it would "make no sense" for the enactment not to apply to them. The rationale given by Ribash for the applicability of the enactment to

VI. SEARCH BY THE HALAKHIC AUTHORITIES FOR THE LEGAL SOURCE OF PARTICULAR RULES

The previous discussion of the various legal sources of Jewish law has noted that the halakhic authorities, especially the *amoraim,* often searched for the precise legal source of particular rules.[66] A number of instances have been cited where the halakhic authorities regarded legal reasoning as the source for particular rules. In the following example, the *amoraim* sought to attribute the origin of a particular rule to various legal sources, until they finally concluded that the source necessarily had to be legal reasoning.

The third chapter of Tractate *Bava Batra,* chapter *Ḥezkat ha-Battim,*[67] deals for the most part with the subject of possession (*ḥazakah*),[68] specifically the rule that possession for a number of years (*ḥezkat shanim*) may serve as proof of ownership. For example, if A is in possession of real property, B claims ownership of the property and proves by means of witnesses or a deed that he had been the owner (the "first owner"), and A contends that he purchased the property from B or received it from him as a gift but the deed of purchase or gift was lost, then the law is that if A produces witnesses who testify that he has been in unchallenged possession of the property for at least three years, A's contention that he bought the property or received it as a gift must be credited. The possession of that property for a period of three years serves as proof, in place of the lost deed, that the

---

the unborn is not valid for minors, since, as far as minors are concerned, the legal problem is: How is it possible to bind one who is not legally competent? Even if we assume that the enactment will apply to those born later, it is possible that it will apply to them only from the time they reach majority and not before.

Resp. Maharashdam, ḤM, #327 presents another instructive example of *sevarah* as a direct legal source in a ruling that all transactions previously entered into by Marranos were valid even after the Marranos returned openly to the Jewish faith. Maharashdam reasoned that "otherwise, life for the Marranos will be unbearable. . . . [If the previous transactions are held invalid,] they will all now come to reclaim from one another the real and personal rights that were created not in accordance with Jewish law but in accordance with the practice of their place. This is simply unthinkable. . . ." *See* M. Elon, EJ, V, p. 885, s.v. Conflict of laws (reprinted in *Principles,* p. 718).

Still another interesting example involved the question of the validity of a will made by a Marrano in Majorca. Ribash (*Resp. Ribash* #46–52) and Rashbeẓ (*Resp. Tashbeẓ,* I, #58–61) differed on this question; and the view of Ribash was based entirely on legal reasoning. For details, *see* Elon, *supra* at 889–890 (reprinted in *Principles,* pp. 722–723).

For a detailed discussion of the use of legal reasoning in the development of Jewish public law in the post-Talmudic period, *see* Elon, *Samkhut ve-Oẓmah,* pp. 25–27; *id.,* "Darkhei ha-Yeẓirah ha-Hilkhatit be-Fitronan Shel Ba'ayot Ḥevrah u-Mishpat ba-Kehillah" [The Methodology of Halakhic Creativity in Solving Social and Legal Problems in the Jewish Community], *Yitzhak Baer Memorial Volume, Zion,* XLIV (1979), pp. 250–264.

66. *See, e.g., supra* pp. 298–299, 886–890.

67. TB Bava Batra 28a *et seq.*

68. For the various legal meanings of the term *ḥazakah, see supra* pp. 79–80.

property does belong to A and came into his possession legally.[69] This rule is stated as follows in the Mishnah:[70]

> [The period of] possession [needed to prove ownership] of: houses; pits, ditches, and caves [used as receptacles for water]; dovecotes; bathhouses; olive presses; irrigated fields [fields that are irrigated by hand and produce crops several times a year]; slaves [whose legal incidents are analogized to the law of real property]; and anything that is continually productive [*i.e.*, not just once a year]—is three years from day to day [*i.e.*, possession by the occupier for three complete years is sufficient to constitute proof that the property belongs to him]. In the case of a field not under irrigation [a field that uses only rainwater and therefore produces crops only once a year], [the period of] possession is three years, which need not be from day to day [*i.e.*, although the field must be occupied for three years, it need not be worked for the entire year since it produces crops only once a year].[71]

The Talmud contains a comprehensive discussion as to the original legal source of the rule that possession for three years is sufficient to constitute proof of ownership:[72]

> R. Johanan said: "I have heard from those who went to Usha[73] as follows: 'What is the source of the rule that possession [of real property to prove ownership] must be for three years? It is the goring ox: just as the goring ox, after goring three times, ceases to have the status of an ordinary animal and acquires the status of a habitual gorer, so too after one has eaten from a field for three years it ceases to be owned by the seller [the "first owner"] and

69. The rules relating to possession for three years are thus a part of procedural rather than substantive law. Maimonides therefore included them in *MT*, To'en ve-Nit'an [The Laws of Plaintiff and Defendant].

70. M Bava Batra 3:1; *see also* 3:3. For this law in *MT*, *Tur*, and Sh. Ar., *see infra* pp. 1331–1335.

71. This is the interpretation of Rashba (Novellae to Bava Batra 28a, s.v. Sedeh ha-ba'al *et seq.*; *Shittah Mekubbeẓet, ad loc.*, s.v. Sedeh ha-ba'al) and Ritba (Novellae to Bava Batra 28b, s.v. Le-rabbanan mai, and to Bava Batra 36a, s.v. Matnitin), *i.e.*, that the field must be occupied for three years although it need not be worked for the full three years. According to Rashi (*ad loc.*, s.v. Sedeh bet ha-ba'al), however, "which need not be from day to day" is interpreted as meaning that the field need not be occupied or worked for three years but only for three crops—either eighteen or fourteen months.

72. TB Bava Batra 28a–29a.

73. "Those who went to Usha" (*holkhei Usha*) refers to R. Meir, R. Judah, and the other disciples of R. Akiva who followed the Sanhedrin to its place of exile in Usha, in the middle of the second century C.E. *Cf.* M Avot 5:14: "There are four types among those who go to the House of Study (*holkhei le-vet ha-midrash*)." The text presents a difficulty, since R. Johanan lived in the middle of the third century C.E. and could not possible "have heard" from the disciples of R. Akiva. TJ Bava Batra 3:1, 7b (3:1, 13d) reads: "R. Johanan said: 'We have heard . . .'" in the plural, which means "we have a tradition" and not that he personally heard from them. *See* Epstein, *Amoraim*, p. 251.

acquires a new status as the property of the buyer [the present occupant who claims to have bought it].'"

The law of the goring ox is as follows:[74] If an ox has gored once, twice, or three times, its owner does not pay for the entire damage caused by its goring, but only for half of the damage. The reason is that with the first and second goring, the ox still has the status of an ordinary ox that is not a habitual gorer. Since an ox is a domesticated animal that does not normally gore, its owner need not have foreseen that it would gore, and he is therefore not guilty of negligence in failing to restrain the ox. The purpose of imposing liability for half the damage is to motivate the owner to exceed the minimum standard of care in protecting against harm caused by the ox.[75]

However, once an ox has gored three times, it no longer has the status of an ordinary animal, but has become a "goring ox"; this imposes on the owner a duty to take special care, since he has been forewarned that the ox will gore and cause damage. Therefore, if it gores a fourth time, the owner must pay for the entire damage.

The Sages at Usha sought to deduce by way of analogy from the law of the goring ox the rule relating to three years' possession of real property. Just as the Torah established the principle that goring three times changes the status of an ox from an ordinary ox to a goring ox, so three years' possession of real property changes the status of the property: it no longer belongs to the "first owner," but to the occupier, who claims to have acquired it.

The Talmud then examines the force and quality of this analogy and concludes that the analogy is indeed valid with regard to the establishment of the basic principle that a threefold repetition may be sufficient to change a status. However, how do we know that the threefold recurrence with regard to possession must be a period of three years? May not three months be sufficient when three complete crops can be produced in three months? For instance, the Talmud asks, when one occupies a field that produces clover, which has a period of growth of one month, so that it is possible in the normal course to gather three crops in three months, why should three months not be a sufficient period of possession? Indeed, a view is expressed that possession for three years is unnecessary, and that three crops are sufficient, even if they are produced in less than three years; and this view may certainly be derived just as plausibly by analogy from the threefold goring by an ox. What then is the source for the requirement of possession of at

74. Exodus 21:35–36.
75. TB Bava Kamma 15a.

least three years,[76] which is held to be necessary by the first *tanna* in the *mishnah* quoted above, as well as by other Sages?[77]

When it was determined that the method of analogy—*i.e.*, interpretation—could not be considered the source of the rule of three years' possession, the Sages turned to another legal source—tradition or ancient custom:

> R. Joseph said: "It is derived from the Scriptural verse: 'Fields shall be purchased, and deeds written and sealed,'[78] for the prophet is speaking in the tenth year and warns of the eleventh year."

Chapter 32 of the Book of Jeremiah states that in "the tenth year of King Zedekiah of Judah," the prophet cautioned the people that when they buy a field they should write a deed and have witnesses sign it. The reason was that in the eleventh year of Zedekiah's reign they would be exiled to Babylonia after occupying the field for less than three years; and without a deed, they would not be able at the appropriate time to prove ownership. They would not be able to prove ownership by possession, because the minimum period for proof by possession is three years, and only about two

76. According to the original version of R. Johanan's statement, there is no basis for this question. That version is in TJ Bava Batra 3:1, 7b (3:1, 13d):

> What is the source of the rule concerning possession [of real property as proving ownership] (*minayin le-ḥazakah*)? R. Johanan said: "We have heard from those who went to Usha that they derived it from the goring ox."

In this version, the number of years is not mentioned at all; the reference is to a cycle of three with regard to possession. However, the Babylonian *amoraim* added and explained: "Just as the goring ox . . . ceases to have the status of an ordinary animal . . . so too after one has eaten from a field for three years . . ." (TB Bava Batra 28a; it should be noted that this addition is in Aramaic), and this turned the discussion into one regarding the requirement of three years. This is also the view of *Tosafot,* Bava Batra 28b, s.v. Ella me-atah ḥazakah she-ein imah ta'anah: ". . . Those who went to Usha said only that we analogize from the goring ox and nothing more."

Some texts of TJ (*see* ed. Venice, and *Penei Moshe, ad loc.*, whose commentary to this begins: "*Minayin le-ḥazakot*") read: "*Minayin le-ḥazakot*" ("What is the source of the law relating to *ḥazakot* [in the plural]?") This might very well not be a reference to the possession of real property as proving ownership at all, but rather to *ḥazakah* as meaning a legal presumption, which is derived from the goring ox, to the effect that, when a new quality repeatedly manifests itself, it is presumed to be permanent. This is the central notion of various presumptions, such as the presumption that a person is still alive, the presumption of propriety, and the like. The matter requires further study. *See supra* pp. 79–80 for the various meanings of *ḥazakah.*

77. *See* TB Bava Batra 36b: "The Sages say: 'There must be possession for three years from day to day. . . .' The Sages say: 'Until he harvests three crops of dates, grapes, or olives.'" *See also* Rashbam, *ad loc.*, s.v. De-amar Rav Yehudah amar Shemuel zo divrei R. Yishmael ve-R. Akiva; Rashi, Bava Batra 28b, s.v. Le-rabbanan mai, and Ritba, *ad loc.*, s.v. Le-rabbanan mai.

78. Jeremiah 32:44.

years remained before the impending exile.[79] According to R. Joseph, we may deduce from this passage that in Jeremiah's time the practice of proving ownership by possession for three years was already in existence and had its source in an ancient tradition.

However, the Talmud rejects this conclusion as well: "Abbaye said to him [R. Joseph]: 'Perhaps all that this means is that he was giving good advice.'" That is to say, how do we know that the prophet is saying that if they did not have a deed, they would be unable to prove their ownership by means of possession? Perhaps under the law at that time they could have proved their ownership through possession; perhaps possession for only one year would have sufficed, and Jeremiah was advising the buyers of the fields that it would be preferable, out of abundance of caution, to have a deed because it might be difficult for them to find witnesses after the exile to prove their occupancy for one year. Perhaps the prophet was not speaking of the legal impossibility of establishing ownership by proof of possession, but of the practical difficulty of proving possession, and for this reason, and for this reason alone, he advised them to obtain a deed. The Talmud then demonstrated that this indeed was the intent of the prophet:

> For if you say otherwise, what is the intent of the verse, "Build houses and live in them, plant gardens and eat their fruit"?[80] Just as in that verse the prophet was merely giving good advice, so here too he was also giving good advice.

The Talmud points to the fact that the prophet had previously turned to "the priests, the prophets, the rest of the elders of the exile community, and to all the people"[81] exiled to Babylonia during the reign of Jeconiah eleven years before the exile of Zedekiah and told them that in their exile in Babylonia they should build houses and plant gardens because the exile would last for seventy years[82] and they would still have time to eat the fruit of their labors. He also warned them to pay no heed to the false prophets who were assuring them that they would return from their exile before that time. This message certainly contains no legal rules; it was simply good

79. *See* Ritba, Novellae to Bava Batra 28b, s.v. U-mihu kasheh, explaining that R. Joseph agreed that the "cycle of three" is derived from the goring ox, and that what we learn from Jeremiah 32:44 is that the unit of which a minimum of three is required cannot be days or months—since nearly two years remained until the exile. Thus, the minimum period must be three full years. *See also* Rabbenu Hananel in *Tosafot, ad loc.*, s.v. Ve-dilma eẓah tovah ka mashma lan; *Yad Ramah*, Bava Batra 28b, s.v. Ve-daikinan le-rabbanan mai, #20; Maharsha, *ad loc.*, s.v. Be-oto dibbur ve-od.

80. Jeremiah 29:5.

81. *Id.* 29:1.

82. *Id.* 29:10.

advice, and since that is all it was, so too his message to the people of Jerusalem with regard to the writing of deeds of acquisition was only meant as good advice, to make it easier for them to prove their ownership.

The Talmud adduces additional proof that this was what the prophet really meant: "The proof is that it states 'put them into an earthen jar, so that they may last a long time.'"[83] Thus, in that very same message to the people of Jerusalem that contains the prophet's advice to write deeds and have them properly witnessed, the prophet went on to advise that those deeds should be put into earthenware vessels for long-term protection against the ravages of time until the return from exile. There is certainly no legal duty to keep deeds in an earthen vessel. The prophecy as a whole thus indicates that all of the prophet's admonitions with regard to the purchase of fields were intended only as good advice, and no legal rule with regard to three years' possession can be deduced from them.

After the verse in Jeremiah was also rejected as a legal source, the Sages turned to legal reasoning, anchored in the observations of actual conditions, as the legal source for the rule of three years' possession. It was Rava who took this approach. At first, he sought to base the rule on the likely conduct and characteristics of the "first owner" of property occupied by someone else. For the first and second years, a person will waive his rights if someone else is enjoying the benefit of his property; but an owner will not waive his rights to the extent of permitting someone else to take the produce from his property for as long as three years. Therefore, the passage of three years is proof that the property no longer belongs to the "first owner," but belongs to the occupier as a result of either purchase or gift.

As an alternative, it could be reasoned that even though during the first and second years an owner will not waive his rights so as to allow someone else to benefit from his property, he may not be diligent about enforcing his rights against such a person for a relatively short period, but he will not look on indifferently for as long as three years while another takes the produce of his property. Therefore, occupancy by another for three years is proof that the property no longer belongs to the "first owner" and that the occupier obtained it legally either through purchase or gift.

These two explanations were also rejected by the Talmud because the conclusions that flowed from them were not consistent with various accepted rules of the law of three years' possession. Therefore, Rava concluded that if indeed the original source of the rule is legal reasoning, the rule is grounded not on the conduct of the "first owner" but on the logic of

83. *Id.* 32:14.

how the occupier, a reasonable buyer, conducts himself in relation to his property:

> Rather, Rava said: "For the first year a person takes care of his deed, and he takes care for two and three years, but beyond that, he does not take care."

That is to say, reason grounded in observation of actual conduct tells us that a person who buys property is careful and preserves his deed for three years in order to be able to prove his purchase if anyone challenges his ownership. However, after three years pass without any challenge to his legal right to the property, he is no longer careful to preserve the evidentiary material in his possession, since he is confident in his ownership and does not anticipate a future challenge to it.

This reasoning with regard to the limitation of the time for preserving evidentiary material—a principle that serves as one of the decisive rationales in the law of limitation of actions in various legal systems[84]—was accepted in the Talmud as the source for the rule that if a person occupies property for three years, this possession is sufficient to prove that he obtained the property legally even if he does not have a deed or other proof.[85]

This discussion in the Talmud is instructive as to the way the Sages, especially the *amoraim*, searched for the original source of halakhic rules. At first, they sought to analogize from a law of the Torah itself; they next turned to tradition—ancient custom. When it became clear that neither of these two could have been the original source, the actual source was found to have been legal reasoning grounded in the observation of actual conduct.[86] The discussion also demonstrates the great importance and re-

84. *See* M. Elon, "Al Hityashenut ba-Din ha-Ivri" [On Limitation of Actions in Jewish Law], *Ha-Praklit,* XIV (1958), pp. 179–189, 243–279; M. Elon, EJ, XI, pp. 251–254, s.v. Limitation of actions (reprinted in *Principles,* pp. 596–599).

85. According to R. Judah in M Bava Batra 3:2, the rationale of the three-year period is to provide for the case when the "first owner" is away in "Aspamia" (Spain). This is to allow the time for the land to be occupied for one year; during the second year the "first owner" will hear of it, and a third year will give him time to return to evict the occupier. *See also* TJ Bava Batra 3:1, 7b (3:1, 13d). *Cf.* Code of Hammurabi, secs. 30–31, which also establishes a three-year period for possession of another's property. Under Hammurabi's Code, the three-year period does more than evidence ownership—it creates ownership even where the possession was not under claim of right. *See* D.H. Müller, "Die Gesetze Hammurabis und die Mosaische Gesetzgebung" [Hammurabi's Laws and Mosaic Legislation], *Jahresbericht der Israelitisch-Theologischen Lehranstalt* [Jewish Theological Seminary Annual], Vienna, X, pp. 16–17, 92.

86. The law as to possession for three years may have originated in an enactment based on the premise that people preserve their documents for three years. If so, the legal source for this rule is legislation and not legal reasoning. However, Talmudic sources nowhere present the law as a rabbinical enactment, and we are therefore bound to conclude that the Sages saw legal reasoning as the direct legal source of the law. *See further infra* n. 87.

spected position the Sages accorded to legal reasoning as the original source for a rule of broad and significant scope.

In short, *sevarah,* the legal reasoning of the halakhic authorities based on their observations of the life and processes of society, was an important and respected legal source for the creation of Jewish law. Legal reasoning was the legal source of various specific rules in matters of both *mamon* and *issur.* It played an important role especially in the creation and development of general legal principles that guide and determine the character of the halakhic system as a whole. These rules and principles based on legal reasoning were, as a general rule, accorded the status of Biblical law because their source was the reasoning of the halakhic authorities, and the Torah was entrusted to them and their power of reason.[87]

87. To conclude the discussion of the legal sources of Jewish law, it is important to stress that it is entirely possible that the laws concerning certain subjects may have had more than one legal source. An interesting example is the large body of laws concerning the *agunah.* The primary legal source of these laws was legislation (*see supra* pp. 552–530), but interpretation and *ma'aseh* also played an important role. As to interpretation, *see supra* p. 402; as to *ma'aseh, see supra* pp. 528–529. M Yevamot 16:4, 6 discusses a number of laws on this subject for which the legal source is *ma'aseh.*

Some rules have two legal sources, *e.g.,* the rule in M Yevamot 16:7 that a single witness to a man's death is sufficient to permit his widow to remarry. The sources of this rule are both legislation and *ma'aseh* (*see supra* pp. 525–526). It is impossible to ascertain definitively whether the *ma'aseh* occurred first and served as the basis for the legislation (in which case two separate legal sources would have operated sequentially) or whether the legislation came first and the *ma'aseh* constituted merely the application of the legislation. (The case in TB Yevamot 116b, discussed *supra* pp. 523–524, did not involve a ruling on this point, since it was found that the woman's claim was factually correct. That case is therefore irrelevant to our present discussion.)

In some instances, different legal sources operated in different historical periods in the various stages of the development of a legal principle. Imprisonment for debt is an interesting example. The law on that subject originated as custom. Later there were communal enactments, and still later there was interpretation (by Ribash) designed to refine and complete the development to accord with the spirit and general principles of Jewish law. For details, *see* Elon, *Ḥerut,* pp. 140–148, 262; *supra* pp. 709–710.

Finally, it should also be pointed out that any attempt to determine the legal source of a given law requires research necessarily limited to extant material. This means that even where, as far as we can ascertain, *ma'aseh* is the legal source, the *ma'aseh* may very well have been preceded by a custom of which there may presently be no record. The opposite may also be true: a law, the legal source of which we see as custom, may very well have first entered Jewish law through legislation, through *ma'aseh,* or otherwise. For various views on this question, *see supra* pp. 880ff.

The foregoing discussion has attempted to discover the direct legal sources of the laws as indicated by the extant materials. Even as so limited, the task calls for the most penetrating and painstaking investigation. Tracing the chain of legal sources culminating in a particular law is even more difficult and requires the utmost caution to avoid unjustified conclusions reached on the basis of unsupported conjecture.

GLOSSARY

aggadah ("telling") the non-halakhic, non-normative portion of the *Torah she-be-al peh* consisting of historical, philosophical, allegorical, and ethical rabbinic teachings

aginut the state of being an *agunah*

agoria, *pl.* **agoriot** non-Jewish court

agunah ("anchored" or "bound") a woman unable to remarry because she is "bound," *e.g.,* to a husband who has disappeared and cannot be legally proved dead or who has abandoned her or who refuses to divorce her

aḥarei rabbim le-hattot "follow the majority" of a court or of legislative representatives

aḥaronim ("later ones") later halakhic authorities, generally referring to those from the sixteenth century onward. *See also rishonim*

am ha'areẓ ("people of the land") (1) national council; (2) hoi polloi; (3) ignorant, unlearned person; (4) a person not punctilious in observance, opposite of *ḥaver* and *ḥasid;* (5) the assembled public

amora, *pl.* **amoraim** (1) rabbis of the Talmudic period (220 C.E. to end of the fifth century C.E.); (2) *meturgeman,* which *see*

Anshei Keneset ha-Gedolah ("Men of the Great Assembly") Ezra, Nehemiah, and those who entered with them into the covenant to observe the laws of the Torah after the return of the Babylonian exiles. The Great Assembly was the supreme institution of the Jewish people during the time it was active, from the latter half of the fifth century B.C.E.

arba'ah shomerim ("four bailees") the four types of bailees in Jewish law—the unpaid bailee (*shomer ḥinam),* the borrower (*sho'el*), the paid bailee (*shomer sakhar*) and the hirer (*sokher*)

arev kabbelan one who has undertaken to be a surety by a declaration that entitles the creditor to look to him for payment without first pursuing a claim against the principal debtor

arka'ot (shel goyim) non-Jewish courts

arvit evening prayer

asharta judicial "certification" that a legal document has been properly authenticated

asmakhta ("something to lean on," "supportive device") (1) an action or transaction without an unqualified and deliberate intention to take the action or enter into the transaction; (2) a transaction involving a penalty or forfeiture; (3) exegesis identified by the Sages as integrative, not creative; (4) according to some, a strained and far-fetched (symbolic and figurative) exegesis that is necessarily only integrative

avak ribbit ("dust of interest") any form of benefit (other than actual stipulated interest) received by a lender that exceeds the value of the money or property lent; it is not expressly prohibited by the Torah, but is rabbinically proscribed because it partakes of the nature of interest

av bet din ("father of the court") (1) one of the two national leaders during the period of the Zugot; (2) presiding judge

avot nezikin ("fathers of damages") primary categories of causes of damage, namely, "ox" "pit," "grazing animal," and "fire." *See bor, mav'eh,* and *shor*

Bagaẓ acronym for *Bet Din Gavo'ah le-Ẓedek,* which *see*

bal tigra ("you shall not take away") the prohibition (Deut. 4:2, 13:1) against taking away from any commandments (*miẓvot*) set forth in the Torah; antonym of *bal tosif*

bal tosif ("you shall not add") the prohibition (Deut. 4:2, 13:1) against adding to the commandments (*miẓvot*) set forth in the Torah

baraita, ***pl.*** **baraitot** tannaitic *dictum* not included in the Mishnah (capitalized if referred to collectively)

be-di-avad ("after the fact," ***ex post*****)** usually employed in connection with the question whether an act in violation of a prohibition is not only a transgression but also without legal effect. *See also le-khateḥillah*

bein adam la-Makom ("between man and God") (1) involving human relationships with God; (2) pertaining to "religious" law as distinguished from civil law; (3) pertaining to matters of private conscience

bein adam le-ḥavero ("between a person and his fellow") (1) involving relationships between people; (2) pertaining to civil as distinguished from "religious" law

berurim ("selected ones," "arbiters") (1) members of the community council; (2) representatives for enacting legislation; (3) arbitrators selected by the parties; (4) lay judges; (5) communal leaders

bet din, ***pl.*** **battei din ("house of law")** (1) a court or panel of judges who adjudicate in accordance with the *Halakhah;* (2) a Jewish arbitral tribunal

Bet Din Gavo'ah le-Ẓedek "The High Court of Justice," the capacity in which the Supreme Court of Israel sits as a court of original jurisdiction to review administrative or governmental action claimed to be arbitrary or in excess of jurisdiction

bet din shel hedyotot ("a court of ordinary people") (1) a court lacking a rabbinic judge who is ordained; (2) a court composed entirely of laymen not knowledgeable in the law

Corpus Juris (Civile) ("Body of the [Civil] Law") (1) The Code of Justinian; (2) a comprehensive legal code that has achieved ultimate authoritative status

corpus juris the total body of law in a given legal system

darkhei shalom ("the ways of peace") the social and religious interest in peace and tranquillity

darshan (1) "exegete"; (2) preacher, homilist

dat (1) religious faith; (2) law, particularly law based on custom; (3) established practice

dayyan ("judge") a judge according to the *Halakhah;* a judge of a rabbinical court

de-oraita "Biblical"; the precise contours of this concept cannot be indicated in a glossary. *See* vol. 1, pp. 207ff.

de-rabbanan "rabbinic"; for the precise contours of this concept, *see* vol. 1, pp. 207ff.

derishah va-ḥakirah ("inquiry and examination") thorough interrogation of witnesses by the *dayyanim* of a *bet din*

din, *pl.* **dinim ("law")** (1) law generally; (2) "interpretation," particularly analogical or syllogistic interpretation or *a fortiori* reasoning; (3) sometimes, law included in the Order of *Nezikin;* (4) law based on a source other than custom or legislation

din Torah (1) Jewish law generally; (2) a case before a rabbinical court

dinei issur ve-hetter ("laws of prohibition and permissibility") laws governing religious and ritual matters, *i.e.,* matters involving relationships with God

dinei kenasot ("law of fines") (1) laws in civil cases pursuant to which the prescribed payment is not equivalent to actual loss suffered; (2) in modern usage, also a criminal fine or civil penalty

dinei malkot or **makkot ("laws of flogging")** laws relating to offenses punishable by flogging

dinei mamonot ("monetary laws") the body of Jewish law generally, but not completely, corresponding to civil law in contemporary legal systems

dinei nefashot ("law of souls") the body of Jewish law involving (a) capital crimes, (b) crimes punishable by corporal punishment, or (c) criminal law

din emet le-amito ("a judgment that is completely and truly correct") a judgment that combines principled decisionmaking with individualized fairness and equity based on thorough understanding of the particular circumstances as well as the law and the general background

divrei kabbalah ("matters of tradition") (1) the writings of the Prophets and the Hagiographa; (2) teaching transmitted orally by teacher to disciple, from one generation to the next; (3) Jewish mysticism (a much later meaning)

divrei soferim ("words of the Scribes") (1) equivalent to *de-rabbanan;* (2) matters essentially rooted in the written Torah but explained by the Oral Law; (3) enactments of the Scribes

divrei Torah ("words of the Torah") equivalent to *de-oraita* ("Biblical")

ed sheker "false witness"

edim zomemim ("scheming witnesses") witnesses who conspire to testify falsely

ein li ("I have nothing") an oath by a debtor attesting inability to pay the debt and undertaking to fulfill certain stringent requirements as to future earnings

erusin ("betrothal") (1) synonym for *kiddushin;* creates the personal status of husband and wife *vis-à-vis* the whole world, but marital rights between the couple do not arise until after *nissu'in, i.e.,* entry under the *ḥuppah* (marital canopy); (2) (in modern Hebrew) engagement

eruv ("merging") a method or device to (a) extend the boundaries within which one may walk or carry on the sabbath, or (b) permit food to be cooked on a festival for consumption on the sabbath immediately following

Even ha-Ezer one of the four principal divisions of the *Sefer ha-Turim* and the *Shulḥan Arukh,* dealing mainly with family law

exilarch the head of the internal Jewish government in the Babylonian diaspora

gabbai, *pl.* **gabba'im** (1) collector of dues, charitable contributions, or assessments; (2) director of a craft guild; (3) manager or director of a synagogue, with particular reference to the religious service

gaon, *pl.* **geonim** *see geonim*

garmi (geramei, gerama) (1) indirect causation; (2) harm other than by direct physical impact

GeFeT Hebrew acronym for "Gemara, Ferush, and Tosafot," *i.e.,* Talmud, Rashi, and Tosafot

Gemara ("completion" or "study" or "tradition") that part of the Talmud that contains discussion of the Mishnah

gematria a method of reaching or supporting conclusions on the basis of the numerical equivalents of letters of key words

gemirut da'at serious, deliberate, and final intent, without reservation, to enter into a legal transaction or perform a juristic act

geonic pertaining to the *geonim* or the gaonate

geonim heads of Talmudical academies (*yeshivot),* (the most famous being Sura and Pumbedita in Babylonia), from the end of the sixth or middle of the seventh century C.E. to the middle of the eleventh century C.E. in the west and the thirteenth century in the east

get bill of divorcement

get me'usseh ("a compelled divorce") a divorce that is invalid because given not voluntarily but rather as a result of improper compulsion

gezel mi-divreihem ("robbery by their words") theft under rabbinic law, *i.e.,* acts designated by the Rabbis as theft, although they do not constitute theft under Biblical law and were not prohibited by the Bible at all

gezerah ("decree") legislative enactment by the halakhic authorities; in the technical sense, as used by some authorities, limited to an enactment that extends or adds prohibitions beyond preexisting *Halakhah,* as distinguished from *takkanah,* an enactment prescribing performance of designated acts

gezerah shavah ("[comparison with] similar matter") inference from similarity of words or phrases. One of the thirteen canons of Biblical interpretation

guda ("wall") a ban

ha'anakah ("bonus," or "gratuity") a sum given to a Hebrew slave upon attaining freedom after six or more years of service; *see* Deuteronomy 15:11–18

haftarah, *pl.* **haftarot** prophetic reading that supplements the weekly Torah portions read during the synagogue service on sabbaths and other holy days

ḥakham, ***pl.*** **ḥakhamim ("sage")** (1) through the Talmudic period, rabbinic Sage; (2) in subsequent periods, halakhic authority, Talmudic scholar

halakhah le-ma'aseh a legal norm intended to be applied in practice, as distinguished from a theoretical or academic statement

Halakhah the generic term for the entire body of Jewish law, religious as well as civil

halakhah, ***pl.*** **halakhot ("the law")** (1) a binding decision or ruling on a contested legal issue; (2) a statement of a legal rule not expressly based on a Biblical verse, made in a prescriptive form; (3) in the plural, a collection of any particular category of rules

halakhah le-Moshe mi-Sinai ("law given to Moses at Sinai") (1) a law specifically given to Moses at Sinai, not indicated by or deducible from the Biblical text; (2) a law unanimously accepted by the Sages, having a tenuous connection with the Biblical text, given the designation to emphasize the law's authority; (3) a law so well settled that it is as authoritative as if it had explicitly been given to Moses at Sinai

halanat ha-din ("deferring judgment") deliberation in judgment

ḥaliẓah ("removal," "pulling off") release from levirate marriage by a rite whose central feature is removal of a sandal from a foot of the *levir. See* Deuteronomy 25:7–10. *See also levir*

ḥasid (1) pious; (2) equitable, more generous than the law requires; (3) punctilious in observance; synonym for *ḥaver*

haskamah, ***pl.*** **haskamot** (1) "agreement"; (2) (as the term was used by Spanish halakhic authorities) enactment

hassagat gevul (1) "removing a landmark" [*i.e.*, boundary marker]; (2) copyright infringement; (3) unfair competition; (4) unfair interference with contract or economic advantage

ḥaver (1) "friend," "comrade, "fellow"; (2) one punctilious in observance of the laws of ritual purity, (3) generally a halakhic scholar

ḥazakah (from ***ḥazak,*** **"strong")** (1) a mode of acquisition of property; (2) a legal presumption; (3) possession; (4) the rule that possession of real property for three years under claim of right is equivalent to a deed as proof of ownership; (5) an act of dominion such as putting up a fence or locking the premises

hedyot ("ordinary") (1) pertaining to mundane affairs, as distinguished from matters of Torah; (2) layman; (3) one untutored in the law

hefker bet din hefker ("ownerless [declared by] a ***bet din*** **is ownerless")** a halakhic court has the authority to expropriate property; the principle was later used as authority to legislate

hefker ẓibbur hefker ("ownerless" [declared by] the community is ownerless") the community has the authority to expropriate property and legislate

hekkesh ("analogy") analogical reasoning, a method of Biblical interpretation

hekkesh ha-katuv ("Scriptural analogy") analogy made by the Bible itself

henpek same as *asharta,* which *see*

ḥerem, ***pl.*** **ḥaramim ("ban")** (1) a ban as a sanction for transgression; (2) in its most severe form, total excommunication, an enforced exclusion from communal Jewish religious, social, and civic life; (3) oath; (4) sanctification

ḥerem ha-yishuv ("ban with respect to settlement") an enactment prohibiting settlement in a town without the consent of the townspeople, and providing penalties for violation

ḥezkat kashrut "presumption of propriety," *i.e.*, the presumption that persons behave correctly and that what should have been done has been properly done

ḥezkat shanim "possession for [a specified number of] years," which may serve as a substitute for proof of ownership

ḥiddushim, *sing.* **hiddush ("innovations")** novellae, *i.e.*, new legal interpretations and insights

hilkheta Aramaic for *halakhah*

hilkheta gemiri (1) "a determined [settled and accepted] rule"; (2) a rule handed down by tradition; (3) equivalent of *halakhah le-Moshe mi-Sinai*

hilkheta ke-vatra'ei "the law is in accordance with [the view of] the later authorities"

ḥiyyuv (1) contract; (2) obligation; (3) debt

ḥok (1) law; (2) statute; (3) regulation

hora'at sha'ah ("a directive for the hour") a temporary legislative measure permitting conduct forbidden by the Torah when such legislation is a necessary precaution to restore people to the observance of the faith; some legislation originally adopted or justified as a temporary measure has become an established part of Jewish law

Ḥoshen Mishpat one of the four principal divisions of the *Sefer ha-Turim* and the *Shulḥan Arukh*, dealing mainly with matters of *mishpat ivri*

ḥuppah the nuptial "canopy," under which bride and groom join in the concluding phase (*nissu'in*) of the marriage rite

innuy ha-din ("torture of the law") delay of justice, the law's delays

issur, also **issura ("prohibition")** and **issur ve-hetter ("prohibition and permission")** "religious" or ritual law; laws other than *dinei mamonot*

Jerusalem Talmud the Talmud of the *amoraim* of the Land of Israel

jus cogens ("compelling law") a mandatory legal norm not subject to variance or modification by agreement of the parties affected

jus dispositivum ("displaceable law") a legal rule that can be varied by agreement, as distinguished from *jus cogens*, which may not be varied by agreement

jus naturale ("natural law") law whose source is "in nature" and which is therefore common to all humanity; sometimes called "higher law," superior to law pronounced or enacted by human agency. *Cf.* Noahide laws

jus non scriptum ("unwritten law") in Roman law, law not reduced to writing, *e.g.*, custom. Not synonymous with the Jewish Oral Law

jus scriptum ("written law") in Roman law, law that has been reduced to writing. Not synonymous with the Jewish Written Law

kabbalah ("tradition") *See divrei kabbalah*

kabbalat kinyan assumption of an obligation made binding by exchange of a symbolic object (*sudar*) as "consideration" for the obligation

kallah (1) semiannual assembly of scholars and teachers at a *yeshivah*; (2) bride; (3) daughter-in-law

kal va-ḥomer ("easy and hard," "minor and major") inference *a fortiori* (one of the thirteen canons of Biblical interpretation)

karet, *pl.* **keritot** or **keretot ("extirpation"** or **"excision")** premature death by divine action as punishment for sin

kasher ("fit") (1) kosher; (2) competent (as applied to a witness)

kashrut ("fitness") dietary laws as to permissible and forbidden foods and food preparation. *See also ḥezkat kashrut*

kehillah the organized Jewish community, especially when possessed of juridical autonomy

kelalei ha-Talmud ("principles of the Talmud") methodology and rules of halakhic decision making

kerem be-Yavneh ("the vineyard in Yavneh") the academy of the Sages in Yavneh (also called Jabneh and Jamnia)

ketubbah, *pl.* **ketubbot ("writing")** marriage contract prescribing a wife's economic entitlements during the marriage and in the event of divorce or the husband's death, in addition to such other provisions as may be agreed by the parties

Ketuvim ("writings") the Hagiographa; *i.e.*, the third division of the Hebrew Bible, the other two being the Torah (Pentateuch) and the Prophets

kim li ("it is established for me") a plea that the defendant's position is supported by a halakhic authority, and that therefore the defendant is not liable. The plea lost its effectiveness with the acceptance of the *Shulḥan Arukh* as the authoritative code of Jewish law

king's law (*mishpat ha-melekh*) the legal authority of the Jewish king (later extended to other forms of Jewish governance), which includes the power to temper the *Halakhah* to meet social needs

kinyan ("acquisition") (1) a formal mode of acquiring or conveying property or creating an obligation; (2) ownership; (3) contract; (4) abbreviation of *kinyan sudar*

kinyan agav karka ("acquisition incident to land"); also **kinyan agav** a conveyance of land in which chattels are incidentally transferred without limitation as to quantity, kind, location, or value

kinyan ha-guf ownership or acquisition of property as distinguished from the right to income

kinyan ḥalifin ("acquisition by barter") exchange of one chattel for another, in which each party acquires the other's chattel

kinyan meshikhah ("acquisition by pulling") a mode of acquisition created by an enactment pursuant to which ownership is not acquired upon payment of the purchase money (which is sufficient under Biblical law to transfer ownership to the buyer) but is acquired only when actual possession is taken

kinyan perot (1) the right to income; (2) acquisition of the right to income

kinyan sudar ("acquisition by kerchief") symbolic barter. The transferee gives the transferor a symbolic object such as a *sudar* (kerchief) in exchange for the object that is the subject of the transaction. The *sudar* is returned to the transferee upon completion of the transaction. This mode of acquisition is also used to create a contractual obligation

kiyyum shetarot ("validation of legal instruments") judicial authentication and certification of legal instruments

Knesset the Israeli parliament

kohen "priest," a member of the tribe of Levi descended from the branch of the tribe authorized to perform the Temple service and other sacred duties

kol de-alim gaver ("whoever is the stronger [of claimants to property] prevails") whoever obtains possession by self-help when self-help is permissible may retain the property

kol di-mekaddesh ada'ata de-rabbanan mekaddesh ("all who marry do so subject to the conditions laid down by the Rabbis") a principle upon which the Rabbis were empowered to annul marriages

kum va-aseh ("arise and do") a category of legislation permitting the performance of an act prohibited by the Torah

laẓeit yedei shamayim ("to fulfill a duty in the sight of Heaven") fulfilling a moral, but not legal, obligation

le-hatnot al mah she-katuv ba-Torah ("to contract out of a law contained in the Torah") by agreement between the parties, varying or rendering inapplicable a rule of the Torah

le-khateḥillah ("in the beginning") *ex ante*, in the first instance. *See also be-di-avad*

le-ma'aseh ("for action") in actual practice, or for practical application as distinguished from *"le-halakhah"* ("for law," *i.e.*, as theoretical doctrine, not practical application)

le-migdar milta ("to safeguard the matter") the principle that authorizes the halakhic authorities, as a protective measure, to adopt enactments in the field of criminal law that prescribe action the Torah prohibits

lefi sha'ah ("temporarily") a principle authorizing legislation permitting conduct contrary to the Torah as a temporary measure under exigent circumstances

leshon benei adam ("colloquial usage of the people") (1) the principle that terms in a legal document should be construed according to their colloquial meaning, not in the sense used in Scripture or by the Sages; (2) according to R. Ishmael, the principle that the Torah speaks as people speak, and therefore there are redundancies in the Torah and not every word has midrashic significance

letakken olam ("to improve [or mend] the world") to promote the public welfare

levir brother-in-law of the widow of a man who has died leaving no children; he must marry the widow unless the rite of ḥaliẓah is performed (Deut. 25:5–10). *See also ḥaliẓah*

lifnim mi-shurat ha-din ("on the inside of the line of the law") acting more generously than the law requires

ma'amad sheloshtan ("a meeting of the three") a method of assignment of property rights or obligations: the creditor-assignor, in the presence of the debtor and the assignee, states that the ownership of the property or obligation is assigned to the assignee

ma'aseh, *pl.* **ma'asim** "act," "incident," "event," or "case" that is the source of a new halakhic norm or declarative of a preexisting norm

ma'aseh adif ("a *ma'aseh* takes precedence") a *ma'aseh* is entitled to particular deference

ma'aseh ha-ba ba-averah a transaction involving illegality

ma'aseh rav "a *ma'aseh* is [of] great [significance]"

ma'aseh yadeha "her [a wife's] handiwork," *i.e.*, the domestic services to which a husband is entitled from his wife in consideration of his obligation to support her

mah lo leshakker ("why should he lie") *see migo*

makkot mardut disciplinary flogging

malkot flogging; stripes

malshinut (1) "slander"; (2) informing, betrayal, *i.e.*, a slanderous accusation against a Jew of a kind that, if heard by a non-Jew, would likely cause harm to the person accused

mamon; also **mamona** "money" matters, *i.e.*, civil-law matters, as distinguished from religious-law matters

mamzer ("misbegotten") offspring of an incestuous or adulterous union that is subject to capital punishment by a court or extirpation (*karet*) by God; often mistranslated as "bastard," in the sense of one born out of wedlock

Mappah ("Tablecloth") the title of the commentary by Moses Isserles (Rema) on Joseph Caro's *Shulḥan Arukh* ("Set Table")

mattenat bari ("gift of a healthy person") a form of disposition of property essentially equivalent to a will, whereby the donor "gives" property to his beneficiaries but retains possession and control during his lifetime

mattenat shekhiv me-ra ("gift of one facing imminent death") gift in contemplation of death made by a *shekhiv me-ra*, or the last will and testament of a *shekhiv me-ra*, for which the usual formal requirements are relaxed

me-aḥar ("since") *see migo*

Megillah "scroll," usually referring to the Book of Esther

meḥusar amanah ("lacking in trustworthiness") a description applied by a court as a sanction to a person who reneges on a transaction as to which there is only an unenforceable oral agreement

me'ilah ("sacrilege") unlawful use of consecrated property

Mejelle the Ottoman code of civil law, based on Mohammedan principles and formally repealed in the State of Israel in 1984

melog, also **nikhsei melog ("plucked [usufruct] property")** property belonging to a wife, of which the income belongs to the husband and the principal remains the wife's; the husband is not responsible for loss or diminution in value of *melog* property as he is for *ẓon barzel* property

memrah, *pl.* **memrot ("statement")** a law originated by the *amoraim*

meshikhah ("pulling") *see kinyan meshikhah*

meturgeman (1) spokesman; (2) one who repeated aloud the words of a speaker to a large audience for whom it would be difficult to hear the speaker directly; (3) interpreter

me'un ("refusal") disaffirmance by a woman of a marriage entered into when she was a minor

meẓavveh meḥamat mitah "a testator on the brink of death," for whose will the usual formal requirements are relaxed

mezuzah (1) parchment scroll containing Deuteronomy 6:4–9 and 11:13–21, affixed to the right doorpost in a wooden, metal, or other case; (2) doorpost

mi-de-oraita *see de-oraita*

mi-de-rabbanan *see de-rabbanan*

middah, *pl.* **middot** (1) canon of interpretation; (2) desirable quality of character

middat ḥasidut ("the quality of piety or benevolence") pious or altruistic behavior

mi-divrei soferim ("from the words of the Scribes") *see divrei soferim*

midrash (1) interpretation of Scripture and *Halakhah;* (2) exegesis; (3) a particular midrashic text (when used in this sense in this work, *midrash* is italicized)

midrash ha-Halakhah interpretation of *Halakhah*

midrash mekayyem ("confirming exegesis") integrative exegesis, by which existing law is "integrated" or connected with a Biblical text

midrash yoẓer ("creative exegesis") exegesis that is the legal source of new law

migo ("since," "because" [Aramaic]) a procedural rule to the effect that a claim, despite insufficiency of proof, is deemed valid "since" (or "because") if the claimant had desired to lie, he could have stated a more plausible case that would have been accepted as true, and therefore the weaker claim actually made should also be accepted; also called *me-aḥar* and *mah lo leshakker*

mikveh ("collection of water") ritual bath

minhag (1) "custom" (in modern Hebrew, custom operating as an independent legal norm), *cf. nohag;* (2) legislative enactment (*takkanah*); (3) prescribed practice, *i.e.*, a legal rule for which the Torah itself is the source

minhag garu'a ("bad custom") custom deemed undesirable, which some halakhic authorities held for that reason legally ineffective

minhag ha-medinah ("custom of the region") local custom

minhag le-dorot ("a prescribed practice for the generations") a law for all time

minhag mevattel halakhah ("custom overrides the law") the principle that in monetary matters, custom controls even if contrary to the *Halakhah*

minḥah afternoon prayer

minyan ("number") a quorum of ten, the minimum number for public congregational prayer

mi she-para ("He Who punished . . .") an imprecation by the court addressed to a party who has violated a moral obligation for which there is no legal sanction

Mishnah the code of R. Judah Ha-Nasi, redacted about 200 C.E., which is the basis of the Gemara

mishnah, *pl.* **mishnayot** the smallest division of the Mishnah; the Mishnah is divided into Orders, tractates, chapters, and mishnayot (paragraphs)

mishnat ḥasidim ("standard of the pious") a higher ethical and personal standard than the law requires

Mishneh Torah Maimonides' Code, also called *Yad ha-Ḥazakah*

mishpat (1) adjudication, the act of judging; (2) decision; (3) justice; (4) a system of laws; (5) a legal right; (6) custom, usage, or practice

mishpat ivri ("Jewish law") that part of the *Halakhah* corresponding to what generally is included in the *corpus juris* of other contemporary legal systems, namely, laws that govern relationships in human society

mishpat ha-melekh *see* "king's law"

mishum eivah ("because of enmity") a principle of legislation to the effect that laws should be designed to prevent strife and enmity

miẓvah, ***pl.*** **miẓvot ("commandment")** (1) religious obligation; (2) good deed

miẓvah ha-teluyah ba-areẓ ("precept dependent upon the land") a precept directly relating to the Land of Israel, *e.g.*, the sabbatical year and the law of the firstfruits

mored a "rebellious" husband who refuses to cohabit with his wife

moredet a "rebellious" wife who refuses to cohabit with her husband

mu'ad ("forewarned") having given notice of propensity for causing harm. Opposite of *tam;* if the cause of harm is *mu'ad,* damages are higher than if the cause is *tam*

na'arah ("girl") a female minor, *i.e.*, a girl who is more than twelve years and one day old but has not reached the age of twelve years, six months, and one day

na'arut ("girlhood") the legal status of a *na'arah*

nasi, ***pl.*** **nesi'im ("patriarch")** president of the Sanhedrin

naval bi-reshut ha-Torah ("scoundrel within the bounds of the Torah") one who keeps within the letter but violates the spirit of the Torah

nekhasim benei ḥorin ("free [*i.e.*, unencumbered] property") property fully subject to execution of a judgment against the owner

nekhasim meshu'badim ("encumbered property"); nekhasim she-yesh lahem aḥarayut ("property bearing responsibility") real estate, which is responsible for and secures the owner's contractual obligations by virtue of an automatic lien created by entry into the contract

nekhasim she-ein lahem aḥarayut ("property bearing no responsibility") personal property, as to which no lien arises upon the creation of a contractual obligation

Nevi'im the Prophets, *i.e.*, the second division of the Hebrew Bible, the other two being the Torah and the Ketuvim (Hagiographa)

nezikin (1) damages; (2) torts; (3) injuries

niddui ("banning") semi-ostracism, a less severe ban than total excommunication

nikhsei melog *see melog*

niksei ẓon barzel *see ẓon barzel*

nissu'in ("marriage") joinder under the *ḥuppah* (wedding canopy). *See also erusin*

nohag (1) "usage," "conventional custom"; (2) in modern Hebrew, custom given operative effect not as an independent legal norm but because parties are presumed to have acted pursuant to it. *Cf. minhag*

nos'ei kelim ("armor bearers") commentaries and glosses to a legal code

novellae *see ḥiddushim*

ona'ah ("overreaching") taking unfair advantage, as by fraud or deception, in a legal transaction (Lev. 25:14)

ones, pronounced **o-nes ("force")** (1) coercion; (2) duress; (3) act of God (*vis major*); (4) rape

Oraḥ Ḥayyim ("The Way of Life") one of the four principal divisions of the *Sefer ha-Turim* and the *Shulḥan Arukh,* generally dealing with ritual and religious matters outside the scope of *mishpat ivri*

Oral Law (Torah she-be-al peh) all of Jewish law except the part explicitly written in Scripture

parshanut ("explanation") (1) commentary; (2) synonym for midrash

pasul unfit; opposite of *kasher*

pe'ah, *pl.* **pe'ot** "corner" of a field, where a portion of the crop must be left for the poor by the reapers

perat u-khelal ("specification and generalization," "particular and general") inference from a specification followed by a generalization. One of the thirteen canons of Biblical interpretation

peri eẓ hadar ("product of hadar trees") the *etrog* (citron)

perushim "commentaries"

pesak, *pl.* **pesakim** (1) legal ruling; (2) judgment in a litigated case

pesharah "compromise," "settlement"

peshat "plain meaning," as distinguished from midrash

pilpul a method of halakhic study characterized by subtle dialectics and finespun distinctions

piskei ba'alei battim ("judgments of householders") lay judgments

posek, *pl.* **posekim** (1) authoritative decisionmaker, decisor; (2) codifier

praesumptio juris a legal presumption whereby the law assumes the existence of a fact or condition unless the presumption is rebutted by proof to the contrary

prosbul a legal formula authorized by an enactment of Hillel whereby a debt would not be released by the sabbatical year, notwithstanding Deuteronomy 15:1–12, which prescribes such release

rabbinic period the period following the *geonim* to the present time. There are three subperiods: (a) the period of the *rishonim* (eleventh to sixteenth century C.E.), (b) the period of the *aḥaronim* (sixteenth century to the beginnings of the Jewish Emancipation in the late eighteenth century), and (c) the post-Emancipation period

regi'ah ("rest," "allocation of time [rega]" an agreement in restraint of trade allocating time for work and rest (*margo'a*)

resh galuta exilarch

rishonim (1) in prior historical periods, "earlier" halakhic authorities who lived longer ago than in the then recent past; (2) in contemporary usage, halakhic authorities from the eleventh to the sixteenth century. *See also aḥaronim*

rosh yeshivah head of a talmudical academy

Sanhedrin (1) the assembly of 71 ordained scholars constituting the supreme legislative and judicial authority of the Jews during the period of the Second Temple and some time thereafter; (2) the name of a tractate of the Talmud

savoraim ("reasoners") rabbinic Sages from the end of the fifth to the beginning of the sixth or middle of the seventh century C.E.

seder, ***pl.*****, sedarim ("order")** (1) one of the six major divisions of the Mishnah; (2) the ritual meal on the first night of Passover

sefer halakhot a code that includes a discussion of the range of views of the various authorities

Sefer ha-Turim the code of Jewish law written by Jacob b. Asher

sefer keritut "bill of divorcement"; *see also get*

sefer pesakim a code written in prescriptive terms, without discussion of legal theory or conflicting opinions

semikhah ("laying on of hands") rabbinic ordination

sevarah "legal reasoning"

shali'aḥ "agent"

she'elot u-teshuvot ("questions and answers") responsa

Shekhinah Divine Presence, the "immanent" or "indwelling" aspect of God

shekhiv me-ra one who is dangerously ill and faces or otherwise reasonably apprehends imminent death

Shema three Biblical passages recited twice daily, beginning with "Hear (shema) O Israel" (Deut. 6:4), constituting the confession of the Jewish faith

shetar, ***pl.*** **shetarot** (1) legal document; (2) contract; (3) deed

shev ve-al ta'aseh ("sit and do not do") a category of legislation directing that an affirmative precept, obligatory according to Biblical law, not be performed

shevi'it ("seventh [year]") the sabbatical year

shevu'at ha-edut ("witness's oath") an oath by one formally called upon to bear witness, to the effect that the affiant has no knowledge of the matter about which he is called to testify

shevut ("[sabbath] rest") (1) work rabbinically forbidden on the sabbath; (2) the rabbinical prohibition of such work

shi'bud nekhasim ("encumbrance of property") (1) lien, security interest; (2) the general lien on the real estate of an obligor that arises automatically upon creation of the obligation

shi'buda de-oraita "Biblical lien"

shiddukhin an agreement to enter into marriage

shikkul ha-da'at (1) [judicial] "discretion"; (2) decision on a moot point of law; (3) the zone of permissible latitude of a *dayyan* to disagree with other authorities

shimmush (1) "service" to the Torah; (2) attendance upon a halakhic scholar; (3) apprenticeship to a halakhic authority

shi'ur (1) prescribed measure; (2) "lesson," talmudic lecture

sho'el ("borrower") a bailee in possession of property as a result of borrowing it from another

shofet (1) "judge"; (2) magistrate, ruler

shomer ḥinam "an unpaid bailee," *i.e.*, one who undertakes without compensation to preserve property of another

shomer sakhar a "paid bailee" who is compensated for his service in connection with the bailment

shufra de-shetara ("adornment of the *shetar*") clauses designed to enhance the effectiveness of a legal document, *e.g.*, waiver of certain defenses otherwise available

Shulḥan Arukh (the "Set Table") the code of Jewish law written by Joseph Caro in the sixteenth century; the most authoritative of the Jewish legal codes

sitomta ("seal") mark placed on a barrel or other large container identifying the owner; placing the mark was recognized as a mode of acquisition

sofer, *pl.* **soferim ("counter," "scribe")** (1) a halakhic authority of the period of Ezra the Scribe; (2) a scholar of the Talmudic period. *See divrei soferim*

sof hora'ah ("the end of instruction") the completion of the Talmud

sokher ("hirer") a bailee or lessee who pays for the right to possession of the bailed or leased property

sudar ("kerchief") the instrument used in the most widespread mode of acquisition in Jewish law. *See kinyan sudar*

sugyah, *pl.* **sugyot** (1) passage; (2) discussion; (3) issue; a Talmudic subject or area

sukkah "booth" or "tabernacle" erected for the festival of *Sukkot*

supercommentary a commentary on a commentary

takkanah, *pl.* **takkanot ("improvement," "repair")** legislative enactment by halakhic or communal authorities. *See also gezerah*

takkanah kevu'ah ("established enactment") legislation permanently in effect, as distinguished from a temporary measure. *See also hora'at sha'ah*

takkanat ha-kahal "communal enactment"

takkanat ha-shavim ("enactment for the encouragement of penitents") a category of enactments to encourage penitence and rehabilitation, *e.g.*, an enactment providing that a thief may be relieved of the obligation to return stolen property and may pay its value instead, when the property has been incorporated into a building and would be very expensive to retrieve

takkanat ha-shuk ("enactment for the market") an enactment to promote the security of transactions in the open market ("market overt") by protecting the purchaser from a thief at such a market against claims by the owner of the stolen property

takkanat medinah "a regional enactment," intended to be applicable to many Jewish communities (*kehillot*)

talmid ḥakham ("wise scholar") (1) halakhic scholar; (2) learned and pious person

Talmud the Mishnah and the discussion of the Mishnah by the *amoraim* of Babylonia (comprising the Babylonian Talmud) and the *amoraim* of the Land of Israel (comprising the Jerusalem Talmud)

talmud ("learning") (1) academic study; (2) midrash; (3) the colloquy between *tannaim* on a specific law

Talmud Bavli Babylonian Talmud

talmud lomar ("the text teaches") a statement introducing a conclusion derived by implication through exegesis

Talmud Yerushalmi Jerusalem Talmud

tam ("innocuous") not chargeable with notice of propensity to cause harm (opposite of *mu'ad*); if the cause of harm is *tam*, damages are less than if the cause is *mu'ad*

tanna, *pl.* tannaim rabbi of the Mishnaic period (first century to approximately 220 C.E.)

tanna kamma ("the first *tanna*") a *tanna* whose opinion is stated first, without attribution, in a *mishnah*

tenai, *pl.* tena'im (1) "condition"; (2) legislative enactment (*takkanah*); (3) in plural, (a) marriage contract, (b) formal betrothal contract

tenai bet din ("stipulation [or requirement] imposed by the court") a legislative enactment (*takkanah*); the term indicates that the legislation is based on prior private agreements that have become more or less standard

terumah ("contribution") (1) priestly tithe, which only priests and their families are permitted to eat; (2) in modern Hebrew, a donation

teshuvah (1) responsum; (2) "return," or repentance; (3) refutation

tikkun (ha-)olam ("improvement [or mending] of the world") promotion of the public welfare; the verb form, "to promote the public welfare," is *letakken olam*

tofes ("template") the main body of a legal document, containing basic and generally standard provisions relating to the type of transaction involved

tom lev ("purity of heart") (1) good faith; (2) wholeheartedness; (3) integrity; (4) sincerity

Torah ("teaching") (1) the five books of Moses (Pentateuch); (2) the entire Hebrew Bible; (3) doctrine; (4) custom; (5) the prescribed procedure; (6) divine revelation; (7) all Jewish study, the entire religious and ethical and cultural literature of Judaism

Torah min ha-shamayim ("Torah from Heaven") divine revelation, the article of Jewish faith that the Torah was given by God to the Jewish people

Torah she-be-al-peh ("Oral Law") (1) all Jewish law that is not set forth in Scripture; (2) the entire Teaching of Judaism, including aggadah

Torah she-bi-khetav "Written Law," *i.e.*, the law explicitly set forth in the text of the Torah

toref ("blank") the parts of a legal document relating to the individual aspects of the transaction, filled in as to the details of the particular transaction

Tosafot ("additions") critical and explanatory glosses on the Babylonian Talmud written by a school of scholars in France and Germany in the twelfth and thirteenth centuries

tosefet ketubbah ("addition to the *ketubbah*") an optional supplement to the mandatory minimum amount of the *ketubbah*

Tosefta ("additions") a collection of tannaitic statements supplementing the Mishnah

tovei ha-ir ("the good citizens of the town") lay judges or communal officials. Sometimes called "the seven *tovei ha-ir;*" they were the political and economic heads of the community

uvda Aramaic for *ma'aseh*—an act, incident, event, or case that gives rise to new law or is declarative of an existing norm

Va'ad Arba (ha-)Araẓot ("Council of the Four Lands") the central institution of Jewish self-government in Poland and Lithuania from the sixteenth to the eighteenth century

Written Law law explicitly set forth in Scripture

Yad ha-Ḥazakah the *Mishneh Torah,* Maimonides' Code

Yavneh (Jabneh, Jamnia) a town in Judea where R. Johanan b. Zakkai established an academy for teaching and studying the law after the destruction of the Temple in 70 C.E. *See kerem be-Yavneh*

yeshivah ("a place of sitting") academy for Talmudic study

yeẓe din ẓedek le-ẓidko ("let a righteous judgment justly issue") a judgment must do justice, let justice be done

Yom Tov ("good day") festival, holiday

Yoreh De'ah ("it will teach knowledge") one of the four principal divisions of *Sefer ha-Turim* and the *Shulḥan Arukh*

zaken mamre ("rebellious elder") a rabbi who adjudicates contrary to the ruling of the Sanhedrin

zav, *pl.* zavim ("bodily issue") *Zavim* is the title of a tractate of the Talmud in the Order of *Tohorot*

ẓavva'at shekhiv me-ra a deathbed will, or a will of one who apprehends imminent death. *See shekhiv me-ra*

ẓon barzel ("iron flock") assets of a wife over which a husband has almost complete dominion; he is responsible for any loss or diminution in value of these assets, as distinguished from *melog* property, since he has undertaken to preserve "like iron" the value of the *ẓon barzel* property at the time of the marriage

Zug, *pl.* Zugot ("pair") the *Zugot* consisted of the *nasi* and the *Av Bet Din,* who were the acknowledged leaders of the Jewish people from 160 B.C.E. to the beginning of the common era